# International Marketing Strategy

# International Marketing Strategy

**Frank Bradley**

*University College Dublin*

PRENTICE HALL

New York London Toronto Sydney Tokyo Singapore

First published 1991 by
Prentice Hall International (UK) Ltd
66 Wood Lane End, Hemel Hempstead
Hertfordshire HP2 4RG
A division of
Simon & Schuster International Group

Typeset in 10/12 pt Palacio
by MHL Typesetting, Coventry

Printed and bound in Great Britain
at the University Press, Cambridge

---

Library of Congress Cataloging-in-Publication Data

---

Bradley, Frank, 1942–
    International marketing strategy/Frank Bradley.
       p.    cm.
    Includes bibliographical references and index.
    ISBN 0-13-317892-7
    1. Export marketing — Management. I. Title.
  HF1416.B72  1991
  658.8'48 — dc20          90-47584
                                        CIP

---

British Library Cataloguing in Publication Data

---

Bradley, Frank 1942–
  International marketing strategy.
  1.  International marketing
  I.  Title
  658.848

ISBN 0--13-317892-7

---

3 4 5  95 94 93 92

*This book is dedicated to my wife Breda,
my sons Jonathan and Simon, and my
daughters Siobhán and Maedhbh with love.*

# Contents

# *Acknowledgements*

Several people helped with this book. I am grateful for the stimulation and challenge provided by my students at University College Dublin. I also acknowledge the contributions of students at the University of California at Berkeley in the United States, the University of Gothenburg in Sweden and the National Institute for Management Studies in Beijing, the People's Republic of China, where early versions of parts of the book were tested. I owe University College Dublin and my colleagues there a great degree of gratitude for their professional and personal support over many years. I am also indebted to a number of reviewers who provided very useful contributions regarding content and structure at various stages in the preparation of the book. My editor, Cathy Peck, at Prentice Hall International provided extensive and continuous advice and support at all stages. The talent and patience of Anne Woods were very much in evidence as she typed the many drafts. Thanks are also due to Máire Quinlan-Pluck who helped type some of the material. A number of other people helped with various aspects of the preparation of the book: Emer Ní Bhradaigh, Rita Byrne, Rachel Condon, Aidan Connolly, Dennis Geary, and Frank Moran. While these and others have helped, I remain responsible for any errors and other shortcomings in the book. Nevertheless, I hope that students and managers will find the book valuable as they prepare for the challenge of international markets.

Frank Bradley
University College Dublin

xix

# Introduction

International marketing strategy is a management topic of the 1980s and 1990s. In preceding decades international business was the preserve of large commodity traders and a few pioneering marketing companies. Now companies in most industries are concerned with developments in international markets: banks, communications and transport; manufacturing; and retailing. Small and large companies are affected, as are companies in traditional and high-technology industries. There are very few businesses that are not affected by trends in international markets. Growth in international marketing opportunities and competition creates new challenges, for students and managers alike, to develop appropriate strategies to compete successfully in dynamic international markets. This book has been prepared for them.

A study of international marketing strategy is concerned with the strategic and operational marketing issues arising in the management of the firm's international operations. The firm in international markets develops its marketing strategies and implements them in the context of a complex and changing environment. In doing so it must also respond to the needs and demands of its customers while coping with competition. Of special interest, therefore, is the role of the firm in mediating the international environment through corporate marketing strategies. The material in this book is presented from the perspective of the firm which is attempting to develop and grow in international markets.

## International marketing strategy

The distinctive attribute of the strategic development of the firm in international marketing is that the firm transfers packages of tangible and intangible assets or resources across national boundaries. In some circumstances it does so by selling the assets abroad. In other situations it retains ownership or management control over them by entering into alliances with like-minded companies, or it may invest directly in foreign markets to transfer the assets or resources. In making this transfer, the firm in international markets responds to many pressures, among which the most important are pressures originating in the home country, such as saturated markets or the opportunity to exploit new products; the attraction of incentive packages offered by host country governments; the attraction of large and growing foreign markets for the firm's products; and shortening product and technology life cycles, and growth aspirations in the firm.

In more recent years, the function of the firm in international markets has been to combine international marketing decisions with newer forms of resource transfer, thus blurring the distinction between the equity and contractual form of international asset transfer. What is thus needed is a way of examining the activities of the firm which encompasses the selling activities associated with exporting and the investment activities associated with the other modes of resource transfer such as licensing, joint ventures and other forms of competitive alliance and foreign direct investment.

This book examines the unique and changing role of the firm in international markets and seeks to judge how established firms, firms new to international marketing and policy makers in home and host countries approach the evolving modalities of international resource transfer. The primary unit of enquiry is the firm and the effect on it of the changes required in response to internationalization.

## Objectives

Having studied this book the reader should be better equipped to understand the interaction among the methods of entering and competing in international markets, and the firms and institutions involved. It is important to attain this understanding in the context of influences emanating from the marketing environment, from customers, competitors, and the technological and public policy environments. The reader should be able to integrate the various market entry strategies into a series of decisions which reflect an interplay of the international marketing environment, technological forces and the strength and weaknesses of the firm.

Hopefully, the book will also enable the reader to examine and develop international marketing strategies for consumer products firms, industrial products firms, and services firms, irrespective of size or ownership structure. The reader should be able to integrate a wide range of material written on various aspects of management with an emphasis on the international dimension. The principal objective is to assist students and managers to develop analytical frameworks suitable for the design and implementation of international marketing strategies. Consequently, students and managers, having studied the material, should be able to analyse management problems facing the firm in international markets, select and evaluate appropriate conceptual frameworks, identify courses of action, develop appropriate international marketing strategies, and know how to implement them.

## Target audiences

The text is designed for students interested in understanding the changing international business environment, in particular the question of how international business affects our daily lives and the unique and changing role that the firm in international markets has played. Included in this readership would be senior undergraduate students of marketing, international marketing and international business and postgraduate students specializing in international business or international marketing who are likely to work with firms active in the international arena. In addition, students in business, economics, and organizational behaviour with research interests in the evolution and growth of the firm in international markets would have a general interest in the book.

The book should be of special interest to the manager who thinks strategically about the development and growth of the firm in international markets. It should also interest the manager who wishes to keep abreast of the most recent thinking in his specialized field.

## Features

This book has four important features. First, the recently developed body of knowledge related to the discipline of international marketing has been consolidated and integrated, with a focus on the strategic development of the firm in international markets. Second, the conceptual and theoretical aspects of the book are illustrated in two ways: examples of the practice of international marketing by actual companies are used throughout the book; and a series of chapter exhibits, drawn from actual reports of international marketing in action, provide further detail. Third, the material is developed from the perspective of the firm in international markets. The circumstances facing the firm at various stages of its development are examined: international marketing opportunity analysis; market entry strategies; and the development of appropriate marketing programmes for consumer products firms, industrial products firms and services firms. The final section of the book deals with issues of implementation and control in international markets. The focus is on the firm, not on individual elements of the marketing programme. Fourth, the book is international both in terms of the sourcing of its material and in the treatment of the subject matter. It is not a book on marketing management to which an international emphasis has been added. The material has been written from the point of view of the firm competing in international markets irrespective of country of origin.

## Outline

There are twenty chapters divided into five parts, as follows:

(a) the decision to internationalize: Chapters 1–4;

(b) deciding which markets to enter: Chapters 5–9;

(c) how the firm enters international markets: Chapters 10–14;

(d) the international marketing programme: Chapters 15–18;

(e) implementation of the international marketing programme:Chapters 19 and 20.

The following schematic outline of the book shows how each of these chapters and parts fit together.

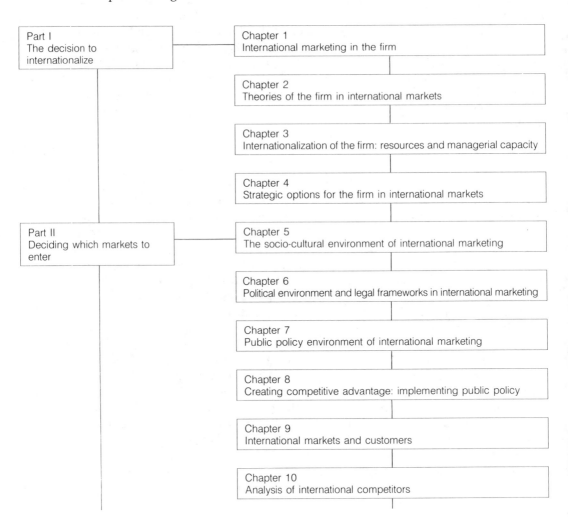

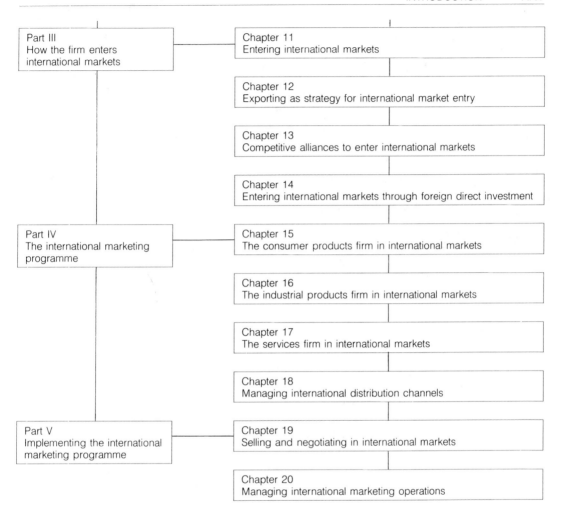

Part III
How the firm enters
international markets

Chapter 11
Entering international markets

Chapter 12
Exporting as strategy for international market entry

Chapter 13
Competitive alliances to enter international markets

Chapter 14
Entering international markets through foreign direct investment

Part IV
The international marketing
programme

Chapter 15
The consumer products firm in international markets

Chapter 16
The industrial products firm in international markets

Chapter 17
The services firm in international markets

Chapter 18
Managing international distribution channels

Part V
Implementing the international
marketing programme

Chapter 19
Selling and negotiating in international markets

Chapter 20
Managing international marketing operations

# *The decision to internationalize*

# International marketing in the firm

The corporate context of international marketing involves understanding how the firm responds to environmental opportunities and threats in markets of very different configurations and underlying behaviour. In such circumstances the firm responds by developing new products or by adapting existing products to the needs of consumers in domestic and international markets. International marketing also means deciding which markets to enter and develop and the sequence and timing of entry. A most important issue is the firm's decision as to how to enter international markets. The nature of the firm in international markets is described in this chapter, as is the role of strategic thinking in the development of the firm. The expansion process followed by the firm is examined in the context of the firm as a co-ordinator of international markets. Finally, the performance and growth of the firm as it diversifies into new international markets is also examined. Of special interest is the role of competitive marketing strategies for success in international markets.

## The firm in international markets

Firms exist where an organizational solution to the allocation of resources is superior to a market solution. Firms come into existence when markets fail. The growth of the firm may be conceived as the replacement of markets or the creation of an internal market within the firm where none existed previously. The motivation for growth by internalization of markets may be attributed to a number of factors.

Production and distribution take time, and delays in the provision of inputs or services when and where necessary may require control of the market for these inputs and services: backward integration of raw materials markets; the forward integration into distribution and marketing of branded products; and the control of information by financial institutions across national borders, are good examples.

Internalized markets avoid the bilateral concentration of marketpower; instability is avoided in a joint venture or internal market.

The buyer uncertainty problem which adversely affects the market transfer of information is avoided in internal markets. This is particularly true in international markets where marketing information is such a vital asset. In such circumstances the buyer is unaware of the value of information until he has possession of it, at which point he has no incentive to pay for it. Such outcomes are avoided when the buyer and seller join together in an internal market formed as a joint venture, licensing arrangement, or full equity participation in foreign direct investment. In an internal market within a firm, transfer prices may be adjusted to achieve the firm's objectives; arm's length pricing is only one alternative.

Other price factors must also be recognized. Price discrimination among foreign subsidiaries may be used by firms to increase profits or minimize the impact of national taxes. Firms also shift funds between currency areas to avoid the adverse effects of changes in currency values. While these activities may be legitimate, the discretion left to the international firm is a major cause of concern to governments and transnational regulatory bodies (Buckley, 1987, pp. 16–17).

There are costs, however, of establishing an internal market within the firm. The market is an economizer of information, only price and quantity signals are necessary. The information burden of an internal market in the firm is greater and communications costs are higher than those experienced in the open market. Skilled management is required to run an internal market and skilled management is expensive. The cost of foreignness, including lack of knowledge of local conditions and costs of adverse discrimination, is a disadvantage.

## Nature of the international firm

Until the mid-1960s, there was little treatment in the literature of the firm in international markets. Nor was there much examination of internationalization as a process culminating in foreign direct investment (Teece, 1986). Teece suggests that the international company is one that exports capital, moving products and equity from countries whose returns are low to markets whose returns are higher, earning the profits of arbitrage while simultaneously contributing to the more efficient worldwide allocation of capital. But the predictions of capital arbitrage theories are quite different from the resource transfer activities of international firms. International firms invest, borrow, buy and sell in different markets and there are considerable cross-flows of investments and products between markets, which make the task of the international firm both interesting and challenging (Exhibit 1.1).

A more plausible theory of foreign direct investment appeals to oligopoly theory and suggests two major reasons why firms should operate beyond their borders (Hymer, 1970). The first reason is to by-pass competition by acquiring it or displacing it, and the second is to employ the firm's special competitive advantages abroad, such as financial skills, access to capital, entrepreneurship

**Exhibit 1.1 Growth in international marketing means cross-flows of investments and products**

*Coals to Newcastle and sand to Saudi*

When certain countries are immediatly associated with a certain product — like Germany with beer, Holland with cheese or even Ireland with potatoes — the last thing you would imagine is that they would be a substantial import market for such products.

But many countries usually import their "national" product because there is such an insatiable demand which domestic producers can't fill or because the consumers are seeking a bit of variety.

Sending beer to Germany may seem like a classic "coals to Newcastle" example, but it is a huge and obvious market for beer makers everywhere. Germans like all kinds of beer, the same way the Americans like all kinds of automobiles. Detroit may be the natural home of the motor car, but Americans have developed a real fondness for the ones made in Japan.

The "coals" sent to the "Newcastles" of the world — aside from beer to Germany — include Gouda cheese to Holland, bacon to Denmark, knitwear to Italy, deer to Scandinavia and even sand to Saudi Arabia. Years ago, we even exported spiral staircases for minarets to Arab countries, but the company in question, Crescent Staircases, unfortunately went out of business. Whatever the product, the common denominator is the quality of the "substitute" which is either as good as or superior to the home-grown variety.

**Source:** *The Irish Times*, Tuesday, 9 February, 1988.

and marketing skills. There are various ways to ensure that the benefits accrue to the firm. The product in which the competitive advantage is embodied could be exported, or the technology used to make the product could be licensed to a foreign firm or produced under a joint venture with a foreign firm. The firm will, however, prefer to invest abroad in many situations to avoid technological misappropriation and to prevent the costly bargaining between licensor and licensee, on the one hand, and the inherent instability and danger of technological misappropriation of joint ventures, on the other (Hymer, 1970; Killing, 1982). It is the costs associated with these forms of transfer and the extent of control under each which decides the hierarchical mode of organization. These insights shift emphasis away from international trade and finance toward industrial organization.

## Marketing orientation for the international firm

Marketing means starting with customer needs to focus the firm's resources on these needs to serve them at a profit. Profit, profit growth and cash flow are normally the objectives of the firm, not just sales. Marketing is different from a production or a sales orientation in that a production orientation is captured in the oft-quoted phrases:

> We have a good product — the world will beat a path to our door to buy it. (The "mousetrap" syndrome),

Or

> They don't appreciate my product. (They're all out of step except our Johnny!)

Similarly, a sales orientation is implied in the claim:

> We can produce lots of widgets: get out there and sell them.

Implied in the sales approach are the needs to fix a sales target and get down to the business of selling. A marketing orientation helps to define the firm's business since marketing is concerned with problem solving and customer benefits. Customers face problems and seek solutions in products and services which are of value to them. A marketing orientation also means matching the firm's resources with the needs of the market (Figure 1.1).

The marketing function identifies and manages the area of overlap between resources and needs to ensure that the customer gets:

> The product and service benefits desired when and where wanted at an acceptable price while producing a profit for the firm.

It is important, especially in regard to international markets, to recognize that needs and wants are not the same thing! Needs are often universal but the means of satisfying them are frequently parochial. Wants reflect the customer's education, culture and personality. The housewife may need the carpets cleaned but may or may not want an Electrolux to do the job! Depending on the country and circumstances she may not even have carpets to clean, other forms of floor covering being more common. The international marketing environment is a complex mixture of macro and micro forces which must be considered by the firm. The environment facing the international firm consists of the constellation of

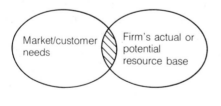

= the area of overlap between the firm's resources and market needs

**Figure 1.1**   Matching the firm's resources with market needs

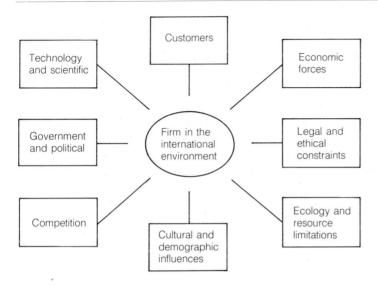

**Figure 1.2** The international marketing environment

demands and constraints to which the organization must adjust in order to survive and grow. This environment consists of a number of elements, the underlying characteristics of which are that they lie outside the domain of the control of the firm (Figure 1.2).

The successful firm caters for its customers within the context of a competitive environment which has become increasingly international. It is not the marketing environment itself that is important but the firm's ability to cope with it. In the rapidly changing technological environment that characterizes international markets there are few isolated market niches. Attention must be focussed on the missing link in developing a competitive strategy for success in international markets: investment in marketing to produce an international orientation; and an ability to compete successfully in international markets.

A standardized approach to the domestic market is frequently adequate because buyers and conditions are homogeneous. To succeed in international markets it is necessary to develop multidimensional strategies. It is usually myopic to consider exporting as the only or primary way of entering foreign markets. By ignoring licensing, joint ventures and direct investment as ways of entering foreign markets, many firms effectively limit their strategic options to those markets which are best served by exporting. Increasingly, however, other foreign market entry modes are being used. Foreign direct investment and equity joint ventures, licensing and other alliances are now quite common.

The internationalization of the firm and industry tends to redefine what it takes to be successful. The conventional wisdom of growth through exporting only may not be very meaningful for the longer-term development of the firm, but it continues to be emphasized in public policies at national level in many countries. Herein lies a potential for conflict between macro and micro policies aimed at supporting internationally competitive firms. It is because competitiveness has different meanings for the firm and for the national economy that such conflict may occur.

## Research and development in the international firm

While it may be possible to organize the research and development function, so necessary in the development of an industry, as a series of market transactions, each with a unique arm's length price, it is infinitely more efficient and less costly to organize such activities within a firm. Here research and development is interpreted to be that which creates the firm's differential advantage and thereby provides an incentive to the entrepreneur to organize within a firm. Research and development consists of technical research and development and marketing research and development.

The inputs of research and development are highly skilled labour, sophisticated durable equipment, and information obtained from the scientific and busines community. The outputs of research and development are new or improved products or new or more efficient durable equipment, managerial methods or processes. A list of the better-known assets which create a firm's differential or competitive marketing advantage are shown in Table 1.1.

We must distinguish further between technical research and development and marketing research and development because of implications for the changing role of the firm. By their very nature, technical inventions and innovative products are easier to define and separate from the firm, i.e. establish a market price, than are marketing or product co-ordination advantages. It may not be easy to find a buyer for a new product, but it is not difficult to determine what is being priced; the contract for using the product is not difficult to draw up and the expectations of seller and buyer are not difficult to specify.

**Table 1.1**  Assets which create competitive advantage for the firm

1. *Proprietary technology*: product or process technology held by a firm that others can obtain only through new research and development or licensing/purchase from the possessor
2. *Management know-how*: skill for managing multicountry operations, usually gained through experience in different countries
3. *Multinational distribution network*: sales subsidiaries in many countries allowing a firm to serve a portfolio of markets
4. *Access to scarce raw materials*: ownership or long-term purchase contracts for minerals, forest products, etc.
5. *Production economies of scale*: large-scale production facilities that lower per unit-costs of production
6. *Financial economies of scale*: access to funds at a lower cost for larger firms than for smaller firms
7. *Possession of a strong brand or trade name*: continuing reputation for quality, service, etc. developed through experience by some products/firms

Source: Grosse, Robert E. (1980) *Foreign Investment Codes and the Location of Direct Investment*, Praeger Publishers NY.

In contrast, those firms whose competitive advantage or uniqueness derives from marketing skills or product co-ordination resort to very few joint ventures or licences — "product bundles" — and constantly changing marketing strategies are difficult to contract out and, hence, are likely to be performed within the firm. This places the firm under pressure to expand when it wishes to serve international markets.

## Competitive advantage in the firm

Where the capacity and incentive to innovate are strong enough, innovators are likely to concentrate on those products that seem in most demand in the home market in which the innovators operate. Later the advantage is exploited internationally in a series of stages. This is the life cycle model first enunciated by Vernon and Wells (1976). Once a firm establishes a technological lead in some product it will be faced with the question of how best to exploit the lead. Exporting the product will sometimes be sufficient. Exporting to exploit a technological lead is likely because at the early stage of the development of a product, managers are not acutely concerned with production cost. Later on, however, costs do become a concern.

Firms that place heavy weight on research and development as a basis for their strategy typically adopt very different patterns in the way they enter foreign markets (Vernon and Wells, 1976, Chapter 1). Successful firms with very narrow product lines (IBM, SKF) are generally committed to an effort to maintain their lead in a limited, well-defined market. Confined to that market they have a high stake in maintaining quality standards, in holding their technological skills close to the chest, and in maintaining *tight* control over market strategy to be applied to their products. Strategic decisions may be relatively few but each is highly important and each affects the firm as a whole. Such firms show a strong preference for wholly owned subsidiaries. They usually enter and stay in foreign markets through foreign direct investment.

Successful firms with very broad product lines which exploit technological leads see themselves as comparatively efficient at developing technological leads. Because they know such leads are perishable, their strategy is to make the widest and presumably the quickest, application of any technological lead they may develop. Since such leads can be exploited over many products in many markets, these firms rely on others to provide the specific market information and specialized distribution machinery needed to exploit them. Because of the need to penetrate markets quickly, these firms are more tolerant of joint ventures as the means of entering and staying in international markets.

An alternative means of internationalizing the firm is to exploit a strong trade name. In the modern world of easy international movement and communication, brand names can sometimes gain strength without much conscious effort on the part of the firm that owns the name. Strength of a foreign brand name is associated with the fact or illusion of superior or predictable performance. The expectation of this performance is often strengthened and fortified by extensive promotional expenditures, as is commonly the case for branded pharmaceuticals and foods, beverages, and tobacco products. In regard to predictable performance, the strong brand may rest on some technological capability, e.g. delivering a packaged food product such as Nestlé or Jacob–Suchard confectionery in a reasonably standardized condition on a reasonably reliable basis can be a technically exacting job that has been mastered by only a limited number of firms.

While brand names endure, their ability to command a premium erodes with time. If the product underlying the brand in packaged foods, soft drinks, cosmetics, and similar products does not change, national producers learn either to match the performance of the foreign product or to overcome the illusion of a difference that was never there. Foreign firms tend to lose market share or face a complete shut out of the market in time unless they continue to innovate.

A trade or brand name applied to a very narrow range of products such as cars, e.g. Ford, Fiat, Nissan, is intended to convey a narrow and explicit set of expectations about a particular product. A brand name applied to a broad range of products, e.g. 3M, Heinz, Hoechst, Heinkel, is intended to convey only a general aura of reliability. Firms with a broad product range have less need for tight control of production and marketing. For such firms, the risks of weakened control associated with operating through joint ventures and even looser alliances are more tolerable.

Even narrow product range companies may use joint ventures and other "less control oriented" modalities. Coca-Cola takes on local interests as partners in its foreign bottling plants because Coca-Cola, until recently, totally controlled the vital marketing functions — trade name, advertising programme, flavour, and the bottles.

## Strategic thinking in international marketing

For most firms, marketing may be interpreted at three levels: as a concept; as a process; and as the subject of decision-making. Marketing as a concept refers to a strategic focus on the environment to produce company and stakeholder benefits, a way of thinking about the company which produces profitable exchanges. Marketing as a process refers to the managerial direction of resources to realize environmental opportunities while recognizing that customers have limitless needs and wants. Marketing decisions arise as a set of programmed actions to ensure co-ordinated and targeted marketing operations.

In regard to the corporate context of international marketing the key issues for management include the direction and behaviour of competitors on domestic and international markets, the needs and wants of customers, and how to gain sustainable competitive advantage in those markets in which the company decides to operate. For the firm in international markets the strategic thinking menu consists of carrying out an analysis of the industry or industries in which the firm competes, determining the best sources for components, raw materials and other resources, identifying and specifying the firm's competitive advantage, and analysing the strengths and weaknesses of competitors. The firm must then determine an appropriate competitive position in each of its markets, evaluate the strategic alternatives open to it, and specify a set of operational and concrete courses of action.

## Strategic marketing process

The strategic marketing process is a six-step procedure: specifying objectives; analysing opportunities; segmenting and targeting markets; deciding the marketing programme; implementing a profitable exchange; and controlling the programme.

There are a number of preconditions for successful marketing in the international firm, for which successful marketing means recognizing that marketing exchanges are characterized by the convergence of the company's marketing process and the customer's purchase decision process. In this context it is important to recall that a market is the total of the actual and potential buyers of a product, service, or idea, and that marketing is about understanding the behaviour of people and firms on the buying and selling sides of the equation. Also implied is the expectation that marketing deals with existing and potential products and services.

The firm must, therefore, be outward looking. It must attempt to understand its own strengths and limitations in a world of customers with different needs and wants and in a world of competition from other firms located in the domestic market and, increasingly, abroad. Firms must maintain an orientation which accounts for customer and competitor behaviour. A customer orientation means directly appealing to customers by offering a better match of products to customer needs.

A competitor orientation views customers as an ultimate prize gained at the expense of rivals. Sources of competitive advantage also include: strong distribution, preferential treatment by suppliers; and lower costs.

Pursuing competitive advantage in marketing means accepting five propositions. First, competition consists of the constant struggle of firms to develop, maintain or increase their competitive or differential advantage over other firms in the business. Second, competition for differential advantage is the primary force for innovation in marketing. Third, the foundations of competitive advantage are: market segmentation; selection of appeals; product improvement; process improvement; and product innovation. Fourth, over time competitors will attempt to neutralize the differential advantage of an entrant to the business or market and, finally, the existence of a differential advantage may give the firm a monopoly position within a market niche known as an "ecological niche." Some firms are very astute in exploiting technological leads in such specialized niches (Exhibit 1.2).

There is growing consensus among managers and academics that the

---

## Exhibit 1.2  Exploiting a technological lead

*UK and West German manufacturers of kitchen cabinets compared*

"The use of computers is very important in our plants. Orders go into the computer and production is organised in the most efficient way. Every day at 9 am we know how many units were sold the previous day and whether we have made a profit." Hans Grabs, Head, Work Planning, Wellmann Kuchen, Enger, West Germany.

> "The Germans tend to produce very small batches of kitchens and they need highly sophisticated computer machinery to enable them to do that. We mass produce and do not need computers because the machines are running all day." (Mike Runak, Production Director, Ram, H.I., Sowerby Bridge, West Yorkshire)

The National Institute of Economic and Social Research Study (November 1987) Report found that UK manufacturers were weak due to:

- Acute skills shortages exacerbated by superficial training programmes
- Restricted use of computers for production scheduling
- Inadequate and outdated equipment, frequent breakdowns.

Results of such weaknesses on the competitive position of UK firms were:

- Output per employee in West German plants is twice that in the UK in some processes
- Productivity in the West German furniture industry as a whole is 66% higher
- West German manufacturers export about 33% of their output; UK companies only 4%.
- Though profitable now, UK industry is threatened by developing countries able to exploit low cost labour and by West Germans who offer high quality at competitive prices.

Source: *Financial Times*, Friday, 20 November, 1987

---

marketing function: initiates; negotiates; and manages acceptable exchange relationships with key interest groups or constituencies in the pursuit of sustainable competitive advantage within specific markets on the basis of long-run consumer and channel franchises (Day and Wensley, 1983).

Marketing strategies may be developed for all stages of the value added chain. Understanding how best to apply marketing to the firm, irrespective of how many stages of the value added chain are included within the scope of the firm or where in the chain the firm operates is facilitated by understanding that firms have points of vulnerability and points of leverage (Figure 1.3).

While most successful international firms attempt to operate in the context of strategies developed for international markets, some will also successfully exploit opportunistic markets.

In working in opportunistic markets successful firms attempt to avoid

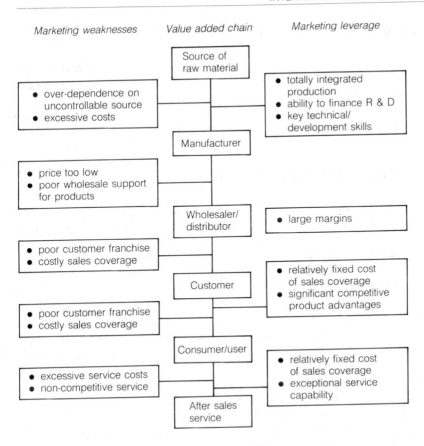

**Figure 1.3**   Points of marketing vulnerability and leverage in the value added chain

opportunistic cost traps, which usually involves providing customized capacity, high front end design and engineering costs to obtain the first order, the opportunity cost of unsuccessful bidding, and the opportunity cost of resources devoted to opportunistic business. Firms operating in such markets avoid opportunistic cost traps by setting conservative capacity levels for such business; separating core markets both organizationally and procedurally, and implementing tight screening processes throughout.

Summarizing, the meaning of strategy for the international firm refers to an integrated set of actions taking account of the firm's resources, aimed at increasing the long-term well-being of the firm through securing a sustainable advantage with respect to its competition in serving customer needs in domestic and international markets. The key words in this definition of strategy are: integrated; actions; sustainable; and competition. Within this approach to describing strategy, marketing mix strategy refers to the development of specific marketing mixes geared to the unique characteristics of selected target markets to achieve marketing objectives.

## Performance and growth of the firm

Ways of improving the marketing performance of the firm and growth in the firm over time are factors closely monitored by management. The more important dimensions of growth and the meaning of growth in the context of the firm in international markets are, therefore, key considerations for the profitable expansion of the firm in international markets.

### Improving marketing performance in the firm

The international firm has a number of choices available as it attempts to improve marketing performance. First it may adapt existing products or develop new products. Second, it may develop new markets. Third, it may decide on a combination strategy of new products for new markets. In examining these issues firms sometimes fail to recognize that they must make another set of decisions which are central to success in international marketing: decisions on the modes of entry to international markets. There are many ways of entering international markets but for our purposes it is sufficient to consider three broad sets of circumstances: those where licensing or joint ventures are appropriate; those where exporting is appropriate; and those where foreign direct investment, acquisitions or mergers are appropriate.

The mode of entry decision reflects the level of commitment and investment by the firm to international markets, as moving from licensing to foreign direct investment means a much greater investment in the market. The international firm may improve its marketing performance by considering options regarding product development, marketing development and the means of entering new markets (Figure 1.4).

The firm in international markets attempts to improve marketing performance through decisions on any of the above three dimensions, i.e. product, market, and mode of market entry. The firm may improve its performance by examining ways of achieving improved sales or improved profits or a combination of both. Four distinct ways of obtaining sales growth have been identified: market penetration; product development; market development; and forward integration in the market (Figure 1.5).

Market penetration would mean selling more products to existing customers. This may be difficult where the firm is already strong or where there are entrenched competitors with very large market shares. An aggressive strategy would be to take shares from competitors by attracting away their better customers. The nature of the industry may make it difficult for the firm to discourage competitors by raising the stakes. Big brand companies frequently raise the advertising stakes or use pre-emptive pricing and announcements of capacity additions to discourage competitors. In regard to new product development a firm might use its own people or consultants. Alternatively, it could license or joint venture from overseas where appropriate.

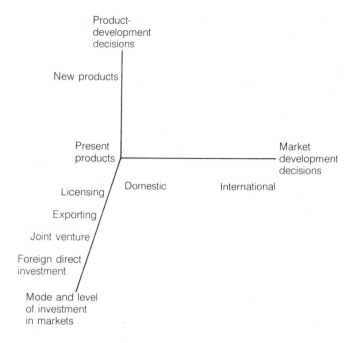

**Figure 1.4**  Product-market mode of entries decision for the international firm

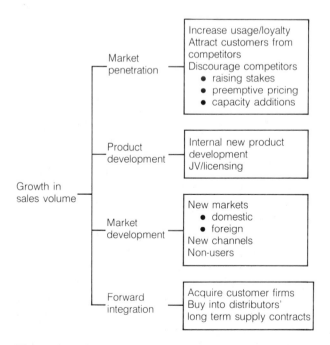

**Figure 1.5**  Improve marketing performance: sales growth

Market development strategies might mean identifying new segments not yet properly served in the domestic market, or segments in nearby or psychologically close markets. Forward integration would probably mean taking over distributors or retail outlets, which may or may not be feasible. Very often successful international firms start by selling through agents, subsequently taking an equity position in those agents and, later still, acquiring the agency and its customer base to give the firm a strong competitive presence in the market.

A firm could also decide to attempt to improve profitability which would mean increasing yield, reducing costs, integrating backwards, reducing investment intensity or focussing on key segments (Figure 1.6). Yield increases may come about through an improvement in the sales mix, e.g. pushing the high margin lines, increasing price or reducing margin. This last approach may not be possible for smaller, weaker firms in a highly competitive and fragmented market. Many firms would appear to have room for manoeuvre in regard to the mix of items they sell. At the other extreme the firm may decide to rationalize its product line and rationalize segments of the market served or distribution. Selective distribution in foreign markets, an option not often considered by the firm new to international markets, would seem well within the scope of possibility in this respect.

Clearly, any firm may pursue a number of the strategies outlined and it is important that those selected serve to promote the well-being of the company overall. In deciding the best way forward, the firm is constrained by the market, by growth in the market, and by its competitors.

## Meaning of growth for the international firm

The international firm has aims which it attempts to achieve independently of the state of the environment. These aims consist mainly of motives or a desire for prestige. The firm formulates aims in terms of those elements which satisfy the motives identified, e.g. a large share of the market or active participation in dynamic foreign markets will generally enhance prestige for most managers. Within the firm such aims are treated as objectives at managerial level but goals at firm level. The borderline between motives, objectives and goals is not always precise. These dominant motives have been identified in the western world as income, status and power, and it is with these three factors that success in western and western style countries is usually associated.

There is less agreement about the objectives and goals arising from the motives discussed. The salary—sales relationship has been well studied, showing in general that the main reason for pursuing a sales objective is its effect on status, power and security. The status derived from managing a very large, well-known company is almost certainly greater than that derived from high profitability, provided profits are reasonable. Power over resources, people, machines and finance is determined primarily by size, and the power that comes from market dominance increases with company size. A related factor, especially in circumstances of publicly quoted firms, is the fact that managers face an

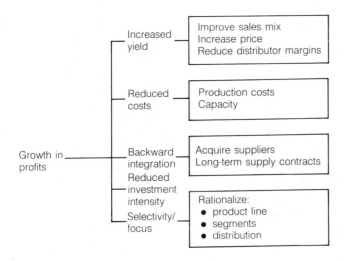

**Figure 1.6**   Improve marketing performance: profit growth

asymmetry in their rewards: very good performance makes very little difference, but poor performance results in criticism and even dismissal. This means that there is a tendency to increase size among publicly quoted firms because it tends to reduce the variability of the returns to the firm. An increase in size in such circumstances frequently means sales growth.

A desire for size naturally implies a desire for growth. But growth of the firm requires growth of available funds, capital, people, and demand, and the appropriate integration of these over time (Hay and Morris, 1985). Growth, even from a small base, may well be more attractive to the firm than large size with no growth. In a situation of no growth, new opportunities can be realized only at the expense of some entrenched position, and where this means the reduction in status or power it will be resisted strenuously. Growth permits new opportunities to be exploited without bringing negative forces into play. Frequently, existing operations become institutionalized to the point where new ventures can only occur against the background of company growth. Pressure for growth emanates naturally from the norms of professional competence among managers, which includes the drive for organizing (Marris, 1964, pp. 58–9). In a static business environment, therefore, by reducing the need to organize, the status of the executives in the firm is greatly reduced.

## Marketing objectives and firm growth

The emphasis on profit, size, growth and security does not imply that no other objectives exist. Other objectives are frequently found, e.g. market share, innovation, new product development and, more recently, cash flow. Companies and their managers sometimes cite as objectives the need to "stay ahead of the competition," the need "to be technically efficient," and the need "to be a good corporate citizen." In general these goals are frequently contained by broader objectives. For example, technical efficiency and share of market may be encompassed by profits, and in the way these are outlined above they are suspect because of the public relations aspects involved in providing acceptable answers to questions about objectives. Unless good working definitions can be established there is not much value in referring to many of the above as objectives. It is necessary to operationalize the concept in measurable terms.

In studying the growth of the firm it must be recognized that the firm can sometimes manipulate the competitive environment rather than act as a passive player whose performance depends on a number of environmental and structural characteristics of the market. It is thus necessary to identify the constraints which operate on the firm given that those such as consumer preferences, competition, costs and technology may be manipulated to some extent by the firm itself.

In examining growth in the firm we must also recognize that the predominance of large multiproduct firms suggests that there may not be any limit to the size of firms. Quoted firms must be concerned with performance not just in their product markets but also in capital markets. The possibility of take-over of such firms creates opportunities and constraints on their behaviour.

As the firm grows, over the long term it requires an increased amount of all inputs to match increases in demand for its products. Firms try to avoid both spare capacity and excess demand and to do so the manager spends a lot of time attempting to co-ordinate existing and future rates of growth in resources and demands. In the context of growth, good management will mean seeking a balance in the growth in resources and in the growth of demand to produce products and services desired by the market. We are concerned with longer-term growth even if in the short run the growth in resources and market growth is not balanced.

In order to be precise regarding the meaning of growth it is necessary to specify its meaning for both sides of the equation. The growth rate of productive resources may be measured by the rate of growth of the firm's asset base, by which is meant physical assets, i.e. fixed assets and inventories, net financial assets including cash, goodwill generated through marketing expenditures, and know-how arising from R & D expenditures.

On the market side the situation is not so clear. For any one product with a specified price, growth may be defined in terms of growth in demand in physical units. This approach cannot be used where firms decide on growth by diversification. In such circumstances growth may be measured as growth in sales revenue. Measures of growth in the market are reflected in growth in sales and growth in profits.

## Market resources and profit growth

As noted in a preceding section, one of the principal determinants of market and sales growth is the extent to which the firm is able to diversify into new products

and new markets. Many successful international firms are multiproduct organizations managing a portfolio of products for a variety of international markets. Any
new product introduction must contain an innovation as perceived from the
customer's viewpoint, and these customers are located in domestic and international markets. For successful innovations, sales of new products tend to rise
quite rapidly since the firm meets customer needs competitively. In such circumstances the firm is rewarded with a valuable share of the product market and
the successful introduction becomes a regular line within the firm. This is shown
on the vertical axis in Figure 1.4 above.

Alternatively, sales growth may be achieved through market diversification.
Such products follow the normal expected pattern of the life cycle framework
(Figure 1.7). Eventually market share and growth will tend to stabilize, primarily
because of imitation and greater competitive pressures. Afterwards, sales tend
to grow only as fast as the overall market. The life cycle framework shows such
sales growth as continuing but at a slower rate once market share has stabilized.

Alternatively, for products which do not contain any significant innovation
or are not perceived as innovative by customers, sales will initially rise as
customers try the product and as a result of promotional efforts at the launch
stage, but then fall off rapidly as potential customers become aware that the
product is not sufficiently competitive or attractive. Such products are failures
(Figure 1.7).

In order to grow faster than the rate of growth in the market as a whole
the firm must carry out further successful diversification. Sales growth is,
therefore, related to the role of successful diversification achieved by the firm,
whether this diversification is achieved through product or market diversification
as was seen above. Given the preceding argument this relationship obtains even
if the diversification results from objectives other than growth, e.g. the exploitation
of higher profits in new foreign markets and the need to diversify into new foreign
markets in order to provide more security against deterioration of business
conditions in the domestic market.

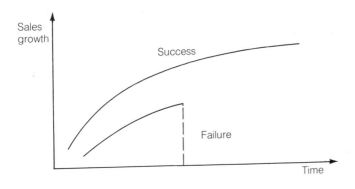

**Figure 1.7** Market growth and the life cycle

## Exhibit 1.3   Effect of adverse foreign exchange movements in international marketing

*Japanese managers alarmed in land of the rising yen*

Rapid appreciation of a currency tests the ability of companies to respond to pressure on margins, loss of market share, falling orders. For two decades, Japanese companies have dazzled the West with their ability to conquer foreign markets.

But now, with the yen soaring to dizzying heights, that strategy is backfiring. The 57 percent appreciation of the yen against the dollar in a little more than a year since September 1985 has erased Japan's labour cost advantage and made it extremely tough for Japanese companies to price competively.

Endaka, as the high yen is called, is clobbering many of the big blue chip companies. Endaka's bite has spurred Toshiba and scores of other companies to step up offshore production and procurement dramatically. Hardly a day passes without announcements of plans to expand existing manufacturing facilities or build new plants abroad.

Sony Corp will next year begin making 1 million compact discs monthly in Salzburg. In the United States, Sony will spend $30 million to expand output of colour TVs in San Diego. Sony aims to boost overseas manufacturing from 25 percent to 35 percent of sales in three years.

Canon Inc is shifting production of desktop calculators from Japan to Taiwan, will make office equipment in the United States from next spring, and will expand output in France.

Nissan will more than quadruple production of cars at its new plant in Britain to 100,000 units annually by 1991.

Toshiba is investing in a plain paper copier factory in France and VCR operations in West Germany, and will buy-in conventional TV sets from Korea and Taiwan.

**Source:** *International Management*, December 1986, pp. 58–66

The firm's management, concerned for its security and wishing to avoid the loss of its control, salary, status and power will settle for a lower profit retention rate. This lower rate reflects the risk adverse views of management, the shareholders' view of risk associated with the financial structure of the firm, and management's assessment of a potential take-over. Many internal and external factors such as changes in the economic and financial environment can adversely affect the performance of the firm. In such circumstances managers pay particular attention to adverse movements in foreign exchange markets and may respond with decisions affecting a number of areas of international marketing (Exhibit 1.3).

### The costs of company growth

The expansion of the firm is not, however, costless. We recognize that there are significant costs associated with successful diversification and these expansion costs reduce the firm's rate of return on capital. These factors are dominant in seeking growth through product or market diversification. First, larger expenditure on promotion generally results in a higher growth rate for a firm by making an increase in diversification more successful than otherwise. Second, greater expenditures on new product development would, by making products more appropriate and reliable, have a similar effect. Third, lowering price below that of other firms would normally also enhance growth by attracting more customers. These are costs of expansion and if they are regarded as capital costs then they result in a higher capital–output ratio. If they are regarded as current costs they result in a lower profit margin.

Fourth, there are limits to the organizational and decision-making capacity of managers. If managers attempt to carry out a high rate of diversification then fewer management resources can be devoted to each, which will result in the technical, financial, marketing and development aspects of each being less well researched or implemented so that the proportion of product-market failures may increase. When this occurs there will be excess capacity in the firm, thus raising the capital–output ratio. Recruiting new managers at a faster rate does not solve the problem since the additional managers lower the managerial efficiency of the firm. In such circumstances the rate of return on capital associated with faster diversification is lower.

## International market expansion process

There are various ways to internationalize: direct exporting; licensing; agency representation; and foreign sales subsidiaries. By slowly deepening its involvement in international markets the firm learns from its mistakes and successes so that it can control its continued growth through internationalization. Learning by exporting means that the firm becomes familiar with the demand conditions in the eventual host country: the selling methods; distribution system or mode of transfer of products and services. By agency representation, the firm learns how to do business with a host country organization. Agencies also allow the firm to cope with legal and cultural constraints.

In a sales subsidiary the firm learns how to control a foreign firm in the host country. It begins to co-ordinate its policies with the home firm and thereby obtains the experience of management at a distance. Only then does the internationalizing firm have to cope with the problem of organizing foreign production through foreign direct investment.

### International exchange of assets

All forms of international business involve the international exchange of assets and rights, either through the market mechanism or within an international firm. The transfer of assets between organizations requires the transfer of a property right. There are two kinds of asset which are regularly exchanged in international marketing: diffusable assets, the exclusive rights to which are difficult to control; and non-diffusable assets over which the firm can more easily exert its control. In the case of non-diffusable assets such as finished products or raw materials and components the property right transferred necessarily includes the right of access, i.e. the right to use the asset and the right of exclusion, i.e. the right to prevent others from using it except at the holder's discretion.

Where a diffusable asset is being exchanged the capacity to supply users is theoretically infinite and so the right of exclusion must be separately upheld. Information, production and marketing know-how are diffusable assets and legally enforceable rights of exclusion over them are known as patents.

Where the exchanged asset is easily identified and vested in exclusive and freely transferrable property rights, then market transfer through licensing may be appropriate. This is the case when the asset being exchanged is embodied knowledge in a patent, brand name, machine or separate process. When it is not embodied knowledge in a patent, it may be impossible to transfer the asset: difficulties tend to arise in agreeing the limits within which the asset can be used. In fragmented markets within uncertain and changing boundaries and, given uncertainty about the life of an asset, firms frequently restrict their attention to specific markets and time periods. Consequently, the licensing firm needs to be assured that the terms of the agreement will be adhered to. The enforcement of such agreements involves considerable policing costs.

Rights of ownership are frequently ill defined and difficult to enforce in international markets, and to publicize possession is often to invite imitation or replication or to encourage rival claims. In such circumstances possession is often maintained through secrecy. This gives rise to a serious problem for the firm — to sell the asset requires publicity, with the consequence that ownership may be lost. The problem is avoided by integrating forward into the use of the asset in the foreign market and so internalizing the market across national borders.

In many cases, the most efficient institution (the institution which minimizes transaction costs) for transferring production and marketing technology internationally is the international firm.

## Firm as co-ordinator of international markets

When the value of certain assets in one country is dependent on the actions of decision makers in another country, gains will be made by a co-ordination of the activities of the independent parties through which each accounts for the international effects of the actions taken. The more completely each decision maker within an interdependent group takes into account the effects of actions on others in the group the higher will be the combined wealth of all of the members, so long as the costs of co-ordination are less than the gains from more efficient allocation of resources. The international firm is one way in which the activities of interdependent parties in various countries can be co-ordinated; the price mechanism and contractual arrangements are other ways. "The international firm is an alternative means of attempting to maximize the joint wealth of interdependent parties in different countries." (McManus, 1972, p. 83).

The function of the firm is to co-ordinate the actions of resource owners. To examine its efficiency we must consider the costs of using markets or the price mechanism. The market costs or costs of transacting are the costs incurred by the parties to an exchange to enforce their exclusive rights to the assets or services being exchanged.

Because of transaction costs the market may be an expensive way to effect some forms of exchange or to constrain some form of interdependence. This is especially true for international markets. In such markets it is a consequence that potential partners to an exchange will seek means to reduce the costs involved in allocating services and assets through market exchange or in co-ordinating behaviour through the price mechanism (McManus, 1972, p. 76). Transaction costs reduce the effectiveness of price constraints on behaviour by creating opportunities for one partner at the expense of others.

## Dynamics of the international firm

Many international firms shift slowly to foreign direct investment after first establishing a sales branch abroad which in turn commonly precedes the establishment of a contractual relationship with a foreign sales agent (Nicholas, 1983). Agency contracts are frequently unsatisfactory, containing vague and difficult to enforce performance criteria. Attempts to support these by attempting to specify quantitative budgets for travelling, advertising, engineering and support, as well as certain inventory levels in the agent's premises, often prove unsatisfactory.

The transition from agency to branch sales office is facilitated by the manufacturer's gradual accumulation of information about the foreign market, acquired through monitoring its foreign agents and by expansion in sales volumes to levels which would support a facility of minimum economic size. The establishment of a sales branch also demonstrates to customers a more solid commitment on the part of the manufacturer to support the market in question.

Often triggered by the failure or termination of an agent, the establishment of a foreign sales subsidiary subsequently becomes the platform upon which a manufacturing investment may be made (Chandler, 1977, p. 369). Looking at the cost side of the equation the transition to manufacturing, however, depends upon the relationship of production costs abroad to production costs at home plus tariffs and transportation, as well as control considerations.

The foreign direct investment process is stimulated by more than just economic incentives. An initiating force, which galvanizes the firm into action is often required. The presence of a sales office also assists information collection and a better understanding of the market opportunities, thereby significantly lowering perceptions of uncertainty and raising the probability that the firm will engage in foreign direct investment if the underlying cost conditions permit.

---

**Exhibit 1.4  Firms have multiple and changing objectives for entering foreign markets**

---

*Why Philips sees Singapore as vital link in its worldwide network*

Philip's strategic decision to invest in Singapore in the late 1960s — and subsequently expand there — was based on the following objectives:

- To produce for Europe, and later also for North America and Asia's open markets.
- To source cheaper components.
- To gain valuable information and experience by meeting Far East competitors head on in their home markets.
- To assist affiliates in closed Asian markets.
- More recently, to be part of the trendsetting electronic industry in the Far East.

Philips initially was drawn to Singapore by its then relatively low wage levels, productive labor force, working hours, and efficient infrastructure. Other attractions included political stability, a responsible union movement, and the free flow of goods, people, and money. In the early 1980s, however, Philips grew increasingly concerned by what it perceived as an antimanufacturing bias among government officials. By 1985, the firm was on the brink of opting for other investment sites.

But now that the 1985–86 economic recession has fostered what Bonno Hylkema, Philip's Singapore Managing Director, terms a "return to reality," manufacturing is again getting due consideration as a key economic growth engine. This change in attitude is manifest in government efforts to restrain wage costs, cut employers' Central Provident Fund contributions, and lower corporate taxes.

These measures have enhanced Philips's competitiveness in export markets and restored its confidence in Singapore as an investment site. Yet, while acknowledging these improvements, Hylkema notes some drawbacks as well. The most obvious is, of course, the city-state's small domestic market and dependence on exports, which could become a liability in today's protectionist environment.

**Source:** *Business Asia*, 1 June, 1987, p. 171.

---

Clearly, transaction cost economics must be married to organizational and marketing decision theory if the dynamics of international markets are to be better understood.

Foreign direct investment stems from the possession by a firm of a competitive advantage or of certain unique assets. The ability to develop and protect the profits associated with these assets often requires the extension of some kind of control structure over productive assets which are distributed internationally. The implications of such control for the location of manufacturing facilities and the marketing of its output vary from time to time and may be unique to the firm in question (Exhibit 1.4).

Within this hierarchical structure, technology and other assets which are intangible and difficult to protect and exchange can often be used more economically and securely. The result is that when contracting problems arise, the existence of the international firm facilitates the technology and transfer process and enables the asset in question to work in combination with foreign factors of production, according to the dictates of cost minimization.

## Summary

This chapter examines the performance and growth of the firm as it diversifies into new international markets with particular emphasis on the role of competitive marketing strategies. In seeking to improve marketing performance the firm must consider its options with regard to the development of products and markets and modes of entry to new markets in order to improve sales and/or profits. In attempting to improve the growth in sales the firm can pursue one of, or a combination of, the following strategies: market penetration; product development; forward integration to increase profits or reduce costs.

Power over resources derives principally from size. Firms seek to grow to gain power and market dominance. It is important that the firm achieve a balance between growth in resources and growth in demand. An important determinant of market and sales growth is the firm's capacity to diversify into new products and markets. There are, however, four principal determinants to a firm's growth: market constraint; managerial constraint; financial constraint; and the objectives pursued by the firm. Growth in a firm is essentially the creation of an internal market where none previously existed. This internalization by means of backward or forward integration or joint ventures/licensing gives the firm greater control of the market for inputs and services and reduces uncertainty. Costs of this process, however, include higher communication expenses and the need for skilled management. Firms internalize to overcome competition and to exploit their competitive advantages in new markets. In order to succeed they must adopt multidimensional competitive strategies more suited to the complexities of the international marketing environment.

Innovative firms, having penetrated the domestic market, are keen to exploit their leads in foreign markets. Initially, this is done through exporting. As demand grows in foreign markets the firm may increase its commitment progressively by moving through the spectrum of foreign sales subsidiaries, joint ventures or direct investments. In order to survive, however, they must continue to innovate. Firms internationalizing through the use of a strong brand name must be aware that while brand names endure, the ability to command a premium erodes over time.

With regard to strategy, most international firms operate with customized international strategies. The key issue for the firm is the gaining and retention of competitive advantage in the markets in which it operates. The firm must focus its strategic marketing efforts internationally on achieving the greatest possible match between its marketing efforts and the customer's purchase decision process. To accomplish this it is necessary to focus closely on the customer and competitors.

## Discussion questions

1. The improvement of marketing performance in the international firm can be visualized in terms of product decisions, market investment decisions and market development decisions. Discuss.

2. Explain the importance of research and development and innovation as determining factors in the choice of international market entry mode.

3. The predominance of large multiproduct firms in international markets suggests that there may not be any limit to the size of the firm. Would you agree?

4. What are the principal factors to consider when examining the growth of the firm through internationalization? Refer to market inefficiencies in your answer.

5. Identify and describe the nature of assets transferred in international marketing. What are the key characteristics of these assets and how do they affect their mode of transfer between one country and another?

6. Many factors affect the environment facing the international firm. Identify and describe the more important of these. How does the international firm cope with its environment?

## References

Buckley, Peter (1987) *The Theory of the Multinational Firm*, Acta Universitatis Upsaliensis, 26, Uppsala.

Chandler, Alfred (1977) *The Visible Hand*, Harvard University Press, Cambridge, MA.

Day, George S. and Wensley, Robin (1983) 'Marketing theory with a strategic orientation,' *Journal of Marketing*, **47**, 79–89.

Grosse, Robert E. (1980) *Foreign Investment Codes and the Location of Direct Investment*, Praeger Publishers, NY.

Hay, Donald A. and Morris, Derek J. (1985) *Industrial Economics*, Oxford University Press, Oxford.

Hymer, Stephen (1970) 'The efficiency (contradictions) of multinational corporations,' *American Economic Review*, **60**, 441–8.

Killing, Peter J. (1982) 'Technology acquisition: license agreement or joint venture,' *Columbia Journal of World Business*, **15** (3), 38–46.

Marris, Robin (1964) *The Economic Theory of Managerial Capitalism*, The Free Press of Glencoe, NY.

McManus (1972) 'The theory of the international firm,' in Gilles Paquet (ed.) *The Multinational Firm and the Nation State*, Collier Macmillan Canada Ltd, pp. 66–93.

Nicholas, Steven, (1983) 'Agency contracts, institutional modes and the transition to foreign direct investment by British manufacturing multinationals before 1939,' *Journal of Economic History*, **43** (3), 675–86.

Teece, David (1986) 'Firm boundaries, technological innovation and strategic management,' in Lacy Glen Thomas III (ed.) *The Economics of Strategic Planning: Essays in honor of Joel Dean*, Lexington Books, MA, pp. 197–9.

Vernon, Raymond and Wells, Louis T. (1976) *Manager in the International Economy*, 3rd edn, Prentice Hall, Englewood Cliffs, NJ.

# 2 Theories of the firm in international markets

An analytical assessment of the international marketing literature shows that researchers are preoccupied with the description and conceptualization of international marketing problems. But because little endeavour is devoted to research which is more scientifically advanced, the literature continues to be descriptive, repetitive and non-analytical. Researchers have concentrated on descriptive studies of the interaction between participants in the system and the products and services transferred. Less attention is given to the international marketing environment and the transfer modes used. Little attention has been given to specifying the goals and objectives of the system.

This chapter attempts to integrate the considerable body of knowledge available to the international marketing scholar and manager. It also attempts to interpret the literature and our understanding of the discipline within a framework which allows both the researcher and the manager to systematically draw from and contribute to the body of knowledge that we refer to as international marketing.

## Recent interest in international marketing

Two sets of factors are thought to contribute to the recent interest in the discipline: the curriculum in business schools; and the contributions made in the field of strategy. As a consequence of the first, there are now many text-books with "international marketing" in the title, and many editors of established journals prepared to give more space to the subject. Indeed, interest has been so intense that journals devoted entirely to the subject have appeared.

### Theory and practice in international marketing

While welcoming the recent interest in international marketing, a number of authors have called for more critical work in the area and have identified the need to examine the firm's competitive position in world markets and the allocation of resources to these markets. Furthermore, the issue of critical mass and sequenced market development in international market expansion strategies and the mode of foreign market entry are key decision areas facing the international firm and yet are poorly addressed in the literature. Wind and Robertson (1983) have called for direction for the firm in making decisions regarding the most desired portfolio of countries, by mode of entry, by market segments, by products and by marketing programmes. International marketing is still a very broad, pluralistic, and not well integrated field of study.

Managers and firms have for a long time given explicit attention to the international marketing dimension of business and have recognized it as a separate field in regard to strategy formulation and the structural requirements resulting from internationalization. Academics have until recently ignored it as a field of study. A reason for the neglect according to Robock and Simmonds (1988) arises from the fact that earlier theories and generalizations, developed in response to the requirements of such large domestic oriented markets as that of the United States, were neither general nor universal. In contrast to purely domestic operations, marketing activities which take place across national boundaries require considerable familiarity with multiple marketing environments, international exchange rate determination and the various geo-political pressures which from time to time affect the firm. International marketing involves new elements of risk, conflict, environmental adjustments and the influences of socio-economic change. Few of these elements are covered in traditional economics and trade texts and they receive only minor treatment in traditional books on marketing and management.

## Impact of strategic thinking

Regarding the second set of factors alluded to above, the recent literature on strategy is of considerable importance (Chandler, 1977; Lawrence and Dyer, 1983; Porter, 1980). These authors have focussed interest on examining the position of the firm within its environment, its industry position, its technology, its marketing and competitive positions, and the role of government and public policy. These are dimensions which have a very powerful impact as the firm internationalizes.

Much of the literature on strategy has, however, ignored the marketing dimension. Because of the dependence by some scholars and managers on the simple matrix of some measure of firm advantage against a selected strategic customer group, Wind and Robertson (1983) argue that the outcomes ignore the fact that all markets are heterogeneous and thus a non-segmented strategy is inevitably sub-optimal. A strategy for international marketing which assumes a non-differentiated approach is prevalent in this literature (Bartels, 1968; Buzzell, 1968; Levitt, 1983). These authors have argued that markets are global and that marketing strategies should also be global and, therefore, standardized and non-differentiated.

The underlying issues associated with these different views of the world stem from very different and somewhat myopic perspectives on the origin of the work. While the recent thinking on strategy is very useful there is, nevertheless, a tendency to see problems as two-dimensional, whereas we believe them to be multidimensional. The "matrix models" have been weakest in predicting outcomes in complex, turbulent environments which characterize international marketing.

## Trade theories of the firm in international markets

In this section we examine a number of theories which attempt to explain international business patterns. These patterns include the worldwide flow of imports and exports, the pattern of joint ventures and licensing arrangements, and the location and direction of overseas investment.

### *Absolute advantage and the international firm*

This theory is used as a framework for understanding and predicting international business patterns where trade between independent buyers and sellers in different countries is the predominant form of inter-nation transactions. For economists, trade between countries arises because of the possession of an absolute or comparative advantage in the basis for trade. Absolute advantage as a basis for trade explains trade between two countries, the first with an absolute advantage in the production of one product, and the second in the production of a different product. Absolute advantage may arise because of differences in factors such as climate, quality of land, natural resource endowments, labour, capital, technology, or entrepreneurship. According to this theory it is sensible for each country to specialize in the product in which it has an absolute advantage and secure its needs of the products in which it has a disadvantage through foreign trade. The extent of benefit from specialization and trade will depend, of course, on the prices at which trading takes place. This brings in the concept of "opportunity cost," meaning what a country will have to give up of one product in order to secure another.

### *Comparative advantage and the international firm*

However, if a country possesses an absolute advantage in the two products traded, there may not be any trade since the country with the absolute advantage in producing both products has nothing to gain from trade. An alternative explanation may be sought in the possession of a *comparative* advantage. Under this theory, a country may have an absolute advantage in producing both products but so long as the weaker country has a comparative advantage in the production of one of the products, trade will occur.

**Table 2.1** Absolute and comparative advantage contrasted — hypothetical example

| Product group | Production per one hour labour | |
| --- | --- | --- |
| | Country A | Country B |
| | Bottles | |
| Wine | 20 | 16 |
| Soft drinks | 40 | 24 |

Consider two countries, Country A and Country B, with wine and soft drinks being the two products that these countries produce. The assumed output from one labour hour input for the two products in each country is shown in Table 2.1. Note that Country A has an absolute advantage in the production of both products, but comparative advantage lies predominantly in soft drinks. Country B has a comparative advantage in wine.

A company in Country A can only get 20 bottles of wine for 40 bottles of soft drinks at home. If the company brought the 40 bottles of soft drinks to Country B it could exchange them there for 27 bottles of wine (ratio of exchange in Country B is 1.5 bottles of soft drink = 1 wine (40/1.5 = 27). The company would then take the 27 bottles of wine back to Country A and realize a profit equal to 7 bottles of wine.

If the Country B firm ships wine to Country A it would receive 32 soft drinks for it (40/20 = 2; 2 × 16 = 32) (compared to 24 at home). On return, the firm's profit would amount to 8 bottles of soft drinks. Both countries benefit, even though Country A can produce both products more efficiently.

## Exchange rates and trade theory

It is necessary to introduce exchange rates to show that *real* cost differences in comparative advantage actually translate into monetary price differences (as was the basis for our simple trade model above). Assume that wage rates in Country B are 5 Marks per hour and $10 per hour in Country A. Then, using the information in Figure 2.1 it is possible to derive the cost of producing wine and soft drinks in both countries (Table 2.2).

Note again that the relative prices of the two products differ between countries. But what about absolute prices? To see the effect of absolute prices we must introduce exchange rates. Assume that the $ exchanges for the Mark at the exchange rate of $1 = 1.50 Marks or 1 Mark = $0.67. At the start of trade Country A soft drinks exporters would realize about $0.32 (0.21 Marks × 1.50 = $0.32) from every bottle of soft drinks exported to Country B at a profit of $0.07 per bottle. Country B wine exporters would receive 0.33 Marks ($0.50/1.50 = 0.33 Marks), thereby realizing a profit of 0.02 Marks per bottle. At that

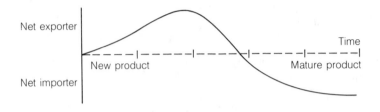

| Phase I | Phase II | Phase III | Phase IV | Phase IV |
|---|---|---|---|---|
| All production in United States | Production started in Europe | Europe exports to DCs | Europe exports to United States | DCs export to United States |
| US exports to many countries | US exports mostly to DCs* | US exports to DCs displaced | | |

*DCs = developing countries.

**Figure 2.1** The product life cycle framework applied to international markets: a US perspective (Source: Vernon, Raymond and Wells, Louis T. (1976) *Manager in the International Economy*, 3rd edn, Prentice Hall, Englewood Cliffs, NJ)

**Table 2.2** Cost of production: wine and soft drinks compared — hypothetical example

| | Cost per bottle | |
|---|---|---|
| | Country A | Country B |
| | $ | Marks |
| Wine | 0.50 | 0.31 |
| Soft drinks | 0.25 | 0.21 |

exchange rate trade would occur just as shown under the barter situation above. Trade will continue until prices are equalized.

Suppose Mark/$ = $1.15, i.e. a considerable hardening of the Mark or depreciation of the $; then at the start of trade Country A soft drink exporters would realize about $0.24 from every bottle exported (0.21 Marks × 1.15 = $0.24) — a loss of $0.01 per bottle. But the Country B exporter makes a relatively large profit — receiving 0.43 Marks per bottle of wine exported ($0.50/1.15 = 0.43 Marks) and realizes a profit equal to 0.43 Marks − 0.31 Marks = 0.12 Marks. There is unlikely to be any two-way trade for $ exchange rates greater than 1.61 Marks or less than 1.19 Marks. The lower limit break-even exchange rate is $1 = $1.19 Marks (i.e. $0.21 × 1.19 = $0.25 = domestic price).

If trade is limited to wine and soft drinks then the $ value of Country A's soft drink exports *must* equal the $ value of Country A's imports and similarly for Country B in Marks. This can only occur at exchange rates *between* the limits $1.00 = 1.19 Marks and $1.00 = 1.61 Marks, rates at which traders in both countries find it profitable to do business.

The comparative advantage concept, especially with exchange rates incorporated, is the less restrictive and more general. It also serves the useful purpose of demonstrating the importance of exchange rate movements on the marketing strategies of the firm in international markets. An adverse movement in exchange rates could easily wipe out the benefits of an otherwise excellent international marketing programme.

## Limitations of trade theory

There are a number of limitations in the trade theory interpretation of the firm in international markets. They flow in part from the simplifying assumptions of the model. Some key assumptions are that factors of production, land, labour and capital are immobile between countries, that perfect information exists as to international trade opportunities, and that trading firms in different countries are independent entities. Also the model assumes perfect competition and does not allow for oligopoly or monopoly. Nor does it explicitly recognize technology, know-how or management and marketing skills as significant factors of production which can be the basis for comparative advantage. Probably the most important limitation of trade theory is that it assumes that traditional importing and exporting is the only way of transferring products and services across borders. Nor does it recognize that the firm may supply foreign demand through, for example, licensing or foreign production.

It also misses the rationale behind the twentieth century development of marketing by assuming that products sold in the international marketplace are standard, basic and transferable — wheat, cotton and wine, for example.

Efforts are under way, however, by trade theorists to reconstruct international trade theory in order to allow for the implications of the firm in international markets. The emphasis of the reconstruction efforts is more on ways of making traditional theory relevant than on developing a theoretical framework for explaining the behaviour of the international firm.

## Foreign direct investment theories

While some theorists have been working to extend trade theory to include foreign direct investment, others have been making important contributions under the rubric of theories of foreign direct investment or theories of the multinational enterprise.

In classical economic theory, the issue of geographical horizons for the business enterprise does not arise. The firm is assumed to have perfect and costless knowledge of, and be prepared to take advantage of, attractive opportunities wherever they exist. The firm is usually born with a geographical horizon limited to a locality, a region, or a home country. However, as part of the growth process of the firm, geographical horizons change. The change may be a result of internal forces such as the influence of a senior executive, the development of a new technology or product, observed need for a larger market and so on, or it may be the result of external forces such as customers, governments, the foreign expansion of a competitor, or a dramatic event such as the formation or enlargement of a trade bloc such as the EC or the opening of new markets such as those of Eastern Europe. These factors explain the awareness of business opportunities. Other factors are needed to explain how the firm responds to perceived opportunities.

## International firm and market imperfections

This approach assumes that the firm has a complete global horizon, that is, it is constantly aware of foreign opportunities. The firm's decision to invest abroad is explained as a move to take advantage of certain capabilities not shared by competitors in foreign countries (Hymer, 1970).

To operate successfully abroad, the firm must have certain compensating advantages that more than offset the innate advantages of local firms. These innate advantages include an intimate knowlege of the local economic, social, legal, and public policy environment, the avoidance of foreign exchange risks, and the risks of possible misunderstandings and errors from cross-cultural operations. The compensating competitive advantages of foreign firms are explained by imperfections in markets for products or factors of production. In the theoretical world of perfect competition, firms produce homogeneous products and have equal access to all productive factors.

In the more realistic world of imperfect competition, as explained by industrial organization theory, firms acquire competitive advantages through product differentiation, brand names, special marketing skills, economies of scale, and other factors which accord them a competitive advantage.

The market imperfections approach attempts to explain both horizontal and vertical investments. The objectives of horizontal investments in international markets are to produce in foreign locations the same products manufactured in the home market. Vertical investments are supply oriented, intended to produce abroad raw materials or other production inputs which are then supplied to the firm at home or to other subsidiaries. The foreign firm may have privileged access to raw materials or minerals because of firm specific advantages such as an established marketing system, managerial capacity, control over transportation, or access to capital.

The market imperfections framework helps to identify the industries in which firms are likely to expand their direct operations, either domestically or internationally. The framework assumes that the firm is constantly aware of foreign opportunities. The market imperfections approach to understanding the behaviour of the international firm fails, however, to explain why foreign production is the preferred means of exploiting the firm's advantage. This advantage could also be exploited through exporting or licensing.

## Internationalization approach

This aspect of investment theory is concerned with the firm's incentive to create its own internal markets whenever transactions can be carried out at a lower cost within the firm. This internalization involves extending the direct operations of the firm and bringing under common ownership and control the activities carried out by intermediate markets which link the firm to customers. There are a number of aspects of this approach: the introduction of markets within the firm; the location of production internationally; and the movement of resources, which relates to trade theory.

The creation of an internal market permits the firm to transform an intangible piece of research or understanding of the market into a valuable property specific to the firm. The firm can exploit its advantage in all available markets and still keep the use of the information internal to the firm in order to recoup its initial expenditures on research and knowledge generation.

The internationalization approach goes a long way towards synthesizing the various explanations of the motives for foreign direct investment. The theory focusses on the motives and decision processes within the firm but gives only such limited attention to the potential of public policies and other external factors as they can affect the benefits and costs of internationalization.

## International production theory

The various foreign direct investment theories help to explain which firms go international — those with a competitive advantage and the motivation for engaging in foreign production. They do not explore to any extent the pattern of location for exploiting these advantages. The theory of international production addresses the issue of where foreign production takes place by integrating location theory into theories of the multinational enterprise. An example of such a theory is the "eclectic theory of international production" (Dunning and McQueen, 1981), which argues that the propensity of a particular enterprise to engage in foreign production will also depend on the locational attractions of its home country's endowments compared with those offered by other countries including financial and other inducements to locate there. Fayerweather (1982) expands the concept of resources embodied in trade theory to include technological, managerial, and entrepreneurial skills, as well as natural resources, capital, and labour. He then argues that differentials in the supply—demand relationship of resources among countries generate basic economic pressures for the international flow of resources and create opportunities open to the multinational firm. In sum, three groups of factors: resource differentials; governmental actions; and characteristics of the business enterprise determine the way in which the international firm plays a role in the international exchange of resources. This aspect of direct investment theory assigns a major role to governments in influencing international business patterns through actions that affect resource differential relationships and the entry conditions for foreign enterprise.

These aspects of international investment theory are general enough that they can incorporate most dimensions of international management. They do not, however, address the process by which essentially domestic firms acquire their global horizons. Furthermore, they appear to be predominantly concerned with manufacturing activities and the role of markets in motivating international expansion.

## Product cycles in international markets

The product cycle model relates trade and direct investment as sequential stages that follow the life cycle of a product. The model suggests that firms innovate new products at home for the home market. Such a product life cycle approach was discussed by Vernon and Wells (1976), who offered an explanation of trade patterns in US manufactured products. These authors believe that, from a US point of view, the United States is more likely than other countries to initiate the production of certain types of items — those that appeal to high-income consumers or those that are labour saving. The effect on the US trade of the eventual movement of efficient production facilities from the United States to less developed countries is shown in Figure 2.1. Initially, manufacture will take place in another advanced country such as the United Kingdom or Germany because, initially, the US entrepreneur is under little pressure to reduce costs by using cheaper foreign labour. Also, the innovator decides to manufacture close to the market at the early stage of a product's life so that market information can quickly and easily be translated into rapid product changes. For a period, US producers are likely to have a virtual monopoly in the manufacture of new products which are introduced there. Some foreigners demand the new products and US exports begin.

As foreign incomes grow, as lower income consumers abroad begin to buy the older product, and as prices begin to fall, US exports increase. However, at some point, a market abroad is large enough for manufacturing to begin there. Either a local entrepreneur sees that he can undersell imports if he manufactures locally, or a US firm invests to preclude a local firm taking the market that the United States has been supplying by exporting. At this stage, US exports to that market cease to grow as rapidly as before; they may even decline. However, US exports continue to go to markets where production has not yet begun.

In the third phase of the cycle, US exports to non-producing countries begin to be displaced by exports from other nations. In the fourth phase, foreign production in some countries reaches a sufficient scale that costs are low enough to overcome the transportation and tariff protection which the US manufacturer possesses. The United States becomes a net importer of the product. A further stage has been hypothesized in which the less developed countries become exporters of the mature product.

In summary, according to the life cycle hypothesis managers initially pay attention to the following characteristics:

1. Maintaining effective communication among the key development engineers,

production specialists, sales people and prospective customers. If the product passes the development stage, the first units will be produced where developed.

2. Even if managers could choose locations, they would have difficulty in determining the least cost production and distribution points. Managers also cater to markets whose ultimate size and geographical boundaries cannot easily be determined in advance.

3. No real pressure to reduce costs exists because of the innovative nature of the product and customers. The product is not price elastic. At a later stage costs do become a consideration:

4. As the product matures it begins to assume characteristics that permit easier comparison from one manufacturer to the next.

5. As the product matures, the special knowledge and skills of the original producers are shared with others at home and abroad. With the dissipation of proprietary product knowledge the threat of price competition becomes very tangible.

6. As demand for the product grows, late users are more price elastic. Furthermore, differences in the prices between brands (cross-price elasticities) generally matter more with later customers.

7. As demand grows and volume of sales in some foreign markets increases, the possibility of producing from a location in the host country grows. A formal analysis to determine least-cost production points is more likely to suggest foreign production sites than it would in earlier stages. The timing depends on (a) scale economies in production and (b) transportation costs.

8. As the product matures, import restrictions and formal requests to establish abroad usually arise, thus forcing the hand of the international firm.

The product life cycle model provides a useful framework for explaining the early post World War II foreign manufacturing investment by US companies. But its explanatory power has waned with changes in the international environment, especially the rise of Japanese competition and innovation. Vernon (1979) has recognized these limitations, noting that many international companies have developed global networks of subsidiaries and a global scanning capability. Furthermore, the US market is recognized as being no longer unique among national markets either in size or factor cost configuration. Also, initial production does not necessarily occur in the market which inspired the innovation. Production may be located wherever costs and other factors are advantageous. The life cycle framework does not address the strategy issue of why multinational firms undertake investment abroad instead of, say, licensing. Nor does it seem to explain supply-oriented raw materials foreign direct investments.

## *Limitations of foreign direct investment*

Most of the above explanations are partial in that they focus on only one method by which international business patterns change. They may throw light on either trade movements or direct investment but not on both as inter-related activities. Nor do they indicate when firms might collaborate through joint ventures, licensing or other forms of competitive alliance to enter and grow in international markets. Foreign direct investment theories also have a limited view of the international strategies that may be adopted by the firm and most theories are one way; they offer explanations of investment and not of divestment, which is also an important and growing feature of the firm in international markets.

We saw previously that trade theories concentrate on explaining the movement of undifferentiated commodities under conditions of comparative advantage in a simple exporting framework. In international direct investment we observe behaviour at the other end of the continuum, where the firm is involved in direct investment. Options in between are ignored by these approaches, which are very restrictive. For the wider objective of explaining overall international marketing patterns the underlying framework of these theories must be broadened to include all forms of exchange performed by the firm in international markets.

## Transactions costs in international markets

Since Hymer (1970), the internalization school has emerged which emphasizes the benefits and costs associated with internalizing business activity (Buckley and Casson, 1976; Rugman, 1981). The principal conclusion of this school is that

> markets will tend to be relatively more efficient than firms in handling transactions between a large number of buyers and sellers. Markets will be at a comparative disadvantage when transactions are subject to a high degree of uncertainty and when they consist of long-term exchanges of complex and heterogeneous products between a relatively small number of traders. (Buckley and Casson, 1976, pp. 167–8)

In order to provide unambiguous normative criteria useful to management and policy makers, the nature of the transactions which are being internalized must be examined. The unit of analysis is the transaction rather than the firm (Williamson, 1979, 1981). A major assumption of this approach is that the purpose of business is to reduce the costs of doing business over time. It regards firms, markets and mixed modes as alternative control mechanisms. The selection of one or another mode of market depends on their efficiency properties.

The most important attribute for assessing whether a transaction requires a special control mechanism other than unassisted markets is the degree to which the parties to the exchange must invest in assets dedicated to the proposed exchange of products and services (Williamson, 1979). If dedicated assets are required, then the parties to an exchange will become locked in once the assets are used. With transaction specific assets there is the strong possibility that in the absence of safeguards, one or both parties will try to take advantage of the fact that the other can no longer get out of the arrangement except at great cost

(Williamson, 1981; Monteverde and Teece, 1982). To avoid such situations, some form of control mechanism is required: "The parties have an incentive to develop control mechanisms that help prevent opportunistic behaviour and infuse confidence." (Williamson, 1984, p. 1203)

The internal controlling mechanism provided within the firm is one such possibility. The transaction is taken out of the market and the specialized control mechanism of the firm can be used to protect it and ensure that the full benefit of the specialized asset in question accrues to the firm. But internalizing the transaction substantially changes the incentives of the parties since, from the perspective of the firm's worldwide profits, there is nothing to gain and possibly something to lose by having a foreign subsidiary gain or lose at the expense of the domestic firm. The point is, however, that transactions cost economics provides a framework for discriminating between those transactions which need to be internalized and those which do not (Teece, 1986).

Practically every firm, by virtue of its history, possesses some kind of unique asset which is the potential source of a stream of profits to the owner. These assets may consist of a technological, marketing, managerial capability or a natural resource position not fully possessed by other firms.

## Role of transaction costs

Suppose that for any reason a firm cannot export, then it must sell its special assets or services — licensing in the case of know-how — to a foreign firm or it must establish a foreign affiliate.

Suppose the source of the firm's competitive advantage is its technological know-how. If the regime of appropriability in which the firm operates permits only weak legal enforcement of rights over intellectual property, transactional problems will abound, and alternative control modes are likely to be preferred. (Teece, 1981). Know-how often cannot be codified since it has an important tacit component. Even when it can, it is not always readily understood by the receiver. Such know-how is tacit and is extremely difficult to transfer without intimate personal contact involving teaching, demonstration and participation. Even when transaction difficulties are apparent, establishing a foreign subsidiary is an extreme response to the needs of a one-off transfer.

The above arrangements, though expressed in the context of assets which are based on technological know-how extend to many different kinds of asset which are difficult to trade, e.g. managerial and organizational know-how, goodwill, or brand loyalty. These represent types of assets for which markets may falter as effective exchange mechanisms. Accordingly, the existence of high transaction costs is one of the major issues which lies behind foreign direct investment, especially horizontal investment.

Various attempts have also been made to examine the role of specialized managerial know-how as a driving force behind the international expansion of US firms. Pugel (1978) and Swedenborg (1979) have shown that the influence of managerial skill levels is statistically significant. So far the empirical tests have failed to disaggregate down to the level of the individual transaction; so support for transaction costs considerations is only indirect. There is good evidence for internalization in low-technology businesses also, especially where quality control is important for success, e.g. hotels (Dunning and McQueen, 1981).

## International marketing theories

Marketing in the late 1980s and early 1990s has taken on a strong strategic orientation reflected in a shift in the firm's focus away from the customer and the product to the external environment facing the firm. It has been argued that to succeed, the firm must cater for its customers within the context of its environment (Hayes and Abernathy, 1980; Simon, 1984; Wind and Robertson, 1983). This environmental emphasis is important in the development of an incentive for business to cross national boundaries.

### Product-specific variables

These variables are concerned with the competitive advantages possessed by the foreign firm. They include product development, product differentiation, production processes, managerial skills, economies of large-scale production and other characteristics of the product, the firm, or the industry. It should be remembered that these variables are also found in purely domestic markets.

International marketing is a discipline which contains a number of paradigms which draw upon a number of theories. Theories in international marketing are operationalized through the decisions taken by managers in dealing with the international environment. The issue of identifying suitable paradigms is important since a paradigm indicates what a discipline should study, what questions it should ask and what rules should be followed in interpreting the answers obtained (Cateora, 1990).

Consequently, we may deduce, by extending Carman (1980), that an international marketing paradigm would serve as the basis for theory formulation by suggesting units of analysis, constraints and similar necessary elements to form the basis of a calculus of theory in the discipline. The task is, therefore, to determine which paradigms will lead to useful theories.

### Definitions in international marketing

Many writers have offered different suggestions as to what the discipline of international marketing should study. Cateora (1990) defines international marketing as the performance of business activities that direct the flow of a company's goods and services to consumers or users in more than one nation. For Cateora it is the complexity and diversity found in international marketing operations which distinguishes the discipline. Terpstra (1983) also stresses the complexity of international marketing. Keegan (1984) distinguishes between domestic and global marketing and states that the differences between the two derive entirely from differences in national environments, company organization and strategies in different national markets. For Kahler and Kramer (1977) international marketing is broader and consists of exporting or producing and marketing in more than one country without the goods crossing national borders. This definition begins to recognize the key role of the firm in international marketing.

Fayerweather (1982) recognizes the dominant factor in the international marketing process as the firm: the firm must be significantly involved in international business having permanent operations in two or more countries. This broad definition refers to marketing associated with business processes intersected in some way by national borders. The business processes identified by Fayerweather are: (a) economic transactions; (b) cultural and socio-psychological interactions; and (c) political interactions. An important aspect of Fayerweather's view is that the concept "national borders" should be interpreted flexibly to include the multidimensional nature of inter-nation contact as implied in the three business processes.

This brief review of some of the definitions of international marketing suggest that the discipline is a broad one encompassing many aspects of management. Indeed, for many scholars of international marketing the discipline is perceived so broadly that they do not attempt a definition, claiming by implication that the discipline defies definition. This is poor guidance to scholar and manager alike. As an alternative working definition the following is offered:

> International marketing processes and decisions require the firm to identify needs and wants of customers, to produce assets to give a differential marketing advantage, to communicate information about these assets and to distribute and exchange them internationally through one or a combination of exchange transaction modalities.

The correspondence between this definition of international marketing processes and decisions and well-known definitions of marketing is intended (Ohio State University Marketing Staff, 1965; Sweeney, 1972). Following Carman (1980) the study of these processes is called the discipline of international marketing which contains a number of paradigms, each paradigm drawing on a number of theories. Clearly, therefore, international marketing is not a single theory but, rather, a discipline containing a number of theories which when applied become the operating technologies of practitioners engaged in the international marketing process (Carman, 1980).

## Search for an international marketing paradigm

Two important paradigms in current use in the international marketing literature are the geobusiness and interaction paradigms. The first paradigm is most closely

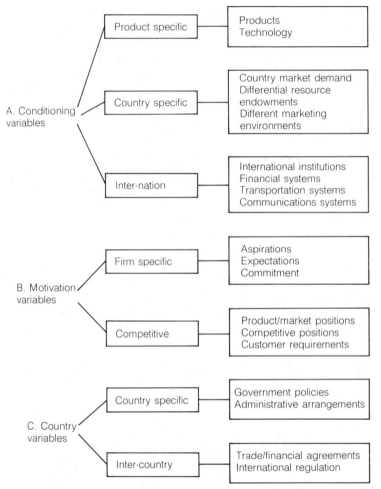

**Figure 2.2**   Constructs of the geobusiness paradigm (Source: Adapted from Robock, Stefan H. and Simmonds, H. (1988) *International Business and Multinational Enterprises*, 4th edn, Irwin, Homewood, Ill.)

associated with research initiated at Uppsala University and the Stockholm School of Economics in particular, but is developed and added to by others with widespread affiliation. These researchers recognize that the individual firm is "the motive force and that international business patterns are shaped by the adjustments of specific enterprises, operating competitively over a range of national environments to survive and grow." (Robock and Simmonds, 1988, p. 50) These authors propose the geobusiness model which suggests a paradigm based on a set of conditioning and motivation variables. The extended version of this paradigm accommodates much of the literature alluded to in Figure 2.2.

## The geobusiness paradigm

Because they are also interested in how the overall system is governed, Robock and Simmonds include as constructs a set of control variables, some of which are country specific. Central to the work of many of the writers working within the geobusiness paradigm is the role of key conditioning and motivation variables in the growth of the firm through stages of internationalization (Bilkey, 1978; Bilkey and Tesar, 1977; Cavusgil and Nevin, 1981a; Johanson and Vahlne, 1977; Reid, 1981; Wiedersheim-Paul, Olson and Welch, 1978). The kinds of issues examined at length by these authors include items which are country specific such as differences in the economic, technological, cultural, and political environments. Motivation variables examined are those which are firm specific and classified as internal determinants of the firm's internationalization behaviour. Other variables, such as the firm's competitive position in the international arena, are classified as external determinants of internationalization.

## The interaction paradigm

The second paradigm focusses on the interaction which occurs when two firms engage in an exchange transaction. The origins of this paradigm, most closely associated with the International Marketing and Purchasing Group, is based on two schools of thought: (a) interorganizational theory (Reve and Stern, 1979; Sweeney, 1972; Van de Ven, Emmitt and Koenig, 1975); and (b) markets as hierarchies (Teece, 1983; Williamson, 1975). The interaction paradigm is based on three major assumptions: (a) that buyers and sellers are active participants; (b) that the relationship between buyer and seller is frequently long-term and complex; and (c) that the links between buyer and seller often become institutionalized (Hakansson, 1982). Four sets of constructs underlie the interaction paradigm (Figure 2.3).

The key roles accorded to the firm and the manager are evident in the interaction paradigm. The strengths, weaknesses and motivations of firms and managers play a central role. Similarly, the exchange transaction process itself is also seen as a key dimension. Noteworthy is the fact that the paradigm includes the examination of myriad exchange transactions and not just those associated with products and services.

The environment is also examined and explicit treatment is given to a number of constructs which directly relate the firm to its international markets: the structure of markets; the changes occurring in these markets; and the extent to which they are internationalized. The interface between the firm and other firms in the manufacturing and distribution channel is treated in the context of a hierarchical marketing structure within a socio-political environment.

The interaction paradigm views marketing operations as taking place in the

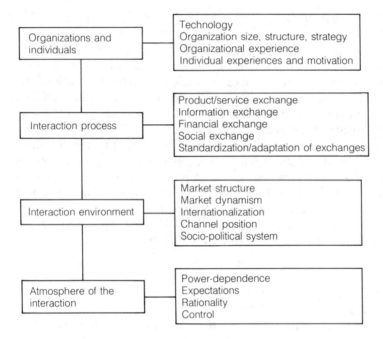

**Figure 2.3**   Constructs of the interaction paradigm

context of a power dependence relationship where firms have varying expectations regarding outcomes. When environmental uncertainty, which typifies international markets, is coupled with market failure accompanying the international transfer of high technology or knowledge-based assets, then the transfer modality might best be controlled through a firm with a decentralized, non-formal and specialized structure (Ruekert, Walker and Roering, 1985). The context of the exchange is conditioned, therefore, by the atmosphere surrounding the transaction according to the interaction paradigm.

## Markets and networks

By observing that the industrial system in society comprises firms engaged in production, distribution, and consumption, Swedish researchers concluded that the interaction which arises among firms in the system can be examined as a network of relationships (Johanson and Mattsson, 1986, pp. 242–3). Firms are seen as dependent on each other in the system, and their activities are co-ordinated through interaction between firms in the network. Each firm in the network has relationships with customers, distributors and suppliers.

Transactions between firms take place within a framework of established relationships. According to this view marketing activities in networks serve to establish, maintain, develop, and sever relationships with the objectives of determining exchange conditions and expediting the exchange itself. In the markets as networks paradigm, the international firm establishes and develops positions in its network relative to counterpart firms in foreign networks. Internationalization of the firm according to this view means integrating networks across national boundaries. Markets as networks paradigm continue to be developed by researchers at the Stockholm School of Economics, the University of Uppsala and others in the Industrial Marketing and Purchasing Group.

## Systems exchange paradigm

There is some overlap between the interaction paradigm, the markets as networks paradigm, and the geobusiness paradigm. Central to the three paradigms is the firm, the role of the manager, and products and services. The interaction and markets as networks paradigms specifically examine the exchange process in the context of the marketing environment facing the firm and give explicit treatment to the conditions surrounding the exchange. In contrast, the geobusiness paradigm acknowledges the important role of government and public policy in international marketing and especially the roles played by international institutions including financial, transportation and communications networks.

Many features of these paradigms are captured in the systems-exchange paradigm (Carman, 1980). By modifying and extending the systems-exchange paradigm it is possible to incorporate the geobusiness and interaction paradigms while also addressing issues neglected by both.

A justification for using the systems-exchange paradigm arises from its foundation in the general systems paradigm which focusses on inter-relationships between institutions in a system which is "a set of regularly interacting groups co-ordinated in such a way as to form a unified whole and organized so as to accomplish a set of goals." (Carman, 1980, p. 4) These constructs are captured as the first heading in Figure 2.4. Three other sets of constructs comprise the systems-exchange paradigm: (a) environmental constraints; (b) participants in the system; and (c) the assets exchanged and transfer modality used. In international marketing we limit the types of systems and exchanges studied to those involving individuals, households, firms and governments.

Goals in the system in which the international firm operates are usually multiple and conflicting. In pursuing one goal other goals are sacrificed, or achievement of them is diminished either because means are too scarce to achieve all goals or because achievement of all goals is logically inconsistent.

Opportunistic behaviour as a motivating principle by a firm new to international markets may lead to short-term profits but prevent the correct response for longer-term profits to ensure the development and growth of the firm. In this respect the orientation of senior management and culture are thought to be of paramount importance (Bradley, 1984). Nor is any set of goals pursued single-mindedly; there are always constraints. Foreign market entry and expansion

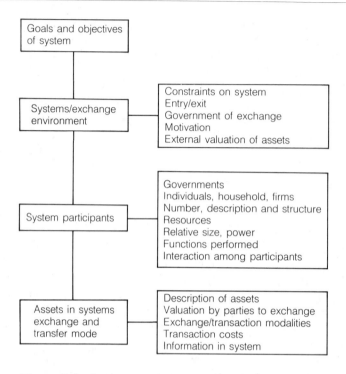

**Figure 2.4** Constructs of a systems-exchange paradigm applied to the firm in international markets (Source: Adapted from Carman, James M. (1980) 'Paradigms for marketing theory', *Review in Marketing*, **3**, 1–36)

are highly resource dependent and are affected by legal codes. Many firms have only limited options as they attempt to enter foreign markets or expand from existing markets. At times the goals of firms in the system may be too narrow, thereby concentrating on optimizing some sub-system, e.g. export sales, which if achieved may be detrimental to the interests of the total system. Finally, the goals of a system are usually shifting as environmental circumstances change.

Firms change products, markets, and modalities of entry as the marketing environment demands. Changing the focus of marketing from a domestic to an international orientation also requires a full recognition of the interdependence between marketing and other management disciplines, e.g. finance, manufacturing, and human resources management, to name the more obvious.

## Framework for understanding the international marketing process

A critical view of the nature and significance of international marketing up to 1973 has been provided by Schollhammer (1973) who, though dealing with international business and comparative management research, divided research studies into empirical work and theoretical–abstract work.

Schollhammer concluded that the theoretical–abstract frameworks which he found did not provide the focal point for extensive empirical research and they had not been used as frameworks for integrating or synthesizing the multitude of empirical research findings then extant. His second major finding was that much international management research was merely descriptive and lacked analytical rigour. Third, he found that empirical research frequently suffered from substantial methodological deficiencies. His fourth major finding was that researchers were reluctant to direct their investigations to the task of establishing empirically verifiable generalizations and to develop a body of knowledge from which predictions could be derived. Almost a decade later reviewers concluded that while international marketing was well on its way to becoming a respected sub-discipline there were still a number of criticisms to be made: (a) the absence of conceptual and theoretical frameworks to guide research; (b) lack of interest among researchers in the findings of previous studies; and (c) confirmation that Schollhammer's conclusions on the methodological weakness of much of the research still obtained (Cavusgil and Nevin, 1981b).

For international marketing scholars and managers, the interesting question is to determine how much has changed since the two literature reviews cited were completed. The extended systems-exchange paradigm suggests *what* should be studied as international marketing. Guidance on *how* such studies might be performed requires a research process framework. Because it addresses research questions as a progression from the scientifically relatively simple to the scientifically extremely complex, an adaptation of the Zaltman, Pinson and Angelmar (1973) framework is appropriate (Table 2.3). Recent literature on international marketing has been cross-classified using the systems-exchange paradigm and this research process framework (Bradley, 1987). As may be seen, not much has changed in the past two decades in the research approach adopted by writers in the better known journals (Table 2.3).

Regarding the research process followed by writers, a number of striking features are apparent. Almost three-fifths of all articles were devoted to assessing existing knowledge. A considerable proportion of these studies was devoted to profiling and describing firms and markets for further detailed work.

The second and striking result regarding the research process is that 33 per cent of the literature falls in the category of exploratory and inductive research. Writers have been mainly concerned with the selection and clarification of hypotheses but not with anything scientifically more advanced. Very few studies progress beyond this point. Only 6 per cent of articles were devoted to the testing of research hypotheses.

Finally, just over 2 per cent of articles were concerned with data gathering instruments such as questionnaires, psychological tests, statistical techniques and other research instrumentation.

Taking the systems-exchange perspective of the research content it is evident that, though less skewed than before, there still remains a strong preference for

**Table 2.3** Classification of international marketing literature: research process and systems/ exchange paradigm*

| Research process | Systems/exchange paradigm process | | | | |
|---|---|---|---|---|---|
| | Goals and objectives of system (%) | Systems/exchange environment (%) | Systems/exchange participants (%) | Assets and transfer mode (%) | Total (%) |
| Assessment of relevant existing knowledge | 3 | 19 | 25 | 11 | 58 |
| Exploratory and inductive research | 2 | 7 | 12 | 11 | 33 |
| Hypotheses testing | — | 1 | 2 | 3 | 6 |
| Instrumental investigations | — | 1 | 1 | 1 | 3 |
| Total | 5 | 28 | 40 | 27 | 100 |

*Articles reviewed: 1,014 articles in 32 journals in the period 1980–5 were classified which represented 12.8% of all articles in these journals.

Source: Adapted from Bradley, M. Frank (1987) 'Nature and significance of international marketing: A review,' *Journal of Business Research*, **15**, 205–19. The figures represent the proportion of articles in each category.

certain types of study. For example, very little work, only 5 per cent of the articles surveyed, is being carried out in the area of assessing the goals and objectives of the international marketing system. Two areas of the systems-exchange paradigm, the environment and the assets exchanged and mode of transfer receive about equal attention, with slightly greater endeavours being devoted to the participants in the system — 40 per cent of papers reviewed. Consequently, research in international marketing to date is largely descriptive and exploratory.

## Dominance of the firm in the international exchange of assets

Firms are established and grow with: (a) increases in the spatial distribution of the exchange transactions organized; (b) increases in the similarity of the exchange transactions; and (c) increases in the likelihood of changes in prices and costs of assets being transferred (Coase, 1937). All three conditions are much more likely to occur in international markets than in purely domestic operations. Spatial distribution of exchange transactions is usually greater for international marketing.

As the volume of transactions rises with the development of international business and as a determined move by the firm away from opportunistic exporting occurs, the second condition comes into play. With differential interest rate regimes, different inflation rates and fluctuating exchange rates, which typify international markets, the third condition comes into play.

Interest by the scholar and manager in the behaviour of the firm in international markets arises when the firm transfers assets internationally, where an asset is defined as something that is owned by a specified person or firm on which it confers a competitive advantage which may or may not be capable of being objectively valued. Successful firms in international marketing possess one or more assets which may be tangible, such as finished products. In such cases the international transfer modality is usually through exporting. Where the assets are intangible, i.e. where the asset represents technological know-how, marketing know-how or brand loyalty, the transfer is normally performed through one of the other exchange modalities.

Observing these differences enabled Levitt to coin the phrases "high-tech" for the intangible assets and "high-touch" for the product categories (Levitt, 1983). Consequently, it is possible to conceive of the international firm as exchanging a firm specific rent yielding asset giving the firm its competitive advantage which may be found somewhere on a scale from high-touch to high-tech.

## Foreign market entry mode

Possession of a firm specific rent yielding asset of the kind described may provide the *raison d'être* for international marketing operations (Teece, 1983). Furthermore, it is possible to specify the international exchange transaction modality by determining the extent to which the knowledge or know-how embedded in the asset being transferred is explicated. The greater the codification or explication of the knowledge and know-how associated with the assset being transferred the more likely will the transfer be through exporting. There are, however, a number of organizational, transaction costs and strategic marketing factors which become more pronounced as knowledge and know-how in the asset being transferred is tacit and difficult to codify or explicate as a finished product, which favours an international exchange modality other than exporting.

These pressures are shown as a movement in transfer modality from exporting through licensing and joint ventures to the establishment of a full international firm (Table 2.4). Again, the modality dimension is also perceived as a continuum parallelling the market asset continuum already described.

By their very nature commodities, mature products and innovative products are high-touch, easy to define and separate from the firm (Levitt, 1983). In contrast, technical inventions, product co-ordination competences, technical skills and strategic marketing skills are to be found more toward the high-tech end of the continuum. Firms whose competitive advantage or uniqueness derives from technical skills, product co-ordination skills or marketing skills seldom resort to exporting activities, joint ventures or licences since product bundles and constantly changing marketing strategies are difficult to contract out and hence are likely to be performed within the firm.

**Table 2.4**  Competitive advantage in international markets: exchange of assets

| Market asset | Exchange transaction | International exchange transaction modality |
|---|---|---|
| High-touch assets explicated knowledge | Market determined | Export modality |
| ↑ | ↑ | ↑ |
| | | Licensing |
| | | | |
| | | Joint venture |
| | | ↓ |
| ↓ | ↓ | |
| High-tech assets tacit knowledge | Firm determined | International firm |

and constantly changing marketing strategies are difficult to contract out and hence are likely to be performed within the firm.

## Role of international marketing

To understand the role of international marketing in the firm it is necessary to consider decisions being made on the continuum outlined above and not the discrete components corresponding to the various modalities used to transfer assets internationally. It is limiting, therefore, to examine exporting behaviour as something very different from licensing, joint ventures or foreign direct investment through the establishment of an international firm.

The literature is deficient in this regard since it is divided very much along the lines of that dealing with exporting decisions and that dealing with the other modalities. This division of the literature along these lines is a reflection of the "production–selling" versus "marketing" syndrome evident among managers and scholars. A "marketing" approach, as proposed here, is the more comprehensive as it integrates all the international exchange modalities, as opposed to the "production–selling" approach associated with the separation of decisions into exporting decisions and decisions involving the other exchange transaction modalities.

Some of the more obvious conclusions concerning the nature and significance of international marketing have already been outlined. There is a great deal of interest among researchers and managers in describing international marketing activities, but little attention has been given to understanding the decision and implementation aspects. It would appear that researchers are busy learning from practitioners who are much further developed in their understanding of the discipline since they have been engaged in international marketing activities for much longer than have the researchers who have only recently begun to pay attention to it as a research and teaching area to be developed. The flow of knowledge seems to be from what managers do to what researchers think. Undoubtedly this situation will change with the growth of interest in the firm in international markets. The systems-exchange paradigm could be useful in directing researchers' attention to the goals and objectives of the system.

## Summary

Interest in international marketing as a sub-discipline of marketing is a relatively recent phenomenon. It appears that practitioners of international marketing are much further advanced in their thinking about the discipline than are researchers. Research in the area has built upon theories and paradigms developed in other areas, especially international trade theory, industrial organization and strategic marketing. Valuable insights into the conditions under which international exchange of assets occurs may be gleaned from international trade theory, especially the effect of fluctuating exchange rates on marketing programmes. From industrial organization theory the role of the firm in the internationalization process, and especially the reasons for foreign direct investment, may be understood.

Because the firm in international markets must deal with relatively high transaction costs it is necessary to consider various ways of transferring assets abroad. The different modes of foreign market entry identified are exporting, competitive alliances based on licensing, and joint ventures and foreign direct investment. It is necessary to examine each in the context of a theory or set of paradigms.

A number of marketing theories and paradigms were identified and discussed, many of which have components which are relevant to the firm in international markets. The interaction paradigm in the context of a systems-exchange framework appears to hold high promise, as with this it is possible to identify the transactions costs of international marketing and measure the attainment of other non-financial marketing objectives. The chapter ends with a section outlining the dominant position of the firm in international markets. This dominance stems from its ability to complete the international marketing task in an effective way.

## Discussion questions

1. Explain what is meant by a theory of international marketing. What is meant by a paradigm? Why is it important to have a suitable paradigm for the study of international marketing in the firm?

2. What is the significance of the systems/exchange paradigm as applied to the firm in international markets?

3. Describe and evaluate the principal constructs of the interaction and the geobusiness paradigms.

4. How relevant is the life cycle model to the understanding of international marketing?

5. What are the principal contributions of international trade theory, if any, to the study of the firm in international markets?

6. Describe the international marketing task facing the firm and outline an approach to the study of international marketing.

## References

Bartels, Robert (1968) 'Are domestic markets and international markets dissimilar?', *Journal of Marketing*, **32**, 56–61.

Bilkey, Warren J.(1978) 'An attempted integration of the literature on the export behaviour of firms', *Journal of International Business Studies*, **9** (1), 33–46.

Bilkey, Warren J. and Tesar, George (1977) 'The export behaviour of smaller sized Wisconsin manufacturing firms', *Journal of International Business Studies*, **8** (1), 93–8.

Bradley, M. Frank (1984) 'Effects of cognitive style, attitude towards growth, and motivation on the internationalization of the firm', *Research in Marketing*, JAI Press, **7**, 237–60.

Bradley, M. Frank (1987) 'Nature and significance of international marketing: A review', *Journal of Business Research*, **15**, 205–19.

Buckley, P.J. and Casson, M. (1976) *The Future of the Multinational Enterprise* (Holmes and Meier, London).

Buzzell, Robert, (1968) 'Can you standardize multinational marketing', *Harvard Business Review*, November–December, pp. 103–13.

Carman, James M. (1980) 'Paradigms for marketing theory', *Research in Marketing*, **3**, 1–36.

Cateora, Philip R. (1990) *International Marketing*, 7th edn, Irwin, Ill.

Cavusgil, S. Tamer and Nevin, John R. (1981a) 'Internal determinants of export marketing behaviour: An empirical investigation', *Journal of Marketing Research*, **18**, 114–19.

Cavusgil, S. Tamer, and Nevin, John R. (1981b) 'State of the art in international marketing: An assessment', in Ben M. Enis and Kenneth J. Roering (eds.), *Review of Marketing*, American Marketing Association, pp. 95–216.

Chandler, Alfred D., Jr (1977) *The Visible Hand*, Harvard University Press, Cambridge, Mass.

Coase, Ronald H. (1937) 'The nature of the firm', *Economica*, **4** (New Series) (16), 386–405.

Dunning, John and McQueen, M. (1981) 'The eclectic theory of international production: A case study of the international hotel industry', *Managerial and Decision Economics*, **2**, 197–210.

Fayerweather, John (1982) *International Business Strategy and Administration*, 2nd edn, Ballinger Publishing Company, Cambridge, Mass.

Hakansson, Hakan (1982) *International Marketing and Purchasing of Industrial Goods*, Wiley, Chichester, England.

Hayes, Robert H. and Abernathy, William J. (1980) 'Managing our way to economic decline', *Harvard Business Review*, **58**, 67–77.

Hymer, Stephen (1970) 'The efficiency (contradictions) of multinational corporations', *American Economic Review*, **60**, 441–8.

Johanson, Jan and Vahlne, Jan Erik (1977) 'The internationalization process of the firm: A model of knowledge development and increasing foreign market commitments', *Journal of International Business Studies*, **8 (1), 23**–32.

Johanson, Jan and Mattsson, Lars Gunnar (1986) 'International marketing and internationalization processes — a network approach', in Peter W. Turnbull and Stanley J. Paliwoda (eds.) *Research in International Marketing*, Croom Helm, London, pp. 234–65.

Kahler, Ruel and Kramer, Roland L. (1977) *International Marketing*, 4th edn, Southwestern Publishing Co., Cincinnatti.

Keegan, Warren J. (1984) *Multinational Marketing Management*, 3rd edn, Prentice Hall International, London.

Lawrence, Paul R., and Dyer, Davis (1983) *Renewing American Industry*, The Free Press, NY.

Levitt, Theodore (1983) 'The globalization of markets', *Harvard Business Review*, May–June, pp. 92–102.

Monteverde, K. and Teece, D.J. (1982) 'Appropriable rents and quasi-vertical integration', *Journal of Law and Economics*, **25**, 321–8.

Ohio State University Marketing Staff (1965) 'A statement of marketing philosophy', *Journal of Marketing*, **29**, 43–4.

Porter, Michael E. (1980) *Competitive Strategy*, The Free Press, NY.

Pugel, T.A. (1978) *International Market Linkages and U.S. Manufacturing: Prices, profits, and patterns*, Ballinger, Cambridge, Mass.

Reid, Stan D. (1981) 'The decision maker and export entry and expansion', *Journal of International Business Studies*, **12** (2), 101–12.

Reve, Torger and Stern, Louis W. (1979) 'Interorganisational relations in marketing channels', *Academy of Management Review*, **4** (3), 405–16.

Robock, Stefan H. and Simmonds, Kenneth (1988) *International Business and Multinational Enterprises*, 4th edn, Irwin, Homewood, Ill.

Ruekert, Robert W., Walker, Orville C., Jnr and Roering, Kenneth J. (1985) 'The organisation of marketing activities: A contingency theory of structure and performance', *Journal of Marketing*, **49**, 13–25.

Rugman, Alan M. (1981) *Inside the Multinationals: The economics of internal markets*, Croom Helm, London.

Schollhammer, Hans (1973) 'Strategies and methodologies in international business and comparative management research', *Management International Review*, **13** (6), 17–32.

Simon, Herman (1984) 'Challenges and new research avenues in marketing science', *International Journal of Research in Marketing*, **1** (4), 249–61.

Swedenborg, B. (1979) *The Multinational Operations of Swedish Firms: An analysis of determinants and effects*, Industrial Institute for Economic and Social Research, Stockholm.

Sweeney, D.J. (1972) 'Management technology or social process', *Journal of Marketing*, **36**, 3–10.

Teece, David (1981) 'The market for know-how and the efficient international transfer of technology', *Annals of the American Academy of Political and Social Science*, **458**, 81–96.

Teece, David J. (1983) 'Technological and organisational factors in the theory of the multinational enterprise', in Mark Casson (ed.), *The Growth of International Business*, Allen and Unwin, London, pp. 51–62.

Teece, David (1986) 'Firm boundaries, technological innovation and strategic management', in Lacy Glen Thomas (ed.), *The Economics of Strategic Planning: Essays in Honour of Joel Dean*, Lexington Books, Lexington, Mass., pp. 187–99.

Terpstra, Vern (1983) *International Marketing*, 3rd edn, The Dryden Press, Chicago.

Van de Ven, A.H., Emmit, D.C. and Koenig R. (1975) 'Frameworks for interorganizational analysis', in A.R. Negandhi (ed.), *Interorganizational Theory*, Kent State University Press, Kent, Ohio.

Vernon, Raymond and Wells, Louis T. (1976) *Manager in the International Economy*, 3rd edn, Prentice Hall, Englewood Cliffs, NJ.

Vernon, Raymond (1979) 'The product cycle hypothesis in a new international environment', *Oxford Bulletin of Economics and Statistics*, **41** (4), 255–67.

Wiedersheim-Paul, Finn, Olson, Hans C., and Welch, Lawrence S. (1978) 'Pre-export activity: The first step in internationalisation', *Journal of International Business Studies*, 9 (1), 47–58.

Williamson, Oliver E. (1975) *Markets and Hierarchies: Analysis and antitrust implications*, The Free Press, NY.

Williamson, O.E. (1979) 'Transactions cost economics: The governance of contractual relations', *Journal of Law and Economics*, **22**, 233–61.

Williamson, O.E. (1981) 'The modern corporation: Origins, evolution, attributes', *Journal of Economic Literature*, **19** (4), 1537–68.

Williamson, O.E. (1984) 'Corporate governance', *The Yale Law Journal*, **93**, 1197.

Wind, Yoram and Robertson, Thomas, S. (1983) 'Marketing strategy: New directions for theory and research', *Journal of Marketing*, **47** (2), 12–25.

Zaltman, Gerald, Pinson, Christian R.A. and Angelmar, Reinhard (1973) *Metatheory and Consumer Research*, Holt, Rinehart and Winston, NY.

# Internationalization of the firm: resources and managerial capacity

This chapter is divided into two parts. The first part examines the firm as an organization and deals with the products it makes and the firm's advantages. The second part focusses on the people in the firm, especially the characteristics of those people who make the strategic decisions in the firm — the management.

## Resources and aspirations

### Excess capacity in the firm

A major incentive for internationalization develops from the presence within the firm of excess or unused resources. These may be physical resources such as money, excess capacity in production or special knowledge, highly specialized labour and machinery, or by-products from existing operations. In moving into a new field, a firm may develop new strengths and may find another set of underused production resources, which sets the stage for another round of expansion that may be in a domestic or international market.

### Identifying the firm's competitive advantages

These advantages can be derived from the nature of the firm's products, markets, technological orientation or resources (Table 3.1). Examples include competitively priced products, technically superior products and technological intensity in the firm's production. Products produced at very competitive prices will often find success in international markets because of the features they offer at low prices. Thus, high-quality calculators and digital watches produced in huge numbers led to the rapid internationalization of many Japanese companies.

Though these differential advantages "are not sufficient, by themselves, to

55

**Table 3.1**  Resources
required for
internationalization

Excess capacity
- financial
- physical
- knowledge

Competitive advantage
- products
- markets
- technological orientation
- resources
- knowledge

initiate export marketing, these unique advantages are important in preparing
the firm and in providing initial motivation for management." (Cavusgil and Nevin
1981, p. 114) Thus, firms which produce competitively priced and technically
superior products have clear marketing advantages which can be exploited on
international markets.

Likewise, the greater the technological intensity of the firm's output, the
greater the likelihood that the firm will distinguish itself on international markets.
The possession of these advantages presupposes that the firm also has an
abundance of another key resource: knowledge. Knowledge of opportunities or
problems is assumed to initiate decisions. Furthermore, the evaluation of
alternatives is based on some knowledge about relevant parts of the market
environment and about performance of various activities (Johanson and Vahlne,
1977). By market knowledge these authors mean information about markets and
operations in these markets which is somehow stored and reasonably retrievable,
in the minds of individuals, in computer memories, and in written reports.
Knowledge is considered to be vested in the decision-making system which may
be the firm or business unit (Johnson and Vahlne, 1977, p. 26).

Knowledge can be divided into two types: objective knowledge which can
be taught; and experience or experiential knowledge (Penrose, 1959). These two
forms of knowledge underlie the firm's differential advantages. One important
outcome of this is that there is a direct relation between knowledge and
commitment. Knowledge is a resource and, consequently, the better the
knowledge about a market, the more valuable are the resources and the stronger
is the organizational commitment to the market.

This is especially true of experiential knowledge, which is usually associated
with the particular conditions of the market in question and thus cannot be
transferred to other individuals or markets. Experiential knowledge is also an
important determinant of management expectations. The implications of
knowledge acquisition are obvious in the case of large-scale indigenous firms in

most countries. Many of these firms have been criticized for their lack of international marketing orientation and it has been suggested that policy makers direct their attention to reorienting these firms. This is not an easy task.

In many cases this kind of experience is not for sale; at the time of entry to a market the experience may not even exist. It has to be acquired through a long learning process in connection with current business activities. This factor is an important reason why the internationalization process often proceeds so slowly.

## Characteristics and aspirations of the firm

A number of factors, including the firm's objectives and goals, its technology, its products, its location and its size, are believed to influence its performance on international markets (Table 3.2).

**Table 3.2** Factors influencing internationalization in the firm

- Goals and objectives of the firm
- Technology
- Product line
- Location
- Size

    availability of resources
    knowledge
    attitudes

### Goals and objectives of the firm

Managers are concerned with the goals of the firm and the extent to which they are achieved. Avoiding undue instability in sales performance is related to a basic goal of the firm, i.e. security and survival. The more unpredictable the firm perceives variations in its sales performance to be, the more concerned it will be to find other sources of sales and growth in order to insulate it from potential disturbances. Two forms of diversification — creating and marketing a new product and selling internationally — provide the firm with a degree of insulation ensuring that if the firm suffers a loss in one market it is less likely to experience losses in all markets. Thus, where the basic security of the firm is threatened by market fluctuations, a powerful reason for export operations may be developed.

The strategies that the firm is capable of adopting will be constrained by its past behaviour and actions. A firm may have to pass through a type of internationalization process or a similar process within the domestic market before it is prepared for the international market.

The value system and past history of the principal decision maker is also important. The decision maker's international outlook, i.e. the extent to which the decision maker perceives and considers as interesting events occurring outside his own country, is of central importance (Wiedersheim-Paul, Olson and Welch, 1978, p. 48). These authors suggest that it may be more relevant to distinguish between a local market and a distant market than between the domestic market and the export market. To ensure that their goals and objectives for the US market were achieved Korean industry was prepared to change its entire senior management structure in order to stay competitive and to recognize the new competitive environment in the United States, which was increasingly becoming protective. A shift to sourcing more components in the United States still allowed Korean firms to maintain dominance in certain key market segments (Exhibit 3.1).

## Product range in the firm

Another important factor is the type of product line produced by the firm. Products can be described in different dimensions: degree of standardization; complexity; and the software—hardware relationship in sales. The most important dimension is the software—hardware relationship since it stresses that a product is, in effect, "a package of services." The higher the hardware content — given the degree of technical complexity — the smaller the information flow needed between seller and buyer and, therefore, the greater the chance for a potential seller of being exposed to export stimuli. Products which include a more comprehensive package of software demand a more extensive flow of information and closer contacts between seller and buyer. This tends to favour already established business connections and consequently tends to decrease the possibility of an "outside" firm getting an order.

## Location of the firm

As a firm expands its operations into more distant regions, it is moving into less familiar territory — more "foreign" markets. Communication is more difficult and costly than for the local region. But as these barriers are overcome, the relative "foreignness" of distant markets is reduced. Also, the firm is likely to develop skills in marketing a product at a distance.

As the firm expands into additional regions in the domestic market, it will extend its communication network. From the extended network, there is a greater likelihood of exposure to attention evoking factors — those influences which cause a firm to consider an international strategy, e.g. an overseas enquiry. This process is probably more likely to operate in a large country such as the United States or Australia than it is in a small country such as Belgium or New Zealand.

The location of the firm affects the transport costs of products and also, more importantly, information flows. One of the reasons given for the high efficiency in urban regions is that a large number of firms and places of work, concentrated in a small area, improves the conditions for production and creates a favourable "enterprise environment." This is especially true in the case of "information

## Exhibit 3.1 A change of tactics to maintain strategic market objectives

### *Korea's new bosses: made in America*

Just as South Korea's leading conglomerates are taking advantage of the strong yen to dramatically increase exports to the US, they are promoting a new generation of managers to carry out their strategies. The elder generation may have launched the Korean export miracle. But it will be their younger brothers and sons who attempt to maintain Korea's growth in the face of heightened international competition and protectionism.

Korea's older entrepreneurs, who founded the powerful conglomerates, or chaebol, have relied on Japanese-style export strategies, leading to charges that Korea is "another Japan". These groups are largely responsible for Korea's trade surplus with the US. To avoid a backlash, Seoul is pressuring them to shift their component and technology purchases from Japan to the US. "Many of their parents are fluent in Japanese and have Japanese friends", says Y.S. Chang, director of the Asian Management Center at Boston University. "These new people are fluent in English and have friends in America. That's the big difference".

The pressures building on the chaebol have made this year's traditional round of New Year's management changes more sweeping than usual. The ageing chairmen of the Samsung and Hyundai groups announced plans to retire. The Lucky-Goldstar group, the third-largest conglomerate, and Daewoo, the smallest of the Big Four, also are promoting younger, US-educated executives. The ruling families hold only minority shares, but their control is unchallenged. Achieving that will be the task of the new managers.

The shifts at Hyundai are particularly sensitive because the Chairman Chung Ju-Yung, 71, the founder, is trying to engineer smooth succession. At Hyundai, Chung has named himself honorary chairman, turning over the chairmanship to his brother Chung Se-Yung, 58, who studied at the University of Miami. The younger brother, as president of Hyundai Motor Co., has been responsible for the success of the company's Excel subcompact in the US and Canada. Unlike the elder Chung, he speaks English fluently and tries to draw subordinates into decision-making.

His skill in dealing with the Americans will be important because Hyundai, of all the Korean exporters, has achieved the greatest visibility. To prevent Hyundai from becoming a protectionist target Chung Se-Yung is stepping up the purchase of US components. "I buy tires, glass, and carpets from America", he says. "If I were not educated in the US I wouldn't think about it."

As the new breed takes power, will Korea become a better economic ally? The new executives understand why their trade surplus is so sensitive in Washington, and they may invest more in the US. But they also come equipped with far better knowledge of how to penetrate the US market. "They are going to become better partners", says Phillip D. Grub, a Korean expert at George Washington University, "but also better competitors." If that's true, the new generation could be even tougher than their predecessors.

**Source:** *Business Week*, 23 February, 1987, pp. 18–19

production" that contains a high proportion of face-to-face contacts, since direct personal contacts are often more efficient than other means of contact. Direct personal contacts are preferable when the exchange of information involves uncertainty or when it is impossible to foresee what will happen when the information transmitted creates new situations demanding a new exchange of information.

## Size of the firm

When a firm's horizons are very limited, even if it has an excellent product, it will have little knowledge of the market. In general, small firms are:

- less aware of the potential of exporting;
- less confident of their ability to export;
- less knowledgeable about how to export or where to find the relevant information.

Many small businesses wrongly believe that only a large enterprise can handle the technical details of exporting, but frequently find that the only significant difference between small and large firms concerns the area of documentation. This is due to the fact that the small firm has less elaborate systems than the large firm and in most cases one person has multiple responsibilities. Large firms have the organization to handle all the extra form-filling and co-ordination work involved in dealing with overseas clients. Company size may, however, dictate the size of a business opportunity that can be undertaken. Thus small companies frequently find the risks too great and the financial demands too high to undertake very large research projects. Bilkey and Tesar (1977) report that size was relatively unimportant for export behaviour, but in a later paper Bilkey (1978) suggests that a possible intercorrelation of firm size may exist between exporting behaviour and the quality of management. The extent to which this correlation exists may alone cause firm size to vary directly with a firm's propensity to export. Reid (1981) states that the size of a firm "predominantly" affects the export entry into foreign markets.

The belief that small size is an indisputable disadvantage overseas inhibits many small firms from entering export markets (Cannon and Dawson, 1977). There may, therefore, be three main considerations with respect to size, as follows:

(a) resources
(b) lack of market knowledge; and
(c) perceived inability to survive in international markets.

The availability of resources, particularly those critical for successful exporting such as managerial and foreign marketing know-how, adequate financing and research and development tend to be limited in the small firm, which has less spare resources to devote to internationalization activity. The larger firm's needs for financial assistance may be met by corporate funds and by venture capital. Small firms do not have ready access to these sources. They usually have less money, therefore, for development of new products and production capacity. Furthermore, the small firm generally does not have adequate management personnel to devote to overseas markets. The small firm also typically lacks expertise in market research and planning. Finally, the smaller firm is usually not as expert as a large firm in processing documentation, the complexity of which increases manifold in overseas dealings.

On the second point, the small firm will have less knowledge and information about markets than the larger firm with "market scanning" ability. This may be alleviated slightly if the firm is positioned in a favourable enterprise environment. By interacting with neighbouring firms, information about markets and market needs may be easily assimilated. A major deterrent for internationalization is a belief by small firms that they are not capable of carrying out business overseas. Managers of small firms adopt generally conservative patterns of business behaviour and attitudes which undermine the effectiveness with which they can operate in a competitive environment. Exporting is perceived as risky just as any major diversification on the home market is seen as risky.

## Management of the firm

There are three characteristics of management responsible for simulating internationalization behaviour: managerial aspirations; commitment by the firm to international market development; and management expectations (Johanson and Vahlne, 1977). These factors interact with the firm, its resources and charcteristics to produce a certain international marketing behaviour in the firm (Figure 3.1).

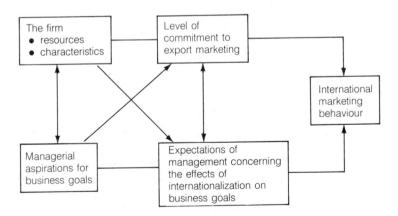

**Figure 3.1** Internal determinants of international marketing behaviour: causal relationships (Source: Adapted from Johanson, Jan and Vahlne, Jan-Erik (1977) 'The internationalization process of the firm — model of knowledge development and increasing foreign marketing commitments,' *Journal of International Business Studies*, **8** (1), 23–30)

## Managerial aspirations for internationalization

Aspiration levels are widely discussed in the literature on the theory of the firm as a determinant of risk-taking behaviour. The importance the decision maker places on the achievement of various business goals such as growth, profits and market development is believed to be a direct determinant of decision-making behaviour. Some empirical studies, like that of Simmonds and Smith (1968), support this assumption by revealing a positive relationship between export marketing behaviour and the decision maker's preference for business goals.

Very frequently there is a tendency for non-exporting firms to believe that someone outside the firm should be responsible for proving that exporting would be successful for them. The reluctance of firms to export may be attributable to senior management's determination to internationalize (Cavusgil and Nevin, 1981). A general willingness among the decision makers to devote adequate resources to export-related activities appears to be critical, because in carrying out the export marketing function many tasks are new to the firm and involve a commitment of financial and managerial resources.

Another aspect of managerial aspirations relates to the concept of international orientation which is specific to the individual manager (Reid, 1981). An international orientation appears to be important in regard to aspirations. Cunningham and Spigel (1971) report that successful exporters recognize that growth and long-term improvement in profitability are achievable only through the adoption of an international marketing outlook. Differences between individuals in international orientation may explain differences in behaviour. It is likely that an individual with a high degree of international orientation will have a higher probability both of being exposed to attention-evoking factors and of perceiving them. Aspirations in international marketing are affected by many factors including the orientation of management. An accurate assessment of the firm's strengths and weaknesses and an assessment of how it should respond helps the firm to develop realistic aspirations for international markets (Exhibit 3.2).

## Commitment to internationalization

The more specialized the resources are in respect of the specific international marketing endeavour, the greater is the firm's commitment to international marketing. The degree of commitment is higher the more the resources are integrated with other parts of the firm. Their value is derived from these integrated activities (Johanson and Vahlne, 1977). An example of resources which cannot easily be directed to another market or used for other purposes is a marketing organization which is specialized around the products of the firm and which has established an integrated system for maintaining good customer relations.

The other aspect of organizational commitment to international marketing refers to the amount of resources committed. Here we refer to the size of the investment in the market including investment in marketing, organization,

**Exhibit 3.2   Effect of international orientation on management aspirations**

*Most US companies are innocents abroad*

Why don't US companies export more? The government estimates that just 250 companies account for approximately 80% of US exports.

Chrysler's strategy is to export cars made in America. "We're a healthy company, the products are right, and the currency has moved in our favour", says David W. Lowsley, director of international sales and market development at Chrysler Motors. Chrysler doesn't plan to set the world on fire as an exporter, but put the emphasis on "the products are right", and you begin to understand why it's heading back overseas and why there's more than money at stake.

Chrysler is pinning its highest hopes on its minivans and on the Jeep models it acquired when it bought American Motors Corp. Jeeps have long had a slight presence in France and Italy, and Chrysler has shown off its minivans at recent auto fairs.

Those products can't be shipped as is. Chrysler will have to modify them by, among other things, tinkering with emission systems to run on leaded gasoline and by replacing regular outside mirrors with ones that break away on impact. By 1990 the company hopes to include such features in its cars at the factory.

Lowsley estimates that Chrysler is 75% to 80% of the way to putting its export plan in motion. Already, though, the team is thinking of how to approach Asia and other markets after Europe. That may involve shipping parts for assembly abroad, as Jeeps now are assembled in Venezuela and China, or linking up with other overseas manufacturers.

Some of those links already are in place. Besides increasing its stake in Mitsubishi Motor Corp to 24%, Chrysler recently bought fabled carmaker Lamborghini and holds 15% of Maserati. In a world where isolation in a single market can leave a company like Chrysler painfully vulnerable to bigger competitors, Lowsley says Chrysler decided: "We're going to be a survivor. We're going to be in that international arena."

Nevertheless, "this is no huge invasion", admits (chief executive) Iacocca. By the mid-1990s, say executives, Chrysler's shipments to Europe may climb as high as 100,000 vehicles a year. That's a respectable 8% or so of current annual sales but hardly enough to put the company in the big leagues of exporting. Unless Chrysler finds an even warmer reception than it expects overseas, it's likely to remain typical of the vast majority of US companies, which have long been content to mine the rich market in their own backyard. "I'd question whether America in general is or ever will be export-oriented", says Lowsley, "We do not have that mission that the Japanese do."

**Source:** *Business Week*, 16 November, 1987, pp. 54–5.

---

personnel and other functional areas. Included are the gathering of foreign market information, assessment of foreign market potential and formulation of basic policies towards international marketing and planning.

## Managerial expectations and internationalization

Many factors influence management expectations about the effects of exporting on business goals. Expectations reflect the decision maker's present knowledge, as well as his perceptions of future events. Managers tend to form expectations or opinions about the profitability and riskiness of export marketing on the basis of their own and/or the experience of other firms. Environmental variables, e.g. unsolicited orders from foreign buyers or fluctuations in the exchange rate, play an important role in management's subjective assessment of the desirability of internationalization.

There is a degree of conflict regarding the role of profits from international markets as an influence on expectations. Classical economic theory implies that a firm's probability of exporting will vary directly with the profit its management expects from exporting. It is generally believed that the firm's attitudes towards exporting varies directly with the perceived profitability of exporting and inversely with the perceived intensity of domestic competition (Bilkey and Tesar, 1977). Experimental exporting seems to relate primarily to non-profit considerations (Bilkey, 1978).

In an attempt to measure the firm's motivation to export, Bradley and Keogh (1981) draw on expectancy valence theory to develop a model of export motivation based on the following four assumptions:

1. Managers of firms have preferences among the various results which are potentially available if the firm decides to internationalize.
2. Managers have expectancies about the likelihood that an effort on their part to internationalize will lead to the intended international marketing behaviour and performance.
3. Managers have expectancies about the likelihood that certain results will follow their behaviour.
4. The decisions a manager makes are determined by the expectancies of him and his preferences in a given situation.

In simple format, the expectancy valence theory of motivation reflects the following pattern: effort leads to performance/behaviour which in turn leads to certain results which may or may not be attractive to the growth and development of the firm (Figure 3.1).

The single most important determinant of a manager's expectations regarding the performance and behaviour of the firm for a certain level of effort committed to the internationalization process is the actual business situation facing the firm. As managers gain more experience of a given situation, they are better able to develop more accurate expectations regarding the behaviour and performance of the firm in international markets. Herein lies the role of experiential knowledge. Government sponsored programmes which promote experience of international markets are quite valuable in this regard.

The second aspect of the model, Performance Behaviour Outcomes (P/B → O) shows that expectations about the consequence of performing a task

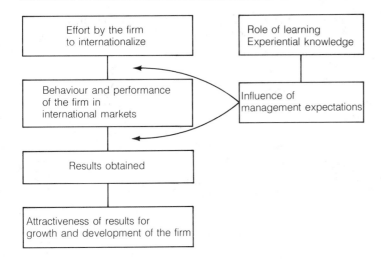

**Figure 3.2**   Motivation to internationalize

also influence motivation. Since successful task performance can lead to a number of possible outcomes — various degrees of success or failure — this part of the model shows a number of expectations which reflect the manager's subjective probability regarding various results. These expectations are strongly influenced by the actual business situation, the manager's previous experience, and advice received by the manager. They are, therefore, also experientially determined.

The third aspect of the model concerns the attractiveness of the various possible results, which can be thought of as varying from very desirable to very undesirable. The model suggests, therefore, that a manager's motivation to perform or behave in a particular fashion will be influenced by his expectations regarding results and the attractiveness of the outcomes involved. This theory of motivation suggests that managerial behaviour is, to a considerable extent, a function of the interactive processes between the characteristics of the manager, such as attitudes towards growth, and personality traits such as cognitive style and the manager's perceived environment (Figure 3.2).

## Attitude towards company growth

In this and the following sections we examine the relationships among attitudes to company growth, motivation to internationalize, the intellectual or cognitive style of managers and the stage reached in international markets (Table 3.3).

Attitudes towards the growth of the firm are determined largely by the perceptions of senior management regarding the opportunities and barriers to expansion. For instance, if it is accepted that the basic goal of the firm is security for its assets and survival, then the attitude towards growth through expansion

**Table 3.3**  Relationship among company growth, motivation to internationalize, cognitive style and stage of internationalization

A.  Attitude towards company growth

    internal incentives:
        unused resources
        special knowledge
        motivation of management

    external incentives:
        increasing demand
        changes in marketing environment
        changes in product/technology environment
        changes in institutional environment

B.  Cognitive style

    reflects manager's innovativeness and open-mindedness towards new foreign markets

    people high on dogmatism unlikely to exhibit a high propensity to export

C.  Three stages of internationalization

    potential exporter — firms not having any record or knowledge of ever having received a direct export order

    passive exporters — firms responding to unsolicited export orders

    active exporters -- firms exhibiting a continuous pattern of winning foreign businesss through direct sales and marketing efforts

into new products and new markets will be strongly influenced by the degree of variation perceived by managers in such variables as future sales and profits.

Where the degree of variation is high, the manager's attitude towards growth will be positive, keeping in mind the insulation of the firm from potential disturbances (Wiedersheim-Paul, Olson and Welch, 1978). Consequently, a strong motive for growth exists where the basic security of the firm is threatened by market fluctuations, and the manager's attitude towards growth becomes a powerful reason for developing diversified operations. Market changes, therefore, constitute a major force in forming attitudes towards growth of the firm.

At all times, the firm faces a variety of incentives to grow in one or more directions, but at the same time there are barriers to be overcome in implementing an expansion programme. The incentives to expand or grow may originate outside the firm or within it. The external incentives to growth include increasing demand for a particular product or service, reflecting changes in the marketing environment and changes in the product technology environment which call for exploitation. External incentives in the institutional environment to grow internationally might include new or improved government-assisted exporting schemes, or favourable changes in tariffs and other policies designed to encourage new and existing exporters.

Internal incentives to grow arise largely from the existence within the firm of a pool of unused productive services, resources, and special knowledge. In many cases the firm will have a supply of these resources, but in other cases some resources may have to be acquired or somehow introduced into the firm. The presence of unused management services or their ready availability to the firm means that the firm can grow by increasing total investment. Clearly, then:

> Whenever a firm's management feels that the firm's capacity for growth is greater than that permitted by existing market and existing products, it will have an incentive to diversify. The possibility of producing new products and acquiring new markets frees the firm from the restrictions on its expansion imposed by the demand for its existing products, although not from the restrictions imposed by its existing resources. (Penrose, 1959, pp. 144–5).

Consequently, the critical restriction on growth is that imposed by existing resources, including management. It is important, therefore, to examine management attitudes toward growth of the firm in general separately.

Attitudes toward growth are also thought to be influenced by the dynamics of learning or experience and the motivation of management. The firm possesses the unique capacity to initiate its own growth; new staff may be hired; demand for the firm's products induced to expand; and suppliers of capital persuaded to provide the necessary finance. "Such growth must be based on past success and the rate is, therefore, subject to considerable dynamic restraint." (Marris, 1964, p. 114) It has been shown further that motivation and learning are two constructs which are precursors of management's attitude toward growth. The stronger the firm's motivation to grow, the greater will be the activity it generates, including search activity for new opportunities. In this connection Marris's dynamic restraint has been recognized by others: "Over time the firm's attitude toward growth will be influenced by the type of feedback which it has received from past expansionary efforts." (Wiedersheim-Paul, Olson and Welch, 1978, p. 50) Consequently, attitudes toward growth are to a certain extent also determined by management perceptions of opportunities, and these opportunities are environmentally determined.

## Cognitive style of managers

International outlook, foreign market orientation and dynamic firm management all refer to the same underlying aspect of management — a cognitive style which gives rise to an attitudinal propensity towards internationalization, reflecting the manager's innovativeness and open-mindedness toward new foreign markets. The more open-minded the cognitive style of the manager, the more favourably will he treat negative exporting outcomes (Welch and Wiedersheim-Paul, 1980). Bradley (1984) uses the term "dogmatic" to refer to a closed cognitive style, the opposite of open-minded managers. Dogmatic managers display a closed cognitive style and are unlikely to adapt to a changing ill-structured international business environment. Firms with a high proportion of such managers are, therefore, less likely to export than their less dogmatic or more open-minded counterparts.

Finally, environments, business frameworks, and management tasks which are highly structured, as they are in a well-established domestic market, tend to be favoured by the highly dogmatic manager (Faschingbauer, Moore and Stone, 1978). It is thus likely that highly dogmatic managers will not exhibit a high propensity to internationalize. International markets are demonstrably unstructured, involve considerable risk, require considerable innovation and adoption of new ideas and management processes, and are characterized by the need for information and the assistance of external support agencies. It is expected, therefore, that active exporters will be much less dogmatic than their passive counterparts.

## Preventing internationalization failure

There are many factors which are believed to influence the pre-internationalization stage. These include managerial time and expense which must be devoted to sales, visiting foreign markets and collecting market information. As a result of these search and information gathering activities, the manager is more likely to develop a balanced positive attitude towards internationalization. The experience thus gained allows the manager to perceive problems as a series of small manageable issues that are more easily resolved.

The investment of managerial time is especially important for smaller firms. This initial stage in the internationalization process "warrants careful study as it represents a key establishment phase in the process of international growth." (Welch and Wiedersheim-Paul, 1980, pp. 333–4)

The firm new to international marketing has, however, no previous experience or measure of performance in international markets on which to base a level of aspiration regarding the outcomes of this new activity. For this reason the objective criterion of successful feedback will vary widely from company to company and is likely to be highly related to the perception and expectations of the key decision makers in each instance (Welch and Wiedersheim-Paul, 1980, p. 338). If the manager has a well-developed international outlook on the environment, the negative aspects of feedback are likely to be accorded less importance than the positive elements (Wiedersheim-Paul, Olson and Welch, 1978, pp. 48–9).

The likelihood of withdrawal from international markets as a result of perceived negative early experience of such markets is thought to be strongly related to the degree of commitment to the internationalization process. Many authors on the subject argue that psychological commitment as manifested through changes in attitude are more important than financial commitment. Lack of such commitment frequently shows itself as passive performance in international markets responding to unsolicited requests from foreign potential customers instead of actively seeking new foreign business. A passive disposition usually results in the firm eventually withdrawing from international markets.

Discussing exporting as a primary form of internationalization, Wiedersheim-Paul and Welch (1980, pp. 341–3) state "firms displaying an active form of export marketing behaviour may fail as exporters for some period of time. Usually this comes about because of developments in the firm's external environment which are beyond its immediate control ..." and the likelihood of success of the new venture "is not assisted by the adoption of a relatively passive degree of export marketing activity in response to the initial involvement — failure almost becomes a self fullfilling exercise as the marketing effort is not sufficient to maintain or expand export sales."

In new ventures such as exporting, growth is not spontaneous or self generating — it requires the co-ordination of decisions and actions to carry the firm beyond the stage of mere experimentation.

## Motivation to internationalize

The way in which managers are motivated to internationalize their firm's activities was discussed above under management expectations. It is possible to measure the manager's motivation to internationalize by using proxy measures. This may be done by understanding the manager's cognitive or intellectual style, his or her attitude towards business growth, and how he or she is motivated to continue in business in stressful situations.

There appears to be no significant difference between passive exporters and active exporters in regard to attitude towards growth (Bradley, 1981). This study, though dealing with a restrictive situation, also concluded that there is a strong positive correlation between exporting experience and motivation to export. Potential exporters, having no experience of exporting, are least motivated to export, whereas the most experienced group were highly motivated. Active exporters are also much less dogmatic about their environment and their role in business than are potential exporters.

## Strategic and opportunistic approaches to internationalization of the firm

A major difficulty facing many firms in attempting to internationalize is that they respond to the environment and international competition by trial and error or as a process of incrementalism based on an opportunistic response to market development. As a result, beneficial small changes are gradually adopted in a process of adapting to the existing situation, an evolutionary, expedient process. Because it is expedient and evolutionary it frequently produces meagre short-term results which are opportunistic and, therefore, not coupled with their long-run consequences. In contrast, the requirement for firms seeking to survive in international markets is to adopt a revolutionary or strategic perspective on international competition. Strategic competition is comprehensive in its commitment; it involves the dedication of the whole firm (Mitchell and Bradley, 1986).

## Strategic approach to international markets

For firms new to competing in international markets the reluctance to compete on strategic terms rather than on the basis of increments is understandable for two reasons. First, strategic failure can be as widespread in its consequences as strategic success (Welch and Wiedersheim-Paul, 1980). Second, incumbents in foreign markets frequently possess a competitive advantage over new entrants. Strategic success frequently depends upon the culture, perceptions and attributes of the firm and its competitors. The basic elements of strategic competition refer to the firm's ability to understand competitive interaction as a dynamic system that includes the activities of competitors, customers, finance and the resources of the firm itself (Bradley, 1985). It also includes the ability to use this understanding to predict the consequences of a given intervention in that system.

Strategic competition also means that there are uncommitted resources which may be dedicated permanently to uses which have a long-term payoff (Penrose, 1959). It also implies that management has the training and skill to predict risk and return with sufficient accuracy and confidence to justify the commitment of such resources. Finally, it means that firms must be willing to act deliberately to make the commitment to invest in marketing and markets (Johanson and Mattsson, 1984).

It is this lack of commitment to developing marketing resources within the firm and to developing markets which has recently come to be recognized as a central management concern. To counteract some of the problems which arise firms spend considerable sums of money developing staff. Recently there has been a trend towards internationalizing the staff of the firms themselves. This is done by attracting internationally oriented managers to work for the company (Exhibit 3.3).

## International market experience

Much of the literature on export marketing refers to the activity just described as a process of internationalization by which firms gradually increase their international involvement (Johanson and Vahlne, 1977). The incrementalism of this process has been stressed. In this section we suggest that management behaviour differs from one export stage to another. This suggests a learning process whereby experiential knowledge is obtained through the firm's international experiences. This learning process, through its effect on perceptions, knowledge and confidence, results in either increased or decreased commitment to the internationalization process (Yaprak, 1985). The essence of these arguments

---

**Exhibit 3.3   Finding skilled managers and workers**

---

*Japanese enterprises begin hiring foreigners*

The number of enterprises actively hiring foreigners for full time employment is increasing these days. Honda Motors hired six new college graduate foreigners for the first time this spring. All six of these foreign employees majored in such liberal arts subjects as marketing and advertising theory. The company has always been technology oriented but it has decided that in order to make a new leap ahead in the future as an international enterprise, it is absolutely imperative that it expand its staff with personnel who possess thorough-going knowhow in such areas as foreign business practices and market characteristics.

The same situation prevails among not only manufacturers, but with trading companies and banks as well. For instance, in order to cope with the sudden internationalization of the financing market, Fuji Bank hired four foreigners at one time in April 1986. Mitsubishi and Marubeni corporations have also begun hiring newly graduated foreigners studying in Japan as full time company members.

It appears that one of the aims of this movement is to introduce into the company the heterogeneous ways of thinking of foreigners in order to give new life to the organization as a whole. At the same time, in the high-tech industries, there is a movement toward hiring employees with no question as to nationality in order to obtain superior technicians.

**Source:** *Focus Japan*, September, 1987, p. 3.

---

is that the firm evolves through sequential phases of export commitment. Firms further along the path are likely to have greater knowledge and are likely to possess more sophisticated management skills than non-exporting and passive firms.

Lack of knowledge in respect of foreign markets and operations is an important obstacle in the development of international operations, but the necessary knowledge can be acquired through repeated foreign operations (Johanson and Vahlne, 1977). These authors distinguish between objective market knowledge from which it is possible to formulate theoretical foreign market opportunities and experiential knowledge which allows the manager to perceive concrete export marketing opportunities (Johanson and Vahlne, 1977, p. 26). The internationalization process through which the firm proceeds depends, therefore, on obtaining experiential knowledge. By obtaining additional knowledge the firm moves through a process of increasing foreign market commitment. The identification of an internationalization process in international market development has encouraged the formulation and testing of the concept of stages in export market development. One of the important early stages is referred to as the export initiation stage (Bilkey, 1978). Movement through this stage depends on both external change agents such as the firm's top management as reflected in its international orientation and its perception of the attractiveness of exporting *per se*.

Confidence in regard to successful competition in foreign markets is also stated to be an important influence. The second important stage occurs when the firm begins to experiment with exporting. Critical to this stage is the receipt of an unsolicited export order (Bilkey, 1978, p. 42). The third critical stage is reached when the firm is an experienced exporter. Management expectations with respect to the effect of exporting on the firm's profits, growth, and objectives are the most important determinants of exporting behaviour at this stage. The key point in Bilkey's model and those of his colleagues is that export development is a process in which each stage has its own unique influences and expectations.

An alternative way of examining firms in the process of internationalization is to consider a three-stage process: potential exporters; passive exporters; and active exporters (Cannon and Dawson, 1977). Firms in the first group correspond approximately with the pre-exporting and export initiation stages already identified (Bilkey, 1978). A firm not having any record or knowledge of ever having received a direct export order (i.e. an order initiated by a foreign buyer) is classifed as a potential exporter. The second group, passive exporters, are those who have some experience of exporting, having responded in the past to unsolicited export orders. While passive exporters have some history of meeting export orders, they do not devote any direct sales or marketing effort to winning foreign business. Firms in this group correspond with firms in Bilkey's experimental exporting stage. The third group, active exporters, are those exhibiting a continuous pattern of winning foreign business through direct sales and marketing efforts. In the literature cited, such firms are classified as experienced. This three-stage model has been used in a number of circumstances and is believed to be particularly appropriate in analysing the internationalization behaviour of smaller firms (Bradley, 1981; Bradley and Keogh, 1981).

## Commitment to internationalization

Commitment to international markets requires that the firm devotes financial and human resources, as well as management attention to carrying out tasks that are new to the firm, and for building the infrastructure required for export marketing. Commitment to international market development means devoting resources to understanding the market and to developing it. The firm's resources and characteristics are interwoven and influence the level of commitment, aspirations and expectations which among them determine how the firm behaves in international markets.

Commitment is also related to risk and uncertainty perceptions, where instability or a decline in the domestic market may increase the firm's search for diversification possibilities, thus decreasing the risk previously associated with exports. This, therefore, results in a more favourable attitude and probably increased commitment.

Firms classified as "committed exporters" exhibit a higher propensity to engage in certain planning activities than do non-committed or passive exporters (Cavusgil, 1984). These activities include budgeting, the statement of specific export goals and the creation of a distinct structure or responsibility centre for export management. However, empirical studies have produced disappointing results, even for companies regarded as aggressive exporters (Tesar and Tarleton, 1982). There is little evidence to support the hypothesis that all stages of the exporting process result from a carefully developed strategy devised to achieve the maximization of specified goals. Given the way in which firms commit resources to international marketing, it is more reasonable to conclude that for some stages in the process, at least, international marketing activity tends to be unplanned, reactive and opportunistic.

## Measuring commitment to international markets

While commitment is not directly measurable, certain proxies can be used to indicate commitment (Daniels and Robles, 1982). The first is determination of whether firms are engaged in exporting. Many firms decide not to export even when unsolicited orders come to them (Simpson and Kujawa, 1974). Export activity, therefore, however slight, marks an important decision in the commitment process. The second proxy, length of export experience, is based on the theory that exporting is a development and learning process. Even if firms have commenced exporting, however, and have some involvement over a prolonged period of time, there is no assurance that there will be high commitment.

Sales may be so small, cyclical or treated passively that management does not incorporate foreign market conditions into its overall strategy. For this reason a third proxy, export volume as a percentage of total production, is sometimes used as the basis of the premise that a greater dependence on exports indicates a greater commitment.

Similarly, other proxies such as visits to foreign markets, time spent abroad in a given year, attendance of trade fairs, purchase of reports, percentage of the telephone or telefax bills accounted for by foreign communications and other similar measures may be used as indicators of export commitment.

An important finding of a study of thirty-seven companies, representative of each of the stages outlined above, was that commitment to internationalization was greatest among firms which had displayed some strategic thinking by actively exploring the feasibility of exporting. Second, commitment was also very high among firms pursuing the feasibility of exporting to new distant country markets (Mitchell and Bradley, 1986). Here we see experimentation followed by commitment.

The firm in international markets is mainly motivated by internal factors such as a desire to increase profit, achieve company growth, gain experience and spread risk. These motivations did not, however, seem to shift dramatically over the stages of the exporting process described but were rather stable.

Regarding expected profitability of exporting, optimism tended to increase by stage of internationalization. This probably exhibits the role of experience and its effect on the perceived risk of the exporter during the process. Statistical tests showed that this optimism and decreased risk perception translated into greater commitment, as hypothesized. On the basis of this finding there is strong support for a determining relationship among exporting motives, exporting expectations and aspirations and subsequent commitment to exporting activities.

Export motives when filtered through the organization and mediated by management result in certain expectations and aspirations which in turn translate into positive or negative commitment to exporting.

## Internationalization of the firm: integration and application

It is possible, in most countries, to classify firms as large and small. In addition, many countries have a third category which may be large or small. These latter are the subsidiaries of multinationals. This categorization is used to classify firms in relation to the common weaknesses found in internationalizing their activities (Table 3.4). In many countries there is a predominance of large indigenous firms which are slow to change and loath to adapt to the needs of international markets. In general these firms do not possess many competitive advantages, their managers are poorly motivated, myopic in their marketing, and they suffer from the tyranny of short-term profit expectations. Many such firms are satisficers which do not commit themselves to internationalization strategies and invest very little in marketing or markets. These are the weak firms for whom industrial policies in many western economies are now geared to rejuvenate so that they can employ more people, grow and internationalize.

The second group of firms are the production subsidiaries of multinationals which by and large lack marketing clout and serve the needs of the parent or sister firms in the international marketing system. These firms tend to be functionally myopic, being production units accountable to headquarters. They frequently lack the autonomy required to plough the risky furrow of international markets.

The third group of firms are the small and medium firms which, because of their size and lack of resources, are dependent on the assistance of government sponsored support systems. These firms often serve the larger firms and do not grow for various reasons which include management, but a considerable number relate to weak structure and difficult environmental circumstances which prevent growth through internationalization. Such firms are beginning to benefit from the management skills of senior executives who for many reasons decide to leave the large marketing multinational firms and bring to the smaller firms the

**Table 3.4**  Determinants of internationalization in the firm: common weaknesses

| Large-scale indigenous firms | Foreign-owned firms/ subsidiaries of multinationals | Small and medium firms |
| --- | --- | --- |
| Competitive advantages/disadvantages: | | |
| Old products | Poor marketing skills | Weak management |
| Domestic markets | Decisions made externally | High dependency on State Support |
| Weak technology | Little exporting experience | System |
| | | Lack marketing skills |
| Managerial aspirations: | | |
| Myopic marketing | Functionally myopic | Lack export market experience |
| Supply conditioned | Profit/growth goals given | High-risk perceptions |
| Motivational barriers | Institutional barriers | Opportunistic goals |
| Management expectations: | | |
| Short-term pressures | Expectations clearly defined | Mixed and unrealistic |
| Motivational barriers | but limited | Lack relevant international knowledge |
| Satisficing business | | |
| Organizational commitment: | | |
| Short-term resources | No marketing investment, | Inadequate financial/personnel resources |
| Few strategic resources | but access to key skills | Lack commitment required to reach |
| Little marketing investment | Lack independence in | critical mass threshold |
| | resource commitment | Unaware of deficiencies |

accumulated experience of their former employment. This transfer of marketing technology is particularly welcomed by European firms (Exhibit 3.4).

In each of the three groups it is possible to find many exceptions to the above. The weaknesses found, however, can be summarized, as outlined, and serve to characterize the internationalization problems faced by firms attempting to grow by entering international markets.

## Summary

This chapter focusses attention on the resources and managerial capacity required for successful internationalization. Resources are linked to aspirations in the firm and also determine the extent of the firm's competitive advantage in international markets. The characteristics of the firm in terms of objectives, technology, product location and size influence the aspirations of managers and hence the success of the firm. The principal resource available to the firm which is attempting to internationalize is open-minded management which seeks to develop the firm in international markets. By committing resources in a strategic way the firm can succeed in international markets. There are, however, many kinds of firm, many

---

**Exhibit 3.4    Strengthening management in smaller firms**

---

*The hidden benefits of "management transfer"*

... a growing number of European managers who have left high-flying careers at US and European multinationals to join indigenous firms and transformed their new companies' fortunes by importing a more sophisticated management culture and a clear view of world markets. This "management transfer" effect is beginning to rank alongside technology transfer and job creation as one of the important long-term impacts of multinationals on the national economies in which they operate. Especially in Europe, multinationals have become a prime source of modern management training, probably more effective in practical terms than business schools.

What the escapees bring from their multinational experience besides the strategic outlook is an understanding of organizational structure, international perspective, a grasp of the innovation process, a respect for financial controls, and a structured approach to problem-solving.

Perhaps as important, the multinational veterans — especially those from US companies — have developed a taste for open communication, unconventional behaviour, marketing flair, candid performance evaluation, and a willingness to be hard-nosed about business ventures that underperform.

**Source:** *International Management*, May 1986, pp. 24–32.

---

of which never succeed abroad. Only a small proportion of firms successfully internationalize.

## Discussion questions

1. A major prerequisite for success in international markets is possession by the firm of a competitive advantage. Identify and discuss the most common sources of competitive advantage found in international firms.

2. While most firms pay close attention to the importance of external factors as they internationalize, many firms fail to consider internal factors adequately. What are these internal factors and how important are they to the firm in international markets?

3. Is it necessary to adopt a specific business outlook for success in international markets? Is such an outlook a prerequisite for the motivation in firms to internationalize?

4. Many commentators have suggested that firm size and motivation to succeed in international markets are closely correlated. Discuss. Is there a possible conflict in this relationship?

5. The process of internationalizing the firm can be seen as a sequential process of increasing knowledge and foreign market commitment. Discuss.

6. Distinguish clearly between opportunistic and strategic international marketing. Is there a relationship between opportunistic international marketing behaviour and a commitment to compete in international markets?

# References

Bilkey, W.J. (1978) 'An attempted integration of the literature on the export behaviour of firms,' *Journal of International Business Studies*, **8** (1), 33–46.

Bilkey, W.J. and Tesar, G. (1977) 'The export behaviour of smaller-sized Wisconsin manufacturing firms,' *Journal of International Business Studies*, **8** (1), 93–8.

Bradley, M. Frank (1984) 'Effects of cognitive style, attitude toward growth and motivation on the internationalization of the firm,' *Research in Marketing*, 7, JAI Press, pp. 237–60.

Bradley, M. Frank (1985) 'Key factors influencing international competitiveness,' *Journal of Irish Business and Administrative Research*, 7 (2), 3–14.

Bradley, M. Frank and Keogh, P. (1981) 'Export management: Motivated-openminded,' *Journal of Irish Business and Administrative Research*, October (2), pp. 29–40.

Bradley, M. Frank (1981) 'Attitudes to export marketing growth among small scale enterprises: A discriminant analysis,' *Proceedings, Dublin: Marketing Education Group, (United Kingdom), Annual Conference*, St. Patrick's College, 7–9 July.

Cannon, T. and Dawson, G. (1977) 'Developing the export potential of small firms,' *Industrial and Commercial Training*, **8** (7), 292–5.

Cavusgil, S. Tamer (1984) 'Organisational characteristics associated with export activity,' *Journal of Management Studies*, **21** (1), 3–9.

Cavusgil, S. Tamer and Nevin, J.R. (1981) 'Internal determinants of export marketing behaviour: An empirical investigation,' *Journal of Marketing Research*, **18**, 114–15.

Cunningham, M.T. and Spigel, R.I. (1971) 'A study in successful exporting,' *British Journal of Marketing*, **5** (1), 2–12.

Daniels, John D. and Robles, F. (1982) 'Choice of technology and export commitment: The Peruvian textile industry,' *Journal of International Business Studies*, pp. 67–87.

Faschingbauer, T.R., Moore, C.D. and Stone, A. (1978) 'Cognitive style, dogmatism and creativity: Some implications regarding cognitive development,' *Psychological Reports*, **42**, 795–804.

Johanson, Jan and Mattsson, Lars-Gunnar (1984) 'Marketing assets in networks,' *Proceedings, Second International Marketing Strategy Seminar*, University of Manchester Institute of Science and Technology, Manchester, United Kingdom, 2–4 September.

Johanson, Jan and Vahlne, Jan-Erik (1977) 'The internationalisation process of the firm — model of knowledge development and increasing foreign marketing commitments,' *Journal of International Business Studies*, **8** (1), 23–30.

Marris, Robin (1964) *The Economic Theory of Managerial Capitalization*, The Free Press of Glencoe, New York.

Mitchell, O. and Bradley, Frank (1986) 'Export commitment in the firm — strategic or opportunistic behaviour,' *Journal of Irish Business and Administrative Research*, 8, Part 2, 12–19.

Penrose, E. (1959) *The Theory of the Growth of the Firm*, Basil Blackwell, Oxford.

Reid Stan D. (1981) 'The decision maker and export entry and expansion,' *Journal of International Business Studies*, **12** (2), 101–12.

Simmonds, K. and Smith, H. (1968) 'The first export order: A marketing innovation.' *British Journal of Marketing*, **2**, (Summer), 93–100.

Simpson, C.L. and Kujawa, D. (1974) 'The export–decision process: An empirical inquiry,' *Journal of International Business Studies*, (Spring), pp. 107–17.

Tesar, George and Tarleton, Jesse S. (1982) 'Comparison of Wisconsin and Virginia small and medium sized exporters: Aggressive and passive exporters,' in Michael R. Czinkota and George Tesar (eds.), *Export Management*, Praeger, New York, pp. 85–112.

Weidersheim-Paul, F., Olson, H.C. and Welch, L. (1978) 'Pre-export activity: The first step in internationalization,' *Journal of International Business Studies*, **9** (1), 47–58.

Welch, Lawrence and Wiedersheim-Paul, Finn (1980) 'Initial exports — A marketing failure?,' *Journal of Management Studies*, October, pp. 333–44.

Yaprak, Attila (1985) 'An empirical study of the differences between small exporting and non-exporting US firms,' *International Marketing Review*, Summer, pp. 72–82.

# *Strategic options for the firm in international markets*    **4**

In this chapter we outline a framework for analysing international marketing entry strategies and discuss a number of options open to the firm. The manager needs a framework to assist in making a selection among such strategies. The international competitive environment which directly affects the performance of firms in the various product markets is becoming increasingly complex and dynamic. Successful international firms first examine the competitive environment before determining the appropriate marketing response. In implementing such responses a clear indication of how to combine the various product-market options available with the appropriate means of foreign market entry is clearly desirable.

## Marketing orientation in international competitive environment

It is the marketing orientation that counts. Marketing attempts to free the firm from the shackles of competition by identifying and developing a competitive advantage for the firm. Competitive advantage derives from the firm's orientation to its environment and the competition. A marketing orientation means starting with customer needs and focussing the firm's resources on these needs at a profit. It also means matching the firm's resources with the needs of the market. Good marketing means identifying and managing the area of overlap between resources and needs to ensure that the customer obtains:

- the benefits desired when and where wanted at the acceptable price, while
- producing a profit for the firm.

Frequently used marketing strategy options include:

- new products;
- new markets;

79

- more intensive new distribution channels;
- better production facilities;
- increased marketing expenditures;
- price reductions;
- acquisition of other companies.

In this chapter we are concerned with developing and entering new foreign markets and the role of marketing strategy in assisting the firm in so doing.

Developing foreign markets means treating the world market as a series of segments, each with different needs and wants. Successful market segmentation means careful selection of country markets, regions and customers. A related decision refers to market sequencing to acquire product experience and customer ranking, distribution penetration and market expansion (contiguous vs distant markets) as the firm develops its various product markets. Consideration of market flexibility involving variation in the marketing mix across markets and by stage of development of product markets is, therefore, central to the growth of the firm. The key decision area examined in this chapter is that of entering foreign markets successfully.

Ideally, entry costs should be reasonable with the cost of error acceptable, and the industry structure should be favourable with little chance of competitive retaliation. This means entering the markets in the right manner which often involves product-market studies, new product features, less product at lower price, built-in quality and reliability, smaller versions of standard products, better customer relations, or sequenced distribution and selective promotion.

New market entry should support other aspects of the firm's business. This means entering the right markets resulting from accurately targeted industries to accommodate company resources while recognizing the stage of product-market evolution. Consideration must also be given to scale effects on the marketing mix while accounting for the strength of competition. In this context, as noted below, markets become fragmented and firms attempt to consolidate them by various means. The process of market fragmentation followed by consolidation presents firms with growth and development opportunities in the context of foreign product-market development. Market fragmentation is caused by low entry costs and high exit costs, no experience curve effect, atypical cost structures and government interference in the market. Consolidation of markets is achieved when low-cost, standardized products are introduced, marketing expenditures are systematically raised, a spate of acquisitions occurs and large capital investments raise the minimum scale to be efficient. Until recently the consumer electronics business in Europe was very fragmented. In recent years there has been an attempt, principally by Philips, to consolidate the market to compete with the Japanese. The growth of the firm in international markets is conditioned by these factors.

# Required international marketing response

Since the mid-1970s, rising foreign competition, from the Far East in particular, turbulent financial markets and new technologies have created an era of rapid and painful change for many companies. Many European and US managers, educated to operate in less volatile times with protected and virtually guaranteed markets under relatively fixed exchange rates, have faltered in the past decade.

## *Product-market development*

In order to avoid opportunistic responses there are a number of things that successful firms do and a number they eschew. In a period of rapid change and discontinuity in the environment, the successful firm avoids knee-jerk reactions to difficulties in the marketplace. Successful product markets can only be developed with patience and careful planning. Firms should, therefore, avoid attempting to introduce instant new products. Only products or product attributes with a very short life cycle can be introduced at short notice and without due strategic thinking.

Creating a permanent and successful challenge in most markets is very difficult. The most difficult task is to develop a new product which will permanently avoid the attention of direct competitors. Examples of many such successes may be cited:

- Polaroid instant camera;
- General Foods soluble decaffeinated coffee;
- Hewlett-Packard scientific calculators;
- Honda lightweight motorcycles;
- Baileys Original Irish Cream.

Eventually, competition may become direct as competitors imitate the strategy, e.g. Kodak, Nestlé, Texas Instruments, Kawasaki, and Emmetts and the many other cream liqueur imitators. The more recent battle in the international marketplace between Fuji and Kodak also serves to illustrate this point (Exhibit 4.1).

Successful companies also avoid attempting to develop instant new markets. In this context it should be realized that there are very few left and those that are left must be treated in a deliberate and strategic way. It is usually wrong to jump into markets; since markets follow certain rhythms the company may miss the opportunity. A more powerful strategy is to get in ahead of the crowd and enjoy the benefits of a developing marketing infrastructure. In this way the firm avoids the bandwagon effect when the costs of serving the market begin to increase and the market then declines or disappears.

---

**Exhibit 4.1   Imitating strategy to compete directly**

---

*Kodak fights Fuji with "me-too" tactics*

After decades of belittling the company that takes its name from the sacred Japanese mountain, Kodak is now offering Fuji Photo Film Co the highest form of flattery — its undivided attention.

In the Kodak laboratories where modern photography was born, researchers now methodically analyze Fuji films to uncover their magic. "It's me-too technology", says one researcher distastefully. "We do what Fuji does. We're obsessed with Fuji." For years, Fuji sold film with brighter colors. Kodak researchers thought the colors looked unrealistic but they soon discovered customers liked Fuji film. Last year, Kodak came out with its series of VR-G films that feature the same vibrant colors found in Fuji. More realistic color reproduction "is not what people prefer", concludes Judith A. Schwan, director of Kodak's Photographic Research laboratories.

The concern with Fuji's products pales, however, in comparison with the effort to match Fuji's productivity. Fuji's sales per employee last year were about $370,000, nearly four times Kodak's. To close the gap, Kodak studies every aspect of its rival's performance... In the photo paper coating plant Kodak brought in specialists to train the workers in Japanese-style quality control. The result: Last year the factory increased productivity by 20 percent. "Now", says factory superintendent, Robert M. Ward, "we are ahead of Fuji." Kodak is trying to extend that experience to other factories.

Kodak is making even faster headway against Fuji in marketing. After watching the green Fuji blimp attract the eyes of millions of spectators at sports events in Europe and the US, Kodak decided to use the same tactic in Japan. Last August, Kodak leased the only available blimp in Japan and now floats supreme above Fuji's home turf.

To rub it in, Kodak's customary New Year's greeting cards in Japan showed the Kodak blimp with Mt Fuji in the background.

The blimp will be plugging Kodak film in Seoul during the 1988 Summer Olympics. After its embarrassing loss of the 1984 Los Angeles Olympics sponsorship to Fuji, Kodak plunked down about $8 million to get an early grip on the rights to use the five-ring emblem. Kodak hopes to use the Olympic sponsorship to rout Fuji's aggressive moves into such fast-growing markets as Taiwan, India, and China.

**Source:** *Business Week*, 23 February, 1987, p. 82.

---

## Segmenting and targeting international markets

Marketing is performed in three dimensions which relate to the technology embodied in the product, the customer segment served and the function performed (Figure 4.1). The successful firm segments its markets and targets them to provide benefits for the firm and the customer. The two key considerations here are the extent to which customers or customer groups seek different benefits

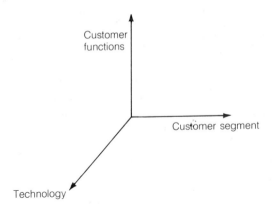

**Figure 4.1**   Marketing performed in three dimensions

in the products and services purchased and the ability of the firm to differentiate its products on attributes of importance.

Targeting international markets means selecting market segments for separate marketing mixes. Market segmentation, on the other hand, means dividing a market into consumer groups who might merit separate marketing mixes. A market segment is a consumer group whose expected reactions is expected to be similar to a given marketing mix. Usually market segments refer to contiguous but separate groups. Segmentation means identifying buyer characteristics which are correlated with the probable purchase of the firm's products, services, or ideas. Examples include purchasers of beer vs spirits and original purchasers of electronic components vs. replacement purchasers. All are in the market for alcoholic beverages or electronic components but will buy different product benefits for different reasons. Firms recognize four major reasons for segmenting markets (Figure 4.2).

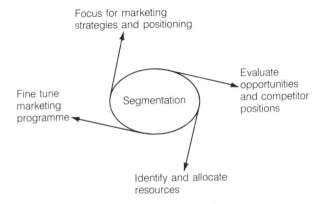

**Figure 4.2**   Why segment the market?

Usually, market segments are obvious to someone who knows the industry well! Even in such cases, it is important that the marketing strategist challenges traditional wisdom by testing different bases for segmentation, e.g.

- buyer demographics/socio-economics;
- size of purchase;
- motivation for purchase;
- manner of purchase;
- tender, list price, barter.

The relevance and suitability of the above approaches are increasingly being questioned. Perhaps there are better ways of segmenting the market — life style? family circumstances? product/innovation cycles? Researchers are examining ways of grouping some of the segmentation methods into management-oriented approaches. Other criteria for selecting segmentation strategies include:

- company resources;
- type of product;
- stage in life cycle;
- buyer homogeneity;
- competitor's strategy.

By identifying customer benefits and differentiating products to serve the associated segments the firm attempts to position itself competitively against its rivals in its served product markets. To do so successfully the firm must develop products to produce customer benefits desired by different market segments (Figure 4.3).

| Customer benefits | Market Segments | | |
|---|---|---|---|
|  | Segment 1 | Segment 2 | ----- Segment n |
| Benefit 1 |  |  |  |
| Benefit 2 |  |  |  |
| Benefit 3 |  |  |  |
| Benefit n | Product 1 | Product 2 | ----- Product n |
|  | Firm's products | | |

**Figure 4.3**   Benefit segmentation and differential products

Benefit segmentation and differentiating products means obtaining answers to a number of questions: How important is each benefit to each segment? How much better than competitors does the firm provide those benefits for each segment? This is the marketing task referred to as "positioning," which involves market segmentation analysis and product differentiation analysis to determine the degree of fit between the two. To successfully position the firm and its products it is necessary to examine its technology, its products and the international markets being considered.

## Technology, product, and market decision

The firm must also consider in which direction it should innovate when considering an internationalization strategy. The simplest move, as was seen above, is to sell existing products abroad. Rarely does such a simple strategy work. Usually the firm must adapt its products, and sometimes even its technology, when considering entry to new international markets. The firm thus innovates on three dimensions: product innovation; technological innovation; and market innovation (Figure 4.4). The origin in this diagram, Point 1, represents present circumstances and any distance in any of the three directions specified represents an innovation (Carroad and Carroad, 1982). Selling an existing product overseas without any change is represented by Point 2 which is itself an innovation since it involves a whole new marketing programme for a different market.

The firm might also innovate by developing a new product based on existing technology, Point 3. An example of this would be the introduction of a private

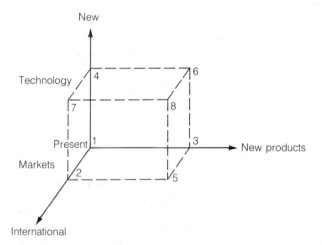

**Figure 4.4**  The technology–product–market decision (Source: Adapted from Carroad, Paul A. and Carroad, Connie A. (1982) 'Strategic interfacing of R&D and Marketing,' *Research Management*, January, pp. 28–33)

label brand of whisky to position against brand leaders. The firm may reduce the cost of producing its products by introducing new technology. A change to computer process technology in the food industry, Point 4, could mean improved product and or lower product cost. Here the product is unchanged and so are the markets but the technology is modernized.

Frequently, firms develop new products for new international markets but based on present technology, Point 5. The introduction to Greece of branded regato cheese by Bord Bainne (the Irish Dairy Board) under its Kerrygold brand would fit this situation. In this case product development was substantial but a large lucrative market in Greece was discovered and developed. The technology of regato cheese manufacture was known as the Irish Dairy Board had previously exported similar, but unbranded, cheeses to other European countries, especially Italy.

When Guinness developed its alcohol free beer, Kaliber, it required a new technology to remove alcohol from the beer, which resulted in the development of a new product for an existing market, Point 6. Alcohol free beers have successfully entered the beer market. For some beer consumers alcohol free beers have replaced ordinary beers, especially under certain circumstances, e.g. before driving, after a long drinking session or for health and dietary reasons. Television is a good example of a new product based on a new technology which entered the existing entertainment market, displacing radio in the process, Point 7. Finally, Baileys Original Irish Cream was a new product based on a new technology, aimed at a new market, Point 8. It was a new product in that it is whiskey and cream but with lower alcohol than the one it was designed to replace. It was based on a new technology since it is very difficult to mix spirits and cream successfully. The product was developed in Ireland but from the start it was developed for the large lucrative international markets throughout the world, especially the US.

Clearly, any innovation which takes the firm along two or more of the dimensions discussed above requires considerable planning and company resources. Innovating on any one dimension requires considerable care. The difficulty arises when firms attempt to minimize the extent of the innovation when the customer requires innovation on more than one dimension and perhaps on all three dimensions.

## Strategic corporate response: general considerations

There is considerable debate in the marketing literature on the appropriateness of niche vs global strategies (Levitt, 1983; Quelch and Hoff, 1986). This is the old standardization debate in new clothes, which is not very different from the issue as debated in the late 1960s (Bartels, 1968; Buzzell, 1968). Conceptualization of the problem is the key to understanding the behaviour of international firms but so too is the actual behaviour of firms which is often much further advanced than the prescriptions of theoreticians. Many European firms expect to respond to these internationalization questions by developing a global image for their products

**Table 4.1**  Planned internationalization strategies by European firms*

| Firms/regions | Improved global image (%) | Customized products (%) | Standardized products (%) |
|---|---|---|---|
| EC firms | 63 | 59 | 48 |
| of which: | | | |
| Big Five** | 61 | 63 | 48 |
| Small | 64 | 55 | 47 |
| EFTA firms | 59 | 59 | 54 |
| Average | 62 | 60 | 51 |

*There were 825 respondents in this survey who were asked to provide their responses compared with five years before.
**The Big Five are France, Germany (FRG), Italy, Spain and the United Kingdom. The Small countries refer to the remainder of the EC.

Source: Adapted from data provided in *International Management*, November, 1986, pp. 24–31.

and company, by customizing products for specific markets, and by standardizing products for all major markets (Table 4.1).

Quite a number of EC companies have begun to foster a global image for their products and company. Companies in the smaller markets appear to be somewhat keener to do so. Both groups are equally disposed to producing standardized products: less than half of those surveyed. In general, EFTA countries appear less disposed to the idea of developing a global image and customizing products for niche markets but they are more favourably disposed to producing standardized products than are EC companies.

## Cost cutting and restructuring the firm

Cost cutting and restructuring the firm are not strategic responses to the market but reflect failure to develop the appropriate marketing response (Porter, 1987). Sometimes firms do not recognize this and engage in simple or serious cutbacks. Successful firms avoid cosmetic cutbacks. Expenses may be cut back but this type of response frequently focusses and occupies managers' minds and shifts them from the main thrust of the business. Successful firms also avoid the situation whereby very deep surgery is required. Deep surgery is a last resort all too frequently used by a number of European companies, in which significant parts of the firm are cut away and can damage the firm's ability to perform in relation to its market. Situations arise whereby what remains of the firm becomes risk averse and resists any new ventures because of the fear of further deep surgery.

In these circumstances only a revival of the economy at large or the world economy will pull the firm back from collapse. This partly explains the weakness of many firms meeting the international marketing challenge and also explains some of the diversification activity of many firms having reorganized as holding companies.

Some companies are more successful at cutting costs than others. In recent years, due to the high Yen, Japanese companies have been forced to cut costs, some with considerable success. Successful companies frequently respond on a number of dimensions, however, not just on costs (Exhibit 4.2).

---

**Exhibit 4.2   Move production off-shore to cut costs**

---

*Matsushita: a giant learns how to step smartly*

Matsushita Electric Industrial Co in many ways symbolizes how Japan is beating the high yen. Although it's the world's largest and richest consumer electronics company, with $38 billion in sales, it is often regarded as slow-moving. When the strong yen hit hard in 1986, a third of Matsushita's sales were overseas, but only 10% of its goods were produced outside Japan. Export earnings dwindled, and a flat domestic market failed to compensate. The company had also made little progress shifting away from consumer goods, where the video-cassette recorder was quickly approaching market saturation.

But the giant is bouncing back. Accelerating a carefully calibrated strategy that had been in place since the early 1980s, Matsushita slashed production costs to the bone, a tactic mastered over 70 years as a low-cost producer. It also hoisted overseas production to protect its margins on sales overseas, but without undermining its hold on the domestic market. And it stepped up its drive into industrial electronics fields, such as robots.

Keeping costs down while moving offshore and upscale, Matsushita President, Akio Tanii, says he can still turn a profit at 115 yen to the dollar. Some Tokyo analysts say the company could still operate in the black at an incredible 110. At Matsushita's Osaka headquarters, the cost-cutting pressure is still on. The resulting price edge helps the company hold its leading 30 percent share of all Japanese microwave production.

Although Matsushita is a relative newcomer to large-scale offshore production, it is catching up fast. Last year total offshore production increased to $3.3 billion, from $2.4 billion in 1986. By 1995, Matsushita hopes to have 25 percent of its production overseas, compared with only 11 percent now. In North America, the company now has nine manufacturing facilities in operation or in planning, assembling everything from Panasonic VCRs to Quasar microwave ovens.

Letting smaller companies, such as Sony, take the risks and then moving in with superior resources is "the typical Matsushita way", says Yoshi Tsurumi, a business specialist at New York's Baruch College. "They let the Sonys act as guinea pigs."

Matsushita does not intend to plunge as deeply as Sony has. Sony estimates that 30 percent of its production could be offshore by 1990, but Matsushita is determined to retain some key manufacturing activities in Japan.

**Source:** *Business Week*, 18 January, 1988, pp. 16–17.

## *Company growth and discontinuity*

To be sustaining, growth and development must come from within the company. It cannot be foisted on companies directly through grants and favourable loan terms or other public policy initiatives. The environment facing companies in the 1990s is completely different from that of the 1980s. Policy makers, working at the macro level, provide the necessary framework for competition in the 1990s. The hardware of such support might consist of financial and other incentives. This software, the more attractive option, consists of, among other things, providing through the education system the right people to manage. Winners cannot be picked but must be developed (Storey *et al.*, 1987).

The question of overcoming these problems must be addressed. Successful firms recognizing periods of discontinuity introduce a range of corporate changes realizing that cost cutting is not enough. In such circumstances the basic philosophy of the firm is questioned. Corporate change means introducing new strategic thinking with institutional support within the company for a new environment. This means a thorough review of the risks facing the company, which begins to react to discontinuity by tightening its risk review process and developing or strengthening strategic thnking within the company. This should be a continuing process and should be quite specific.

## Foundation for strategy development

Much interest has been shown recently by strategy and policy theorists in the whole area of strategy development, the formation of contingency theories and the categorization of companies into particular strategy archetypes. Much of this research has the objective of specifying and defining the relationship between variables under the firm's control, such as marketing, production and investment decisions, and those variables generally outside the firm's control, usually referred to as environmental variables. Many models have been developed which suggest a limited number of identifiable strategies, each of which involves a different pattern of competitive positioning objectives, investment strategies and competitive advantages in order to be successful.

It is apparent that strategy at a corporate level represents the cumulative direction of the organization given the nature of the industry, the competitive environment and internal factors related to production, finance, marketing and personnel. The firm may follow one of three options: to build; to hold; or to harvest (Buzzell, Gale and Sultan, 1975); or it may be a performance maximizer, a sales maximizer or a cost minimizer (Utterback and Abernathy, 1975); or it may manage its resources with one of six options in mind: to increase share; to grow; to produce profits; to encourage market concentration; to introduce a turnaround; or to liquidate (Hofer and Schendel, 1978).

Strategies at this level of an organization have been described as "master strategies" and the later function or operational strategies as "programme or sub-strategies." (Steiner and Miner, 1977) These would include plans for the specific use of resources, physical and intangible, formulated to achieve the overall purpose. The lines of demarcation are blurred; however, despite inevitable overlap it has continued to be standard practice that strategic alternatives at the programme level be detailed and analysed dependent on the overall strategy (Thompson and Stickland, 1983). Hence, at the corporate level, for example, management may decide that an aggressive growth strategy is required for which it will then be the responsibility of functional management to develop appropriate programmes. One such functional strategy may be marketing, where management would need to formulate plans on how the organization would compete in given markets with given technology in order to meet a given objective. Concern here rests on such a functional marketing strategy or basis of competition for international markets.

## Competitive strategies

Porter (1985) has done much to narrow the gap between the strategy domain of marketing and corporate planning by introducing the powerful notion of the value chain. The notion of competitive strategy — how a firm competes for customer loyalty and franchise — has shifted from being purely fought on the "shelf space" offering to now being a competitive battle of all aspects of a firm's operations. Porter's "value chain" stems from the notion of value being added progressively to a product as it passes through the stages of inbound logistics, operations, outbound logistics, marketing, sales and service. Value may also be added by the support activities of the firm's infrastructure, human resource management, technology development and procurement. At each stage of the value chain there exists an opportunity to contribute positively to the firm's competitive strategy, by performing some activity or process in a way that is better than competitors, and so providing some uniqueness or advantage to the firm. If a firm attains such a competitive advantage which is sustainable, defensible, profitable and valued by the market, then that firm may earn high rates of return even though the industry structure may be unfavourable and the average profitability of the industry modest. Even though a firm may have a myriad of strengths and weaknesses in comparison to competitors, there are only two types of competitive advantage that a firm may possess: low cost or differentiation (Porter, 1980). These will result from a firm's ability to cope with the forces of the value chain better than its rivals. Combining these two types of competitive advantage to a firm's scope of activities provides three general competitive strategies for above average performance in an industry: cost leadership, differentiation and focus. The focus strategy may be of two types: cost and differentiation focus (Figure 4.5).

In seeking cost leadership a firm sets out to become the low-cost producer in its industry. Such a firm will have a broad scope, serve many industry segments and may operate in related industries. The sources of cost advantage may include economies of scale, proprietary technology, access to raw materials, and process design. A firm following a pure low-cost strategy will utilize its advantage to attract custom by offering lower prices, while still maintaining industry comparable returns.

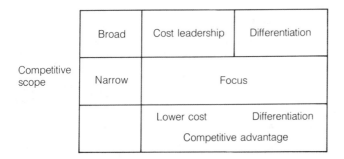

**Figure 4.5**  Generic competitive strategies (Source: Porter, Michael E. (1980) *Competitive Strategy*, The Free Press, NY)

The firm which seeks to be unique in its industry along some dimension which is widely valued by buyers follows a strategy of differentiation and obtains a premium price. Uniqueness may be product design, service, spare parts availability or a distributor network. The firm that achieves and sustains such a difference will be an above-average performer in its industry if its price premium exceeds the extra cost incurred in being unique. A differentiator, therefore, cannot ignore its cost position and must aim at cost parity or proximity relative to its competitors by reducing costs in all areas that do not affect differentiation.

The firm that selects a segment or group of segments in the industry and tailors its strategy to serving them to the exclusion of others follows a focus strategy. As already stated, either a cost or differentiation strategy could be followed; the choice depends on differences between the firm's target segment and other segments in the industry. Narrow focus in itself is not sufficient for above average performance.

A firm is "stuck in the middle" according to Porter when it engages in each generic strategy but fails to achieve any of the designed positions, unless the firm is fortunate enough to be in a favourable industry or its competitors are also stuck in the middle this is a weak option. Such a strategic position is usually a recipe for below-average performance. Porter argues that no room exists for combining the strategies, as each requires mutually exclusive actions or investments and any attempt to be "all things to all people" will lead to a loss of sight of the company's competitive advantage and ultimately its success.

## Combined approaches to competition

While still maintaining that each generic strategy requires a fundamentally different approach, Porter accepts that under the following three conditions a firm may simultaneously achieve both cost leadership and differentiation:

(a) where competitors are themselves stuck in the middle and thus are not strong enough to point out where cost and differentiation strategies become inconsistent;

(b) where cost is heavily determined by market share, rather than by product design, level of technology, service provided or other factors; and where

(c) a firm pioneers a major innovation thus enhancing its cost and differentiation position simultaneously.

The view that a cost leadership strategy or differentiation strategy should be absolute and are incompatible is rejected by Phillips, Chang and Buzzell (1983). Their research, which utilizes PIMS measures, shows:

(a) a positive relationship between relative product quality and a business's return on investment;

(b) only in capital goods businesses is there any evidence that higher relative quality results in higher relative direct costs per unit. Hence, attaining widespread differentiation by superior product quality need not be incompatible with a low-cost position.

Most industries compete with a range of factors. The European motor industry has identified five sets of factors which are believed to lead to competitive superiority. These factors include structural considerations, assembly issues, marketing matters, R & D, and competing on international markets (Figure 4.6).

The industry is still relatively fragmented, however, and competes on a small number of factors. In 1988 Fiat and Volkswagen each had 5 per cent of the 13 million European car market. Peugeot had 13 per cent, Ford and General Motors had 11 per cent and Renault had 10 per cent of the market (*The Sunday Times*, 12 March, 1989). The Japanese held 10 per cent which is expected to increase significantly with the completion of the internal market in 1992 (Exhibit 4.3).

Other researchers have also provided evidence which shows a high-quality and low-cost position as compatible (Hayes and Wheelwright, 1984). The research evidence of Phillips, Chang, and Buzzell (1983) is strong and refutes the traditional received wisdom that the attainment of a high-quality position would involve strategic trade-offs, such as higher relative direct costs or marketing expenditures.

## Analysing competitor strategies

Every firm has a marketing programme which it uses to attract and hold customers. The best competitors use their marketing skills to obtain a competitive advantage in the market by meeting customer requirements more efficiently than other firms. Some firms compete on the basis of product superiority, product innovation, prices, product availability, image and reputation and service. Firms must identify these customer advantages as well as determine competitor weaknesses. In this regard there is a close relationship between the firm's competitors and their strategies. The more a firm's strategy is similar to the strategy of another firm, the more they compete.

In many situations it is possible to separate competitors into groups that pursue different strategies. A group of firms in an industry following the same

**Exhibit 4.3  Compete with them by joining them**

*No clear road into Europe for Japanese cars*

The continuing deadlock over French restrictions on imports of British-built Nissan cars is set to escalate into a fierce battle over European Community policy towards Japanese car plants planned in Europe.

Continental carmakers are horrified by suggestions that the Japanese, left unhindered, could capture 25 percent of Europe's booming car market by the mid-1990s, compared with 11 percent today. They want Nissan to be a test case — as do the Japanese.

"The belief that cars built in Britain would be allowed to circulate freely in the European Community is the very purpose for the Japanese coming", says Garel Rhys, professor of motor industry economics at Cardiff Business School.

The European industry is aware that it faces a two-pronged assault. Japanese motor manufacturers plan to build a string of plants in Europe and at the same time are looking to export to Europe from new car plants in America. France and Italy stand to lose most in open competition with the Japanese — they have severely constrained Japanese imports so far.

Lord Young, the industry secretary, is hoping that Martin Bangemann, the West German EC commissioner in charge of the internal market, will move quickly against the French. But the Nissan dispute may become embroiled in wider talks in Brussels on new rules for the industry after trade barriers fall in 1992.

These talks centre on common standards for the industry as well as rules on state aid and — crucially — a common European approach towards the Japanese.

They have been heavily lobbied by the big European motor manufacturers, with the hard-liners pushing for tough rules on local content, aimed at making the Japanese production in Europe as costly as possible. Many would like to see local content more tightly defined, as well as rules for local manufacturing of key components, such as engines or transmissions, or high-technology electronics.

The continental manufacturers are aware that Britain is an attractive, low-cost base for the Japanese — who will have been pleased by Young's support for Nissan. Toyota favours Britain in its search for a plant while Honda already co-operates with Rover and owns land at Swindon, where it has an engine plant.

If all the Japanese plans materialize, more than half the cars that are assembled in Britain by the end of the century could be from Japanese companies.

**Source:** *Sunday Times*, 12 March, 1989.

or similar strategy along key dimensions is known as a strategic group. In a study of the Irish food industry Dignam (1984) identified the characteristics of successful firms which could survive and grow in international markets. Two important strategic dimensions identified were new product development and productivity measured as sales turnover per employee. In this way Dignam identified five

**Table 4.2**  Factors
leading to competitive
superiority in the motor
industry

Cohesive industry structure
Improved assembly methods
Meeting market needs
Research and development
Internationalization

Source: *The Financial Times,*
Thursday, 8 December, 1988.

strategic groups in the sixty-one firms studied in the food industry (Figure 4.6).

Only two firms were highly successful on both dimensions whereas a further fourteen firms were successfully pursuing a niche strategy based on innovative product development programmes. Their recent entry into international markets resulted in low productivity rates. A second strategic group of eight firms appeared to be attempting to imitate the preceding new product development strategy but were still operating in many segments. A further group of eight firms consisted of commodity producers providing little value added. These firms were, however, very successful on commodity export markets due in part to a low-cost structure. They employed few people, however, which placed them in the high-productivity category.

The group which caused greatest concern were the nineteen firms which operated with low prices, indifferent quality and old products. These firms were threatened by imports and competition from others in the industry. Dignam (1984) suggests that these firms are "stuck in the middle" and should endeavour to move to one of the other positions. The optimum position is the high new product development, high productivity position but the niche strategy and low-cost strategies are both viable.

## Investing in manufacturing and marketing

The attainment of any strategic position is not only a question of good analysis or commitment but also involves a number of specific investment decisions (Cook, 1983). The construction of efficient scale facilities and the vigorous pursuit of cost reduction through accumulated experience is associated with cost leadership. Research and design, quality control and customer service facilities are more important when differentiation is pursued. These discreet instruments are generally not mutually exclusive. A level of exclusivity will exist, however, in managerial co-ordinating capacity, and the need to select a system of internal organization, evaluation and reward that will be designed for optimal pursuit

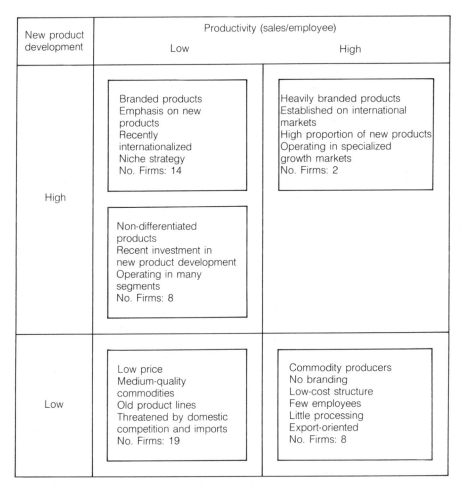

| New product development | Productivity (sales/employee) | |
|---|---|---|
| | Low | High |
| High | Branded products<br>Emphasis on new products<br>Recently internationalized<br>Niche strategy<br>No. Firms: 14 | Heavily branded products<br>Established on international markets<br>High proportion of new products<br>Operating in specialized growth markets<br>No. Firms: 2 |
| | Non-differentiated products<br>Recent investment in new product development<br>Operating in many segments<br>No. Firms: 8 | |
| Low | Low price<br>Medium-quality commodities<br>Old product lines<br>Threatened by domestic competition and imports<br>No. Firms: 19 | Commodity producers<br>No branding<br>Low-cost structure<br>Few employees<br>Little processing<br>Export-oriented<br>No. Firms: 8 |

**Figure 4.6** Strategic groups in the food industry (Source: Adapted from Dignam, Loretta M. (1984) New Product Development in the Irish Food Industry, unpublished Master of Business Studies Dissertation, Department of Marketing, University College Dublin, pp. 134–50)

of the chosen strategy. Different managerial talents and organizational measures of success will be needed depending on the strategy followed (Porter, 1985).

The essence of global competition is the management of international cash flows through the strategic co-ordination of manufacturing operations and marketing systems (Prahalad and Doz, 1987, Chapter 3). This statement applies equally to small and large firms irrespective of the extent to which the firm has expanded its marketing internationally and the extent to which it has located its production abroad. Managing cash flows emphasizes both costs and prices.

## Managing costs and prices

In managing the cost side the successful competitor is concerned with factor costs, scale and technology effects and exchange rate fluctuations. Factor costs refer to the location specific advantages that accrue to a manufacturer, e.g. labour cost differentials, availability of cheap raw materials and components, access to low-cost capital, and government sponsored industrial promotion incentives. Size, location, and technological sophistication of manufacturing plants in different countries can present the firm with significant cost advantages. This is most apparent in comparing a single plant firm which exports to serve international markets and a multiplant firm serving a selected portfolio of markets.

Exchange rate fluctuations can eliminate cost advantages or make certain locations more attractive. Successful competitors learn how to manage these three elements of cost: labour costs; manufacturing scale; and technology and exchange rate fluctuations (Figure 4.7). The successful competitor does not attempt to reduce the impact of any one of these elements while ignoring the others. It is a question of seeking a balance among the three factors while maintaining flexibility. To do so the firm must have a portfolio of manufacturing locations that allows it to exploit both factor cost advantages and exchange rate differentials (Prahalad and Doz, 1985, p. 43).

On the price side the firm usually attempts to obtain the highest net price possible. A number of factors influence the ability of the firm to derive such prices: market structure; access to distribution channels; brand power; and the product line. In regard to the first issue, the market in each country is unique in terms of its competitive structure; the intensity of competition determines the level of prices and is dependent upon the number and type of competitors in the market. In order to exploit the resulting price differentials, especially when competitor costs are the same as those of the firm, it is valuable to be present in a portfolio of markets.

Access and command of distribution channels is also a well-known competitive advantage. Well-known brands with a quality image command a premium. Established reputations allow for a price premium. Control over the distribution channels due to a broad product line also gives rise to a premium which, according to Prahalad and Doz (1985, p. 46), suggests that in addition to being present in a portfolio of markets a firm should attempt to develop a brand and distribution presence in its key markets. Finally, a wide product line can be as effective in allowing the firm to compete on price as being present in many markets. The Swatch story is a good illustration of how the Swiss watch industry responded to Japanese competition by reorganizing, cutting costs and introducing new sophisticated technology to compete on price where the retaliation would produce the greatest damage (Exhibit 4.4). Just as a firm can use its portfolio of markets to cross-subsidize competitive battles, so it can cross-subsidize among products within a market.

Managing net prices is critical to managing the firm's overall cash flow. The

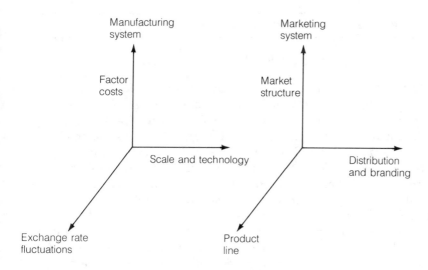

**Figure 4.7**  Managing the manufacturing and marketing systems for international competitiveness (Source: Adapted from Prahalad, C.K. and Doz, Yves, L. (1987) *The Multinational Mission*, The Free Press, NY)

firm must, therefore, manage the marketing system which comprises a portfolio of markets to respond to price differences arising from different market structures, a brand presence which allows for a price premium and a product line to leverage economies of scope, control distribution channels and to allow cross-subsidization among products within a single market (Prahalad and Doz, 1985, p. 47). The firm attempts to balance these three sources of price advantage (Figure 4.7).

The discussion on approaches to managing international cash flows suggests that the firm should develop a strategic infrastructure to allow it to compete successfully in international markets (Prahalad and Doz, 1987, p. 48). The strategic infrastructure comprises five elements (Table 4.3). The portfolio of manufacturing locations provides the firm with the opportunity of leveraging factor cost advantages with the objective of integrating them into a global network which

**Table 4.3**  Strategic infrastructure for international competition

Portfolio of manufacturing locations
Improvements in manufacturing technology and productivity
Portfolio of markets
Strong branding and distribution network
Wide product line

Source: Adapted from Prahalad, C.K. and Doz, Yves L. (1987) *The Multinational Mission*, The Free Press, NY.

---

**Exhibit 4.4   Using price, quality and segmentation to compete**

---

*Hayek: the "Napoleon" of the Swiss watch industry*

No matter how many times he has told it, the loquacious chairman of SMH AG, makers of the fabulous Swatch, still relates its phenomenal success story with the gusto of a kid telling how he beat up the school bully. "They were expecting us to launch our attack in the medium- and high-price watch segments", he says, chalk slashing across the blackboard. "But we hit them with a quality watch in the low priced segment, where they were strongest, where they would be hurt the most and where we had the highest risk." That it came off is now one of the great corporate marketing epics of the 1980s, and Hayek played no mean role in making it happen.

The 58-year-old Hayek was already a self-made millionaire and established as Switzerland's leading management consultant when he was initially brought in by a lender bank in 1981 to help sort out the country's two largest watchmakers, ASU AG and SSIH. He drew up a plan to merge the two foundering companies, makers of such famous brands as Omega, Tissot, Longines and Rado. He also took an active part in implementing it, forming SMH. Then, last June, after putting together a Swiss consortium that acquired the bank's 56 percent equity stake in SMH, he took over as chairman.

The ambitious Hayek is also pushing SMH into such high-technology niche businesses as microelectronic wafer production, lasers, robots, quartz measuring systems and bonding machines. These diversifications already account for more than one-sixth of group sales. "Five years from now, I'm aiming to double the volume of our watch sales and increase the diversifications three fold so that we move towards a 66−33 breakdown", says Hayek.

To do that, he makes clear that there's no time for an armistice in the Swiss watch industry's onslaught to regain its lost market share in the medium- and lower-price segments. "The competition is now hiring French and British designers to copy our models", he says, scribbling on his blackboard and talking at breakneck speed.

"The Japanese price strategy worked as long as they were the cheapest. But now they're no longer cheapest, and they're in trouble. So we have a new strategy — to open up a new front every eight months. Attack, attack, attack," he declaims.

**Source:** *International Management*, January, 1987, pp. 18−19.

---

would also consider exchange rate fluctuations. The infrastructure also permits the firm to pay constant attention to the need to seek improvements in technology and productivity.

The portfolio of markets allows the firm to leverage differences in competitive market structures to exploit the resulting price differentials. Strong branding and control of distribution allow the firm to develop markets and to have almost guaranteed access to the firm's customer base for existing and new products. Finally, a wide product line allows cross-subsidization across products in a given market. Most firms do not possess such a strategic infrastructure but seek to develop elements of it to suit circumstances. The more developed, balanced and flexible the infrastructure the more likely is the firm to maximize international cash flows and compete successfully in international markets.

## International competitive strategies

The literature relating to the strategies that firms follow in international markets has been limited according to Porter (1986) by an overemphasis on the problems of becoming an international company rather than on strategies for establishing international firms. The fact that a firm is an international competitor says very little about its international strategy except that it operates in several countries. Many of the strategic issues facing firms competing internationally are very much the same as those competing in domestic markets only. A checklist which may serve to assist in the analysis of competitors and their positions would cover the principal areas of marketing (Table 4.4). The firm still needs to analyse its industry structure and competitors, understand its buyers and sources of buyer value, diagnose its relative market position and seek to establish a sustainable competitive advantage with a broad or industry segment scope. However, there are questions peculiar to international competition which can affect the success of an international competitive strategy profoundly.

## Pattern of international competition

The questions "can you standardize multinational marketing?" and "are domestic and international markets dissimilar?" were raised in the late 1960s (Buzzell, 1968; Bartels, 1968). In a literal sense this involves the offering of identical product lines at identical prices through identical distribution systems, supported by identical promotional programmes, in several different countries. This would contrast strongly with completely "localized" marketing strategies which contain no common elements whatsoever. These approaches are at extreme ends of a

**Table 4.4**  Analysing competitors and positions

Who are the firm's competitors
- current competitors
- potential entrants

What is their position in the market
- segments served
- benefits offered
- strategy followed

What is the principal competitive advantage/weakness of each competitor in each position

How are competing products positioned relative to
- each other
- customer needs

continuum and the firm may decide to avail of only some of the cost savings as a result of standardization. While Buzzell ultimately suggests that a balanced consideration of the benefits and costs of standardization is required, he favours a single marketing strategy. Levitt (1983) is even more hard hitting, suggesting that a new reality has emerged which consists of global markets. This is based on increasingly similar consumer desires throughout the world. Even more apparent is the presumed Europeanization of markets with one single internalized market which directly affects EC countries and indirectly affects neighbouring countries. Levitt points out that the firms that are prepared for the single internal EC market will benefit from enormous economies of scale in production, distribution, marketing and overall management, which will provide these firms with a cost competence and potential competitive advantage, thereby beating competitors that still live in the disabling grip of old country centred assumptions.

Indeed, the EC Commission views the strategy of focussing on country centred needs as one of the enormous costs of a non-Europe (Commission of the EC 1987). If this were to continue it would be to the advantage of Europe's competitors, Japan and the United States, who may carry out R & D work more economically, based on large home markets, and also produce for all markets in bulk. A failure by firms to follow a single European market outlook and use the collective resources of such a market will contribute to the uncompetitiveness of these firms, their low productivity and poor innovation record.

Not all companies will be able to adopt a standardized strategy as its appropriateness will vary from industry to industry. At one end of the spectrum Porter (1986) suggests, will be the multidomestic industry, in which competition in each country, or a small group of countries, will be essentially independent of competition in other countries. In these industries a firm may enjoy a competitive advantage from a one-time transfer of know-how from its home base to foreign countries. The firm may adapt its intangible assets for each country, however, and accordingly, the competitive advantage of the firm will be largely specific to each country. Examples of industries operating in this mode would be: retailing; distribution; insurance; and retail banking. At the other end of the spectrum are what are termed global industries. The term global, like the word strategy, has become overused and perhaps misunderstood; it should not be taken literally but, rather, should be applied to a collection of markets or a region of markets. A global industry is one in which a firm's competitive position in one country is significantly influenced by its position in other countries. In these industries firms do not operate with a collection of individual markets but a series of linked markets in which rivals compete against each other across these markets.

A firm may choose to compete with a country centred strategy thus focussing on specific market segments or countries, when it can carve out a niche by responding to whatever local country differences are present. The firm which follows this approach does so at considerable risk to itself from competitors that follow a global strategy. It also misses opportunities for cost savings and scale economies. The purest global strategy would be to concentrate as many activities as possible in one country and serve markets from this base with a tightly co-ordinated market offering. This type of strategy is not only the domain of companies like Toyota or Xerox, but smaller international firms could clearly also gain by co-ordinating their international marketing endeavours through joint ventures and other alliances. As a result of such a strategy, clear advantages may accrue in the rapid attainment of scale and learning thresholds, the sharing of development and commercialization costs and establishing significant if shared positions in international markets.

## Approaches to internationalization

One of the most significant developments in business practice in recent years has been the rapid growth of international activities. Exports, foreign direct investment and sourcing of products and components abroad have expanded dramatically. In a 1986 survey of European firms, the extent of the internationalization process was explored in general terms (International Management, 1986). For the study, International Management selected participants at random from its top executive subscriber categories in companies with more than 200 employees. A total of 440 executives returned usable questionnaires, representing a 14 per cent response. Some of the more significant aspects of this survey are worth recounting as they indicate how European firms are changing their competitive positions.

The data provided in the International Management Survey were reanalysed to seek categories of company response. On average 51 per cent of respondents in the survey stated that their companies were attempting to focus on the production of standardized products. At the same time 60 per cent of respondents reported that their companies were giving emphasis to customized products. By taking the average as the cut-off between high and low it is possible to classify respondents as high standardization—low customization (Table 4.5). Thus 61 per cent of Austrian respondents report a desire to compete with standardized products, while the average for all respondents in the survey was 51 per cent. At the same time 56 per cent of Austrian respondents reported a desire to compete with customized products while the average for all firms was 60 per cent. Swiss and Turkish firms appear to compete at a high level on both factors while neither factor seems to hold great appeal for respondents in Greece, Norway, Portugal and Spain (Table 4.5).

A similar classification comparing the desire of managers to establish a global image and the extent of perceived protectionism in markets yields similar results (Figure 4.13). Belgian, Danish, French and Italian firms scored high on global image and low on protectionism. For these firms, establishing an image of global intent is very important. These firms do not appear to be overly concerned about protectionism. The average for all firms on global intent was 62 per cent while it was 28 per cent for protectionism. In contrast German firms appear not to be overly concerned about creating an image of global intent as many are already well established in world markets. They are, however, concerned with protectionism. The same is true for Norwegian, Spanish and UK firms (Table 4.6).

**Table 4.5**  Competing with standardized or customized products among European firms

| Country and classification | Standardized products Respondents (%) | Customized products Respondents (%) |
|---|---|---|
| High standardization–low customization | | |
| Austria | 61 | 56 |
| Italy | 65 | 58 |
| Netherlands | 63 | 56 |
| Sweden | 52 | 59 |
| Low standardization–high customization | | |
| Belgium | 46 | 63 |
| Denmark | 50 | 64 |
| France | 42 | 81 |
| Germany (FRG) | 50 | 61 |
| United Kingdom | 40 | 60 |
| High Standardization–high customization | | |
| Switzerland | 57 | 68 |
| Turkey | 65 | 61 |
| Low standardization–low customization | | |
| Greece | 41 | 41 |
| Norway | 46 | 54 |
| Portugal | 33 | 52 |
| Spain | 42 | 55 |
| Average | 51 | 60 |

Based on responses from 440 European executives.

Source: Derived from survey data in *International Management* November, 1986.

This raises the question regarding niche strategies as opposed to global strategies. Some firms are content to serve lucrative niche markets while others believe it is important to have open markets and a global strategy. For firms in Greece, Sweden and Turkey, levels of perceived protectionism were high but these firms were content to operate in niche markets. Firms in two of these countries are new to international markets while Swedish firms remain outside the EC and may therefore be very sensitive to issues of protection. A word of warning is necessary here. These comments are highly speculative as they are based on survey data of a broad range of firms in many markets, and sample sizes varied greatly. In the absence of better data they provide a broad indication of the response of European firms to internationalization issues.

## Summary

This chapter is concerned with the role of marketing strategy in assisting firms entering foreign markets successfully. When developing new products for a

**Table 4.6**  Creating an image of global intent hindered by non-tariff barriers

| Country and classification | Image of global intent<br>Respondents (%) | Perceived protectionism<br>Respondents (%) |
|---|---|---|
| High global intent—low perceived protectionism | | |
| Belgium | 79 | 13 |
| Denmark | 71 | 14 |
| France | 69 | 27 |
| Italy | 68 | 27 |
| Low global intent—high perceived protectionism | | |
| Greece | 53 | 35 |
| Netherlands | 50 | 28 |
| Sweden | 41 | 45 |
| Turkey | 57 | 44 |
| High global intent—high perceived protectionism | | |
| Austria | 69 | 42 |
| Portugal | 67 | 30 |
| Switzerland | 76 | 32 |
| Low global intent—low perceived protectionism | | |
| Germany (FRG) | 58 | 22 |
| Norway | 50 | 4 |
| Spain | 52 | 26 |
| United Kingdom | 60 | 20 |
| Average | 62 | 28 |

Based on responses from 440 European executives.

Source: Derived from survey data in *International Management*, November, 1986.

market it is necessary to emphasize that marketing is performed along three dimensions: technology; customer segment; and customer function. As with domestic markets, foreign markets must be segmented and targeted to provide customer benefits in gaining a competitive advantage. The firm must innovate in a number of directions when entering international markets. General considerations of firms entering foreign markets are niche versus global strategies, cost cutting and company restructuring.

There are a number of different master and sub-strategies that a firm can pursue as a basis for competition in international markets. At the broad generic level competitive strategies may be based on the "value chain" concept. It is important, however, to keep in mind that industries compete on a range of factors.

It may be possible to group competitors into strategic groups when analysing competitor strategies in an industry. There tends to be a close relationship between the firm's competitors and their strategies. The more similar the strategies the more they compete. Many firms compete on the basis of cost and non-cost factors.

Strategies pursued by firms also involve investment decisions such as managing the cash flow based on manufacturing and marketing decisions. Managing costs and prices is an important aspect of this decision area.

## Discussion questions

1. The world market is really a series of market segments, each with different needs and wants. Successful international market segmentation requires a careful selection of country markets, regions and customers. Discuss.

2. What are the advantages and disadvantages of competing directly with strong rivals in international markets? When would you recommend a direct competitive response?

3. International market expansion usually means innovating in a number of directions simultaneously. Discuss the value to the firm of the technology−product−market framework in deciding how to proceed.

4. The firm in international markets must manage manufacturing and marketing costs. What are these costs and how do they affect the fortunes of the firm?

5. An international marketing strategy is based on market considerations and competitive factors. How should the firm analyse and cope with these issues in formulating a strategy for international markets?

## References

Bartels, Robert (1968) 'Are domestic and international marketing dissimilar?,' *Journal of Marketing*, **32**, 56−61.

Buzzell, Robert D. (1968) 'Can you standardize multinational marketing?,' *Harvard Business Review*, November−December, pp. 102−13.

Buzzell, R.D., Gale, B.T. and Sultan, R.G.M. (1975) 'Market share: A key to profitability, *Harvard Business Review*, January−February, pp. 97-106.

Carroad, Paul A. and Carroad, Connie A. (1982) 'Strategic interfacing of R & D and marketing,' *Research Management*, January, pp. 28−33.

Commission of the European Communities (1987) *Europe Without Frontiers — Completing the Internal Market*, official publication.

Cook, Victor J., Jr (1983) 'Marketing strategy and differential advantage,' *Journal of Marketing*, **47**, 68−75.

Dignam, Loretta M. (1984) New Product Development in the Irish Food Industry, unpublished Master of Business Dissertation, Department of Marketing, University College Dublin.

Hayes, Robert H. and Wheelwright, Steven C. (1984) *Restoring Our Competitive Edge*, John Wiley and Sons.

Hofer, G.W. and Schendel, D.E. (1978) *Strategy Formulation: Analytical Concepts*, West Publishing, St. Paul, Minn.

Levitt, Theodore (1983) 'The globalization of markets,' *Harvard Business Review*, May–June, pp. 92–102.

Phillips, Lynn, Chang, Dae R. and Buzzel, Robert D. (1983) 'Product quality, cost position and business performance: A test of some key hypotheses,' *Journal of Marketing*, **47**, 26–43.

Porter, Michael E. (1980) *Competitive Strategy*, The Free Press, NY.

Porter, Michael E. (1985) *Competitive Advantage*, The Free Press, NY.

Porter, Michael E. (1986) 'Changing patterns of international competition,' *California Management Review*, **2**, 9–37.

Porter, Michael E. (1987) 'The state of strategic thinking,' *The Economist*, 23 May, pp. 21ff.

Prahalad, C.K. and Doz, Yves L. (1987) *The Multinational Mission*, The Free Press, NY.

Quelch, John A. and Hoff, Edward J. (1986) 'Customizing global marketing,' *Harvard Business Review*, May–June, pp. 59–68.

Steiner, G.A. and Miner, J.B. (1977) *Management Policy and Strategy*, Macmillan Publishers Inc., NY.

Storey, David, Keasey, Kevin, Watson, Robert and Wynarczyk, Pooran (1987) *The Performance of Small Firms*, Croom Helm, London.

Thompson, A. and Strickland, A.J. III (1983) *Strategy Formulation and Implementation*, Business Publications, Inc., Plano, Texas.

Utterback, J.M. and Abernathy, W. (1975) 'A dynamic model of process and product innovation,' *OMEGA*, **3**, 639–56.

# *Deciding which markets to enter*

# The socio-cultural environment of international marketing

International business has always been recognized as an activity involving investment decisions or the exchange of products and services across national boundaries. It is only in recent years, however, that socio-cultural influences have been identified as critical determinants of international management behaviour. International business, and especially international marketing, is seen as a cultural as well as an economic phenomenon. The basic argument behind the need to examine the socio-cultural dimension of the internationalization of the firm is that the management view tends to be culture bound and therefore inward looking and subject to the dictates of the self-reference criterion (Lee, 1966). Writers on the subject have recognized this need by moving away from the narrow perspective of economic analysis of the internationalization process. The growing use of anthropology, sociology and psychology in international marketing analysis is an explicit recognition of the non-economic bases of marketing behaviour (Cateora, 1990, pp. 2–19; Terpstra, 1978, p. 86).

It is accepted, for example, that it is not enough to say that consumption of a product is a function of income; it is also a function of many other cultural factors. Furthermore, only non-economic factors can explain the different patterns of consumption of two different countries with identical *per capita* incomes. Culture is so pervasive yet complex that it is difficult to define: each scholar seems to have a separate definition. Culture has been called "the integrated sum total of learned behavioral traits that are manifest and shared by members of a society" (Hoebel, 1960, p. 168). For present purposes culture may be considered the man-made part of our environment, or the distinctive life style of a people. Culture is not biologically transmitted; any given culture or way of life is learned behaviour which depends on the environment and not on hereditary factors (Terpstra, 1978, p. 87).

In the present context, therefore, the term "socio-cultural environment" is used to refer to all those factors behind a country's international marketing prowess which are of a learned nature. This makes it a rather omnibus term, covering attitudes, sociology, behaviour, psychology and cultural development of, and within, the country as a whole, and the various sub-populations which go to make up that country. Just as there is more to Japan's prowess in international marketing than the strict application of the techniques identified in some text-book or manual, so, too, is there for other countries with different cultural backgrounds. It is the objective of this chapter to focus on factors which may not be as obvious as text-book techniques, i.e. those emanating from the socio-cultural environment.

## Socio-cultural environment

The socio-cultural environment consists of those physical, demographic and behavioural variables which influence business activities in a given country (Figure 5.1).

Among human variations, the most noticeable are physical attributes or appearance. While most differences in appearance are readily apparent, there are a host of subtle variations that, although important to people within a given society, may be easily overlooked by non-discriminating outsiders. Size of individuals would seem to be one of the most noticeable differences, but many firms make mistakes in this respect. For example, one US company attempted to sell men's trousers in Japan based on US patterns for tailoring, only to realize that they fitted few Japanese men because of their narrower hips.

Not only must actual physical differences be taken into account, so also must traits that a country has idealized. Various populations have created wishful stereotypes of themselves that must be considered when creating imagery. For this reason, advertisements in the United States typically depict individuals who are somewhat younger and thinner than the bulk of the people toward whom the product is aimed. In West Germany there has been an idealization of the tall Nordic type, who is actually no taller than the average Pole, Frenchman or Dutchman.

Demographic changes also influence the international firm. Certain population characteristics are important to the international firm. For many products, population size may be used as a broad preliminary indicator of market potential. However, population size should only be used in conjunction with income levels and other measures, as a large population may represent little potential where income levels are quite low.

It is important to study population growth rates: low population growth rates are more typical of countries generally regarded as more highly developed economically. This arises from an historical tendency of both birth and death rates to decrease following, rather than preceding, economic development. In most developing countries in recent years, the death rate has fallen markedly because of medical advances, while the birth rate has remained high. This has caused an unprecedented population explosion that has hampered efforts to raise living standards.

Not only is the world's population growing rapidly, but the population density is shifting from the industrial countries of the North to the developing countries of the South. By the end of this century, population in the developed world is expected to increase by about 200 million, whereas the developing areas of Africa, Asia and Latin America are expected to increase by two billion. By the

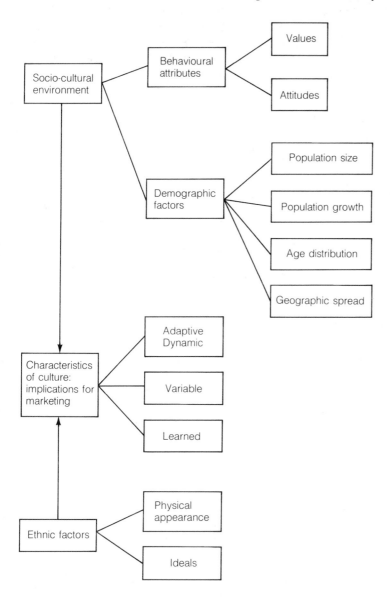

**Figure 5.1**  The socio-cultural environment and marketing implications

year 2000, the World Bank predicts that over four-fifths of the world's population will be concentrated in developing countries.

The age distribution in a foreign country is yet another factor which affects both sales and investment opportunities. A country with a larger proportion of people in the older age brackets would have a smaller market for items such as maternity and infant goods, and school equipment. Conversely, a more elderly population would represent a larger market for healthcare products. The age distribution of selected populations is shown in Figure 5.2.

Generally, employable people are considered to be those between the ages

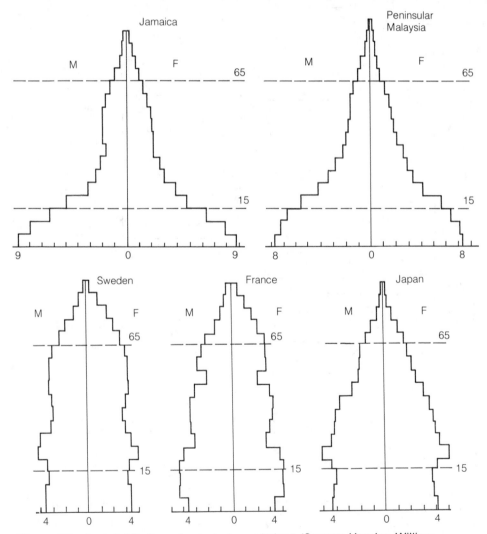

**Figure 5.2**   Age distribution of selected populations (Source: Hornby, William F.(1980) *An Introduction to Population Geography*, Cambridge University Press, Cambridge)

of twenty and sixty years. If a population consists largely of very old or very young people, then a smaller than normal number will be available to do productive work. This may lead to a shortage of skilled or manual labour and greatly increased wage rates.

Overall, country data obscure differences that exist within individual nations. Within developing countries there are, typically, fairly substantial groups that have the characteristics of advanced countries. Of course, it is also possible to find backward areas or groups within the most developed countries. It is important to note, however, that the socio-cultural environment varies greatly from country to country.

## Interpreting culture for the international firm

Culture may be defined as the ways of living built up by a group of human beings which are transmitted from one generation to another. Culture includes both conscious and unconscious values, ideas, attitudes and symbols which shape human behaviour and are transmitted from one generation to the next (Terpstra, 1978).

In this sense culture does not refer to the instinctive responses of people, nor does it include one-time solutions to unique problems. Hall (1960) has stated that "culture is man's medium; there is not one aspect of human life that is not touched and altered by culture. This means personalities, how people express themselves (including shows of emotion), the way they think, how they move, how problems are solved, how their cities are planned and laid out, how transportation systems function and are organized, as well as how economic and government systems are put together and function."

That which gives man his identity no matter where he was born is his culture — the total communication framework of words, actions, posture, gestures, tones of voice, facial expressions, the way he handles time, space and materials and the way he works, plays, makes love and defends himself and his property (Hall, 1960). All man's actions are modified by learning. Once learned, habitual responses and ways of interacting gradually sink below the surface of the mind and operate from the unconscious.

It is important to remember that some managerial functions are more sensitive to culture than others. Sensitivity of a particular function to cultural influence depends upon the importance of direct exchange between that function and the cultural environment. Functions such as marketing and public relations generally demand more interaction with local culture than, for example, the functions of finance or production.

### Characteristics of culture

There are two ways in which a person develops norms and values (Engel, Warshaw and Kinnear, 1983). The first is called socialization, in which a person learns a culture when he or she is very young. Two different forces operate here. The first source of values is referred to as the institutional triad — families, and religious and educational institutions. The second source is early lifetime experiences which may include war, social disturbances and family upheavals. Values and norms formed at this stage will lead to differences between the generations, when the population as a whole is being considered.

The second process is termed acculturation, and is the process of learning a culture of which one is not native. For example, if a firm wishes to invest in, or sell to another country, it must learn the culture of that country. For the firm in international markets the characteristics of culture are learned, interrelated and adaptive. These operate at times as sub-cultures involving language, religion, values, attitudes and other aspects of social organization (Table 5.1). Patterns which govern behaviour and perception come into consciousness only when there is a deviation from the learned pattern as can happen in intercultural encounters which may lead to cultural bias.

To transcend this bias the manager of the firm in international markets must achieve awareness of the structure of his own system by interacting with others who do not share that system. This awareness may be achieved through the acquisition of the relevant language and of its associated conceptual frameworks.

In attempting to understand the impact of culture on the firm it is important to recognize that parts of culture are interrelated and that culture is adaptive and may change rapidly or slowly. The various parts of culture are interrelated. Cultural systems have a unity which, as a result of the interaction among the

**Table 5.1** Characteristics and elements of culture

Characteristics of culture:

1.    Learned
      • socialization
      • acculturation
2.    Interrelated
3.    Adaptive
      • discontinuity
      • evolutionary
4.    Sub-cultures
      • nationality
      • religion
      • age
      • occupation

Elements of culture:
   • Language
   • Religion
   • Values and attitudes
   • Social organization
   • Education
   • Technology and material culture

parts, is different from a simple sum of the parts. To achieve understanding of any culture, one must not only understand the content, but also how the system is put together and how its parts are interrelated. Culture is also adaptive, either through a discontinuous or evolutionary process (Engel and Blackwell, 1982). Culture responds to the physical and social environment in which it operates and has contact (Exhibit 5.3). It is especially important for the firm in international markets to monitor the change in the physical and social environment as such changes can in a relatively short period result in either positive or negative effects on the demand for the company's products (Exhibit 5.1).

A very sharp discontinuity occurs in the pattern of cultural change when the value system of a culture becomes associated with the gratification of only one class. Other classes reject the logic of the value system and replace it with a new value system. In an evolutionary process, change comes, but is a process of modification and adaptation. The adaptive nature of culture is an important consideration in developing an understanding of behaviour in that culture. In the past, cultural change was usually slow and gradual. The accelerated technological changes that characterize contemporary society, together with rapid changes in the institutional triad mentioned above, have created a situation where change is quicker and more unpredictable.

Most cultures are also characterized by a series of sub-cultures which involve sets of learned beliefs, values, attitudes, habits and forms of behaviour which are shared by subjects of a society and are transmitted from generation to generation within each subset (Bennet and Kassarjan, 1972). Members of sub-cultures typically conform to many of the norms of the dominant culture and deviate from others which are not compatible with the norms of their sub-culture.

There are a number of variables upon which sub-cultures are based. Some are based upon nationality, such as the Turkish immigrants in West Germany, who represent 6 per cent of the total population. Religion is often the base for sub-cultures, such as the Catholic minority in Northern Ireland. In the United States race is an important base of sub-culture. Age can also represent an important basis for recognizing sub-cultures with, for example, teenagers and older age groups exhibiting quite different patterns of consumption.

Often the values of a sub-culture will be passed on to the dominant culture. Denim jeans, which were originally worn by the youth sub-culture, are now worn by all age groups.

## Elements of culture in international markets

Language is perhaps the most obvious difference between cultures, and has been described as a cultural mirror which reflects the content and nature of the culture it represents. Language is human behaviour, not just a collection of words and sounds. It is the spoken and not the written language which most accurately describes and reflects the contempory behaviour and values of members of a

## Exhibit 5.1    Socio-cultural environment: some elements change, some don't

*Cultural assessment for international marketing: case study — Japan*

Notable physical features

- average height at 20 years: 169.7cm (men); 156.9cm (women)
- Japanese people growing taller over past decade
- compared to Northern Europeans, Japanese have:
  shorter legs and larger heads
  women have smaller bustlines
  men have smaller chests and narrower hips
  shorter and wider feet

Notable demographic features:

- 118 million consumers
- average monthly income of ¥424,025 ($1796) of which 86% is disposable
- ageing population
- largest segment of population in early to mid 30s in the late 1980s
- by 2025, largest proportion 55 years or older
- impact of the "bulge generation"
- large proportion of population live in densly populated urban belt running from Tokyo to Osaka
- life expectancy longest in the world for men and for women is second only to Iceland

Notable cultural features:

- lifetime employment system (selective)
- income rises more with age than performance
- bonuses paid in mid-summer and December (prime period for increase in purchases)
- on average 20% of disposable income saved
- wife determines family spending patterns. Husband "surrenders" salary and in return receives allowance
- individualization, while maintaining high quality and reasonable cost, a feature of Japanese demand
- consumer highly "fashion" and "brand" conscious
- diet characterized by high consumption of cereals, particularly rice and of fish, and by low consumption of dairy products
- high standard educational system
- read regularly, and keeping up to date is a point of pride
- low crime rate (14 murders per million people per year compared to 102 in US)
- 90% Japanese people classified as middle class

**Source:** Compiled from the Japanese External Trade Organization (JETRO): *The Japanese Economy and Industry* (1987); *The Japanese Market in Figures* (1980); *The Japanese Consumer* (1988).

culture. Some countries are linguistically homogeneous while others are heterogeneous. There is a preponderance of linguistically heterogeneous countries in Asia and Africa. Europe and the Middle East are about evenly balanced, while Latin America is almost homogeneous linguistically (Table 5.2).

In addition to differences in official languages, nations also differ in the number of languages used within their boundaries. Looking at just national official languages can give a misleading picture of the linguistic uniformity within countries. There are only about 100 official languages for all countries in the world, whereas there are at least 3,000 languages currently spoken throughout the world. Well under half of the countries of the world are linguistically homogeneous in the sense that 85 per cent or more of the population speaks the same native tongue. The degree of linguistic heterogeneity varies greatly between countries. Some countries are almost "pure" linguistically, with nearly all the citizens speaking the same native tongue. A complicating factor in most countries, which is not easily resolved, is the issue of dialects. In countries where more than one language is spoken widely the issue of dialects is, of course, much more complicated. Switzerland is a good example of a small country in which there are a number of official languages but a range of dialects based on these languages.

## Language, communication, and values in international marketing

Language, as the primary means of communication among civilized peoples, is perhaps the most important single cultural input. Language is the medium we all use to make meaning from environmental stimuli. Clumsy or careless language use may result in inaccurate communication (Cundiff and Tharp Higler, 1984). The nuances of meaning for particular words may vary from language to language, and a literal translation may change the entire meaning. Poor translation and the misuse of language are among the common traps of international marketing, but no aspect of international marketing is insulated from the problems associated with the management of cultural issues (Ricks, 1983).

Managers who find it necessary to communicate in a foreign language should make use of a truly bilingual interpreter who will make certain that the meaning is not lost in translation. It can be dangerous for people with an elementary knowledge of a foreign language to act as their own interpreter. They can miss subtle meanings in written correspondence that may affect interest in a product, or even a possible sales contract. The same kind of traps exist in oral communication of which examples abound. The international manager should therefore be aware of the more obvious differences in languages and general behaviour as well as the more subtle influence it has on thinking and cultural identities (Exhibit 5.2).

Regarding the religion and values in society, we are dealing with man's deepest convictions. For Terpstra (1978) religion is a mainspring of culture. A person's religious beliefs influence consumption behaviour, social behaviour, manner of dress, ways of doing business, general societal values and harmony and conflict in society. Religion also affects our attitudes toward time, wealth,

**Table 5.2** Linguistic characteristics of selected countries

| Region of world | Linguistically homogeneous countries | | Linguistically heterogeneous countries | |
|---|---|---|---|---|
| Asia | Korea<br>Mongolia<br>Japan | | Afghanistan<br>Burma<br>Cambodia<br>China<br>India<br>Indonesia<br>Laos<br>Malaysia | Nepal<br>Pakistan<br>Philippines<br>Sri Lanka<br>Syria<br>Thailand<br>Vietnam |
| Africa | Burundi<br>Rwanda<br>Somalia | | Benin<br>Cameroon<br>Chad<br>Congo<br>Ethiopia<br>Gabon<br>Ghana<br>Guinea<br>Ivory Coast<br>Liberia<br>Mali | Mauritania<br>Niger<br>Nigeria<br>Senegal<br>South Africa<br>Sudan<br>Tanzania<br>Togo<br>Uganda<br>Zaire |
| Europe | Albania<br>Austria<br>Denmark<br>France<br>Germany<br>Greece<br>Hungary<br>Iceland | Ireland<br>Italy<br>Netherlands<br>Norway<br>Poland<br>Portugal<br>Sweden<br>United Kingdom | Belgium<br>Bulgaria<br>Cyprus<br>Czechoslovakia<br>Finland | Romania<br>Spain<br>Switzerland<br>USSR<br>Yugoslavia |
| North America | | | Canada<br>United States | |
| Latin America | Argentina<br>Brazil<br>Chile<br>Colombia<br>Costa Rica<br>Cuba<br>Dominican<br>   Republic | Haiti<br>Honduras<br>Jamaica<br>Mexico<br>Nicaragua<br>Paraguay<br>Trinidad<br>Uruguay<br>Venezuela | Bolivia<br>Ecuador<br>Panama<br>Peru | |
| Middle East | Egypt<br>Jordan<br>Libya<br>Saudi Arabia | Tunisia<br>Yemen | Algeria<br>Iran<br>Iraq | Israel<br>Morocco<br>Turkey |
| Oceania | Australia<br>New Zealand | | | |

Source: Adapted from Banks, Arthur S. and Textar, Robert B. (1963) *A Cross-Polity Survey*, MIT Press, Boston, pp. 72–5.

---

**Exhibit 5.2   Cultural sensitivity requires a subtle approach**

---

*Protocol errors cost big bucks*

An American attorney employed by a large US corporation arrived at a meeting to close a deal with a Minister from Saudi Arabia. The lawyer rushed in, sat down, crossed his legs and watched, to his complete bewilderment, as the Minister gathered his papers and stalked out.

What went wrong? The American inadvertently turned up the sole of his shoe, a grave insult to Arabs. As a result, the company he represented lost a $4 million-dollar account.

The lack of awareness of many American executives about the rules, protocol, and manners involved in doing business with foreign nationals is increasingly alarming to many companies. They are seeking better ways to educate their managers and court foreign clients and prospects.

Sondra Snowdon, managing director of Snowdon International, a firm that helps companies address these problems by setting up international protocol desks, delivering "VIP services", and training managers in the customs and character of foreign business, feels that the mistakes that cause Americans to lose international business generally spring from these sources:

1. American executives do not recognize the social status the foreign businessperson holds, above and beyond personal wealth.
2. Foreign businessmen and women place a very high priority on personal relationships with the people with whom they do business.
3. Companies don't have the formal structure to handle the needs and requests of the foreign client, investor, or prospect.

**Source:** *Management Review,* June, 1985, p. 6.

---

change and risk. All these factors are fundamental to marketing and understanding of consumer and buyer behaviour.

Not only does religion establish taboos and moral standards within a culture affecting behaviour, it also reflects the principal values of a people. Social mobility and the achievement ethic in the West are supported by the Christian values of self-determination and the importance of work. The Hindu religion emphasizes reaching Nirvana through a combination of inherited status and a contemplative life. Where religion is important in a society, the religious institutions usually play an important role in either promoting or discouraging change.

Much of human behaviour depends upon values and attitudes. Our values and attitudes help determine what we think is right and wrong, what is important and what is desirable. Consumption and business behaviour may be directly related to values. For instance, achievement and success are regarded as being very important in some countries which can act as a justification for the acquisition of material wealth.

Attitudes towards time are also culturally distinctive: they vary from culture to culture and occasionally within the same culture. In some countries, for instance, an executive knows what is meant when a client lets a month go by before replying to a business proposal.

In Arab countries time does not generally include schedules as they are known and used in western countries. The time required to get something accomplished depends upon relationships. In Latin America, to be kept waiting does not necessarily mean one is not getting anywhere. Even in neighbouring European countries attitudes to time can be very different, causing conflict in management relations. In international marketing it is very important that we understand attitudes to time in different cultures (Exhibit 5.3).

## Social organization and education

Social organization concerns the way in which people relate to one another and organize their activities in order to live in harmony with one another. Social classes, the family, positions of men and women, group behaviour, and age groups are interpreted differently within different cultures (Table 5.3).

Social classes tend to have quite different consumption patterns, which affect, among other things, the purchase of housing and home furnishings, food and alcoholic beverages. The degree of social mobility is also an important dimension of class structure, as is the relative size and number of distinct classes within a society. Figure 5.3 illustrates five different societies in terms of the relative sizes of different social classes; the top rectangle shows the size of the upper class relative to middle and lower classes. In some societies only a small number of distinct social classes can be identified, whereas in others, such as the United States or India, many different social classes exist side by side, each with its own unique needs and wants.

Upper classes in almost all countries seem to be more similar to each other than they are to the rest of their own society. Lower classes tend to be more culture bound, i.e. they are less aware of other cultures, whereas middle classes are more apt to participate in cultural "borrowing." Therefore, the larger the upper and middle classes the more likely a market is to buy products and services that are not cultural bound.

The role of the family may also vary among cultures. In primitive and rural societies, the family is the all-important social focal point, providing food, clothing, shelter, education, acculturation and a social centre.

In some of the more sophisticated urban societies the family may provide little more than food and basic acculturation. All other activities are partially or totally transferred to other groups, especially peers and educational institutions.

The role of women varies widely from society to society. In many societies women do not enjoy parity with men as participants in the economy. The extent to which they participate affects their role as consumers, consumption influencers, and workers in the money economy.

## Exhibit 5.3 Understanding the concept of time in different cultures

*Swatch vs the sundial: a study in different attitudes towards time*

Certainly we all have a general awareness of the contrasting attitudes of different nationalities towards time. The Belgians, Swiss and Germans, for example, are perceived as punctual with a sense of time that communicates urgency. The Latin nations and the Irish have a more relaxed sense of time with a tolerance of the "mañana" tradition. But what happens when these attitudes meet in business?

A recent experience provides some lessons. A major Italian manufacturing company commissioned a specialized Swiss software and engineering company to design, create and install computerized materials-handling equipment.

Two project teams, one Swiss and one Italian, were formed to develop the programming. The early project meetings were courteous and formal as each side struggled towards mutual cooperation, using English as their lingua franca.

After three months of meetings, however, relationships deteriorated markedly. The Swiss engineers complained that their Italian colleagues were always changing their minds, that they never met the deadlines and did not seem to think time was important.

The Italians, meanwhile, complained that their Swiss colleagues were inflexible, always insisting on receiving documents by fixed dates.

Was it not better to get the best possible performance from the equipment by delaying a few days, and allowing better ideas to emerge?

Central to most of the complaints, when analysed in detail, was a conflict over the "sense of time." The Swiss team were heavily steeped in their cultural understanding of time as a commodity of precise and specific measurement.

The Italians, separated geographically by a solid wall of snow-covered peaks, have endured and enjoyed a more casual attitude towards time. Like their moods, their sense of time is more fluid, and is imbued with a temporary and transitional flavour.

To learn how strongly their behaviour was tied to cultural traditions, the Swiss and Italian teams decided to experiment with each other's ways. They agreed to live short periods according to the sense of time dominant in each other's culture. From this exercise, the Swiss engineers learned how to be more flexible about time and to subordinate deadlines to other values. The Italians realized how the discipline of precise time commanded respect in Swiss daily life.

By the end of the exercise, each project team understood how the other marched to the tick of different cultural clocks; one no better than the other, only different.

Project work resumed with the Italians committing themselves to an agreed specification on a fixed date. The Swiss team agreed to deliver a provisional programme, to which traditional Italian inventiveness and improvization could be applied.

**Source:** *International Management*, December, 1987, p. 80.

**Table 5.3**  Social organization and class structure

Social class
- Upper classes in different countries more similar to each other than to the rest of their society
- Middle classes more apt to "cultural borrowing"
- Lower class more culture bound

Role of the family

Role of women

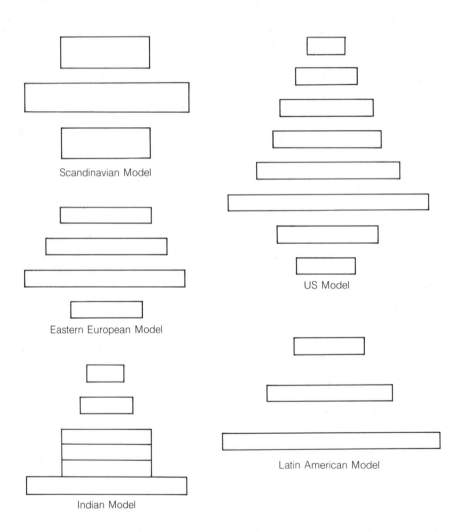

**Figure 5.3**  Relative importance of social class structures in different societies (Source: Cundiff, Edward W. and Tharp Higler, Mary E. (1984) *Marketing in the International Environment*, Prentice Hall, NJ)

In the industrialized world the educational system is synonomous with schools and these play a major role in passing on cultural values to the individual. In many developing countries, however, elders and oral historians play a greater role in the transmission of cultural traditions and values to young people. Formal education through schools has a strong relationship to literacy levels within a society. In those countries where schools are provided for the broadest possible group, literacy levels tend to be highest. Well-educated people tend to want more sophisticated information about products and tend to use more sources of information when making purchase decisions. It is important, therefore, for the international firm to understand the nature of the formal educational system, to whom it is available, and its relative importance in transmitting cultural values compared to other institutions.

## Technology and material culture

Technology includes the techniques used in the creation of material goods, it is the educational and technical know-how possessed by the people of a society (Table 5.4). Material culture affects the level of demand, the quality and types of products demanded and their functional features, as well as the means of production of these goods and their distribution (Cateora, 1990). The marketing implications of the material culture of a country are many. Electrical appliances may sell in England or France, but may find few buyers in a market where less than 1 per cent of the homes have electricity. Economic characteristics such as the level and distribution of income may limit the desirability of certain types of products. Electrical toothbrushes and electrical carving knives, which are acceptable in the West, would be considered a waste of money in countries where income could be better spent on clothing or food.

Closely related to a country's material culture is its aesthetic values or preferences in the arts, music and design. For example, Americans often feel that Japanese homes are barren while the Japanese comment on the sterility of the American home. Similarly, Hoover, the large washing machine manufacturer serving the British, French and German markets, found that the generally accepted ideas about what constitutes good design were different in each market. The

**Table 5.4** Technology and material culture

The techniques used in the creation of material goods; the technical know-how possessed by the people of a society which affects:

- level of demand
- quality and types of products demanded
- means of producing goods
- means of distributing goods

and is related to:

- aesthetic values or preferences in the arts, music, or design

German homemaker preferred a design that was larger and more sturdy in appearance, that gave a feeling of sound engineering and durability. The French homemaker preferred a smaller, lighter machine that did not overly dominate a small kitchen. No single compromise design would allow maximum penetration in all three markets.

In the same way a visual advertising appeal that may seem attractive to potential buyers in some countries, may seem dull or imcomprehensible in others. Guinness, when advertising in West Germany, used the same advertising copy as in Ireland and Great Britain. The commercial consisted of a small humorous story involving Guinness. It was not successful because Germans do not read the small print in advertising, considering it as a waste of time.

## Analysis of culture influence

The task of interpreting culture's impact on a group can be difficult. Cultural influence is both pervasive and subtle. Furthermore, our own culture always gets in the way of our understanding of another culture because we must understand the other culture in terms of how it is similar to or different from our own. This is called the self-reference criterion (Lee, 1966). There are several barriers to be overcome in estimating cultural impact on a group. The need to recognize the influence of one's own culture in interpreting another is one of the more important of these barriers. The firm must also acknowledge that cultural differences tend to stand out more than similarities; yet it is the similarities that may be more important. Similarities may be analysed across factors referred to as cultural universals (Table 5.5).

A cultural study for international marketing decisions may be carried out on a macro and a micro level (Figure 5.4). This section draws heavily on Cundiff and Higler (1984) and Terpstra (1978). The purpose of the macro study is to identify the general sociological climate towards business in a country, its attitudes towards foreigners and new products. The micro study is concerned with interpreting culture's impact upon a specific group of people in a country (Cundiff and Higler 1984). Both levels of cross-cultural analysis are concerned with a search for cultural "universals." A universal is a mode of behaviour existing in all cultures. To the extent that aspects of the cultural environment are universal as opposed to unique, it is possible for the international firm to standardize some aspects of marketing the programme such as product design and communications, which are two of the major elements (Keegan, 1980).

### *Macro analysis of the cultural environment*

The elements of a macro analysis of the cultural environment include an examination of variability, complexity, cultural hostility, heterogeneity and interdependence. Cultural variability refers to the degree to which conditions

**Table 5.5** Analysing similarities and differences using cultural universals

The following phenomena are found in most cultures and are considered as universals:

| | | |
|---|---|---|
| age grading | feasting | marriage |
| athletic sports | folklore | mealtimes |
| bodily adornment | food taboos | medicine |
| calendars | funeral rites | modesty |
| cleanliness | games | mourning |
| cooking | gestures | music |
| cooperative labour | gift giving | personal names |
| courtship | government | population policy |
| dancing | greetings | property rights |
| decorative arts | hair styles | religious rituals |
| education | hospitality | residence rules |
| ethics | joking | status |
| etiquette | language | trade |
| family | law | visiting |

Source: Murdock, George P. (1945) 'The common denominator of cultures,' in *The Science of Man in the World Crises*, (ed.) Linton, Ralph, Columbia University Press, NY, 123–42.

within a culture are changing at a low or high rate or are constant. As cultural environments become more turbulent, i.e. more variable, the unpredictability of operations increases. Facing unpredictability, the organization will need to become more receptive to change. Internal structures and processes will need to be altered in order to cope with change. Open channels of communication, decentralized decision making, and predominance of local expertise should help improve the firm's capacity for perceiving and adjusting to rapid change.

Cultural complexity refers to the degree to which understanding of conditions within a culture is dependent on the possession of background data which places it in its proper context. Cultures, according to Hall (1960) differ widely in the extent to which unspoken, unformulated, and unexplicit rules govern how information is handled and how people interact and relate to each other. In "high-context" cultures, much of human behaviour is covert or implicit, whereas in "low-context" cultures much is overt or explicit. For a foreigner, the ease of understanding and communication in a culture is inversely related to the importance that culture places on "silent language" and "hidden dimensions." The amount of contexting required therefore extends from low in some cultures to high in others (Table 5.6). Hall places the Federal Republic of Germany, Switzerland, Scandinavia and the United States at the lower end of the continuum, France in the middle, and China and Japan at the high end of the scale.

Cultural hostility refers to the degree to which conditions in a culture are threatening to organizational goals. The extent of hostility depends upon the perceived acceptability and legitimacy of the firm. Hostility means that the firm

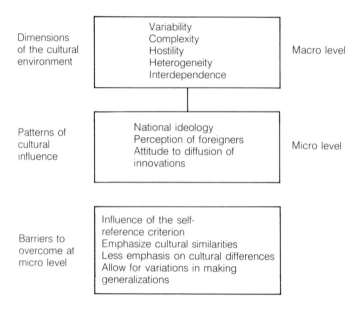

**Figure 5.4**    Analysis of cultural influence

will be less able to acquire raw materials, capital, personnel, information, goodwill, political favours, and other resources. Hostility may also reduce the firm's ability to dispose of its products and services.

Cultural heterogeneity refers to the degree to which separate cultures are similar or dissimilar. The cultures in which a firm operates can range from relatively homogeneous to extremely heterogeneous. Increasing heterogeneity means that there is greater variety which the organization must take into consideration in centralized decision making. Organizations functioning in diverse

**Table 5.6**    Characteristics and context of culture

Low-context cultures:

- much information contained in coded, explicit, transmitted messages
- fragile bonds and low involvement between people
- fewer distinctions made between insiders and outsiders
- change easy and rapid
- Examples: Federal Republic of Germany, Switzerland, Scandinavia, United States

High-context cultures:

- much information implicit in the physical context or internalized within people
- strong bonds and high involvement between people
- greater distinctions between insiders and outsiders
- cultural patterns long lived and slow to change
- Examples: China, France, Japan

Source: Hall, Edward T. (1960) 'The silent language of overseas business', *Harvard Business Review*, May–June, pp. 88–96.

environments typically seek to identify homogeneous segments or "sub-environments." They may then establish decentralized, semi-autonomous operating units to deal with them. In addition to structure, management practices may also tend to become differentiated with heterogeneous environments.

Cultural interdependence refers to the degree to which conditions in one culture are sensitive to developments in other cultures. Interdependence of cultures operates by way of contact. Advances in communication and transportation, growth or cross-border economic exchange, expansion of regional and international institutions, and the emergence of transcultural interest groups all serve to increase the volume of transactions between different cultures. Given increasing cultural interdependence, the actions of the firm in one culture are likely to be exposed to the scrutiny of governments and interested groups in others. For example, in cases as diverse as bribery, operations in South Africa, sale of powdered infant milk in developing countries, and ecological destruction, international firms have been faced with transcultural interest groups and demands.

Each of the above factors is best interpreted as part of a continuum from low to high. Within and among cultures it is possible to find high and low expressions of each of the dimensions of culture discussed above.

## Micro analysis of the cultural environment

We now turn to an examination of the patterns of cultural influence at the micro level in the market. The national ideology represents the way the citizens of a particular country think about and react to various stimuli (Table 5.7). Frequently we wish to predict how the typical French person, an Italian or a Portuguese will act in certain situations. Even though all three of these countries are predominantly Roman Catholic, the Portuguese is likely to react more strongly to infringements on the role of the Church than will the Frenchman or Italian. The French have a much stronger sense of national pride and unity than the Italians or the Portuguese. As a consequence they tend to be less willing to substitute a foreign-made product for a French product, at least in areas that reflect national expertise.

**Table 5.7** National ideology and attitude toward foreigners

National ideology:

- attitudes
- economic philosophy
- length of cultural identity.

Attitude toward foreigners:

- Foreign products may be perceived as
- different and/or inferior
- interesting and/or of high quality

Sometimes such sterotyping is valuable, sometimes it is a great hindrance to understanding the micro cultural environment.

Economic philosophy is an important element in national ideology. Sweden has a strong national commitment to socialism and has for several decades permitted extensive government involvement in business and economic affairs. This is in contrast to the United States and other countries operating under a capitalistic ideology, where massive government involvement in economic affairs has been strongly resisted.

The national ideology is strongest and most consistent in countries that have a long cultural identity. For example, there is a strong, easily identifiable national ideology in a country such as Egypt, which, even though it has not consistently had political independence in recent centuries, posesses a long and consistent cultural history. However, some of the newer black nations in central Africa have not had separate identities long enough to have developed strong national ideologies. Instead, different sub-groups within these nations reflect the ideologies of the sub-groups or tribes from whch they descend. However, even in countries with strong national ideologies, these ideologies represent a general cross-section or average. Not all individuals fit the pattern. Nevertheless, it is important for the international firm to know the general national ideology so that it can fit the product and its marketing strategy into the local environment.

Allied to the preveding point is the observation that people may view that which is foreign as different and potentially threatening to existing patterns of action and behaviour. In some countries this reaction toward foreign peoples and ways is reflected in a fear of contamination or change from outside. An extreme example of this fear was the policy of the Chinese government in early years when foreigners and foreign products were not welcome. Yet even when foreigners and foreign products are not perceived as a threat to the local economy, they may still be perceived as different and/or inferior. It is for this reason that international firms often play down their foreigness and try to blend in with the local scene.

Not all attitudes towards foreigners and foreign products are negative, however. Highly sophisticated and talented individuals may be perceived as interesting rather than just "different" by nationals of other countries. Foreign products of high quality are often viewed in the same light. Belgian lace, French wine, Japanese cameras, and German microscopes are all viewed as distinctive and of extra high quality in world markets. In these instances, the foreign identification actually provides an advantage in the marketplace. Success in a foreign market, then, may depend upon the firm's ability to blend in with the local scene and develop a domestic identity, or it may depend on the firm's ability to convince local buyers that foreign means better.

Attitudes toward innovation diffusion influence the success or otherwise of the international firm (Table 5.8). Frequently when a foreign firm enters a market, it is introducing a product or service that represents an "innovation" in that market. If a product is sufficiently different from other products in a market, local consumers may see it as something entirely new. Hence, the firm must try

**Table 5.8**  Influences on diffusion of innovations

Rate of adoption is influenced by:

- resistance to change
- perceived superiority of product
- can product be "tried" or "explained"
- cost of product
- product compatibility with cultural values and tradition

to anticipate how consumers in that market will react to change. If local people show a strong resistance to change, some other less resistant market may prove to be more promising. Even where the introduction of a new product seems promising, it is important to understand the process through which changes are introduced and accepted. It is generally believed that the principles of diffusion, as applied to new products and services, also apply in international markets.

A consumer's perception of an innovation may have a strong impact on how quickly it is adopted. An innovation that consumers see as being clearly superior to other ways of meeting their needs will be adopted faster than those products or services which do not have such relative advantages. If it is easy for consumers to understand the functions of an innovation and it can be "tried" or "explained," this product or service will also be adopted quickly. It follows that products or services that are less costly and more compatible with cultural values and traditional ways of doing things will be adopted faster than others. International firms need to be aware that they must communicate these qualities to markets when the product or service is seen as new.

## Techniques for micro cultural assessment

Since culture is learned behaviour, it is, by definition, specific to the individual. Therefore, any generalizations about a culture must recognize the variations within a culture as much as the differences or similarities between that culture and any other. Because of the numerous intangible dimensions involved it is difficult to apply a cultural analysis at product or service level. A number of attempts have been made to apply a cultural analysis at the micro level. Robock, Simmonds and Zwick (1989) using Hall's (1959) framework developed a cultural analysis for a hypothetical toy manufacturer. A brief review of the method is worthwhile as it appears to have value in application.

The technique for micro cultural assessment as proposed by Hall (1959) provides a detailed set of guidelines which may be used by the firm in international markets. Hall's basic premise for understanding culture is that it consists of systems for structuring the interaction with a society. Interaction can be person with person, person with things, person with the environment, person with outsiders, man with woman, and so on. Hall has organized this view of culture into a framework which identifies primary message systems or cultural rules for human activity (Table 5.9).

**Table 5.9**  Hall's primary message systems

| Primary message | Depicts attitudes and cultural rules for: |
| --- | --- |
| 1. Interaction | The ordering of man's interaction with those around him, through language, touch, noise, gesture and so forth |
| 2. Association | The organization (grouping) and structuring of society and its components |
| 3. Subsistence | The ordering of man's activities in feeding, working and making a living |
| 4. Bisexuality | The differentiation of roles, activities and function along sex lines |
| 5. Territoriality | The possession, use and defence of space and territory |
| 6. Temporality | The use, allocation and division of time |
| 7. Learning | The adaptive process of learning and instruction |
| 8. Play | Relaxation, humour, recreation and enjoyment |
| 9. Defence | Protection against man's environment including medicine, warfare and law |
| 10. Exploitation | Turning the environment to man's use through technology, construction and extraction of materials |

Source: Adapted from Hall, Edward T. (1959) *The Silent Language*, Doubleday, Garden City, NY, pp. 61–81.

By exploring each of the ten areas identified above, the international manager is better able to isolate him or herself from the self-reference criterion and to understand the complexities of another culture. However, in most cases such intense cultural understanding is not necessary; international firms need only know the culture's impact on their specific concerns; demand or use of a product; influences in the purchase decision; organization structure and relations with employees.

To perform this level of analysis, Hall suggests that we investigate the "interaction" of message systems. If we wish to understand how people's attitudes about work are formed in a culture, for instance, work messages are related to each of the other messages systems: How do people interact in work situations? How do work roles structure the way people interact? How do people learn about work and so on?

## Socio-cultural distance as a barrier to internationalization

Normally, distance is thought of as the spatial difference between two or more points. Distance in this sense, which takes account only of physical or geographic characteristics, is a unidimensional concept and limiting when attempting to understand the internationalization process of business. In the present context, distance is also taken to include economic and socio-cultural distance. It is possible to measure the separation of countries in terms of all three distance concepts to derive a separation of markets based on what is referred to in the literature as business distance (Luostarinen, 1980, pp. 124–52). Consequently, it is important to examine the effects of economic and socio-cultural distance on the internationalization process in addition to purely physical considerations.

The importance of distance may be gauged by observing that companies tend to be more knowledgable and have more information about foreign markets which are culturally near to them than for more distant markets. The implication of this statement is that companies will tend to favour markets which are culturally close and which are known to them. Companies new to exporting or contemplating the internationalization process will tend to avoid those markets which are unfamiliar. So far the discussion has only considered the flow of information or knowledge. The same argument holds for the movement of products and people. For all three flows, therefore, cultural distance is an impediment and restricting force which predisposes the company to closer markets (Goodnow and Hansz, 1972). In these studies countries are classified on the basis of various measures of socio-cultural distance. In marketing terms, the analysis based on socio-cultural distance normally suggests the hypothesis that experience in international marketing, increasing levels of tourism, increases in holidays abroad, improvements in the educational system, television, journals and increases in the number of foreign-owned companies constitute the principal explanatory factors in bringing about an openness of management attitudes and attitudes of the population at large towards the international dimension. In a direct business context, of course, international marketing and tourism are probably the most directly effective. In terms of analysis of the socio-cultural environment it may be concluded that while it is difficult without proper historical data to observe any improvement in openness of attitudes to other nations, it is possible that experience in dealing with foreign nationals has a major impact on bringing about such an improvement. In a business context, this means international marketing, including service marketing activities such as tourism.

## Cultural influences on the international firm

Because of their multiple influences and difficulty of prediction, behavioural attributes or cultural variables may be regarded as the most important elements of the socio-cultural environment.

Culture is best understood as the total way of life of a society; the ways of acting, thinking and feeling about the whole range of human experiences which people living in a particular society share. Culture is that "complex whole which includes knowledge, belief, art, morals, laws, customs and any other capabilities and habits acquired by men as a member of society." The elements of culture are shared and learned, transmitted from one generation to the next, and are ignored by the international marketing firm at great peril. As societies differ so do their cultures. It is important, therefore, to understand the basic elements of culture. As was seen above, culture is best understood as based on three elements: norms and behaviour patterns; ideas; and material culture. As each has a direct effect on the marketing of products and services internationally it is important to understand them.

## *Norms and behaviour patterns and the international firm*

Norms are standards shared by a society to which members are expected to conform. They are rules that specify appropriate and inappropriate behaviour. For the international firm it is important to note that some norms are more important than others. Some norms in a society are considered by the members as not being extremely important and, therefore, may be violated without severe punishment. These are referred to as "folkways" and may be the target for innovative marketing on the part of the international firm. For example, Sunday opening of fast food restaurants in a traditionalist society may contravene folkways but be welcomed by a growing middle class wishing to entertain the family and give the housewife some relief from the drudgery of the kitchen. Other norms of society, referred to as mores, are those which are seen as extremely important to the welfare of society and whose violation reaps severe punishment. A marketing practice which contravenes the mores of a society would be met by product failure, withdrawal from the market and even forced closure. An understanding of the distinction for each international market between its folkways and mores is an important managerial responsibility for the international firm.

A behaviour pattern is a uniformity of acting and thinking that regularly recurs among a plurality of people. The behaviour pattern, besides being a *form* of conduct, is also a norm of conduct. The international firm must also make a distinction here; this time between ideal norms, those to which people give their verbal allegiance, and real norms, those with which people comply. Many people consider themselves to belong to a particular religion but do not follow its practices or dictates.

The manager of the international firm must realize that ideal norms are what the individual says or believes he would like to do which may coincide with the real norms, but which may at times have only an indirect and remote relationship to actual behaviour. Even when ideal norms do not coincide with real norms, they provide guides to behaviour in the sense of being remote goals which are to be reached indirectly.

## *Cultural ideology and the international firm*

By a rather general consensus a society arrives at a body of meanings and beliefs that every "right thinking" member is supposed to hold. This body of meanings constitutes the principles of thought in the society. Social scientists refer to these principles of thought as the ideology of a society, which derives from ideas which are classified as cognitive, expressive, and evaluative (Chinoy, 1967). For Chinoy, cognitive ideas "includes the beliefs men hold about themselves and the social, biological and physical world in which they live, and about their relations to one another, to society and nature and to such other beings and forces as they may discover, accept or conjure up. It embraces the whole vast body of ideas by which men account for their observation and experience." Cognitive ideas include knowledge, skills and practical know-how. Knowledge comprises all we know about man and reality from the social and natural sciences including theories and hypotheses yet to be proved. Language is probably the most important of all human skills since it is by means of language that man is able to exchange ideas which makes organized social life possible.

In this context language and perception are intimately intertwined. Culture influences what we perceive. We never really see the physical world around us. The world we perceive is a product of the interaction between the physical aspects of the universe and what we have learned from previous experience. Language plays a considerable part in what we perceive and to a large extent it also determines what we experience.

Expressive ideas encompass "the forms by which men express their feelings about themselves and others and their responses, emotional and aesthetic to the world around them." (Chinoy, 1967) Expressive ideas are manifested in the arts, music, literature and painting of a society.

Evaluative ideas help a society to define the criteria by which it lives: "men also learn and share the values by which they live, the standards and ideals by which they define their goals, select a course of action and judge themselves and others." (Chinoy, 1967)

These factors: language; ideology; and intellectual styles in particular, affect the way people think and behave and also determine the disposition of managers in the international firm. Unfortunately, how we see ourselves and how others see us may be very different due to different cultural backgrounds. Frequently, too, we do not have full information about others, especially if they come from a distant country. In such circumstances we rely on what others tell us or on limited information which may produce a stereotype rather than a true interpretation of the situation. However, it may be very dangerous to use stereotypes in international marketing (Exhibit 5.4).

## Material culture and the international firm

By material culture is meant those material things which humans create and use, e.g. buildings, works of art, tools, machinery and transportation equipment. These things constitute a human created environment interposed between people and the material environment and greatly influence human behaviour. By considering the importance to international business of the improvements in transportation and logistics which have occurred in the past ten to thirty years we obtain a good measure of the effect of material culture on the international firm.

## Summary

The analysis of the socio-cultural environment with the help of anthropological, sociological, and psychological frameworks is increasing in importance for the firm in international markets. This socio-cultural environment involves the following:

- the learned behavioural features shared by people of the same culture;
- real physical attributes or appearances;
- physical idealized traits, i.e. advertisement stereotypes;
- demographic characteristics such as population size, age distribution, etc.,

---

**Exhibit 5.4  Don't rely on stereotypes, insist on accurate cultural analysis**

*Organizational renewal: can you change horses in mid-stream?*

Is national character like a stereotype? "Italians either belong to the Mafia or a relative does." "The problem with this country is that the Jews control everything. Worst of all, they're cheap and sneaky." "Blacks are lazy and think they've got everything coming to them." "The French are nationalistic and dislike all foreigners." "The Japanese are hard-working and intelligent, but they're also sly."

These statements are stereotypes and contain "pictures in our heads" that are exaggerated beliefs and oversimplifications. Stereotypes often originate from the experiences of others and are used to complete the pictures in our heads about unknown situations.

Stereotypes merely contain a kernel of the truth. Descriptions of national character, on the other hand, are accurate descriptions of a culture. Take the Swedes, for example, and let them speak for themselves. In repeated lists of words, the following are usually accepted by Swedes as Swedish cultural characteristics: honest, punctual, efficient, low risk-takers, lacking social confidence, serious, having strong technical knowledge, polite and well mannered.

A 1986 survey by the Stockholm School of Economics and a US organization found, in terms of teamwork and communication when working with Americans, both Swedes and Americans believe that the Swedish strengths as managers are that they are used to and seek consensus, that they are good listeners and loyal.

As for business strategy, the same study found that Swedes and Americans believe the Swedes take a long-term perspective, see the importance of company values and care for quality.

Gunnila Masreliez-Steen, a Swedish management consultant, describes Swedish business people at home and abroad as "concerned about people". "For example, because terminations of employments are very restricted, a manager must learn to work with his people. Abroad, however, Swedes use technical subjects almost exclusively as a way of getting to know their counterparts. Social discussions are rather rare and this is a liability."

Abroad, the Swedish negotiator is also often perceived as "cold" when discussing areas outside the technical. But he possesses another quality I would add — a strong desire to learn in all areas.

**Source:** *International Management*, March, 1987, p. 58.

---

which when related to given income levels can help in definite the market potential.

Culture is a complex concept which includes specific knowledge, beliefs, morals, laws and customs shared by a society. Culture is broadly based on the following three elements:

(a) norms, which are hierarchical rules specifying behavioural and thinking patterns according to varying situations. A distinction must be made at this stage between ideal norms to which they give verbal allegiance and real norms to which people actually comply;

(b) ideology, which involves beliefs, physical and empirical knowledge, cognitive and aesthetic ideas, aesthetic forms of expression and evaluative ideas which help define standards and judgements about oneself and others;

(c) material culture, which covers all buildings, tools, machinery, etc., created and used.

Cultural interpretation for the international firm in the sense that it is a learned process differs in essence from instinct. There are two main ways, as follows, to develop cultural norms and values:

(a) socialization, referring both to life experiences and the influences of institutions such as family, religion and education systems;

(b) acculturation, which refers to a voluntary process of learning.

It is important to note that cultural elements are all interrelated and adaptive and therefore subject to change.

The elements which go to make up culture in the international marketing environment include the following:

- language, the "cultural mirror";
- religion, which deals with intimate convictions;
- varying attitudes towards time, wealth acquisition and risk taking;
- organization of relationships in the form of social and cultural stratification, family units;
- level of education;
- technology and material culture development in general;
- aesthetic values.

Through the analysis of cultural influences, an attempt has been made to determine international modes of behaviour. At the macro level the elements of the cultural environment involve the following:

- cultural variability, which is a function of the rapidity of change and stability in a given environment;
- cultural complexity, in the broad sense the sum of implicit rules;
- cultural hostility, the attitude of specific markets towards the firm;
- cultural heterogeneity, the multiplication of sub-cultures;
- cultural interdependence, the related sensitivity of a specific culture to the development of others.

At the micro level, the main patterns of specific cultural attitudes include the following:

- national pride;
- economic philosophy;
- national identity and fear of foreign influences;
- attitudes towards innovation.

Socio-cultural distance as a barrier to internationalization involves the notion of business distance which is multidimensional in nature. It takes into account not only the geographical distance and physical characteristics but also economic and socio-cultural differences. The greater the business distance and subsequent lesser information flow from the market, the fewer movements of products and people. This business distance has to a certain extent been diminished in recent years as a result of increased use of the media as a means of communication and increased travel.

Cultural analysis can, however, only be made in reference to one's own situation and thus tends to be subjective in nature. Despite these restrictions it is essential for a firm to fully understand the socio-cultural environment in which it operates in order for it to succeed.

## Discussion questions

1. What is culture? Why is an understanding or culture important in international marketing?

2. Outline and discuss the principal elements of culture as they affect the behaviour of the international firm.

3. The scope of culture is very broad and covers many aspects of behaviour within a country or culture. Describe the implications of this observation for the firm in international markets.

4. It is not possible to understand how markets evolve and how buyers react to marketing programmes developed by the firm without accepting that markets are based on individual and group behaviour determined by cultural conditioning. Discuss.

5. What role has the firm in international markets as an agent of cultural change? Is the role different in different countries?

## References

Banks, Arthur S. and Textar, Robert B. (1963) *A Cross-Polity Survey*, MIT Press, Boston.
Bennett, Peter and Kassarjan, Harold (1972) *Consumer Behaviour*, Prentice Hall, NJ.
Cateora, Philip R. (1990) *International Marketing*, Irwin, Homewood, Ill., 7th edn.

Chinoy, E. (1967) *Society — An Introduction to Sociology*, 2nd edn, Random House, NY.

Cundiff, Edward A. and Tharp Higler, Mary E. (1984) *Marketing in the International Environment*, Prentice Hall, Englewood Cliffs, NJ.

Engel, James and Blackwell, Roger (1982) *Consumer Behaviour*, 4th edn, Dryden Press, NY.

Engel, James, Warshaw, Martin and Kinnear, Thomas (1983) *Promotional Strategy*, 5th edn, Irwin.

Goodnow, James D. and Hansz, James E. (1972) 'Environmental determinants of overseas market entry strategies,' *Journal of Business Studies*, **3**, 33–50.

Hall, Edward T. (1959) *The Silent Language*, Doubleday, Garden City, NY.

Hall, Edward T. (1960) 'The silent language of overseas business,' *Harvard Business Review*, May–June, pp. 88–96.

Hoebel, Adamson (1960) *Man, Culture and Society*, Oxford University Press, NY.

Hornby, William F. (1980) *An Introduction to Population Geography*, Cambridge University Press, Cambridge.

Keegan, Warren (1980) *Multinational Marketing Management*, Prentice Hall, NY.

Lee, James A. (1966) 'Cultural analysis in overseas operations,' *Harvard Business Review*, March–April, pp. 106–14.

Luostarinen, Reijo (1980) *Internationalization of the Firm*, Acta Academiae Series A: 30, The Helsinki School of Economics, Helsinki, 260 pp.

Murdock, George P. (1945) 'The common denominator of cultures,' in Ralph Linton (ed.) *The Science of Man in the World Crises*, Columbia University Press, NY, 123–42.

Ricks, David A. (1983) *Big Business Blunders*, Dow Jones-Irwin, Homewood, Ill.

Robock, Stefan, Simmonds, Kenneth and Zwick, Jack (1989) *International Business & Multinational Enterprise*, 4th edn, Irwin, Homewood, Ill.

Terpstra, Vern (1978) *The Cultural Environment of International Business*, South-Western Publishing Company.

# 6 *Political environment and legal frameworks in international marketing*

In this chapter we discuss the political environment facing the international firm and the manifestations of political policies and concern at the level of the firm. Political policies are manifested through laws and regulations which affect the flows of products, services, people, technology, investment and money. The management issues which arise are examined from the point of view of the firm in the source country involved in the transfer and from the point of view of the recipient firm in the host country. Circumstances arise occasionally in which firms in international marketing find themselves in dispute over some aspect of marketing. In such situations arbitration is frequently used but the law is referred to quite frequently. For this reason the legal framework in which disputes may be settled is examined.

## Political environment of international marketing

A crucial aspect of doing business in a foreign country is that permission to conduct business is controlled by the government of the host country. The host government controls and restrict a foreign company's activities by encouraging and offering support or by discouraging and banning its activities, depending upon the interests of the host. Reflected in its policies and attitudes towards foreign business are a government's ideas of how best to promote the national interest considering its own resources and political philosophy. An analysis of the political environment should include a number of factors: the type of government in the host country; its philosophy; its stability over time; and its disposition to international business.

The type of government: democracy; dictatorship; monarchy; socialist or communist; gives an insight into the business—political environment. The type of government is determined by the procedure through which the citizens form and express their will and the extent to which their will controls the composition and policy of government. Under parliamentary government the people are consulted from time to time to ascertain the majority will, and, therefore, policies of the government theoretically reflect the majority opinion of the population. Under absolutist governments (monarchies and dictatorships), the ruling regime determines government policy without specifically consulting the needs and wants of the people. Though the absolutist form of governments is uncommon, it may be found in some countries in the Middle and Far East and in some developing countries.

The philosophy of the government towards business in general and foreign business in particular should also be taken into account. Conservative governments usually promote a broad role for private business with a minimum of restrictions. Socialist governments, on the other hand, may encourage public ownership of business with an emphasis on restrictions and a more comprehensive regulatory environment.

Because of the different political viewpoints, international firms are often treated in a very different way than local businesses. Japan is perhaps the most obvious example of a government that supports domestic industry but erects barriers to foreign firms wishing to penetrate the Japanese market. In some countries the prevailing philosophy is that imports are to be discouraged but foreign investment in manufacturing encouraged, e.g. Greece. In other countries, only joint ventures find government support. The international firm must discover what the perceived role is for foreign business activity in a country.

## *Importance of political stability*

Stable governments are more likely to ensure continuity in government policy as it affects business. Stable systems allow firms to plan their affairs with some degree of certainty. Political instability arises from political risks of doing business in a foreign market, political harassment and excessive nationalism (Figure 6.1). Change is the main source of political risk, and radical change causes the most difficulty for business adjustment. Because change in a government or its political philosophy can lead to unknown consequences for business, it is more disruptive than other business constraints. The situation in developing countries may be somewhat less predictable due to extra constraints. Nevertheless, a cabinet reshuffle or a change in policy can seriously affect the business environment facing the international firm (Exhibit 6.1). The international firm should become aware of the processes whereby policy changes are instituted.

There are several sources that the international firm can use to measure political instability, the most common simple mechanism is to use one or more of the stability indices developed by political scientists. A good example of a political instability index is the one developed by Feierabend and Feierabend (1965). The index is actually a three-digit score based on the severity of the most destabilizing event in recent political history and the frequency of destabilizing activities within the country. Examples of political events covered in this index

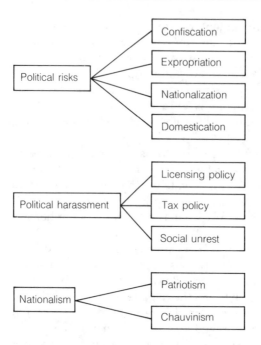

**Figure 6.1**   Analysing political instability in host country: risks, harassment and nationalism

are shown in Table 6.1. It should be noted that the index must be interpreted for applicability to the specific risks the individual firm faces. Very often these indices reflect the political philosophy of the country in which they are developed and, therefore, have only limited applicability to decision makers in other countries.

## Common political risks

The risks an international firm faces from the political environment can be significant. A range of political risks exist depending on the countries in question, the firm and the nature of its business. At one extreme, the firm may lose all control, ownership of assets and market access; on the other hand, the firm may simply face customs delays or problems in getting working visas for headquarters staff.

A firm can lose ownership of foreign assets in one of four ways: confiscation; expropriation; nationalism; or domestication. Confiscation requires nothing more than a government decision to take control of a foreign firm's assets in its country: no payment is made to compensate the firm for its loss. Expropriation differs only in that compensation is given for the firm's assets. Very few firms feel satisfied with the compensation given when their assets are expropriated. In most cases

---

**Exhibit 6.1   Political change and the business environment**

---

*India: politics in command*

India's October 22 cabinet reshuffle points to a growing political element in New
Delhi's decision making process that will raise entry barriers and may lead to a slight
deterioration of the business climate. The halcyon days of 1985, when Prime Minister
Rajiv Gandhi was able to largely ignore political factors, are gone. Potential fallout
from policy decisions will become more important, especially as the 1989 elections
near. But firms prepared to act swiftly and able to identify the right constituency can
still find opportunities.

Political primacy becomes clear by noting who was excluded from the cabinet.
Gandhi previously preferred proven industry or government technocrats. None of the
new entrants fall into this category, most are state-level politicians.

These realities will make it more difficult for MNCs to gain access to the Indian
market. Forces opposed to their entry will have an easier time politicizing the issue
and either blocking or delaying approval. The approach of elections will heighten
political sensitivities; economic factors (e.g. the worsening balance-of-payments
position) will accentuate them. Thus, MNCs interested in the Indian market should act
as fast as possible; entry will become more difficult the longer it is put off.

Companies would also be well advised to build ties with politically influential
groups — e.g. the state governments — that can help lobby the central government.
Although it failed in an earlier attempt, US-based Pepsi Co is taking another stab at
market entry. This time, Pepsi has made some concessions, such as agreeing to
manufacture its concentrate in India; the key difference is Pepsi's decision to team up
with Punjab Agro-Industries Corp, a public sector corporation. Pepsi has promised to
locate its plant in Punjab, which is eagerly courting new investors. Getting the Punjab
government on its side should substantially boost Pepsi's prospects.

**Source:** *Business International,* 17 November, 1986, p. 362.

---

the payment is not negotiable: but even when a government is willing to discuss
compensation with a firm, there is likely to be disagreement on the basis for
valuing the firm's assets. Confiscation and expropriation usually arise due to the
development role of international firms in a country. Both forms of risk are higher
in resource-based industries such as oil exploration and refining and in the
extractive industries.

Nationalization is the process whereby a government decides to take over
ownership of an industry for its own control. Both local and foreign owned firms
may be affected. Government ownership and management of an industry may
give it more control over the country's economic life and is usually tied to issues
of economic sovereignty, national defence, or control of strategic industries.

Domestication represents a variety of pressures that can be placed on a

**Table 6.1**  Political events included in the Feierabend index

| | |
|---|---|
| 1.  Elections | 16.  Arrests of significant persons |
| 2.  Vacation of office | 17.  Imprisonment of significant persons |
| 3.  Significant change of laws | 18.  Arrests of few insignificant persons |
| 4.  Acquisition of office | 19.  Mass arrests of insignificant persons |
| 5.  Severe trouble within a non-governmental organization | 20.  Imprisonment of insignificant persons |
| 6.  Organization of opposition party | 21.  Assassinations |
| 7.  Governmental action against significant groups | 22.  Martial law |
| 8.  Micro strikes | 23.  Executions of significant persons |
| 9.  General strikes | 24.  Executions of insignificant persons |
| 10.  Macro strikes | 25.  Terrorism and sabotage |
| 11.  Micro demonstrations | 26.  Guerrilla warfare |
| 12.  Macro demonstrations | 27.  Civil war |
| 13.  Micro riots | 28.  Coups d'état |
| 14.  Macro riots | 29.  Revolts |
| 15.  Severe macro riots | 30.  Exile |

Source: Feierabend, Ivo K. and Feierabend, Rosalind L. (1965) *Cross-national Data Bank of Political Instability Events (Code Index)*, Public Affairs Research Institute, San Diego, pp. 2A–10A.

foreign-owned firm to transfer ownership and or control to local citizens. At one extreme, a foreign investor may be forced to sell shares of stock to local investors at a predetermined price.

Alternatively, the firm may be asked to develop a plant for sale to locals over a certain time period, but the business is allowed to determine how the transfer of ownership will occur. Other examples of domestication policies include pressure to employ nationals at top decision-making levels, permits required for importing equipment, parts, personnel or technology.

Political harassment may affect exporters as well as firms that enter foreign markets through foreign production, joint ventures, or licensing. Harassment can take many forms and can affect all areas of business operations, from labour relations to customer relations, to product design or pricing. The foreign firm may be singled out for harassment, or an entire industry may be the target of new, restrictive regulations.

A government's power to license may be used to harass. A licence may be required to establish a business, acquire foreign exchange, purchase imports, change prices, hire or fire personnel, or sell to government agencies. Changes in tax policy can also be used to capture more revenue and penalize businesses.

Another form of harassment for the foreign firm is social unrest. Political terrorists in Europe, Latin America and the Middle East have increasingly used kidnappings of business executives to publicize their demands and fund their causes. Damage to property from riots and insurrections can also be significant.

Nationalism can have similar effects to those discussed above. Citizens of every nation typically have some sense of national identity. This manifests itself in national feelings, pride and attitudes towards foreign firms and products. The respectable form of nationalism is called patriotism. The excessive form is called chauvinism. Today, nationalism is considered a divisive force, hindering regional and international co-operation. This is especially true for major policy issues within the EC. When the residents of one country see themselves as a "we" group and all other nations as a "they" group, there is an implicit feeling that "they" are somewhat of a threat to us.

The existence of nationalism has several implications for the firm in international markets. First, home country nationalism should not colour the firm's marketing programme. Its task is to sell products, not carry the flag. Second, the firm as a foreigner in its international markets may be the victim of local nationalism. A strategy to avoid this might be to develop as local an image as possible, which will affect policies on branding, promotion, distribution, as well as other elements of the marketing mix. Indeed, one of the challenges facing the firm in international markets is finding how best to adapt to the demands of local nationalism without diminishing the international strengths of the firm.

The effect of nationalism on foreign production is the same whether the country is industrialized or is a developing country. Most variations would be in degree of intensity, but all countries will demand control of profits and borrowing within the host country, control over foreign investment in established and locally owned business, local ownership of equity, in part at least, by nationals and the replacement of expatriate management by local citizens.

Firms attempt to reduce political risks by identifying points of political vulnerability, establishing positive political–business interaction and promoting among government officials the need to regulate international transfers of various resources and assets. Governments attempt to regulate the political environment within a legal framework which forms the basis of control (Table 6.2).

**Table 6.2** The political environment of international business

Political environment

- Analysis of political environment
- Identifying political vulnerability
- Establishing a positive political–business interaction

Regulation and control of international transfers

- Rationale for regulation
- Transfer of goods
- Transfer of money
- Transfer of persons
- Transfer of technology

International legal framework

- Existing international law
- Major world legal systems
- Minimizing international legal problems
- European Community law

## Identifying political vulnerability

Some products appear to be more politically vulnerable than others. Favourable political attention can mean protection, reduced tax rates, exemption from quotas, control of competition, and other concessions. Political vulnerability, however, can also lead to labour agitation, public regulations, price fixing, quotas and other forms of government harassment if, for any reason, the product is considered to be undesirable.

A change in attitudes towards politically vulnerable products does not always come from obvious instability in the political system. Even an orderly change of government, or a change in existing government attitudes can lead to a drastic change in public policy towards certain products.

## Positive political–business interaction

The safest long-term strategy for minimizing political risk is to acknowledge the importance of positive interaction with host governments. Some firms implement this by reminding personnel that they are "guests" in foreign markets and that continued permission to operate is contingent on showing the benefits the firm brings to host countries. Benefits arise in four ways: resource or product transfer; balance of payments effects; employment or income contributions; and social or cultural benefits.

International firms use a variety of techniques to ensure a supportive political environment. For example, in many developing countries large importers in developed countries have designed programmes to assist local industry. Frequently, importers insist on buying up to 25 per cent of their supplies from local manufacturers in developing countries. On the social and cultural side, Pepsi-Cola has sponsored opera and ballet in Argentina and Gulf Oil has fought smallpox in Nigeria.

In spite of efforts at being a "good citizen," different modes of entry or modes of investment which render the venture less risky may be the only long-range solution to hostile political environments. These include joint ventures with locals but controlling marketing and distribution of the products outside the country. Licensing technology is also employed as it is especially effective where the technology is unique and the risk is high.

Another approach towards establishing a positive political–business interaction may be the political payoff or bribe. The political payoff has been used in many countries to avoid confiscatory taxes or expulsion, to ensure agent acceptance of sales contracts, and to provide monetary encouragement to an assortment of people whose actions can affect the effectiveness of a company's programmes. The definition of bribery can range from the relatively innocuous payment of a small sum of money to minor officials or business managers to expedite the processing of papers or the loading of a truck, to the extreme of paying large sums to top ranking government officials to ensure the company gets

---

## Exhibit 6.2  Legitimacy of payments to government officials

*Bofors armaments and the Swedish government*

The armaments maker Bofors and the Swedish Government continued to pass the ball back and forth on the question of whether bribes or other illegal payments were made in connection with a SEK 8.4 billion artillery deal with India that Bofors won in 1986.

An investigation by the Swedish National Audit Board determined that Bofors, now a subsidiary of Nobel Industries, had made payments of between SEK 170–250 million in "winding up costs" to agents in India.

Bofors said it wound up operations by agents, who provided local administrative services and other assistance, after the Indian government insisted that there be no middlemen in the artillery negotiations.

But the company declined to disclose details of these and other payments, claiming that secrecy is normal practice in such deals. Sweden's Foreign Trade Minister Anita Gradin said it was up to Bofors to waive company secrecy and explain payments on an individual basis. The company has refused and stated repeatedly that it didn't pay any bribes to obtain the Indian deal.

Allegations of bribery were first made in a Swedish radio report and led to a political crisis in India as well as tension between New Delhi and Stockholm over what some Indian officials thought was the inability of the Swedish Government to get all the facts in the case and the unwillingness of Bofors to disclose them.

Sweden's Foreign Minister, Sten Andersson, went so far as to angrily declare that expatriate Swedish financier Erik Penser, who controls Nobel Industries, should pressure Bofor to disclose all the facts surrounding the India artillery order.

**Source:** *Sweden Now*, 4, 1987, p. 19.

---

preferential treatment. It is not always clear when bribery actually does occur (Exhibit 6.2); bribery is very much an ethical issue, being dependent upon the country and circumstances in question.

## Regulating international transfers

The issue of international transfers covers the physical transfer of products through importing and exporting, financial flows, the transfer of people, the transfer of technology and cross-border data flows. The question arises as to why, in view of the widely espoused benefits of free trade, countries sometimes attempt to control such international transfers. There are numerous reasons why governments attempt to control international transfers (Table 6.3).

It is more convenient to classify these political controls under four headings: attempts to control the transfer of products and services; the transfer of money; the transfer of people; and the transfer of technology.

**Table 6.3**  Reasons for
controlling international
transfers

Revenue goals
Employment protection
Development goals
Balance of payments objectives
Sectoral adjustment policies
Health and safety protection
National security
International political goals

## Regulating transfers of products and services

The most common type of trade control is the tariff or duty, a government tax
levied on goods shipped internationally, most commonly in the form of an import
tariff but there are numerous others which can be equally effective (Table 6.4).
Import duties serve primarily as a means of raising the price of imported products
so that domestic products gain a relative price advantage. A duty may be classified
as protective in nature even though there is no domestic production in direct
competition. For example, if a country wishes to reduce the foreign expenditures
of its citizens because of balance of payments problems, authorities may choose
to raise the price of some foreign products, even though there are no domestic
substitutes, in order to curtail consumption temporarily.

Tariffs also serve as a means of government revenue. Although of little
importance to the large industrial countries, the import duty is a major source
of revenue elsewhere. A tariff may be assessed on the basis of a tax per unit,
in which case it is known as a specific duty. It may also be assessed as a percentage
of the value of the item, in which case it is known as an *ad valorem* duty.

Although countries sometimes use direct payments to producers for losses
they incur by selling abroad, governments most commonly give other types of
assistance to their firms to make it cheaper or more profitable for them to sell
overseas. An example here would be the services provided by export promotions
boards, found in many countries, which include the provision of information,

**Table 6.4**  Mechanisms used to restrict
international transfer of products and
services

Tariffs on imports
Subsidies on domestic production
Exchange rate manipulation
Customs valuation practices
Quantity controls — quotas
Buy local legislation, standards and licences
Restrictions on services

sponsoring trade exhibitions and overseas visits, providing advice, and establishing overseas contacts for exporters and potential exporters.

In order to attract investment, especially from abroad, many countries provide incentives to companies. These are frequently in the form of tax holidays, duty-free imports of materials and equipment, training of personnel, offering low-cost loans, conducting feasibility studies, and building the required infrastructures.

Sometimes a country holds the value of its currency so that it buys less of a foreign currency than might be the case in a free market. This is referred to as exchange rate manipulation. In such circumstances, its products will have a relative cost advantage. For example, if New Zealand and West Germany each produce identical widgets at a cost of $2 and DM4 respectively, the costs are identical as long as the exchange rate is $2 = DM4. If West Germany devalued the DM so that $1 = DM4, New Zealand could buy widgets from West Germany at half the price of available widgets produced in New Zealand at $2. There is much evidence that artificially maintained exchange rates have been major influences on world trade in the last few years. US Government officials and business commentators frequently accuse Japan of manipulating the exchange rate.

Through multiple exchange rates, a country sometimes sets high import charges in order to get foreign exchange to purchase certain products abroad, or, conversely, an exporter receives more in his or her own currency. In 1978, for example, Peru, in an effort to increase manufactured exports, gave exporters 180 Soles for each dollar worth of exports instead of the official rate of 130. This had the effect of encouraging producers to divert output abroad as well as to charge lower export prices in order to be more competitive.

In order to determine the value of an imported product for affixing an *ad valorem* duty, customs officials formerly had fairly wide discretion. Even though the invoice value of a shipment might be $100, customs officials might use the domestic wholesale or retail price or even an estimation of what it would cost if the product were produced domestically. This meant that they might charge a 10 per cent duty on a value much higher than the $100. This practice was frequently applied on imports in the United States where domestic wholesale prices, the yardstick in such comparisons, were much higher than the comparable import price of the product in question. Such policies were seen as being quite discriminatory. Since 1980, however, most industrial countries have agreed on a sequence for assessing values ("Tokyo round: New customs valuation rules," *Business Weekly*, 10 March, 1980). They must first use the invoice price. If there is none or if there is doubt of authenticity, they must then assess on the basis of value of identical goods or on the basis of similar goods coming in about the same time. If these techniques cannot be used, then customs officials can compute a value based on final sales value or reasonable cost.

The most common form of import or export restriction, from a quantity point of view, is the quota. From the standpoint of imports, a quota most frequently sets a limit on the quantitative amount of a product allowed to be imported in a given year. The amount frequently reflects a guarantee that domestic producers will have access to a certain percentage of the domestic markets. In the case of import tariffs, the gains from price increases to consumers are received in the form of government revenue in the importing country. In the case of quotas, however, the gains are most likely to accrue to producers or exporters in the producing country, although windfall gains could accrue to middlemen in the importing country if they bought at a lower open-market price and then sold at the higher protected domestic price.

Import quotas do not necessarily protect domestic producers. Japan, for example, maintains quotas on twenty-five agricultural products, most of which are not produced in Japan. Import quotas are used as a bargaining ploy in establishing contracts for Japanese exports. They are also used as a means of avoiding excess dependence on any one country for essential food needs, which could be cut off in the case of adverse climatic or political conditions.

Export quotas may be established in order to ensure that domestic consumers have sufficient supplies at a low price to prevent depletion of natural resources, or to attempt to raise an export price by restricting supply in foreign markets, e.g. OPEC restrictions on oil output.

A specific type of quota that prohibits all trade is known as an embargo. Embargos may be placed on either imports or exports, on whole categories of products regardless of destination, on specific products to specific countries, or on all products to specific countries.

"Buy Local" legislation may restrict purchases by government agencies to local suppliers, or ensure that a certain percentage of the product for governmental purchase must be sourced locally. Aside from direct legislation, campaigns are sometimes conducted by governments to persuade their nationals to buy locally made products and services rather than those of foreign origin. Indeed, in some countries government agencies have been established to promote buy local campaigns, many of which are increasingly being questioned at international level. In recent years the EC Commission has taken a keen interest in such campaigns and seeks to limit their application.

It has not been uncommon for countries to set classifications, labelling and testing standards in such a manner as to allow the sale of domestic products but to inhibit the sale of foreign-made products. These are sometimes ostensibly for the purpose of protecting the safety and health of domestic consumers; however, imports have often been tested under more onerous conditions than have domestic products. For example, before an American car may be sold in Japan, the Japanese government requires six volumes of documents on standards for each car, plus local testing of nearly every vehicle. This adds as much as $500 to the retail price of a US car in Japan. Under EC legislation such practices are being eliminated for the twelve member countries.

Many countries require that potential importers or exporters secure permission from government authorities before they conduct trade transactions. In order to gain permission it may be necessary to send samples abroad in advance. The use of such permits may not only restrict imports and exports directly by denial of permission, but may also result in a further deterioration of trade because of the cost, time, and uncertainty involved in the process.

Internationally traded services have not been exempt from restrictions. There are reported incidents of widespread discrimination by countries which favour their own firms. Among the complaints have been that Japanese Airlines obtain cargo clearance more quickly in Tokyo than do foreign airlines, that Argentina requires car imports to be insured with Argentine firms, and that West Germany requires models for advertisements in West German magazines to be hired through a West German agency, even if the advertisement is made abroad. Similarly, extensive industry regulation in Australia prevents international advertising agencies growing in that market.

## Regulating money transfer

Countries influence international transfers of money through foreign exchange controls, capital controls, policies of tied aid, supervision of the foreign operations of domestic banks and other financial institutions, and taxation.

Taxation laws are used in many ways to influence international financial transfers. Taxation levied on remittances of profits, for example, encourages reinvestment and discourages remittance back to the tax jurisdiction. In both the United States and the United Kingdom, the policy is shifting from taxation on remittances towards taxation on income, whether or not remitted. Taxation laws are also being created to discourage tax deferral through transfer of funds to corporations owned but registered in other tax jurisdictions.

Control over funds granted for foreign aid has at times been attempted through tied aid or tied loans. The granting country sometimes requires that funds be utilized in purchasing goods or services from the granting country, hoping to avoid balance of payments problems from the outflow of funds. An increasing number of countries are beginning to tie their aid in this fashion.

## Regulating people transfers

National policies controlling the entry and exit of people from a country are generally not motivated primarily by international business considerations. Broader political, economic, and social considerations invariably underlie such policies, which generally distinguish between people entering a country for a temporary stay such as tourists or, at the other end of the spectrum, people who want to enter a country on a permanent basis. Passports and visas are the basic means of controlling this form of international movement.

Generally speaking, restrictions on exit are regarded as morally less defensible than restrictions on entry. Apart from a small number of Eastern European countries only a few countries make it very difficult for people to depart. However, restrictions on the export of personal capital, are common. Nationals of India, for example, are not normally granted any foreign exchange facilities for emigration purposes. In cases of exceptional hardship, up to 100,000 rupees in 1987 (about US$13,000) may be released at the time of emigration. Many poorer countries follow a similar policy.

Most countries, anxious to expand their tourist industry, impose minimum restrictions on the entry of persons on temporary visits. The most restrictive policies are applied to persons who wish to seek employment in a foreign country or become permanent residents. The general world pattern in the late 1980s, apart from free internal movement within the EC and the Arab states, has become one of selected and limited immigration. For most countries the basis for admitting immigrants has increasingly favoured those professionally trained or highly skilled, with resources and able to join the workforce so that they do not create a burden on social welfare systems. For the underprivileged of any country, the opportunity to gain admission to another country is steadily decreasing.

From the standpoint of international business, national controls over the transfer of persons are more likely to be burdensome than prohibitive. Yet there are cases where countries have not granted work permits to foreign managers and technical staff of an international enterprise, as part of a policy of reserving such positions for nationals. Some countries delay the issue of visas and work permits in order to protect or favour local people. In many reported instances of such delays, however, the situation arises more from inefficient administrative systems than deliberate protectionist policy.

## Regulating technology transfers

The concept of technology encompasses technical and managerial know-how that is embodied in physical and human capital and in published documents, and is transmitted across national boundaries in various ways. In recent years governments, especially those in developing countries, have encouraged inflows of technology as a major means of achieving national development goals (Table 6.5).

In industrially advanced countries, there are few controls over the international transfer of technology or even the price received for such transfers. This is so even when the international sale of technology can produce major social costs in the shape of unemployment and redundant production facilities. Even taxation authorities have little say on transfer prices as long as they are determined

**Table 6.5**  Controlling technology transfer to developing countries

Developing countries are interested in controlling technology transfer to:
- ensure imported technology is appropriate to their needs
- ensure technology will actually be transferred to local nationals
- ensure charges for technology are not excessive
- minimise restraints on transfer agreements
- develop a code of conduct for technology transfer

at arm's length. However, attitudes in the developing countries differ markedly. They are predominantly buyers rather than sellers of technology. The objectives of the developing countries are ambitious. They want to ensure that imported technology is appropriate to their needs, which generally means smaller-scale and labour-intensive technology, and that it will actually be transferred to local nationals.

Developing countries in particular wish to ensure that charges for technology are not excessive and that the technology transferred is appropriate. "Excessive" is usually defined as any price above the lowest possible cost for obtaining the technology in any other way. Another common objective is to minimize the restraints in technology transfer agreements, such as limiting the markets in which the licensee can sell or the quantity that can be produced. Such restrictions have been common in order to protect the licensor from competition from the licensee, or to ensure that the licensed subsidiary fits into a global strategy.

Since 1976 the developing countries have been attempting to improve the terms for international transfers of technology through pressures by UNCTAD for a code of conduct. As a result of subsequent negotiations with the industrialized countries, progress has been made towards a possible convention. Industrial countries, however, have resisted attempts to apply better terms to intrafirm transactions.

## Political concerns of managers in international firms

Political matters arise in many ways which affect the functioning of the firm in international markets. Countries jealously guard their freedom of action within their own borders and are slow to give up rights to supranational organizations such as the United Nations, the IMF, the OECD or the EC. For this reason, it is important to examine the workings of the international political system as it applies to the international transfer of products, services, ideas, and investments. The managerial manifestation of political concerns in the international firm arises in four ways, as follows:

(a)  source country concerns;
(b)  host country concerns;
(c)  the politics of dependent capitalism; and
(d)  restrictive business practices.

### Source country considerations

There are many and varied arguments against the transfer of technology from developed to developing countries (Dunning, 1981, Chapter 12). The principal interest of policy makers in developed countries, the source countries for much of the technology being transferred internationally, is the effects such technology exports might have in slowing down international economic growth, in dampening technological innovation, in stagnating productivity, in producing inflation, and, most of all, in increasing unemployment in the source country. For these reasons the politics of international technology transfer are never far from the mind of the manager of the international company.

In addition to the fears listed, another more fundamental objection is frequently raised. Because technology transfer is designed to improve the international competitiveness of firms in host countries, it is argued that this can only occur at the expense of firms in source countries. This in turn erodes the market base in the source country of the technology exporting firms, making it more difficult to recover R & D and other investment costs.

The political and legal issues arise since there is frequent conflict between macro policy matters and welfare factors affecting individual firms at the micro level. To the international company transferring technology through the foreign direct investment mode, ownership is central as the firm maintains full control or believes it does. A conflict frequently arises, however, when a company in one country sells technology to another country which in turn uses that technology in products or components for sale to a third country, an enemy or potential enemy of the first. These situations usually involve sensitive technologies which can be used in military applications (Exhibit 6.3).

## Host country considerations

The traditional theory derived from economics that foreign investment depends on the yield of the investment no longer holds much sway. Trade in the same product groups flows between markets. There are extensive cross-investments between countries and many companies seek a presence in certain markets for strategic marketing reasons. For these reasons, it is the political economy of international markets which exists in a particular country which determines the level and nature of investment in that market.

Writing about foreign direct investment, the international activity which so exercises the political mind in most countries, Long (1977, p. 179) reports that governments, especially in small open countries, provide the necessary political and economic climate for the inflow of foreign direct investment. It is through the coalescence of this interplay of societal and business forces that a meaningful explanation of foreign direct investment among host countries may be found.

## Restrictive business practices

It is possible to divide restrictive business practices as applied internationally into three groups. International firms are often charged with applying horizontal, vertical or intra-company restrictive business practices (Davidow, 1980). An example of horizontal restrictions would be any form of international cartel such

---

**Exhibit 6.3  Affiliate sales of technologies with military applications**

---

*The Toshiba scandal has exporters running for cover*

Manufacturers all over Japan are suddenly jittery about doing business with Communist nations. Trade between Japan and the Soviet Union was already on the decline, but the scandal surrounding Toshiba Machine Co's illegal sale of milling machines to Moscow is slowing it further.

Although Japan's Ministry of International Trade & Industry (MITI) barred Toshiba Machines from exporting to Communist countries for a year, it was the severity of the US reaction that was most alarming. First, the Senate voted to bar any Toshiba imports, prompting the July 1 resignations of both the chairman and president of Toshiba Corp, the parent company. Japanese companies were then flabbergasted by the televised spectacle of US members of Congress smashing a Toshiba boom box on the Capitol lawn. "The US retaliation is terrifying", says an official of a large textile company. "It's terrifying to think that we could be held responsible for an affiliate's wrongdoings." Toshiba and the Japanese government have begun a damage control effort. "My first and biggest assignment is to figure out how to restore the trust in Toshiba that has been damaged by the actions of Toshiba Machine", Joichi Aoi, the company's new president and CEO, said in an interview. The key to Toshiba's attempt to head off congressional sanctions is devising new rules and procedures that, it argues, will prevent leaks in the future.

Getting the Japanese to recognize possible military uses of their exports lies at the core of the US-Japanese dispute. Public opinion in Japan still is strongly against enacting an espionage law or giving the military greater influence over exports.

**Source:** *Business Week,* 20 July, 1987, pp. 48–9.

---

as OPEC. Vertical restrictive business practices usually refer to restrictions in distribution and licensing agreements. It is thought that these are the most damaging when they take the form of demands by distributors who use the manufacturer as an accomplice. US anti-trust law, however, usually condemns horizontal restrictive business practices but applies the rule of reason to vertical restrictions. These latter frequently provide attractive briefs to US lawyers. The third kind of restriction refers to activities in a market between different members of the same business groups. Grey markets and parallel imports often arise in the absence of such restrictions. The usual rule in the United States and the EC is that a firm has the right to dictate policy to its branches and divisions to ensure that they do not compete with each other.

In addressing possible approaches to control Davidow (1980) mentions three and favours the third:

(a) extra-territorial application of developed country anti-trust law;
(b) strengthening of host country restrictive business practice law;

(c) development of international rules including voluntary or binding international codes of conduct.

## International legal framework

The legal environment for international business consists principally of the laws and courts of the individual nation states. Increasingly, international firms, especially high-technology firms, are going to court to resolve claimed infringement (Exhibit 6.4). Since no single international commercial legal system exists, the international firm is confronted with as many legal environments as there are countries. The national systems differ significantly in philosophy and practice, and each nation-state maintains its own set of courts in complete independence of every other nation. The closest approximation to an international legal framework is a patchwork system of treaties, codes and agreements among certain nations that apply to selected areas of international business activity.

What is normally called international law is more accurately described as international public law or the law of nations. It consists of a body of rules and principles that nation-states consider legally binding. It can be enforced through the International Court of Justice, international arbitration, or the internal courts of the nation-states. It is mainly concerned with the relationship between states, the delimitation of their jurisdictions, and control of war. In recent years, international law has also emphasized the protection of individual human rights, even against the individual's own state.

Apart from EC institutions, the only international court is the International Court of Justice at The Hague. It is the principal legal organ of the UN, and all members of the UN are parties to the statute establishing the court. The function of the court is to pass judgment on disputes between states. Private individuals or corporations do not have direct access to the International Court.

From the standpoint of international business, the most important approximation to international law is the growing number of treaties and conventions covering commercial and economic matters. The more important international agreements are referred to as treaties. Those of lesser importance are called conventions, agreements, protocols or acts. All these forms are agreements between two or more nation states which normally become legally enforceable through the municipal courts of the participating countries and an international court is not essential. Very frequently such agreements, enshrined in the laws of one of the countries, are bilateral and result from political pressure.

Since there is no "international law" covering commercial transactions, where necessary the international firm must have recourse to the laws of the countries concerned. A first step here would be to understand the world's major legal systems. It is also important to understand how the international firm can minimize legal problems. It has also become increasingly important to understand the interplay of national law and international law, especially EC law.

## Major world legal systems

Two major structures have guided the development of legal systems in most countries of the world (Table 6.6). Common law is the basis of law in countries that have been at some time under British influence. Common law countries do not attempt to anticipate all areas in the application of a law by writing it to cover every foreseeable situation. Instead, cases in common law countries are decided

---

**Exhibit 6.4   Patent protection returns**

---

*When the going gets tough, the tough go to court*

Until recently, high-technology companies like TI were a uniquely unlitigious lot . . . mostly chipmakers and their brothers in the computer business were too busy getting new products out the door to do more than grouse about knockoffs. No longer in just the last year:

- The US District Court for the Southern District of New York ruled that Sumitomo Electric Industries Ltd had "willfully infringed" two of Corning Glass Works' patents on its optical-wavelength fibres. In addition, Corning was awarded unspecified damages . . .
- Chipmaker Zilog Inc based in Campbell, Calif., got the US Customs Service to stop imports of a chip made by Japan's Sharp Corp on the grounds that Sharp was using technology it had licensed from Zilog in versions of chips it was not licensed to produce
- Intel and NEC continued their long-standing court battle over whether NEC had copied the microcode in one of Intel's microprocessors. And in February Intel created a new position within the company, chief counsel for intellectual property.

Some changes in the legal system also explain the increased litigation. During the 1960s and 1970s the courts were generally very anti-patent, making patent litigation highly unpredictable. Judges were often uncomfortable with arguments that centered on complex technology. Then, in 1982, a special court, called the Court of Appeals of the Federal Circuit Court, was created to hear all patent appeals coming from district courts. At least one patent lawyer serves on this court.

The Copyright Act of 1976, which clarified software copyrighting, and the Semiconductor Chip Protection Act of 1984, which created a new form of protection for the designs etched on chips, also have helped. And Polaroid's successful suit against Eastman Kodak, which forced Kodak to abandon the instant photography business, showed companies how much could be gained by vigorously defending their inventions.

**Source:** *Forbes*, 28 December, 1987, pp. 36–7.

---

**Table 6.6**  Major world legal systems

Common Law

- countries at one time under British influence or former colonies of Britain
- law not written to cover all foreseeable situations
- cases decided on basis of tradition, common practice and interpretation of statutes
- precedents important in understanding common law

Code Law

- codes of conduct inclusive of all foreeseable applications of law
- codes developed for commerical, civil, and criminal applications
- laws themselves important factor in understanding code law

upon the basis of tradition, common practice and interpretation of statutes. Civil or code law countries have as their premise the writing of codes of conduct that are inclusive of all foreseeable applications of law. Codes of law are then developed for commercial, civil and criminal applications. Precedents are important in understanding common law as it is or has been interpreted. The laws themselves are the key to understanding the legal environment in civil or code law countries.

Even in common law countries there are often codes of law. The Uniform Commercial Code in the United States is a good example of a code of law governing business activity. However, common law does not differentiate between civil, criminal and commercial activities, and thus a business may be liable under any of these laws. Code law countries separate the three types of activity, but there are always areas where codes are not sufficiently specific and must be interpreted by the courts. Hence, most countries use common or code law as the basis for their legal system, but they rely on a combination of the two in applying the legal system to actual disputes.

Perhaps the best example of how common and code law differ is in the recognition of industrial property rights. These include trademarks, logos, brand names, production processes, patents, even managerial know-how. In common law countries, ownership of industrial property rights comes from use. In code or civil law countries, ownership comes from registering the name or process. The implications of this difference are obvious; a company may find itself in litigation in a code law country to gain the rights to use its *own* names or logos, and it may not win! The EC Commission is taking a keen interest in developing directives regarding such property rights which will have applicability throughout the community and will also affect firms outside the EC.

## Minimizing international legal problems

The international firm should always be aware of the different legal systems to be abided by when doing business in more than one country. The international firm should also appreciate the elements of a good contract, make provision for arbitration, and have a detailed knowledge of international conventions as they affect its business (Table 6.7). The problem is especially troublesome for the firm that formulates a common or standardized marketing plan to be implemented in several countries. Although differences in languages and customs may be overcome, legal differences between countries may still prevent a standardized marketing programme. Each country has laws regulating activities in promotion, product development, labelling, pricing and channels of distribution.

Anti-trust laws can affect territorial restrictions on distributors and agents or the granting of exclusive territories. In the EC, these activities are covered by Articles 85 and 86 of the Treaty of Rome which are effectively concerned with the abuse of a dominant position, or concerted practices which may affect trade between member states. Another example would be that exclusive territory provisions in US contracts are not enforceable, but they are allowable under most conditions in Latin American countries. Other distribution activities such as tying

**Table 6.7**  Minimizing international legal problems

Awareness of commercial law within countries:

- Commercial activities may be affected by differing legal environments for:
  - distribution
  - pricing
  - promotion
  - product development and introduction
  - product liability

Elements of a good international contract:

- Use of contract terms which are not bound to one culture
- Clear units of measurement
- Avoidance of standard/domestic contracts
- Provision for jurisdiction in event of a dispute

Provision for arbitration:

- Arbitration clause commits all parties in a contract to an agreement to take disputes to an arbitrator before pursuing other legal recourses

- Reasons for arbitration:
  - expense of facing foreign legal and/or court system
  - foreign firm may face prejudice in another country's courts
  - difficulty of enforcing, in one country, decisions made in another country
  - time consuming nature of litigation
  - possible damage to firm's image

Knowledge of international conventions:

- There has been a concerted effort worldwide to standardize and co-ordinate regulations related to customs, labelling, quarantines, units of measurement, and taxes.

- International conventions which protect industrial property rights in foreign markets should also be noted.

contracts, resale restrictions on dealers, full-line forcing, franchising or other forms of vertical integration may be prohibited in some countries and permissible in others.

Pricing by the international firm is likely to be affected in a variety of ways by the legal environment in different countries. Price maintenance laws may prevent the firm from using discount stores or from offering quantity discounts or other price concessions. Some countries have minimum price laws and others may require licences for price increases. Pricing may have to be pegged to inflation indices in some situations; in others the firm may be prevented from raising prices in a highly inflationary environment, and thus will face declining profitability.

## Legal aspects of marketing claims

Promotion is the area of marketing strategy where the impact of varying legal rules is particularly obvious. In Germany, for example, advertisements cannot claim that the firm's products are the "best," since that is interpreted as violating a law that forbids disparaging competitors, whereas such practice has been quite common in the United States but is now on the wane. In Austria, premium offers to consumers come under the discount law which prohibits any cash reductions that give preferential treatment to different groups of customers. In France it is illegal to offer a customer a gift or premium conditional on the purchase of another product. Furthermore, a manufacturer or retailer cannot offer products that are different from the kind regularly offered. For example, a detergent manufacturer cannot offer clothing or cooking utensils. The typical premiums or prizes offered by cereal manufacturers would be completely illegal under this law.

The development and introduction of new products must conform to laws that regulate units of measurement, quality or ingredient requirements, safety or pollution restrictions, and industry standards. This may force the firm to modify its products in every national market in order to meet varying legal rules. Labelling and branding also face many laws regulating their use. Product liability is yet another area of concern; the differences in interpreting implied and explicit warranties and product returns are special areas of concern to the international firm.

The use of specific terms which are not bound to one culture is most important for the international firm when writing a contract for business in a foreign market. Consider the problems that might be caused by terms such as "premium," "first rate quality" and "commercial grade" when a different country's cultural and legal perspectives are used to interpret such terms.

Conflicts can also arise when units of measurement such as weight and length are not sufficiently clear. Standard contracts used in domestic markets are often inadequate in international marketing because they make too many assumptions about the interpretation of terminology, e.g. garment sizes as small, medium or large. Another example which caused considerable difficulty for a food exporter to the United States was liquid measure based on the imperial measure of the pint; in Europe a pint contains 20 fluid ounces of liquid, whereas in the United States it contains 16 fluid ounces, and the US pint is smaller.

## Use of arbitration agreements

A good international contract should also specify jurisdiction in case of a dispute. The jurisdiction clause should state which country's laws will apply, as well as which court system will be used to judge the case. Both these phrases are important because they facilitate enforcement of a decision. For example, in contracts offered by the EC Commission, Dutch law is often specified as the basis for resolving any dispute which might arise.

Many firms engaging in international business further protect themselves from legal problems by including an agreement for arbitration in their international contracts. An arbitration clause commits all parties in a contract to an agreement that they will take disputes to an arbitrator before pursuing other legal recourses.

In international business there are clear reasons for preferring an independent, third party arbitrator to litigation: since, as we have seen, there is no court for international commercial conflicts, at least one of the parties will have to face a foreign legal and/or court system, and such litigation can be extremely expensive. The foreign firm may face prejudice in the courts of another country simply because the firm is foreign owned. It may be difficult to enforce judgements that are made in another country; and legal proceedings may be even more extensive than anticipated. Litigation is very time consuming and expensive. If the dispute involves a shipment of fashion clothing held in a customs warehouse, the clothing may be worthless by the time the case is decided. Legal proceedings often generate the kind of negative image that an international firm seeks to avoid in foreign markets.

There are several sources of arbitrators for international business contracts, i.e. International Chamber of Commerce, Inter-American Commercial Arbitration Commission and London Court of Arbitration. There has been a concerted effort worldwide to co-ordinate, if not to standardize, the regulations related to customs, labelling, guarantees and units of measurement. Perhaps most important to international firms are the international conventions that help protect the firm's industrial property rights in foreign markets. The Convention of Paris established the International Bureau for the Protection of Industrial Property. This convention gives the person or firm which has files for a patent in one country twelve months' priority in applying for that patent in about eighty other member countries. The European Patent Office allows a firm's patent to be automatically registered in sixteen European countries. Even so, the ability of the firm to protect its intellectual property rights in the area of high technology can be circumscribed due to the difficulty of proving infringement on the one hand and waiting for a worthwhile result on the other. Legal cases can often take so long that the technology is displaced by newer versions. These two factors, proving infringement and technological obsolescence, sometimes give firms an opportunity to reconsider litigation. In many cases neither party is the winner, as was seen in the case taken by Intel against NEC Corporation in the US some years ago.

In the Intel vs NEC Corporation microcode copying case mentioned in Exhibit 6.4 the US District Court in February 1989 ruled that chipmakers can copyright so-called micro code, i.e. the software embedded in microprocessors and similar chips. On other issues Intel, the US company, lost to NEC Corporation, the Japanese company. The judge ruled that Intel had invalidated copyright protection on its 8088 and 8086 chips since some of its licensees had shipped millions of chips without copyright notice on their labels. The similarities in the software produced by the two companies stemmed from the relatively few options available in writing microcode instructions to produce a particular result (*Business Week*, 20 February, 1989). Intel argued that NEC had exploited a licence from Intel to product the 8088 and 8086 chips to develop clones for which it would not have to pay royalties. The judge ruled, however, that the final version actually used by NEC was sufficiently different to avoid infringement. Although NEC won every issue that might have required it to pay royalties the victory was hollow. The trial dragged on so long that the chips in dispute were largely displaced by the 80286 and 80386 generation chips. In 1989, the year the case was resolved, the disputed designs represented only about 1 per cent of Intel's $2.9 billion annual revenues (*Business Week*, 20 February, 1989).

## Growth and application of European Community law

As seen earlier, international law, or law of nations, is the traditional name for the "customary and treaty rules which are considered legally binding by states in their intercourse with each other" and it is therefore generally accepted that individuals can claim no rights nor assume obligations under international law. By signing the European treaties the member states have, on the contrary, in the opinion of the court attributed to Community law, "an authority which their citizens may evoke in the national courts." Furthermore, when referring to Community law, one is not confined to the provisions of the various European Treaties (primary Community law), but one should also include the decisions of the Community's institutions.

Once it is admitted that Community law is an independent legal order existing within the Community, several questions arise as to the relations between this Community law and the national legal orders.

The precedence of Community law over the national laws of the member states is based not upon any national provision, but on the very nature of the Communities themselves, whose very existence and functioning requires identical applicability of the Community law in all the member states. Hence, where there is a conflict between a national and a Community legal provision, the Community provision will rule (Exhibit 6.5).

A Common Market depends upon the elimination of trade barriers and of distortions of free and equal competition. This necessarily requires

---

**Exhibit 6.5   EC legal provisions supersede national law**

---

*EC Commission and competition in chemicals*

In a bitter dispute with the West German chemicals giant Hoechst AG, the Commission of the European Community has sent an unmistakable signal that it intends to assert its authority to enforce competition laws throughout the EC. The outcome of the dispute will establish a far-reaching precedent, confirming or invalidating the principle that Community law supersedes national law.

In mid-January, Commission inspectors armed with EC warrants staged dramatic dawn raids on eight European companies suspected of price-fixing in polyethylene and PVC, two plastics materials, in violation of Community anti-cartel laws. In a similar case last year, the EC fined 15 companies £37 million ($55.5 million) for price fixing in polypropylene.

The current investigation involves companies in France, Belgium, Italy, Spain, The Netherlands, and West Germany. Hoechst refused to recognize the Commission's search warrant, though the EC inspectors were accompanied by officials of the West German Federal Cartel office. The company obtained a restraining order from an administrative court in Frankfurt on the grounds that the investigators did not have a warrant approved by a West German court and refused to hand over requested documents.

It was the first time a local court had issued an injunction against the Commission though EC warrants have been used in hundreds of investigations over the years. The Commission considers the dispute a test case of its jurisdiction and of the very credibility of Community law, a view with which legal experts do not quibble.

In 1964 the European Court ruled that law stemming from the EC treaty could not "be overridden by domestic legal provisions, however framed, without being deprived of its character as community law and without the legal basis of the Community itself being called into question." The current case will be the first specific test of that ruling. A decision against the EC could call the very purpose of the Community, and therefore its existence, into question.

**Source:** *International Management*, April, 1987, p. 7.

---

rules made centrally and operating in identical terms throughout the area of the market to secure fairness and consistency. (Mr Rippon, House of Commons, Hansard, 15 February, 1972)

## Summary

In this chapter concern rested on analysing the political environment as it affects the firm in international markets. The key questions examined were the importance of political stability in providing a basis for international marketing activities, irrespective of the mode of entry used. The political risks of operating abroad are much greater than operating in the familiar domestic market. The political philosophies, cultures and laws are different which affects the way business is done. Attitudes to property and contracts are therefore very different.

In some markets the political–business interface is quite strong and positive, whereas in other countries business is seen as a basis for taxation and control. For these reasons some markets are more open and dynamic than others. Governments in all countries, however, attempt to regulate cross-border flows of products, services, people, money and other assets. Furthermore, the regulation of technology transfers is of increasing interest in recent years. Regulations provide a source of anxiety to some firms, especially those seeking open markets and freer competition. To other firms regulation is seen as a source of protection and monopoly power.

Countries, separately and together, attempt to co-ordinate regulation and controls through a legal framework. To date, the legal framework which applies to business transactions tends to vary from country to country. The code of law which applies in an individual country can complicate matters. Increasingly, transnational bodies, including the EC, are taking a greater interest in providing a co-ordinated legal framework within which the firm in international markets can operate. Because of cost and the time factor involved, international firms prefer arbitration as a means of settling disputes.

## Discussion questions

1.  What aspects of international marketing are most affected by political instability in a country?

2.  How can you measure political instability? Is political instability also a matter of perception?

3.  Some countries have been more successful than others in developing a positive political–business interaction. Discuss. Evaluate the situation in your own country.

4.  Regulation of international transfers of any kind is invidious and should be banned by the recognized international authorities. Discuss.

5.  The manager of the international firm can cope with regulations once they are clear and unambiguous. Do you agree?

6.  Regulations which remove restrictive business practices in major world markets should be favoured. Discuss.

7.  How do firms minimize international legal problems?

8.  European-based firms are increasingly faced with EC directives, laws and regulations. How will this affect the role of national law and how will it affect

the marketing of products and services in Europe? What effect will it have on firms outside the EC?

# References

Davidow, Joel (1980) 'Multinationals, host governments and regulation of restrictive practices,' *Columbia Journal of World Business*, Summer, pp. 14–19.

Dunning, John H. (1981) *International Production and the Multinational Enterprise*, George Allen and Unwin, London.

Feierabend, Ivo K. and Feierabend, Rosalind L. (1965) *Cross-national Data Bank of Political Instability Events (Code Index)*, Public Affairs Research Institute, San Diego.

Long, Frank (1977) 'Towards a political economy framework of foreign direct investment,' *American Journal of Economics and Sociology*, **36**, 171–85.

# 7 Public policy environment of international marketing

There have been very many changes in the international competitive environment in recent years. Competition for US, European and other Western countries now comes from resource-poor countries especially Japan, countries in South East Asia, Brazil, and Mexico. These countries have consistently achieved more rapid increases in productivity, output, and exports than the more established countries. Such changes have forced the older competitors to question their approach to competing internationally and to examine the role of advanced technology developed through creative industrial and commercial policies. The critical element of the response by older countries has been to seek effective participation by national governments in shaping the business environments through national planning and strategies.

## Marketing challenge of open markets

Among the more significant responses by successful companies worldwide to the removal of protective barriers and globalization of markets has been the almost frenetic search for new ways of entering and staying in foreign markets. The strategic concern lies in seeking ways of establishing effective equity and non-equity ways of entering and developing foreign markets through exporting, foreign direct investment and corporate alliances based on joint ventures and licensing. For many firms, some or all of these approaches to competing in international markets represent new challenges and opportunities.

The challenge in a competitive environment is corporate survival and the opportunity is growth through internationalization. A new boost for the internationalization of European firms occurred in 1985 with the publication of the EC White Paper on Industrial Policy "Completing the Internal Market." The signing of the Single European Act in 1987 added impetus to this process. In addition the "Delors Plan" agreement finalized at the February 1988 EC summit meeting in Brussels provided the EC with a secure financial base for the following five years. The question facing managers was to what extent they were preventing the development and growth of their firms by adhering to the delusion of protected markets instead of adapting to a changing world which was becoming increasingly international. Industry in neighbouring Switzerland has long recognized the importance of a global orientation and when, from time to time, the focus is temporarily lost Swiss firms are prepared to make the required change.

## *Impact of global competitors*

Competitiveness for the firm refers to its ability to increase earnings by expanding sales and/or profit margins in the market in which it competes to defend market position in a subsequent round of competition as products and processes evolve. Competitiveness in this sense is almost synonymous with the firm's long-run profit performance relative to its rivals. An analogue exists at the national level, but it is much more complicated (Cohen *et al.*, 1984). A country's competitiveness is the degree to which it can produce goods and services that meet the test of international markets while simultaneously expanding the real incomes of its people.

International competitiveness at the national level is based on superior productivity performance and the economy's ability to shift to high-productivity activities, which in turn can generate high levels of real wages. Competitiveness is associated with rising living standards, wealth, expanding employment opportunities, and the ability of a country to maintain its international obligations. It is the country's ability to stay ahead technologically and commercially in those product markets likely to constitute a larger share of world consumption and value added in the future and not just the ability to sell abroad to maintain a trade equilibrium that is the key to national competitiveness (Cohen *et al.*, 1984).

To understand the issues, the dynamics of competition in international markets must be clarified. Three different competitive situations are encountered (Cohen *et al.*, 1984). The newly industrialising countries (NICs) have entered European markets by combining, in varied formulas, low-cost labour, government promotion and standard mature technologies. European firms have responded in three ways to such competition: off-shore production to match foreign labour costs; speciality products to move competition away from price; and innovative automation to reduce the labour content in manufacturing to become low-cost producers. The second competitive situation arises in industries where product quality and costs depend on dominating complex manufacturing processes; success depends on factors such as the quality and speed of product design, the organization of production and services, e.g. cars and TVs. Competition in such industries tends to be concentrated among the advanced industrial countries of Europe, North America and Japan.

In the third situation are high-technology industries where advances in product performance based on research and development are critical. As advanced products are copied, however, holding markets in high-technology competition depends on sophisticated manufacturing and marketing skills since the pace of imitation is faster because competitors are closer to the same technology frontier and because design processes can be accelerated.

The common feature of these three forms of competition is the importance of manufacturing and marketing systems in retaining industrial competitiveness in international markets, and the ability of firms to understand and cope with the interaction between them. Even in the so-called haven of high technology, the long-run competitiveness of firms will rest on their ability to translate product advantage into enduring market position through the application of sophisticated marketing expertise. In this respect the traditional method of attempting to support exporters and reduce import competition by manipulating the exchange rate can sometimes produce ambiguous results (Exhibit 7.1). The position of the firm relative to its competitors is important. Some European, and many Japanese and other Far Eastern firms continue to spend large sums in marketing investments. Treated creatively, marketing investment should be included on the balance sheet as an investment and not treated as an expense to be minimized.

## Challenge facing the international firm

The successful firm caters for its customers within the context of the firm's competitive environment which has become increasingly international (Hayes and Abernathy, 1980, p. 68; Simon, 1984; and Wind and Robertson, 1983, p. 15). The competitive milieu consists of domestic and international customers and competition, and national and public policies and regulations. It is influenced by social, cultural and educational trends throughout the world. The international marketing environment directly affects the strategic options open to the firm and, as a consequence, affects the kind of structure most appropriate for international marketing operations (Bradley, Hession and Murray, 1985). It is not the marketing environment itself that is important but the firm's ability to cope with it (Bradley, 1987). In the rapidly changing technological environment that characterizes international markets there are few frozen market niches (Abernathy, Clark and Kantrow, 1983).

Furthermore, the "most endangered companies in the rapidly evolving world tend to be those that dominate rather small domestic markets with high value added products for which there are smaller markets elsewhere." (Levitt, 1983, p. 94) Attention must be focussed on the missing link in developing a competitive strategy for success in international markets: investment in marketing to produce an international orientation and an ability to compete successfully in international markets. A standardized approach to the domestic market is frequently adequate because buyers and conditions are homogeneous. To succeed in international markets it is necessary to develop multidimensional strategies. It would be myopic to consider exporting as the only or primary way of entering foreign markets.

---

**Exhibit 7.1  Using the exchange rate to support exporters**

---

*A weak dollar: scant help for many US products*

Despite the dollar's sharp descent, chances of a rapid turnaround in the US trade balance are relatively slim, warns Deborah Allen Olivier of the Claremont Economics Institute in Claremont, Calif. In a paper presented at the Western Economic Association's recent annual conference in Vancouver, she estimated that "only about one-quarter of the US's major trade categories will benefit from the weaker dollar . . . [while] others will deteriorate further."

Like other analysts, Olivier notes that the dollar has declined only against the Japanese yen, the West German mark, and a handful of other currencies, while holding steady or rising against the currencies of the many other major US trading partners. But she uses this analysis to develop "product-dollar indexes" that indicate how shifting exchange rates have affected the competitiveness of specific products — many of which are heavily traded with countries whose currencies have actually weakened against the dollar.

Olivier calculates, for example, that the dollar index for the broad category of food and livestock has actually strengthened by 35% over the past two years, while her manufactured goods dollar index is up 9.4%. On a more detailed level, she finds that US animal feed producers should benefit from a 17.7% drop in their dollar index, while suppliers of steel and iron proudcts are better off by 13.3%. But wheat growers will be hampered by a rise of almost 23% for their dollar, and makers of semi-manufactured goods face a 19% increase.

Olivier is now revising her indexes so that they reflect differences in inflation rates by country and product line — a process she believes will alter the numbers, "but not the broad trends.".

**Source:** *Business Week*, 27 July, 1987, pp. 11–12.

---

By ignoring licensing, joint ventures and direct investment market entry modes, many firms effectively limit their strategic options to those markets which are best served by exporting.

Other foreign market entry modalities are increasingly being used by successful firms. Foreign direct investment and equity joint ventures are now quite common. With joint ventures, licensing and other alliances, as with other aspects of internationalization, the relevant measure of the character of competition is not a simple calculation of market share but a careful determination, at a given point in time, of the precise relationships among market preferences, technical configuration and competitive focus (Abernathy, Clark and Kantrow, 1983, p. 50). The internationalization of the firm and industry tends to redefine what it takes to be successful. The conventional wisdom of growth through exporting only may not be all that meaningful for the longer-term development of the firm.

## *Marketing implications of single European market*

The creation of a large internal market in Europe is expected to create opportunities for production and distribution scale effects which have not been feasible to date. An internal market with 320 million people is larger than the domestic markets of either the United States or Japan.

However, the nature of the internal market is not comparable to a large domestic market. Linguistic and cultural divergences remain intact and are likely to continue for a considerable period. Scale effects in production do not necessarily mean scale effects in marketing — or at least in all aspects of marketing. It will be necessary, for example, to continue to tailor many products, especially low-technology products such as food and clothing, packaging, and promotion to individual country-market requirements.

A single European market may pave the way for cross-border mergers and joint ventures. New modes of co-operation between firms may be developed. It is likely that existing distribution channels will change in nature and size in response to the elimination of physical, technical and fiscal barriers. Many of these changes are already in evidence but their full impact has not yet been felt.

Among the major requirements for proper preparation for the completion of the single European market will be the development of a capacity to adapt to rigorous technical and marketing standards and the development of flexibility and adaptability in the modes of market entry chosen. The narrow interpretation of exporting as a sales mode may well diminish in importance as the other modes mentioned above gain in strategic significance. In a large internal market, segmentation strategies will become increasingly important. Opportunities for imaginative segmentation are likely to emerge. It is almost certain that success will accompany those firms which, through strategic thinking on the consequences of the internal market, are prepared for it, while those that continue to operate in an opportunistic fashion are likely to be eliminated by the brute force of competition. Already there is a great deal of evidence that restricted markets are a thing of the past (Exhibit 7.2).

It is important, therefore, to ensure in the lead up to, and for a period after, the completion of the internal market that companies do not suffer from retrograde policies and ill-conceived management decisions.

## **Industrial and commercial policy environment**

Industrial and commerical policies may be regarded as tools which are used to affect the speed of the process of resource allocation among and within industrial sectors. This implies that, for a variety of reasons, public authorities may not accept the way the market allocates resources and achieves major structural changes (Bradley, 1983). According to the goals pursued by public policy, the process of reallocation may be retarded or accelerated, facilitated or impeded. For example, the national security argument might justify the maintenance of otherwise

---

**Exhibit 7.2    Policies to open EC markets**

---

*Landmark ruling by EC on restrictive practices*

EC Commissioner Peter Sutherland yesterday welcomed what was generally regarded as a landmark ruling by the European Court of Justice. The judges upheld the powers of the EC executive to take legal action and impose fines against companies based outside the EC.

A group of 41 wood pulp firms from Canada, the United States and Scandinavia had claimed that the EC Commission had no such "extra-territorial" powers in relation to companies which had no base within the EC and in relation to pricing policies decided outside the Community.

But yesterday the Court ruled that the decisive factor was the place where the alleged restrictive practices were put into effect, not where the companies were based or where they decided their policies.

Mr Sutherland said: "This landmark judgment confirms the Commission's policy of applying EC competition rules in a coherent and non-discriminatory manner to restrict practices, wherever initiated, which have an impact on competitive conditions and Trade within the Community. This is of particular significance in the light of the completion of the internal market and the development of international trade."

Yesterday's ruling on the territoriality issue is now to be followed by a ruling on whether the wood pulp firms were actually guilty of forming a price fixing cartel.

**Source:** *The Irish Times*, Wednesday 28 September, 1988, p. 15.

---

uneconomical production facilities, e.g. small, inefficient oil refineries. Employment measures may be needed because labour markets are imperfect. Manpower policies can also reduce the costs of adjustment, hence increasing the speed of reallocating human resources.

Similarly, growth-oriented science and technological policies can ensure a socially sufficient flow of resources. There may also be a case for subsidizing R & D in high-technology industries affected by large fixed costs. Hence, industrial policy may be regarded as a positive response to the imperfections of modern markets — whether capital markets, labour markets, or product markets.

A much wider role than that for correcting market distortions may, however, be suggested. Industrial and commerical policy may deal with such issues as the continued rise in the cost of economic adjustment and the social resistance to it. Industrial and commercial policies in some countries frequently address the necessity of simultaneously safeguarding social peace, especially in a society deeply divided by class. Industrial policy may be used to shift resources out of activities which have become uncompetitive due to the pressure of international economic forces. Finally, it is increasingly being recognized by governments that, for a wide range of manufacturers, competitive advantage may be relatively malleable instead of rigidly predetermined by national endowments of resources (Exhibit 7.3).

At the present time the last argument is critical as there are several economic and political reasons for an industrial and commercial policy which reflects the need to help domestic industries respond to the challenge of international competition. Contrasting with traditional trade theory, which treats the determinants of national factor endowments and national technological developments as exogenous, it is argued that, in many sectors, comparative advantage rests on relative capital endowments, which result from accumulated investment. Government policies can alter the process of physical and human capital accumulation over time to improve the country's strategic position in international competition.

## *Nature and formation of industrial and commercial policy*

Industrial policy may be applied at three levels: macro-economic policy; sectoral policy; or company level policy (Defraigne, 1984). Macro economic policy is the least interventionist and leaves the functioning of industries and firms to the market mechanism. Industrial policy is therefore seen as something to improve the general framework within which producer activities and consumer choices take place, and to facilitate an automatic process of industrial adjustment. Such an approach requires a high-quality infrastructure, a professionally adapted labour force, and accessibility to capital and credit. This type of policy is closest to the "invisible hand" policy in vogue in the United Kingdom and the United States in the late 1980s. It is the traditional policy of equilibrium economics which relies entirely on market mechanisms for resource allocation.

Sectoral policies aimed at certain industries are justified when market imperfections, or "market failure", affect specific industries. The precise reason for the market imperfection or market failure must be identified and a policy designed to solve the specific problem directly. Industrial policy is then viewed as being able to provide non-market mechanisms that improve the response given by the market forces existing in the relevant industry. Much of the work of the General Agreement on Tariffs and Trade (GATT) deals with sectoral policies and trade barriers that affect sectoral development in many countries. Because of the impact that open markets might have on key industrial sectors governments frequently oppose the liberalization of trade in key products and commodities (Exhibit 7.4).

Public policy is increasingly designed to produce various forms of actions directed towards specific companies or industrial groups. Such micro level policies are now quite common in Western Europe and particularly in the newly industrialized countries. Policies aimed at attracting foreign firms or developing small indigenous businesses are a clear illustration of this type of industrial policy. There are many instances of direct intervention by governments in the operational

---

**Exhibit 7.3   Using public policy to improve competitive advantage**

---

*From NAFTA to CER*

From 1965 through 1982, trade between Australia and New Zealand was carried out under the New Zealand–Australia Free Trade Agreement (NAFTA), which provided for the gradual reduction and eventual elimination of tariffs between the two countries. NAFTA was replaced by an agreement for "Closer Economic Relations" (CER). The CER treaty calls for tariff restrictions to be removed in five stages. This process started on January 1, 1983, when goods with a tariff of 5% or less became duty-free; tariffs of 5–30% were reduced by five percentage points initially and will be cut by five percentage points a year; and tariffs of more than 30% will drop to zero over a five-year term.

   Because Australian tariffs are generally lower, most New Zealand exports to Australia move to duty-free status faster. New Zealand's import restrictions on Australian goods will be removed progressively until 1995 and export incentives will be eliminated in trans-Tasman trade by the end of the 1986/87 tax year (March 31 for New Zealand, June 30 for Australia). A final agreement will ensure that restrictive trade practices legislation standards, technical specifications, testing procedures, and domestic labeling requirements do not hinder free trade.

   The CER timetable is right on track. Given the New Zealand government's efforts to speed up dismantling the country's import-licensing system, the two neighbors are likely to achieve an effective free trade area well before 1995.

**Source:** *Business Asia*, 19 January, 1987, p. 20.

---

and strategic affairs of specific firms. Government policies of this type are found throughout the EC, particularly in France, Spain, Greece, Ireland, Scotland, Wales and other regions where large-scale industry never took hold.

## Approaches to industrial and commercial policy

The following four approaches to industrial and commercial policy making have been recognized (Eliasson, 1984):

   (a)  the positive approach;
   (b)  the subsidy approach;
   (c)  the planning approach; and
   (d)  the market approach.

This section draws heavily on a number of sources on industrial and commercial policy, particularly that of Eliasson (1984) whose framework is used here.

## Exhibit 7.4   Impact of trade liberalization on industrial sectors

### Key issues at GATT talks

Here are some of the proposals being made and some of the countries making them in Montreal at the midterm review of the Uruguay round of the General Agreement on Tariffs and Trade.

*Issue*: Freeze domestic and export agricultural subsidies and roll back restrictions on market access.

*Supporters*: United States and 13-member Cairns Group, including Canada, Argentina, Australia, Brazil, Philippines.

- European community says subsidies are necessary to protect its farmers and save the rural way of life.

*Issue*: Liberalize trade in services such as banking, insurance, advertising, legal services and tourism.

*Supporters*: United States, Japan, European Community.

- India, Brazil, Nigeria, Egypt and others, fearing harm to their own service sectors, say services should not be made part of the GATT talks.

*Issue*: Protect intellectual property by harmonizing and enforcing copyright, trademark and patent laws.

*Supporters*: United States, European Community.

- Brazil, India and others fear that stringent laws would restrict their technological development.

*Issue*: Streamline methods for GATT to resolve disputes between member nations.

*Supporters: United States, Japan, European Community, others.*

- Agreement on some kind of streamlining considered highly likely.

*Issue*: Cut tariffs on textiles in the United States and other developed countries.

*Supporters*: Developing nations.

- United States, concerned about protecting its domestic textile industry, does not favour changes in the existing multi-fiber agreement, which is separate from GATT.

*Issue*: Better access in developed countries for tropical products such as citrus, coffee, cocoa.

*Supporters*: Brazil, Colombia, Malaysia, Thailand.

- United States says its market is already the most open and says marketing openings for tropical products should be linked to progress on agriculture in general.

**Source:** *Arab News*, Riyadh, Saturday, 3 December, 1988.

## Positive approach to industrial development

The positive approach to developing industrial policy is concerned with supporting and stimulating new technological industrial activities by direct involvement in the process of company operations. A key concept in this regard, particularly among European policy makers, has been direct government technological support of industry to improve international competitiveness. For example, the computer, electronics, nuclear and aircraft industries have the highest priority in French industrial policy. France uses direct subsidies and government research as a means of implementing this policy.

Similarly, the UK government has supported local firms in developing their own very large-scale integration (VLSI) capabilities. It also supports the use of micro electronics in industry. The Federal Republic of Germany has allocated vast amounts of money to a select group of companies, notably Siemens, to achieve a catch-up effect in micro electronics hardware production. In one important field, telecommunications, the government purchasing agency, in an attempt to protect domestic industry, insisted on domestic specifications that virtually excluded foreign competitors. At the European level much of this development has been supported by the mainly privately funded EC Eureka joint research programme, practical results of which have already appeared on the market (Exhibit 7.5).

There are drawbacks, however, to the positive approach to the formation of policy. First, when technological ventures are publicly supported by government agencies which specify what should be done and how it should be done, the venture frequently tends to leap beyond what the market is prepared to absorb. Projects tend to be technologically ambitious but economically non-viable. Concorde is a case in point. Second, public policy support of this nature may introduce slack or commercial sloppiness into the internal operating procedures of firms. R & D departments may grow into institutions remote from the discipline of the market. If there is insufficient government funding, technically "interesting" projects may be terminated on commercial grounds. Finally, government intervention and guidance of industrial technological development in an advanced industrial economy may be a policy trail towards obsolescence. The argument is that central government agencies cannot be as informed about the commercial and technological frontiers as can the advanced companies actively operating in the field.

## Subsidy approach to industrial development

Because of difficulties with the positive approach, some governments have attempted to apply the subsidy approach which is directed towards either reorganizing commercially failing businesses or simply prolonging their lives in order to attend to certain social issues, such as employment. Steel and ship building are the recipients of enormous government support throughout Europe and, indirectly, through defence spending in the United States. As a rule, these basic industries and other supported industries as a rule do not engage in sophisticated forms of production by western standards. Product design and marketing are also small parts of total value added. Many state operated companies in Europe exist as a result of governments having had to bail out ailing industrial firms.

Such policies also seem to be extremely costly in terms of misallocated resources and lost growth (Eliasson, 1984). To enforce this point, Eliasson cites Sweden's extremely costly industrial subsidy programme — up from one of the

---

**Exhibit 7.5   Cross-country company research to compete internationally**

*Eureka has found it — the "fragile idea" for bolstering high-tech R & D in Europe*

When the Japanese proposed adoption of their system for the next generation of television technology 18 months ago, the Europeans refused to agree. Acceptance would have opened the way for Japanese domination of yet another global market for the foreseeable future. High-definition television (HDTV) is the sharp-image system that could replace many of the 600 million television sets now in use worldwide as well as revolutionize production and transmission equipment. Eureka, the initiative launched by French President Francois Mitterrand in 1985 is designed to encourage cross-border industrial linkups and thereby help the Europeans compete with the United States and Japan in the high-tech sectors that increasingly underpin the global economy.

After the successful European move to postpone any decision on HDTV until 1990, four major European manufacturers — Philips, Bosch, Thomson and Thorn EMI — joined up in October 1986 in a $200 million, three-year Eureka project to develop a competing European HDTV standard.

By last August, less than one year after starting, the crash research programme had produced a result: A European HDTV that is by all accounts the equal of its Japanese rival. Eureka has become an important feature on the European industrial landscape. It has become a giant clearinghouse for 165 cross-border research and development projects worth more than $4 billion, and dozens more are under consideration.

Over 600 companies and research organizations from 19 European countries are participating, including most of Europe's top industrial groups. The projects run the gamut from telecommunications, lasers and robotics to biotechnology, new materials, futuristic transport systems and space-based manufacturing.

To qualify as a Eureka project, companies or research organizations from at least two European countries must devise a collaborative programme to develop marketable technologies and submit a detailed business plan to their national Eureka representatives.

**Source:** *International Management*, December, 1987, pp. 38–9.

lowest rates in the industrial world in the early 1970s to a record breaking 16 per cent of value added in manufacturing in 1982 — as being a major explanation of the complete collapse of manufacturing output growth in Sweden since 1973.

With few exceptions, the stated ambitions of these rescue operations have been the positive reconstruction of companies from within, with the objective that business units, once in trouble, can be reorganized where they happen to be located, using the same human resources and causing a minimum of intermediate unemployment. However, it is felt that the odds are heavily weighted against success in such ventures (Eliasson, 1984). Entry and exit is the normal vehicle for rejuvenation of industries. Rejuvenation from within usually involves a major change in the corporation and type of management.

## Planning approach to industrial development

The third approach, the planning approach, has as its central instrument a policy agency which sees itself as possessing a superior overview of the business environment and, hence, believes it should interact with all firms to achieve an orderly and efficient group action. The theory behind this approach is that improved information and overview make an analytically explicit operational solution possible. This is the way indicative planning as practised in France has often been presented.

In Japan, MITI has been regarded as combining the planning approach with the positive approach, i.e. stimulating innovative activities. The planning approach, however, has three requirements: that the necessary information can be obtained, that the information can be interpreted in terms of a policy, and that the economy adjusts to the stimulus of policy members.

## Market approach to industrial development

Finally, the market approach is concerned with non-interference in the internal management process of firms. The market-oriented approach is in contrast to the first three kinds of policy which may be termed selective. The market approach involves policy action only through the business environment of the firms, by making it more competitive, encouraging free trade, anti-trust and providing similar incentives; by building the right infrastructure through education, transport and communication; or by providing the right cultural climate through stimulating entrepreneurial attitudes, honouring property rights and accepting risks (Abernathy, Clark and Kantrow, 1983; Bradley, 1983). The market approach is based on the assumption that the more interventionist forms of industrial policy do not percolate down to the level of the firm. In this regard it is similar to the traditional equilibrium approach but here the emphasis is on a market led approach to development, whereas the former depended more on production adjustments.

## Dynamic comparative advantage

Some of the successful Far Eastern countries such as Taiwan, South Korea, Singapore and Hong Kong — the Tiger Economies — have applied a revised theory of comparative advantage as well as resources. Instead of focussing on static factor endowments and rising short-run costs these economies have focussed on factor mobility and the possibility of declining long-run costs based on the learning curve and scale economies. This is a dynamic theory of comparative advantage which focusses on the opportunities for change through time.

To place the issue of dynamic comparative advantage in context let us assume that we are dealing with a small open country such as New Zealand or Denmark. Call this country Country X for convenience. In terms of Chapter 2, the short-run advantage for Country X might arise from specializing in producing commodity foods: the long-run advantage might arise from making a success of industrial electronics, the high-technology, high-growth rapidly changing industry. If Country X follows the theory of comparative advantage it sacrifices long-term growth for short-term gains and implicitly accepts a lower standard of living than its neighbours. Concluding otherwise implies that for some reason Country X is unable to compete in industrial electronics, a proposition much like the once popular notion that it was not possible to sell coal to Newcastle, the centre of the UK coal industry! As was seen in an earlier chapter it is possible to sell coals to Newcastle. A world of static comparative advantage and free trade favours the rich and the strong. It also favours those with natural resources and high levels of productivity in major growth industries.

In a world of technological change, differential rates of growth in volume and productivity across industries, and declining costs, the rational choice for a small country such as Country X is to select growth industries and to use public policy to supplement market forces in order to organize the resources necessary for entry and successful participation in the international marketplace. Country X needs to think in terms of acquiring or creating strength in promising sectors rather than simply attempting to exploit the short-run comparative advantage as efficiently as possible.

Following this line of reasoning we are led to the conclusion that Country X should specialize in industrial electronics, not commodity foods, regardless of whether their costs are lower or higher than those prevailing in its rich neighbouring countries. Following the dictates of the dynamic theory of comparative advantage, Country X, or any other growing economy, has a considerable measure of freedom to create the comparative advantages it wishes, provided it has the will and ingenuity to create or borrow the necessary mix of policies and institutions to achieve the cost and quality positions required for success.

The criterion used by the Japanese in selecting which industries to promote is often described as higher value added. But as Scott (1985) suggests, their selection criteria appear to have been more subtle, less mechanical and above all appear to require sophisticated judgements about the future. In this respect MITI has relied on two basic criteria: an income elasticity criterion; and a comparative technical progress criterion. The income elasticity criterion suggests that industries with comparatively high demand elasticities with respect to world real income should be developed as export industries. The comparative technical progress criterion attempts to ensure that technical progress in the future of the selected industry is guaranteed, even though this may mean relatively high investment costs (Shinohara, 1982, pp. 24–5).

## Growth and productivity strategies

It is possible to identify five different public policy initiatives which governments use to promote growth and productivity in their countries (Figure 7.1). Macro economic policies can contribute to long-term economic growth in a variety of ways. One approach is to maintain an undervalued exchange rate, which makes exports cheaper on world markets and boosts profit margins, investment, and productivity. Undervalued exchange rates were part of the success of Japan and Germany in the 1950–1970s. Using tax policy to promote savings and investment is a well-known alternative way of increasing supply. Tax free savings accounts are an example of promoting individual savings, and accelerated depreciation is a way of promoting both savings and investment by companies.

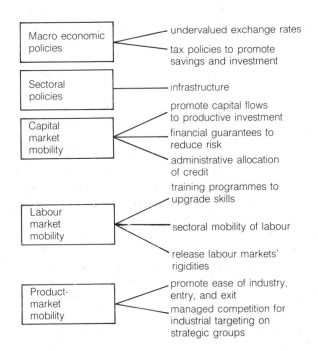

**Figure 7.1**  Public policy initiatives to promote growth and productivity

Familiar sectoral approaches to promoting productivity and growth include the development of infrastructure: airports, seaports and roads, the educational system, and active promotion of R & D. Public policy can also promote mobility in capital markets, labour markets, and product markets. A high capital gains tax retards the mobility of capital by exacting a high penalty from those who would move their capital from one successful investment in search of another. Sometimes countries promote capital mobility by taxing real gains, not nominal gains which may be artificially high due to inflation. Financial guarantees, implicit or explicit, are a means of reducing risk, reducing cost, and increasing the mobility of capital. In some countries there are administrative as well as market criteria for the allocation of credit. There may, therefore, be aspects of administrative credit rationing in the system which is part of a national development plan, the effect of which is to promote capital mobility on administrative terms.

Public policy is frequently and extensively used in European countries to promote labour mobility, both in terms of up-grading of skills and to higher performing sectors and hence better paid employment. Government-approved employment agencies and training programmes are familiar elements of such policies. It may be argued, however, that within Europe in particular, the very high unemployment payments have provided income security which in turn has had the effect of reducing labour mobility.

The above policy matters have their principal effect outside the realm of marketing. Mobility in product markets can be assisted by promoting the ease of entry and exit. Deregulation of airlines in the United States and Europe has brought new, low-price entries into the industry which in turn have provided a wider, better and cheaper service to customers. The same is beginning to happen in other industries, e.g. insurance, banking, telecommunications and road transport. The effect is to add new competitors and to change the nature of competition (Exhibit 7.6).

In a similar vein, governments and common markets such as the EC sometimes encourage managed competition instead of promoting maximum competition. In a regime of managed competition, a firm might be encouraged to give up marginal products or product lines to concentrate on what it does best, while other domestic firms in the same industry would be encouraged to make similar concessions. The result is a narrower line for all firms, permitting a higher level of resource commitment behind each remaining product market. Managed competition requires the government, or, in the case of a common market such as the EC, the EC Commission, to play a role in mediating decisions about who would give up what, and compliance would be monitored by the public body or an industry association. Restructuring policies in countries such as Japan are good examples of the industrial targeting of strategic sectors using managed competition as a guiding principle. Successful management of competitive forces brings to mind the relative success of countries such as France in telecommunications and rail transport, Brazil in aircraft and motor vehicles, and Scotland and Ireland in electronics.

For governments to intervene successfully usually does not depend on how

---

**Exhibit 7.6  Deregulation benefits consumers as nature of competition changes**

---

*Telecoms liberalisation: EEC sets mobile phone standards*

Mobile phone manufacturers can organise their production and sales pitch for the next generation of mobile phones with the knowledge that a mass market is about to open up in the EC, as a result of agreement on a single standard for mobile phones.

The EC ministers' decision follows hard on the heels of the agreement between the German, French, Italian and British governments to introduce a common mobile phone system by 1991 and is part of the technical backup to that agreement. In fact, the standards will be applied by the six EFTA countries as well as the 12 Community countries, since they are based on CEPT recommendations.

According to Commissioner Karl-Heinz Narjes, the standards will enable mobile phone manufacturers to develop a "continental European strategy, which will mean that the most expensive product available in 1995 will be less expensive than the cheapest on the market in 1987." There are currently 150,000 mobile phones in the EC, but by 1995 this figure could rise to 2.5 million.

The next generation of mobile phones will permit voice and data transmission as well as access to data banks and special services. The standard directive is designed to make certain frequency bands available exclusively to the new European system. From 1991, two 9 MHz frequency bands will be allocated to the new services with an extension to 25 MHz ten years later.

**Source:** *Business Europe*, 29 June, 1987, p. 7.

---

refined the plans are or how knowledgeable the executives in the government sponsored industrial development agencies are, but on the broad strategy that is implemented. Public policy can only provide the framework within which business operates. It cannot pick winners.

## Industrial policy, growth, and welfare

According to Scott (1985) countries may be divided into two groups; those that place emphasis on measures to promote productivity and growth; and others which are concerned with the allocation of wealth by redistributing income through transfer payments. In the latter countries there has been a shift of responsibility away from the individual, the family and the firm and toward the government. There are welfare states where the people expect more from government. As a result the public sector continually assumes new roles, thus becoming responsible for a greater share of aggregate demand. Wages, too, absorb a greater proportion of GNP and investment falls. Finally, to sustain domestic demand and expanding social programmes in slack economic conditions, these governments resort to deficit financing. This was the situation which faced many European countries during the 1970s and most of the 1980s. There is evidence now that public policy is beginning to redress this situation. Governments are not as keen to intervene to support social causes and do so only for viable economic or political reasons.

Over time an inordinate concern for income distribution appears to lead a country not only away from a concern for productivity but toward an increased dependency on the state to provide a living for a growing segment of the population.

The typical roles and institutional responsibilities adopted by income redistributive and development-oriented countries have been specified by Scott (1985). A public policy based on income or wealth distribution emphasizes national economic security in which the government takes responsibility for full employment among all members of society. Government policies focus on providing full employment and are complemented by unemployment compensation programmes, the liability for which is passed on to the tax payer. In contrast, a public policy based on industrial development emphasizes job security in which the government takes responsibility for the stability and growth of the firm. Policies in such countries are complemented by programmes which support retirement and health care needs. Not all society members would benefit as a right under such policies. Performance in the economic arena would be the principal criterion for obtaining any benefits which arise. The costs of any support programmes are usually funded by the beneficiaries through their contributions.

The impact of public policy on income distribution and savings in society is also important. A public policy based on income or wealth distribution emphasizes high minimum wages, transfer payments, taxes and borrowings. Savings policies are dominated by subsidized borrowing and situations where saving is actually penalized. The responsibility for income and savings policies rests with the government, and all members of society benefit. In contrast, a public policy based on development emphasizes a market clearing minimum wage, salary and profit sharing, and corporate earnings. Savings policies are dominated by subsidized savings and penalties or restrictions on borrowings.

Over time these two extreme approaches to public policy produce very different results. Under a public policy based on income and wealth distribution, savings will tend to be low, wages rigid, labour mobility low, greater dependence on the state and political priorities focussed on due process (Table 7.1). In contrast, under a public policy based on industrial development savings will be high, wages flexible, labour mobility high, responsibility for income levels retained by the family or firm, and political priorities focussed on performance.

## Classifying country development strategies

The basic priorities of major national competitors may be compared by placing public policy as a vehicle for redistribution on one axis of a single diagram and

**Table 7.1** Impact of public policy over time

| | Alternative strategies | |
| | Distribution | Development |
| Intervention factors | Redistribution by the state results in: | Distribution through the firm results in: |
|---|---|---|
| Savings | Low savings | High savings |
| Wages | Rigid wages | Flexible wages |
| Labour mobility | Low mobility | High mobility |
| Responsibility for incomes | Increasing dependence on state | Family and firm retain high level of economic responsibility |
| Political priorities | Focus on due process | Focus on substantive performance |

Source: Adapted from Scott, Bruce R. (1985) 'National strategies: Key to international competition,' in Scott, Bruce R. and Lodge, George C. (eds.), *US Competitiveness in the World Economy*, Harvard Business School Press, Boston.

public policy as an agency for development on the other. In this framework it would be possible for a country to have balanced priorities either in the upper left quadrant or in the lower right, or unbalanced strategies in the other two quadrants (Figure 7.2). Acknowledging the need for further research to enhance the descriptive power of the framework, Scott (1985, pp. 125–7) places the major western OECD countries in the lower left quadrant indicating a low priority to the role of public policy in promoting industrial development and a high priority to a more direct role in income distribution. The reverse appears to be the case for Japan and the Tiger Economies.

As indicated above, there is evidence that this approach to industrial policy is rapidly changing in many western countries, especially in the EC. It still remains strong, however, in the United States and other developed countries such as Australia and Canada. Many developing countries are to be found in the low–low quadrant, a situation in which public policy regarding saving and investment is designed to create job security through an export competitive society.

In theory, the case for industrial targeting or a sector selective industrial policy is simple and compelling. Familiarity with one of the strategy matrices, for example the Boston Consulting Group growth/share matrix, helps to recognize the above framework as promoting winners and cutting back on investments in low-growth areas. Or, using the scheme that organizes industries from high technology to low, it would be a strategy of systematically upgrading the portfolio as in the "Japanese model." (Scott 1985, p. 132). Conceptually, it can be likened to the application of product portfolio theory at the level of the country.

Industrial targeting has been successful on a sustained basis only when it has been a part of a productivity-oriented development strategy. Each country needs to turn its attention to comparing its strategy with those of its most successful competitors and to think comprehensively about reforms that are

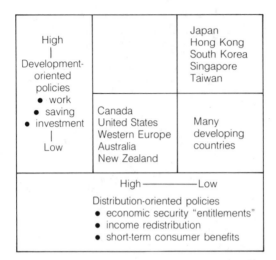

**Figure 7.2** Classification of country development strategies (Source: Adapted from Scott, Bruce R. (1985) 'National strategies: Key to international competition' in Scott, Bruce, R. and Lodge, George C. (eds.), *US Competitiveness in the World Economy*, Harvard Business School Press, Boston)

necessary to get its house in order. Excessive concern with the targeting issue is likely to lead policy makers to focus their attention on retaliating against other countries for unfair trade practices, or to create a social welfare programme introduced as a courageous new way for public policy to help build competitiveness. It should not require financial or technical wizardry to recognize that in an increasingly interdependent world, the economy of each country cannot meet its various commitments unless there are significant changes in political priorities, i.e. a new emphasis on growth and productivity rather than on redistributing existing wealth.

## *Future of industrial and commercial policies*

International competition in the preceding 30 years has been envisioned as competition among firms, with governments establishing the rules and enforcement processes. International competition was based on the concept of free markets, the invisible hand, and a limited role for the state as the framework for domestic competition. This peculiarly Anglo Saxon and American view of the world derived from Adam Smith has been challenged by a group of competitors that has found a positive role for the visible hand of government in creating comparative advantages and in promoting mobility of capital and labour in exploiting these advantages. Indeed, the whole thrust of the concept of dynamic comparative advantage is:

that the competitive challenge comes from well-managed companies based in countries characterized by developmentally oriented national strategies. How one views this challenge frequently tends to be influenced by whether one is positioned with the challengers or the challenged. (Scott, 1985, p. 138).

The central issue for Scott and other policy writers is that international competition is now influenced by national strategies as well as by the strategies of firms. A developmental strategy based on mobilizing the resources of a country to create comparative advantage in growth industries and industries in which technological change is rapid has been shown to yield higher growth over the medium term than simply accepting advantages as "given." The implications of this analysis for international competition according to Scott (1985, p. 140) are threefold. First, the welfare states might realign their priorities and become much more competitive. Second, the development-oriented countries might become increasingly security oriented, and somewhat less competitive, thereby progressing into the upper left quadrant (Figure 7.2). Third, the welfare states might take the lead in restricting access to their markets, thereby reducing the competitive threat by restricting the roles of the most competitive players. The evidence to date seems to suggest that countries emphasizing welfare considerations are developing competitive strategies and the development-oriented countries such as Japan are beginning to show signs of becoming more distribution conscious. Evidence on the third factor points toward continuation of pressure to keep markets open, opening them further, and avoiding a regression to closed economies.

The only stable, mutually beneficial, and supportive outcome would seem to require that the major competitors find broadly similar strategies in the upper left quadrant, the one area that is now almost empty. This would require that the leading developmental countries take on more distributional responsibilities as direct government functions, and that the distributional countries make many changes to achieve more balanced strategies. These are issues underlying the frequent meetings of GATT which are rarely resolved to the satisfaction of any of the participating countries.

## Summary

The international competitive environment has changed enormously over the past decades. Consequently, both government and firms have had to adapt their policies so as to ensure survival and growth through internationalization. National competitiveness is essential to enable the firm to stay ahead both technologically and commercially in important market segments.

Three competitive situations are evident in the world today: (1) newly industrialized countries which focus on low-cost labour, government promotion and standard mature technologies; (2) advanced industrial countries which rely on complex manufacturing processes to increase quality and reduce costs, and (3) high-technology industries which concentrate on R & D in order to achieve advances in product performance. Essential to competitiveness in the firm in all three situations is a strong emphasis on manufacturing and marketing systems and on the ability to grasp the interaction between them.

It is not the marketing environment *per se* which is so important but, rather, the firm's ability to cope with it as it directly influences its strategic options. It is imperative to adopt an international orientation and multidimensional strategies.

The Single European Act will act as a major force in this respect. Firms will have to examine more closely the option of cross-border mergers and joint ventures and adapt to new technical and marketing standards.

Industrial and commercial policies are used to influence the allocation of resources in industrial sectors so as to achieve structural changes in capital, labour and product markets and to help domestic industries respond to international challenges by addressing economic and political issues. Industrial policies may be applied at three levels: macro economic policy; sectoral policy; and company level policy. In each instance the government may adapt a positive approach, a subsidy approach, a planning approach, or a market approach to the formulation and implementation of public policy.

There are three likely outcomes for the future. Welfare states may realign their priorities and become more competitive. The development-oriented countries may become more security oriented and less competitive. The welfare states might take the lead in restricting access to their markets. Evidence to date supports these outcomes, e.g. the Japanese are showing signs of being more distribution conscious, while the Europeans are beginning to become more developmental in thinking and practice.

## Discussion questions

1. What is meant by international competitiveness? Distinguish between country-level competitiveness and company-level competitiveness.

2. The text describes industrial and commercial policies in international markets as falling into one of four categories. Describe and evaluate each approach and discuss the relevance of each to your country.

3. Industrial and commercial policies can provide the framework in which the firm in international markets operates. Public policies cannot be used to pick winners. Discuss.

4. Judging from the success of the Japanese economy and the recent take-off of the Tiger Economies there is much to recommend in a policy of industrial targeting. What would be your advice to policy makers in your own country?

# References

Abernathy, William J., Clarke, Kim B. and Kantrow, Alan M. (1983) *Industrial Renaissance*, Basic Books, NY.

Bradley, M. Frank (1983) 'A public policy for international marketing,' *Journal of Irish Business and Administrative Research*, **5** (2), 57–75.

Bradley, M. Frank, Hession, Enda, and Murray, John A. (1985) 'Public policy intervention and the growth and development of the firm in a changing technology–product–market environment,' a paper presented at the *Second Open International IMP Research Seminar on International Marketing*. University of Uppsala, Sweden, 4–6 September 1985.

Bradley, M. Frank (1987) 'Nature and significance of international marketing: A review,' *Journal of Business Research*, **15**, 205–19.

Cohen, Stephen, Teece, David J., Tyson, Laura and Zysman, John (1984) *Global Competition: The New Reality*, Working Paper of the President's Commission on Industrial Competitiveness, Vol 3.

Defraigne, Pierre (1984) 'Towards concerted industrial policies in the EC,' in Jacquemin, Alexis (ed.), *European Industry: Public policy and corporate strategy*, Clarendon Press, Oxford, pp. 368–77.

Eliasson, Gunnar (1984) 'The micro foundation of industrial policy,' in Jacquemin, Alexis (ed.), *European Industry: Public policy and corporate strategy*, Clarendon Press, Oxford, pp. 295–326.

Hayes, Robert H. and Abernathy, William J.G. (1980) 'Managing our way to economic decline,' *Harvard Business Review*, **58**, 67–77.

Levitt, Theodore (1983) 'The globalization of markets,' *Harvard Business Review*, May–June, pp. 92–101.

Scott, Bruce R. (1985) 'National strategies: Key to international competition,' in Scott, Bruce R. and George C. Lodge (eds.), *US Competitiveness in the World Economy*, Harvard Business School Press, Boston, pp. 71–143.

Shinohara, Miyohei (1982) *Industrial Growth, Trade and Dynamic Patterns in the Japanese Economy*, University of Toyko Press, Toyko.

Simon, Herman N. (1984) 'Challenges and new research avenues in marketing science,' *International Journal of Research in Marketing* **1** (4), 249–61.

Wind, Yoram and Robertson, Thomas S. (1983) 'Marketing strategy: New directions for theory and research,' *Journal of Marketing*, **47** (2), 12–25.

# 8 *Creating competitive advantage: implementing public policy*

In this chapter we attempt to describe how governments and transnational public sector organizations apply industrial and commercial policies in an endeavour to promote the well-being of enterprises. There are four sections. The first examines strategies adopted by countries and trading communities for development. The second section considers industrial and commercial policies in selected countries and how public policy is designed to create competitive advantage. The third section deals with industrial and commercial policies in the EC, while the fourth section contains a brief discussion of the internationalization of business in the EC in recent years.

## Strategies for development: countries and communities

As may be seen in later sections of this chapter, a national strategy consists of goals, a view regarding the attainment of these goals in a competitive environment, and a set of policies and institutions to implement the approaches adopted. It is argued that the similarity between firms and countries is even stronger (Scott, 1985, pp. 71–2). Just as some firms are growth oriented, with a low dividend payout to permit a maximum level of reinvestment in the business, so too are some countries. Similarly, some countries are growth oriented with strong incentives to promote savings and investment and thereby reduce short-term consumption in favour of greater future returns. Other firms may have more modest growth aspirations and a higher payout of earnings. In the same vein, there are countries which give a high priority to short-term consumer benefits and choose to promote consumption rather than savings. Indeed, just as there are companies which change their behaviour without much regard for a strategic position, so too are there countries which switch from one set of industrial and commercial policies to a contrasting set, often on the whim of the government in office.

It is more important, however, to consider the broad thrust of government policies over the longer term rather than worrying about internal consistency in policies in the short term. On this criterion, as was seen in preceding chapters, there are two very different types of country strategy: the invisible hand variety; and the strongly interventionist variety. An alternative view of country strategies may be found in the degree to which countries are resource oriented rather than marketing opportunity oriented. Countries which are resource oriented tend to see markets and competition guided by the invisible hand as the most effective way to develop those resources. Governments in such countries are expected to play the role of benign regulators and observers, entering the fray only when state security or the national currency is threatened. In contrast, countries that are market led acknowledge a role for the visible hand of government in supplementing market forces. Such countries provide incentives to promote savings and investment in certain kinds of industries (Exhibit 8.1). They discourage consumption through heavy sales taxes, promote the mobility of resources and alter the risk—reward relationships. Many such countries actively promote the establishment of new industries and the attraction of foreign-owned industry through well-funded industrial development boards.

## Trends in comparative advantage

In the past twenty to thirty years a number of countries have improved their comparative advantage through a process of upgrading their industrial product portfolio. It is possible to classify trade between countries and trading blocs using a variety of schemes. One attractive classification ranks products traded by research and development intensity (Kelly, 1977). In this scheme industries form a continuum from high technology to low technology. Using this scheme it is possible to analyse a country's specialization and adjustment over time.

Export specialization is revealed by those sectors having higher shares of world export markets than the country average. If all sectors cluster around the average, there would be little specialization, indicating that the country or area in question was not significantly stronger in any sector. In the remainder of this section we examine the industry base for global competitiveness. Three major trading powers are analysed: the EC, the United States, and Japan. Export statistics are used to identify the sectors of industry in which a number of countries are likely to prove strong and those where they are expected to continue to be weak. The analysis is carried out through an examination of each area's revealed advantages compared with those of its major competitors.

While there is no precise way of measuring comparative advantage, export data allow us to observe revealed comparative advantage. An ideal pattern of adjustment over time would show Country X adding relative market share in high-technology sectors and losing share in low-technology products (Figure 8.1). Over time the curve might be expected to shift clockwise with gains in high-technology products and declines in low-technology sectors.

---

**Exhibit 8.1    Visible head of government supplements market forces**

---

*New Australian R & D incentives*

Companies doing research and development work in Australia will benefit from legislation that will be introduced in the February/March session of Parliament: 150% of eligible R & D spending may be deducted from income for tax purposes.

R & D is defined as "the systematic investigation or experimentation involving innovation or technical risk, the outcome of which is new knowledge, with or without a specific practical application, or new or improved materials, products, devices, processes or services."

Eligible R & D essentially covers basic and applied research and experimental development from July 1, 1985 on — including salaries, wages, and other labor costs directly associated with R & D work; other current spending exclusively for R & D purposes; and payments to contractors for the use of special facilities — but excluding spending on production and marketing activities or activities otherwise directly assisted by the government.

As now, the cost of buildings used exclusively for R & D may be fully written off over three years, but expenditure on plant and equipment wholly attributable to R & D will qualify for the 150% tax deduction over three years. Expenditures of pilot plants not operated as commercial units, nor intended to be so operated, will also benefit from the concessions, but only up to the first A$10 million (A$1.41:US$1).

If deductions under the scheme result in a firm's incurring a loss for tax purposes, that loss may either be carried forward or transferred to another company in the group under existing group taxation arrangements.

Because the government feels a meaningful R & D programme requires a minimum amount of expenditure, a company must spend at least A$50,000 to qualify for the full concessions.

**Source:** *Business Asia,* 24 February, 1986, p. 61.

---

The vertical line represents the average Country X share of the world market in a given year. The arrows show relative share, above or below the average, for the year $t$ and the year $t + n$. When the arrows point to the right Country X has gained share; when they point left Country X has lost share. In the illustration, aircraft are assumed to be in sectors of export specialization. In year $t$ Country X reported exports of aircraft equal to about twice Country X's average share of world exports. By the year $t + n$ this performance had reached nearly 2.5 times Country X's average share of world exports. Finally, the hypothetical situation shows Country X to be gaining in the high-technology sectors, losing out in medium- and low-technology sectors and beginning to gain again in the lowest-technology products such as animal and vegetable oils and fats and paper products.

Using this framework the revealed comparative advantage for the EC, Japan

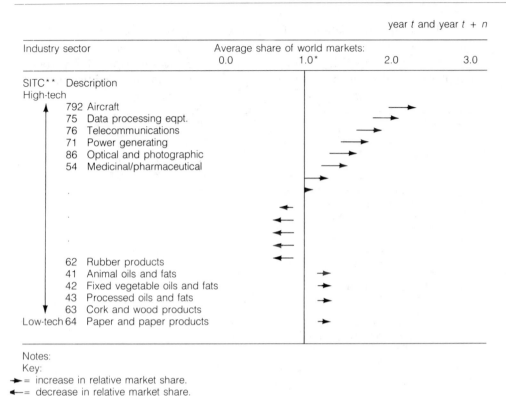

**Figure 8.1**  Hypothetical revealed comparative advantage for country X in the early 1990s

and the United States was calculated using OECD statistics. The base year chosen was 1977 and it was compared with the performance in 1986. A ten-year period should be long enough to detect shifts in comparative advantage and it should present us with a good indication of the relative positions as we move into the 1990s. The results of this analysis for the EC are shown below (Figure 8.2).

The results shown in Figure 8.2 resemble the hypothetical pattern in Figure 8.1 in some respects only. The EC is gaining in many sectors, with improvements in fixed vegetable oils and fats, animal oils and fats, cereals, tobacco and iron and steel being especially pronounced. The EC is losing share in quite a number of sectors, especially solid fuel, gas, manufactured fertilizers, electrical machinery, telecommunications, and data processing equipment. The overall pattern is one of small improvements, mostly at the lower end of the technology spectrum, with a number of losses at the top end. Considerable change in the underlying competitive structure of industry in the EC is occurring at present, viz. the series of S-shaped patterns around the average market share line.

The competitive situation facing the United States is radically different (Figure 8.3). The results also resemble the hypothetical pattern in Figure 8.1 in some respects. The US is gaining in a number of sectors, especially medicines and pharmaceutical products, manufactured fertilizers, and fish and fish products.

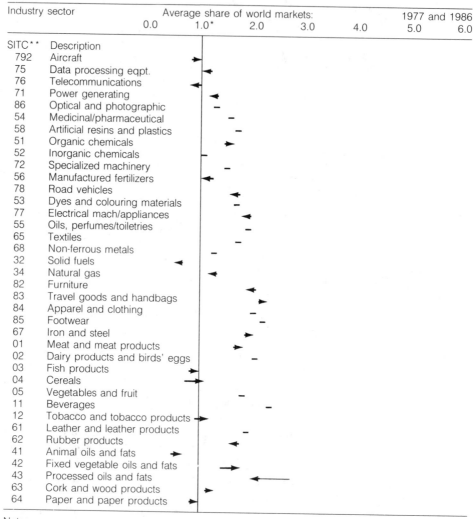

Notes:
Key:
⟶ = increase in relative market share between 1977 and 1986.
⟵ = decrease in relative market share between 1977 and 1986.
— = no change between 1977 and 1986.

\* Average share of world export markets in 1986.    -
\*\* Ranked by technological intensity using criteria similar to those used in Scott and Lodge (1985, p. 78).

**Figure 8.2**  Revealed comparative advantage: EC exports

It is losing in many sectors and substantially so in cereals, fixed vegetable oils and fats, processed animal and vegetable oils and fats, organic chemicals, paper and paper products, textiles, telecommunications, and road vehicles. It is noteworthy that a number of these declines correspond directly with

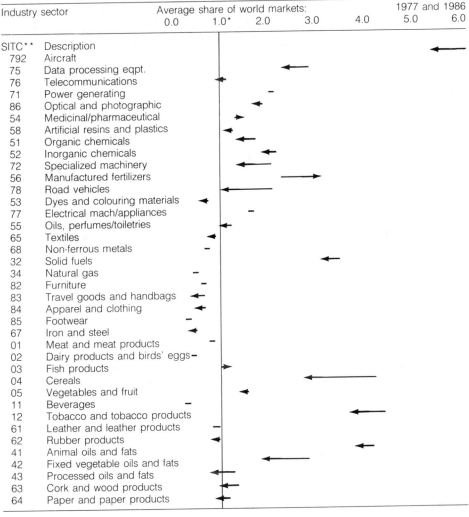

| Industry sector | | Average share of world markets: | | | | | 1977 and 1986 | |
|---|---|---|---|---|---|---|---|---|
| | | 0.0 | 1.0* | 2.0 | 3.0 | 4.0 | 5.0 | 6.0 |
| SITC** | Description | | | | | | | |
| 792 | Aircraft | | | | | | | |
| 75 | Data processing eqpt. | | | | | | | |
| 76 | Telecommunications | | | | | | | |
| 71 | Power generating | | | | | | | |
| 86 | Optical and photographic | | | | | | | |
| 54 | Medicinal/pharmaceutical | | | | | | | |
| 58 | Artificial resins and plastics | | | | | | | |
| 51 | Organic chemicals | | | | | | | |
| 52 | Inorganic chemicals | | | | | | | |
| 72 | Specialized machinery | | | | | | | |
| 56 | Manufactured fertilizers | | | | | | | |
| 78 | Road vehicles | | | | | | | |
| 53 | Dyes and colouring materials | | | | | | | |
| 77 | Electrical mach/appliances | | | | | | | |
| 55 | Oils, perfumes/toiletries | | | | | | | |
| 65 | Textiles | | | | | | | |
| 68 | Non-ferrous metals | | | | | | | |
| 32 | Solid fuels | | | | | | | |
| 34 | Natural gas | | | | | | | |
| 82 | Furniture | | | | | | | |
| 83 | Travel goods and handbags | | | | | | | |
| 84 | Apparel and clothing | | | | | | | |
| 85 | Footwear | | | | | | | |
| 67 | Iron and steel | | | | | | | |
| 01 | Meat and meat products | | | | | | | |
| 02 | Dairy products and birds' eggs | | | | | | | |
| 03 | Fish products | | | | | | | |
| 04 | Cereals | | | | | | | |
| 05 | Vegetables and fruit | | | | | | | |
| 11 | Beverages | | | | | | | |
| 12 | Tobacco and tobacco products | | | | | | | |
| 61 | Leather and leather products | | | | | | | |
| 62 | Rubber products | | | | | | | |
| 41 | Animal oils and fats | | | | | | | |
| 42 | Fixed vegetable oils and fats | | | | | | | |
| 43 | Processed oils and fats | | | | | | | |
| 63 | Cork and wood products | | | | | | | |
| 64 | Paper and paper products | | | | | | | |

Notes:
Key:
⟶ = increase in relative market share between 1977 and 1986.
⟵ = decrease in relative market share between 1977 and 1986.
── = no change between 1977 and 1986.

*  Average share of world export markets in 1986.
** Ranked by technological intensity using criteria similar to those used in Scott and Lodge (1985, p. 78).

**Figure 8.3**  Revealed comparative advantage: US exports

improvements in the EC position, e.g. cereals, fixed vegetable oils and fats, and processed animal and vegetable oils and fats. Perhaps a contributory factor in this development is EC external protection through tariffs or subsidies applied in these sectors. The overall S-shaped pattern is there but in general the US is losing share across the technology spectrum with heavy losses at the top and the bottom.

The competitive situation facing Japan is different from the other two regions (Figure 8.4). The results fit the general hypothetical pattern in Figure 8.1 in many important respects. Japan has made gains in equipment, data processing equipment, telecommunications and road vehicles and electrical machinery. There have been some very substantial declines as well, especially in fish products, manufactured fertilizers, cork and wood products, and textiles.

Overall, Japan has gained considerably in the high-technology sectors represented by power generating equipment, data processing equipment, telecommunications and road vehicles and electrical machinery. It has lost ground in manufactured fertilizers, a low-technology sector, but it has gained substantially in data processing and telecommunications, sectors noted for high R & D and marketing expenditures. The United States has lost ground in a wide range of low-technology sectors, especially cereals, oils and fats, and organic chemicals. It has also lost ground in road vehicles and telecommunications equipment. The EC has gained in low-technology sectors such as cereals, tobacco, animal oils and fats, and iron and steel. The EC has lost ground in some low-technology sectors such as solid fuel and gas and processed animal fats and oils and manufactured fertilizers. It has lost ground in the high-technology sectors of telecommunications and electrical machinery.

This revealed comparative advantage data indicate that all three regions face key industrial development and corporate strategy decisions as their commercial enterprises face the 1990s. The 1977–86 data represent the economic structure of enterprise in each of the three regions. This economic structure changes only slowly so that the present circumstances are likely to obtain for a number of years. These data would indicate the very strong and growing position of Japan, the relatively strong position of the EC and the weaker position of the United States.

## Industrial and commercial policies in selected countries

In this section the approaches to industrial and commercial policies in a number of very different countries are discussed to demonstrate the variety which exists and to show that no single approach fits all circumstances. Here we discuss the policy framework for marketing asset development within the country and within the firm. Changes in the international environment are very clearly manifested when the firm attempts to transfer technology or capitalize on new international marketing opportunities (Figure 8.5). Government policy operating as industrial or commercial policy attempts to mediate the influences arising in the international environment.

Governments attempt to modify the environment facing firms through direct policies; monetary, fiscal, foreign exchange policies, which operate through the price mechanism. Policy assistance is also provided indirectly through the State Support System: advice; executive support; grants provided through a structured

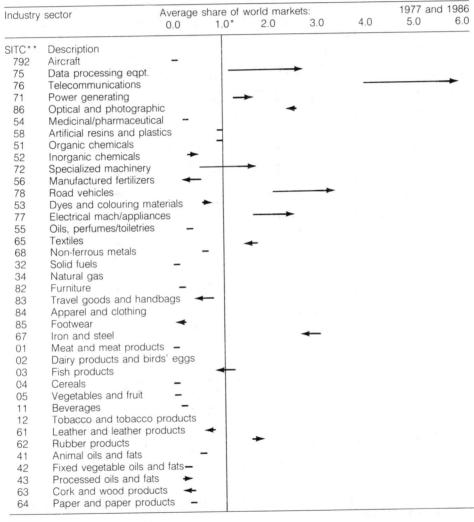

| Industry sector | Average share of world markets: | | | | | 1977 and 1986 | |
|---|---|---|---|---|---|---|---|
| | 0.0 | 1.0* | 2.0 | 3.0 | 4.0 | 5.0 | 6.0 |

| SITC** | Description |
|---|---|
| 792 | Aircraft |
| 75 | Data processing eqpt. |
| 76 | Telecommunications |
| 71 | Power generating |
| 86 | Optical and photographic |
| 54 | Medicinal/pharmaceutical |
| 58 | Artificial resins and plastics |
| 51 | Organic chemicals |
| 52 | Inorganic chemicals |
| 72 | Specialized machinery |
| 56 | Manufactured fertilizers |
| 78 | Road vehicles |
| 53 | Dyes and colouring materials |
| 77 | Electrical mach/appliances |
| 55 | Oils, perfumes/toiletries |
| 65 | Textiles |
| 68 | Non-ferrous metals |
| 32 | Solid fuels |
| 34 | Natural gas |
| 82 | Furniture |
| 83 | Travel goods and handbags |
| 84 | Apparel and clothing |
| 85 | Footwear |
| 67 | Iron and steel |
| 01 | Meat and meat products |
| 02 | Dairy products and birds' eggs |
| 03 | Fish products |
| 04 | Cereals |
| 05 | Vegetables and fruit |
| 11 | Beverages |
| 12 | Tobacco and tobacco products |
| 61 | Leather and leather products |
| 62 | Rubber products |
| 41 | Animal oils and fats |
| 42 | Fixed vegetable oils and fats |
| 43 | Processed oils and fats |
| 63 | Cork and wood products |
| 64 | Paper and paper products |

Notes:
Key:
⟶ = increase in relative market share between 1977 and 1986.
⟵ = decrease in relative market share between 1977 and 1986.
— = no change between 1977 and 1986.

*   Average share of world export markets in 1986.
** Ranked by technological intensity using criteria similar to those used in Scott and Lodge (1985, p. 78).

**Figure 8.4**  Revealed comparative advantage: Japan's exports

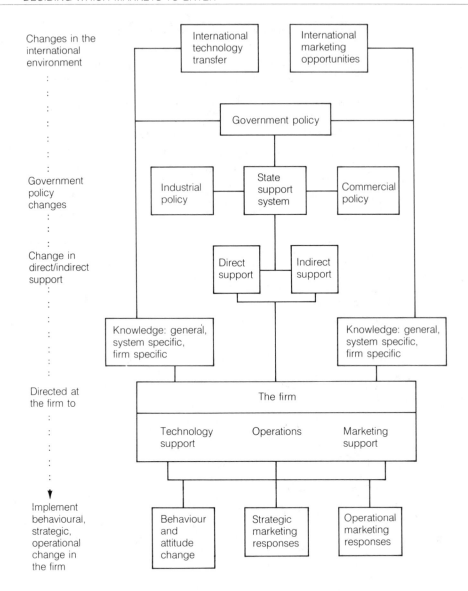

**Figure 8.5** International competitiveness: impact of public policy on marketing asset development in the firm

network of agencies such as development boards; and export promotion bureaux. Knowledge or the resources to acquire knowledge is the basis of all such support. Knowledge may of course be general in nature; it may be specific to particular systems such as a franchise systems or marketing systems or operating systems, or it may be firm specific as would arise in the transfer of knowledge in a licensing or joint venture arrangement. In all circumstances the support is directed to the firm by way of technical or marketing assistance (Figure 8.5). Industrial and commercial policies usually have as objectives the implementation of change within firms. This change may arise at the level of changing behaviour and attitudes, at the strategic level or at the operational level.

Intervention by the State Support System should promote effective firms while maintaining efficiency within industrial sectors. Increasingly, it is being recognized that governments, acting through the State Support System, cannot pick winners. In circumstances of limited resources, intervention by the public sector bodies tends to be focussed on important industrial and commercial policy interests. The Australian government, with a very specific objective in mind, was prepared to modify trade policy to encourage industrial development in a key sector (Exhibit 8.2).

## Creating competitive advantage in Japan

Japanese industrial policy has been discussed widely in the literature. This section draws heavily on a well-known work dealing with international industrial policies

---

**Exhibit 8.2   Trade policy modified to encourage industrial development**

---

*Australia to waive offsets for MNC investment, R&D in information industries*

Canberra has just put the finishing touches on a multipronged strategy to plug Australia's information industries into international markets. For MNCs, the key point is a proposal to waive offset requirements on government contracts in exchange for corporate commitments to boost local R&D and exports significantly. The catch: if companies refuse to sign up, they risk being shut out of the lucrative public sector market for information technology, hardware, and services.

Since 1971, Canberra has required overseas suppliers to the government and its agencies to use the equivalent of 30% of their sales to buy Australian goods, invest in domestic industries, or transfer technology to Australia. In the 16 years the program has been in effect, local firms have won A$1.02 billion (A$1.41:US$1) in nondefense offset orders against a total obligation of A$1.38 billion. Information industries got the lion's share of the booty, discharging A$445 million in obligations since 1971.

Now, to encourage MNC participation in developing information industries down under, the government plans to waive offset requirements for firms that sign so-called corporate citizenship agreements. Chances are the waiver will be extended to state offset obligations as well.

Firms interested in becoming "corporate citizens" should expect to spend 5% of their annual turnover on R&D and export enough products to equal 50% of their imports in value-added terms within seven years. The timetable for meeting these levels will be negotiated on a case-by-case basis.

**Source:** *Business Asia*, 5 October, 1987, p. 315.

---

(Behrman, 1984). Japanese business—government cooperation began in the mid-nineteenth century with the Meji revolution to industrialize the country. The government sold state enterprises to the private sector which felt a responsibility for growth and security of the country. Following the post World War II breakup of the Iaibatsu, the companies formerly associated, regrouped into Keiretsu.

The Keiretsu are not holding companies, as were the Iaibatsu, but are separate companies, commonly held, with their own boards of directors but using the same tradename; the heads of each of the operating companies used to meet periodically to decide strategy. This concentration, and the connection of each Keiretsu with one of the major banks made co-ordination with the government relatively easy compared to the situation in other countries. In the late 1950s, Japan had established a list of priority sectors including textiles, shipbuilding, steel, cars, and chemicals for which it restricted imports, prohibited foreign investment, except as minority partners, and encouraged imports of foreign technology.

The present approach to industrial policy in Japan is based on the government's national industrial plan, which identifies the best prospects for technological advance and international competitiveness. Under the policy each company is in principle free to respond in its own way, but industry officials are members of an advisory board, the Industrial Structure Council. The council meets frequently and is composed of individuals personally known to each other in many other contexts so that they are able and willing to make compromises where necessary. The mutual concern is to achieve consensus, if feasible, without endangering company survival. Agreement is not always reached but the process is a continuing one. Japanese mechanisms for industrial policy co-ordination involve parties from many different levels in Japanese society (Table 8.1).

Japanese industrial policy is very different for growth and declining sectors in the economy. For growing sectors the objective of industrial policy is to anticipate and accelerate signals from the market. Consequently, the Japanese government supports R & D activities, capital expenditures and export efforts, but maintains a highly unrestrained competition for market share among the companies within the domestic market. Financial assistance is provided by both MITI and the Ministry for Finance and through the Japan Development Bank, Industrial Bank of Japan, and indirectly through commercial banks. The government also provides tax incentives, low-cost financing, plus accelerated depreciation to encourage R & D activities of any qualifying firms.

The emphasis of Japanese industrial policy tends to change over time. In the industrial machinery sector, the policy emphasis has shifted from the improvement of individual company efficiency in the late 1950s to a consolidation of the sector in the early 1960s, and, in the late 1960s and 1970s, to the encouragement of greater specialization and economies of scale. In the mid-1970s, policy shifted towards R & D assistance and sales of entire plants abroad. In 1988 about 60 per cent of export—import bank loans were directed to exports of entire plants. As found in other areas, a number of Japanese institutions work together to promote these exports. In regard to marketing, the Japanese government has aided firms in the purchase of computers and it has aided firms to expand the

**Table 8.1**  Japanese mechanisms of industrial policy co-ordination

| Organization | Policy instruments and implementation |
| --- | --- |
| Ministry of International Trade and Industry (MITI) | Tax incentives, anti-trust, lending, price and capacity price and capacity controls, export–import measures, environmental regulations, raw material price setting and procurement, technology subsidies, dislocation subsidies, regional policies. Anything affecting sectors or firms, judged on a differential basis according to priorities. |
| Ministry of Finance | Tax incentives, low-cost loans, subsidies, tariffs, foreign exchange rate changes |
| Research Development Corporation | Subsidy for R & D, joint private/government research, licensing of technology |
| Ministry of Post and Telecommunications | Guidance to telecommunications sector |
| Ministry of Health and Welfare | Guidance to pharmaceutical sector |
| Keidanren (Federation of Economic Organizations) | Co-ordination of industry views on industry policies |
| Shoko Kaigesho (Chamber of Commerce and Industry) | Co-ordination of the views of industry, including medium- and small-sized companies, commerce, and banking |
| Keizai Doyukai (Committee on Economic Development) | Position papers on economic and industrial policies by companies |
| Nikkeiren (Federation of Employers Associations) | Co-ordination of industrial relations among industries and companies |
| Zaikai (Friday Club) | Small group of chief executive officers, close to prime minister and parties |
| Industry Associations | Co-ordination with MITI on specific sectoral policies and formation of industry cartels as desired |
| City Banks | Linked with Keiretsu (conglomerate enterprises) as financial sources and directors; linked with Bank of Japan and other government banks (Industrial Bank, Development Bank) |

Source: Behrman, Jack N. (1984) *Industrial Policies: International Restructuring and Transnationals*, Lexington Books, Lexington, Mass., p. 17.

national market. It offers financial assistance and has established a joint venture with private enterprise to lease computers. The government also reserves 90 per cent of its purchases of computers for Japanese producers. In semi-conductors, much of the private market is closed to foreigners, and in telecommunications it has been extremely difficult to open up purchasing to foreign bids.

Nippon Telephone and Telegraph Corp. (NTT) has not only given a preference to Japanese suppliers, but has directly supported the R & D programmes of the major telecommunications equipment suppliers, and has helped to finance their exports. As a result of such trilateral cooperative efforts among the government, private enterprises, and financing institutions, the

Japanese companies have a high degree of flexibility in pricing and in competitive efforts both in the domestic and international markets.

Traditional businesses such as aluminium, fertilizers, ferro-alloys, plywood, sugar refining, shipbuilding and other sectors where demand has been declining have been recognized as such. If a sector is declared structurally depressed, it may receive support for reconstruction. To be so classified an industry must have substantial overcapacity, be in serious financial difficulty, and two-thirds of the firms must sign a petition for such a designation. MITI then develops a stabilization plan, forecasting supply and demand; it calculates excess capacity, and it identifies marginal plants and those to be cut back or eliminated. During the process, MITI consults with the industry, and labour unions are given a voice. A workable plan is then agreed upon and reorganization measures are put into effect.

As witnessed in the aluminium smelting and shipbuilding sectors, however, all firms may not necessarily agree on the specific measures to be taken to bring about rationalization, not wanting to cut capacity permanently and looking for strong temporary financial support. This indicates the relative difficulty of gaining consensus on measures to adjust a declining sector, as distinct from the ease of distributing benefits in a growing sector. This approach to the application of industrial policy is fundamental to the new departures in policy initiatives recently adopted in the EC.

## Creating competitive advantage in France

Prior to the mid-1970s, French industrial policy was aimed at preventing the take-over of French industry by foreign firms and at strengthening it through consolidation, in order to compete more effectively with European firms in anticipation of further European integration. This section is based on material in Behrman (1984, pp. 21−6). The French government selected certain sectors for encouragement through R & D assistance; support of mergers and consolidation; creation of investment banking, facilities to provide risk capital; and protection of industry from international competition. It deliberately exposed some sectors to international and domestic competition to force efficiency and competitiveness. In addition, it sought to promote high-technology industries through government investment in national champions, sometimes a state-owned company, and through the selective admission of foreign firms that could accelerate technological innovation in cooperation with French companies.

One major departure from pre-1976 policies was that success was to be judged on achieving international competitiveness, preferably without, but if necessary with, technological assistance from abroad, even so far as accepting joint ventures with foreign firms. The policy approaches that followed shifted somewhat from direct guidance by the government to specific sectors and firms towards greater reliance on market signals, enterprise strategy and other approaches to hasten market processes.

French financial assistance for industrial objectives is channelled through government controlled institutions viz the Caisse and Postal Savings, which are the savings and loans institutions that mobilize individual and small company savings of the economy. These funds are accumulated and disbursed through the Bank of France and the state-owned banks. The control by the government of access to credit has restricted the ability of commercial banks to lend and has permitted the government to specify the ultimate recipients of loan funds.

Despite the liberal measures adopted in the latter half of the 1970s, France has not relinquished its historical policy orientation of state intervention. Only France and Japan publicly announced the selection of target industries for government support in the 1980s and the lists are virtually identical. French policy is also critically dependent on the existence of state enterprises in key sectors: particularly petroleum; computers; and aerospace. These enterprises are used to subsidize customer companies, through preferential orders. These activities give the government a strong influence, if not complete control over the relevant sectors.

In 1982, France expanded the scope of industrial policy by the adoption of the *Filière* concept, referring to vertical lines of production which are intimately tied. Four large industrial sectors have been identified, with government policy extending beyond these sectors to the support elements and secondary and tertiary industries related to them. These four sectors: chemicals; electronics; health; and materials, have within them the five large state-owned complexes. Thus state enterprises are relied upon to lead in these four priority areas. The government's objective in each case is to consolidate enterprises, particularly the state-owned ones, so that they will be stronger, better integrated in terms of raw materials, and have more effective control over their markets.

## Creating competitive advantage in small open economies

As an example of industrial policy in a small open economy, we discuss industrial and commercial policy as implemented in Ireland, a small open economy on the periphery of Europe, not well endowed in natural resources, and formerly a colony of a larger industrial country, the United Kingdom. As an independent nation, Ireland has embarked upon a road to industrial development dependent upon strong public policy interventions. Like France, Ireland is a full member of the European Community.

By the early nineteenth century, Ireland had a substantial industrial sector by the standards of most countries at that time, apart from England. This is indicated by the fact that, according to the 1821 census, more than one-third of the Irish counties had a larger number of workers in manufacturing, trade or handicraft, than in agriculture. But, with the exception of the north-east, the numbers employed in industry declined during the nineteenth century. By the 1920s, the industrial labour force of the Irish Free State, which became an independent Republic in 1948, was little more than 100,000 or 7 per cent of those employed.

Modern Irish industrial policy has its origins in the 1950s. The goal was the creation of new employment in industry with increased incomes. The methods of accomplishing this goal have been consistent since the 1950s: encouraging industrial investment by Irish and foreign companies through general industrial promotional activities and financial incentives; and opening the Irish economy to free trade. The first strategy was initiated in 1950 with the creation of the Industrial Development Authority (IDA), and the second was initiated with the publication of the government's White Paper "Economic Development" and the introduction of the first "Programme for Economic Expansion" in 1958: an indicative approach to planning along French lines. The government of Ireland had long accepted the need for an industrial strategy. In the proposal accompanying the creation of the IDA in 1950, the then Minister for Industry and Commerce stated.

> The Government is certain that in the national interest the development of industry should not be let follow a course set by the unco-ordinated activities of individuals, companies and groups working to cater for the market requirements as determined by themselves. . . there is a need at Government level for assisting and supplementing the efforts of private enterprise. . . .

Measures to provide financial incentives for industrial investments have been continually increased during the past thirty years. The first grants were provided in 1952. Since then there has been a steady increase in grant aid. Concurrent with the expansion of these direct grants was the steady increase in tax incentives given by the government to encourage industrial investment. These included the granting of a 100 per cent tax remission on the profits earned from export sales. This policy incentive expired in 1990. Also included were the free depreciation on plant and machinery, and the introduction in 1980 of a standard 10 per cent corporation tax.

The progressive increase in grants and tax incentives represented one of the two strategies used to attain Ireland's goal of increasing industrial employment and real incomes. The other main strategy has been the opening of the economy to free trade, which was seen as necessary for developing higher productivity in Irish industry. The major steps accompanying this effort included the relaxation of controls on foreign ownership of Irish industry, the 1965 Anglo–Irish Free Trade Area Agreement, and the introduction of free trade following Ireland's membership of the EC.

Because industrial policies developed in the 1960s and implemented in the 1970s did not work as well as expected, governments and industrial bodies completed a series of reports, many of which suggested a redirection for industrial policy away from the "grants for all" dependency approach to an approach which was much more self-reliant and which left much of the executive control with the managers in the firm. As a result, the industrial policy objectives and incentives outlined above were implemented in a controlled fashion. Future directions for

**Table 8.2** Redirection of industrial policy in small open economy

- Industrial incentives and state advisory services will be applied selectively; involving the concentration of resources on internationally traded manufacturing and service industries, particularly Irish owned firms
- A shift in state resources from fixed asset investment to technology acquisition and export market development
- Priority will be given to the attraction of foreign projects which will perform their key business functions in Ireland
- A risk capital market for investment in internationally traded manufacturing and service sectors shall be developed through tax incentives
- The government will take all measures within its powers to improve the business environment with the aim of increasing the competitiveness and profitability of industry
- Effective education, training and worker mobility measures will be promoted
- Wealth generated by industrial development to be retained within the country

Source: *White Paper on Industrial Policy*, Government Publication Office, Dublin, 1984.

industrial policy in Ireland were set out in the 1984 White Paper on Industrial Policy (Table 8.2).

Clearly, Irish governments are beginning to recognize that concern for employment is not the immediate function of enterprise, but of greater wealth. The creation of wealth in international markets by competitive enterprises is expected to deliver growth and development for the country at large. Also, there is a recognition that it is the software factors which are important: management and attitudes rather than hardware factors such as grants, factories and other subsidies (Bradley, 1985).

## Industrial and commercial policies in the EC

The European Commission has every reason to view with concern the proliferation of national industrial policies in the Community. It is argued that in addition to failing in their objectives, such national industrial policies are also likely to result in a revision to nationally divided markets within Europe (Defraigne, 1984). The drawbacks of individual national industrial policies in the EC as seen by Defraigne include unwillingness to harmonize laws and regulations, failure to promote European industrial companies, failure to achieve scale economies and continued support for industrial policies geared to support the public sectors in member countries.

Inadequate harmonization of laws and regulations refers to the problems which arise in regard to company law, taxation, various consumer protection and environmental conservation arrangements, and lack of progress in opening up public sector purchases, creating European standards in place of national ones, and unifying export credits, leaving a whole armoury of non-tariff trade barriers in the hands of member states (Exhibit 8.3).

---

**Exhibit 8.3   Countries use non-tariff barriers to protect industry**

---

*Germany: Liberalization dribble*

MNCs should not expect the latest move toward PTT liberalization in Germany to produce a bonanza for foreign firms. Pressure from the EEC helped persuade Bonn to end the Bundespost's monopoly over the supply of modems by year-end. In essence, MNCs will be free to compete for business that traditionally went to Siemens AG and ITT's Standard Elektrik Lorenz AG. Companies will not find a big market: There are roughly 95,000 modems in use in Germany, which is one half the number in France and one third of the UK total.

In addition, there are several strings attached to the deal. First, the Bundespost will continue to outline specifications and test and approve any modem connected to its network. Second, technology will limit sales prospects to a few years at most. Germany plans to begin introducing a new integrated services digital network in January 1988. The system, to be phased in over five years, will eliminate the need for modems.

It would thus be more practicable for MNCs to see the changes as a precursor of more substantial market-opening moves. The EC will continue to exert pressure on Germany to liberalize telecommunications, and, despite the Bundespost's reputation for blocking market-opening initiatives, more contracts are being led to foreign suppliers. Sony, for example, provided the equipment for nine out of the 12 video conference centers built by the Bundespost. The Bundespost is also the main domestic customer for the Corning Glass/Siemens JV in fiber optics.

**Source:** *Business International,* 11 August, 1986, p. 256.

---

Failure to create European transnational groups such as Shell, Unilever and Philips, which existed prior to the EC, stems from the failure of firms to cut the close links they have forged with their home governments lest they forgo the protectionist umbrella and/or the privileges which may be accorded by national governments, e.g. public sector purchasing, R & D support, major export contracts and tax relief. Consequently, as long as Europe fails to grant trans-European groups preference at least equivalent to that which individual members accord their major industries, there are unlikely to be any major European groups. In this context EC and national merger policies come under scrutiny. Mergers between two European firms, irrespective of whether they are in the same EC country, to compete on world markets would appear to make sense but national and EC policy differences make it difficult to establish such strong enterprises through mergers.

Linked to this issue is that of economies of scale which may require the company to go beyond the national market. Since national policies are unable to use the combination of creating demand pull and regulating competition in the wider European markets, the firm may not be able to attain the necessary sales and hence economies in the wider markets. Many national markets are too small to achieve economies. Thus the government has to rely on "technology push" and "pick the winners" operations, which are much more risky and often fail because they are incomplete and because it is inherently difficult for public officials to pick winners.

Industrial policies based on extending public sector industry further increases the risk of returning to national markets. National industrial policies may put too much weight on maintaining *all* stages of a particular process within the country, rather than in the EC as a whole. In practice it is impossible, within the limits of EC markets, for an average-sized national industry to excel in all stages of production. Attempting to do so may well prove very costly in terms of public resources.

Given the above circumstances, the EC Commission has attempted to identify the preconditions for successful national measures which may differ widely in both their means and ends. Defraigne (1984) summarizes and discusses the three following such preconditions:

1. major restructuring and stimulation schemes which would proceed via the EC Community, since they necessarily involve commercial policy, national aids and cooperation relating to at least the whole Community;
2. recognition that cooperation between government-owned and private enterprises is necessary at EC Community level, e.g. ESPRIT involves cooperation between Thomson, ICL, Siemens, Olivetti, Plessey and others;
3. there should be no threat of domination by a partner in a position to call on the backing of the public authorities and funds from the national budget.

It was recognized that such country-level measures could be supported at Community level by removing non-tariff barriers, by promoting European products and by defining new ground rules for mixed economies. By the first is meant the unification of the EC by removing non-tariff barriers between member states in the sector in question, and ensuring that the various forms of extra-Community protection introduced by individual member states are "communitized." Promoting EC products means establishing community preference for European industry through European NTBs, co-ordinated public sector procurement, R & D, export credit, and access to the Community's financial instruments.

The EC Commission has already stated that it will not impose external EC barriers greater than those already in place and, further, it is likely to reduce these external barriers. Many of these developments are already being implemented as a result of the signing of the Single European Act and the move toward completing the internal market by 1 January 1993.

The third factor implies the definition of new ground rules for mixed economies in the EC where the sovereignty of members would be subject to certain rules with regard to the following:

- the criteria and conditions for nationalization and de-nationalization;
- transparency in dealings between governments and public corporations e.g. funding, public sector purchasing, aid of various kinds;
- non-discrimination between nationalized corporations and private enterprise; and
- Community arbitration in the event of disagreements between public authorities and enterprises.

## Internationalization of business in the EC

### Policies for international competition

The pressures from each of the forms of competition described previously are moulded by the concerted strategies of such governments as Japan, Korea, Brazil and the United States, through its Department of Defense, to promote national industrial development and to enhance the competitive position of their firms. As seen above, the Japanese government's systematic policies have helped to move the economy from labour intensive manufacturing such as textiles, to income elastic products such as televisions, motor vehicles, computers and aircraft. Similar competitive pressures are present in countries such as Brazil which has managed to penetrate the US steel and light aircraft industries. Clearly, therefore, comparative advantage is dynamic and can be created, and it is the belief in such creation that has encouraged many countries to play an active role in the development of local firms.

Increasingly battered by competition from the United States and Japan, European companies have been preoccupied with achieving the critical mass that will give them R & D strength, economies of scale and marketing strength to meet the challenge. The EC still does not, however, have the catalytic influence on industrial development as is exerted by the public authorities in the United States, Japan or the NICs. In these situations governments have the power to sponsor business development. The EC has only a fraction of the leverage over industrial R & D enjoyed by the government departments in the United States, especially the US Department of Defense. Neither does the EC possess the scope for industrial targeting coupled with a systematic cooperation between all the economic actors needed to achieve such targeting, which is the hallmark of Japan's MITI. Cooperation with business seems to be the foundation of Japan's industrial strategy. Cooperation and sponsorship appear to be the key policy issues of the late 1980s and 1990s.

Underscoring the EC Commission's new role is the need to integrate policies on trade, industry, competition and R & D, at present pursued separately, into a welded single competitive strategy designed to improve the performance of European business. Progress on such matters often seems to be very slow (Exhibit 8.4).

The need is for an effective European response in the form of high-

---

**Exhibit 8.4 Progress on EC integrated industrial policy is slow**

---

*Deregulating Europe's phones: the talk so far is just static*

Talk that Europe will deregulate its hidebound PTTs is stronger now than at any time since the US government broke up American Telephone & Telegraph Co's monopoly in 1983. Since August alone, France has begun to break its PTT's stranglehold on data communications, a German commission has recommended Bundespost reform, and the European Commission has pledged to force Europe-wide competition by 1992. AT&T and the Baby Bells are already itching for a piece of the action when US-style deregulation hits.

But Europe's goverments fear deregulation would spark a backlash from the PTTs' powerful unions. Moreover, argues Michel Noir, France's Foreign Trade Minister, it would be "suicidal" for Europe to open up to foreigners now because its industry is too weak.

Trans-European leased lines, used for corporate communications, are priced up to five times higher than in the US. In Italy and Spain, phone service is downright awful, but there's no competition in sight. No one expects much change in Germany, and even in Britain, where competition is encouraged, British Telecommunications Plc's main rival, Mercury Communications Ltd, has only a fraction of the market.

Yet Europe's communications services need a drastic overhaul. By the year 2000, the European Community estimates that telecommunications will have jumped from the current 2% to 7% of Europe's gross domestic product. But unless governments agree on common standards and permit more competitive pricing, this growth in better service and equipment won't happen.

**Source:** *Business Week*, 2 November, 1987, p. 37.

---

technology alliances and cooperation. This is beginning to happen independently of the Commission as evidenced by the many and varied cross-border alliances and joint ventures at the corporate level in Europe (Bradley, 1988). The lessons from these industrial developments and corporate alliances have not gone astray in Europe. The French have been successful in promoting internationally competitive firms in telecommunications, aerospace, nuclear energy, off-shore engineering and transportation equipment. It is noteworthy that European successes have not been tied to the inimitable cultural and social peculiarities of Japan, especially its management traditions. It will be interesting to see how the EC Commission responds to these country initiatives.

There are two clear signals regarding the approach of the EC to industrial policy. First, since the publication of the EC Commission's White Paper, the Commission appears to be moving close to business and in so doing it is distancing itself from the formal EC decision-making process (Commission of the European Communities, 1985). The White Paper is designed as a charter for business involvement in the attainment of EC market goals in a variety of sectors including foodstuffs, pharmaceuticals, tobacco, motor vehicle manufacturing, banking and insurance. The cause of European integration is carried forward, drawing on and deliberately fostering a new constituency: European international business. The second factor which is expected to assist in bringing about industrial and commercial integration is the Single European Act which permits majority voting in the Council of Ministers in many circumstances. From the various utterances and from the White Paper itself it would seem that the Commission has adopted a strong interventionist role in the area of industrial policy.

The turbulent change in the environment implied by the completion of the internal market in the EC will bring with it very dramatic consequences for the unprepared. Because of the magnitudes involved, the 1990s must be viewed as a period of marketing discontinuity whereby it will be very difficult, if not impossible, to predict environmental change. Hence, it is likely that governments will continue to intervene in the system to support the growth and development of firms in their jurisdiction.

## Response of European firms to the new competition

In the competitive milieu of international markets the practice of management should acknowledge no frontiers other than those imposed by laws, cultural mores, and the personal limitations of managers. The older generation of managers in Europe has been characterized as operating in a protected system and closed network whereby many deals were done with one another and with trade unions which benefited neither customer nor supplier. As a result the orientation of such managers is local and nationalistic in the extreme. A new type of manager has appeared in recent years, however, who is energetic, assertive, financially sophisticated and committed to progress through merit rather than connections or protection. The challenge for these managers is whether they develop their firms into internationally competitive enterprises.

Recognizing that a key strength of the United States and Japan is a large uniform domestic market, European businesses are beginning to discard the antiquated idea that prosperity derives from protected markets. For many European firms this means large organizational changes, while for others it means cross-border alliances to create global companies. A typical organizational response arises when firms observe the growth of EC markets and the new ease in advertising across borders. Under such circumstances it makes sense to switch from country based subsidiaries to a system organized along product lines. The recent spate of organizational change in many of the world's largest marketing companies is evidence of this phenomenon (*International Herald Tribune*, 20 November, 1987, p. 15). The new organizational structure would require multilingual product line managers sensitive to cultural differences.

These kinds of change are already beginning to occur in Europe and their impact is manifest, especially on the management of foreign-owned international companies. It will be difficult for policy makers and executives in business and export development agencies to counteract the inevitable impact that these pressures will have on the product portfolio of such firms. European firms have, therefore, become more international in the past decade and continue to do so.

Internationalization of the European firm has arisen through a unique combination of management strategies and tactics (*International Management*, November, 1986). Successful European firms have achieved international status through a concentration on a six-stage process (Table 8.3).

Other studies have reported that the most striking difference between high-performance European firms and average companies is not just their professed commitment strategic thinking but, rather, the emphasis that these firms give to implementation. For high-performance firms five factors were found to be highly correlated with success, the most important being quality (Table 8.4).

Contrary to the conventional wisdom that perceives finance as the primary factor behind corporate success, marketing factors tend to be more critical among high-performance firms. Perhaps the frequent complaint by some firms about the lack of finance should be read as a symptom of a problem arising under one of the above headings rather than as a shortage of finance.

In a survey of 825 executives ranging from owners, chairmen and presidents

**Table 8.3**  Successful European firms achieve international status in six steps

| | |
|---|---|
| 1. | Increased efforts to foster a global corporate image |
| 2. | International alliances to expedite the acquisition of new technologies, products and new foreign markets |
| 3. | Sourcing more products and components from foreign firms |
| 4. | Increased foreign market budgets |
| 5. | Customizing products to specific foreign markets |
| 6. | Changing the international executive's work habits to shorten his/her learning curve for going international through: |
| | — improving fluency in at least one foreign language |
| | — more frequent foreign travel |
| | — reading more foreign publications |
| | — attending more foreign conferences |
| | — greater use of worldwide telecommunications |

Source: Adapted from *International Management* (1986) 'Expansion abroad: The new direction for European firms,' November , pp. 22–31.

**Table 8.4**  Success factors for high-performance firms*

| | | | |
|---|---|---|---|
| 1. | Quality of product/service | — | a marketing concern |
| 2. | Efficient technology | — | a manufacturing concern |
| 3. | Efficient marketing systems | — | a marketing concern |
| 4. | Ability to recognize market gaps | — | a marketing concern |
| 5. | Effective educational programmes | — | marketing and other functional area concerns |

*Ranked in order of importance.

Source: Adapted from *International Management* (1986) 'Expansion abroad: The new direction for European firms,' November, pp. 22–31.

to directors, general managers and financial controllers in the twelve EC countries in September 1987, it was found that there was extensive support for political as well as economic unity in Europe (*International Management*, January, 1988). A high proportion of managers believed that the EC internal market is a realistic goal.

European firms are unwilling to wait for EC politicians to reach agreement on potentially conflicting national interests and have developed strategies to cope with competition from Japan and the United States. The nature of the response to the new marketing environment among EC firms emphasizes self-reliance, management development programmes, and the formation of competitive alliances.

Regarding the benefits of an open EC market, a new, larger, more open internal EC market would present some firms with the opportunity of larger markets for existing products; firms would be able to sell more and there would be certain marketing and distribution scale effects as well as production effects. The increased orientation toward the EC would possibly, however, damage relationships with customers in non-EC markets and it would be important to assess increased competition both from within and from outside the EC.

Consideration of the implications of 1992 among many firms seems to have arisen more from fear of the competition which the single market is expected to bring to national and sectoral pockets of inefficiency than from any strategic thinking on the part of such firms. The decision to merge the insurance operations of Compagnie du Midi and Axa in France is a case in point (*The Financial Times*, 3 May, 1988). France's protected insurance industry faces liberalization and both companies felt they are too small to compete on their own in a freer market. The choice was clear: merge or let Compagnie du Midi fall to Italy's Assicurazioni Generali. The distorted financial markets of Spain and Italy are other markets where price competition could lead to a severe decline in profitability. It is expected that these markets will secure a great deal of attention from aggressive market consolidators during the next few years.

## Summary

This chapter describes how governments and public sector organizations apply both industrial and commercial policies to promote the well-being of enterprises. Similarities of behaviour between firms in relation to their growth orientation and incentives for saving and investment were discussed briefly. Different government policies were also examined, i.e. invisible hand vs heavy interventionist role of government. In the former approach governments play the role of benign regulators and observers, in the latter the government supplements market forces. Trends in comparative advantage were examined using a classification that ranks products traded by R & D intensity. Three trading regions were analysed, the EC, the United States, and Japan. The analysis concluded that the three regions face key industrial development and corporate strategy decisions as their enterprises face the 1990s.

In the second major section of the chapter the industrial and commercial policies of three very different countries were examined. In Japan the government attempts to identify the best prospects for technological advance and international competitiveness. It supports implementation through policy initiatives specifically tailored to the situation and it supports R & D and anticipates and accelerates market signals.

In France the government selects certain sectors for R & D assistance. It also supports mergers and acquisitions and facilitates the provision of risk capital and protection of industry from international competition. The government deliberately exposes some sectors to international and domestic competition to force efficiency and competitiveness; it also uses a procedure of national champions to promote high-technology firms.

In Ireland, a small open economy, public policy encourages industrial investment through general industrial promotional activities and financial incentives such as grants and tax incentives. Having examined the three different situations it was concluded that both direct and indirect policies should be used to promote effective firms while maintaining efficiency within industrial sectors.

In the early 1980s it was argued that existing national industrial policies among EC countries were a revision to nationally divided markets within Europe. There was a problem of a lack of harmonization of laws and regulations and a failure to promote European companies. Industrial policies based on extending public sector industry further increased the risk of returning to national measures. Since then, however, there have been a number of positive developments including restructuring and stimulation schemes under support from the EC and a recognition of the necessity of cooperation between government-owned and private enterprises at EC Commission level.

Comparative advantage is dynamic and can be created. Belief in such creation has encouraged many countries to play an active role in the development of local firms. The EC does not yet have a major influence on industrial development as is exerted by public authorities in the United States, Japan or the NICS. What is needed is an effective European response in the form of high-technology alliances and cooperation.

## Discussion questions

1. An essential prerequisite for a firm attempting to succeed in international markets is that it should be market oriented and aware of competitors. If such a firm is located in a resource-oriented country, however, public policy is likely to take the form of the invisible hand strategy, with government providing little support to supplement market forces. Discuss.
2. In the chapter OECD statistics were used to compute the revealed comparative advantage of the EC, Japan and the United States. From these data each region was seen to face key industrial development and corporate strategic issues in the 1990s. Comment on these claims and say whether you

accept the framework and analysis. If a similar framework were applied to data for your country what would the outcome be?

3. Examine the three different approaches to industrial policy as described in the chapter and state how relevant each would be to the circumstances in your country. Can you identify your country's industrial development strategy?

4. Now that the EC is beginning to formulate and implement industrial policies which affect the firm in international markets is there any value in individual EC countries pursuing their own individual country policies?

## References

Behrman, Jack N. (1984) *Industrial Policies: International Restructuring and Transnationals*, Lexington Books, Lexington, Mass.

Bradley, M. Frank (1985) 'Key factors influencing international competitiveness,' *Journal of Irish Business and Administrative Research*, **7** (2), 3–14.

Bradley, M. Frank (1988) 'The marketing challenge of 1992,' *Irish Marketing Review*, **3**, 97–112.

Commission of the European Communities (1985) *Completing the Internal Market*, White Paper from the Commission to the European Council, Brussels, July.

Defraigne, Pierre (1984) 'Towards concerted industrial policies in the EC,' in Jacquemin, Alexis (ed.), *European Industry: Public Policy and Corporate Strategy*, Clarendon Press, Oxford, pp. 368–77.

*International Management* (1988) 'Fortress Europe finally takes shape,' January, p. 48.

Kelly, Regina (1977) *The Impact of Technological Innovation on Trade Patterns*, US Department of Commerce, Bureau of International Economic Policy and Research, ER-24, December.

Scott, Bruce R. (1985) 'National strategies: Key to international competition,' in Scott, Bruce R. and Lodge, George C. (eds), *US Competitiveness in the World Economy*, Harvard University Press, Cambridge, Mass., pp. 71–143.

# International markets and customers

This chapter describes the various factors the firm must consider when selecting international markets to enter for the first time. A process approach is adopted in the context of trial and error to assist in making decisions at various stages in that process. Two approaches are discussed: the opportunistic approach; and the systematic approach. It is also shown how some firms start in the opportunistic mode and gradually shift to a more systematic approach. Five major influences or constraints on the market selection process are examined and an integrated view of the entire process is provided.

## International market selection process

For many firms, internationalization is increasingly becoming an important end in itself, as corporate objectives become those of survival and growth. It follows, therefore, that the degree of success in selecting international markets influences not only future growth potential but in many instances it affects the company's ability to survive.

### Importance of international market selection

The issue of international market selection is important for a number of reasons (Papadopoulos, 1983). Errors in the international environment can be far more costly in both monetary and psychological terms than at home. The wrong choice of market is a frequent source of two types of cost: the actual cost of unsuccessfully attempting to enter the wrong market; and the associated opportunity costs, i.e. the missed opportunity of entering markets where the product might have been successful. Choosing the right markets and the right sequence of entry is an integral part of competitive strategy. Many foreign firms now compete in terms of operating a balanced portfolio of markets, grouping markets according to their similarity, having a deliberate policy of concentrating or diversifying marketing efforts, and sequencing market entry to ensure optimum international competitive advantage.

The firm that ignores such strategies may find itself in a weak competitive position. A careful approach to international market selection is essential because of the vast diversity that exists in international markets. Within a given country, it may be assumed that a reasonable degree of inter-segment cohesiveness exists. At the international level, however, there are enormous differences in income, culture, and politics. Discovering meaningful similarities between various markets can help standardize strategies, reduce costs, and allow maximum advantage from common experience. It is not easy to do, however.

Approaching international market selection in an intuitive rather than a methodical manner can cause many problems of co-ordination due to country differences. The decision to internationalize is a major commitment to enter a new field of business and should clearly be taken in a systematic way (Tookey, 1975). This involves the acquisition of information, its analysis and the generation of alternative courses of action, and the best possible estimates of the likely results of each of these alternative approaches.

Frequently it is possible to find firms which have drifted haphazardly into international markets — perhaps a machine has been seen by a foreign buyer at an exhibition or an enquiry has come from overseas for some of the firm's products, giving the firm a basis on which to develop international markets. One of two consequences is likely as a result of this haphazard approach. The firm will pursue each enquiry and may quote, and perhaps deliver, some orders abroad. However, because of the lack of preparation and the lack of international market knowledge and skills in the firm it will soon become clear that operating in this casual way is neither practicable nor profitable. The excessive amount of managerial time taken up in co-ordinating these diverse sales orders may disillusion management and eventually lead to a decision to discontinue selling in international markets.

On the other hand, the number of enquiries and the firm's business may increase but this will be in such a random way that profitability may be substantially reduced. The firm may become involved in a large number of markets all over the world, but in none of these markets will it have planned its marketing efforts, so that sporadic orders will result and the scale of business and the amount of adaptation required will make this business essentially a casual exporting business, much less valuable to the firm that it could have been.

It is important that the firm consciously selects international markets as opposed to reacting to short-term opportunities (Attiyeh and Wenner, 1981). These authors identify hidden cost "traps" in the opportunistic approach: providing excessive production capacity for opportunistic business; agreeing initial design and engineering costs to obtain the first order; the additional costs stemming from low initial production efficiency, and repeat orders which do not materialize; the cost of unsuccessful bidding for opportunistic business and the dissipation of the company's efforts that may result from constantly pursuing opportunistic business abroad. For these reasons it is generally advisable to avoid such an opportunistic approach to the selection of international markets.

## Approaches to international market selection

It may be possible to determine an approach to international market selection which enhances the decision maker's understanding of the decision; stimulates creativity in the search for possible solutions to the problem, and aids evaluation of alternative courses of action. Such an approach to market selection may be viewed in terms of examining the nature of competition in various markets, specifying the mechanics of the endeavour and identifying the influences upon the selection process.

## Competitive characteristics of the market

The kind of market the firm operates in is an important determinant of success. When entering new international markets for the first time it is essential that firms take care in making their choice. Economists have developed a useful way of classifying markets which may serve the firm as a starting point in its investigations. Markets are purely competitive when there is a very large number of competing suppliers of undifferentiated products in markets with no entry barriers where information flows are very rapid and accurate. Examples of purely competitive markets include unorganized farming and commodity trading.

Sometimes firms operate in monopolistic markets. In such markets there are many suppliers of slightly different products facing few entry barriers where information flows are imperfect. Examples of monopolistic markets include machine tool manufacturing and unbranded clothing companies.

Companies which have successfully branded their products and services or which have otherwise differentiated themselves from the competition in the eyes of customers operate in oligopolistic markets, where there are usually suppliers of significantly different products facing some entry barriers and imperfect information flows. Examples of oligopolistic markets include detergents, fuel and oil, tobacco and, increasingly, other packaged consumer products.

Finally, some firms operate in monopoly markets where there is only one supplier of a totally differentiated product in a market with very high entry barriers and perfect information flows. An example of a monopoly market would be a utility, e.g. gas or electricity. Sometimes products classified as "non-traded" have a certain amount of monopoly protection within a market. It is significant, however, that all markets experience competition; the issue is to determine the source and strength of the competition. With the removal of protection and the deregulation of industries and the opening of markets, few firms can rely on monopoly protection.

## Mechanics of international market selection

In the absence of an incentive to internationalize, it is unlikely that the company will respond favourably to foreign market opportunities. Without a strong incentive it is unlikely that the company will make a conscious decision to expand internationally. The market selection decision can, therefore, be traced back to the incentive to internationalize. Six major incentives to internationalize may be identified (Table 9.1).

The incentive to internationalize is not enough in itself, however; it must be coupled with an awareness of specific market opportunities. This awareness may arise in three ways (Figure 9.1). The first situation arises where certain stimuli bring a foreign market opportunity to the attention of the firm and it responds by entering the market; the firm may be said to choose its market opportunistically. The search and market identification is random or casual. The second situation arises when awareness of specific market opportunities results from a systematic comparison of prospective markets and the firm expands by entering the market; this approach to market selection would be termed "systematic." The third situation involves a combination of these: an opportunistic approach which on refinement and testing evolves into a systematic approach.

## Opportunistic selection of international markets

If a firm is expanding internationally on an opportunistic basis, certain stimuli are required to bring market opportunities to its attention. The receipt of an

**Table 9.1**  Incentives to internationalize

- Compensate for lack of growth in saturated domestic market
- Reduce dependence on domestic market, especially if it is in decline
- Use excess capacity and/or spread overheads over greater volume
- Dispose of products no longer attractive on the domestic market
- Exploit unique competence in the firm
- Match domestic competitors entering foreign markets

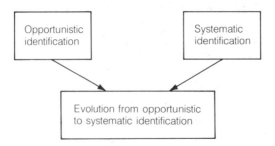

**Figure 9.1**  Identification of international market opportunities

unsolicited order or enquiry for product, price or distribution information from a potential customer may result from advertising in trade journals, by observation of competitors' activities in a particular market, and through information obtained from magazines, newspapers, TV or radio. Occasionally the firm becomes aware of opportunities from the activities of market consultants engaged to identify export market opportunities consistent with the firm's ability to serve these markets. This approach is, however, more in keeping with a systematic approach to export market selection.

Sometimes governments supply information on export opportunities. In such circumstances this function would be mainly performed by a government sponsored export promotions board. These promotion bureaux may also perform overseas market investigations, organize selling missions, trade fair participation, store promotions, sales presentations in overseas offices and at home, and buying missions for groups of overseas buyers.

The firm's response to an international market opportunity which has arisen will be governed by a number of factors. The degree to which the company is affected by foreign country legislation, tariff and non-tariff barriers (NTBs), health regulations, or industrial standards, is likely to influence its reaction. For instance, many companies avoid the Japanese market because tariff and NTBs there are perceived as difficult to overcome. Also, because of stringent West German technical standards, many foreign electrical and engineering manufacturers find it difficult to enter the German market. These latter barriers are beginning to fall under pressure to complete the internal EC market.

The extent to which a company is sensitive to competitive pressure may influence its reaction to foreign market opportunities that come to its attention. Because of a fear of foreign competition many firms may ignore promising opportunities and take a "walled city" approach, concentrating on home markets or culturally close markets with a defensive intent (Ayal and Zif, 1979). An example here would be Norwegian companies exporting predominantly to Sweden and Finland or US companies concentrating on the US market or perhaps also selling to Canada or Mexico depending on location.

The value to the company of adequate distribution in a foreign market may also influence its reaction to market opportunities. A company may be required to adapt its product to different tastes in each export market. In this regard it is quite possible that the company will react more favourably to export market opportunities which need a minimal degree of product adaptation (Jaffe, 1974). Alternatively they may show a tendency to enter markets which are as similar as possible to those with which they are already familiar (Carlson, 1975).

Finally, the reaction to a market opportunity which has arisen may be influenced by the business distance phenomenon examined at length in Chapter 5. Recall that the concept of "psychic distance" comprises all those factors which weaken internationalization incentives. These factors may be seen as an amalgam of the physical distance, language and cultural differences between any two countries (Vahlne and Weidersheim-Paul, 1977; Hallen and Weidersheim-Paul, 1982). The concept of "geocultural distance" is quite similar and is defined as "barriers created by geographical separation, cultural disparities between countries, and problems of communication resulting from differences in social perspectives, attitudes and language" (Goodnow and Hansz, 1972). According to these two concepts, a company should react more favourably to opportunities with a shorter psychic or geocultural distance from the home market.

## Systematic selection of international markets

Instead of merely responding to foreign market opportunities as they arise, the company may adopt a logical procedure for market selection (Figure 9.2). In principle, this is concerned with establishing criteria for selection, researching the potential of markets, classifying them according to the agreed criteria and selecting those which should be addressed first and those which are suitable for later development (Tookey, 1975).

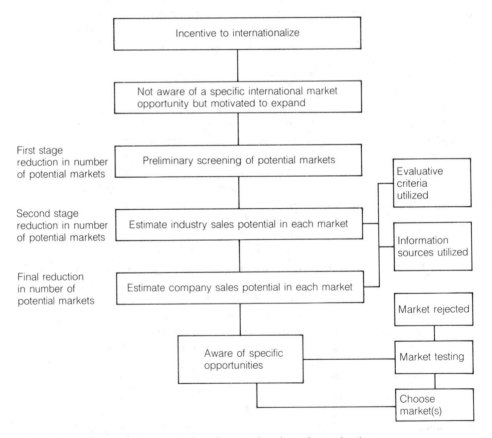

**Figure 9.2**  Systematic approach to international market selection

We first examine what happens at Stage 1 during which preliminary screening of the market is carried out. According to Root (1982) the purpose of preliminary screening is to identify country markets whose size warrant further investigation. Root believes that preliminary screening tries to minimize two errors: the error of ignoring countries that offer good prospects for the firm's product type; and the error of spending too much time investigating countries that are poor prospects. Preliminary screening thus requires a "quick-fix" on the market potential facing the candidate product in many countries. The criteria used in preliminary screening would, therefore, tend to be quite broad in their nature and include quantitive economic and social statistics which should be readily available for most countries and be comparable across countries. Many such multicountry indicators appear in publications of the UN, World Bank, OECD and Eurostat. These economic and social statistics cover areas such as GNP, GNP growth, income per capita, private consumption and population in each foreign market. These data are sometimes provided for regions and areas within countries, which is very useful.

The criteria that should be applied to preliminary screening may be found under three major headings (Figure 9.3). First, physical and geographic features, including the physical distance of each market from the home country and the climate in each market, is taken into account. Quantitative economic and social statistics, including GNP, income per capita, private consumption and similar measures, would be used. Second, population statistics including total population figures, geographical concentration and distribution by age group, the number of people of different sexes and level of literacy may be used to indicate the quality, concentration, current responsiveness of the market and its future growth potential. Third, local economic conditions must be considered. A large population may represent little potential if income per capita is extremely low. Aside from income per capita, Deschampsneufs (1967) suggests other measures of the wealth and purchasing power of potential foreign markets. These measures may be obtained in many ways, such as by finding out the number of cars owned per

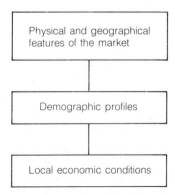

**Figure 9.3** Preliminary screening of international markets (Source: Based on Deschampsneufs, Henry (1987), *Marketing Overseas*, Pergamon Press, 1967)

family, the number of homes with telephones, washing machines and other consumer durables.

Also related to local economic conditions is the financial economy of a country. This may be an overriding factor when considering its possibilities as an export market since if the country cannot pay for its imports then business cannot be done under normal circumstances. Other modes of entry such as foreign direct investment, licensing or countertrade may have to be considered if entry is desirable.

As an aid to preliminary screening, Deschampsneufs (1967) suggests that a company might examine existing home country sales to markets under consideration. This does not mean that the search should ignore an examination of new markets. Having completed the preliminary screening process, the company is now in a position to begin a more detailed evaluation.

## Industry market potential

The next stage of the systematic market selection process is to examine the total potential for the product category in each promising market. This may be defined as the "Industry Market Potential" and involves an examination of the most probable total sales of a product by all sellers in a designated country over a strategic planning period (Root, 1982). The markets with the most promising Industry Market Potential should be examined to see if the firm could gain a share of that potential in each case. This fine distinction is important, as it is clearly a waste of time and money for the firm to investigate how it will gain access to a market if there is no market for its product category in the first instance. There are several criteria by which the Industry Market Potential may be examined: imports of the product category; apparent consumption (local production added to imports less exports); or actual sales figures of the product category. In forecasting sales the firm must also take account of social habits, local tastes and preferences and consumer trends in the market. Because of a possible historical bias, it is important when using sales or apparent consumption data that managers estimate their likely values in the future or make the necessary adjustments for foreseeable changes in the quantities (Root, 1982). Two approaches may be used here: the so-called naïve model which involves a simple projection of historical sales data into the future; or a causal model. The latter involves the construction of product sales forecasts for each prospective market on the basis of certain variables which have a known relationship with product sales.

Social habits play an equally important part in determining the total sales potential of a product in each market. For example, in Italy the potential for DIY car maintenance products tends to be limited because the idea of asking a garage to care for the family car is firmly entrenched in the Italian mind. However, one should realize that such local tastes and preferences may be either short or long term because markets change continually.

Another aspect of examining Industry Market Potential ís the study of consumer trends. For example, in many countries the leisure market is a growing one and anything which is designed to increase the profitable use of leisure time may have worthwhile potential.

Consumer habits are, of course, becoming rapidly more international and individual markets tend to show fewer national differences, except in so far as there is a gulf between those markets where industry is sufficiently far advanced to create a demand for particular raw materials and industrial equipment, and those where it is not.

Having identified countries with greatest total sales potential for the product category, the firm is then in a position to consider its own ability to gain a share of that potential in each case.

## Company sales potential

During the third stage it is necessary to estimate the firm's sales potential. Company Sales Potential is defined as the most probable sales that the firm's product in a designated country can attain over a strategic planning period. Company Sales Potential may also be viewed as the company's most probable share of a country's Industry Market Potential (Root, 1982). When investigating its most probable share of high Industry Market Potential countries, the company will examine a number of factors. Local import legislation, which may take several forms such as prohibition on importing certain products, the imposition of high tariffs, or legislation affecting the composition of a product, is among the more important. For example, Japan refuses to accept that American pharmaceutical exports are safe. In most instances, import regulations add to the cost of foreign market entry; at the other extreme they render international market entry impossible or unprofitable.

Competition in prospective markets is also a major concern. First, the firm must examine its own product in relation to those of its competitors in each market, and decide if the company's product offers any real advantage. It is of little use trying to sell in a foreign market if the firm cannot offer the consumer something which has some edge on the competition. Second, competitors have to be carefully studied from the point of view of their share of the market, their size and resources and pricing policies. This helps to indicate what opportunities there are for the firm's product and what sales may be possible.

Another element of competitor analysis is an appraisal of market structure. Here one should investigate the degree of monopoly in the market and whether competition is rigorous or loose. Market structure bears directly upon ease of entry for a newcomer. Some country markets have strong associations of local producers who lend their collective efforts to keeping foreign firms out. Other country markets are dominated by a few large firms with a host of small followers. Still other country markets have no dominant firms and a loose competitive structure which facilitates entry.

Distribution channel structure in each market also influences the Company's

Sales Potential. Here the company should concentrate on its ability to obtain adequate distribution in each foreign market and the degree to which it can match the distribution of the market leaders. The terms of distribution are also important, since it may be possible to improve them. If this is so, considerable success may be achieved.

Although it may have been considered initially in preliminary screening, the physical distance of each high Industry Market Potential country from the home country may again be evaluated, albeit in greater detail. Here the firm may attempt to calculate transportation and other logistical costs to move the product from the home country to each of the foreign countries in question.

Language and cultural differences between the home country and each of the foreign markets may also be considered at this stage. For example, it may not be feasible for a telecommunications systems manufacturer to enter a small foreign market if all technical literature has to be translated specifically for that market, although in many such instances English is increasingly accepted. Cultural differences would have greater implications for the consumer products manufacturer.

At this stage of the systematic international market selection process, the firm should be able to estimate its sales potential with some accuracy in a number of the most promising foreign markets. It should then be possible to place the most favoured markets in order of priority. The next set of questions is how many of these markets should be addressed, how to enter them and whether to do so simultaneously or in sequence.

## Role of information sources

Systematic market selection is essentially an evaluative process. It is now appropriate to consider the information sources which may be used in applying these criteria. The principal information sources available may be found under six headings (Table 9.2).

The use of management knowledge and experience accumulated within the firm is very much dependent upon the product category and upon the individuals

**Table 9.2**  Information sources used in international market selection

Internal:
- Knowledge and experience within the firm
- Company data

External:
- Published reference materials
- Trade journals, magazines, newspapers
- Government or industry advisers and support services
- Trade associations, business clubs, consultants, market research agencies and market intelligence

involved in the market selection process, but it can be important if the product category is quite specialized. Greater emphasis may be placed upon management knowledge and experience in market evaluations where there is a lack of information from other sources. This emphasis, however, is influenced by the amount of experience and knowledge actually possessed by company managers, the length of time they have worked in the product area, their education and training, and degree of international exposure.

Some firms maintain extensive internal company data bases relevant to key export markets. These data bases may be found in firms which have previously carried out investigations into prospective new markets or where the firm has established an internal international market information system for the product category. The existence of such data tends to vary in accordance with the size and structure of the company. Although a small- to medium-sized company may have some reports on past market investigations, the larger company or subsidiary of a large company is more likely to possess such reports or to maintain an export market information system. Many firms have access to commercially available computer maintained data bases which may be used as required.

Externally published reference publications on foreign markets are also available. The sources of information such as status reports and trade intelligence include central and commercial banks, chambers of commerce, embassies and consulates, trade associations and research institutes. It would be expected that although externally published reference sources would play a role in preliminary screening and in the estimation of Industry Market Potential, they would be of less importance in the firm's estimation of its own potential in each market.

It is quite possible that valuable articles aiding systematic market selection may appear in trade journals, magazines or newspapers, but such articles are likely to play a greater role in the opportunistic identification of export markets. In recent years, however, the business pages of well-known business and financial journals publish in-depth market and industry analyses and profiles and provide information on country markets which may be used successfully by the exporting firm.

Services provided by government and industry sponsored promotion agencies which are related to systematic market selection may be grouped under two headings: advice and facilities; and support services. Under the first heading the agency may provide a firm with information and advice on many aspects of foreign markets such as market size, patterns of demand, costs and prices, local standards, servicing requirements, purchasing and distribution methods, competition from domestic and other imported products and choice of representatives.

Under the second heading the firm would be provided with market reports and surveys, profiles of foreign countries and other library facilities. Such support services would, therefore, have more in common with externally published reference sources than with direct contact with advisers.

The principal role played by marketing consultants and market research agencies in systematic market selection would involve the identification and investigation of opportunities at each stage of the selection process. Involvement with these firms may change from total dependence to their use in conjunction with the firm's own research and marketing personnel (Cateora, 1990).

The influence of non-company business colleagues or members of a trade association upon systematic market selection depends on the industry. In some sectors, there may be a lot of inter-company cooperation and sharing of market information, while in others, competitive pressures may be intense, with little contact between companies. In some countries company executives are very open about sharing non-competitive information, while in others they are much more circumspect. This is a highly culture-bound matter and only in specific circumstances would its true outcome be known.

Once management has satisfied itself that a relatively attractive demand exists for the company's products, that the firm can cope with the competitive conditions in the market, and that the marketing costs are manageable, the next step is an on-the-spot survey. Various approaches for on-site market surveys have been used (Table 9.3). Among the most important and fruitful are: measuring responses to exhibitions at local trade fairs; professional meetings and world trade centres; sampling customer responses by questioning; pretesting the market through free samples; and, in the case of highly culture-bound markets, consulting local anthropologists familiar with the area.

## *Evolution from opportunistic to systematic market selection*

In some situations market awareness initially involves an opportunistic approach to market selection. Rather than solely evaluating the specific market opportunity, however, the firm compares the opportunity to other markets not already entered (Figure 9.4). This comparison may resemble the systematic selection procedure already discussed.

## Influences on selection of markets

There are a number of influences which may affect the market selection process. Influences can hinder the process, but they can also facilitate, stimulate and expand it. Influences on the market selection decision may be discussed under five headings.

**Table 9.3**  Research in international markets: approaches to market surveys

- Measuring responses to exhibitions at local trade fairs, professional meetings and world trade centres
- Sampling of customer response by questioning (mailed, telephoned, or face-to-face)
- Pre-testing the market via free samples
- Consulting local anthropologists and sociologists familiar with area

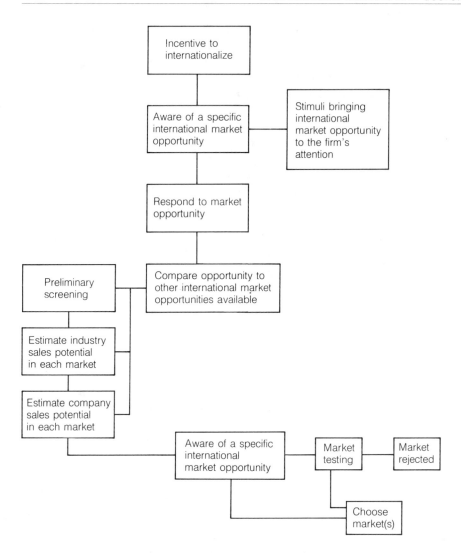

**Figure 9.4** Evolution from opportunistic approach to systematic approach (Source: Adapted from: Bowers, A.M. (1986) Towards an Understanding of the Export Market Selection Process, unpublished Master of Business Studies Dissertation, Department of Marketing, University College Dublin)

## Company size and market selection

Because of a greater resource base, it is possible that a larger company may prefer to use more comprehensive market selection procedures than its smaller counterpart. The possible interconnection between firm size and quality of management may also result in the "higher-quality" management of larger companies showing a greater tendency to engage in systematic market selection (Bilkey, 1978). There is no evidence that "higher-quality" management is the prerogative of all large firms. Indeed many smaller high-technology firms possess excellent managers with relevant international experience.

## Influence of export sales

A company which exports a greater proportion of annual sales tends to be more dependent upon international markets as a source of profitability and stability. Such a company may tend to exercise greater care in market selection as opposed to a company which exports a smaller proportion of total sales.

Companies which only export or have available for export less than, say, 5 per cent of total sales are unlikely to give much attention to the method of selection of markets unless they see a strategic opportunity in their development.

## Corporate goals and market selection

It has been argued that many, if not most, influences on organizational decisions that define acceptable activities are associated with an organizational goal (Table 9.4). Corporate goals for exporting may cover non-maximizing behaviour and non-profit aims as seen in early literature on the subject (Tookey, 1964; Hunt, Froggatt and Hovell, 1967). These goals include the disposal of surplus production as opposed to profit objectives. Where these non-maximizing goals exist it is unlikely that the firm would use a systematic export market selection procedure with a view to identifying optimal opportunities.

In the more recent literature, however, more emphasis is placed on growth in turnover and profitability as goals for international sales. In a survey of UK firms, Piercy (1980) found that the vast majority of companies pursued the same goals in the domestic and export markets, and very few companies reflected the traditional view advanced by the above authors, where domestic business involves the pursuit of profits and exporting the pursuit of volume. Other goals discussed

**Table 9.4**  Influence of company goals on international market selection

Corporate goals for international markets include the following:
- non-maximizing behaviour and non-profit aims, e.g. disposal of surplus production
- desire for sales stability with growth
- growth in profit from international sales
- percentage profit on international sales
- growth in international sales turnover
- growth in share in each international market

in the literature include the following: desire for sales stability with growth (Weidersheim-Paul, Olsen and Welch 1978); growth in profit from export sales; percentage profit on export sales, i.e. profit from sales in each market after deducting all costs; growth in export sales turnover; and growth in share of each export market.

The importance the firm places on the achievement of certain goals may also influence the market selection process. For example, Japanese strategic behaviour in the United States and many world markets suggests the following three goals (Kotler, Fahey and Jatusripitak, 1985):

1. Build market share over a long time period.
2. Disregard profits as market share is being obtained.
3. When a significant market position is established challenge US and other foreign competitors head-on in their principal product markets.

The aim is to build market position and then worry about profitability. This will lead to quite different criteria for evaluating international markets, compared to those employed by US and European firms which focus on maintaining profitability levels or other goals where short-term financial returns dominate.

## Influence of company strategy

Three possible strategic influences on market selection may be considered: the strategy of market concentration; the strategy of grouping similar markets; and the strategy of sequencing entry to different markets.

The strategy of market concentration is examined first. A company may have a deliberate policy of concentrating its sales efforts on certain key markets. Such a strategy will provide an important guiding influence upon both the systematic and opportunistic approach towards market selection. A company which selects markets on an opportunistic basis may decide to concentrate upon a limited number of the market opportunities which have come to its attention. In the process of deciding whether or not to pursue a market opportunity which has arisen, a concentration strategy would lead the company to carefully consider its ability to obtain a minimum penetration level in the market in question.

With regard to a concentration strategy and the systematic selection process, the degree to which each market facilitates a concentrated selling effort by the firm is emphasized throughout the selection procedure. Hence, the company may place more emphasis on evaluating marketing costs, competition, distribution channel availability, and "depth" of prospective markets. From the point of view of market concentration, for example, many Belgian companies find France a more attractive proposition than Far Eastern countries.

In general, a policy of market concentration would tend to result in a more critical evaluation of prospective markets, while dissipation of effort may lead to less background research prior to market entry.

## *Value of market information*

The systematic, and to some extent the opportunistic, approach towards market selection is dependent on the availability of sufficient information on international markets. The information required for evaluating foreign markets may be classified as country- or market-level or company- or product-level information. Country-level information consists of broad cross-comparable statistics as would be used in preliminary screening or some stages of estimating Industry Market Potential. Product specific information, on the other hand, is concerned with a detailed profile of individual markets and would be required in estimating Company Sales Potential or in deciding whether or not to pursue an export opportunity which has come to the attention of the company.

With regard to country or market information, the services of international organizations, e.g. UN, OECD, EC, coupled with computerization and the information explosion, make it possible to collect reasonably comparable data where none existed before. By using UN publications, OECD Economic Reports, the Reports of UNCTAD-GATT including those of the International Trade Centre in Geneva, Eurostat, and the publications and other data bases provided by commercial organizations, the firm should be able to obtain a comparable view of countries at the country or market level.

Unfortunately, the collection of company or product specific information is far more difficult. Apart from selective reports from organizations such as EIU, Predicast or Mintel, and Dialog, international reports on specific industries may be non-existent. As stated by Papadopoulos (1983), however, there is a surprising amount of secondary data which provides product specific information. This ranges from the purchase or consumption patterns of larger purchase items, e.g. cars, TVs, white goods, usually available through national statistical bureaux, to information on industrial or consumer small purchase items, e.g. soft drinks and detergents, which can be purchased from private research agencies. Hence, by examining the market for similar products, the company may estimate sales potential for its own category.

As information on prospective markets is required in more detail, it may be necessary to secure primary data on the product category. Hence, executives of the firm may research overseas markets under consideration themselves, or they may commission the services of a market research agency.

## Segmenting international markets

Strategic approaches to grouping international markets raise a different set of problems. Arranging things in classes according to some system allows the firm to generalize about problems rather than face the endless or impossible task of dealing with each one on an individual basis (Liander *et al.*, 1967). An appropriate system of classifying or grouping markets can therefore be an important element in clarifying a firm's understanding of its international operations.

The grouping principle may also direct the selection of markets. Prior to a discussion of the possible relationship between market groups and market selection, it is necessary to consider the various techniques for classifying or grouping countries.

## Market segmentation: geography and zones of influence

An approach based on geographical groups and the groupings of countries on the basis of trading patterns has a number of attractions. Trading pattern groups would include Eastern Bloc countries, the EC, the dollar markets of North America and the Pacific and the pound sterling areas. Such an approach leads to the concept of zones of influence and the marketing consequences which arise as a result of such groups. An alternative approach based on a geographical form of grouping, but dependent on the levels of economic development, political and socio-cultural factors, size of the firm's business in a country, the firm's ownership or distribution pattern in a country, sales growth potential in the country, or the stage of development of the country concerned may be used (Liander *et al.*, 1967).

## Market segmentation: business distance

Countries have also been grouped on an environmental "temperature gradient scale" (Goodnow and Hansz, 1972). "Hot" countries are those which are politically stable, are economically well developed, are culturally homogeneous and provide many market opportunities but have few legal and physiographic barriers, i.e. obstacles to the development of efficient business operations created by the physical landscape, or landforms of a country. This method of grouping markets also uses as a key variable geocultural distance, i.e. barriers created by geographical separation, cultural disparities between countries and problems of communication resulting from differences in social perspectives, attitudes and language.

A hierarchical clustering computer program was used by Goodnow and Hansz (1972) to classify countries into similar groups which lie along a "country temperature" continuum. Three clusters of countries resulting from this analysis are shown in Table 9.5. The temperature scale used in this study reflects the perspective of firms in the United States. A different ranking would be likely to arise if the same analysis were carried out for a firm located elsewhere. It may be concluded, therefore, that the firm may have to develop its own profile, comprising those variables which it considers significant for its own operations, and generate its own alternatives and clusters.

## Linking market segmentation to market selection

The link between market grouping and market selection is clearly indicated by Liander *et al.* (1967). These authors discuss two main approaches towards developing country clusters and investigate the impact of each approach upon

**Table 9.5** Market groups and the "country temperature continuum"

| Sample hot countries | Sample moderate countries |
|---|---|
| Australia | Caribbean countries |
| Canada | Central American countries |
| European countries | Mexico |
| Japan | South American countries |
| | South Africa |
| Cold countries | South Korea |
| African countries | Israel |
| Middle East countries | Hong Kong |
| Far East countries | |

Source: Goodnow, James D., and Hansz, James E. (1972) 'Environmental determinants of overseas market entry strategies,' *Journal of International Business Studies*, **3**, 33–50. The above selection of countries and areas was made from a much larger list provided in Goodnow and Hansz (1972).

market selection: the developmental approach through cluster analysis; and the regional typological approach. The first classifies countries into groups depending upon their level of development. The technique emphasizes the degree of similarity between markets based upon the number of attributes they share. In using this approach, a company would proceed to select markets as follows:

1. Assess the "fit" between its products and each of the clusters, and select the most promising cluster.
2. Select the most promising country from that cluster and, assuming favourable results from on-site research, introduce the product.
3. In deciding to enter additional countries, select from the same cluster before moving on to another.

The regional typological approach is similar to the first, except that countries are grouped by geographic location instead of by degree of development. The underlying assumption in this case is that countries of the same region display similar characteristics, e.g. culture, religion. Liander *et al.* (1967) used a rank order system at one of four levels of development within each region. As with the preceding approach, a company proceeds by selecting a region, then a development level, then a country within it. In future market entries, the firm would first consider those within the same development level as the preceding country, then those at different levels of development within the same region.

Other classification approaches have a similar impact upon market selection; a company which groups markets on the basis of trading patterns may initially choose the more favourable trading pattern areas, and then enter the most promising markets in those areas in order of priority. The company may subsequently develop several marketing approaches, each tailored to the characteristics of the respective group. This matching of the marketing approach to group characteristics greatly reduces problems of co-ordination and control, and may produce economies in production and reduce marketing costs (Sorenson and Wiechmann, 1975).

## Systematic selection of customers

The most attractive customers depend on the firm's position. A low-cost firm can sell successfully to powerful, price sensitive buyers. A firm without cost advantage or product differentation must be very selective in the selection of customers. In responding to these basic principles successful firms attempt to develop attractive buyers by building up switching costs, increasing value added and redefining the buyer's way of thinking about the product or service on offer. These firms are quick to estimate high-cost buyers especially marginal customers in the growth phase of industry and product life cycles.

In these circumstances successful firms choose their customers with care. It is necessary to match the company's resources and capabilities with customer requirements. Convergent customer needs and company competences permits greater product differentation and lower costs in servicing such buyers. Changes in demographic profiles and quantities purchased influence the growth potential in consumer markets while industry related factors influence the growth potential in industrial markets. Buyers are not passive actors: they frequently spread purchases, qualify alternative sources, avoid switching costs, promote standardization, threaten backward integration or use tapered integration through contracts and other commitments. Some buyers have little intrinsic buying power while others are not very price sensitive. The cost of serving buyers can also vary greatly. Hence, it is important to evaluate each customer market thoroughly before committing resources to its development.

In evaluating alternative markets and customer segments within these markets the firm must assess its own strengths and weaknesses relative to those of its competitors, and it must also consider market developments. Following the broad framework provided above, this analysis will lead the firm to the selection of target countries and to an evaluation of segments within these countries. A systematic way of proceeding further which emphasizes the importance of evaluating market opportunities and business strengths segment by segment within each target country is needed. By using the basic principles of segmentation analysis it is possible to proceed from country selection to customer selection. By relating segmentation and positioning in the context of the firm's strengths and weaknesses, opportunities and threats (a SWOT analysis), Wind and Robertson (1983) are able to evaluate individual segments and positions which might be the focus of the firm's attention (Figure 9.5).

In order to apply the framework, the firm at Stage 1 develops an evaluation of the alternative market segments and it also develops appropriate positioning strategies for each segment. For example, $S_3P_4$ represents the light user segment that is satisfied with a particular product-service offering and that is motivated to purchase by the status and image associated with the product-service. At stage

2 the firm would carry out the SWOT analysis for each segment-position. When the analysis reaches stage 3 the firm develops an evaluation of market opportunities in relation to the firm's business strengths. In this regard the $S_3P_4$ segment provides an attractive market opportunity (high) but the firm's strength to match this opportunity is questionable — between high and low in the diagram.

## Integrated view of market selection process

Firms use two very different approaches to the market selection process: an opportunistic approach; and a systematic approach. The elements of these approaches are brought together in Figure 9.6. On the right-hand side of the diagram the opportunistic approach is outlined, while on the left-hand side the more detailed systematic approach is described. Some firms use a combination of these approaches, starting in the opportunistic mode and evolving into a systematic approach. In a recent study of market selection practices Bowers (1986) discovered that a systematic approach to international market selection was followed by a significant proportion of the firms surveyed (Exhibit 9.1).

## Summary

The objective of this chapter was to provide an understanding of the dynamics of international market selection. A simple trial and error approach was developed to provide a benchmark against which to measure the selection of international markets.

The market selection model begins with the incentive to internationalize. The essence of the international market selection approach involves the company becoming aware of market opportunities. It is suggested that this awareness may arise in three ways, as follows:

1. Opportunistically — where certain sources would bring market opportunities to the firm's attention. A number of factors would be taken into account in deciding whether or not to pursue these opportunities.
2. Systematically — where the company would become aware of certain opportunities as a result of exploring and evaluating many alternative markets.
3. A third option allowed for a combined opportunistic and systematic approach.

Emphasis was placed upon the role of certain information sources throughout the above evaluative procedures. The possible influence of certain constraints upon the selection process was also discussed. These include company size, proportion of sales exported, export goals, certain strategic considerations, and the availability of international market information.

In selecting international markets the firm must have access to various kinds

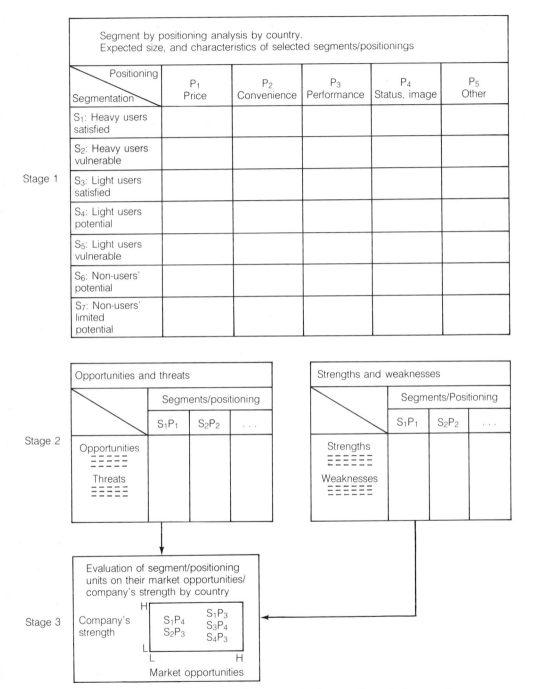

**Figure 9.5** Systematic selection of customers, matching positions to segments (Source: Adapted from Wind, Yoram and Robertson, Thomas S. (1983), 'Marketing strategy: New directions for theory and research,' *Journal of Marketing*, **47**, 18)

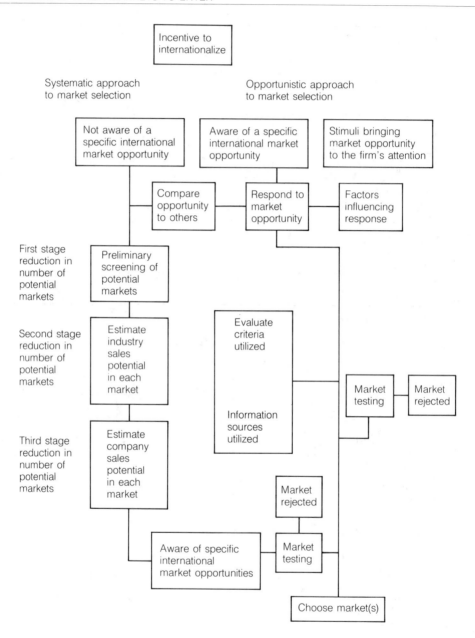

**Figure 9.6**   Integrated view of the international market selection process.
(Source: Adapted from Bowers, A.M. (1986) 'Towards an Understanding of the Export
Market Selection Process,' unpublished Master of Business Studies dissertation,
Department of Marketing, University College Dublin)

---

## Exhibit 9.1   Understanding the international market selection process

---

*International market selection practices*

In a study of international market selection among firms Bowers (1986) reports that firms which identified increased sales, greater profits and the spreading of overheads over larger volumes adopted a systematic approach to market selection. An opportunistic approach to market selection was common among firms in traditional sectors like clothing and textiles and among firms attempting to avoid competition on the domestic market. These firms also believed that margins obtainable abroad were higher.

An opportunistic approach toward market selection was the most common approach used by 36 percent of the firms surveyed. Unsolicited orders from abroad and obtained at trade fairs were the main sources of these opportunities. A systematic approach towards market selection was the most common among 64 percent of the firms surveyed. These firms used very broad preliminary screening techniques. In determining industry potential these firms used product specific criteria such as:

- apparent consumption of the product
- imports of the product category
- product sales growth

In estimating the sales potential for the firm, an assessment of competitors and distribution channels was carried out.

The systematic approach toward market selection also meant that in the early stages of the search externally published sources and internal company data were used but ceased to be important at the later stages. These firms relied heavily on the knowledge of company executives throughout the selection process. Some use was made of market research agencies and consultants. On-site field research increased in importance as market information was required in greater detail. This occurred as the firm moved closer to the selection of a particular market or group of markets.

Companies which strongly advocated the selection of markets similar to the domestic market attached considerable importance to incentives related to the use of excess capacity where such existed and the spreading of overheads over greater sales volume. These firms also found that specific product-market information was frequently unavailable.

Companies which agreed with the principle of market concentration attached greatest importance to goals of growth in market share and the elimination of sales fluctuations.

On the issue of strategic grouping of markets 56 percent of the firms reported that they grouped foreign markets based on product specific criteria. These companies tended to enter the most attractive markets in each group in order of priority.

**Source:** Adapted from Bowers, Anthony M. (1986) Towards an Understanding of the Export Market Selection Process, unpublished Master of Business Studies Dissertation, Department of Marketing, University College Dublin.

of information. There are numerous sources, as follows:

- management knowledge and experience;
- internal company data;
- publications, trade journals and magazines;
- government and industry sponsored information agencies and marketing consultants.

There are several influences on the selection process, some of which hinder and others which facilitate selection:

- Larger firms are more likely to be systematic in their selection of international markets.
- Companies dependent on international markets for a large proportion of their revenues are more likely to adopt a systematic approach.
- Company goals and the relative importance placed on them may influence selection by concentrating on a limited number of options.
- A systematic approach places emphasis on evaluating costs, competition, distribution and customer needs in prospective markets.
- Availability of information influences market selection.

The firm is also faced with the decision of segmenting chosen international markets. Two general approaches are used: geographic areas or regions and zones of cultural influence and a selection of markets based on business distance. Market choices may be linked or embedded in each other which introduces the notion of sequencing the selection of international markets.

There are two principal forms of market sequence: market diversification by which the firm carries out fast penetration into a number of markets and allocates limited resources to each; and market concentration by which the firm concentrates on a few markets and gradually expands. In the latter approach resources are allocated to a small number of markets initially.

## Discussion questions

1. What are the advantages and disadvantages of an opportunistic selection of international markets?

2. Before the firm can take a decision to enter a specific foreign market there must be an awareness of opportunities in that market. How does the firm become aware of such opportunities?

3. How is it possible to obtain the relevant information to carry out a systematic analysis of markets prior to selection?

4. Outline and discuss the factors which influence the international market selection process.

5. Discuss the most common forms of international market expansion strategies. What are the key variables used in deciding between the two?

6. Identify an appropriate set of criteria to be used in evaluating and comparing country markets in terms of opportunities.

# References

Attiyeh, R.J. and Wenner, D.L. (1981) 'Critical mass: Key to export profits,' *The McKinsey Quarterly*, Winter 1981.

Ayal, Igal and Jehiel, Zif (1979) 'Market expansion strategies in multinational marketing,' *Columbia Journal of World Business*, Spring, pp. 84–94.

Bilkey, Warren J. (1978) 'An attempted integration of the literature on the export behaviour of firms,' *Journal of International Business Studies*, 9 (1), 33–46.

Bowers, A.M. (1986) Towards an Understanding of the Export Market Selection Process, unpublished Master of Business Studies Dissertation, Department of Marketing, University College Dublin.

Carlson, Sune (1975) 'How foreign is foreign trade?,' *Acta Universitatis Upsaliensis, Studia Oceonomiae Negotiorum*, Bulletin No 15, Uppsala.

Cateora, Philip R. (1990) *International Marketing*, 7th edn, Irwin, Homewood, Ill.

Deschampsneufs, Henry (1967) *Marketing Overseas*, Pergamon Press.

Goodnow, James D. and Hansz, James E. (1972) 'Environmental determinants of overseas market entry strategies,' *Journal of International Business Studies*, 3, pp. 33–50.

Hallen, Lars and Weidersheim-Paul, Finn (1982) 'The evolution of psychic distance in international business relationships,' *Working Paper 1982/83*, Department of Business Studies, University of Uppsala.

Hunt, H.G., Froggatt, J.D. and Hovell, P.J. (1967) 'The management of export marketing in engineering industries,' *British Journal of Marketing*, Spring, pp. 10–24.

Jaffe, E.D. (1974) *Grouping: A strategy for international marketing*, American Management Association, NY.

Kotler, P., Fahey, L. and Jatusripitak, S. (1985) *The New Competition*, Prentice-Hall, Englewood Cliffs, NJ.

Liander, B., Terpstra, V., Yoshino, M.Y. and Sherbini, A.A. (1967) *Comparative Analysis for International Marketing*, Boston, Allyn and Bacon 1967.

Papadopoulos, Nicolas G. (1983) 'Assessing new product opportunities in international markets,' *Proceedings, ESOMAR Seminar on New Product Development*, Athens, Greece, 2–5 November 1983, 69–88.

Piercy, Nigel (1980) 'Export marketing management in medium sized British firms,' *European Journal of Marketing*, 17 (1), 48–67.

Root, R.F. (1982) *Foreign Market Entry Strategy*. Amacom, NY.

Sorenson, Ralph, Z. and Wiechmann, Ulrich E. (1975) 'How multinationals view marketing standardization,' *Harvard Business Review*, 53, 38–56.

Tookey, Douglas A. (1964) 'Factors associated with success in exporting,' *Journal of Management Studies*, 1, pp. 48-66.

Tookey, Douglas A. (1975) *Export Marketing Decisions*, Penguin Books, England.

Vahlne, J.E. and Weiderscheim-Paul, F. (1977) 'Psychic distance: An inhibiting factor in international trade,' *Working Paper 1977/2*, Department of Business Administration, University of Uppsala.

Weidersheim-Paul, F., Olsen, S.C. and Welch, L.S. (1978) 'Pre-export activity — the first step in internationalisation,' *Journal of International Business Studies*, **9** (1), 47–58.

Wind, Yoram and Robertson, Thomas S. (1983) 'Marketing strategy: New directions for theory and research,' *Journal of Marketing*, **47**, 18.

CHAPTER

# Analysis of international competitors

**10**

The firm in international markets must deal with competitors in its own domestic market and in each international market it enters. Some of these competitors will be the same while others will be different and encountered for the first time. In order to prepare itself for such competition the firm must understand the behaviour of its competitors. The number, size, quality and origin of the competitors affects the firm's ability to enter and compete profitably in a particular market. In general, firms devote more resources to understanding their customers than their competitors. There is no valid reason, however, why firms should not devote considerable time and resources to understanding their competitors in international markets since the fortunes of the firm are determined by an interplay of what the firm itself does, what its customers want and what competitors do. It is not just a matter of only one or two of these elements.

In general it is more difficult to determine the competitive structure of international markets than it is to obtain information on market opportunities and environmental factors — topics discussed in preceding chapters. In the situation where the firm faces the same competitors in many markets it is clear that strategy must be integrated in some way as a certain response in one market may have competitive repercussions in several. Where the firm meets several different competitors it is important to understand how each behaves so that initiatives and responses may be made.

Because of these changes, a dual competitive milieu arises. For some firms, marketing has become global and integrated decisions are required. For other firms, especially the smaller ones, marketing has shifted toward an emphasis on niche strategies. Of course these two approaches frequently meet. The dimensions of these two broad approaches to competition and their interaction are described and evaluated in this chapter.

## Meaning of competition

Preceding chapters have examined environmental considerations and the ability of the firm to compete internationally. Some markets are attractive; it depends

237

on the firm's competitive position. Attractiveness is influenced by market factors, such as size and growth in the market and customer bargaining power; by economic and technological factors, such as the nature and intensity of investment, the technology used and mobility barriers; by competitive factors, such as the structure of competition, substitutes; and perceived differentiation and environmental factors such as social acceptance and regulations.

The firm's competitive position is influenced by its market position — share, differentiation, product range and image; by its economic and technological position — cost structure, capacity, patents; and capability — management and marketing strengths, channel power and its relationships with labour and government. The general framework, developed by Day (1984), is used to link the analysis of competitors to marketing planning for international competition (Figure 10.1).

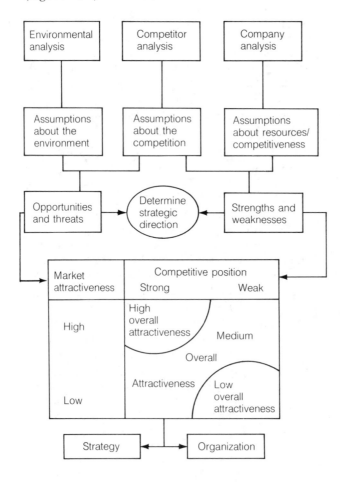

**Figure 10.1**  Linking competitor analysis to marketing planning (Source: Adapted from Day, George (1984) *Strategic Market Planning*, West Publishing Company, St Paul, Minn.)

In the following sections we examine the competitive structure of international markets, the determinants of international competitiveness, approaches to understanding international competitors and strategic control for successful competition.

## Nature of competition among firms

The argument in this chapter is not that the firm should only focus on the competition. In the preceding chapter it was shown how important it is to focus on the customer as well. Indeed, a balance between the two is desirable. As was seen in earlier chapters some firms focus on the product only and exclude consideration of customers and competitors. A firm focussed on customers pays great attention to customer issues in the development of strategy. In contrast a competitor-oriented firm reacts to the behaviour of competitors. Both approaches have advantages.

A customer-oriented approach is better when the objective is to identify new opportunities, whereas the competitor-oriented approach is preferred when it is important to monitor strengths and weaknesses in other firm's endeavours. A market-oriented approach combines both approaches (Figure 10.2). Furthermore, the firm in international markets must also consider the international repercussions of the way it treats customers and responds to competition — the international market focus.

## Establishing competitive positions of international markets

The success of any marketing strategy depends upon the strength of the competitive analysis on which it is based (Henderson, 1983). Porter (1980) has developed a formal industry structure model for such analysis which consists of a review of all key industry players, new entrants, suppliers, substitutes, buyers and industry competitors themselves. Henderson outlines a number of competition principles drawn from biological theory and sets out to show that business is equally a question of the "survival of the fittest." Henderson makes the observation, drawn from Darwin's *The Origin of Species*, that the more similar competitors are to each other, the more intense their competition will be. This serves to underline the need for competitive analysis and advantage. Characteristic by characteristic, Henderson proposes that competitors should be compared in order to identify the unique advantage that will set a company apart and allow it to win in the competitive marketplace.

The rules of good market competitive positioning are for the firm to attempt to create long-term sustainable positions. The distinction between contestable and sustainable is a matter of degree but, clearly, sustainability will be greatest where the advantage is based on a number of factors, where the advantage is large and when few environmental threats to it exist. In this context Ghemawat (1986) makes two suggestions for the firm. First the firm should not ignore contestable

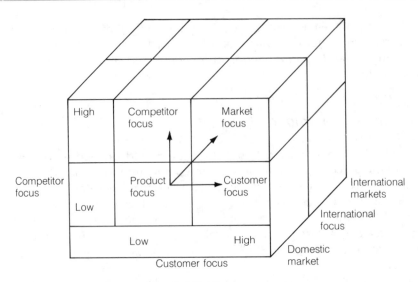

**Figure 10.2**  Changing focus of the firm

advantages, and small moves can be made if they avoid creating a competitive disadvantage. Second, as sustainability is also a function of management and organization resource commitment, the firm must decide to what extent it wishes to compete in a particular way and invest accordingly while maintaining the flexibility to compete effectively in other ways.

## Hierarchy of competition

There is a hierarchy of competition facing the firm depending on the substitutability of products. Products which are close substitutes have a high cross-elasticity of demand. Products which are not so close as substitutes would have a low cross-elasticity of demand. The hierarchy of substitutability is shown in Table 10.1.

In addition to the concept of product substitution it is important to understand the nature of the dynamics of the industry. To understand the competitive dynamics of an industry the firm must understand the conditions underlying supply and demand. These factors influence industry structure which in turn influences the behaviour of firms in the industry. The behaviour of firms in regard to product development, pricing, advertising and distribution determines industry performance such as the efficiency, growth, and profitability of firms in the industry. This framework, known in the economics literature as the study of structure conduct and performance, allows the firm to examine the nature and source of competition in an industry (Figure 10.3).

An examination of the structure of the industry gives the firm much of the information it requires to understand the conduct or behaviour of its competitors.

**Table 10.1**  Identifying competitors by product substitution criteria

| Product substitutability | Level of substitution |
|---|---|
| Low ↑ | Firm considers all firms that compete for the same consumer funds in different markets as competitors |
| | Firm considers all firms producing products that provide the same service as competitors |
| | Firm considers all firms making the same product or class as competitors |
| High ↓ | Firm considers all firms providing a similar product to the same customers under similar commercial conditions as competitors |

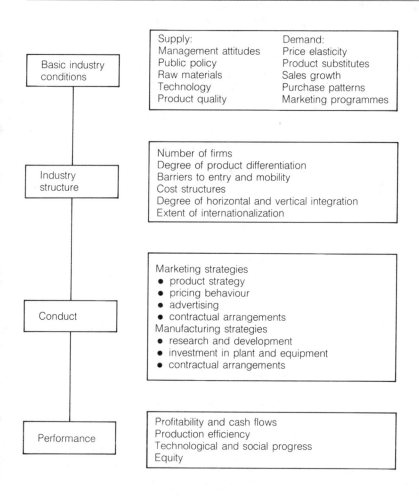

**Figure 10.3**  Analysis of industry competition (Source: Adapted with modifications from Sherer, F.M. (1980) *Industry Market Structure* and *Economic Performance*, Rand McNally, Chicago, p. 4)

There are a number of points to consider. First, it is necessary to specify the number of firms in the industry and whether the product is standardized or highly differentiated. Second, firms desire to enter industries that offer attractive profits. Some industries are easier to enter than others. The major barriers to entry are: brand strength; access to distribution; large capital requirements and scale economies; and international agreements. Some of these barriers are intrinsic to certain industries such as petroleum, coffee and tin, while others are established by the actions of firms already in the industry, e.g. the branded consumer products firms. Third, in an ideal world firms should be able to exit an industry freely but frequently there are barriers to exit such as obligations to customers and employees, government restrictions and lack of alternatives.

When it is in the interests of firms they can be induced to lower the exit barriers for others, e.g. taking over the provision of employment in a town or taking responsibility for serving an established customer base.

The fourth consideration refers to cost structures which determine the strategic behaviour of firms in the industry. Firms with heavy manufacturing and raw materials costs behave differently than firms with heavy distribution and marketing costs. Firms tend to focus on activities associated with their greatest cost which gives rise to competitive opportunities. Fifth, the ability to integrate backwards, forwards or horizontally can lower costs and provide more control of the market and the value added chain. In industries which are thus integrated, firms may be found which manipulate their prices and costs in different segments of their business to earn profits where taxes are lowest. Transfer pricing to exploit the incentives provided by governments to attract foreign direct investment is an example of such behaviour. Firms that cannot integrate operate at a disadvantage. Finally, the extent to which the industry has internationalized affects structure and competition in the industry. Some firms compete only in the domestic market while others have the choice of competing in many markets which affect the nature and extent of competition in the industry.

## Impact of competition on market and firm

Competition has positive and negative effects which the firm must consider. It also affects the market and the firm itself but if carefully monitored and managed can be to the firm's benefit.

The product-market innovator has a lonely and expensive time in the market since it must educate consumers and other users of the value of the new product. Competition in this case can expand market opportunities for all firms in the industry which serve the market. The marketing programmes of all competitors when taken together usually help customers gain a better understanding of the product or service and encourage more people to enter the market. The world market for cream liqueurs is a good example, as is the market for new financial services in most western style countries.

Competition also has a negative side for the firm which arises when competitors seek greater shares of the market. In this situation each firm tries to persuade customers to buy its product, service or brand rather than the offerings of competitors. In unregulated markets, as found for most products and services in western style economies, competition is essential to ensure that customers receive the best on offer.

## Benefits of competition

Successful firms recognize the value of competitors in the market for additional reasons. In general, the presence of competitors benefits the firm in three ways: they contribute to increase the firm's competitive advantage; they improve the structure of the industry; and they help to develop the market (Porter, 1985, Chapter 6). The presence of competitors allows the firm to increase its competitive advantage in a number of ways. First, fluctuations in market demand can be shared, thus avoiding the necessity of providing enough capacity for peak demand. The firm must, however, ensure that there is sufficient industry capacity to serve the most important buyers while not attracting new entrants. Second, product and service differentiation are easier where there is a credible competitor to provide a benchmark for measuring relative performance. It is, of course, presumed that buyers can perceive the claimed differences in the product attributes. Third, a high-cost competitor may provide a cost umbrella which allows a low-cost firm to enter international markets or increase profits if already there. Finally, a viable competitor may be an important motivator to reduce costs, improve products and keep abreast of technological and environmental change.

Competitors also help to improve industry structure in a number of ways. First, competitors can help to expand overall industry demand. This benefit frequently accrues to the innovator who is first in the market with a new product, especially in situations where the firm's sales are related to total industry advertising. At the growth stage of the life cycle followers frequently spend disproportionately on advertising which tends to benefit the innovator who is better able to service the market. Second, buyers, especially industrial buyers, seek a second and third source in an endeavour to reduce the risk of interruption to supply. This is especially true in industries such as the motor components industry as the presence of a number of suppliers may prevent buyers from inviting the participation of more aggressive competitors. It may also prevent motor firms from integrating backwards. Third, competitors may contribute to an attractive industry structure. A competitor that emphasizes product quality, durability and service in industrial product markets may help to reduce buyer price sensitivity and mitigate price competition in the industry. In consumer product markets a competitor who spends a lot on advertising may hasten the evolution of the industry into one with a few strong brands and high entry barriers (Porter, 1985, p. 208).

The cost of developing new markets, especially for radically new products and where product and process technology is still evolving, can be prohibitive for many firms. There are three considerations: competitors can help by sharing the cost; reducing buyer risk; and standardizing the technology (Porter, 1985, p. 209). First, market development frequently involves the cost of market testing, legal and technical compliance and perhaps providing repair and service facilities in a market. Competitors can lower these costs, especially if the market development efforts are in areas that deal with problems common to all firms in the industry. Second, competitors lend credibility to an innovator's product. Buyers are frequently reluctant to purchase a new product where only a single source exists since the buyer could be adversely affected if that supplier failed to provide the product or service or if the supplier went out of business. Third, having competitors that use the same technology as the firm can accelerate the process by which the technology becomes the standard.

## Determinants of competitiveness in international markets

Competitiveness for the firm means its ability to increase earnings by expanding sales and/or profit margins in the market in which it competes. This implies the ability to defend market position as competition in products and production processes evolve. The extent to which a firm proves successful in defending its position will clearly be dependent upon its ability and the competitive strategy it chooses to follow. Where the markets involved are international in scope, then so also is the concept of competitiveness.

The competitiveness of firms depends upon the quality and quantity of the physical and human resources they possess, the manner in which these resources are managed, the supporting infrastructure, and the politics of the nation.

One great myth, which must be dispelled, regarding competition in international markets is that price explains all differences in competitiveness. While price is an important element in marketing strategy it is of course not the only element, as competitive advantage may be gained in price, speed of delivery, design or service provided and brands developed, to name the more obvious.

A tendency to place too much emphasis on the importance of costs, inflation and exchange rates in international markets is tantamount to recognizing no other form of competition than price. While costs and price factors have an important role to play, other factors influence the purchase decision, and this applies no less in international markets than at home. Finally, to survive and grow in international markets a dimension often neglected is manufacturing. For example, it is generally believed that Japanese firms continue to win the technology and manufacturing race, a feature which is beginning to attract much comment in Europe and the United States (Exhibit 10.1).

## Measuring competitiveness in the firm

While conventional economics recognizes the importance of non-price factors, the abundance of economic data which facilitate the measurement of price factors

**Exhibit 10.1   Success in international markets also means close attention to manufacturing**

*Have Western manufacturers gone back to sleep?*

By the late 1970s many Western manufacturers began to understand that the "secret weapon" of their fiercest competitors was simple manufacturing prowess. Yet too many of them had been systematically neglecting their own manufacturing organizations.

The years 1980 to 1983 witnessed an amazing resurgence, however. Company after company came to grips with the challenges facing them and embarked on dramatic and effective programmes to address these challenges; new plants, advanced manufacturing technologies, imaginative quality improvement and inventory reduction programmes. Astonishing progress was reported. Some companies saw their labour productivity more than double in the space of 2 or 3 years. The crisis had been averted many thought.

Alarmingly, many managers saw the good times as evidence that the crisis had never really existed, that it had been more apparent than real. They subsequently began to reduce investment in manufacturing and as a result productivity, quality levels and other measures of effectiveness stagnated in many companies and regressed in others. Unfortunately, while many Western manufacturers rested on their oars, those in Asia were still rowing hard. Japanese manufacturers for instance, are not as worried that their Western competitors will catch up with them as they are of pressure from the "new Japans" such as South Korea and Taiwan. These countries have observed Japan's success very closely and are following its example with remarkable results.

The Japanese understand very clearly that no company can long prevail against a competitor that makes the same product as it does, using a similar manufacturing technology, and employing workers having comparable skill and imagination, but who pays those workers only a fraction of the amount you pay your own workers. Such a company may be protected for a while by tarrif barriers, local content laws and favourable exchange rates. But such barriers will eventually disintegrate, and the game will be over. The only way one can prevail against low-wage competitors is by developing better products than theirs, by introducing manufacturing processes that are superior to theirs or by building the capabilities of your workforce to the point where they can coax more and better output from a comparable manufacturing process.

Understanding this, and recognizing that Japan's wage rate will continue to increase rapidly over the foreseeable future, Japanese managers are putting renewed emphasis on product development, factory automation and worker training. Their Western competitors, who seem oblivious to the underlying causes of their problems, are lagging behind on all three fronts.

**Source:** *International Management Europe*, September, 1985, pp. 88–90.

has created a not unexpected bias toward price variables. Price competitiveness may be measured by relative export prices and cost competitiveness by such indices as labour costs relative to a weighted average of the principal international competitors.

In attempting to assess the relative competitiveness of an industry or a firm on any other factor than price or cost factors, there is a data problem. Buzzell, Gale, and Sultan (1985) in their PIMS work have identified six factors which allow an evaluation of competitiveness (Figure 10.4). The most powerful factors have been shown to be relative product quality, level of innovation and marketing expenditure. Relative product quality refers to product attributes which are considered superior to those of competitors offset by attributes considered inferior. Product innovation refers to sales from products introduced in the preceding three years as a proportion of current sales.

Marketing effort refers to marketing expenditures as a proportion of market sales. Relative service quality refers to the possession of superior or inferior attributes compared to competitors. Research and development is measured as a proportion of sales, and product availability refers to finished products inventory as a proportion of sales.

Day and Wensley (1988) suggest that two methods of evaluating a firm's competitive superiority are available: competitor-centred methods, and customer-focussed methods. The former relies on a comparison of the firm's key resources against those of its target competitors, and evaluations of the success factors attributed to those competitors that hold winning positions in the market. In this situation competitors are viewed as part of the same strategic group pursuing a strategy identical or similar to that being pursued by the firm and having basically the same resource configuration. The differences by which strategic groups are identified depend on circumstances and include the stage of the product life cycle, whether firms are consolidating or growing, the distribution channels used, their position on quality and the technology used.

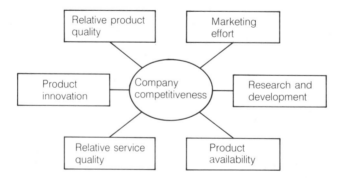

**Figure 10.4**  Evaluative factors in assessing company competitiveness (Source: Adapted from Buzzell, R.D., Gale, B.T. and Sultan, R.G.M. (1975) 'Market share: A key to profitability,' *Harvard Business Review*, January–February, pp. 97–106)

Customer-focussed methods used customer comparison models whereby the firm is compared to its competitors. It also uses customer satisfaction surveys and loyalty measures. In many cases direct competitors in international markets are highly visible or easily identifiable. Most firms know who their competitors are but not always. For example, R & A Bailey and Company should be able to identify sets of products, alcoholic and non-alcoholic, with which its brand Baileys Original Irish Cream competes. It is likely that the brand competes in the overall beverage market. Substitute products can range from wine to beer. Because of consumption patterns, in Germany coffee may be a possible substitute, whereas in the United States soft drinks have a greater possibility of being a substitute. Also within the alcohol beverage market itself, Baileys is competing with beer, spirits and wines. Again, "beer culture" countries would have more of a tendency to substitute beer whereas "wine culture" countries would tend to substitute wine. The products competing with Baileys Irish Cream could therefore be visualized as: soft drinks, coffee and tea at one level, beers, wines and spirits at another level and liqueurs at a third, more focussed, level.

Two lessons emerge from these observations (Aaker, 1988, p. 71). In nearly all industries the competitors can be usefully portrayed in terms of how intensely they compete with the business that is motivating the analysis. There are usually several very direct competitors, others that compete less intensely, and still others that compete indirectly but are still relevant. A knowledge of this pattern can lead to a deeper understanding of the market structure. The competitor groups that compete most intensely may merit the most in-depth study, but other groups may still require analysis.

The identification of the most competitive groups will depend upon a few key variables, and it may be strategically important to know the relative importance of these variables. After entering the Japanese market Kodak learned the lesson that attention to the detail of marketing practice was as important as the strategic thrust of its original entry into that market to compete with Fuji on its own ground (Exhibit 10.2).

Before a clear competitive strategy may be formulated, it is suggested that a fully researched understanding of the sources and positions of advantage, as well as the performance measures of success, will be required. Piercy (1982) has outlined a general measure of export competitiveness which is based on comparisons of the firm's relative strengths on price and non-price grounds, compared to each competitor.

## Understanding competitors in international markets

There are two sets of reasons why a firm should attempt to understand its competitors. Understanding current and likely future strategies of competitors and their strengths and weaknesses may suggest opportunities and threats for the firm which allow it to identify a strategic position which might be adopted. From Porter (1980) and Aaker (1988) it is possible to identify a set of six groups

---

**Exhibit 10.2  Competing with attention to detail**

---

*Developing a positive image in Japan*

If Japanese companies are among your major competitors, then you had better have a presence in the Japanese market. "We have a plan, we are moving to that plan aggressively, but we are not where we want to be," admits David Biehn, executive vice president of Kodak Japan. Kodak's Japanese competitors, Fuji Film and Konica, were beginning to make an impact in Western markets. Fuji, in particular, had moved aggressively into overseas markets.

Although Kodak still dominated in all of these markets and its products were recognized by the majority of the world's photographers as being of the highest quality, the growing competition was beginning to hurt.

The real shock for Kodak came in 1984 when Fuji marched brazenly onto the US company's home ground and captured the sponsorship for the Los Angeles Olympic Games. From that point, Kodak very quickly decided it had to retaliate, and part of that retaliation involved taking on Fuji seriously in Japan.

At that time, Kodak was running a dismal third in the Japanese market with about a 10 per cent share against Konica's 20 percent and Fuji's walloping 70 percent. Whereas in every other market in the world, the Kodak name alone is worth a lot, it meant nothing to the average consumer in Japan. Thus, in addition to improving its customer service, the company would have to make big efforts to build its image.

The company decided it had to shed its American image and become more like a Japanese company. "We want the Japanese to feel more familiar with us", says Biehn. It began putting Japanese characters on its film packaging, sponsoring local fairs and flying a publicity blimp designed to look like a carp, a fish close to the hearts of the Japanese people.

Such changes in its image and a strong emphasis on its commitment to the local community were considered necessary steps in a country where close business relationships are often crucial to success and loyalties are much stronger than in the West.

However, image is no substitute for good service. Shop-owners were not going to carry Kodak film unless they could be sure that they would not receive angry calls from customers whose prints did not meet expectations. Kodak must respond to customers more quickly and more thoroughly than it does elsewhere. "In Japan, if you don't react quickly you're not committed", Biehn says. It is not enough to answer consumer complaints by dealing with a problem in-house as Kodak was accustomed to doing. A consumer problem in Japan calls for immediate action, such as a visit to the film store or the customer himself.

> "Kodak has become aware that it has to conform to Japanese ways", says an official at Fuji. "We are keeping a close eye on the aggressive moves."

**Source:** *The Financial Times*, 1 June, 1989, p.13.

---

of factors, an analysis of which allows the firm to understand its competitors (Figure 10.5).

## Competitor objectives, future goals and assumptions

Successful firms attempt to identify and understand objectives that competitors set for themselves and the assumptions they make about the future. Some firms, especially those in the United States, frequently operate on short-run financial objectives, whereas their Japanese competitors are known to operate on longer-term objectives. This also affects the market share objectives that a firm can set and how they are likely to respond when entering markets for the first time or when threatened by a competitor in an established market.

Where the competitor is part of a larger organization it may also be important to understand the objectives held by the parent. The competitor may be seen by the parent as a growth unit or it may be expected to produce a cash flow to fund other areas of the business. For example, leading car manufacturers such as Saab, Daimler-Benz, Chrysler and General Motors have attempted to create a degree of synergy between automobile and aircraft manufacture using overlapping aircraft and electronic engineers and joint aircraft and automotive R & D to stay in the forefront of automotive technology. Hence, the automobile manufacturers appear to attach greater importance to their automotive facilities than might seem justified.

The competitor may have assumptions about itself or its industry which may or may not be true but which can still influence its strategy. For example, the competitor may perceive itself as having a high-quality premium product which might lead it to ignore a price cut by competitors. Or it may be overly optimistic about the competition in the industry and make decisions accordingly. For example, in 1979 it was forecast that the automotive industry within a decade would consist of fewer than a dozen giants making so-called world cars using

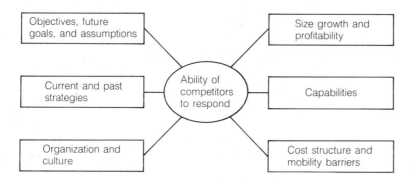

**Figure 10.5**  Understanding competitors (Source: Adapted from Aaker, David A. (1988) *Strategic Market Management*, 2nd edn, John Wiley and Sons, NY, p. 77; and Porter, Michael E. (1980) *Competitive Strategy*, The Free Press, NY)

similar bodies and power units. While there has been a discernible trend towards convergence in car styles, types and configurations, Saab at that time expressed the optimism of the specialist car manufacturer and ignored such forecasts. The company subsequently invested heavily in specialist facilities which for a number of years worked well until a softening of the US dollar and a number of internal company factors caused a downturn in the fortunes of the firm.

## Review of competitor strategies

In general the firm will wish to monitor, at a minimum, competitors' approaches to new product development and the basis for competition. In particular an analysis of strategies which work and do not work in particular circumstances would seem valuable.

## Competitor organization and corporate culture

An understanding of the way in which managers in competing firms think and work together provides valuable information for the likely future activities of such firms. The choice of manager for a particular position can tell a great deal about the strategic thinking in the competitor firm. In addition, the way the firm organizes itself can give good clues as to its likely competitive behaviour and strategy.

A cost-oriented, highly structured organization that relies on tight controls to achieve objectives and motivate employees may have difficulty innovating or shifting into an aggressive marketing-oriented strategy. A loose, flat organization that emphasizes innovation and risk taking may similarly have difficulty in pursuing disciplined product-refinement and cost-execution programmes. These two systems contrast markedly with that of Atlas Copco, a Swedish industrial equipment manufacturer. Here one finds a consensus-oriented system where the company president sees himself as the leader of a closely knit team that he coaches by asking questions rather than dictating answers. He does not force people to accept solutions but makes them feel they have taken part in the decisions themselves, while maintaining a top management rein on the decision process. It is felt that this has greatly facilitated cost reductions, improved efficiency and the elimination of wastage. This approach is in marked contrast to Atlas Copco's most important international rivals, US based companies such as Ingersoll-Rand and Presser Industries, where the organization structure demands that orders come down from the top. Many of these US companies suffered huge losses in the early 1980s, in contrast to the Atlas Copco dramatic increase in profitability.

## Size, growth, and profitability of competitors

If there are many competitors in a market, it is usually necessary to identify the few most significant firms or strategic groups. One measure is their size and associated market share, both domestically and in each of the foreign markets under consideration. Firms that have achieved a recent and substantial increase in market share are also of interest even if they are relatively small. Growth rates, in addition to reflecting the success or failure of strategy, can suggest the possibility of organizational or financial strains that could affect future strategies.

Profitability rates associated with competitors can be very relevant. A profitable firm will generally have access to capital for investment. For example, the West German car manufacturer Audi increased annual sales by 75 per cent between 1980 and 1984 to $2.8 billion, facilitating a $650 million investment programme over the same period, designed to completely overhaul the company's plants at Ingolstadt and Neckarsulm. This had a major impact upon other West German competitors such as Daimler-Benz and BMW, as Audi became a major competitor with an image as a maker of distinctive models that were sharp in styling, impressive in performance and highly economical for their size. A very different situation could also exist. For example, profitability might not lead to increased investment in situations where a subsidiary is expected to produce profits to be transferred to a parent. Such might be the situation were Audi profits to be transferred to its parent, Volkswagen.

## Competitor capabilities

Knowledge of a competitor's strengths and weaknesses can provide insights into how capable it is in pursuing various types of strategies. It also forms an important input into the process of identifying and selecting strategic alternatives (Aaker, 1988, pp. 80–5). One approach is to attempt to exploit a competitor's weakness in an area where the firm has an existing or developing strength. The desired pattern is to pit a strength against a competitor's weakness. Conversely, a knowledge of the competitor's strength is important so that it can be by-passed or neutralized.

## Cost structure and mobility barriers

A knowledge of a competitor's cost structure, especially for a competitor that is relying on a low-cost strategy can provide an indication of its probable future pricing strategy and its staying power (Aaker, 1988, p. 79). The goal should be to obtain a feel for both direct costs and fixed costs which will determine break-even levels. In some circumstances a great level of detail is required: labour and material costs; investment levels; and sales. In other circumstances, especially for international labour cost comparisons, it may not be necessary to carry out such an exhaustive analysis for many countries. Due to economies of scale, superior technology, and lower wage rates, the cost advantages of certain countries, e.g. Japan, Korea, and Taiwan, may be quite evident. High mobility barriers, especially if they are exit barriers, experienced in a few countries, tend to increase competitive pressures within an industry. These barriers include specialized assets; fixed costs such as labour agreements, and leases; relationships to other parts of the firm due to shared facilities, distribution channels, or the sales force; government and social barriers; and managerial pride and emotional factors.

## Assessing potential competitors

In addition to current competitors the firm should assess the potential of competitors who are likely to enter the market. Potential market entrants are motivated to enter a new international market for three reasons: product-market expansion; market integration; and the possibility of exploiting unique competences in international markets.

### Product-market expansion

There are many examples of firms which seek to expand through the introduction of new products. In recent years in attempting to address a serious decline in profits, IBM developed a new product range. The products included a more powerful PC, with some hard-to-clone features, and the 9370 mini computer designed to run the same software as IBM mainframes. The development of a new mini computer, added to the attempts towards reduced cloning, has had major implications for competitors such as Digital and Ericsson.

In regard to market expansion there is a lot of evidence of firms moving into new foreign markets. An example here would be the Finnish company Nokia which manufacturers Mikko computers, Salora TVs, Moriba mobile telephones and Luxor satellite TV reception dishes. Nokia considers itself to be too big for Finland and other Scandinavian countries and believes that the rest of the world is its market.

The restructuring of Nokia has involved weaning the group away from erratic Comecon markets and giving it a new international orientation skewed more towards high-tech trade with the West. Like many of its oriental competitors, Nokia shows a long-term commitment to growth at the expense of short-term profit and shareholders' gratification. Such a company represents a major competitive threat to firms with similar products selling to Western Europe or other markets at present.

## Market integration

Customers and suppliers are potential competitors. In Europe, as for many years in the United States, General Motors, a major customer for components, absorbed many auto component manufacturers to ensure that delivery and quality standards of vital components were met. Suppliers are also potential competitors. Texas Instruments began making watches, calculators, and computers that use its components. Suppliers, feeling they have the critical ingredients to succeed in a market, may be attracted by the margins and control that come from integrating forward. For example, having established the Virgin record company in the United Kingdom in the early 1970s, the Virgin retail empire expanded rapidly both in the United Kingdom and abroad.

## Motives associated with unique competences

An existing small or insignificant competitor with critical strategic weaknesses can turn into a major entrant if it is purchased by a firm that can rescue or eliminate those weaknesses. For example, the Electrolux take-over of the debt-ridden Zanussi company promised a new lease of life to the Italian appliance manufacturer by injecting fresh capital and managerial resources (*International Management*, Sepember, 1985, pp. 24–8). Hence European competitors such as Siemens-Bosch, AEG-Telefunken, Philips-Bauknecht, Thomson-Brandt and Thorn had to seriously re-evaluate the competitive threat from Zanussi.

## Information on international competitors

Sources of information on international competitors can be divided into field data and published data. Field data sources include feedback from the company's own sales force and engineering staff, distribution channel members, personnel hired from competitors, and security analysts. Meanwhile, published sources include articles in newspapers, trade journals and magazines, advertisements for management positions, promotional materials, annual reports, and advertising. Competitors may also be examined from the point of view of what they say about themselves and what others say about them (Table 10.2).

It is unlikely that data to support a full competitor analysis could be compiled in one massive effort. Data on competitors usually come in small flows and must be put together over a period of time to yield a comprehensive picture of the competitor's situation.

Compiling the data for a sophisticated competitor analysis needs an organized mechanism and a competitor intelligence system to ensure that the process is efficient. Data obtained in the market and published data are the two sources of general information about competitors (Figure 10.6). A small firm may

**Table 10.2**  Specific sources of information for evaluation of competitors

| | | Source of information | |
| Public | Trade professionals | Government | Investors |
| --- | --- | --- | --- |
| *What competitors say about themselves* | | | |
| Advertising | Manuals | SEC reports | Annual meetings |
| Promotional materials | Technical papers | FIC | Annual reports |
| Press releases | Licences | Testimony | Prospectuses |
| Speeches | Patents | Lawsuits | Stock/bond issues |
| Books | Courses | Antitrust | |
| Articles | Seminars | | |
| Personnel changes | | | |
| Want ads | | | |
| *What others say about them* | | | |
| Books | Suppliers/vendors | Lawsuits | Security analyst reports |
| Articles | Trade press | Antitrust | Industry studies |
| Case studies | Industry study | State/federal agencies | Credit reports |
| Consultants | Customers | National plans | |
| Newspaper reporters | Subcontractors | Government programs | |
| Environmental groups | | | |
| Consumer groups | | | |
| Unions | | | |
| "Who's Who" | | | |
| Recruiting firms | | | |

Source: Rothschild, W.E. (1979) 'Competitor analysis: The missing link in strategy,' *Management Review*, **68** (7), 22.

not have the resources or staff to attempt some of the more sophisticated approaches, whereas a company with a large stake in monitoring key competitors should probably be following each approach.

## Strategic control for competition

The assumption that firms in different countries behave in the same way and operate with the same set of values is delusory in the extreme. At a minimum, firms in different parts of the world have different views regarding the time horizon of their investments, as has already been noted. Not all firms emphasize short-run earnings. A concentration on quick returns may sacrifice the future for the present.

The television industry is a good illustration of how different approaches to competition have resulted in the fragmentation of the European consumer electronics industry, the virtual disappearance of that industry in the United States, and the emergence of Japan as a most formidable competitor in world markets. Alliances and rationalization through inter-firm sales of consumer electronics business units are now seen as part of the response by European and US companies to the Japanese onslaught (Exhibit 10.3).

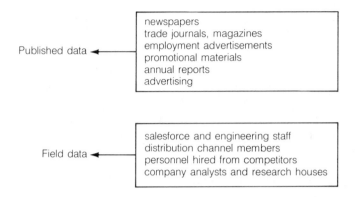

Published data ◄────

- newspapers
- trade journals, magazines
- employment advertisements
- promotional materials
- annual reports
- advertising

Field data ◄────

- salesforce and engineering staff
- distribution channel members
- personnel hired from competitors
- company analysts and research houses

**Figure 10.6**   General sources of information on competitors

The recent spate of leveraged buyouts in many western markets also indicates a shift in emphasis in the underlying criteria by which the performance of firms is judged. It means that return on investment is losing favour as a criterion in evaluation of a business, while cash flow has become the key variable.

Many firms have recently reorganized themselves into small flexible business units to respond to a changing world market. Such changes recognize the necessity for strategic control and not just bureaucratic control in the firm. Firms differ in regard to how they view the need for strategic direction, rapid decisions and good communications. For some firms, especially older firms in more traditional industries, strategic control tends to be diffuse and unfocussed. In consequence, such firms are slow to adapt and are very bureaucratic. Many European and US firms in particular have turned strategic control into tactical control which allows headquarters to understand the market and the competition, but it severely inhibits initiative and decision making. This is a special problem for the firm operating in several markets where central management attempts to impose direction on all details of the firm's endeavours to compete. The result is bureaucratic control, inflexibility and a limitation on the firm's ability to compete.

Many more firms have recognized this torpor recently and have changed, and newer firms are being established with flexibility and strategic positions central to their thinking. Strategic strength in these firms also derives from a consensus within the firm regarding the firm's mission and strategy which is manifested as a strong corporate culture. The behaviour of Japanese firms is often cited as an example where there is infinite care in digesting market and manufacturing data to produce a consensus (Kotler, Fahey and Jatusripitak, 1985, Chapter 2).

These lessons have been learned by many firms in Europe and the United States and their fruits are beginning to be seen in the competitive behaviour of the smaller high-technology firms and the reorganized large electronics firms especially. Such a process results in a deep understanding across all organizational levels which makes close tactical control unnecessary. Firms operating in this culture become a strong competitive force.

**Exhibit 10.3   For marketing clout in consumer electronics, you must be big**

*Thomson can take on the Titans*

For the past two years, vicious price-cutting has pushed Zenith into the red; it lost $10 million last year. And Zenith's share of the US color-TV market has slipped from 20 percent in 1981 to an estimated 14.5 percent in 1987, behind a combined 23 percent for RCA and General Electric Co. All of the American companies have been steadily losing ground to imports.

To make matters worse, Zenith recently lost a 13-year law suit that charged Japanese manufacturers with dumping TV sets on the American market at prices below cost.

The bloodletting helped convince GE Chairman, John F. Welch Jr, that a consumer electronics company needs a sizeable presence around the world to make money these days. He agreed in July to sell 80 percent of GE's consumer elecronics lines, including the RCA brand, to Paris-based Thomson.

By selling Thomson 80 percent of its consumer electronics business, including the RCA brand acquired in late 1985, GE made Thomson a consumer electronics giant overnight, doubling its sales to $6.2 billion and catapulting it into the ranks of such industry leaders as the Netherlands' Philips and Japan's Matsushita.

Up to now, the US TV market has been dominated by the key American producers, RCA, Zenith, and GE, although Japanese rivals have been moving in fast. Meanwhile, Philips has waged the battle against Japanese competition in Europe and other world markets. Now, with Zenith Electronics Corporation remaining the only major US TV maker, Japanese consumer electronics companies must contend with two big European rivals, Thomson and Philips, in Europe and the US.

Gomez, a 48-year-old former paratrooper who has run Thomson since 1982, has set his sights on Japan's giants. If Thomson can develop and make more of its own products, Gomez says it will reap its reward in the 1990s, when high-resolution and digital televisions and stereos will replace today's models. "The industry is going through a shakeout that will not be over until the end of this decade", he says.

**Source:** *Business Week*, 10 August, 1987, pp. 6–14, and 17 August 1987, pp. 36–7.

---

Large bureaucratic firms which once dominated many markets are no longer protected. Three elements have changed the situation: the proliferation of small firms; increased competition; and rapidly changing technology. The low cost of entry to some markets and the declining advantages of scale give rise to the need for rapid responses, integrated decisions, and specialist managers in all areas of activity. The recent spate of hirings of marketing specialists by traditional engineering-focussed firms illustrates the point. The low cost of entry and the ability to produce small batches at low cost shows that for some industries size is not important. In such circumstances it becomes very difficult to differentiate products. The firm with the strongest position will be the one able to develop flexibility and from that a successful competitive strategy.

The question of rapidly changing technology is another matter. Rapid changes in technology have meant shorter life cycles and numerous product changes within the life cycle. For this reason firms which traditionally depended on patents now find the value of patenting is severely limited. Furthermore, many countries now produce their own patents, causing some overlap since inventions are frequently discovered simultaneously. There is also the difficulty of enforcing patent rights and in some markets there is an ideological objection to the payment for intangible benefits.

## Competing on quality

Successful international competitors are successful because they compete through quality focussed on the needs of customers. A customer orientation is an attitude fostered as corporate culture and not a series of discrete responses to customer enquiries or complaints. At the heart of competing on quality is a serious commitment to the production of quality products augmented with quality service, sometimes through a heavy brand-marketing programme. These firms are dedicated to ensuring long-term customer loyalty through products and brands. The degree to which an emphasis on quality results in competitive advantage is a function of how well the various activities within the firm and between the firm and its customers work together.

For many businesses success arises from a series of small steps rather than being dependent on a few very large developments. Both approaches to competing are found in practice. Some firms follow the route of strategic leaps, making a few major steps forward at critical points in the development of the product market. These leaps may take a number of forms: a product redesign; new product development; entering a new international market; an alliance or joint venture with another firm to compete internationally; a change in technology; or the acquisition of a supplier. At the opposite end of the continuum the firm could· develop itself through a series of relatively small steps with the same cumulative effect. This would mean a constant effort to strengthen the firm's competitive position through an incremental approach: improved products; better delivery; reduction of rejects; and better order processing.

Firms which grow through strategic leaps are highly visible because such developments require a great deal of money and many people at all levels of the organization. The champions of each major development are also exposed to a great deal of risk. In such firms the job of middle and lower managers is to implement decisions taken by the firm's leaders. In contrast, growth through incrementalism is rarely visible, requiring less funds but higher skill levels at lower management levels which takes longer to develop and accumulate.

Few firms choose such extreme positions as those outlined but, rather, choose positions along the continuum. Among international competitors, however, it is generally believed that German and Japanese firms seek incremental improvements within an existing technology, whereas US, and to a lesser extent UK firms, adopt approaches which are more strategic in nature.

**Table 10.3**  Incremental growth or strategic leaps

| Incremental growth | | Strategic leaps |
|---|---|---|
| Not very visible | | Highly visible |
| Lower risk | | Higher risk |
| Low financial requirements | | High financial requirements |
| Gradual process | Characteristics | Immediate, rapid |
| Implementation skills and initiative required at middle management level | | Vision and leadership required at senior management level |
| Improved products and services | | Product redesign |
| Better delivery | | New product development |
| Lower product rejects | Forms | New international markets |
| Better order processing | | Acquisitions and competitive alliances |
| Improve existing technologies | | New technologies |
| Germany and Japan | Country examples | United States and United Kingdom |
| Possibility of being left behind | Risks | New breakthroughs do not materialize when required |

The risk of the incremental approach is that the firm will be leapfrogged and left behind by a competitor who abandons its traditional technology, moves to a new lower-cost manufacturing location, or develops a new more successful market strategy. Conversely, the risk of the strategic leap approach is that the new anticipated breakthrough may not be available exactly when required. A response to this predicament is to adopt an incremental approach until a breakthrough comes. But firms following the different approaches are usually organizationally very different and firms which operate on the expectation of repeated breakthroughs cannot easily change. Firms which adopt the incremental approach, however, can eventually accommodate themselves to profound changes, i.e. the ability to progress through incremental change does not preclude a firm's ability to master a major change (Hayes and Wheelwright, 1984). These authors further suggest that developing the capablities to make regular incremental improvements may enhance a firm's ability to make occasional leaps.

## Competing through manufacturing

Manufacturing strategy for international competition at IBM may be seen on two dimensions. First, manufacturing strategy may be viewed in terms of the emphasis given to seven factors (Hayes and Wheelwright, 1984, pp. 406–7). IBM believes it must be the low-cost producer in each of its businesses if it is to be successful, where success is defined as being regarded by customers as having the best product quality, growing as fast or faster than the market it serves, and being profitable. Another of IBM's objectives is to reduce inventories through the adoption of just-in-time philosophy and the standardization of components. The firm also emphasizes product quality where this is measured as the total cost of quality including prevention, detection and appraisal. Automation is pursued because it is expected to contribute quality improvements.

To provide better linkages between manufacturing and other aspects of management, especially marketing, IBM installed an extra layer of line management to take responsibility for all plants that manufacture a particular product line. This is also one of the outcomes of a global view of the market where production managers take responsibility for a product line serving a number of different markets. IBM also developed integrated systems which provide information to all its managers linked directly to strategic business variables. Finally, evaluation by the market of manufacturing performance through the provision of desired products for separate customer groups is a company objective.

Three themes support IBM's strategy (Hayes and Wheelwright, 1984, pp. 407–8). The first is an emphasis on activities that facilitate, encourage and reward the effective interface between manufacturing and marketing as well as between manufacturing and design. Second, IBM expects product technology and process technology to interact to exploit state-of-the-art products and processes in meeting customer needs in a competitive environment. Third, the firm focusses attention and resources on only those factors that are essential to the long-term success of a business.

A study of the three major computer manufacturers supplying the markets in the United Kingdom and Ireland reveals the strong competitive position of IBM on most factors analysed (Littler and Wilson, 1988). These researchers were interested in comparing IBM to DEC and ICL on a range of manufacturing and marketing variables to determine the perception of competitiveness of the three firms among the twenty-four buyers surveyed (Table 10.4). Although the sample is small and the research is preliminary the findings show how IBM competes on the key dimensions discussed above and how these are manifested in competitive markets.

## Competing through flexibility

In some businesses, particularly those with a high fashion content such as apparel, there is a very clear trade off between lower labour costs which can be obtained in some Far East countries and the need for faster turnarounds and deliveries to respond to the changing whims of fashion. For many years clothing makers in the United States and the Federal Republic of Germany, in particular, relied on cheap manufacturing in Asia. The time lag, three to six months between order and delivery, has forced these firms to bring production back to the domestic base. Indeed, there is evidence of some companies from traditionally low-wage countries in Asia, particularly Taiwan and South Korea, moving their production to the United States and Europe to avoid rising costs and quotas and to get closer to their customers to avoid obsolescence.

Until recently US and European apparel companies were locating abroad

**Table 10.4**  Perceptions of competitiveness among computer buyers and users

| Evaluative criteria | Poor . . . . . . . . . . . . . . . . . . . . . . Excellent |
|---|---|
| | 0  1  2  4  5  6  7  8  9  10 |
| Breadth of product line | |
| Strength of R+D | |
| Product reliability | |
| Delivery time | |
| | |
| Value for money | |
| After sales support | |
| Marketing professionalism | |
| Addresses customer needs | |
| | |
| Management professionalism | |
| Product design | |
| Ease of product integration | |
| Availability of software | |
| | |
| General competitiveness | |
| Product user-friendliness | |
| State of the art products | |
| General reputation | |

Source: Adapted from Littler, Dale and Wilson, Dominic (1988) 'Strategic management in nascent product markets: A suggested perspective,' paper presented at the *British Academy of Management Annual Meeting*, University of Cardiff Institute of Science and Technology, 7–9 September

since they could afford to make incorrect predictions about the market and still win because labour in the Far East was very cheap and customers were less demanding. Now labour costs in the East are rising and computer aided design systems can lay out patterns with minimal waste which are directly sent to automated cutting machines. Consumers have become more demanding regarding fashion and many retailers have found that they must discount heavily to move older merchandise. In the United States, discounts which absorb at least 10 per cent of net sales are frequently inevitable on clothing which must be ordered in bulk and far in advance because it comes from abroad (*Business Week*, 7 November, 1988). Items made closer to the market in smaller lots for faster delivery allow quicker reaction to fashion and reduce the effect of the markdown (Table 10.5).

## Innovating to compete internationally

Even successful innovators occasionally feel it is necessary to cut costs. In 1985 when he took over the chief executive position at 3M in the United States, Jake Jacobson announced a 35 per cent cut in labour and manufacturing costs to be accomplished by 1990. But competing by cost cutting alone is not enough. The

**Table 10.5** Changing competitive conditions in the apparel industry: payoff from US production

| Costs and margins | Domestically produced $100 dress ($) | Imported $100 dress ($) |
| --- | --- | --- |
| Material | 22.5 | 16.0 |
| Labour | 15.0 | 6.0 |
| Overhead and manufacturer profit | 12.5 | 4.0 |
| Duty, shipping, quota charge, brokerage | 0.0 | 14.0 |
| Retail costs | 34.5 | 44.5 |
| Retail profit margin | 15.5 | 15.5 |
| Total | 100.0 | 100.0 |

Source: Derived from data in *Business Week*, 7 November, 1988, p. 25.

company also required that a quarter of the sales of its many divisions be derived from products introduced in the preceding five years. Company bonuses were related to this 25 per cent yardstick. To encourage the development of new ideas and new products 3M encourages anyone in the firm to spend up to 15 per cent of the work time on anything desired so long as it is product related. To succeed in a very competitive business 3M follows a few basic rules (*Business Week*, 10 April, 1989):

- Keep divisions small.
- Tolerate failure.
- Motivate the champion.
- Stay close to the customer.
- Share the wealth with other divisions in the company.
- Promote new projects.

All 3M divisions are relatively small. Division managers soon get to know everybody personally. When a division grows beyond a certain point it is split up.

The company believes in experimentation and risk taking since the chances of product success are thereby likely to be increased. Product champions recruit their own action team to develop and commercialize new product ideas. Researchers, marketing people and managers visit customers and routinely invite them to brainstorm product ideas. Technology developed and exploited in one division becomes the property of everybody working in the company. Seed money by way of grants is also provided. In these ways 3M is known and respected worldwide as a major competitor in the adhesives business.

## Organizational change for competition

Many successful firms reorganize themselves when changing their competitive stance on world markets. In recent years such reorganization for large firms has taken the form of shifting from rigid, centralized management structures towards smaller, independent business units. Such firms find that more bureaucratic structures are quite adequate for national and even regional markets but flexible organic structures are required for global competition.

In this respect, in 1988 Siemens launched the largest reorganization in its history, the first stage of which was to cut central operations, remove two management layers and reassign 9,000 staff at headquarters (*Business Week*, 20 February, 1989). The second stage is designed to divide Siemens' seven very large operating divisions into fifteen smaller, more flexible business units with separate decentralized sales and marketing staffs. In preparing the reorganization Siemens realized that it was overly dependent on its domestic and regional markets; only 50 per cent of overall sales come from outside of the Federal Republic of Germany and only 10 per cent from the United States. Siemens began to place greater emphasis on international competition, especially in the micro electronics sector, where, compared to its major competitors worldwide, it invested heavily to compete with the Japanese in micro chips and computer memories (Table 10.6).

In 1988 Siemens produced 3.5 million 1-megabyte chips and it was expected that by the end of 1989, only four months behind the Japanese, its 4-megabyte chip would be in full production thus making Siemens one of the leaders in Europe (*Business Week*, 20 February, 1989, p. 18). Siemens is stronger in some of its divisions than others, which enables it to be a world competitor. In the very competitive medical imaging business, Siemens is No. 1 in Europe, No. 2 in the United States after General Electric and No. 4 in Japan. The medical equipment business developed its flexibility long before the present reorganization. Cut-throat price competition, short product cycles and the necessity of targeting global markets to sustain high levels of R & D have for decades demanded a different corporate culture. Seventy five per cent of Siemens' medical products are less than five years old compared with 50 per cent for the company as a whole. Here is a good example of how a firm can successfully develop a competitive posture by studying one of its own divisions and transfer the lessons to other parts of the organization.

**Table 10.6**  R & D expenditures and profit margins among selected global competitors

| Company | R & D expenditure (% of sales) | Profit margin (% of sales) |
|---|---|---|
| AT&T | 7.2 | 6.5 |
| CGE | 8.3 | 3.0 |
| Fujitsu | 9.2 | 2.2 |
| GE | 10.0 | 8.6 |
| IBM | 10.0 | 9.8 |
| NEC | 7.8 | 1.0 |
| Siemens | 10.4 | 2.4 |

Source: Derived from data in *Business Week*, 20 February, 1989, p. 18.

# Summary

This chapter is divided into four parts. In the first part the meaning of competition was discussed from the point of view of the firm attempting to compete in international markets. We noted that success depends on good analysis of the competitive environment and a recognition that firms adapt positions in order to compete. It is important that the firm acknowledges that a hierarchy exists in the levels at which competition takes place. Some firms deliberately select positions in the hierarchy in order to compete while ignoring others. Competition brings with it certain key benefits for the firm in terms of developing the market and industry structure and allowing the firm to improve its own competitive advantage by focussing on strong and weak points. Many factors contribute to competitiveness in firms; costs, prices, but also the other elements of the marketing programme including product quality, delivery, and reputation. A number of ways of measuring competitiveness for the firm in international markets were identified and discussed.

The next two sections were devoted to examining how the firm can understand its competitors. Various criteria were identified including size, competitor objectives, strategies, organization, cost structure, and general capability. In examining potential competitors it is important to understand motives for product-market expansion, motives among competitors for integration with suppliers, and customers and their ability to compete.

The final section deals with the need to establish strategic controls for competition in international markets. This means deciding on ways of competing in a structured and controlled fashion in such areas as quality, manufacturing, flexible systems, innovation and organization. Examples of successful international firms are recounted to illustrate the key points.

# Discussion questions

1. What are the principal influences on a firm's competitive position? Do they differ between domestic and international markets?

2. Identify the factors which must be examined in detail in order to give the firm an understanding of the structure of the industry in which it operates. Explain why each factor identified merits attention.

3. Sometimes the presence of competitors in the market can have favourable consequences for the international firm. Discuss.

4. Discuss how you would evaluate competitiveness in a market. Distinguish between price competitiveness and cost competitiveness. What other variables are used to compete?

5. In order to thoroughly understand competitors in international markets, the firm must understand current and future strategies of existing competitors

and also their strengths and weaknesses. The firm must also examine potential competitors. Outline an approach to such an analysis.

## References

Aaker, David A. (1988) *Strategic Market Management*, 2nd edn, John Wiley & Sons, NY.

Buzzell, R.D., Gale, B.T. and Sultan, R.G.M. (1975) 'Market share: A key to profitability,' *Harvard Business Review*, January–February, pp. 97–106.

Day, George S. (1984) *Strategic Market Planning*, West Publishing Company, St Paul, Minn.

Day, George S., and Wensley, Robin (1988) 'Assessing advantage: A framework for diagnosing competitive superiority,' *Journal of Marketing*, **52**, 1–20.

Ghemawat, P. (1986) 'Sustainable advantage,' *Harvard Business Review*, **5**, 53–8.

Hayes, Robert H. and Wheelwright, Steven C. (1984) *Restoring Our Competitive Edge*, John Wiley & Sons.

Henderson, Bruce D. (1983) 'The anatomy of competition,' *Journal of Marketing*, **47**, 7–11.

Kotler, Philip, Fahey, Liam, Jatusripitak, S. (1985) *The New Competition*, Prentice Hall, Inc., Englewood Cliffs, NJ.

Littler, Dale and Wilson, Dominic (1988) 'Strategic management in nascent product markets: A suggested perspective,' A paper presented at the *British Academy of Management Annual Meeting*, University of Cardiff Institute of Science and Technology, 7–9 September.

Piercy, Nigel (1982) *Export Strategy: Markets and Competition*, George Allen and Unwin, London.

Porter, Michael E. (1980) *Competitive Strategy*, The Free Press, NY.

Porter, Michael E. (1985) *Competitive Advantage*, The Free Press, NY.

Rothschild, William E. (1979) 'Competitor analysis: The missing link in strategy,' *Management Review*, **68**, (7), 42–54.

Scherer, F.M. (1980) *Industry Market Structure and Economic Performance*, Rand McNally, Chicago, p. 4.

# *How the firm enters international markets*

# *Entering international markets*

## 11

In this chapter the concept of market entry as it applies to international markets is examined. The various means of market entry are related to the firm's choice of market strategy. The relationship between market strategy, complexity of international markets and market entry is considered in some detail. A series of approaches to market entry is discussed and an attempt is made to integrate them into a form which enables the firm to make an optimum choice of entry strategy.

## International market entry and competition

One of the most significant developments in business practice in recent years has been the rapid growth of international activities. Exports, foreign direct investment and sourcing of products and components abroad have expanded dramatically.

In earlier chapters we have examined broad responses by firms to opportunities and threats arising in the international market. Sometimes individual firms respond in a very different manner especially when they experience a sharp shock. In such circumstances, firms usually respond on a number of dimensions, i.e. they use a number of elements in their strategy when responding to a change in the environment or changes among competitors. A few years ago Japanese firms responded to the strengthening Yen by cutting costs, diversifying product lines, and by increasing overseas production (Exhibit 11.1). In such circumstances Japanese firms are known to enter new international markets to source components more competitively and to enter new product markets not adversely affected by the movement in the exchange rates.

### *Concept of market entry*

The concept of market entry relates to the ease or difficulty with which a firm can become a member of a group of competing firms by producing a close substitute for the products they are offering. The firm must develop a set of products, assets and management activities for new markets entered (Yip, 1982). Concern here rests with new international markets. Successful entry depends on a number of factors. It depends on how the firm:

(a) uses information about opportunities for profitable market entry;

---

## Exhibit 11.1   Movement in exchange rates can upset market entry

*How Japanese MNEs are responding to the strong yen*

In addition to putting the screws on spending, many of Japan's leading firms have closed production facilities, laid off and/or shifted personnel, and slashed salaries and overtime pay.

Squeezing suppliers is another method used by firms trying to prune costs, hold prices down, and protect market share. In one instance, a foreign manufacturer was politely advised by its large Japanese customer to cut the price of a particular component 25 percent if it wanted to keep the business; since the customer accounted for 75 percent of the product's sales, the foreign firm had little choice but to comply. From the Japanese perspective, controlling payments to suppliers is crucial when components account for a sizeable portion of overall costs; in Nissan's case, the figure is 60–70 percent.

The strong yen has made foreign sourcing of raw materials more attractive. Nissan plans to buy 1,500 tons of foundry coke a month, a third of its total needs, from Koppers of Pittsburgh (locally produced coke now costs 20–30 percent more than imports).

Some Japanese MNCs are even importing finished products from overseas subsidiaries. Mazda Motor will ship Ford cars from its Michigan plant in 1988, while Honda is expected to bring in motor cycles from its Italian subsidiary. And Hitachi will start producing software in the US for use in Japan.

Many MNCs are shifting into more competitive businesses and stepping up production of high-value-added, technologically sophisticated goods. Popular targets include information and communications, new materials, fine chemicals, and biotechnology.

Another strategy to remain competitive is to boost overseas output, particularly of lower-end products. According to the Ministry of Finance, overseas direct investment soared 32 percent in 1986 to US$58.1 billion.

In the electronics industry, overseas production already accounts for 10 percent of output. Matsushita Electric Industrial Co plans to hike the value of output abroad from US$2.43 billion in 1986 to US$3.08 billion in 1987. Hitachi has doubled the projected value of annual production of large magnetic disk drives at its new Oklahoma plant from US$25 million to US$50 million. And in 1987 JVC will produce 25% of its output overseas, vs 19 percent in 1986.

**Source:** *Business Asia*, 29 June, 1987, pp. 202–3.

(b) accesses productive resources;
(c) accesses markets; and
(d) overcomes market entry barriers.

Established firms usually perform better than new firms on all four of the above factors. Entry might take place in a number of instances, as follows:

1. The entrant's competitive advantage on cost, selling strategy or product appeal enables the firm to deal a fatal blow to a weak member of the established group of firms.
2. The entrant can obtain sizeable amounts of business from several members of the group, for similar reasons of competitive advantages which rivals cannot match.
3. The group, enlarged by this new entrant, is able to arrive at a new equilibrium at a higher price level, covering the higher unit costs that might come from the reduced scale of operations from each firm.

Or

4. The established outside firm chooses to enter this market as part of a strategy of interfirm relationships involving markets for other products.

Established firms are in almost all respects superior to new firms in their ability to overcome barriers to resources and markets, and to attain scale economies of operation. "Entry is one of the supreme tests of competitive ability. No longer is the company proving itself on familiar ground, instead it has to expose its competences in a new area." (Yip, 1982, p. 85)

## Generic market strategies for international competition

The competitive strategy that an organization pursues depends upon a series of variables over which management may or may not have control. As was seen in Chapter 4 the firm may develop a number of possible marketing strategies. The firm in international markets, however, faces two generic market strategies (Ayal and Zif, 1979): a market penetration strategy, i.e. concentrating in a few select markets; or a market skimming strategy, i.e. spreading over a large number of markets (Figure 11.1).

The objective of a market skimming strategy is to obtain a high rate of return while maintaining a low level of resource commitment. The firm following this strategy selects the more easily available market targets while minimizing risk and investment. As will be shown below, the method of market entry will frequently be some form of exporting or licensing. The success of the strategy depends very much on the choice of agents, distributors or licensees. The responsibility for marketing and distribution falls to the partner abroad. Product modification is unlikely to be more than that required to meet standards and general market preferences. The firm will attempt to charge high prices to produce high margins.

| Countries as markets | Market segments within countries | |
| --- | --- | --- |
| | Segment penetration | Segment skimming |
| Market penetration | | |
| Market skimming | | |

**Figure 11.1** Market expansion strategies: countries and segments (Source: Based on: Ayal, Igal and Zif, Jehiel (1979) 'Market expansion strategies in multinational marketing,' *Journal of Marketing*, **43**, 84–94)

Market penetration or concentration has been described as the purposeful selection of relatively few markets for more intensive development. Such a strategy will be characterized by a slow and gradual rate of growth in the number of markets served. Its advantages, by no means universal to all industries, include: specialization; scale economies; and growth by penetration (Piercy, 1982; Hirsch and Lev, 1973).

A market penetration strategy is based on a longer-term view of opportunities in international markets. In this case the firm supports its entry to the market with a heavy commitment of resources in pursuit of longer-term profitability through market penetration. For some firms this may mean direct investment in local manufacturing facilities or local acquisition of an operating firm. Longer-term marketing relationships are established to ensure that the firm's products and reputation are well known and accepted. Strong contacts with customers, suppliers, distribution outlets and the government are cultivated. Prices are determined with an objective of sales growth. Short-term profits may be sacrificed. The firm adapts its products and services to the precise needs of each international market. A market penetration strategy recognizes that there may be direct competition with local firms and other international firms.

Market skimming or spreading involves the management of the firm's marketing resources in such a way that a relatively equal spread across many markets is achieved. The relative advantages of such an approach include flexibility, a reduced concentration and a way to capitalize rapidly upon some significant competitive advantage. Of course, the firm may pursue a mixed strategy in which it follows neither a pure concentration nor a pure spreading strategy but, instead, sells to a large number of markets while concentrating its resources upon a selection of these. It is easy to see how such a situation could arise as firms often receive what is referred to as opportunistic business, outside the geographic markets in which they are concentrating.

Neither market penetration nor market skimming is a universal remedy to the expansion problems facing the firm. Each strategy has its own strengths and weaknesses which requires the decision maker to find a match between the firm's situation and a possible strategy. Market penetration usually means selling to a small group of markets. Market skimming, on the other hand, involves selling to a large number of markets without concentrating the bulk of efforts on a small number of countries (Piercy, 1982). The optimal number of markets to concentrate upon for a UK firm new to international markets is said to be five to six, while for a developed export international business it is up to twelve countries (Cannon, 1980).

In the longer-term a strategy of diversification will frequently lead to a reduction in the number of markets according to Ayal and Zif (1979). This is a result of consolidation and abandonment of less profitable markets. The different patterns of market expansion are likely to cause the development of different competitive candidates in different markets over time. There will also be different levels of marketing effort and different marketing programmes in each market. With limited budgets and managerial resources, the level of resources allocated to each market under a strategy of diversification will be lower than with concentration.

But a strategy of market expansion is characterized not only by the date of entry into new national markets but also by market segments within national markets and the allocation of effort to different market segments. The modality used to enter international markets can affect the choice of strategy. A small firm, for example, may skim a number of markets through the use of sales agents.

For small firms, agents are an essential ingredient of market access in attempting to expand rapidly into a number of markets in quick succession or simultaneously. The extensive use of agents involves a strategy of market skimming because less resources are devoted to the venture. On the other hand a sales subsidiary implies a market penetration strategy because more resources are devoted to the project.

## Market strategy and competitive strategy

The two strategies of concentration or market spreading should lead to the selection of different levels of marketing effort and different marketing programmes in each market (Ayal and Zif, 1979). Firms have reasonably fixed financial and managerial resources and thus the level of resources allocated to each market in a strategy of market spreading should be lower than under a strategy of concentrating in fewer markets. Specifically, a lower level of marketing effort implies less promotional expenditures, more dependence on agents and a stronger tendency for a skimming approach to pricing. On the other hand, it is argued, concentration involves substantial investment in market share and heavy penetration pricing.

That the competitive strategy should vary at all is rejected by Piercy (1982), who takes the view that price or non-price competition may be combined successfully with market concentration or market spreading. However, it varies according to the situation for each firm, its objectives, its strategic capability and the market characteristics.

The strategic choices facing the firm involve different combinations of country, segment and price decisions (Figure 11.2). A country and segment penetration strategy means concentrating on specific market segments or niches in a few countries and on a gradual increase in the number of markets served. Competition on the basis of non-price factors tends to be very prevalent due to the need to specialize to serve the needs of the segments.

A country penetration and segment skimming strategy means concentrating on markets but spreading the firm's product appeal across a number of different segments. One would still expect competition on non-price factors but the firm seeks a price advantage by capitalizing upon economies of scale in promotion.

A country skimming and segment penetration strategy means concentrating on segments or niches while spreading across many country markets. Firms following such a strategy would be expected to seek a price or cost advantage by economies in promotion or production. Non-price factors, however, would still play a significant role due to the segment specialization. Finally, a country and segment skimming strategy is based on a dual spreading in both segments and markets. This aggressive strategy is sometimes followed by firms with a product line appealing to many segments. Price factors play an important role in the competitive strategy as the firm seeks a fast entry into the market. This strategy may also be applied by smaller organizations by the engagement of commission agents or by a superficial coverage of the markets.

## Linking market strategy, complexity, and entry

One of the hallmarks of successful market entry is the ability to be flexible. Because of the complexity of international markets it may be necessary for the firm to shape its entry strategy to accommodate the specific needs of the marketplace. By complexity is meant the difficulties which arise in dealing with customers, competition, intermediaries and governments. The added dimension of different cultural and competitive situations adds to the difficulty of interpreting signals from such an environment. This issue is referred to by Lawrence and Dyer (1983) as information complexity.

Processing of market signals from diverse situations can be quite difficult for the firm, especially small firms and those new to international markets. This flexibility is essential in adapting to a rapidly changing environment as found in international markets. The various options along the continuum of commitment from exporting through competitive alliances to foreign direct investment indicates the wide range of choice open to the firm seeking to enter international markets.

Two sets of circumstances may be identified related to this choice. There is the issue of market complexity which is discussed here. It is also necessary to combine the issue of market complexity with market strategy which was discussed above. Three possibilities are identified. In situations where market complexity is low the firm intent on market skimming might choose to export.

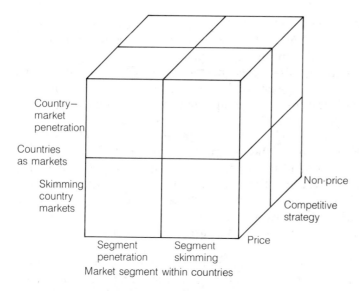

Country–
market
penetration

Countries
as markets

Skimming
country
markets

Non-price

Competitive
strategy

Segment
penetration

Segment
skimming

Price

Market segment within countries

**Figure 11.2**   Market, segment and competitive positioning

In situations of high market complexity it may be advisable to acquire a local firm or directly invest in the market in circumstances where a market penetration strategy is being followed. The firm may form a competitive alliance such as a joint venture or a marketing cooperation agreement with a partner in circumstances where market skimming is the strategy. Similarly, a competitive alliance such as licensing and franchising may be appropriate where market complexity is low and market penetration is the objective (Figure 11.3).

The degree of complexity existing in the market is likely to affect the choice of entry mode. A highly complex market might favour a direct investment mode whereas a situation of low marketing complexity might favour exporting as a means of entering international markets. Competitive alliances will fall somewhere

| Market strategy | | | |
|---|---|---|---|
| | Market skimming | Export | Competitive alliances |
| | Market penetration | Competitive alliances | Acquisition and direct investment |
| | | Low | High |
| | | Market complexity | |

**Figure 11.3**   Market strategy, complexity and entry

between the two extremes. The firm facing a relatively complex marketing environment may form a joint venture or other alliance with a partner firm abroad to reduce the complexity factor. In this regard many firms considering entry to the Chinese or Japanese markets seek local partners since the local culture is so strange to them that they need somebody with similar interests to mediate between themselves and local customers, employees, and government agencies.

A competitive alliance can, however, increase marketing complexity for the firm in certain circumstances. A major cause of failure in joint ventures is the inability on the part of one of the partners to understand the external environmental factors: cultural differences; government rules and regulations; the market; sources of supply; competition; and currency movements. Complexity may also be increased by a failure to understand the decision-making process. In many oriental countries firms place a heavy emphasis on a consensus decision-making process, whereas in the West the emphasis is on the outcome or decision itself.

One of the difficulties of using a competitive alliance to enter international markets arises when firms fail to agree on objectives regarding market strategy. In forming an alliance both partners should clearly and systematically communicate to each other their respective goals and expectations. Top management of the alliance must in turn communicate these to other members of the joint venture. Disagreements over basic objectives spread into disagreements over other issues, such as differences in opinion about dividend pay out policies, debt—equity ratio, marketing policies and quality control methods.

## Entering international markets — modal choice

Entry into foreign markets usually represents a diversification strategy which is expected to provide the firm with a source of profitable growth. Typically, the company going abroad for the first time or entering additional foreign markets does so with a low share of the market having selected rapidly growing markets. Such markets require strong cash flows to finance development. The firm contemplating an internationalization strategy faces two issues, as follows:

(a) which markets to enter: the market choice question; and
(b) how should the firm enter the markets chosen: the market entry question.

Entering new foreign markets may be achieved in a variety of ways, e.g. exporting and its various derivatives, competitive alliances in their various forms including marketing cooperation agreements, licences, franchising and joint ventures, and foreign direct investment and acquisition. Each of these ways of entering the foreign market places its own unique demands on the firm in terms of organizational and financial resources.

## Business development: new product markets

As was seen in Chapter 4, the choice of international strategy revolves around the position that the firm takes regarding the markets it enters and the products and technologies employed. The firm may choose to grow and develop by adapting its strategies to new international markets, developing or adapting products for such markets or a combination of such strategies. The requirements for success may be well known and understood or they may be unfamiliar to the firm. Newness of a technology, process or service embodied in the product to be sold abroad refers to the degree to which that technology, process or service has not been used already in the company's products. Some products require considerable adaptation and modification before they can be sold in most foreign markets.

Newness of a market refers to the degree to which the products of the firm have not been sold in a particular foreign market. It is very much a matter of business distance. The US market for cream liqueurs in 1978 was very new when Baileys Original Irish Cream was the first such cream liqueur to be launched there. Familiarity with the technology or process refers to the extent to which knowledge of the technology or process and its application in differing market circumstances exists within the company. This experience may not already have been incorporated in the firm's products. Familiarity with the market refers to the extent that the characteristics and mores of the market are understood within the company but not necessarily as a result of participating in the market. Here we are referring, for example, to the knowledge that the management of the R & A Bailey Company had of the workings of the US market before the Bailey brand was launched there.

In order to classify the opportunities available to the internationalizing firm it is necessary to draw up a framework. If the domestic market business is referred to as its present business, then competitive market factors associated with internationalization may be characterized as present, similar or distant in the sense of business distance. A similar classification can be applied to products and underlying technologies: present products, similar products and new products.

A checklist developed by Roberts and Berry (1985) helps to distinguish between familiar and unfamiliar technologies, processes, products and services which may be used here. A similar checklist helps to distinguish between familiar and unfamiliar markets (Table 11.1).

By applying the tests described above, it is possible to classify new international marketing opportunities in a 3 × 3 new business development matrix (Figure 11.4). Positions in this matrix may be further classified into those which are more or less demanding on the resources of the firm. In the bottom left-hand corner there is no extra pressure on the firm as this cell represents existing business, i.e. serving existing markets with existing products. As the firm moves away from this point in any direction the strategies become more demanding.

**Table 11.1**  Measuring product-market development constraints

**Technology and Product Experience**

Technological capability used within the firm, processes and components but not embodied in products    Decreasing experience

Main features of the new technology relate to existing corporate technological skills or knowledge

Technological capability exists within the firm but not in products or processes, e.g. at a central R & D unit

Technology has been systematically monitored from within the firm anticipating future use

Relevant and reliable advice is available from outside consultants

**Market experience**

Main features of new market relate to existing product markets    Decreasing experience

Firm participates in the market as a buyer

Market has been monitored systematically from within the firm anticipating future entry

Knowledge of the market exists within the firm without direct participation in the market, i.e. previous experience of credible staff

Relevant and reliable advice available from outside consultants

Source: Adapted from Roberts, Edward B. and Berry, Charles A. (1985) 'Entering new business: Selecting strategies for success,' *Sloan Management Review*, Spring, pp. 5–6.

The most demanding is to develop totally new products to serve distant markets.

The literature supports the view that familiarity of the firm with its products and the market being considered are the critical variables that explain much of the success or failure in approaches to internationalization. Related expansion strategies, i.e. strategies similar to those used in the domestic or existing markets, tend to perform better than other forms of international strategies which frequently result in lower returns for unrelated diversifications abroad and highest profitability for related strategies. Successful international companies typically do not attempt to exploit potentially attractive new opportunities which require skills that they do not possess.

## *Foreign market entry strategies*

A wide range of options are available to the firm wishing to enter foreign markets. In this section the principal means of entry are discussed briefly: exporting; competitive alliances; international direct investments; and acquisitions (Figure 11.5). They are discussed at length in later chapters.

By exporting to a foreign market the firm operates in a selling mode and exploits the internal marketing resources of the firm. Typically, exporting works

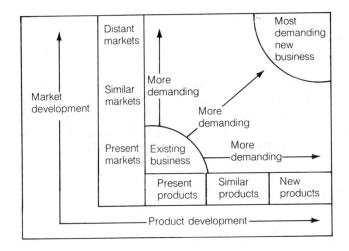

**Figure 11.4**  New business development: markets and products

where an equity participation in the foreign market is either not feasible nor desirable. Patient development of export markets can produce profits but rarely do firms obtain sustained high returns for impromptu effort for opportunistic business. Forcing established attitudes and procedures upon a new foreign exporting business may severely handicap it, which suggests that success may not come until the firm adapts either or both its products and marketing to the international marketplace.

There are various forms of competitive alliance which the firm might develop, the principal ones being licensing and joint ventures. Licensing avoids the risks of product and market development by exploiting the experience of firms who have already developed and marketed the product (Killing, 1980). It is seen as a low-risk, low-reward way of entering these markets that the firm is not really interested in developing or believes to be very complicated and risky. This option is frequently taken as a "better than nothing" strategy.

With very significant international marketing opportunities and expensive technology, the cost of failure becomes too large to be borne by one firm alone. In such circumstances, joint ventures become an increasingly attractive means of entering foreign markets (Killing, 1982). Synergistic new style joint ventures

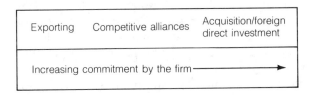

**Figure 11.5**  Generic foreign market entry strategies

in which large companies join small companies to create a new entry in the market are increasingly in evidence. The small company provides the products and technology while the large company provides access to the market (Hlavacek, Dovey and Biordo, 1977).

In some circumstances the firm will prefer to acquire an existing firm or to invest abroad. In such cases the firm may consider building a new plant and developing an entire manufacturing and marketing establishment abroad, referred to in the literature as foreign direct investment. Alternatively, the firm may choose to buy into a firm or acquire the entire assets of a foreign firm (Exhibit 11.2).

## Determining optimum entry strategies

Entry strategies which require high corporate involvement should be reserved for new businesses with similar market characteristics and product requirements. Entry mechanisms requiring low corporate input seem best for unfamiliar sectors (Roberts and Berry, 1985, 10). Large-scale entry decisions outside the sphere of the firm's familiarity are liable to miss important characteristics of the product market, thereby reducing the probability of success.

This suggests a two-stage approach when a firm desires to enter unfamiliar new foreign product markets. The first stage should be devoted to building corporate familiarity with the new area. Once that is done the firm can then decide whether to allocate more substantial resources to the opportunity and if appropriate, select a mechanism for developing the business. Active nurturing of a minority investment in a foreign company allows the firm to monitor new technologies and markets. Over time, active involvement with the new investment can help the firm to move into the not-so-demanding similar product-market positions of Figure 11.4 from which it may be easier to exercise judgement on the commitment of more substantial resources.

Acquisitions of small, high-technology, rapidly growing firms may provide a more transparent window on a new product or market which can assist the transition towards higher familiarity. Before the firm reaches this stage of maturity in international marketing it will normally consider strategies involving less commitment.

In dealing with market entry to existing and similar product markets, the firm is presumed to be fully equipped to undertake all aspects of new business development. The market entry framework used in this section is an adaptation of a much more comprehensive treatment developed by Roberts and Berry (1985). The firm has a number of choices available to it (Figure 11.6). First it may decide to develop existing product markets: the least demanding option. Usually this is done by improving the marketing programme to encourage a greater penetration of the existing markets served by the firm. The firm could choose to develop a range of similar products for sale in existing markets, an option which is slightly more demanding in terms of product development issues. This product development strategy is quite common among firms, especially those in large

**Exhibit 11.2   Acquisition for quick market entry**

*White goods empire: 400 villages crown Electrolux market king*

Pressure from operating in a small home market and within an industry plagued by low profitability forced Swedish-based Electrolux to design a far-reaching global strategy. The foundation of the firm's strategy rests on six pillars: acquisitions, automation, vertical integration, decentralising management, cutting headquarter costs and diversification. This approach has produced some handsome returns — 1985 sales reached $4.6 billion (an increase of 14.8 percent) and profits hit $366 million.

Since 1967, Electrolux has made 125 acquisitions and now counts 400 subs within its global empire. Its European market share is twice as large as its closest competitor. Electrolux specializes in acquiring financially troubled companies in order to get their assets at below-market value. "If you're going to get them cheap, they have to be doing badly", is a maxim for Electrolux Chairman Hans Werthen.

Faced with low profit margins in the white goods industry, Electrolux is a firm believer in plant automation to improve economies of scale. In the search for greater production efficiency, Electrolux is in the midst of forming an integrated global network of automated factories to produce components and products for member firms.

Electrolux plans to produce more standardised products to be sold on a regional and eventually a global basis, beginning with microwave ovens and then moving to washing machines, dishwashers and refrigerators.

While corporate strategy and financial decisions are made at group headquarters in Stockholm, day-to-day decisionmaking for Electrolux subs firmly rests with local management.

Electrolux believes the approach gives it flexibility to deal more successfully with local market conditions. Subs can also sell products under their own brand names. "We are not a city, but 400 villages", says Werthen. Decentralised management enables Electrolux to maintain a lean HQ staff — around 60 people, half of them accountants. There are no intervening levels between corporate staff and foreign subs.

Source: *Business International*, 11 August, 1986, pp. 250–2.

competitive markets. Alternatively the firm may decide to develop new markets close by which are similar in terms of business distance to those already served by the firm: an option slightly more demanding in terms of market development. The firm would normally enter such markets by exporting.

A more demanding strategy in developing the firm's business would be to develop a range of similar products for entry into similar international markets. In such circumstances a competitive alliance may be worth considering: licensing may be a useful alternative since it offers rapid access to proven products. A joint venture may also work since it gives access to a new market for a range of jointly manufactured products which may be similar to the firm's existing range.

A competitive alliance in the form of a joint venture may be an attractive proposition for the firm seeking to enter distant markets with an existing set of products. In this case the firm understands the product technology very well but seeks assistance in a distant market which would normally require a very different approach which could be supplied more readily by a local firm.

A competitive alliance in the form of a licence may be attractive for the firm seeking to develop new products for an existing market which has become more competitive (Figure 11.6). In such circumstances, joint ventures between large firms providing access to markets and small firms providing the technological capability may also be particularly appropriate (Hlavacek, Dovey and Biordo, 1977; *INC*, February 1984).

Finally, for the firm attempting to develop a range of similar products for distant markets, the entry method would favour acquisition or foreign direct investment. The same is true for the firm attempting to develop entirely new products for markets which are similar. The most demanding business development strategy also calls for a heavy commitment by the firm. Acquisition or direct investment seems appropriate for new products in distant markets (Figure 11.6).

From the preceding discussion it is clear that there is no unique combination of product-market situation and entry strategy. There are a number of circumstances where the firm must seek additional support before making a selection of entry strategy. In many situations it was shown that the firm might choose to export, license, joint venture, acquire or invest directly. There are circumstances where one or two of these options are likely to prove better than other choices.

In later chapters additional information is analysed and other constraints

| | Distant markets | Competitive alliance | Acquisition/ foreign direct investment | Acquisition/ foreign direct investment |
|---|---|---|---|---|
| Market development | Similar markets | Export | Competitive alliance | Acquisition/ foreign direct investment |
| | Existing markets | Develop existing product-markets | Develop new products | Competitive alliance |
| | | Existing products | Similar products | New products |

Product development ⟶

**Figure 11.6**  Market entry modes: product-market evolution (Source: Adapted from Roberts, Edward B. and Berry, Charles A. (1985) 'Entering new business: Selecting strategies for success,' *Sloan Management Review*, Spring, pp. 5–6)

are identified which reduces the effective choices available to the firm in specified circumstances. Firms usually respond on a number of dimensions such as costs, developing new products and developing new markets at the same time.

No one strategy is ideal for all new businesses. Within familiar markets virtually any strategy may be adopted and exporting or acquisition is probably most appropriate. In unfamiliar areas, however, these two high-involvement approaches are very risky and greater familiarity should be established before they are attempted. Small-scale investments and small selective acquisitions constitute ideal vehicles for building familiarity and are often the preferred entry strategies in unfamiliar situations.

## Sequencing of international market entry

Strategic sequencing of international market entry raises a different set of problems which must be considered. As a result of long-term objectives, market choices may be linked and embedded in each other. Thus a tactical market choice may be part of a larger strategic framework. Here it is important to examine combination strategies based on sequencing and concentration, sequencing and grouping, and sequencing as a long-run strategy.

A market sequencing strategy based upon concentration or diversification is widely discussed in the literature (Hirsch and Lev, 1973; Ayal and Zif, 1979; Sizer, 1983). These authors highlight the following two alternative penetration strategies for foreign markets:

1.  Enter a small number of the most promising markets initially; only after a "presence" is established in these markets and the potential of the product proved, are new and less lucrative markets entered.

Or

2.  Enter simultaneously as many potential markets as possible; initial wide penetration is followed by a period of consolidation where less profitable markets are abandoned.

These two approaches to market sequencing have implications for different elements of the marketing programme especially pricing.

Ayal and Zif (1979) discuss two market expansion strategies which are similar to those discussed above. The first strategy, market diversification, implies a fast penetration into a large number of markets and diffusion of efforts among them. The second strategy, market concentration, is based upon concentration of resources in a few markets and gradual expansion into new territories. These authors suggest that after a number of years, both strategies may result in the firm operating in the same number of markets. The alternative expansion routes may generate totally different consequences in terms of sales, market shares, and profits over time. A rapid rate of market expansion is usually accomplished by devoting limited resources and time to a careful study of each market prior to entry. With this approach the firm may make more mistakes and may be more likely to enter unprofitable markets.

These are two very different international market expansion strategies in which the focus is on the rate of entry into new markets and the allocation of marketing effort among markets. The strategy chosen usually depends on the nature and extent of the resources that the firm is able and willing to invest in the markets examined. It also depends on the relative attractiveness of the firm's domestic market, in particular its size and growth rate. The strategy of concentration involves dedicating available marketing resources to a small number of markets with the objective of winning a substantial share of these markets. The firm adopts a concentration strategy by focussing its attention on a particular country or on a particular segment within the country.

In contrast, the strategy of diversification allocates resources over a large number of markets and segments using one or more classification techniques. The key factors considered by the firm in choosing a target market are the growth rate of each market, the need for adaptation in the marketing programme and the possibility of distribution scale effects. A high growth rate combined with low distribution scale effects and extensive adaptations to the marketing programme would suggest a strategy of concentration.

An alternative approach is to develop a strategy based on sequencing and market groups. As illustrated earlier, the sequence of market entry may be dependent upon the firm's policy of grouping foreign markets. Hence, the sequence of entry might be as follows:

- clusters of countries selected on the basis of common criteria;
- select the most promising cluster of countries and then selects the most promising country from that cluster;
- in deciding to enter additional countries, the firm selects from the same cluster before moving on to others.

Market groups may also influence the entry sequence in other ways. Many firms find that they need more than one foreign market to provide sufficient volume of sales to justify the modifications to products and production methods involved, and to allow these to be made economically. The firm may, therefore, group markets with similar characteristics, and having adapted a product for a group of markets, all markets in that group may be entered simultaneously or at least rapidly in sequence depending on other characteristics. There are many examples of this approach, as may be observed in firms which manufacture products customized for linguistically homogeneous markets.

## Sequencing as generic strategy

It is now necessary to discuss sequencing as a generic long-run strategy. By utilizing a generic long-run market entry strategy a firm can plan its market entry in a systematic fashion, deriving tactical market choice from an overall strategy

(Ayal and Zif, 1978). These authors identify six possible market expansion strategies which reflect a military approach to markets (Figure 11.7).

The first strategy, based on "concentrated effort," is aimed at the firm's home markets with offensive objectives. With this strategy the firm expands rapidly in the more protected environment of its home market, moving down the experience curve until it competes effectively with international competitors. Many Japanese firms pursue this strategy prior to launching in US and European markets. With a population of 120 million people it is possible to do so in Japan. The relatively small size of the "home" market in many smaller countries, however, means that this strategy has limited applicability.

In the second situation, the "advance base strategy," also an offensive strategy, the firm uses concentrated efforts to gradually capture "neutral" markets, seeing the gradual expansion as one step in a larger offensive plan. One of the implications of the offensive approach is that the firm strives to enter markets that are not only lucrative in themselves, but also prepare it to expand effectively at a later stage. A European firm wishing to enter the US market eventually, for example, may enter the Canadian market first as a preparatory step.

The third strategy, the "Walled City," a defensive strategy, refers to the situation where the firm concentrates on home markets with a defensive intent. This strategy is frequently adopted by small firms whose market offerings have no major advantages over competitors, and where barriers to trade, tariffs and NTBs exist in the home market. When the desire or necessity to internationalize

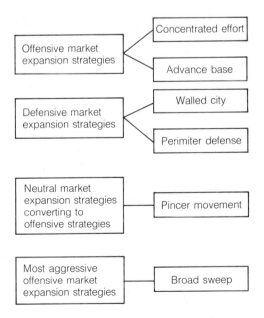

**Figure 11.7** International market expansion strategies (Source: Ayal, Igal and Zif, Jehiel (1978) 'Competitive market choice strategies in multinational marketing,' *Columbia Journal of World Business*, Fall, pp. 72–81)

eventually arises, the firm will be quite exposed and may be forced to enter less attractive markets where reduced competitive pressures apply.

The fourth strategy referred to as a "Perimeter Defense", is a concentrated effort to expand into a few "neutral" markets with defensive aims. Here the firm is recognized to be weaker relative to its competitors, and the markets chosen for expansion are likely to be those closest to the home market. In this case "close" means that there is little or no need for product or communication adaption and there is a high spillover of marketing efforts and goodwill from domestic markets. Often a firm may unknowingly utilize a "perimeter defense" strategy; for example, French firms which predominantly export to Belgium and other French speaking markets with no expressed strategic intent. Other examples would include the approach of UK firms to the market in Ireland or of German firms to the market in the Netherlands or Austria.

The "Pincer movement strategy" refers to the situation where the firm expands rapidly into many neutral markets, rather than capturing them one by one. A typical case of "pincer movement" was the Japanese strategy in the colour TV market. When Japanese manufacturers entered the colour TV market, American firms had a decided experience advantage, and were more advanced than the Japanese both in terms of production cost and product quality (Kotler, Fahey and Jatusripitak, 1985). Because the United States concentrated on the home market, the Japanese were able to adopt a "pincer movement" strategy, using their rapid expansion in the wide-open and neutral world markets to overtake the American firms along the experience curve. Once a cost advantage was achieved through rapid accumulation of production experience in neutral markets they entered the US market, beating their main competitors on their home ground.

Finally, the "Broad sweep strategy" is the most aggressive of all selection strategies discussed by Ayal and Zif (1978). This strategy involves a rapid offensive expansion into a large number of markets, including the opponents' home markets. Such a strategy may be undertaken where the firm itself is very strong, and faces relatively weak, fragmented opposition. Strong multinational enterprises marketing heavily branded products frequently follow such an aggressive strategy.

The Japanese practice of strategic sequencing of international market entry in terms of a "global market expansion path", as discussed by Kotler, Fahey and Jatusripitak (1985), is a good example of the strategic approach to market selection and sequencing discussed in this chapter. The first approach outlined below is a good example of the "pincer movement strategy." These authors describe how Japanese firms follow three global expansion paths (Figure 11.8).

The first approach outlined is the most common expansion path and is commonly found in industries such as steel, automobiles, petrochemicals, consumer electronics, home appliances, watches, and cameras. It involves the following steps:

1. Acquire US or European technology and build products for a relatively protected domestic market. The increased market share brings down manufacturing costs and creates a competitive advantage.

Expansion paths

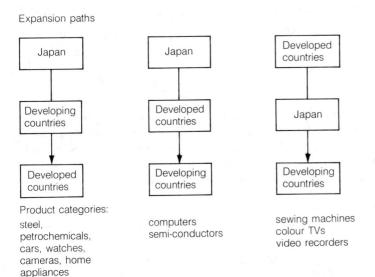

Product categories:

| | | |
|---|---|---|
| steel, | computers | sewing machines |
| petrochemicals, | semi-conductors | colour TVs |
| cars, watches, | | video recorders |
| cameras, home | | |
| appliances | | |

**Figure 11.8** Global expansion paths used by Japanese firms (Source: Kotler, P. Fahey, L. and Jatusripitak, S. (1985) *The New Competition*, Prentice-Hall, Englewood Cliffs, NJ)

2. As domestic markets become saturated, Japanese firms begin to look abroad. Developing countries are first targeted because they are presumed to be less competitive and may be used to build volume and sharpen marketing capabilities before moving into developed countries such as the United States.
3. With marketing experience and cost reductions gained from volume sold to the developing countries, as well as continuous improvements in product quality, Japanese firms begin to penetrate advanced countries such as the United States.

The US market attracted Japanese companies because of its size and high purchasing power. Once Japanese products had been accepted there, the reputation and experience gained made it easier to achieve acceptance in European countries and other western style markets.

The second form of expansion is found in high-technology industries such as computers and semi-conductors. After the Japanese had secured their home markets for these products, their next targets were developed countries such as the United States. Developing countries, on the other hand, had market demands that were too small or non-existent for these products. Later on, when demand in developing countries started to grow, the Japanese moved very rapidly to make strong inroads into these markets.

Although most internationalizing Japanese firms went through this expansion sequence, in some cases they developed products to sell initially in developed countries instead of the home market. These were products for which home-market demand was still not developed or was too small to serve. These products included video tape recorders, colour TVs and sewing machines.

## Summary

The chapter is divided into three sections. In the first section we examined the issue of international market entry from the point of the firm attempting to internationalize. The concept of entry to international markets was discussed in the context of how the firm uses information about opportunities in foreign markets, how it acquires resources, how it accesses the markets, and how it overcomes entry barriers.

Generic market entry strategy is the subject of the second section. Two generic market entry strategies may be used by the firm in international markets -- a market penetration strategy by which the firm concentrates in a select number of markets, and a market skimming strategy by which the firm enters a large number of markets simultaneously or in rapid succession. These strategic alternatives apply to country markets and to segments within each country market. The greater the range of choice the more complex the decision.

In the third section, the choice of entry method is discussed. Entering foreign markets may be achieved in a variety of ways: exporting and its various derivatives; competitive alliances, especially joint ventures, licensing, acquisitions and foreign direct investment. A framework based on market familiarity and product technology familiarity is used to help the firm to decide its optimum choice.

In the third section the important topic of sequencing is examined. The choice of one market may be linked to the choice of another. For this reason it may be important to examine a combination of entry methods involving a sequence of decisions over time for related markets. Two alternatives are discussed — the possibility of entering a small number of promising markets initially or simultaneously entering as many markets as possible. Sequencing may be seen as a generic long-run strategy for the firm in international markets. A range of possible options, as found in the literature, is discussed for their relevance to the firm.

## Discussion questions

1. Why does the international firm often have to combine different levels of market entry to reach world markets effectively?

2. It has been argued that technology is a major determinant of the mode of entry to international markets. Do you agree?

3. What are the strengths and weaknesses of each mode of market entry for a medium-size firm selling a patented sophisticated electronic component.

The firm at present is working close to full capacity and demand for the component is doubling every two years. An immediate decision is required.

4. Discuss the commonly held belief that there is no single market entry strategy which is appropriate in all circumstances.

5. Discuss the market entry decision framework based on market and product familiarity developed in the chapter.

# References

Ayal, Igal and Zif, Jehiel (1979) 'Market expansion strategies in multinational marketing,' *Journal of Marketing*, **43**, 84–94.

Ayal, Igal and Zif, Jehiel (1978) 'Competitive market choice strategies in multinational marketing,' *Columbia Journal of World Business*, Fall 1978, pp. 72–81.

Cannon, Tom (1980) 'Managing international and export marketing,' *European Journal of Marketing*, **14** (1), 34–49.

Hirsch, Seev and Lev, Baruch (1973) 'Foreign marketing strategies — a note,' *Management International Review*, **6/73**, 81–8.

Hlavacek, James D., Dovey, Brian H. and Biordo, John J. (1977) 'Tie small business technology to marketing power,' *Harvard Business Review*, January–February, pp. 106–16.

Killing, Peter, (1980) 'Technology acquisition: License agreement on joint venture" *Columbia Journal of World Business*, Fall, pp. 38–46.

Killing, J.P. (1982) 'How to make global joint ventures work,' *Harvard Business Review*, May–June, pp. 120–7.

Kotler, P., Fahey, L. and Jatusripitak, S. (1985) *The New Competition*, Prentice-Hall, Englewood Cliffs, NJ.

Lawrence, Paul R. and Dyer, Davis (1983) *Renewing American Industry*, The Free Press, NY.

Piercy, Nigel (1982) *Export Strategy: Markets and Competition*, George Allen and Unwin, London.

Roberts, Edward B. and Berry, Charles A. (1985) 'Entering new businesses: Selecting strategies for success," *Sloan Management Review*, Spring, pp. 3–17.

Sizer, John (1983) 'Export market analysis and price strategies,' *Management Accounting*, January, pp. 30–3.

Yip, George S. (1982) 'Gateways to entry,' *Harvard Business Review*, September–October, pp. 85–92.

# 12 *Exporting as strategy for international market entry*

Exporting is one of the quickest ways to enter a foreign market. For some firms it is also a very successful way of internationalizing. There are many firms, however, which attempt to enter foreign markets through exporting but fail. Failure in international markets can be costly in terms of managerial and financial resources and the opportunities forgone. For these reasons, exporting as an entry strategy must be approached with care.

Because of the impact on the balance of payments national policies in many countries focus on encouraging the export of products and services. Very often government-sponsored export promotion agencies encourage firms to export before they are ready for competition on international markets. Herein lies the potential for conflict between the macro economic policies of export-led growth at national level and the policies at the level of the firm in respect of company growth and development in a managed way.

In this chapter a number of topics related to exporting as an entry strategy are examined. In the following section the topic is examined in broad outline to identify the principal issues involved. The export decision process is then documented in detail, ending with a short section on the pre-export situation facing most firms as they prepare for export markets. The impact of firm size on exporting success is examined in the subsequent section and the chapter ends with an outline and discussion of the institutional framework provided for exporting.

## Determinants of export behaviour

The determinants of export behaviour are considered to emanate from three sets of influences on the firm: experience and uncertainty effects; behavioural and firm specific influences; and strategic influences. Before discussing each of these it is necessary to outline the meaning of exporting as a means of entering international markets.

## *Entering foreign markets through exporting*

Exporting is the simplest way of entering a foreign market. The level of risk and commitment is minimized since investment in terms of managerial and financial resources is relatively low. Exporting is often chosen as a means of entry when the following prevail:

1. The firm is small and lacks the resources required for foreign joint ventures or international direct investment.
2. Substantial commitment is inadvisable due to political risk, or uncertain or otherwise unattractive markets.
3. There is no political or economic pressure to manufacture abroad.

Generally, firms export for a number of reasons. Objectives frequently include those associated with geographic expansion, lowering unit costs because of increased volumes and the selling or disposing of surplus production abroad. Food products and commodities often fall into the last group.

Apart from the disposal objective firms which become involved in exporting must consider the question of product adaptation. This subject is treated at length in Chapters 15 and 16. The exporter will have to examine the production facilities to judge whether they are sufficient to meet increased demand and provide prompt delivery. Occasionally it may be necessary to alter designs, which raises issues of technical and design features of the product, packaging, legal requirements, approval and certification and the cost of any modifications required. Finally, the firm must be concerned with sales and technical literature which may have to be made available in a number of languages, in metric and or imperial measure, and aimed at the needs of local markets.

Market potential is a major determinant of the extent to which exporting is used as an effective mode of entry to foreign markets. Successful firms constantly monitor current and potential further demand in export markets. The firm's position, in regard to the suitability of its products against the competition and customer requirements, is also assessed. Here the firm will be concerned with product and service innovation and new product development.

A matter of increasing concern to exporters is the availability of distribution and sales outlets for their products in export markets. Finally, the firm must consider standards and regulations, factors which develop into non-tariff barriers, and the possibility of patent infringements. Consequently, the firm considering exporting as a means of entering foreign markets must prepare itself thoroughly if it is to succeed.

Exporting, as noted already, is part of a continuum of increasing commitment to internationalization. Being a very versatile mode of foreign market entry, firms frequently use it in conjunction with other entry modes (Figure 12.1). Exporting may be found at the initial stages of internationalization and again at the more committed stages where the firm, having taken an equity position in a foreign market, decides to export from there to other third markets.

## Experience and uncertainty effects

There are many schools of thought regarding the way in which the firm begins to internationalize its operations. Many approaches are related to learning and knowledge of markets and marketing. One of the earliest studies declares that the lack of knowledge with respect to foreign markets and operations is an

Exporting is related to other modes of internationalization

```
┌─────────────────┐        Intensity of exporting activity
│ Direct selling  │             High
└─────────────────┘              │
         │                       │
┌─────────────────┐              │
│ Export merchant │              │
└─────────────────┘              │
         │                       │
┌─────────────────┐              │
│  Agent abroad   │              │
└─────────────────┘              │
         │                       │
┌─────────────────┐              │
│ Collaborative   │              │
│ exporting/group │              │
│ export marketing│              │
└─────────────────┘              │
         │                       │
┌─────────────────┐              │
│ Marketing/sales │              │
│ subsidiary in   │              │
│ foreign market  │              │
└─────────────────┘              │
         │                       │
┌─────────────────┐              │
│ Franchising and │              │
│ licensing       │              │
└─────────────────┘              │
         │                       │
┌─────────────────┐              │
│ Joint ventures  │              │
└─────────────────┘              │
         │                       │
┌─────────────────┐              │
│ Manufacturing — │              │
│ international   │          Low
│ direct investment│
└─────────────────┘
```

**Figure 12.1**   Exporting is part of a continuum

important obstacle to the development of international operations and that the necessary knowledge can be acquired mainly through operating abroad (Johanson and Vahlne, 1977, p. 23). However, these authors state that

> By market knowledge we mean information about markets and operations in these markets, which is somehow stored and reasonably retrievable — in the minds of individuals, in computer memories, and in written reports. In our model we consider knowledge to be vested in the decision making system: we do not deal directly with the individual decision maker. (Johanson and Vahlne, 1977, p. 26)

Knowledge and learning in regard to exporting is possessed by the firm and accumulated by it over time so that some firms become established exporters while others with less knowledge of foreign markets have further to go in terms of learning.

The key role of experience in export decision making arises from observing that the firm's involvement in international markets is frequently a gradual process. This behaviour suggests a learning process as the firm adopts successively more complex export structures and as it enters markets of greater business distance over time. This pattern of behaviour has been observed not only for the export mode but also for the international direct investment activities of multinationals (Stopford and Wells, 1972). Indeed exporting may be seen as a stage before foreign production in the firm's internationalization.

One of the most frequently quoted studies of increasing export involvement is Johanson and Wiedersheim-Paul's (1974) study of the foreign operations of four large Swedish firms, Volvo, Atlas Copco, Sandvik and Facit. At the outset four different stages in the development of operations were distinguished in the study:

(a) no regular export;
(b) export via independent representatives or agents;
(c) sales subsidiaries; and
(d) production/manufacturing plants.

This stages model reflects successively larger managerial and financial resource commitments, as well as a more active involvement. The first stage means that the firm makes no resource commitment to the market, while the fourth stage implies a much larger resource commitment than the other three.

In examining the historical international development of the four firms, the study looked not only for evidence of a stages chain but also at the choice of foreign market. Two variables were considered important in this choice, size of market and business distance between the home and foreign markets. In general the study found that the stages chain accurately described the behaviour of the four firms. For instance fifty-six of the sixty-three sales subsidiaries established abroad by the firms were preceded by the use of agents. At the same time the exact pattern did not hold at all times. For Facit and Volvo, for instance, production facilities were found not to have been preceded by sales subsidiaries in some cases. Even here, however, market involvement, in the form of agents, had preceded the production subsidiaries.

In the choice of foreign market, two firms were more influenced by business distance than by market size: they began by exporting to psychologically closer markets. A third firm was more influenced by market size, while the fourth followed no pronounced course with respect to the two variables.

The study supports the hypothesis that a firm's involvement in individual foreign markets is a gradual process. To a lesser extent it supports the hypothesis that a firm's choice of foreign market is influenced by business distance. Similar results were found in other Swedish studies (Johanson and Vahlne, 1977).

The gradual process of involvement in individual markets abroad can be understood as a response by firms to the greater uncertainty and ignorance which is associated with international business: "Foreign operations are different from domestic and the difference is very much related to the problems of knowledge and the cost of information." (Carlson, 1975, p. 20) A firm beginning to export to a foreign market is not only likely to be ignorant of the market itself but is also likely to encounter what Carlson has termed "frontier problems," which include potential problems involving both official procedures related to selling in a foreign market, e.g. customs regulations and also foreign trade technicalities (Carlson, 1975, p. 7). The level of uncertainty and ignorance concerning these elements will tend to increase the greater the business distance between the markets.

## Acquiring knowledge of export markets

As a firm's knowledge of an export market increases, the uncertainty factor diminishes. The key type of knowledge required here, however, appears to be experiential knowledge, i.e. knowledge obtained through operating in the market or, "learning by doing." (Carlson, 1975, p. 8; Olson, 1975) It is this type of knowledge which, according to Johanson and Vahlne (1977, p. 28) gives a decision maker a feel for the market and which allows the identification of concrete opportunities, as distinct from theoretical opportunities which may be apparent from objective or codifiable knowledge. The nature of objective knowledge is such that it can normally be acquired by, or transferred between, individuals relatively easily, e.g. operating manuals, but the acquisition of experiental knowledge is, by definition, a more gradual process.

Carlson has argued that the acquisition of knowledge of foreign operations follows a learning curve: "At first this is a slow and difficult process. But as sales orders start to come in, the rate of accumulation of knowledge will increase, until at a certain point it reaches a peak. Later it will level off." (Carlson, 1975, p. 8)

This gradual acquisition of international experience suggests an explanation for the gradual involvement in foreign markets described above. Johanson and Vahlne (1977) developed the link between these two processes at a theoretical level: the level of involvement; and the nature of the involvement. They then linked these dimensions with the gradual acquisition of experience.

First, increases in the level of financial or resource commitment to the market are likely to be gradual. As uncertainty is gradually reduced through experience the firm may be more willing to increase the level of its commitment to the market. Uncertainty affects risk which affects the level of investment. A firm is therefore likely to be inhibited initially from committing large sums to a foreign market. As the firm acquires more market experience its inhibitions concerning investment expenditure are likely to weaken.

Second, the nature of a firm's involvement will be gradual in the sense that it is likely to be an extension of the firm's existing activities in the market. According to Johanson and Vahlne (1977, p. 29), decisions to commit resources to foreign operations are made in response to perceived problems and opportunities in the market: "the natural solutions to problems will be an extension of the operations in the market to complementing operations. [Such] market operations are searched for in the neighbourhood of the problem symptoms." (Johanson and Vahlne, 1977, p. 229)

The firm's response to ignorance and uncertainty in a foreign market appears to be one of limiting its involvement but to gradually increasing it as market experience is acquired. Despite the theoretical development of the area and notwithstanding the Swedish findings on evolving export structures, there have been few attempts to document both the nature of the process through which experience is acquired and also the way in which increasing experience actually influences specific export decisions. The precise dynamics of the learning process are extremely vague.

## Behavioural and firm specific influences

In general, traditional economic theories of trade have given way to more behaviourally oriented theories as explanations of export behaviour (Bilkey, 1978). Trade theories, while having a function at the national level of analysis, are inadequate at the individual firm level. More recent theories of exporting are strongly influenced by the behavioural theory of the firm which stresses decision-maker characteristics, organizational dynamics and constraints, and ignorance and uncertainty as key variables in decision making.

Exporting has been described as a developmental process based on a learning sequence involving stages (Bilkey and Tesar, 1977). Six learning stages are assumed by these authors (Table 12.1). Others have postulated multiple stages. The Bilkey and Tesar research is one of the few empirical attempts to take account of experience effects and other behavioural influences. Their conclusions are based on an empirical study of 423 Wisconsin manufacturers. The probability of the firm moving from a selected stage to the next stage depends on the firm's international orientation, its perception of the attractiveness of exporting and on management's confidence of competing successfully abroad (Bilkey, 1978). In this framework unsolicited export orders are critical to the firm becoming an experimental exporter. The movement between stages also depends on the quality and dynamism of

**Table 12.1**  Stages in internationalization

Stage 1:    Firm is not interested in exporting; ignores unsolicited business
Stage 2:    Firm supplies unsolicited business, does not examine feasibility of active exporting
Stage 3:    Firm actively examines the feasibility of exporting
Stage 4:    Firm exports on experimental basis to country of close business distance
Stage 5:    Firm becomes an experienced exporter to that country
Stage 6:    Firm explores feasibility of exporting to additional countries of greater business
            distance

Source: Adapted from Bilkey, Warren J. and Tesar, George (1977) 'The export behaviour of smaller Wisconsin manufacturing firms,'*Journal of International Business Studies*, **8** (2), 93–8.

management. For the experienced exporter at Stage 5 the proportion of output sold abroad depends on the firm's expectations with respect to the expected effect of the export operations on the profits and growth of the firm.

Despite the intuitive plausibility of the conclusions, the findings themselves are at best suggestive. The independent variables used in the regression analyses included: managerial expectations; quality and dynamism of management; firm size; perceived barriers to exporting; the existence of an export department in the firm. The authors explained the research approach as follows: "The analytical methodology involved treating each stage of the export development process as the dependent variable of a multiple regression equation. The same dependent variables were tested for each stage by means of step-wise multiple regression analysis, adding variables so long as they improved the (unbiased) coefficient of multiple correlation." (Bilkey and Tesar, 1977, p. 94) Besides the dubious nature of some of the results (export experience was, for example, inversely related to the measure of quality of management), there are clearly methodological limitations in attempting to determine the effects of export experience by measuring large sample responses at a point in time.

A number of more recent export behaviour studies have tended to be more focussed than the Bilkey and Tesar study. Many of these studies have, however, concentrated on the initial stage of the export process. They have been concerned with the question: what prompts firms to export in the first place?

Other studies, however, have suggested that direct stimuli, such as economic incentives and unsolicited orders, may be less important than internal behavioural influences. Cavusgil and Nevin (1981), for instance, concluded from a questionnaire study of a large sample of Wisconsin manufacturers that four groups of variables internal to the firm explain whether firms engage in exporting:

(a) managerial expectations about the effects of exporting on a firm's growth;
(b) the extent to which management systematically explores exporting possibilities and plans for exporting;
(c) the presence of differential firm advantages (including firm size); and
(d) the strength of managerial aspirations towards growth and market security.

These authors argue that it is management's predisposition to exporting which determines how a firm responds to export stimuli.

## Managerial influences on exporting behaviour

In a similar vein Simpson and Kujawa (1974) found that active exporters tended to have higher profit perceptions concerning the effects of exporting and lower risk and cost perceptions than non-exporters. Again, the implication is that any direct stimulus, i.e. economic benefit, to exploit an export opportunity is likely to draw a different response from firms depending on their perceptions of exporting effects. A key question is whether the higher profit perceptions arise from exporting experience itself or whether they stem from other factors as many factors are believed to be associated with export profitability (Bilkey, 1982).

To answer questions like this, a number of researchers have gone a stage further in attempting to identify the influences on managerial attitudes and perceptions. Cavusgil and Nevin (1981), for instance, classified the effects on the initial export decision of four groups of variables discussed above into (a) background influences — managerial aspirations and differential firm advantages, and (b) intervening influences — exporting expectations and export planning. The "background" firm advantage influences included size of firm and uniqueness of product. Czinkota and Johnston (1983) and Abdel-Malek (1978) examined the relationship between firm size and attitudes to exporting and perceived problems in exporting. Both concluded that size was not a significant influence using samples of small- to medium-sized firms. The results of other earlier studies on the effect of size on a firm's propensity to export have been mixed, however (Bilkey 1978, p. 36).

Background influences identified in other studies include personality factors, which are believed to affect the international orientation of small firms:

> A closed cognitive style reflected in the extent to which a manager is dogmatic about the international environment would seem to explain why potential exporters do not get started and are therefore not motivated to export. Because potential exporters are more dogmatic than their exporting counterparts they are less innovative and more reluctant to seek the assistance of outside change agents and more hesitant to request information. (Bradley, 1984, p. 253)

The studies considered so far suggest that there are a large number of variables which potentially influence the initial export decision. Some of these may be regarded as more immediate in the causal process than others.

It is important to know whether the various influences discussed above are active at later stages of the internationalization process. There is some evidence to suggest that the types of influences indicated are active at later stages. Bilkey and Tesar (1977) provide one possible answer: it is possible that the relative strength of the different influences changes as a firm becomes more experienced. It is possible, for example, that purely economic influences become relatively more important at the later stage when exporters are more experienced.

## Strategic influences on exporting

For many years there has been a debate in the literature concerning the degree to which a firm's international marketing activities can be standardized between countries (Levitt, 1983; Buzzell, 1968). Buzzell has argued against what he considers is an overemphasis on the need to adapt to individual markets. As support for his argument he points both to the success of certain multinationals having a high degree of standardization in their international strategies, e.g. Pepsi-Cola, and to the Italian household appliance industry. He also emphasizes the cost economies of standardization. At the same time he concedes that differences between markets may compel a firm to adapt. The market characteristics which he identifies as key influencing factors include stage of economic development, stage of product life cycle, marketing institutions and legal restrictions in the market. In a similar vein Keegan (1970, p. 40) concludes that the degree of product and advertising adaptation in international marketing depends on the following three factors:

(a) the product itself as defined by the function or need which it satisfies;
(b) the foreign market, defined by the conditions under which the product is used; and
(c) the costs of adaptation of these product-advertising approaches.

The point to note here is the emphasis on foreign market characteristics.

Whether firms are actually influenced by environmental factors in deciding on the degree of adaptation is another question. A study of firms in Ireland suggests that many Irish firms adapt only when legally required to do so (Egan, 1981). In a similar American study, Weinrauch and Rao (1974) found that over half of the exporters sampled adapted at least some elements of the marketing mix when selling abroad. Again, however, non-strategic reasons were behind many of these adaptations. Prices were increased because of the need to cover "additional export costs", or products were adapted because of legal requirements in the foreign markets. These studies suggest that environmental factors may not significantly influence export decisions in a strategic marketing sense.

Finally, in formulating an international marketing plan, as in choosing a foreign market or a foreign market entry mode, most writers suggest that firms should engage in a detailed market analysis as a necessary step (Thorelli and Becker, 1980; Root, 1982). Root, for instance, suggests that before committing itself to a foreign market a firm should carry out a competitive audit of that market.

The findings discussed earlier in which firms tend to choose psychologically close markets initially suggests, however, that exporters may encounter difficulties in accumulating and evaluating the type of information required for competitive audits. Instead of rationally choosing between competing markets in the somewhat formal manner suggested by Root, firms may instead be constrained to pick those markets with which they feel most comfortable.

The value of strategic thinking regarding the selection and development of export markets has been established. The export strategy that a firm develops has been shown to be closely linked to the export performance the firm achieves (Cooper and Kleinschmidt, 1985). In a survey of the managers of 142 Canadian firms these researchers found that a marketing orientation rather than a selling orientation was associated with a much stronger export growth and greater export intensity, i.e. export sales as a promotion of the company sales, among the firms. Similarly "a world versus a nearest neighbour orientation is tied to a somewhat stronger export growth ... and ... is associated with a somewhat higher export intensity." (Cooper and Kleinschmidt, 1985, p. 52) It appears, therefore, that a strategic approach to exporting is strongly related to a marketing orientation among managers of firms who also have a strong international marketing orientation.

## Export decision process

### *Preparing for export markets*

A firm's pre-export activities have been identified as an influence on the initial export decision. Wiedersheim-Paul, Olson and Welch (1978) suggest that a firm's domestic expansion pattern, i.e. whether the firm expanded inter-regionally or not, affects its likelihood of exporting. Firms which expand activities into regions outside their immediate region in the domestic market are more likely to export than firms which confine themselves to their home region.

It is suggested that inter-regional expansion forces firms to develop skills in coping with uncertainty and in "marketing a product at a distance" (Widersheim-Paul, Olson and Welch, 1978, p. 51). The acquisition of these skills is more likely to predispose a firm towards exporting. These pre-export activities are believed to have a pronounced influence on subsequent exporting behaviour. Searching, questioning, experimentation and information are fundamental influences on the initial export involvement (Welch, 1982). This author suggests that four groups of factors, pre-export activities, direct export stimuli, latent influences and the make-up of the decision maker influence the initial export involvement (Figure 12.2). A complex mix and interaction among these factors produces a certain level of commitment to exporting.

These include aspirations of management for goals such as growth, profits and market development. Aspiration levels are widely discussed in the theory of the firm literature as a determinant of risk-taking behaviour. The importance that the decision maker places on the achievement of the firm's business objectives is believed to be a direct determinant of decision-making behaviour. Empirical

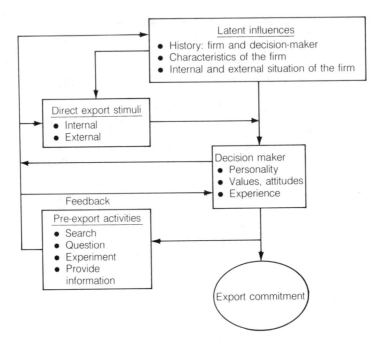

**Figure 12.2** Influence on initial export involvement (Source: Adapted from Welch, Lawrence (1982) 'Decision-making in the international context,' in *Proceedings of the Seminar on Management Decision-Making*, European Institute for Advanced Studies in Management, Oslo, June, p. 96)

studies support this expectation by revealing a positive relationship between export marketing behaviour and the decision maker's preference for certain business goals (Simmonds and Smith, 1968). Definite psychological motivational barriers to the internationalization process exist which may be attributed to the absence of appropriate managerial aspirations.

Much of the research emanating from the Uppsala School (Wiedersheim-Paul, Olson, Johanson, Vahlne) and the Wisconsin School (Bilkey, Cavusgil and Tesar) have focussed their attention on the beginning of the exporting process which they maintain begins essentially with the managerial motivation to export. Among the more frequently examined issues are the relationships between experience, motivation, growth, information, type of firm and exporting behaviour (Bradley, 1984).

## Learning to export

Many small- and medium-sized enterprises wishing to become internationally traded companies seem to exist at either the experimental exporter stage and/or the next stage, i.e. more experienced exporter. Thus it would appear that anything which lowers the perception of risk for the individual company and provides more favourable expectations of profit would be welcomed by these firms. Usually these relationships are treated as independent of one another and subsumed under the rubric of motivation, whereas there is good reason to believe that more complex interactions are involved. Some researchers have sought to demonstrate that a certain cognitive style or international orientation is a necessary prerequisite for the motivation to internationalize. In this context Bradley (1984) maintains that the emphasis in the recent literature on motivation alone is misplaced. In an attempt to address this issue he proposes a framework which integrates the various determinants of internationalization found in the literature (Figure 12.3).

Management expectations about the effects of exporting on the objectives of the firm reflect the decision maker's existing knowledge as well as his or her perceptions of future events. Managers tend to form expectations or opinions about the profitability and riskiness of export marketing on the basis of their own and other experiences. Environmental variables such as unsolicited orders from foreign buyers and fluctuations in exchange rates are also reflected in management's objective assessment of the desirability of exporting.

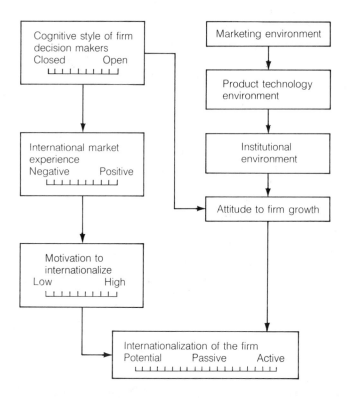

**Figure 12.3**   Determinant of internationalization in the firm (Source: Adapted from Bradley, M. Frank (1984) 'Effect of cognitive style and attitude toward growth and motivation on the internationalization of the firm,' in Jagdish Sheth (ed.), *Research in Marketing*, **7**, JAI Press, Greenwich, Conn., pp. 237–59)

Many firms rely on third parties to take the initiative in developing export markets, which tends to lead to low expectations and passive behaviour. The experience of international markets thus gained by the firm becomes an important determinant of international marketing behaviour. Presumably, successful experience has a positive effect on the internationalization process whereas a poor performance has a negative effect (Bradley, 1983).

During the "experimental involvement stage" favourable expectations of profits appear to be responsible in converting the experimental exporter into one that is more active (Cavusgil, 1984). In a study of UK firms Piercy (1981) examined approaches to export marketing including stages of internationalization reached and the attitude and commitment of management of export business.

Piercy distinguished between active exporters for whom exporting had an important, central growth role, and reactive exporters who sold overseas either to dispose of surplus capacity or as a response to unsolicited orders or external change agents such as regional industrial development boards. The study found that active exporters tended to be larger companies with a higher proportion of their business provided by exports compared to reactive exporters, i.e. smaller firms with a low export sales contribution.

A general willingness among decision makers to devote adequate resources to export-related activities appears to be critical because many tasks in carrying out the export marketing function are new to the firm and involve a commitment of financial and managerial resources (Cunningham and Spigel, 1971; Hunt, Froggatt, and Hovell, 1967). The commitment of marketing resources to the development of a long-term competitive position must be viewed essentially as a strategic investment decision.

The list of external determinants of export marketing behaviour found in the literature is almost endless. The focus of researchers in this area hinges mainly on which school of thought the researcher belongs to. Each school gives different weightings to the impact of external factors influencing the firm and therefore it will differ to some degree in how important external factors are in determining firm export behaviour. The most important according to O'Grady (1987) are government-sponsored export stimulation measures, industry structure and changes in production technologies, including discoveries and inventions. Technology in some instances cause changes in an industry and this can result in increasing demand abroad for small entrepreneurial companies and thus facilitate internationalization sooner rather than later (Abernathy, Clarke and Kantrow, 1983).

## *Size of firm and exporting activity*

Many authors have examined the effect of firm size on exporting behaviour. The literature contains many examples of research which shows that exporting is positively related to firm size, while other research shows that the evidence is inconclusive or that there is no relationship.

**Table 12.2**  Profile of exporting firms in the United States

| Category | Companies |
|---|---|
| | Number |
| Infrequent exporters (9 shipments a year on average) | 86,500 |
| Growing exporters (116 shipments a year on average) | 9,900 |
| Frequent exporters (4,410 shipments a year on average) | 3,600 |
| Total | 100,000 |

Source: *Business Week*, 27 February, 1989, p. 69.

In many countries export-led growth is expected to come from the small-firm sector. The conventional wisdom is that large-scale exporters are so active and have utilized all spare capacity so that little discretion for further export market expansion is left to them. The key issue then becomes one of determining the extent to which the smaller firms possess the critical mass, will, and commitment required to enter and compete successfully in export markets. Research on small exporting companies in many countries shows this sector to be highly unstable. Only a fraction of small exporters become established in export markets. Many treat international markets opportunistically and many are forced out due to competitive pressures (Table 12.2). Small firms face the danger of too much success and not enough success. As was seen in Chapter 3, they frequently overextend themselves. They also spread their managerial and financial resources too thinly across markets (Betro Report, 1975). Other small exporters remain in foreign markets without success and finally resign themselves to inevitable failure before withdrawing.

Advances in all forms of communication help the smaller firm. Improvements in telefax and international airfreight services permit smaller firms to internationalize much more easily than could happen in the past. "A lot of small and medium size companies are finding they can ship to Hong Kong almost as easily as they can to Colorado" stated Mark B. Stringfellow, president of the New Jersey based Environmental Control Group, an exporter of asbestos removal equipment, in an interview (*Business Week*, 27 January, 1989, p. 68).

In larger firms the idiosyncratic preferences of the chief executive have been found to be important in decisions on whether to invest abroad. A senior manager's interest or enthusiasm for exporting may be a key initiating factor.

Many factors appear to influence the decision to export and subsequent exporting activity. Size of firm may be an influencing factor in some circumstances but is not the only factor, nor even the dominant influence in some situations.

## Size of firm and nature of the market

Some authors have argued that it is size in conjunction with other factors which matters. Structural differences in the market due to product differentiation and/or competitive differences in conjunction with size have been reported as significant in explaining exporting behaviour (Auquier, 1980). Auquier seeks to test two distinct hypotheses, that:

> large firms are more efficient at exporting and hence export more of their output, i.e. there are internal differences among firms due to scale economies in production or exporting, and that exporting differences are due to factors external to the firm: structural differences in the market, i.e. product differentation or behavioural differences, i.e. competitive differences.

Differentiation determines the distribution of firm sizes: larger firms manufacture many models or product versions that enjoy widespread appeal or low costs, while small firms produce for niche markets which appeal to smaller proportions of buyers, e.g. speciality products or products which require higher-cost technologies. To support the first hypothesis Auquier states that the only thing which distinguishes large and small firms is "the level of their marginal production costs or the relative height of fixed costs including risk, associated with exporting" (Auquier, 1980, p. 204). To support the second hypothesis Auquier supposes that differentiation tends to reflect national cultural patterns: product versions popular in one country will be less popular elsewhere, although some buyers will prefer them. Under these circumstances smaller firms, if they export at all, will export proportionately more of their output than larger firms. This is also true if demand densities are similar among product versions while technologies or costs differ. Higher-cost firms will be smaller but serve larger areas of demand and hence export more. Auquier concludes that:

1. The proportion of manufacturing firms that export increases strongly with the size of firms within industries. This depends on economies of scale in production, interacting with spatial factors and fixed or variable distribution costs that are higher for international than for domestic transactions.
2. Size cum efficiency, economies of scale, is not the only explanation. The existence of a population of small firms that export shows that where scale economies exist they are not so great as to prevent exports from most firms in most industries.
3. Export participation differs by size of firm in ways that depend on seller concentration. Large firms face lower perceived elasticities of demand in the home market and are better equipped to profit from price discrimination between domestic and foreign markets.
4. The heavily exported versions of products are intrinsically different from those demanded at home. A wide range of small firms export because their product faces a lower demand and requires a widespread market to warrant production in the face of whatever scale economies exist.

## Export marketing groups

There are many reasons why firms come together to form export marketing groups (Bradley, 1985). Frequently, firms form groups to counteract a common external threat such as increased import competition, an entry by a new competitor or a new public policy. Group marketing schemes are frequently found among small-scale firms attempting to enter export markets for the first time. Many such firms do not achieve sufficient scale economies in manufacturing or marketing because of the size of the local market or the inadequacy of the management resources available. The characteristics are typical of traditional, mature, highly fragmented industries such as furniture, textiles, clothing and footwear. Frequently the same characteristics are to be found among recently established, small high-technology firms.

There are good behavioural reasons for collaboration among such firms. It is known that small and medium enterprises working together learn a great deal about international markets, and the experience obtained serves to confirm these firms as established exporters.

Small- and medium-size firms have, however, been accused of unwillingness to collaborate on marketing. Such accusations frequently centre on a belief that each possesses trade and other secrets which they are unwilling to share with others. While this may be the case in competitive situations there are other reasons for unwillingness to cooperate. Managers of smaller firms are frequently not highly motivated to export and are not generally internationally oriented (Bradley, 1984). Consequently, collaborative endeavours may need support from public policy in order to ensure that the benefits accrue to the small firms. Increasingly, small and medium enterprises become positively disposed towards export marketing groups when the benefits of such collaboration are apparent.

In some situations there may be historical or institutional reasons for collaboration. In older industries where integrated trading patterns have evolved within an industry structure, joint ventures in marketing are more common. Such joint ventures tend to be more frequently found in economies which industrialized in the last and earlier part of this century. In economies which have industrialized more recently and continue to industrialize, such historical reasons are rarely an important ingredient of joint exporting venture formation.

Of increasing importance in the formation of export marketing groups is the pervasive role of public policy in the management affairs of small firms. The increasing burden of dealing with the State Support System forces smaller firms to seek new ways of accommodating these demands. In most member countries of the EC there is a plethora of state agencies established with the objective of assisting small firms. Because of the multiple entry points into that system it has become very difficult for the management of the smaller firm to use the system effectively. Increased size through export marketing groups can alleviate part of this problem.

Other factors which influence the firm to join with others in an export marketing group are the opportunities of effectively marketing a complementary product line, the presence of a positive attitude toward collaboration, and the possibility of exploiting a new market opportunity (Figure 12.4). In forming groups firms try, as far as possible, to avoid competitive challenges arising within the group.

Finally, and perhaps the central issue to be discussed in forming export marketing groups, is the matter of common or shared interest among the participating firms. Firms usually have different motivations for joining with others. Sometimes they wish to participate in groups to promote their range of products abroad, or to attend trade fairs, or to sell to particularly difficult markets. Other firms seek more sophisticated participation whereby the product range of all the firms, e.g. a range of furniture, would be manufactured to an agreed design by the different members of the group and distributed using the same marketing programme in the same foreign markets. Frequently, firms have conflicting views as to what the group should do and the area of common interest is thereby reduced. The size of the circles in Figure 12.4 attempts to indicate the extent of desire for three firms to participate in an export marketing group. In this situation the area of common interest, where the circles overlap, is smaller, indicating a restricted scope for the formation of a group.

In general, export marketing groups tend to be successful in situations where firms are already marketing-oriented, financially strong and fully appreciate the benefits and limitations of the group structure (Bradley, 1985). Some of the problems associated with export marketing groups may be avoided through the use of federated marketing, a recent development of export marketing groups (Exhibit 12.1).

## Assessing export competitiveness

### Cost of exporting

Many firms new to exporting fail to realize that the cost of reaching the market can be formidable. Sometimes it is advisable for the firm which does not have adequate funds to seek new outlets in the domestic market rather than enter a foreign market.

Many costs arise in exporting. A number of these are difficult to quantify but are nevertheless important. These include the cost of product modification and any packaging or labelling changes which have to be made. The firm will also incur the cost of researching the foreign market. The cost of obtaining customer and competitor information can be substantial and must be considered.

For the firm new to exporting it is important to realize that it is investing in its development and growth. Cash will be required for the initial research, and for any visits to the market selected. These costs tend to rise as the firm becomes more committed to the export market. Other costs also increase. Extra raw material

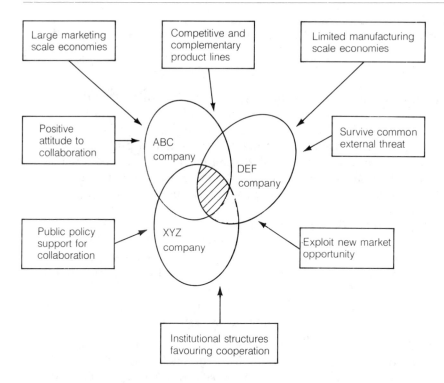

**Figure 12.4** Forming export marketing groups: collaborative pressures and areas of common interest (Source: adapted from: Bradley, M. Frank (1985) 'Market and internal organization in exporting for SMEs,' a paper presented to *Developing Markets for New Products and Services Through Joint Exporting By Innovative SMEs Seminar*, Commission of the European Communities, Luxembourg, 6–7 March)

for the increased demand will cost more money. Finally, the foreign customer may take a long time to pay. All these factors place a severe strain on the firm's cash flow. These are general considerations.

At a more specific level the firm must estimate the cost of sending a consignment of a product to a foreign buyer. First there are the costs of extra people, e.g. an export executive or manager. It would be necessary to add the cost of travel based on a number of visits to the market in a year. Second, one or two sales staff might be required to support the export manager. Third, it is necessary to allow for the cost of custom documentation, labels, samples and promotion. For some product groups these costs tend to be relatively high. Food marketing costs tend to be relatively high in foreign markets because of the cost of label changes, the costs of complying with health regulations and the costs of launching including promotion through in-store testings and promotions.

By far the more important costs are those associated with the services provided by intermediaries such as distributors, wholesalers and retailers and agencies such as transport and insurance companies. Some of these costs are borne

## Exhibit 12.1   Improve export marketing groups through federated marketing

### *The fruits of marketing togetherness*

Federated marketing involves a sales/marketing/service base in a distant market, which is owned in equal parts by a group of cooperating firms with complementary (but not competitive) products and services. What is new is the form this collaboration takes. First, the joint company is set up as an independent operation with profit-centre status. Second, one member of the federated marketing consortium will be a management firm, whose role is to balance the interests of the other stakeholders and adjudicate on contentious issues. This firm controls and carries out all management within the joint operation.

The fundamental difference between the simple consortium approach and federated marketing is the role of this coordinating body. Its contribution to the enterprise is critical. It can manage the team in circumstances where a participating company cannot, because the latter is concerned with its individual priorities and lacks the motivation to combine the efforts of the other partners.

The pioneers of federated marketing have established guidelines for the creation and operation of the system. The most important of these guidelines are:

1. Participants' products must be complementary upstream and downstream if total packages are being offered; and horizontally if a "full-line" range is to be made available (for example, in menswear: suits, overcoats, ties, socks and underwear).
2. Products or services must be compatible in quality and technology: low-technology equipment, for instance, is unlikely to fit comfortably in a range of high-technology products.
3. For horizontally linked products, customer firms and, ideally, individual buyers should be the same for all stakeholders.
4. Each participating member should have one nominee on the sales company board holding a single vote.
5. The coordinator's appointee makes the most effective chairman.

These guidelines are the sine qua non of successful federated marketing. In addition, members must agree, and build into their constitution, rules to regulate the function of the enterprise. Several questions are vital:

1. Are transactions with the sales company to be "arm's length" or at an accepted inter-company transfer price?
2. Is the sales office free to seek other supplies where members are unable to meet customer requirements?
3. Is the sales office free to handle (at a profit) third-party, non-competitive, but nevertheless linked or complementary products or services?
4. Will the sales company handle all sales in the territories, including those emanating from direct enquiries to an individual member?
5. How are profits to be distributed?
6. What criteria will be used to judge success?

The essential ingredient is compatibility of corporate culture and, even more important, of the chemistry of the individuals on the sales company board.

**Source:** *Management Today*, July, 1986, pp. 33–6.

by the exporter while others are absorbed by the intermediaries and covered by their margins. A recent study of the cost of exporting Australian wine to the United Kingdom illustrates many of these points (McDougall, 1989). McDougall estimates that the retail price of a case of Australian wine in the United Kingdom was $A180.41 while the price received by the winery was $A56, less than one-third of the retail price (Table 12.3). The single largest element in the cost of a case of wine in these circumstances was the retail margin.

The example of the cost of exporting wine to the United Kingdom illustrates quite well the cost components that the exporting firm must consider. The information is based on a cost plus approach to the market, i.e. the final retail price is estimated based on identifying each cost element and accumulating them to find an estimated price at retail.

**Table 12.3**  Estimated retail price in 1988 of a case of Australian wine in the United Kingdom

| Cost factors | % | $A | Remarks |
|---|---|---|---|
| Barossa Winery price | 31.0 | $56.00 | Assume selling price of $56 per case |
| Transport to Port Adelaide | | 0.35 | Cost $347 to ship a container from Barossa Valley to Port Adelaide. On average, a container will hold 1,000 cases |
| Port Adelaide to United Kingdom | 1.2 | 2.20 | Adelaide–UK is $2,200/container |
| Landed cost United Kingdom | 32.5 | 58.55 | |
| Import duties and excise tax | 12.1 | 21.90 | As of June 1988, import duties per litre of $0.20 and excise taxes of $2.2/litre or $21.87/case (assume $21.90) VAT |
| Landed with duties and taxes | 44.6 | 80.45 | |
| Value added tax is 15% | 6.7 | 12.07 | |
| Total landed cost | 51.3 | 92.52 | |
| Importer margin | 15.4 | 27.75 | An importer or distributor in the United Kingdom will charge between 25 and 40% margin (assumed 30%) |
| Wholesale price | 66.7 | 120.27 | |
| Retail margin | 33.3 | 60.14 | Retailer margins are approximately 50% |
| Retail price | 100.0 | 180.41 | Equivalent to $15.03/bottle (750ml) |

Notes: 1. The cost to ship a container from Port Adelaide to either the United States or Canada was about $2,500.
   2. Importers in the United States will probably take a 40% margin.
   3. In Canada, agents might be used at a commission of 10% of landed cost.

Source: McDougal, Gordon (1989) 'Barossa Winery: Penetrating the international market,' *International Marketing Review*, **6** (2), 18–33.

## Pricing in export markets

The cost plus approach should be complemented by examining the retail prices
in the market and working backwards. It is necessary, therefore, to examine the
market, the customer's needs and the effect these are likely to have on price.
The successful firm attempts to maintain flexibility and discretion in price
decisions; i.e. too much concentration on the cost side of the equation gives rise
to an extremely jaundiced view of the scope available. The market and the potential
in the market should be the starting point and costs should be used to determine
whether what is desired by the market can be produced at a profit.

One approach to this problem is to attempt to determine the effect of a market
opportunity on profits or on contribution by working backward from the
established or accepted range of market prices and simultaneously working
forward from the cost side. The gap that remains, if there is one, presents the
firm with an estimate of profits or contribution to overheads. Where there is no
gap remaining the firm should examine its costs more carefully or examine the
potential of other market segments or different markets.

An illustration of the procedure demonstrates its value to the exporting firm.
Assume that the firm has been asked by a potential customer in the Federal
Republic of Germany to quote in DM for a quantity of the firm's Deluxe
Honeyspread product. Furthermore, let us assume that initial market research
in Germany indicated that the price bracket for a 12-jar carton of the product was
DM60. There are two things the firm will want to know: will there be a profit;
or will there at least be a contribution to the overheads? The example below shows
how it is possible to price from both ends, the demand side and the cost side,
to see what profits or contribution can be made (Table 12.4).

It is worth noting that there are many charges or costs which at first sight
may not be obvious. Local wholesaler and retailer mark-ups, here assumed to
be 25 per cent, and duties, here assumed not to apply because the business is
being conducted entirely within the EC, are perhaps the two most important.
From the CIF price thus derived it is necessary to allow for freight and insurance
to arrive at the FOB price. Other deductions include dock handling charges in
the exporter's country and the allowances to cover the direct export costs. Two
sets of costs are assumed, direct manufacturing costs and an allocation for
overheads. All figures are in DM to facilitate the discussion of the two approaches.
By following this procedure two sets of residuals are computed: profits or
contribution to overheads depending on circumstances. Many firms find that
when this kind of analysis is performed the profit area disappears and the area
of contribution may not be substantial. The example illustrates the importance
of performing a detailed cost and price analysis before deciding whether to export
to a particular market.

Successful firms in international markets frequently use both costs and prices
in determining their competitive position. An overemphasis on one or other can
lead to trouble. IKEA, the Swedish self-assembly furniture firm recognized the
market opening in many countries for entry level furniture systems which were

**Table 12.4**  Costing and pricing in export markets — hypothetical example

Profitability of exporting one 12 jar carton of Deluxe Honeyspread to the Federal Republic of Germany: hypothetical illustration

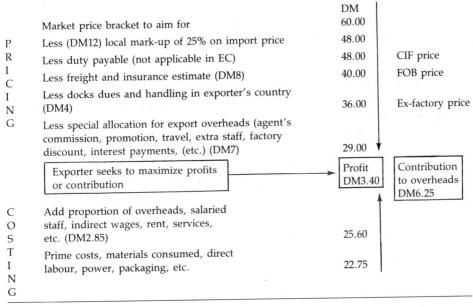

| | | DM | |
|---|---|---|---|
| | Market price bracket to aim for | 60.00 | |
| P | Less (DM12) local mark-up of 25% on import price | 48.00 | |
| R | Less duty payable (not applicable in EC) | 48.00 | CIF price |
| I | Less freight and insurance estimate (DM8) | 40.00 | FOB price |
| C | | | |
| I | Less docks dues and handling in exporter's country | | |
| N | (DM4) | 36.00 | Ex-factory price |
| G | Less special allocation for export overheads (agent's commission, promotion, travel, extra staff, factory discount, interest payments, (etc.) (DM7) | 29.00 | |

Exporter seeks to maximize profits or contribution → Profit DM3.40 | Contribution to overheads DM6.25

| | | DM | |
|---|---|---|---|
| C | Add proportion of overheads, salaried | | |
| O | staff, indirect wages, rent, services, | | |
| S | etc. (DM2.85) | 25.60 | |
| T | | | |
| I | Prime costs, materials consumed, direct | | |
| N | labour, power, packaging, etc. | 22.75 | |
| G | | | |

priced relatively low. By producing self-assembly kits and retailing them through catalogues and retail outlets on the outskirts of large cities IKEA has successfully entered many European markets and has recently opened stores in the United States. The company also keeps costs low by buying components directly from suppliers in many countries. A combination of direct selling and purchasing for a price sensitive market has given IKEA the opportunity to become a successful firm in many international markets (Exhibit 12.2).

## *Export competitiveness*

While the management of costs is very important for success in international markets it is not the only consideration. The firm must consider other factors as well. Costs serve as a bottom line and indicate how successful the firm is in serving the needs of particular customer groups. They do not indicate how that satisfaction might be achieved.

The successful firm usually competes on a number of marketing-related factors such as the product and associated services, quality, design, uniqueness, delivery reliability, business relationships and price. Buyers have many suppliers to choose from in most situations. In large country markets in particular, buyers can choose from among myriad suppliers located in many foreign countries.

---

**Exhibit 12.2   Direct selling and purchasing is a winner for IKEA**

---

*Furniture chain has global view*

Sweden's IKEA, already the world's biggest home furnishings retail chain, is
continuing to expand rapidly in the East and West. IKEA honed its marketing strategy
for two decades in Sweden from its headquarters in the quiet rural town of Almhult
before breaking into the international arena in the mid-1970s. The key to its success is
its ability to offer stylish durable furniture at rock-bottom prices. Armchairs may cost
as little as $60, bookshelves $75 and couches $250 to $300. Costs are kept low by
buying components directly from suppliers in more than 50 countries. The parts are
partially assembled and shipped in flat boxes. Customers do the final assembly at
home.

Founded as a mail-order company in the mid-1940s, IKEA still relies on catalog as
its main marketing tool. Its advertising refers consumers to the catalog. IKEA publishes
45 million catalogs in 10 languages annually, listing roughly 15,000 items. IKEA offers
mail order in Europe and Canada, but the catalogs, which are uniform except for
minor regional differences, are designed primarily to serve as a shopping guide for
customers coming to IKEA's 78 stores worldwide.

IKEA tries to make shopping at its outlets a "fun experience". Bands and clowns
often appear at its stores, which also offer playrooms for children and Swedish-style
food for their parents. The same basic format is followed throughout the world.
Outlets usually are situated outside the city limits of major metropolitan areas, where
land prices are lower.

Despite an initial caution about international expansion, IKEA has found its
greatest success abroad. It ventured outside Scandinavia in 1973 when it opened a
store in Switzerland, used as a test for a planned move into West Germany. Germany
is now IKEA's single largest national market, accounting for one-third of $1.9 billion
world-wide sales in 1986. IKEA stores now stretch from North America through
Europe and the Middle East to Southeast Asia and Australia, attracting 60 million
customers last year and accounting for roughly 70 percent of the chain's total sales.

Source: *Advertising Age*, 26 October, 1987, p. 58.

---

Since 1975 the Irish Export Board has carried out a survey of foreign buyers
to measure the competitiveness of Irish exports in their major markets.
Negotiations between exporters and foreign buyers are monitored by the offices
of the Irish Export Board located in the markets being monitored. The survey
covers various topics concerned with competitiveness, including the main factors
which influence the buyer to place an order with one particular firm rather than
with any other. As an illustration the results of this survey for 1983 are shown
below (Table 12.5).

In the circumstances examined the main influence was quality, though price
was closely associated with it. Export competitiveness is, therefore, a multidimen-

**Table 12.5**  Measuring export competitiveness

| Evaluative factors | UK | Other EC | Other Europe | North America | Other | Total |
|---|---|---|---|---|---|---|
| Quality | 18 | 15 | 1 | 3 | 3 | 40 |
| Price | 17 | 8 | 2 | 3 | 5 | 35 |
| Product uniqueness | 6 | 10 | 1 | 3 | 2 | 22 |
| Design | 6 | 4 | – | 3 | – | 13 |
| Reliability of delivery | 8 | 1 | 1 | 1 | 1 | 12 |
| *Relationship with the exporter | 14 | 10 | 3 | 3 | 1 | 31 |
| Support service/after sales service | 9 | – | 1 | 1 | – | 11 |
| *Other reasons connected with the nature of the product | 9 | 11 | 1 | 1 | 2 | 24 |
| *Other reasons | 8 | 5 | 4 | 8 | – | 25 |

*Denotes amalgamation of a number of different factors with a common theme.

Source: Adapted from CTT — Irish Export Board — Competitive Surveys, Dublin, 1983 (see text for explanation).

sional feature of the management of the firm. Successful firms address the specific elements of competitiveness in preparing their positions for each export market and buyer.

## Summary

Exporting is the simplest way of entering a foreign market, requiring a low level of investment in terms of managerial and financial resources and consequently a low level of corporate commitment and risk. This makes it an ideal first step to internationalization for many firms and a useful strategy for firms in risky and uncertain markets.

The export decision is influenced by three sets of influences on the firm: (a) experience and uncertainty effects; (b) behavioural and firm specific influences; and (c) strategic influences on exporting.

The firm's activities at the pre-export stage have an important influence on the firm's initial export direction. Several factors influence the firm's decision to internationalize: degree of international orientation; previous experience; and perceptions of risk and return. Government-sponsored export stimulation measures, product characteristics, and unsolicited export orders also play an important role at this stage.

Opinion among researchers and managers is divided on the issue of the relationship between firm size and export success. The importance of a positive managerial attitude to exporting and the necessity of committing managerial and financial resources to the internationalization process is emphasized, however, irrespective of the size of the firm.

The costs associated with exporting — market research, product adaptation, market visits, shipping and agency fees — have a strong influence on a firm's export activity and it is in this area that a large firm may have an advantage over a small one. In assessing the cost of exporting and competitiveness in export markets the areas of service, quality, design and product uniqueness are very important. The exporting firm succeeds by being cost competitive and by being competitive in the other areas of marketing as well.

## Discussion questions

1. Why is exporting frequently considered the simplest way of entering foreign markets and favoured by smaller firms?

2. Three sets of factors are believed to influence the firm's decision to export. Identify these factors and discuss their relative importance.

3. The behaviour and activity of the firm prior to exporting is thought to have a very great effect on the degree of success of the firm. Discuss.

4. Size of firm is often cited as a barrier to successful exporting. It is argued that the firm must be large to succeed. Do you agree?

5. What is meant by export competitiveness? How might the firm determine its overall competitiveness in export markets?

## References

Abdel-Malek, Talaat (1978) 'Export marketing orientation in small firms,' *American Journal of Small Business*, 3, 24—35.

Abernathy, William, Clarke, Kim B. and Kantrow, Alan M. (1983) *Industrial Renaissance*, Basic Books, NY. Chapter 4 and Appendix C.

Auquier, Antoine (1980) 'Sizes of firms, exporting behaviour and the structure of French industry,' *Journal of Industrial Economics*, 29 (2), 202—18.

Betro Report (1975) *Concentration on Key Export Markets*, Royal Society of Arts, London, April.

Bilkey, Warren J. (1978) 'An attempted integration of the literature on the export behaviour of firms,' *Journal of International Business Studies*, 9 (1), 33—46.

Bilkey, Warren J. (1982): 'Variables associated with export profitability,' *Journal of International Business Studies*, 13 (2), 39—55.

Bilkey, Warren J. and Tesar, George (1977) 'The export behaviour of smaller Wisconsin manufacturing firms,' *Journal of International Business Studies*, 8 (2), 93—8.

Bradley, M. Frank (1984) 'Effect of cognitive style, and attitude toward growth and motivation on the internationalisation of the firm', in Jagdish Sheth (ed.), *Research in Marketing*, 7, JAI Press, Greenwich, Conn., pp. 237—59.

Bradley, M. Frank (1985) 'Market and internal organization in exporting for SMEs,' a paper presented to *Developing Markets for New Products and Services Through Joint Exporting by Innovative SMEs Seminar*, Commission of the European Communities, Luxembourg, 6—7 March.

Buzzell, Robert D. (1968) 'Can you standardize multinational marketing?,' *Harvard Business Review*, November–December, pp. 102–13.

Carlson, Sune (1975) 'How foreign is foreign trade?' Acta Universitatis Upsaliensis, *Studia Oeconomiae Negotiorum II*, Uppsala, Sweden, Bulletin No. 15.

Cavusgil, S. Tamer (1984) 'Organizational characteristics associated with export activity,' *Journal of Management Studies*, **21** (1), 3–9.

Cavusgil, S. Tamer and Nevin, John R. (1981) 'Internal determinants of export marketing behaviour — an empirical investigation,' *Journal of Marketing Research*, **18**, 114–19.

Cooper, Robert, Elko, G. and Kleinschmidt, J. (1985) 'The import of export strategy on export sales performance,' *Journal of International Business Studies*, Spring, pp. 37–55.

Cunningham, M.T. and Spigel, R.I. (1971) 'A study in successful exporting,' *British Journal of Marketing*, **5** (1), 2–12.

Czinkota, M. and Johnston, Wesley J. (1983) 'Exporting: Does sales volume make a difference?,' *Journal of International Business Studies*, **14** (1), 147–53.

Egan, Barry (1981) Product and Advertising Adaptation for Irish Companies in their Export Markets, Master of Business Studies Dissertation, Department of Marketing, University College Dublin.

Hunt, H.G., Froggat, J.D. and Hovell, P.T. (1967) 'The management of export marketing in engineering industries,' *British Journal of Marketing*, **2**, 10–24.

Johanson, Jan and Vahlne, Erik (1977) 'The internationalisation process of the firm — a model of knowledge development and increasing foreign market commitments,' *Journal of International Business Studies*, **8** (1), 23–32

Johanson, Jan and Wiedersheim-Paul, Finn (1974) 'The internationalisation of the firm — four Swedish cases,' *Journal of Management Studies*, **3**, 305–22.

Keegan, Warren J. (1970) 'Five strategies for multinational marketing,' *European Business*, January, pp. 35–40.

Levitt, Theodore (1983) 'The globalization of markets,' *Harvard Business Review*, May–June, pp. 92–102.

McDougall, Gordon (1989):'Barossa winery: Penetrating the international market,' *International Marketing*, **6** (2), 18–33.

O'Grady, Niall (1987) Openminded Management and Exporting Activity in Small Manufacturing Firms, Unpublished Master of Business Studies Dissertation, Department of Marketing, University College Dublin.

Olson, Hans C. (1975) *Studies in Export Promotion. Attempts to Evaluate Export Measures for the Swedish Textile and Clothing Industries*, Research Paper, University of Uppsala, Sweden.

Piercy, Nigel (1981) 'Company internationalisation: Active and reactive exporting,' *European Journal of Marketing*, **15** (3), 26–40.

Root, Franklin R. (1982) *Foreign Market Entry Strategies*, Amacom, NY.

Simmonds, Kenneth and Smith, Helen (1968) 'The first export order: A marketing innovation,' *British Journal of Marketing*, **2**, 93–100.

Simpson, C. and Kujawa, D. (1974) 'The export decision process: An empirical enquiry,' *Journal of International Business Studies*, **5**, 107–17.

Stopford, J. and Wells, L. (1972) *Managing the Multinational Enterprise*, Basic Books.

Thorelli, Hans B. and Becker, Helmut (1980) *International Marketing Strategy*, Pergamon Press, Oxford.

Weinrauch, J.D. and Rao, C. (1974) 'The export marketing mix: An examination of company experiences and perceptions,' *The Journal of Business Research*, **2** (4), 447–52.

Welch, Lawrence (1982) 'Decision-making in the international context,' in *Proceedings of the Seminar on Management Decision-Making*, European Institute for Advanced Studies in Management, Oslo, June.

Wiederscheim-Paul, Finn, Olson, Hans C. and Welsh, Lawrence S. (1978) 'Pre-export activity : The first step in internationalization,' *Journal of International Business Studies*, **9** (1), 47–58.

# Competitive alliances to enter international markets

In this chapter we examine various forms of inter-firm alliances formed to enter and compete in international markets. In particular, we examine the nature of competitive alliances and how they form part of the continuum of entry methods. The next section examines marketing partnership agreements, followed by sections on licensing, franchising and joint ventures. The last section examines ways of evaluation and controlling competitive alliances in international markets.

## Nature of competitive alliances

### Access to technology and markets

It has been argued in the business press that European industry in particular is being reshaped as a result of strategic alliances between US and Japanese firms on the one hand and European firms on the other. These alliances provide European firms with immediate access to US and Japanese technology and industrial strength. At the same time the alliances provide US and Japanese firms with easy access to the very large European market for their products and services. According to these agreements, European industrialists have realized that the technological distance which has arisen is so great in competitive terms that no firm has the strength on its own to overcome the deficiency. For these reasons strategic competitive alliances, it is believed, will strengthen European firms in technological terms. Technology is defined as know-how relevant to the solution of manufacturing and marketing problems. It is necessary to distinguish between process technology, which relates to functions within the firm such as purchasing, production or marketing and product technology, which relates to product and services manufacturing. It is recognized that independent technological development would result in inferior products and low-entry barriers to non-European firms.

A parallel argument in the business press states that in the late 1980s and 1990s, a trend toward neo-protectionism in markets has appeared. The response of firms in protecting market access is to establish manufacturing operations behind these barriers. Critical to success in these circumstances is access to distribution and the ability to form corporate linkages to exploit technological and marketing developments. These corporate linkages arise, on the one hand, in response to carrying technologies which have resulted in a demand by consumers for fully integrated and compatible lines of equipment which are difficult for single firms to produce alone. The alliances also arise from converging markets due to rising incomes, changing consumer tastes, and the globalization of some consumer and industrial markets. International corporate linkages have been defined as "diverse interorganizational arrangements created by firms based in different countries to obtain strategic advantage in their markets and environments." (Austen, 1987, p. 3)

To understand the nature of the business environment in which the modern firm operates it is necessary to view the international economy as a "network of organizations with a vast hierarchy of subordinate, criss-crossing networks." (Thorelli, 1986, p. 3) An important feature of the international firm is that its choice of network partners may be influenced by the relationship between these partners and other firms, which have a separate relationship which may be competitive or collaborative with the first firm. These pervasive alliances may be viewed as a complex channel of communication through which organizations manage their interdependency and hedge against strategic uncertainty arising from the activities of other firms (Vernon, 1983). The alliances thus formed are seen as part of a process to strengthen the firm's position in an industry and are essential for its survival (Hakansson and Johanson, 1988).

Furthermore, existing and potential competitors may be co-opted or otherwise neutralized by forming a joint venture with a competitor or by entering into a network of cross-licensing agreements. Sometimes, a firm will form joint ventures with a number of other firms to protect against the possibility of a take-over or merger (Gullander, 1976). This is especially true for smaller firms which have entered a joint venture with a larger company.

## Basis for a competitive alliance

Firms may form an alliance to compete in international markets based on the exchange of a range of assets. The possession of product-market knowledge is such an asset. Access to markets and distribution channels are assets also possessed by some firms and sought by others, thereby giving rise to the possibility of a competitive alliance. Similarly, product and process know-how, spare manufacturing capacity, scarce raw materials, and unique management resources may form the basis of a competitive alliance in the markets (Table 13.1).

The competitive alliance may take many forms. It may range from a simple contractual agreement to cross-distribute products to production agreements

**Table 13.1** Immediate complementarity in competitive alliances

| Nature of asset/ nature of alliance | Firm | Product-market knowledge | Market access/ distribution | Know-how Product | Know-how Process | Manufacturing capacity | Raw materials | Management resources |
|---|---|---|---|---|---|---|---|---|
| Marketing partnership | A | x | x | | | | | |
| | B | | | x | | | | |
| Production agreements | A | | | | x | x | x | x |
| | B | | | x | x | | | |
| Franchising | A | | x | | | x | | x |
| | B | x | x | x | x | | x | x |
| Licensing | A | x | x | | x | x | x | x |
| | B | | | | x | | | |
| Joint ventures | A | | x | x | | x | x | x |
| | B | x | | x | x | | x | x |

where the production stages of a product are shared. There are many forms of marketing and production agreement which form the basis of competitive alliances. A partnership which reflects greater commitment may be found under franchising, licensing and joint ventures. These various forms of alliance represent a continuum of increasing commitment to the partnership. The commitment in agreements may refer to one product market for a limited period, whereas the joint venture usually involves the commitment of financial, managerial and technological resources for a considerable period (Table 13.1).

In all competitive alliances there is a reciprocal arrangement in the exchange. This reciprocity may be complementary in the short term and of immediate benefit to the partner firms. For example, in Table 13.1, it is assumed that the competitive alliance involves two firms: Firm A and Firm B. Firm A possesses product market knowledge and market access and a distribution network which is exchanged with Firm B for product know-how.

A similar complementarity between Firm A and Firm B exists in the joint venture arrangement depicted in Table 13.1. Here Firm B possesses product market knowledge which immediately complements Firm A's market access and distribution network. Both firms possess complementary skills in product know-how and have complementary raw materials and management resources. Firm A has spare manufacturing capacity, whereas Firm B possesses process know-how. The complementarity depicted here forms the basis of a competitive alliance and brings firms together in the first place to exploit a mutually beneficial advantage in the market. In Table 13.1 other complementary configurations are shown between the two firms for production agreements, franchising and licensing. As competitive alliances are nurtured and grow over time the partner firms may form closer alliances or bonds. With experience and a better under-standing of each other's capabilities and objectives the form of the alliance may evolve toward a situation where the partners work together to gain access to new third markets and raw materials. Sometimes firms begin to develop and manu-facture new products jointly. This dynamic convergence of resources, capabilities and business objectives may occur quite rapidly but is usually an evolutionary process which takes a number of years. The final stage in the convergence stage arises when the firms decide to form a functional merger (Table 13.2). The evolu-tionary complementarity reflects the strengths of each partner in the key assets to be exchanged. Note the complete matching of resources and capabilities under each heading: each firm possesses strengths of a complementary nature which form the basis of the alliance.

## Marketing partnership agreements

For firms with significant sales and physical distribution systems established in a large market such as the United Kingdom or Germany, there may be opportunities to market the products of, say, US firms suitably adapted for the market through the existing channels of distribution. For the smaller firm particularly, organic internal growth or acquisition may not be an option. A partnership on a complementary basis may be less risky and also potentially more rewarding. Looked at from the opposite perspective there are many small-to medium-sized exporters in the United States who are not active in international markets but who provide a ready made pool of well-equipped, technically sophisticated but internationally inexperienced firms who could serve as partners to European firms with guaranteed market access. A few years ago Belgian sports firms entered a marketing partnership to strengthen their worldwide marketing position (Exhibit 13.1).

## Licensing in international markets

Licensing avoids the risks of product and or market development by exploiting the experience of firms which have already developed and marketed the product. It also provides a good vehicle for the internationalization of small firms that might not have the capital or the foreign experience to establish a joint venture or a wholly owned subsidiary (Carstairs and Welch, 1983). It possesses the advantage of reducing a firm's exposure to financial risk as fixed asset investment is minimized due to the utilization of another firm's existing investment.

The cost of transferring technology is frequently cited as an impediment to such developments. Williamson (1975) and Teece (1981) suggest that criteria based on minimizing transaction costs should be the determinant of the control structures chosen for the transfer of know-how. The greater the possibility of transferring technology in coded or blue-print form the lower the cost of transfer. Uncodified or tacit knowledge requires face-to-face communication for successful transmission and is therefore slow and expensive to transfer. Herein lies a major value of licensing; the costs of knowledge transfer are relatively low.

### Nature of international licensing

Licensing is the purchase or sale by contract of product or process technology, design and marketing expertise. It involves the market contracting of knowledge and know-how, which is "a sleeping asset — it lies hidden in people's heads, their desk drawers and filing cabinets — a potential source of income waiting to be packaged" (Millman, 1983, p. 3).

International licensing arises when a firm provides for a fee or royalty technology needed by another firm to operate its business in a foreign market. Licensing of this form involves one or a combination of the following: a brand name; operations expertise; manufacturing process technology; and access to patents and trade secrets. The licensor firm gains access to a foreign market with very low investment and frequently obtains the investment and market knowledge of a competent local firm. The licensee firm gains access to a foreign technology with very low investment. Lee Cooper, a UK jeans manufacturer, has used

**Table 13.2** Evolutionary complementarity in competitive alliances

| Nature of asset/ nature of alliance | Firm | Product-market knowledge | Market access/ distribution | Know-how Product | Process | Manufacturing capacity | Raw materials | Management resources |
|---|---|---|---|---|---|---|---|---|
| Market access | A | | x | | | | | |
| | B | | x | | | | | |
| Raw material access | A | | | | | | x | x |
| | B | | | | | | x | x |
| New product development | A | x | | x | x | | | |
| | B | x | | x | x | | | |
| Manufacturing | A | | | | | x | | x |
| | B | | | | | x | | x |
| Functional merger | A | x | x | x | x | x | x | x |
| | B | x | x | x | x | x | x | x |

## Exhibit 13.1   Complementary marketing partnership

### Browning—Donnay agreement

Browning and Donnay, the two Belgian sports specialist groups, have signed a co-operation agreement in the tennis and golf fields while retaining their financial independence. The agreement aims to increase the two brands' competitiveness, to turn their complementarity to advantage and to make economies of scale. This is only the first stage in a dynamic process which is to go further, since Browning and Donnay are also to co-operate on the distribution of "racket sports" products.

Four European countries are concerned, namely Belgium, France, the Federal Republic of Germany and the Netherlands. Donnay and its distributors are to handle the distribution of Browning products in these countries. In addition, Donnay and Browning are to set up a services company together in France which will be responsible for all logistics for the French subsidiaries of the two brands. Each will have an equal stake in this joint company, called SGDI (Société de Gestion et de Distribution Integrée). It will have modern logistic resources, including a fully integrated administrative data-processing system to improve customer service. In due course it will also make its services available to other non-competing companies.

The new Donnay—Browning agreement meets the common desire of the two Belgian brands to increase their competitiveness world-wide.

**Source:** *Belgium-Economic and Commercial Information*, **4**, 1986, p. 5.

licensing successfully in Eastern Europe on a number of occasions during the past decade (Exhibit 13.2).

International licensing may be a preferred strategy in some circumstances. It may be attractive in situations where host countries restrict imports and/or foreign direct investments where the foreign market is small, where the prospects of technology feedback are high, where technological change is so rapid that the licensor remains technologically superior, and where opportunities exist for licensing auxiliary processes without having to license basic product technologies (Contractor, 1981, p. 74).

License agreements generally fall into two categories: a current technology licence which gives the licensee access to the technology which the licenser possesses at the time of the agreement; and a current and future technology licence which gives access to technology developed by the licensor in a specified product area during the life of the agreement. Licence agreements vary depending on circumstances but normally contain aspects of a technical, commercial and organizational nature in addition to the patented technology being transferred.

Increasingly, firms in different parts of the world share the development of new technology. Many Japanese, European and American firms have joined together to exploit technological advances in addition to marketing and manufacturing capabilities. They have done so by licensing arrangements involving cross-regional alliances with firms which operate outside their domestic markets.

## Benefits of licensing

There are several reasons why a company might wish to acquire technology or know-how through licensing. The firm in a high-technology industry which lacks resources required for research and development may have no alternative but to license. In an industry where technology is changing rapidly it may also be wise for some firms to consider licensing.

Licensing is especially important in diversification strategies where new markets can be entered by buying not only product technology but also marketing and production know-how. There are a number of very clear benefits to licensing in international markets (Table 13.3). There are a number of disadvantages too.

Licensing can improve the cash flow position of the licensee. Because technology licensing allows the firms to have products on the market sooner than otherwise, the firm benefits from an earlier positive cash flow. In addition, licensing means lower development costs. As Lowe and Crawford (1984) show, however, licensing can mean less profits in the longer term. The immediate benefits of quick access to new technology, lower development costs and a relatively early cash flow are attractive benefits of licensing (Figure 13.1).

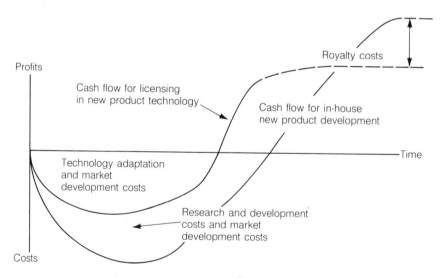

**Figure 13.1**  Life cycle benefits of licensing (Source: Adapted from Lowe, Julian and Crawford, Nick (1984) *Technology Licensing and the Small Firm*, Gower, England)

## Exhibit 13.2   Conditions for successful licensing

### *Lee Cooper signs big licence deal in Czechoslovakia*

In late 1981 Lee Cooper (UK) entered the Czechoslovak market by signing a six-year licensing and production co-operation deal with the OZKN enterprise of Presov covering the manufacture of denim and corduroy jeans. The deal proved so successful that the original targets, spread over six years, were completed in only five.

"The success of the venture was mainly due to the favourable market conditions in Czechoslovakia. Credit must also be given to the professionalism of the OZKN organization, with whom Lee Cooper developed an excellent business relationship", says Mr Cooper. "We encountered no major headaches uncommon to licensing in other parts of the world." This included some initial bureaucracy. But as for garment quality, only the shading of the jeans was at times unsatisfactory.

As a result a new deal has just been signed which is, in terms of production volume, product range and contract longevity, the company's largest foreign licensing agreement to date.

The length of the new deal with OZKN is nine years, a record for Lee Cooper. The agreement foresees doubling production to 2 million garments per year... As with the first deal, the contract includes an option for exports to other Comecon countries.

Payment for the agreement will be as before: hard currency in advance and in arrears. Mr Cooper estimates the value of the agreement over the nine years, including the sale of machinery and fees to the firm, at about $10 million. Denim will continue to be imported from the West until local capacity comes on stream in late 1987. Lee Cooper reserves a say regarding denim quality via control checks.

**Source:** *Business Eastern Europe*, 20 July, 1987, p. 227.

**Table 13.3**   Advantages and disadvantages of licensing in international markets

Advantages of licensing
- Access to difficult markets
- Low capital risk and low commitment of resources
- Information on product performance and competitor activities in different markets at little cost
- Improved delivery and service levels in local markets

Disadvantages of licensing
- Disclosure of accumulated competitive knowledge and experience
- Creates possible future competitors
- Lack of control over licensee operations
- Passive interaction with the market
- Exclusion of some export markets
- Organizing licensing operations: cost of adaptation, transfer and controlling

There are a number of technological reasons why a firm would consider licensing to enter a foreign market. For bulky or heavy products of low value, transport costs may be so high as to make exporting prohibitively expensive. Sometimes a local manufacturer with product knowledge is required, especially when the product requires installation and service support. In such circumstances it is unlikely that an agent could provide the necessary back-up.

Frequently a complementary arrangement may be developed whereby the licensor exports a high-technology component and the licensee provides the less critical assemblies, harnesses, mountings, and cabinets. This arrangement is more like a joint production agreement, however.

There are also a number of territorial reasons why licensing could be an attractive means of entering foreign markets. Few firms have the salesforce necessary to cover wide geographic markets in many different countries, nor do they have sufficient manufacturing capacity to service such large markets. Thus where the potential market is large, licensing partners can be an attractive development.

In addition, developing country governments frequently restrict imports or give preference to local firms, both of which encourage local production. Licensing may be the appropriate means of entering the market in such circumstances.

Financial considerations may be an important determinant of licensing for the smaller firm in possession of advanced technology. Licensing in such circumstances may open foreign markets that might otherwise be beyond its reach. Small- and medium-sized firms which are attempting to expand and grow frequently experience cash flow and liquidity problems. Since licensing income is largely pure profit involving little extra investment, licensing for such firms may speed up the cash flow from new foreign markets. When licensing agreements are successful, the application of many international product markets may be relatively painless and profitable.

## Prerequisites of successful licensing

There are a number of prerequisites for successful licensing. The licensor must have exclusive and easily transferable property rights to the product or process technology being licensed. It must also be possible to identify the benefits associated with the licence, including the value of the licence to the partner firm. The licensing firm should be in a position to control the licensing operation including the geographic market area in which the licence is to apply. At the same time the licensee should have developed a level of technical competence sufficient to cope with the application of the technology in production and marketing.

Sometimes firms are opposed to licensing their technology or, as often claimed, their birthright. Opposition to licensing is usually centred on reluctance to divulge accumulated knowledge and experience that has been hard to develop. The fear stems from the situation where a company may find cheaper or improved versions of its own products competing against it at a later date. Other reasons for the decision not to pursue licensing include: lack of real control over licensee operations; blocking off export areas; doubts about the suitability and transferability of technology; and difficulties of organizing licensing operations in traditional manufacturing-oriented companies.

The major prerequisite of successful licensing is an organizational climate conducive to international business. A separate licensing section under a licensing executive is often preferred, no matter how small, so that it can be clearly seen by people within the licensor and licensee firms that the activity carries status.

## The licence package

Most licensing packages consist of proprietary know-how and patented products or processes specified in great detail. Proprietary know-how relies mainly on secrecy within the licensor company and as a contractural obligation of the licensee. Patented products and processes enjoy a measure of additional legal protection and limited monopoly rights. License packages generally contain elements of the following:

- patents, designs, trademarks, copyrights;
- product and process specifications;
- quality control procedures;
- manufacturing layout drawings and instruction manuals;
- commissioning to achieve a performance guarantee;
- technical and commercial training programmes;
- product literature and other sales support material.

It is difficult to police licences. The difficulty begins during the pre-signing period when a balance is required between whetting the prospective licensee's appetite and not divulging too much information in the event of the negotiation falling through. Some technologies are very concise and the whole licence may depend on disclosure of some novel design or process. This is the problem of information disclosure which can sometimes support the formation of a new international firm (Williamson, 1975).

The form of the licence transaction is fairly well established and involves some combination of the following elements:

- a down payment on release of the written-up part of the technology;
- progress payments leading up to commissioning one or more products to the licensor's performance specification;
- minimum royalty — a guarantee that at least some annual income will be received by the licensor;
- running royalty — normally expressed as a percentage of normal selling price or as a fixed sum of money for units of output.

Other methods of payment include lump sums with no deferred payment related to output, a conversion of royalties into equity, management and technical fees and complex systems of counterpurchase, typically found in licensing arrangements with Eastern European countries.

If the foreign market carries high political risk, then it will be wise for the licensor to seek high "initial" payments and perhaps compress the timescale of the agreement. Alternatively, if the market is relatively risk free and the licensee is well placed to develop a strong market share, then payment terms will be somewhat relaxed and probably influenced by other licensors competing for the agreement.

## Barriers to international licensing

There are a number of limitations in using licenses internationally. The market for licenses is imperfect. The buyer has a weak basis for bidding, especially for undisclosed technology, until the technology has been supplied. It is also very difficult to communicate subtle and complex technologies successfully from one firm to another, especially across cultures. There are heavy costs of knowledge transfer. It is difficult for the licensor to ensure that licensees maintain adequate quality control in production. This is a serious problem when the licensor's brand or trade name is used.

It is difficult and expensive to police other clauses in the agreement, e.g. territorial limits. For these reasons technology leaders are often forced towards an equity involvement to protect their assets. Such pressure may ultimately force them to consider foreign direct investment. In recent years the EC has recognized the need to protect licensing from the adverse effects of competition policy (Exhibit 13.3).

Licensing arrangements generally prohibit or inhibit the flexibility of a later expansion into a sophisticated marketing operation or manufacturing. Licensing contains another risk; if the business is extremely successful the profit potential will be limited by the licensing arrangements. There is also the danger of commitment to an incompetent local firm. Termination clauses rarely prevent a great loss of time and resources.

## Franchising to enter international markets

### Nature of franchising

Despite the rather recent escalation of publicity surrounding it, franchising is not by any means a new phenomenon. Indeed, it is frequently seen as a recent "import" into Europe, particularly from the United States. The real pioneers of modern franchising were almost certainly the British brewers of the eighteenth century who created a system of tied house agreements with their publicans which remains widespread to this day (Stern and Stanworth, 1988). Franchising, a derivative of *Francorum Rex* or "Freedom from Servitude." is now a very significant

---

**Exhibit 13.3   EC promotes licensing**

---

*Licensing to get EEC protection*

Companies concluding licensing deals for nonpatentable, technical know-how will be offered exemption from EEC competition rules once Commission proposals gain approval.

The block exemption for licensing agreement is modelled on the 1984 exemption for patents. Under EEC competition rules (contained in Articles 85 and 86 of the Treaty of Rome), companies are banned from entering into any kind of agreement, except for those specified in exemption legislation...

The regulation will cover both technical information, such as a description of product procedures; industrial designs; software; and mixed know-how involving either a patent or trademark license, and the accompanying information essential for its use.

According to the current proposals, know-how agreements would have to have the following characteristics: they must be secret; involve substantial technological value; and the know-how must be described in the contract.

Once these criteria are respected, the block exemption will allow companies to set the following terms:

- both active and passive territorial protection
- restrictions on a licensee from sublicensing
- restrictions regarding quality standards: and
- the obligation to pay licensing fees even after the know-how has fallen into the public domain.

**Source:** *Business Europe,* 15 June, 1987, p. 5.

---

organizational arrangement in the US economy accounting for approximately 34 per cent of all retail sales and 10 per cent of gross national product in 1988. In contrast the figures for retail sales in Europe are between 2 and 3 per cent and 3 per cent in the United Kingdom (Ayling, 1987). The significance drawn from this by Ayling is that it "highlights the potential for franchising" in Europe.

There are various forms of franchises: job franchises; investment franchises; and business format franchises being the most common (Brandenburg, 1986). Business format franchising is the most common form found in international markets (Table 13.4).

The comparatively recent launching of the Body Shop and Prontaprint on the UK's USM, and the plans being drawn up at Benetton to launch the company on the NYSE and the Tokyo Stock Exchange are powerful indications of what can be achieved with a properly executed franchising strategy. One of the best known examples of international franchising is Benetton (Exhibit 13.4). Franchising

**Table 13.4**  Forms of franchising

Job franchising
- wholesaler–retailer
- Spar, Londis, VG,
- Service Master

Investment franchise
- manufacturer–retailer
  petrol service stations
- manufacturer–wholesaler
  Pepsi-Cola, 7-Up
- Other
  Holiday Inns, Avis Rent a Car
  Coca-Cola

Business format franchise
- Trade marks, trade names
  Kentucky Fried Chicken, Prontaprint
- Licensor–retailer
  McDonald's, Wimpey International

Source: Adapted from Brandenburg M.
(1986) 'Free yourself from servitude,'
*Accountancy*, October, **98** (1118), pp. 82–6;
Stern, Peter and Stanworth, John (1988) 'The
development of franchising in Britain,'
*National Westminister Quarterly Review*, May,
pp. 38–48; and Vaugh, C.L. (1979)
*Franchising*, Lexington Books, 2nd edn.

offers a unique organizational approach to decisions on distribution arrangements and the choices surrounding vertical integration (Norton, 1988a) by providing more control than market exchange (Rubin, 1978) while avoiding some of the negative features of full integration (Harrigan, 1983, 1986).

Franchising is a particular form of licensing of intellectual property rights (Adams and Mendelsohn 1986). Trade marks, trade names, copyright, designs, patents, trade secrets and know-how may all be involved in different mixtures in the "package" to be licensed. Franchising is a form of marketing and distribution in which the franchisor grants an individual or small company, the franchisee, the right to do business in a prescribed manner over a certain period of time, in a specified place (Ayling 1988). A more formal legal definition is provided by Adams and Mendelsohn (1986) who view franchising as a marketing method with four distinct characteristics, as follows:

1. A contractual relationship in which the franchisor licenses the franchisee to carry out business under a name owned by or associated with the franchisor and in accordance with a business format established by the franchisor.
2. Control by the franchisor over the way in which the franchisee carries on the business.

## Exhibit 13.4   Evolution of a franchise

### Benetton — the franchising king

Since 1987, Benetton has opened an average of one of its familiar green and white stores every day. Most of these are franchised. In 1987, the target was to have over 45,000 shops around the world selling only Benetton's range of medium-priced, brightly coloured sportswear.

It has been estimated that Benetton is capable of growing by 15–20 percent each year for the foreseeable future. These shops have been almost exclusively franchised to hasten the Group's expansion and to keep the financial exposure to a minimum; but they differ significantly from most franchises. To avoid the usual quality problems, they are fully owned by carefully screened entrepreneurs.

The franchisees arrange all their own finance, but they pay no fees or royalties. Their obligations are to carry only Benetton clothes, to achieve certain minimum sales levels, to follow guidelines for price mark-ups and to adopt one of the standard shops layouts. The locations are chosen by the company or one of its agents.

Benetton devised a technique of clustering several of its shops in the same area, sometimes as many as three or four on the same street. With more than 1000 designs in each collection, different items are usually on display in each shop. Thus, the failure of a single store is offset by the success of the others, and valuable comparisons and a degree of internal competition are provided as well.

At the heart of the system are the 75 Benetton agents world-wide, all of whom are also shop owners. They have primary responsibility for choosing store owners, teaching them the Benetton business philosophy and supervising operations in their territories. Their commission payments are based on total sales within their territory .

When each new collection is ready, the territory agents arrange a show for their store owners and relay all orders to the company. As shop owners themselves, the agents are also expected to keep a close eye on the market, constantly passing on information and suggestions.

**Source:** Bruce, L. (1987) 'The bright new world of Benetton,' *International Management*, **42** (11), 24–30.

3. Provision of assistance to the franchisee by the franchisor in running the business both prior to commencement and throughout the period of the contract.
4. The franchisee owns his/her business which is a separate entity from that of the franchisor; the franchisee provides and risks his own capital.

A good example of the value of franchising is that of the Swedish furniture manufacturer IKEA which franchises its ideas throughout the western world, especially in Europe and North America. In terms of surface area at retail and the number of visitors to retail stores, this company has experienced very significant growth through franchising in recent years (Figure 13.2).

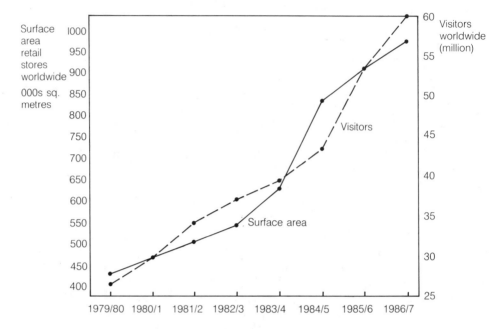

**Figure 13.2** Growth of an international franchisor: IKEA (Source: Götberg, Göran (1989) 'Franchising in international marketing,' in Gustafsson, Karl Erik and Green, Gunella (eds.), *Marketing at the Gothenburg School of Economics: Proceedings from a Symposium for Bo Wickström*, BAS, Gothenburg, Sweden, pp. 83–93)

## *Reasons for growth in franchising*

A number of factors have contributed to the rapid growth rate of franchising (Stern and Stanworth, 1988). First the general worldwide decline of traditional manufacturing industry and its replacement by service-sector activities has encouraged franchising. Franchising is especially well suited to service and people-intensive economic activities, particularly where these require a large number of geographically dispersed outlets serving local markets. Second, the growth in popularity of self-employment is also a contributory factor to the growth of franchising (Ayling, 1988). Government policies of many countries have improved the whole climate for small business as a means of stimulating employment.

As franchising becomes increasingly well known and understood, the chances are that it will appeal to a growing number of people. As a consequence, it can only be expected that there will be a corresponding increase in the number of franchise opportunities. Further, there is an increasing shift by large companies towards divestment from centralized control of an increasing proportion of their business activities. Third, the law surrounding franchising permits its rapid growth. Around the world, particularly in North America, Australia and the EC, franchising has been more or less exempt from legislation concerning competition laws. Finally, the involvement of major clearing banks has lent stability to the franchise industry and has also improved the image of the franchising business significantly. This is especially true in the United Kingdom.

## Advantages of franchising

The major advantage of franchising as a means of rapidly entering a number of international markets is that it is a method of expanding a business activity over a wider area more quickly than is possible if done internally. This occurs because in franchising a business format is sold to someone who will operate it in the manner which has proved to be successful, using the energies of a self-employed person with local knowledge. The franchising formula enables this expansion with minimum capital outlay. It creates additional income to the franchisor in the form of fees and royalty payments. A promising franchise will attract highly motivated operators.

The franchisor's small central organization, consisting of a few skilled experts, does not constitute a heavy overhead (Ayling, 1988). The franchisor is unburdened by day-to-day details which would arise in the case of many wholly owned outlets. In addition, Rubin (1978) highlights the following four specific advantages from a franchise as opposed to operating an independent business:

1. The trademark of a franchise and the product sold are valuable and the franchisee is willing to pay something to sell these products or services.
2. The franchisor often gives managerial advice to the franchisee.
3. The franchisor often makes capital available to the franchisee in some form, e.g. co-signing a bank loan or buying the plant and leasing it to the franchisee.
4. To the extent that franchisees are closer to being employees than entrepreneurs, they may simply lack the requisite human capital to open a business without the substantial assistance of franchisors.

## Disadvantages of franchising

Franchisees are owner-managers who typically bear the residual risk of a local operation because their wealth is largely determined by the difference between the revenue inflows to the operation and the promised payments to the franchisor and other factors (Norton, 1988b). From the point of view of the franchisor, the major risk is the effect the franchise will have on brand names.

Companies involved in franchising generally have identifiable brand names which are an assurance of uniform product quality. The vital importance of this quality assurance in the case of businesses dealing with non-repeat customers has already been noted. A major problem facing companies with valuable brand names is controlling the action of agents throughout the organization to assure the continued value of the trademark.

## Legal aspects of franchising

The market for franchise operations is competitive, with the only monopoly element being the trademark. Hence, Rubin (1978) has difficulty in understanding why courts would want to interfere at all in the franchisor–franchisee relationship. Rubin speculates that perhaps part of the justification for anti-trust intervention in the United States may be that once the contract is signed, the franchisor is in a monopoly position relative to the franchisee, but warns that this argument rests on the misinterpretation of the nature of the relationship between the two parties. Legally, the franchisee is a firm dealing with another firm — the franchisor. But, what Rubin does not recognize is that the economics of the situation are such that the franchisee is far closer to being an employee of the franchisor than an independent entrepreneur.

In Europe, the EC Commission published a new draft of a block exemption regulation in 1988. This was designed to allow franchising exemption from competition laws. The EC's landmark judgement in this area came in the 1986 case of Pronuptia et Paris GmbH in which franchising was deemed exempt from community competition restrictions. The 1988 draft initiative allows franchisors to grant franchisees territorial immunity.

## Joint ventures to enter international markets

A joint venture is formed when two or more firms form a third to carry out a productive economic activity (Harrigan, 1985). A joint venture has also been seen in wider terms: "an equity arrangement between two or more independent firms." (Gullander, 1976, p. 104) The latter definition includes equity alliances between firms to organize production and marketing on a regional rather than a country level, e.g. AT & T's 25 per cent stake in Olivetti. Joint ventures have increased in the variety and form they take and they have become more strategic rather than tactical in nature (Harrigan, 1985). To complicate matters further, Root (1988) categorizes joint ventures not only by their core characteristics along the value added chain but also by geographic scope and dominant mission, i.e. strategic orientation.

Various forms of joint venture are found in practice (Table 13.5). Sometimes firms participate in a spider's-web strategy consisting of many firms. Two dangers are associated with this strategy: (a) indirectly forming a link with a competitor; and (b) the possibility of a take-over. Frequently, firms will cooperate for a period of time and then separate. In contrast, other firms find their bonds with joint venture partners becoming tighter. In these circumstances, full integration may

**Table 13.5**  Alternative joint venture strategies

Spider's-web strategy
- establishing JV with large competitor
- avoid absorption through JV's with others in network

Go-together then split strategy
- co-operating over extended period
- separate
- suitable for limited projects (construction)

Successive integration strategy
- starts with weak inter-firm linkages
- develops towards interdependence
- ends with take-over/merger

Source: Gullander, Staffon (1976) 'Joint ventures and corporate strategy,' *Columbia Journal of World Business*, **11** (1), 104–14.

result. An intricate form of spider's-web joint venture is shown in Figure 13.3. Two intricate and complex joint venture networks are shown for the automotive industry and the telecommunications industry in Figure 13.3 which illustrate the point.

## Benefits of international joint ventures

A joint venture may be considered a mode of interfirm cooperation lying between the extremes of complete vertical integration of business activities within one firm, to the opposite case where stages of production and distribution are owned by separate companies which contract with each other through conventional market mechanisms.

Four major advantages for joint ventures may be identified in the literature: (a) avoidance of inter-firm contracting, transactions and negotiations costs (Williamson 1975); (b) reduction in costs, or economies of scale from combining common administrative, transport and marketing expenses in two or more stages of production or distribution; (c) internalization of technological or administrative secrets within a firm which minimizes the risk of dissipation of competitive advantage arising from these secrets (Teece, 1981; Rugman, 1981); and (d) the ability to implement technological changes more quickly and over more stages of production (Contractor and Lorange, 1988; Contractor, 1986).

The formation of joint ventures is frequently cited as a way of reducing risk to the partners. A joint venture may be attractive in a project involving a large investment. It may also be beneficial in diversifying the portfolio of investments of one or all partners. In this context it has been noted that joint ventures make it possible to access the marketing knowledge of the partner firm active in the market immediately rather than waiting for the internal development of such skills (Exhibit 13.5).

Automotive industry

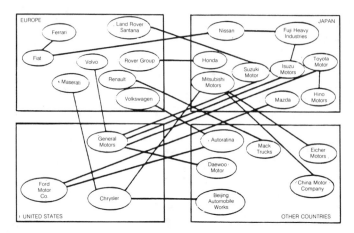

Telecommunications industry

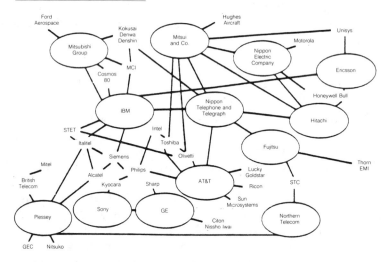

**Figure 13.3** Spider's-web joint ventures in automotive and telecommunications industries (Source: Devlin, Godfrey and Blackley, Mark (1988) 'Strategic alliances: Guidelines for success,' *Long Range Planning*, October, pp. 14–23)

Joint ventures facilitate faster market entry and payback. This is of particular significance in such industries as pharmaceuticals where the certification process consumes a great deal of time. It is often possible in joint ventures to combine slack facilities and expertise in the partner firms. In such circumstances the cost of the joint venture to the partnership may be less than it would be to each partner operating independently. Finally, a joint venture may enable a partial containment of the political risk associated with forming an alliance with a local partner. In

---

**Exhibit 13.5   Co-operating through joint ventures**

---

*New Zealanders discover valuable marketing edge through new LA alliances*

Latin America is beginning to see its share of new corporate alliances that are structured to meet changing global competition. One of the most interesting trends is emerging in Chile, where New Zealand companies with little international presence are moving quickly with investments of the order of $350 million. A look at the rationales of two recent deals offers insight into the possibilities for cross-regional competitive alliances with a Latin flavour.

Carter Holt Harvey, the fourth-largest company in New Zealand, is engaging in a joint venture with Angelini's Cholguan Group to establish a medium density fibreboard (MDF) plant. The 50–50 equity-based project is valued at $25 million and will be CHH's first offshore operating venture. The plant is located in southern Chile and is expected to be operational by early 1988. Annual production capacity will be 100,000 m$^3$ of board, with estimated annual exports of $25 million.

CHH's fundamental motivation in the plan is to change the focus of its relationship with Chilean producers, from competition to co-operation. Executive Chairman, Richard Carter, explains why his company took this approach: "As Chile is poised to become one of the world's largest suppliers of radiata pine products, we must have a strategy to maximize the economic benefit to both countries. The alternative is direct competition, but with Chile having a significant cost advantage against New Zealand."

The JV combines the strengths of its two partners: The Cholguan Group contributes quality raw material and industrial experience, while CHH makes available both its technology and its international marketing experience and presence.

By building the plant with Cholguan, and investing $164 million in related projects with Angelini, CHH will have access to a large and growing source of cheap pine, along with "on the ground" presence to influence the future processing and sale of radiata. It will also gain a bigger share of the world MDF market.

**Source:** *Business Latin America*, 30 March, 1987, **97**, 102–3.

---

such circumstances, the local partner would ensure that negative public policy interference was minimized while meeting host country industrial policy. The benefits of joint ventures are summarized in Table 13.6.

## Access to new resources

Many firms turn to joint ventures as a way of diversifying activities and for company growth. The small company frequently provides entrepreneurial enthusiasm, vigour, flexibility and advanced technology while the large company

**Table 13.6**  Benefits of joint ventures

Facilitates technology transfer
- codification/public knowledge
- converting head knowledge to production
- impact of technology on marketing relationships
- discovery of price of technology

Access to resources
- rapid product diversification strategies as means of corporate growth favours JV's
- provide funds and access to local capital markets
- each partner concentrates resources on an area of greatest advantage
- avoids necessity of developing international management skills
- access to knowledge of local environment and markets
- may reach critical mass for internationalization
- more efficient competitive position

Political pressures
- host country pressure for local participation
- local control of job creation and technology transfer
- preferential treatment (remittance of royalties)
- may avoid local tariffs and non-tariff barriers

Access to markets
- quick and efficient access to distribution
- by-passes trade barriers
- image/attitude to local company

Other reasons
- good public relations
- curbs potential competition
- provides temporary relief for weak product portfolio

provides capital, worldwide channels of marketing, distribution, and service. This combination allows for the rapid diffusion of technology-based product innovation into large international markets. The synthesis implied can create a significant competitive advantage.

Access to valued and scarce human resources with appropriate education and cultural background is a key factor in joint venture formation. One of the critical reasons why European and American companies enter joint ventures in Japan is the inability of companies "going it alone" to attract local management as a result of their "outsider" status (Abegglen and Stalk, 1985). This is supported by Cateora (1990) who states that numerous joint ventures have been formed with the express intention of acquiring nationals with managerial ability. The local partner's participation in the development of the joint venture imposes less of a burden on its managerial capabilities than would a wholly owned or controlled subsidiary (Killing, 1982).

Access to capital is another resource frequently sought when firms enter a joint venture. Capital markets are characterized by significant transaction costs and credit markets are likely to be imperfect for young firms with little or no track record or experience, and for investments in risky projects with no collateral such as research and development (Hennart, 1988). Technology-based firms frequently encounter severe opposition in securing funds for expansion. O'Donoghue (1986) found that 50 per cent of outgoing joint ventures considered access to capital to be important.

Access to distribution channels is also an important motivating factor. Strategic advantages under this heading include an existing marketing establishment, links with buyers, knowledge of the local market and culture, a recognizable brand name and market access. Joint ventures also enable the other partner to reduce its average distribution costs as there is a greater volume throughput (Ohmae, 1989). Equity positions in a partner company can be acquired strategically to strengthen marketing agreements such as Olivetti's agreement to market AT & T products in Europe, where AT & T had relatively little market experience.

Stopford and Wells (1972) found that general knowledge of the local economy was ranked as the most important contribution that a local partner could make to an international firm seeking entry to the market. Anderson and Coughlan (1987) support this view by saying that some form of quasi-integration is likely to occur if the markets under consideration are outside Europe or the United States. In such circumstances a form of internal uncertainty is created by the business distance involved (Anderson and Gatignon, 1986). Uncertainty due to business distance may cause some firms to undervalue foreign investments (Root, 1983), thereby resulting in a lower form of commitment.

## Joint ventures and host country policies

Foreign firms sometimes express reservations over host government ownership restrictions. Imposing a joint venture on a reluctant international firm may curb its contribution to the new company and thereby reduce the venture's productivity. While joint ventures may have narrower product lines, smaller scale and less input of the investor's technology they are especially useful in obtaining access to difficult markets, such as Eastern European markets.

Since Yugoslavia pioneered legislation in 1967 for mixed communist–capitalist arrangements, Eastern European countries, and more recently the People's Republic of China, have forged economic and financial relationships with Western capitalist firms. Companies such as Procter & Gamble, which has argued that this entry mode is inconsistent with its company strategy, have entered into such arrangements in China and other socialist countries. The growth potential of these markets provides the incentive to overcome accepted company philosophies.

Governments of countries such as India, Mexico, China and even France try to encourage joint ventures with local partners through a variety of means. The mechanisms through which joint ventures are encouraged may be quite direct or subtle, such as in France where preferential procurement may occur for joint ventures (Gomes-Casseres, 1989). When asked to state the value of joint ventures to Saudi Arabia, Mahmoud Nasher, Chairman of the Finance Committee of the Arab–British Chamber of Commerce replied:

> I would encourage joint ventures only in industries needing relatively high technologies which we would not be able to get without offering the joint venture and where the Saudis are guaranteed the transfer of technology, and I mean really sophisticated technology, not something you can go and buy in the open market. In my opinion, that's the only justification for having the joint venture. (*Arab News*, Saturday 3 December, 1988)

Joint ventures are useful in any country which restricts market entry by exporting through tariff or non-tariff barriers. The Piper Aircraft Company was forced to enter a joint venture with Embraer, the Brazilian aircraft manufacturer, as the Brazilian government increased tariffs on imported planes from 7 per cent to 50 per cent, thereby effectively prohibiting imports (Moxon, 1987).

## Cost of joint ventures

Joint ventures may be criticized because they are unstable for a variety of reasons, because they may be instrumental in creating a competitor, and because the costs of control become too high. Taking the instability issue first, many studies have highlighted the high break-up rate of joint ventures (Killing 1982). Seventy per cent of the partnerships in studies by McKinsey and Coopers & Lybrand eventually broke up as well as half of those in Harrigan's (1988) sample.

The characterization of joint ventures as inherently unstable may be questioned as it fails to recognize that the joint venture might have been intended as a transitional structure (Harrigan, 1988). Multinational firms are more likely to buy out their partners when they already control a majority of the shares of a company and are more likely to divest when they hold a minority shareholding. In this sense, joint ventures may be viewed as "instruments providing firms with flexibility in responding to trends that are difficult to predict." (Gomes-Casseres, 1987, p. 99) Finally, this author found that the change from joint ownership to wholly owned subsidiary is likely to occur in countries with which the international firm is already familiar. Stopford and Wells (1972) believe that firms tend to reserve proprietary knowledge for modes of entry that they control completely.

Sometimes joint ventures create competitors unnecessarily. According to Lassere (1984), there exists the possibility for long-term opportunistic behaviour from the technology buyer when the technology supplier is no longer needed. This viewpoint may be criticized, however, on a number of grounds. First, the pace of technical change has resulted in shorter product life cycles which means that this risk is minimized by a constantly changing environment. Second, the technology supplier will probably be constantly updating and improving existing products in order to maintain its competitive edge. Third, joint ventures can be dangerous for the technology buyer, particularly when the technology recipient uses the alliance to avoid investment to design and innovation. This short-term orientation can result in a dependency spiral as the technology buyer contributes fewer and fewer distinctive skills. This may force the buyer to reveal more of its internal operations to keep the other partner interested.

Alliances with Japanese companies have resulted in American companies failing to develop essential manufacturing skills, thus preventing them from moving down the experience curve. This failure stems from the US firms taking a short-term orientation and ignoring the organizational learning opportunities that a joint venture affords them. Fourth, the tension between cooperative and competitive strategies varies according to the type of activity. The risks of disclosure are higher for some activities than for others. Government regulation and interlocking directorates carry higher risks of disclosure than do mergers.

On a more general level the difficulties associated with joint ventures may be summarized under three major headings (Table 13.7). As the network of joint ventures becomes larger there is an increased possibility of conflict of interest among the partners. The cost of controlling the joint venture becomes quite significant. The need for control strengthens the argument for the unambiguous control within a single firm as found in foreign direct investment and acquisition modes of entry.

A number of conditions have been identified under which it is easier to operate international joint ventures. These conditions have been classified into dominant partnership and shared partnership arrangements (Killing, 1980). The circumstances under which each works best are as follows:

1. Dominant partnership:

   - The international partner should be dominant when it is important to have long-term control of know-how; the local partner should be passive and outside the industry;
   - The local partner should be dominant when the international partner's skills are needed only temporarily and can easily be transferred.

2. Shared partnership works if the skills of both partners are required over time:

**Table 13.7**  Difficulties with joint ventures

Loss of control over foreign operations
   - large investment of financial, technical or managerial resources favours greater control than is possible in a joint venture

Joint ventures are difficult to co-ordinate
   - lack adequate procedures for protecting proprietary information
   - shared decisions affect global marketing arrangements

Loss of flexibility and confidentiality
   - change in product-market mission may make joint venture a liability
   - unease about sharing technology
   - one partner may form alliance with other partner's competitor
   - managerial dependency between joint venture and one of partners

- Choose a partner with complementary skills;
- Give the joint venture autonomy;
- Allow partners to buy out for a change in conditions.

While many companies have experience of joint ventures, circumstances never remain the same. What starts out as a relatively straightforward plan can change for many reasons. The benefits and risks associated with some joint ventures can be very high for both partners especially where the investment involved is high and the venture involves new technologies and new markets (Exhibit 13.6).

## Evaluation of competitive alliances

Like enterprise in general, there are many risks associated with competitive alliances. The issue for the firm is how it can obtain as much value as possible while maintaining control of its assets and how it can select a partner to attain this objective. Root (1988) classifies risks associated with collaborative agreements on the basis of whether they are fiduciary or environmental. Fiduciary risk refers to the probability that the partner will fail to honour elements of the agreement. Environmental risk is the amount of the firm's assets which would be directly affected by changes in the political, economic, competitive environment. According to Root, there is a trade-off between the two types of risk, the acquisition of control is often at the expense of increased exposure to environmental risk.

### Obtaining value and control in competitive alliances

The issue of obtaining value and control in competitive alliances is especially important for the international firm. A very useful framework, on which this section is based, has been developed by Lorange (1985) which allows these issues to be examined. Marketing partnership agreements tend to be focussed on a specific narrow set of objectives and limited in time. The strategic value of such agreements tends to be high for both partners (Figure 13.11). Time may be critical and so a rapid entry may be essential for success. It may be too expensive and too time consuming for the firm to attain such objectives by itself. Similarly for the local firm, access to the new product may be critical for success. Many such firms have identified gaps in the market and do not possess products in this portfolio to serve the new requirements. A marketing agreement with an international firm may bring temporary respite. While the international firm would wish for as much control as possible, from a practical point of view much of this control may be given to local firms (Table 13.8). Because Partner A — the local firm — is closer to the customer, he will tend to exercise greater control.

---

**Exhibit 13.6   Joint venture when investment is high, technology is new and markets unfamiliar**

---

### *How Philips became an instant leader in medical equipment*

Back in the 1970s, electronics giant Philips was among the world leaders in the $1.5 billion X-ray equipment industry. Then computerized scanners revolutionized the business of helping doctors tell what is wrong with their patients. The leaders in this medical imaging field, General Electric Co. of the US and West Germany's Siemens, left Philips far behind.

But now Philips is striking back. The Dutch company is teaming up in a new 50–50 joint venture with Britain's General Electric Co. (GEC) which is not related to GE.

The venture combines Philips' medical systems business and GEC's Cleveland-based Picker International subsidiary. It is the latest example of a strategy that gives Philips a fighting chance in a broad array of businesses from televisions to telecommunications. The key to the strategy: creating dozens of joint ventures to spread Philips' costs of research, boost market share, and increase the company's political clout in protected markets.

Philips first forged foreign alliances decades ago but the numbers of such linkups — and their importance — have soared in recent years. Says President Cornelis J. van der Klugt: "We are evolving from a European-based company to a global company."

The new medical venture with GEC illustrates the benefits and risks of the joint venture strategy. It will create a company with 17,000 employees and $2 billion in sales, meaning it will rank No 2 in the $5.2 billion world market for diagnostic imaging equipment behind Siemens. In the US, Philips and Picker's combined medical imaging sales totalled an estimated $860 million in 1986, according to Philip G. Drew, president of Drew Consultants Inc., which advises medical equipment makers. That makes the new venture a contender for the No 1 spot in the market currently held by GE.

The venture will also improve Philips' US marketing network and reduce its vulnerability to exchange-rate fluctuations. With 35 percent of its medical sales in the US, Philips saw its margins shrink dramatically last year when the dollar plunged against European currencies.

But the venture poses serious challenges. The companies offer an overlapping range of X-ray machines, CT scanners, and magnetic-resonance imaging equipment. Over time, analysts expect the companies to integrate their product lines and slash their payrolls. Nor is the competition likely to make things any easier: GE, which has been concentrating on the high end of the market, is likely to come up with a lower-cost line of magnetic-resonance imaging equipment before year end.

**Source:** *Business Week*, 11 May, 1987, p. 30

**Table 13.8** Value and control in competitive alliances

| Strategic value \ Desired control | High for partner A Low for partner B | High for both partners |
|---|---|---|
| High for both partners | Co-operation agreements | Franchising |
| High for partner A Low for partner B | Joint ventures | Licensing |

Source: Adapted from Lorange, Peter (1985) 'Co-Operative ventures in multinational settings: A framework,' *Second Open International IMP Research Seminar on International Marketing*, University of Uppsala, 4–6 September.

The strategic value and desired control is high for both partners in a franchising arrangement. For the international firm, Partner B — the franchisor — the strategy is to develop and invest in a franchising concept and package. The local firm, Partner A — the franchisee — develops a business in the local market based on the franchise package. The local firm invests funds and time to develop a local market position.

For the franchisor the degree of desired control over strategic resources tends to be high because of the importance of the contract for the implementation of his internationalization strategy. For that reason the franchisor retains control over the franchising package. For the franchisee the strategic value is also high. For that reason the franchisee retains control over its local organization and the market. Unlike joint ventures, there is no common organization in terms of people. Informed contact between the partners ensures that the value creation process works smoothly. Franchising as an organizational form may be stable and mutually beneficial as it allows both partners to obtain their strategic needs in terms of control and value.

The strategic value of licensing tends to be different for licensor and licensee. For Partner B — the licensor — the alliance is likely to have a relatively low strategic value. The licensor is typically more interested in his own domestic market; his major business interests lie there and not in dealing with foreign firms. The licence agreement is often seen as marginal for Partner B — the licensor. He should acknowledge, however, that through licensing he can obtain rapid diffusion of his know-how and obtain relatively painless pay-offs. For the licensee — Partner A — the strategic value tends to be high. He frequently stakes his own business on obtaining a unique know-how which gives him a competitive advantage in the local market.

The level of control tends to be high for the licensor since he controls the know-how as well as the support organization. Control is also high for the licensee since he controls the commercialization of the know-how. The know-how is typically a small component in the developing the business.

Finally, joint ventures pose a different set of problems for examination. For the sake of argument, assume that Partner B — the international partner — is the majority owner in the joint venture. For him the strategic value of the joint venture tends to be high. The international partner possesses the unique know-how, technology or marketing, and often acquires the missing dimensions in the value creating chain that it does not already possess and offers the minority partner participation in the business in this way (Lorange, 1985, p. 31). The joint venture is strategically critical to Partner B. For Partner A, the local firm, the strategic value tends to be smaller; its position in the joint venture is typically not essential to the implementation of its overall strategy.

For Partner B, control over resources tends to be high. By ensuring a high degree of control over the joint venture, Partner B can exercise control over its own resources and know-how so that they do not leak to Partner A. Partner A has little strategic control over its strategic resources once they have been committed to the joint venture.

The ability of the different forms of competitive alliance to cope with environmental change is a key consideration in regard to developing relationships with firms in international markets. These relationships arise from contact with partner companies. Sometimes such contacts are very much at arm's length but frequently they involve the exchange of personnel for considerable periods of time. In joint ventures it is usual that training would mean the exchange of staff, and the development of joint ventures would need an extended two-way flow of key people between the partners. For these reasons it is important to examine how a particular form of competitive alliance responds to changes in the environment and how the partners in the alliance maintain contact (Table 13.9).

Marketing partnership agreements are frequently established for a particular product market and have a relatively short time scale. Usually an annual contract forms the basis of such a relationship with the option of extension where mutually agreed. In many situations, however, at least one party will not disclose full intentions regarding the longer-term development of the relationship and will reserve position to observe how the arrangement evolves. Sometimes firms see such relationships as a temporary measure until a more permanent arrangement can be found, e.g. a new product developed locally. In such circumstances the relationship may have only a temporary life. The continuation of the relationship depends very much on the two partners to ensure the performance of a specific task. Marketing partnership agreements are usually not equipped, therefore, with significant adaptive or environmental coping mechanisms and it is difficult to develop new business relationships within such partnerships.

In contrast, franchising arrangements have the potential for being stable and mutually beneficial for both partners since they permit both to achieve their respective strategic values. Furthermore, both partners gain from the relationship. The extent of the links between the partners required to attain their respective objectives is low. One of the potential weaknesses of this form of relationship is the relatively low ability of franchising to cope with major environmental changes.

Like franchising, the level of day-to-day contact in licensing required between

**Table 13.9**  Environmental change and organizational links in competitive alliance

| Ability to cope with environmental change | Continuous organizational links between partners | |
| --- | --- | --- |
| | High | Low |
| Low | Marketing partnership agreements | Franchising |
| High | Joint ventures | Licensing |

Source: Adapted from Lorange, Peter (1985) 'Co-operative ventures in multinational settings: A framework,' *Second Open International IMP Research Seminar on International Marketing*, University of Uppsala, 4–6 September.

the licensor and licensee tends to be low. The licence agreement forms the basis of the contact and may require an initial period of training but once the operation is running smoothly, there is little need for extensive further contact between the partners. Because the licensee has obtained a unique know-how which gives a competitive advantage in the local market the licensing arrangement tends to be highly adaptable to changing environmental circumstances. The licensing contract is easily modified to accommodate changes in the environment (Lorange 1985, p. 25).

Joint ventures between two independent partners tend to be able to cope with environmental change as a matter of course. A well-designed joint venture can be well equipped to adapt to a changing environment, particularly if established initially with such flexibility as an objective. A joint venture can sometimes be much more flexible than its parents, while at the same time involving extensive continuous organizational links with the partners. Nevertheless, firms sometimes prefer a licensing arrangement for many reasons. In the early 1980s, Atlas Copco was negotiating an entry into the Peoples Republic of China and faced a choice between a joint venture and a licensing arrangement. To facilitate the decision, Atlas Copco developed a list of thirteen decision criteria (Table 13.10). Having evaluated the situation, Atlas Copco decided to license only. Between October 1983 and May 1985 six licensee agreements were negotiated and signed. One agreement was negotiated but left unsigned.

## Selecting a partner for a competitive alliance

The key to forging mutually satisfactory joint ventures is a realistic assessment of the firm's strengths and weaknesses in the proposed venture (Harrigan, 1985). It is also necessary to assess the commitment of potential partners to the success of the venture and their willingness to contribute resources or provide a market for the products in a manner that accommodates their partners' needs. Search costs are high as major companies do not as a rule wish to sell their technology and smaller companies are more difficult to locate since they do not generally advertise their position (Killing, 1980). It may be necessary to look beyond the obvious candidates engaged in the same business to companies with marketing and manufacturing capabilities in related or complementary product or service areas.

**Table 13.10**  Deciding between a joint venture and a licence agreement in the People's Republic of China: Atlas Copco

| Decision criteria | Joint ventures | Licence |
|---|---|---|
| 1.  Equity contributions of capital or equipment | yes | no |
| 2.  Management responsibility | yes | no |
| 3.  Administrative and production responsibility | yes | no |
| 4.  Responsibility for adapting technology | yes | no |
| 5.  Responsibility for final product | yes | no |
| 6.  Dependent on local infrastructure | yes | no |
| 7.  Buy-back agreements (export) | yes | no |
| 8.  Component deliveries | yes | no |
| 9.  Final customer contacts (service) | yes | yes |
| 10.  Training and other technical assistance | yes | yes |
| 11.  Initial fee | yes<br>export | yes<br>no export |
| 12.  Royalty | yes<br>export | yes<br>no export |
| 13.  Dividend | yes<br>export | no |

Source: Sandberg, Hans (1986) 'Atlas Copco — License Agreements,' a paper presented at the *Chinese Culture and Management Conference*, Economist Intelligence Unit, Intercontinental Hotel, Paris 23–24 January.

In many cases the process of partner selection is not performed thoroughly. The first candidate, generally discovered through contacts established by mail arranged by a banker or a business colleague already established in the country, is often the one with whom the company undertakes discussions. Little or no screening is done, nor is there an in-depth investigation of the motives and capabilities of the candidate.

In more favourable cases, where the firm is already engaged in business in the country, the selected partner may be the agent who is already working for the company. For the foreign partner, there is the advantage of entering into an agreement with someone who is already familiar with the company's products and the parent company. However, the fact that a local company proves to be a good distributor does not guarantee that it will be as good in a joint venture involving manufacturing activities (Lasserre, 1984). To overcome this problem Lasserre proposes a method of assessing a partner based on an analysis of the strategic fit of the firms involved and analysis of the resources fit. This approach has been adapted to accommodate an international firm and a local partner (Figure 13.4).

It is proposed first that potential partners examine their own resources through a detailed resource audit involving the firm's technology, financial and human resources, and experience. Second, the potential partners should then carry out a detailed product-market audit of their respective operations. A comparison of these two sets of audits presents the potential partners with a resources fit and a product-market fit. The next step is to determine the strategy direction for the alliance if there is to be one. The alliance might take the form

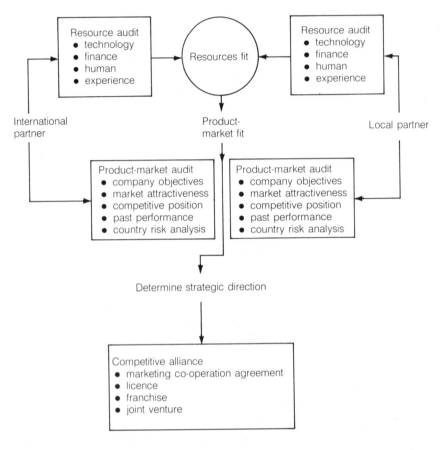

**Figure 13.4**  Framework for partner assessment (Source: Adapted from Lasserre, Philip (1984) 'Selecting a foreign partner for technology transfer,' *Long Range Planning*, **17**, 43—9)

of a marketing partnership agreement, a licence, franchise or a joint venture.

Lasserre maintains that this detailed approach to assessing a potential partner for an alliance is rarely implemented since it requires time, effort and investment in data gathering. A minimum period of one to two years of prior contacts and long-term missions by the foreign company to familiarize itself with the country culture and the business practices of the local company would seem to be required in most circumstances, especially for alliances requiring greater commitment, such as joint ventures.

Because both partners have similar expectations in regard to strategic value and the need for control, it is likely that franchising and joint ventures would produce a better resource and strategic fit than would marketing partnership agreements and licensing. The match in terms of resources and strategy for the latter two is frequently not as harmonious. Circumstances often arise where only one of the partners achieves the objectives established. For these reasons, marketing partnership agreements and licensing arrangements tend to degenerate over time and ultimately dissolve for partners who actively seek to attain their strategic objectives.

## Summary

This chapter examines the various forms of competitive alliance found among firms in international markets. Four distinct forms of competitive alliance are discussed: marketing partnership agreements; licensing; franchising; and joint ventures. Each involves the need to work closely with a firm located in a different market and culture. Greatest commitment to international markets is usually found among equity joint ventures established to transfer product or marketing technology.

The form of alliance varies by product and marketing situation. Some product markets favour one form of alliance while others favour a different form. Marketing partnership agreements are usually established to serve special short-term needs in the market, often involving cross-distribution of the partners' products. Licensing is frequently found as a mode of entry in difficult and distant markets, and is frequently used as a means of transferring product technology. Franchising, in contrast, usually involves a marketing technology transfer to a relatively similar or familiar market. Increasingly, franchising is a versatile means of market entry to secure more distant markets where initial demand is stimulated by international advertising and word of mouth from tourists and other travellers.

Joint ventures are often the only means of entering some markets, especially those where public policy encourages the transfer of technology and know-how to local firms. Joint ventures tend to reduce the risk involved since capital is shared between the partners. The benefits of joint ventures include the ease of technology transfer, access to resources, ability to comply with political pressure, and access to markets.

The chapter ends with a discussion on the circumstances in which one form of alliance might be favoured over another. A simple framework is outlined which highlighted ways in which the value of each form of competitive alliance could be determined.

## Discussion questions

1. Competitive alliances may be described as a set of methods of entering international markets which, in terms of commitment to internationalization, lie somewhere between exporting and foreign direct investment. Discuss.

2. What are the key characteristics of marketing partnership agreements?

3. When would you use licensing as a means of entering new international markets? What are the advantages and disadvantages of licensing?

4. Franchising is a common method of entering services markets abroad. What is the special attraction of international franchising to both partners?

5. Discuss the proposition that no firm should invest in a joint venture to enter an international market as it is always better to export the product or service or establish a plant abroad through foreign direct investment.

6. How can the firm ensure that it continues to obtain value from a competitive alliance?

7. What are the key considerations in selecting a partner for a competitive alliance?

8. Select a firm located near you and assume it is considering entering a distant market. How would you decide the best form of competitive alliance for the firm? Would you suggest some other alternative?

## References

Abegglen, James C. and Stalk, George, Jr (1985) *Kaisa: The Japanese Corporation*, Basic Books, NY.

Adams, J. and Mendelsohn, M. (1986) 'Recent developments in franchising,' *Journal of Business Law*, pp. 206–19.

Anderson Erin and Coughlan, Ann T. (1987) 'International market entry and expansion via independent or integrated channels of distribution,' *Journal of Marketing*, **51**, 71–82.

Anderson, Erin and Gatignon, H. (1986) 'Mode of foreign entry: A transaction cost analysis and propositions,' *Journal of International Business Studies*, Fall, 1–26.

Austen, Ellen R. (1987) 'International corporate linkages: Dynamic forms in changing environments,' *Columbia Journal of World Business*, Summer, pp. 3–6.

Ayling, D. (1987) 'Franchising has its dark side,' *Accountancy*, **99**, 112, 113–17.

Brandenburg, M. (1986) 'Free yourself from servitude,' *Accountancy*, **98**, 11–18.

Carstairs, J. and Welch, M. (1983) 'Licensing and internationalization of smaller companies,' *Management International Review*, **22**, 56–71.

Cateora, Philip (1990) *International Marketing*, 7th edn, Irwin, Homewood, Ill.

Contractor, Farok J. (1981) 'The role of licensing in international strategy,' *Columbia Journal of World Business*, Winter, pp. 73–9.

Contractor, F. and Lorange, P. (1988) 'Why should firms co-operate? The strategy and economic basis for co-operative ventures,' in Contractor, F. and Lorange P. (eds.), *Co-operative Strategies in International Business*, Lexington Books, Lexington, MA.

Contractor, Farok J. (1986) 'International business: An alternative view,' *International Marketing Review*, **3** (1), 74–85.

Devlin, Godfrey and Blackley, Mark (1988) 'Strategic alliances: Guidelines for success,' *Long Range Planning*, October, pp. 14–23.

Gomes-Casseres, B. (1989) 'Joint venture in the face of global competition,' *Sloan Management Review*, Spring, pp. 17–26.

Götberg, Göran (1989) 'Franchising in international marketing,' in Gustafsson, Karl Erik and Gunilla Green (eds.), *Marketing at the Gothenberg School of Economics: Proceedings from a Symposium for Bo Wickströn*, BAS, Gothenberg, Sweden, pp. 83–93.

Gullander, Staffon (1976) 'Joint ventures and corporate strategy,' *Columbia Journal of World Business*, **11** (1), 104–14.

Hakansson, Hakan and Johanson, Jan (1988) 'Formal and informal co-operation in international industrial networks,' in Contractor, F. and Lorange, P. (eds.), *Co-operative Strategies in International Business*, Lexington Books, Lexington, MA.

Harrigan, Kathryn R. (1983) 'A framework for looking at vertical integration,' *Journal of Business Strategy*, **3**, 30–7.

Harrigan, Kathryn R. (1986) 'Matching vertical integration strategies to competitive conditions,' *Strategic Management Journal*, **7**, 535–54.

Harrigan, Kathryn R. (1988) 'Joint ventures and competitive strategy,' *Strategic Management Journal*, **9** (2), 141–58.

Harrigan, Kathryn R. (1985): *Strategies for Joint Venture Success*, Lexington Books, Lexington, MA.

Hennart, Jean F. (1988) 'A transaction costs theory of equity joint ventures,' *Strategic Management Journal*, **9**, 361–74.

Killing, J. (1982) 'How to make a global joint venture work,' *Harvard Business Review*, **60**, 120–7.

Killing, Peter (1980) 'Technology acquisition: License agreements or joint ventures,' *Columbia Journal of World Business*, **15** (3), 38–46.

Lasserre, Philip (1984) 'Selecting a foreign partner for technology transfer,' *Long Range Planning*, **17**, 43–9.

Lorange, Peter (1985) 'Co-operative ventures in multinational settings: A framework,' *Second Open International IMP Research Seminar on International Marketing*, University of Uppsala, 4–6 September.

Lowe, Julian and Crawford, Nick (1984) *Technology Licensing and the Small Firm*, Gower, England.

Millman, A.F. (1983) 'Licensing technology,' *Management Decision*, **21** (3), 3–16.

Moxon, Richard W. (1987) 'International competition in high technology,' *International Marketing Review*, **4** (2), 7–20.

Norton, S.W. (1988) 'Franchising, brand name, capital and the entrepreneurial capacity problem,' *Strategic Management Journal*, **9**, Special Issue, pp. 105–14.

Norton, S.W. (1988b) 'An empirical look at franchising as an organisational form,' *Journal of Business*, **61** (2), 197–218.

O'Donoghue, Deirdre (1986) Joint Ventures as an International Growth Strategy, unpublished Master of Business Studies Dissertation, Department of Marketing, University College, Dublin.

Ohmae, Kenichi (1989) 'The global logic of strategic alliances,' *Harvard Business Review*, March–April, pp. 143–54.

Root, Franklin R. (1983) *Foreign Market Entry Strategies*, AMACOM, New York.

Root, Franklin R. (1988) 'Some taxonomies of international co-operative agreements,' in Contractor, F. and Lorange, P. (eds.), *Co-operative Strategies in International Business*, Lexington Books, Lexington, MA.

Rubin, P. (1978) 'The theory of the firm and the structure of the franchise contract,' *Journal of Law and Economics*, **21**, 223–33.

Rugman, Alan M. (1981) *Inside the Multinationals*, Croom Helm Limited, London.

Stern, P. and Stanworth, J. (1988) 'The development of franchising in Britain,' *National Westminister Quarterly Review*, May, pp. 38–48.

Stopford, J.M. and Wells, Louis T. (1972) *Managing the Multinational Enterprise: Organization of the firm and the ownership of the subsidiaries*, Basic Books NY.

Teece, David J. (1981) 'The market for know-how and the efficient international transfer of technology,' *Annals of the American Academy of Political and Social Science*, **458**, November, 81–9.

Thorelli, Hans B. (1986) 'Between networks and hierarchies,' *Strategic Management Journal*, **7**, 37–51.

Vernon, Raymond (1983) 'Organisational risk and institutional responses to international risk,' in Herring, R. (ed.), *Managing International Risk*, Cambridge University Press, NY.

Williamson, Oliver E. (1975) *Markets and Hierarchies, Analysis and Antitrust Implications*, Free Press. NY.

# Entering international markets through foreign direct investment

## 14

In the preceding chapter the discussion ended with a description and evaluation of joint ventures, the form of competitive alliance involving greatest investment and commitment by the firm. In Chapter 12 we discussed exporting as the mode of entry to foreign markets which is based on organic growth by the firm. In this chapter foreign direct investment, which refers to the acquisition of foreign-based firms and the financing and management of new ventures abroad, is examined. Within the analytical framework adopted, expansion by the firm into international markets through acquisition and new venture investment represents the greatest degree of commitment and requires a greater investment of resources than the other modes of market entry.

## Motives for foreign direct investment

### Nature of foreign direct investment

Investment in foreign markets may take several forms. An important distinction is made between portfolio investment and foreign direct investment. Portfolio investment refers to the purchase of a shareholding in companies, usually through various stock exchanges, with the purpose of obtaining a return on the funds invested. Since portfolio investment is not directly concerned with the control and management of the foreign enterprise we are not immediately concerned with it here. Foreign direct investment refers to participation in the management and effective control of the enterprise in addition. Foreign direct investment also means the establishment of international operations by a firm on the expansion of existing operations. Usually there is a heavy financial commitment involved. More important, perhaps, is the transfer of technology, management skills, production processes, manufacturing and marketing know-how, and other resources.

The choice between foreign direct investment and exporting the knowledge or know-how depends on the additional costs of doing business in the foreign market and on the cost and feasibility of selling the knowledge and know-how.

Classical investment theory suggests that the reason for foreign direct investment is profit maximization, i.e. the factors of production move to where the highest rate of return can be earned. Foreign direct investment is concerned with mobile factors of production. Behind classical investment theory is classical trade theory; the former is an extension of the latter: capital-rich countries tend to export capital intensive products and to invest capital abroad. Labour-rich countries tend to export labour intensive products and experience a migration of workers to better-off countries. Classical investment theory is a macro economic theory which does little to explain the investment decisions of individual firms.

The firm which invests abroad transmits equity capital entrepreneurship, technology or other productive knowledge in the context of an industry specific package. In most investments abroad where the firm replicates what it does well in one market, the importance of some unique asset or competitive advantage in the firm is recognized in another market. It may be a potential invention or a differentiated product which is in demand in the target market. For the possession of some special asset to encourage the firm to invest abroad two conditions must exist: (a) the asset must be a public good within the firm, e.g. knowledge fundamental to the production of a profitable product; and (b) the return attainable must depend, at least partially, on local production (Caves, 1971, pp. 4–5). The essential feature of an asset conducive to foreign direct investment is not that its opportunity cost should be zero, but that it should be low relative to the return available through foreign direct investment.

## Managerial motives for FDI

Many firms which internationalize through the direct investment mode do so to gain better access to scarce raw materials or intermediate products. Many firms, particularly those which use commodities such as oil, bauxite or timber, integrate backwards to ensure an adequate supply of raw materials. Sometimes the reason for foreign direct investment is to develop foreign sources of components. More common is the situation where the firm's intention is to assemble final products for sale in local foreign markets. Investment of this form is often chosen as an alternative to exporting for several reasons.

First, investment in the foreign market may improve the firm's ability to serve that market and nearby markets. By designing products for local conditions the firm provides a better service to distributors and customers. Second, the firm may be forced to establish in a local market to defend it from competitors. Local production may lower the final cost of the product through lower production and distribution costs. Third, local production may be unavoidable where government policies and trade barriers are such as to make exporting unattractive.

Foreign direct investment also occurs where competitive alliances make certain objectives unattainable. Sometimes firms are not in a position to control the use and exploitation of their technology by licences or joint ventures. Firms which depend for their competitive advantage on patents and similar forms of protection fall into this category. Foreign direct investment may provide the opportunity for a more efficient utilization of the technology and greater profits.

There are a number of managerial reasons for entry to foreign markets through foreign direct investment. Many firms capable of investing in foreign markets possess a number of advantages not available to local firms. The foreign firm can sometimes gain a significant share of a local market when local firms do not have adequate management or marketing skills or when the local market has operated on the basis of administered prices. Foreign firms frequently have access to proprietary technology, which gives them an advantage. They may also possess scale economies which allow them to compete aggressively. Frequently firms are forced to merge with others in the same or different market in order to have the critical mass to compete successfully in international markets. Many relatively small branded products firms recognize the threat of such take-overs by large cash-rich companies seeking entry to luxury markets (Exhibit 14.1).

The specific reasons behind a firm's decision to invest abroad are operating efficiency, risk reduction, market development, and host government policy (Figure 14.1). It is frequently possible to manufacture products more efficiently outside the domestic market. A firm increases the efficiency of the production process if it locates where the factors of production are cheapest. For example, in the early 1980s, a number of West German clothing manufacturers established production facilities in the Far East because German labour is relatively expensive.

At the end of the 1980s, other locations especially in the Mediterranean regions, have begun to feature. Efficiency gains may also be possible if operations are closer to the source of raw materials, e.g. oil, ores and timber. Similarly, efficiency gains are possible when the firm produces closer to the market. It is essential for most service industries to locate in the market. This explains the location of many US firms in Europe and Japanese firms in Europe and the United States.

Sometimes firms internationalize through investment to guarantee access to raw materials or cheaper labour. In the latter situation firms are known to twin plants in their network, e.g. a capital-intensive factory in one country twinned with a labour-intensive factory in another. Firms, especially those in services, internationalize by acquisition, especially to protect the domestic market and to hold on to customers there. Advertising agencies frequently follow their clients abroad to protect their domestic operations. Finally, a shortage or restriction on foreign exchange may encourage a firm to locate abroad to protect its profits and sales.

Firms sometimes internationalize through the investment mode to reduce risk. Risk reduction is further enhanced through diversification since it is unlikely that all the firm's investment will perform at the same level of profitability. Because expansions and contractions in different countries do not occur at the same time, the firm should be able to stabilize its earnings by locating in several foreign countries.

## Exhibit 14.1   Brand acquisition for fast market entry

### *"Crazy for European luxury"*

Brilliant marketing has made it possible for European luxury goods makers to ride a tide of affluence and to turn hitherto exclusive products into global brands. Luxury today is big business, and it is a business dominated by the panache of European products.

Along with unprecedented success, however, have come the pressures of growth and size. A wave of mergers has swept through the luxury industry as companies scramble for the capital to fuel world-wide marketing machines. Few luxury firms can survive any longer without the backing of a much larger industrial company or group, a stock market listing or a merger with another luxury producer. The smaller, often family-owned luxury companies are having increasing trouble maintaining control and market share.

Gucci is among the companies vulnerable to take-over, according to luxury industry sources. Others include Hermès, Chanel, Nina Ricci, Bulgari, Lanvin or such champagne and spirit houses as Taittinger and Martell, they say. "The small, family-owned company is condemned to die", warns Cartier's Perrin.

"You must be strong and powerful to develop and survive today in luxury", says Racamier. The 74-year-old former steel industry executive notes that it takes $50–60 million to launch a perfume on the international market.

"The apparition of a unique market in the Western world demands tremendous financial means and a world-wide distribution network", adds Chevalier, of Moët Hennessy, from its gleaming steel and glass offices near Arc de Triomphe. Earlier in the year Moët Hennessy concluded a deal with Britain's Guinness Distillers Ltd to merge world-wide distribution networks.

**Source:** *International Management*, December, 1987, pp. 24–8.

A second cost-related factor is economies of scale. Scale economies arise in several areas of the firm's operations. They are most often associated with production as occurs, for example, in car manufacturing in Europe where different components are produced in different countries. European and even global manufacturing networks are frequently more cost effective than concentrating the production process in one location. Scale economies also occur in financing and marketing. Financial economies of scale may be obtained by a firm with international operations when the firm gains access to several capital markets. Marketing scale economies are evident in many products and services, especially franchised fast foods, soft drinks and clothing.

Foreign direct investment may also be explained by the firm's desire to exploit the market. Some firms possess certain advantages in the design and development of products and services. The source of these advantages lies in the

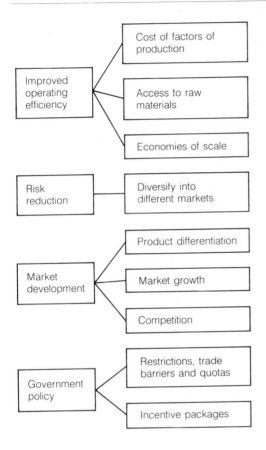

**Figure 14.1**   Reasons for foreign direct investment

ability of the firm to differentiate its products and services. Product differentiation is a strong motive for foreign direct investment (Hymer, 1976). Investment abroad allows such firms to internationalize the product differentiation advantage to other countries where profitable. Because the advantages stem from specialized knowledge, technology and patent protection, foreign-based firms are usually not in a position to compete, hence the reason for foreign direct investment among such firms.

Sometimes foreign markets grow faster than domestic markets or better prices are available due to less competition. There are many markets throughout the world where only a few well-known brands share the market. Foreign markets may also open up to foreign competition due to income growth, population growth or the reduction of ownership barriers.

Governments frequently impose tariffs and quotas which force a firm to locate behind the barrier. In such circumstances foreign direct investment may be the only way for the firm to gain access to a market. Japanese car manufacturers have located in Europe and the United States to avoid import quota restrictions in these markets. Furthermore, as discussed in an earlier chapter, governments frequently provide attractive incentive packages to firms considering foreign direct investment as a mode of entry to international markets.

It is unlikely that exchange rate movements are the dominant factor in foreign direct investment decisions, at least in the short run. Such decisions are typically made in response to long-term market strategy considerations and cannot be implemented so rapidly as to accommodate short-term exchange rate fluctuations. A decision to invest abroad requires several years to come to fruition and it is difficult, in the short term, to reverse such decisions. The possibility of exchange rate changes may, however, be a motivating factor to make or enlarge foreign investments. By locating production in several currency areas the firm can shift some of its production among locations and thus avoid potential exchange rate losses.

The basic motives for foreign direct investment are thus numerous. For some firms they include: securing market positions in foreign markets; overcoming tariff and non-tariff barriers to trade; exploiting new markets; benefiting from government financial incentives; securing supplies; and low wage labour. In addition, firms engage in foreign direct investment because they have superior marketing skills. The firm specific competitive advantages of some firms frequently reside in their excellent marketing skills, their network of distributors, and their well-established relationships with customers.

## Growing importance of market motives

Besides the motives for foreign direct investment outlined above, there are others which are peculiar to certain countries and circumstances. It is believed, for example, that a weak US dollar encourages firms to acquire or build in the United States. Firms in other countries invest abroad for defensive and market development reasons. Enterprise in the Federal Republic of Germany shows that foreign direct investment originating in the FRG is motivated predominantly by market opportunities abroad (Kayser and Schwarting, 1981). The most important motive for investing abroad was to find additional new markets for existing products. This was true in each of the market areas studied (Table 14.1). The second most important motive was to extend an existing domestic market into the international arena.

Other important factors include marketing control, political stability and developing an export base abroad. Foreign direct investment may also function as a stepping stone for exporting activities. In this case foreign direct investment as a mode of market entry acts in a complementary manner rather than as a substitute for exporting. Cost factors and return on investment also feature in the important motives. West German firms are willing to adapt to the economic conditions in the host country as demonstrated by their interest in becoming

**Table 14.1**   Motives for foreign direct investment among firms in Germany

| Foreign direct investment motives | Industrial countries | International markets Newly industrialized countries | Developing countries | All |
|---|---|---|---|---|
| | | Rank | | |
| Extension of activities abroad to new markets | 1 | 1 | 1 | 1 |
| Securing an extension of an already existing market | 2 | 2 | 2 | 2 |
| Securing and controlling marketing in the host country | 3 | 4 | 3 | 3 |
| Political stability in the host country | 5 | 3 | 4 | 4 |
| Export base for products of parent firm | 4 | 10 | 9 | 5 |
| Overcoming trade and export barriers | 7 | 6 | 6 | 6 |
| High return on investment | 8 | 5 | 7 | 7 |
| Suppliers for other firms in host country | 6 | 11 | 12 | 8 |
| Low wages | 12 | 7 | 5 | 9 |
| Securing supplies for the parent firm | 10 | 8 | 8 | 10 |

Source: Adapted from Kayser, Gunter and Schwarting, Uwe (1989) 'Foreign investment as a form of enterprise strategy: On the results of a survey,' *Intereconomics*, November–December, pp. 295–9.

suppliers for other firms in the host country and their interest in securing suppliers for the parent firm (Table 14.1).

Four firms dominate the multinational activities of West German firms: Siemens; Hoechst; Volkswagen; and Bayer. Each of these firms employed at least twice as many foreign-based employees as any other firm in the FRG in 1982 and the value of their foreign production was also at least twice as high as that of any other firm. Daimler-Benz dominates the exporting activities in the FRG (Mettler, 1985, p. A31).

## Determinants of location for FDI

In manufacturing foreign direct investment five sets of factors are thought to be important determinants. First, the size of the market in the host country is likely to have a positive effect on the inflow of foreign direct investment. Since such investment is a commitment of resources in uncertain or unfamiliar markets, firms tend to invest in countries with larger markets to compensate for the risks involved. Second, proximity of the host country measured on a business distance scale results in a general lowering of costs of managing foreign subsidiaries which would have a positive effect on the inflow of foreign direct investment.

Third, the size of the firm is correlated with foreign direct investment. Firm size is frequently taken as a proxy for a number of ownership specific advantages possessed by the firm. Foreign direct investment requires significant funds to establish abroad. Larger firms seem to be more able to cope with the costs and risks involved. Fourth, experience gained through various forms of international operations has a positive effect on foreign direct investment. Previous investments or marketing experience gained in one country assists the firm when investing in another.

The greater the international experience possessed by the firm the greater the learning. Finally, firms in oligopolistic industries tend to mimic each other's foreign direct investment decisions in order to maintain a competitive equilibrium. Such oligopolictic reaction contributes positively to foreign direct investment.

## Trends in foreign direct investment

One of the major reasons for the growth in foreign direct investment in the 1960s which has continued right up to the present is the increased differentiation in the marketing of products and services abroad.

### *Role of marketing and differentiated products*

The lack of a good marketing infrastructure in many countries in earlier years meant that the distribution of differentiated products through agents and other intermediaries was not managed as well as the distribution of standardized commodities. For most differentiated products it is necessary to invest heavily to identify and cultivate customers, to learn how to price the product, to display it, and to demonstrate and advertise it. Most agents or small intermediaries in foreign markets are reluctant to make such heavy investments. There is always the danger that if they are too successful they will be by-passed by the foreign manufacturer or local retailer. Local distributors or agents will only invest in distribution if they control the supply sources or markets through equity participation. Manufacturers or retailers of products which require considerable demonstration and service or require specialized facilities must frequently integrate forward or backward into distribution.

Foreign direct investment activities by all countries in the world is estimated to have reached $67.7 billion in 1960. By 1984 this figure had reached $598.6 billion (Table 14.2). Most of this activity originates in developed countries with the United States being the dominant source of foreign direct investment. Almost 40 per cent of total direct investment originated in the United States in 1984. In 1960, the corresponding figure was 45.1 per cent. The second most important source is the United Kingdom. Two rapidly growing sources of foreign direct investment are the Federal Republic of Germany and Japan, third and fifth most important, respectively, in 1984.

**Table 14.2**   Origin of foreign direct investment activities,
1960–84

| Areas and countries | 1960 (%) | 1980 (%) | 1984 (%) | Rank 1984 (%) |
|---|---|---|---|---|
| Developed countries | 99.0 | 97.4 | 97.0 | |
| France | 6.1 | 4.0 | 5.3 | 6 |
| Germany (FRG) | 1.2 | 8.3 | 7.7 | 3 |
| Italy | 1.6 | 1.4 | 2.0 | 9 |
| Netherlands | 10.3 | 8.2 | 6.8 | 4 |
| Sweden | 0.6 | 1.4 | 1.8 | 10 |
| Switzerland | 3.4 | 4.3 | 4.2 | 8 |
| United Kingdom | 18.3 | 15.6 | 14.3 | 2 |
| Other European countries | 3.7 | 1.8 | 2.2 | |
| Europe | 45.2 | 45.0 | 44.3 | |
| Australia and New Zealand | 0.3 | 0.5 | 0.9 | |
| Canada | 3.7 | 4.4 | 5.3 | 7 |
| Japan | 0.7 | 3.8 | 6.3 | 5 |
| United States | 47.1 | 42.6 | 39.5 | 1 |
| Other countries | 2.0 | 1.1 | 0.7 | |
| Developing countries | 1.0 | 2.6 | 3.0 | |
| All countries (%) | 100.0 | 100.0 | 100.0 | |
| Values $US billion | 67.7 | 516.7 | 598.6 | |

Source: Derived from US Department of Commerce (1988)
*International Direct Investment — Global Trends and the US Role*,
November, p. 87.

## Cross-foreign direct investment

The very large multinational firms have been involved in cross-direct investments
in each others' countries for many years. Firms in the United States continue to
invest heavily in Canada, Europe and Japan. Recently they have begun to invest
heavily in South East Asia. Similarly, European firms have become quite
aggressive in Japan and the United States. Japanese firms have been very active
in foreign direct investment in the United Kingdom and using the United Kingdom
as a base from which to bound into continental European markets (Exhibit 14.2).
Japanese firms are also very active in European office property markets.

There are three reasons for such cross-investments. First, some multinational
firms are in a position to enjoy economies of scale by operating production facilities
in different countries, while still using an integrated system of strategic planning
to monitor and control production for different markets throughout the world.
The Ford Motor Company follows such a strategy in the production of certain
models of car in designated centres for supply to widespread markets. Second,
opportunities for product-market differentiation are increased since it is possible
for the firm to target specific market niches in different countries while supplying

---

**Exhibit 14.2   Entering large markets through foreign direct investment**

---

*Japanese investors successfully avoid barriers*

In the past three years, Japan's major companies have been switching from a direct export strategy to one based on direct investment. In Europe, their investments have grown by no less than 60 percent since 1981. The reasons for this change are not hard to discern. Protectionist pressures have mounted since the onset of the recession. Most auto markets are now subject to controls; but Japanese penetration has passed the 10 percent mark. In consumer electronics, Japanese companies are already operating "orderly marketing arrangements" and other sectors are likely to follow suit.

But on the other side of the equation, something has changed; which is now permitting Japanese companies to continue to profit from Europe's markets. Resistance to direct investment has fallen away as unemployment has mounted. With Europe's economies set for sluggish growth at best, governments have no choice but to welcome the newcomers. Japanese companies have, after all, already created jobs in Spain (15,000), the UK (12,000), France (7,500), Belgium (6,300) and Germany (4,700). They also bring the latest technology; the promise of exports; and new methods that improve quality, productivity and industrial harmony.

Many industry critics still argue that the Japanese presence is equivalent to "putting the fox in the chicken coop." The counter argument, which seems to have been accepted by most of Europe's governments, is that it's better to manufacture products in the country where they are bought and from where they can be exported, rather than import them at the expense of an increase in the trade deficit.

Overall, however, the Japanese industrial foothold in Europe should be viewed in proportion. Although Japan is the world's second industrial power, it is, with only 6 percent of total funds invested abroad, only in fourth place as a foreign investor in Europe, after the US, the UK and Germany.

**Source:** *Business Europe*, 25 January, 1985, p. 26.

---

them efficiently by co-ordinated centralized operations. Third, the convergence of consumer tastes in certain product markets allows the firm to design and produce products and services for global markets. These three sets of factors encourage firms that have the resources to build a presence in each market area. This is usually done by establishing a fully controlled, wholly owned subsidiary.

Developed countries again dominate both inward and outward investment flows. Three-quarters of all inward investment flows in the period 1981–5 involved developing countries, with almost 40 per cent being attracted to the United States. Europe was the recipient of 30.8 per cent of inward investment while Japan received only 0.7 per cent of the total (Table 14.3). The two dominant countries in terms of outward investment were the United Kingdom and the United States,

**Table 14.3**  Capital investment flows, 1981–5

| Areas and countries | Investment flows | |
|---|---|---|
| | Inward (%) | Outward (%) |
| Developed countries | 75.2 | 96.6 |
| France | 4.5 | 6.2 |
| Germany (FRG) | 2.1 | 7.7 |
| Italy | 2.2 | 3.8 |
| Netherlands | 2.7 | 8.6 |
| Sweden | 0.3 | 2.3 |
| Switzerland | 1.1 | 2.5 |
| United Kingdom | 8.6 | 19.5 |
| Other European countries | 9.3 | 3.1 |
| Europe | 30.8 | 53.7 |
| Australia and New Zealand | 4.3 | 3.0 |
| Canada | −0.5 | 1.2 |
| Japan | 0.7 | 11.4 |
| United States | 39.5 | 19.3 |
| Other countries | 0.4 | 8.0 |
| Developing countries | 24.8 | 3.4 |
| Africa | 3.4 | 0.1 |
| Asia | 11.0 | 2.8 |
| All countries | 100.0 | 100.0 |

Source: Derived from US Department of Commerce (1988) *International Direct Investment — Global Trends and the US Role*, November, p. 87.

each with over 19 per cent of the total. The third most important source of outward investment was Japan, responsible for over 11 per cent of the total.

## Forms of foreign direct investment

For most countries engaged in foreign direct investment manufacturing is the most important sector involved. In the four major industrial countries: Federal Republic of Germany; Japan; the United Kingdom; and the United States, manufacturing was responsible for between one-third and two-fifths of foreign direct investment in 1976 and 1984 (Table 14.4). Wholesale and retail trade investment did not experience very significant share changes in any of the countries in the period reviewed. This sector is, however, much more important in terms of foreign direct investment in the Federal Republic of Germany than it is in the others. Petroleum and mining have declined in importance in Japan and the United Kingdom but gained from 23 per cent to 27 per cent of the total in the United States. Significant changes have, however, occurred in financial

**Table 14.4** Composition of outward foreign direct investment in major industrial countries, 1976 and 1984

| Industry sector | Germany (FRG) 1976 | Germany (FRG) 1984 | Japan 1977 | Japan 1984 | United Kingdom 1971 | United Kingdom 1984 | United States 1977 | United States 1984 |
|---|---|---|---|---|---|---|---|---|
| | (%) | | | | | | | |
| Financial services | 8 | 13 | 8 | 10 | NA[a] | NA[a] | 18 | 23 |
| Manufacturing | 48 | 43 | 34 | 32 | 45 | 43 | 42 | 36 |
| Wholesale/retail trade | 19 | 20 | 14 | 16 | 10 | 10 | 11 | 11 |
| Petroleum and mining | 4 | 5 | 25 | 16 | 35 | 29 | 23 | 27 |
| Other industries | 21 | 19 | 19 | 26 | 10[b] | 16[b] | 5 | 4 |
| All industries | 100 | 100 | 100 | 100 | 100 | 100 | 100 | 100 |

[a]Banking and insurance data are not available for either year.
[b]The 1971 figure includes investment only by financial institutions other than banking and insurance. The 1981 figure includes banking and insurance.

Source: Derived from US Department of Commerce (1988) *International Direct Investment — Global Trends and the US Role*, November, p. 87.

services. In Germany they have increased in importance from 8 to 13 per cent, from 8 to 10 per cent in Japan and from 18 to 23 per cent in the United States. Data are not available for the United Kingdom for these years.

## Conditions for success in foreign direct investment

For the firm to be successful in foreign direct investment it must possess a strategic competitive advantage that more than offsets the cost of operating in foreign markets. The competitive advantages must reflect certain characteristics. First the firm should be able to transfer the assets abroad at a low incremental cost without adversely affecting revenues or profits at home. Second, the sale or lease of these assets to an independent firm must involve substantial transaction costs so that the best way of guaranteeing that the benefits accrue to the firm is by internalizing them in a subsidiary rather than by selling or leasing (Buckley and Casson, 1976; Dunning, 1981; Teece, 1981).

The assets in question are intangible, e.g. knowledge and know-how, which may apply to new products and production processes, to the design and implementation of marketing programmes, and to the general management of international operations.

Such knowledge and know-how is very mobile internationally, with the result that arm's length transactions in such assets tend to be subject to high transaction costs and to a high degree of uncertainty. The firm possessing these assets may decide to internalize them within a subsidiary and use them more profitably in foreign markets when relative factor costs, tariffs, transport costs and market size allow.

## International market entry by acquisition

As was noted in the preceding chapter dealing with competitive alliances, acquisitions can be beneficial in situations where firms experience asymmetric access to information or require specific market assets or other resources. In such circumstances a firm may acquire another firm which possesses information, assets, brands, distribution networks or skilled management which can be used to improve the performance of the first firm.

Among EC firms the most important motives for acquisitions lie in the areas of rationalization of production across different locations, restructuring of industry and achieving complementarity of operations. Almost half, 49.4 per cent, of the 1985–6 acquisitions, or 86 acquisitions, were in this group. The importance of these categories declined to 42.1 per cent in the following year and to 36.6 per cent, which was 88 acquisitions in 1987–8 (Table 14.5). The second set of motives are market driven. Market expansion and strengthening of market position were the principal motives in 29.4 per cent of the 1985–6 acquisitions and 33.6 per cent of the 1986 acquisitions. Market expansion and other unspecified motives are becoming more important in acquisition strategies among EC firms. In the most recent year for which data are available, market expansion and strengthening of market position motives represented 45 per cent of the cases reported.

Relying on the market might take a long time, be more expensive or impossible. The lower transaction costs involved means that acquisitions can be a better alternative to competitive alliances or organic growth through exporting. Deciding to enter foreign markets through an acquisition investment mode is akin to the big decision in the build or buy alternatives facing firms as they expand.

Acquiring an established firm in the foreign market presents the firm with

**Table 14.5**  Principal motives for acquisitions[a]

| Principal motives | 1985–6 (%) | 1986–7 (%) | 1987–8 (%) |
|---|---|---|---|
| Rationalization, restructuring | 35.0 | 29.7 | 17.0 |
| Complementarity of operations | 14.4 | 12.4 | 19.6 |
| Market expansion | 18.1 | 22.1 | 19.6 |
| Strengthening market position | 11.3 | 11.5 | 25.4 |
| Diversification | 12.5 | 5.7 | 8.3 |
| Research and development | 2.5 | 5.3 | 0.7 |
| Specialization | 1.9 | 1.3 | 1.8 |
| Other | 4.3 | 12.0 | 7.6 |
| Total (%) | 100.0 | 100.0 | 100.0 |

[a]Percentage of all merger/acquisition cases for which precise information about motives is available.

Source: EC Commission: *Seventeenth Report on Competition Policy*, Brussels, 1988 and *Eighteenth Report on Competition Policy*, 1989.

an established means of entry with institutional support and a working network of suppliers, intermediaries and customers. It is a quick way of entering the market as it by-passes all the planning and negotiation stages which are necessary in building a complete new production facility.

It may, of course, be much more expensive to enter the market in this way. The high cost of entry is frequently offset against the market potential which is presumed to exist. In recent years a number of large European firms have acquired US firms since a strong presence in the growing US market is seen by these firms as an essential ingredient of their worldwide strategy. For example, in 1986 alone, Hoechst of Germany (FRG) agreed to buy the US firm Celanese for $2.8 billion in cash, L'Air Liquide of France paid $1.1 billion to buy Big Three Industries in Texas, a producer of industrial gases, and Electrolux of Sweden acquired White Consolidated Industries for $750 million. Though difficult to value the market accurately, some firms are willing to pay a high premium to enter. Boots Company, the UK chemist chain, paid $555 million, nearly fifty times book value, to buy a drug unit from Boster Travenol Laboratories Inc. (*Business Week*, 24 November, 1986).

A similar pattern has also appeared in Europe, especially in food industries and branded business. Acquisitions frequently have as a central objective the ownership and management of well-known brands. Scarce shelf space in supermarkets and market power resting with supermarket chains has meant that customers have focussed more attention on one or two brands in the market which have become highly valued assets in take-over attempts. In 1988 Nestlé acquired the UK confectionery producer Rowntree Mackintosh PLC for $4.6 billion.

Approximately 232 acquisitions on average occur each year in the EC. In 1982–3 it was 117 and in 1987–8 it reached 383, an unusually high figure (Table 14.6). Most acquisitions are between firms in the same country. During the six-year period under review 62.9 per cent of acquisitions were between firms in the same country. A further 25.0 per cent of acquisitions occurred between firms in

**Table 14.6**  Pattern of acquisitions among EC firms

| | Location of acquisitions | | | | |
| Year | Same EC country (%) | Different EC country (%) | EC and non-EC country (%) | Total (%) | (No.) |
|---|---|---|---|---|---|
| 1982–3 | 50.5 | 32.5 | 17.0 | 100 | 117 |
| 1983–4 | 65.2 | 18.7 | 16.1 | 100 | 155 |
| 1984–5 | 70.2 | 21.2 | 8.7 | 100 | 208 |
| 1985–6 | 63.7 | 23.0 | 13.3 | 100 | 227 |
| 1986–7 | 69.6 | 24.8 | 5.6 | 100 | 303 |
| 1987–8 | 55.9 | 29.0 | 15.1 | 100 | 383 |
| Annual average | 62.9 | 25.0 | 12.1 | 100 | 232 |

Source: Derived from EC Commission: *Seventeenth Report on Competition Policy*, Brussels, 1988 and *Eighteenth Report on Competition Policy*, Brussels 1989.

different EC countries. Just over 12 per cent of acquisitions occurred between EC and non-EC firms. There is, however, considerable variation from year to year in these figures.

Most of the acquisitions involving EC firms in the period 1983–4 to 1987–8 resulted in relatively large merged firms (Table 14.7). For the period as a whole 60.2 per cent of merged firms involved more than ECU 1,000 million. Relatively small mergers were also very important; 26.1 per cent of merged firms fell in the less than ECU 5000 million category. During the period reviewed the trend was toward a greater importance for the larger merged firm.

The major attraction of entry to a foreign market by acquisition is that it is very much quicker than entry through fixed investment in new facilities and internal development of assets. Acquisition has two major advantages. First, the firm obtains assets that are already in use so the return is quicker than from fixed asset investment. Second, acquisition provides the firm with immediate market share without any increase in capacity. Speed may be an important consideration to allow the firm to enter new foreign product markets quickly and thereby to exploit first mover advantage.

Expansion by acquisition can take two general forms. At one extreme are acquisitions which are a complete legal integration of two or more firms. At the other extreme there are acquisitions involving only changes in the ownerships of the firms involved. In the first case the assets and liabilities of two or more firms are transferred into a single firm, existing or new. This form of entry by acquisition involves major reorganization, from changes in the membership of the board to changes in the products sold. Generally legal acquisitions involve the integration of the constituent parts of companies, a process which is not easily reversible. One of the major difficulties of this form of acquisition is that the integration of management functions and the determination of joint strategies may be a long and difficult task.

In the second situation, where a change of ownership allows an acquisition to occur, the take-over of one company by another is the most common form. Here both firms continue to exist as separate legal entities. This form of acquisition

**Table 14.7**  Size of merged firms

| Year | Under ECU 500 million (%) | ECU 500– 1000 million (%) | Over ECU 1000 million (%) | All sizes (%) | All sizes (No.) |
|---|---|---|---|---|---|
| 1983–4 | 22.0 | 13.6 | 64.4 | 100 | 132 |
| 1984–5 | 33.5 | 16.8 | 49.7 | 100 | 185 |
| 1985–6 | 30.9 | 16.2 | 52.9 | 100 | 204 |
| 1986–7 | 33.3 | 10.2 | 56.4 | 100 | 303 |
| 1987–8 | 15.9 | 14.1 | 70.0 | 100 | 383 |
| Annual average | 26.1 | 13.7 | 60.2 | 100 | 241 |

Source: Based on EC Commission: *Seventeenth Report on Competition Policy*, Brussels, 1988 and *Eighteenth Report on Competition Policy*, Brussels 1989.

is performed by a purchase of shares or a public take-over bid. Acquisition in this way unifies the businesses while still maintaining a considerable degree of decentralization between the members of the new entity.

A complicated network of acquisitions of this form can result in a complicated structure even involving subsidiaries large enough to make their own acquisitions. Though complex, acquisitions of this form can be stable and profitable. Success in such firms is frequently due to flexibility and the decentralized management structure which continues.

A network of independent firms, though owned centrally through shareholding arrangements, is likely to be able to adjust better to changing social, political and business considerations in international product markets than are firms which are single legal entities. Decentralized management allows the firm to back out of difficult situations. A change of strategy is easier to implement through the sale of shares than by selling off fixed assets. In decentralized management situations, as occurs, for example, in subsidiaries, managers may have a keener sense of their roles than would occur, for example, in a divisionalized or branch structure. A combination of the advantages of concentration of physical and intangible assets and of a dencentralization of management and responsibility which permits flexibility, occurs in acquisitions involving ownership changes only (Jacquemin, Buigues and Ilzkovitz, 1989). Expansion into international markets by this form of acquisition suffers from problems which arise in the area of human resources. Sometimes working relationships deteriorate to such an extent that managements clash and redundancies and reorganizations occur. The uncertainty thus created can prevent the success of the acquisition.

## Success factors in acquisitions

There are very few firms which deliberately set out to acquire firms which will result in failure. In a study by Coley and Reinton (1988), successful acquisitions had a number of common features. Typically, after acquisition the firms were reorganized to offset the high cost of purchase. The operations of the acquired firms were strengthened by adding new management and sometimes new capital. Most important, the new owners systematically identified and assessed the value created by the acquisition and carefully managed the integration process.

Successful acquisitions normally involve strategies to limit risk to identify and assess elements of synergy, to achieve scale economies, to acquire sequentially and to maintain constant leadership from senior management (Figure 14.2).

A key influence in acquisition strategies is the possibility of reduced unit costs arising from better marketing and distribution arrangements and research and development work as applied to manufacturing. Centrally co-ordinated, such arrangements can produce scale economies. Marketing effectiveness is increased if a standardized approach to positioning can be adopted. Similarly, distribution

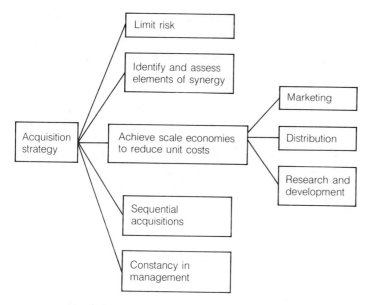

**Figure 14.2**    Components of successful acquisition strategy

economies can be realized by integrating several minor distribution networks and increasing the number of product lines through an existing network. A higher degree of research and development specialization can be achieved through the consolidation of several similar research areas which may lead to shorter development time and quicker commercialization.

A sequenced acquisition strategy can produce dominance in an industry sector or market. By targeting firms for acquisition in a clearly defined sequence a firm can become the dominant player in a region, or even in the world. In the early 1970s Electrolux was just one of several firms with a share in the appliance sector of the electrical products industry. By the end of the 1980s with more than 250 acquisitions behind it, Electrolux was the dominant player in this sector. The firm also maintains a low profile in the industry in that it retains the brand names of the companies it acquires. Electrolux follows a planned acquisition strategy in the five steps illustrated below (Eng and Forsman, 1989):

1. A specific geographic market is targeted.
2. A critical mass in the market is created by buying firms with established brand names.
3. Production is rationalized while taking account of the firm's capacity in other countries. Weak product lines are eliminated in favour of large-volume production lines.
4. Financial management is centralized and country marketing services are co-ordinated.

5. All viable brands are supported to maintain customer loyalty in different markets and to hold shelf and floor space.

Acquiring firms sequentially to enter and dominate industry sectors across many international markets requires a stability of leadership policy in the firm. A mission to develop corporate and marketing strategies through internationalization by acquisition is a long-term strategy achievable only over many years. It is not a short-term strategy: dominance of market position is achieved only with patience, strategic thinking, and a constancy of leadership in senior management. Sometimes the marketing logic is enough to overcome any organizational difficulties which would need to be faced. The marketing and manufacturing complementarity which existed between Electrolux and Zanussi was a large factor in facilitating that acquisition (Exhibit 14.3).

## Success and failure in UK and US acquisitions

In evaluating ways of entering international markets it is worth noting that many, if not most, acquisitions fail if success is defined as adding value above the total cost of analysing, executing and implementing the acquisition strategy. The reasons for such failure may be attributed to acquisition strategies which are unfocussed and insufficient analysis of the targetted industry and company. Furthermore, many firms rely too much on the potential for financial engineering, scale economies, and synergy. Finally, a lack of clear strategy for the acquisition and a thoroughly prepared implementation framework are also contributory factors in failure.

In order to examine the success or failure in acquisition as a corporate growth strategy, McKinsey and Company studied the performance of the "Fortune 250" companies and the top 150 companies in *The Financial Times 500* which had used acquisitions to enter new markets (Coley and Reinton, 1988; *Economist*, 1988, p. 113). McKinsey studied 116 mergers and found that 16 per cent could not be judged a success or failure. Success was measured as the firm's ability to earn back its cost of capital or better on the funds invested in the merger. By this standard 23 per cent were successful and 61 per cent were not. The larger the acquisitions and the greater the diversification the smaller was the likelihood of success (Table 14.8). The major reason for failure was due to companies paying too much for the acquisitions and an inability to introduce operating or financial changes sufficient to offset the premiums (*The Economist*, 1988, p. 113). In this context it is interesting to note that companies frequently have multiple objectives in making acquisitions. The acquisition of the US chemical group, Stauffer, and its division among three of Europe's major chemical companies indicates that the objectives of recent European acquisitions in the United States are buying market share, attaining dominance in strategic businesses and developing corporate synergy (Exhibit 14.4).

## Exhibit 14.3  Marketing and manufacturing complementarity facilitates acquisitions

### Electrolux's acquisition of Zanussi

Italian acquisition makes the cool Swedes world leaders in domestic appliances with a stranglehold on European white goods. Electrolux has shown a talent for devouring competitors, acquiring companies at the rate of one every three weeks in recent years. The acquisitions have transformed Electrolux from a one-product company into a diversified multinational and now the world's largest producer of home appliances.

Electrolux became No 1 by making Industrie Zanussi SpA an offer it couldn't refuse. The new alliance, which will report more than $5 billion in sales this year, controls about 25 percent of the $10 billion-a-year European white goods market.

The flak from European arch-rivals Bosch-Siemens GmbH (which has a 15 percent market share) and AEG-Telefunken AG (seven percent) of West Germany, Holland's Philips-Bauknecht NV (12 percent) and France's Thomson-Brandt SA (6 percent) depends on how quickly the Swedes can modernise Zanussi's outdated manufacturing plant and integrate the Italian firm's white goods and profitable components division into the formidable European network of Electrolux. The main areas of synergy, according to the President of Electrolux, Anders Scharp, are common purchasing, distribution and internal sourcing of components, products swapping and the elimination of production overlaps.

Successfully merging two companies with sharply contrasting cultures is a tall order for any corporation. But Electrolux, with 75% of its sales abroad, more than 300 acquisitions in 40 countries under its belt and 111 manufacturing facilities in 25 of them, has few peers among multinationals in absorbing companies.

Ensuring survival more than anything else is the complementary nature of the acquisition, which fills most of the big geographical gaps in Electrolux's European operations and makes it a full-range white goods producer.

Zanussi, for example, holds significant market shares in Italy and Spain, two countries Electrolux has been unable to crack. It is also strong in France, the only market where the Swedish parent is losing money, and has small but important sales in Germany (it's main OEM supplier of white goods for Quelle, the country's largest mail order house), where Electrolux has no presence aside from vacuum cleaners. As Europe's largest producer of "wet goods" — dishwashers and washing machines — Zanussi gives Electrolux an entree into products where it has always been relatively weak.

Experts believe, however, that the Zanussi acquisition minimises the exposure to foreign competitors on Electrolux's European flanks. More important, the enlarged group is seen as a powerhouse that can orchestrate any further rationalization in the European white goods sector.

**Source:** *International Management*, September, 1985, pp. 24–8.

**Table 14.8**  Success in UK and US acquisitions

| Size of firm acquired | Degree of diversification | |
|---|---|---|
| | Low | High |
| Small | Firms in category 20 | 16 |
| | Success rate 45% | 38% |
| Large | 26 | 35 |
| | 27% | 14% |

| Success | Failure | Unknown | No. of acquisitions |
|---|---|---|---|
| 23% | 61% | 16% | 116 |

Source: Adapted from Coley S. and Reinton, S. (1988) 'The hunt for value,' *The McKinsey Quarterly*, Spring.

In general, the owners of firms which are of potential strategic importance to another firm are aware that they possess valuable assets so they attempt to ensure that a premium is paid for the firm. It is not unusual to witness firms with mediocre performance records and poor prospects commanding price–earnings multiples of over 20. In such circumstances the acquiring firm must use all its skill to structure and negotiate the offer package so that the risk of failure is minimized.

Firms accept a price premium where elements of synergy and scale economies warrant it. A well-planned acquisition can ensure production and marketing synergy. One of the principal elements in the merger of ASEA of Sweden and Brown Boveri of Switzerland was that the new company, ABB, should have the resources to become the low-cost producers in all its businesses, while being the most technologically advanced in the market with sufficient capacity and financial resources to commercialize new technical innovations rapidly.

## Public policy and cross-border acquisitions

Cross-border acquisitions are likely to continue growing and in general to be welcomed by policy makers as in most cases they do not adversely affect competition and the consumer should benefit. Unless the resulting market share held by the new corporate entity is substantial in the relevant market, such acquisitions and competitive alliances are more likely to benefit consumers. A case in point was the take-over battle in the UK confectionery industry. Both Nestlé and Jacob–Suchard had small shares of the UK market and a merger between

---

**Exhibit 14.4   Acquisition for market share, dominance and synergy**

---

*Lessons from European chemical companies' US acquisitions*

The division of the assets of US chemical group Stauffer among three of Europe's major chemical companies ICI (UK), Rhône-Poulenc (France) and Akzo (Netherlands) illustrates the increasingly sophisticated nature of European corporate acquisition strategy.

ICI wanted Stauffer principally for its agro chemicals division and moved quickly to divest the rest. In June, it sold the specialty chemicals division to the US subsidiary of the Dutch chemical company Akzo for $625 million, and in September it sold the inorganic chemicals division to the French chemicals group Rhône-Poulenc for $522 million.

The breakup of Stauffer clearly shows the overall aims of many recent European acquisitions in North America:

- Buy market share in the US to achieve a similar position to competitors. After the Stauffer swops, there was a convergence of the percentage of sales in the US of European chemicals groups: Ciba-Geigy 30%, Hoechst 25%, ICI 25%, Bayer 20%, BASF 19%, Akzo 15% and Rhône-Poulenc 15%.
- Attain world ranking in areas judged "strategic". The division of Stauffer provides each company with substantial positions in closely defined markets.
- Promote synergy with other parts of the corporation. Although the chemicals companies involved in the Stauffer carve-up are fierce competitors in Europe and have interests in each of Stauffer's three main product areas, agro, inorganic and specialty chemicals, they have different strategic needs at present.

ICI wished to strengthen its world-wide agrochemical business, but did not want to strain its balance sheet excessively by acquiring Stauffer's other interests; Akzo has been eager to expand its US specialty chemical businesses: Rhône-Poulenc sees strategic benefits from building a strong presence in basic chemicals.

**Source:** *Business International — Ideas in Action,* 26 October, 1987, pp. 2–3.

---

either and Rowntree Mackintosh would not seriously reduce competition but a merger with Cadbury and Rowntree Mackintosh would.

On purely commercial grounds a cross-border acquisition between either Nestlé or Jacob–Suchard and Rowntree Mackintosh made marketing sense. Rowntree, with world brands such as "Kit Kat", "Rolo" and "After Eight" was a leader in the fastest growing confectionery segment: chocolate coated treats that frequently contain caramel, biscuits or nuts.

In contrast Nestlé and Suchard were concentrated in the shrinking market for solid chocolate. This take-over activity in the United Kingdom reflected pressure to consolidate a fragmented European confectionery market. A number of other mergers are worth noting in this context. Cadbury Schweppes had acquired Poulain, a French chocolate manufacturer. Cadbury itself had been a target of a take-over from the General Cinema Corporation. In 1987, Suchard bought a Chicago company, EJ Brach and Sons, for $730 million. Suchard also bought Belgium's leading chocolatier, Côte d'Or, and Nestlé agreed to pay $1.3 million for the Italian food company, Buitoni, which includes the chocolate maker Perugina (*Business Week*, 9 May, 1988).

Public policy interest in acquisition is frequently concerned with two issues: competition; and efficiency. Governments view acquisitions as providing an opportunity for increased efficiency in industry. At the same time, however, governments are concerned about any reduction in competition which might result from an acquisition. Situations where efficiency gains are large for a small reduction in competition are generally welcomed. In some cases small losses in competition would be traded for small gains in efficiency, depending on circumstances. In general, however, governments and public policy makers resist acquisitions which produce only small efficiency gains for large reductions in competition.

Industry in the EC has been examined to determine the extent of efficiency gains and reduction of competition which would arise if unbridled acquisition activity were to take place (Jacquemin, Buigues and Ilzkovitz, 1989). These researchers have found that large efficiency gains for a small loss of competition would arise if acquisitions were to occur in high-technology industries such as: advanced materials; chemicals; pharmaceuticals; computers; telecommunications and electronics; motor vehicles; aerospace; and specialized instruments (Table 14.9).

Only small efficiency gains but severe loss in competition would occur if acquisitions occurred in low-technology areas such as building materials, metals, paint, furniture, paper, rubber, and tobacco.

## Market entry through new ventures and acquisitions: an evaluation

### Comparison of acquisitions and new ventures

Data which would allow a comparison of mode of entry by firms in international markets is not readily available in published form. Even for the United States, available data are not very precise. It is valuable in such circumstances to report the pattern of entry activity of international firms as they enter the US market. Data reported in Kogut and Singh (1988) based on a survey of 504 firms entering the United States between 1981 and 1985 were reanalysed to identify the importance of the different modes of entry for high-technology firms, low-technology firms and firms in service industries. The proportions of firms in each category entering the United States through acquisitions or new ventures are shown below (Table 14.10).

**Table 14.9** Impact of acquisitions on competition and efficiency

| Reduction of competition | Potential efficiency gains | |
|---|---|---|
| | Small | Large |
| Small | Steel | Advanced materials |
| | Machinery | Chemicals/pharmaceuticals |
| | Leather and leather products | Computers/office automation |
| | Clothing and textiles | Telecommunications |
| | Processed wool | Electronics |
| | Pulp, paper and board | Motor vehicles |
| | Jewellery, toys, musical instruments | Aerospace |
| | | Instruments |
| Large | Building materials | Boilermaking |
| | Metal products | Cables, heavy electrical plant |
| | Paints and varnishes | Railway equipment |
| | Furniture | Shipbuilding |
| | Paper products | Confectionery, chocolate |
| | Rubber products | Flour, pasta |
| | Tobacco | Beer |

Source: Adapted from Jacquemin, Alexis, Buigues, Pierre and Ilkovitz, Fabienne (1989) 'Horizontal mergers and competition policy in the European Community,' *European Economy*, **40**, 27–32.

Overall, acquisitions are the most common form of investment entry mode into the US market. Entry by foreign firms into US high-technology industry was principally through joint ventures followed closely by acquisitions. Acquisition was the dominant mode of entry into low-technology industry. Acquisitions also dominated the services sectors. In terms of entry mode, joint ventures and direct investment are most common in high-technology industries and acquisitions in low-technology industry.

New venture foreign direct investments are frequently less costly than acquisitions since the scale of the firm's involvement can be precisely controlled and the production facility can be expanded exactly in line with achieved market penetration. In general, smaller firms prefer the new venture approach because they lack the financial resources for a take-over. Another reason why the new venture approach is preferred is because the choice of location is open to the entrant and a least-cost site can be selected which frequently comes with an attractive incentive package provided by the host government because of the employment potential of the new facility.

New venture foreign direct investments also avoid inheriting problems which may exist in established firms, while at the same time it is possible to introduce the most modern technology and equipment. For larger firms new venture foreign direct investment can be the best alternative market entry mode when suitable candidates for acquisition are not available.

By acquiring a foreign-based firm, other advantages accrue to the firm.

**Table 14.10**  Industry effect on modes of entry into the United States, 1981–5

| Industry sector | Acquisitions (%) | New ventures (%) | Total (%) | Total (No.) |
|---|---|---|---|---|
| High-technology sectors | 60.6 | 39.4 | 100 | 99 |
| Low-technology sectors | 79.2 | 20.8 | 100 | 173 |
| All industry sectors | 72.4 | 27.6 | 100 | 272 |
| Services industries | 88.4 | 11.6 | 100 | 86 |
| Industry and services | 76.3 | 23.7 | 100 | 358 |

Source: Adapted from data in: Kogut, Bruce and Singh, Harbir (1988) 'The effect of national culture on choice of entry mode,' *Journal of International Business Studies*, **19** (3), 418.

Generally the acquisition route means a quicker pay back and cultural and difficult management problems may be avoided. The major advantage of the acquisition mode of entry is the purchase of critical assets, products, brand names, skills, technology and, above all, distribution networks. This last asset has been central to many of the recent large acquisitions and attempted acquisitions in Europe. Finally, acquisitions do not usually disturb the competitive framework in the host country and for that reason are often not hindered greatly by public policy.

There are a number of thorny problems, however, in pursuing the acquisition route. Firms frequently find it very difficult to value the assets being acquired, e.g. the value of brands. Furthermore, it is often very difficult to determine the degree of synergy which will exist between the firm's existing assets and the acquired assets. As noted above there may be considerable costs associated with integrating a previously independent company into a larger group. Finally, the search costs to find a suitable firm to acquire can be substantial.

## Foreign direct investments in the United States

There are many reasons why the United States is an attractive location for direct investment by companies located in other countries. The size and importance of the US market means that many large international companies with strong brands view it as central to their international activities. In this category are included many of the well-known Japanese companies such as Sony and Toyota. Likewise, European companies have discovered that the size and growth of the US market makes it essential to be active there. Philips, Electrolux and many of the luxury producers of cars have established strong bases in the United States. The confidence of participating in world markets has encouraged these firms to compete with US firms in their home market.

A second major reason for the importance of the United States as a location for direct investment activities is the intermittent fear that protectionism will take hold there. By being behind trade barriers foreign firms can continue to serve the market successfully. Corporate restructuring in the United States has increased the number of US firms available for acquisition. When this is combined with a depreciated US dollar and strong growth in the US economy, the incentive to acquire firms in the United States becomes very attractive. A currency depreciation reduces the foreign currency cost of acquiring assets in the country in question and further protects local production since imports become more expensive. Strong growth improves the earnings of local firms making them more attractive acquisition targets. Finally, foreign investing companies have in recent years been attracted to the United States by financial and other incentives provided by state governments.

## Profitability of foreign direct investment

The value of foreign direct investment at the level of the firm may be judged by the rate of return on the direct investment position. This may be measured by income receipts divided by the average of the beginning- and end-of-year investment positions. One of the difficulties of this approach is that the investment position values are historical book values which tend to understate the real position and overstate the rate of return on older investments compared to more recent investments. Nevertheless, approximate comparisons of relative profitability among countries and industries may be determined. Using this approach the average 1980–6 rate of return accruing to US firms for investment abroad taking all countries together was 13.4 per cent, whereas the average rate of return to all foreign firms investing in the United States was 5.3 per cent in the same period (Table 14.11).

For US firms the highest return was available in developing countries, followed closely by Japan. For non-US firms investing in the United States, Japanese firms were able to obtain the highest return while developing countries

**Table 14.11** Country effect on rate of return on foreign direct investments, 1980–6

| Regions and countries | Average 1980–6 ROI on US FDI (%) | Average 1980–6 ROI to non-US firms for FDI in US (%) |
|---|---|---|
| Canada | 10.0 | 2.3 |
| Japan | 16.0 | 9.8 |
| Europe | 13.3 | 6.1 |
| Developed countries | 12.2 | 5.3 |
| Developing countries | 16.2 | 1.9 |
| All countries | 13.4 | 5.3 |

Source: Adapted from data in: Kogut, Bruce and Singh, Harbir (1988) 'The effect of national culture on choice of entry mode,' *Journal of International Business Studies*, **19** (3), 419.

**Table 14.12**  Industry effect on rate of return on foreign direct investments, 1980–6

| Industry sector | Average ROI on US FDI (%) | Average ROI to non-US firms for FDI in US (%) |
|---|---|---|
| Manufacturing | 10.5 | 2.7 |
| Petroleum | 19.1 | 13.0 |
| Other industries | 11.0 | −1.5 |
| Banking | 26.0 | 12.7 |
| Finance and insurance | 10.7 | 6.5 |
| All industries | 13.4 | 5.3 |

Source: Adapted from US Department of Commerce (1988) *International Direct Investment — Global Trends and the US Role.*

obtained the lowest. It is noteworthy that US firms on average were able to obtain considerably higher rates of return than were foreign firms in the United States.

A similar pattern appears when the effect of industry sales on the rate of return is examined. On average, US firms perform better across sectors than do foreign firms in the United States. The returns to US firms in the banking sector were the highest in the period under review (Table 14.12). The other very high performing sector was petroleum. Banking and petroleum were also the highest performing sectors in the United States for investment there by foreign firms. In the case of both sets of firms, manufacturing industry is a relatively weak performing sector.

## Management view of foreign direct investment

From the point of view of the firm there are advantages and disadvantages associated with the two forms of foreign direct investment. Each can be judged in terms of its effect on the firm's costs and on its product markets (Table 14.13).

**Table 14.13**  Advantages and disadvantages of acquisitions and new venture mode of entry into foreign markets

| Key influencing factors | Advantages | Disadvantages |
|---|---|---|
| Cost factors | Reduced transport costs<br>Scale economies<br>Host government incentives<br>Reduced packaging costs<br>Elimination of duties<br>Access to raw materials and labour | High initial capital<br>Investment<br>High information and search costs<br>Nationalization or expropriation |
| Product-market factors | Management control<br>Market access<br>Effective marketing | Management constraints<br>Loss of flexibility<br>Increased marketing complexity |

The cost advantages of foreign direct investment lie in the areas of reduced transport costs, unit production and marketing costs and access to materials and cheaper labour. The cost disadvantages arise due to the high initial capital investment, high information and search costs and the threat of nationalization and expropriation.

The product-market advantages of foreign direct investment as a mode of entry are threefold: greater management control; better access to markets; and more effective marketing. Disadvantages arise due to increased marketing complexity which arises due to the need to co-ordinate subsidiary and headquarter marketing programmes.

## Summary

Participating in international markets through foreign direct investment is often considered to be the most intense form of commitment to international markets. Foreign direct investment may take the form of acquisitions or new ventures. Acquisitions are by far the more popular of the two forms since market entry is quick and can be very effective. It is an expensive option, however, especially if the acquired firm is already well established in the market through the possession of a well-known branded product.

Foreign direct investment through new ventures is favoured by smaller firms generally and by firms motivated as much by manufacturing reasons as by market reasons. Scale effects can be an important determinant of the new venture mode of entry to international markets.

Foreign direct investment through whichever form generally causes concern at the political level in either the source or host country. In recent years the benefits of foreign direct investment, particularly if motivated for marketing reasons, have been judged to outweigh the costs. Foreign direct investment, even cross-investment, is a feature of international business which is likely to remain with the more open markets of the 1990s.

The advantages for the firm in entering international markets through foreign direct investment may be found in reduced costs, more effective marketing, and tighter control of manufacturing and marketing.

## Discussion questions

1. Foreign direct investment is the most expensive option when considering ways of entering international markets. Discuss.

2. Foreign direct investment is more suited to industrial products firms than to consumer products firms. Discuss.

3. Explain the recent interest by large companies in acquiring branded consumer products firms abroad.

4. Classical investment and trade theory would suggest that foreign direct investment should be one-way. Explain why cross-investment occurs.

5. Some commentators argue that more open markets encourage foreign direct investment while others argue that it is protection which determines such investment. How can you reconcile these contrasting positions?

6. What are the advantages and disadvantages of acquisitions and new ventures as options within foreign direct investment?

7. By what criteria would you judge a particular foreign direct investment activity to have succeeded or failed? Illustrate your answer.

## References

Buckley, Peter J. and Casson, Mark (1976) *The Future of the Multinatinal Enterprise*, Holmes and Meier, NY.

Caves, Richard E. (1971) 'Industrial corporation: The industrial economics of foreign investment,' *Economica*, **38** (149), 1–27.

Coley, S. and Reinton, S. (1988) 'The hunt for value,' *The McKinsey Quarterly*, Spring, 93–100.

Dunning, John H. (1981) *International Production and the Multinational Enterprise*, George Allen and Unwin, London.

*The Economist* (1988) *The World in 1988*, London

EC Commission (1988) *Seventeenth Report on Competition Policy*, Brussels.

EC Commission (1989) *Eighteenth Report on Competition Policy*, Brussels.

Eng, Eva and Forsman, Anders (1989) 'Mergers and acquisitions — Swedish efforts to gain access to the Common Market,' an unpublished paper presented to International Marketing Seminar, Department of Marketing, University College Dublin.

Hymer, Stephen H. (1976) *The International Operations of National Firms: A Study of Direct Foreign Investment*, MIT Press, Cambridge, Mass.

Jacquemin, Alexis, Buigues, Pierre and Ilzkovitz, Fabienne (1989) 'Horizontal mergers and competition policy in the European Community,' *European Economy*, **40**, 13–39.

Kayser, Gunter and Schwarting, Uwe (1981) 'Foreign investment as a form of enterprise strategy: On the results of a survey,' *Intereconomics*, November-December, 295–9.

Kogut, Bruce and Singh, Harbir (1988) 'The effect of national culture on the choice of entry mode,' *Journal of International Business Studies*, **19** (3), 411–32.

Mettler, P.H. (1985) *Multinationale Kenzerne in der Bundesrepublik Deutschland*, Merchen Verlag, Frankfurt-M, **1**, A31.

Teece, David J. (1981) 'The multinational enterprise: Market failure and market power considerations,' *Sloan Management Review*, **22** (3), 3–17.

US Department of Commerce (1988) *International Direct Investment — Global Trends and the US Role*, November.

# *The international marketing programme*

# The consumer products firm in international markets

## 15

In this chapter we examine consumer products and brands in international markets. The chapter is divided into four sections. The first section examines the factors which lead to fragmentation and consolidation in consumer markets. The next section examines how consumer products firms active in international markets respond to such trends. In the third section the ways in which firms implement their brand strategies are evaluated. The last section is devoted to discussing ways of protecting the brand and the firm: brand protection from infringements in the market; and protection for the consumer products firm from take-overs.

## Trends in consumer products markets

### Market fragmentation and consolidation

It has been argued that differences in tastes, languages, culture, and technical standards are among the more serious obstacles to market consolidation. In international markets tariffs and non-tariff barriers force manufacturers to think locally. At the same time retailers are still very much national organizations focussed on one country only, though this is changing. These two factors dictate to a large extent the nature of the consumer products market in many parts of the world. In the regime of international markets characterized by these barriers large firms are deprived of one of their favourite weapons, cost leadership stemming from manufacturing scale effects, while smaller firms proliferate and compete by serving speciality niches. Additional causes of market fragmentation in international markets are low industry entry costs and high exit costs. The absence of experience curve effects in some industries ensures that the industry remains fragmented. The strong determination of national governments to support the development of industries believed to be of strategic importance can also contribute to market fragmentation, which is especially true in telecommunications and was true in consumer electronics in Europe.

In traditional consumer mass markets as found, for example, in the US, population age structures, the increase in the number of women working away from the home and the recognition of a multilingual and multicultural society have forced many companies to cope with fragmented markets by developing niche strategies. Many of the same influences have always existed in Europe. At the same time the media are saturated with claims for standardized products, while consumers seek variety and supermarkets seek higher margins.

Many traditional marketing companies are beginning to exploit the new information technologies to identify customers and determine their motivation. Targeted media are being used to reach these emerging target segments: direct mail; cable TV; and advertisements displayed in areas frequented by the targeted customer segment. Retailers seek higher margins and control of shelf space so they rarely allow decisions in this area to be made without care. Large retailers dictate the amount and type of shelf space and display that a product receives.

These are among the more important factors which have influenced trends towards increased fragmentation in markets. They are more influential in some markets than others and the ability of firms to cope with them varies correspondingly. High culture bound items such as food, clothing, and medicine are more likely to be sold in fragmented markets, whereas consumer electronics and music, especially music aimed at the youth market, will probably continue to serve a standardized consolidated market.

There are a number of ways in which firms attempt to counteract or offset the effects of fragmented markets. Successful international firms frequently introduce low-cost standardized products which can cover most market needs, thereby replacing many specialized products. In the 1970s Philips manufactured ninety TV models for twelve countries but in the 1980s it changed its policy and developed the Matchline Series consisting of twenty-five models to be sold in twelve countries.

Some firms systematically try to raise marketing expenditures to a level where firms that are not well funded are forced out. This is a common strategy in the packaged foods business, tobacco, detergents and breakfast cereals especially. One strategy, already discussed in Chapter 14, involves the firm in acquiring its competitors and rationalizing production capacity. The Swedish firm Electrolux systematically acquired competitors to dominate the European white goods industry and to become a significant competitor through its acquisitions in the United States. Finally, firms will sometimes invest heavily in capital equipment, which raises the minimum scale necessary to be an efficient operator. Companies use various combinations of the above approaches to consolidate markets.

## Convergence of international consumer markets

According to Levitt (1983) consumer markets are converging to such an extent that products will serve world markets. He cites the trend toward a world youth culture fed on rock music, fast food and fashion. The standardization of international marketing practices for consumer products is predicated, according to Levitt, on an international equalization of relative income levels, increasing personal consumption, a convergence of ownership patterns of durable consumer products and increased and better communications.

Following the above line of discussion, companies observe that if they desire a position in the global market they need to brand their products or services. A recent study of worldwide brand power shows some significant departures from traditional patterns (*The Economist*, 24 December, 1988, p. 93). Taking the three market regions, Europe, the United States and Japan and sampling 1,000 consumers in each market this study attempted to measure brand familiarity and brand esteem. Equal weighting was given to consumer familiarity with each brand name. The general results are shown below (Table 15.1). Thus, Coca-Cola ranked first in Europe for familiarity but sixty-sixth in esteem: it finished sixth overall!

The brand itself does not need to be global but the firm will need a global identity to promote its products. General Motors has different brands for different markets, whereas other firms, such as Volkswagen, have one readily identifiable brand for the whole world. It is noteworthy that Volkswagen receives a rating while neither General Motors nor any of its brands featured in the top twelve.

Two additional features of Table 15.1 are worth noting: the country of origin of the brand; and its product class. US brands ranked No. 1 and No. 2. Four of the twelve top brands were of US origin, four were from West Germany and four

**Table 15.1**  World brand leaders, 1988

| Brand | Country of origin | Product class | Europe | Ranking in: US | Japan |
|-------|-------------------|---------------|--------|----------------|-------|
| 1.  Coca-Cola | United States | Beverages | 6 | 1 | 2 |
| 2.  IBM | United States | Computers | 24 | 51 | 8 |
| 3.  Sony | Japan | Electronics | 16 | 68 | 4 |
| 4.  Porsche | West Germany | Motor vehicles | 5 | 7 | 22 |
| 5.  McDonald's | United States | Fast food | 78 | 5 | 26 |
| 6.  Disney | United States | Entertainment | 52 | 11 | 53 |
| 7.  Honda | Japan | Motor vehicles | 29 | 62 | 37 |
| 8.  Toyota | Japan | Motor vehicles | 64 | 64 | 6 |
| 9.  Seiko | Japan | Watches | 47 | 91 | 10 |
| 10. BMW | West Germany | Motor vehicles | 8 | 71 | 96 |
| 11. Volkswagen | West Germany | Motor vehicles | 3 | 112 | 72 |
| 12. Mercedes-Benz | West Germany | Motor vehicles | 1 | 37 | 151 |

Source: Adapted from: *The Economist*, 24 December 1988, p. 93.

were Japanese. As a product class, motor vehicles dominate the group. One of the product groups, computers, might be better classified as an industrial rather than a consumer product. Finally, two of the brands were service brands, McDonald's, and Disney, both US brands.

The strength of these brands in their respective market segments allows the firms behind them to dominate the market and to out-manoeuvre or out-spend potential rivals. The cost of a would be usurper is considerable: a national advertising campaign would probably cost $60 million of the brand builder's money in the United States, $30 million in Japan and $20 million in the United Kingdom (*The Economist*, 24 December, 1988, p. 94).

## Consumer products penetrate world markets

The interesting feature of consumer markets throughout the world, as may be gleaned from the above, is that products and services quickly transfer among markets and the time products and services are left unchallenged in any market has shortened. Convergence of the time factor and of market factors has arisen.

Parallel to these developments have been the developments in communications which also bring about a convergence in consumer markets throughout the world. Post offices and telephone companies report very substantial increases in communications between countries. Sales of telephones, and especially telefaxes, support this claim. In Europe there are twenty-one TV satellites planned for the early 1990s. The footprints of these stations will extend well beyond national boundaries. Already the various European-wide channels are having their impact on which products are sold, from where and to whom. One of the features of this communications explosion is the pressure it places on managers to consider European wide advertising for European brands. In the United States the opposite trend is in evidence. The expense of national TV coverage in the United States, together with a recognition of valuable niche markets, has resulted in market fragmentation there.

For the developing countries the source of the pressure for a world view on consumer products and markets stems from interest in these countries in attempting to raise living standards and modernize. A major contributory factor in this process is technology which has "proletarianized communication, transport and travel. It has made isolated places and impoverished peoples eager for modernity's allurements." (Levitt, 1983, p. 92) According to Levitt, developing countries seek technology transfer to allow them to leap-frog to a better life.

## Branding in international markets

Brands are a relatively new phenomenon in international marketing. But branding in individual countries has existed in a dominant form at least since the start of the present century. Because they are targeted at the mass consumer market, consumer product brands are better known than industrial product brands or service brands. By the late nineteenth century most countries had passed trademarks acts establishing the brand name as a protectable asset. Brands such as Coca-Cola (US), Mercedes-Benz (West Germany), Persil (West Germany) and Cadbury (UK) existed before the passing of the trademark acts.

Brands are usually developed within a country and then introduced to foreign markets as the brand becomes accepted through advertising, word of mouth promotion by visitors, adaptation and strategic development by the company. Another force for internationalization arose from the ease with which colonies could be guaranteed as markets for brands. A more natural expansion path was among countries of the same language and similar culture.

The main growth in international brands occurred, however, after World War II. Troop movements, especially the US military, have been associated with the successful introductions of many US brands to Europe and the Far East. With the resultant expansion of US culture across much of the world and through US business acquisitions and investments in Europe in the 1950s and 1960s, many US brands or US-owned brands became well known internationally: Ford; Opel; Pepsi; and RCA. European brand names also began to spread during the 1950s and 1960s as a result of improved transportation and communications systems.

Japanese companies have also grown into highly developed brand centred firms. Sony, Mitsubishi, Sanyo, Honda, Susuki, Citizen, Seiko, Toyota, Suntory, Sharp, Casio, and Pioneer are brands which are easily recognizable throughout the world. To date Japanese brands have been concentrated in the field of electronics, motor cars, and heavy earth moving equipment. This is changing as a visit to Japan's neighbouring Far Eastern countries proves. Japanese branded foods, cosmetics (Shiseido), and clothing (Kenzo) are now widely distributed in the region and much sought after. They are also available in western markets though they have not dominated their segments yet.

In recent years there have been quite a number of articles written on international branding and the globalization of markets (Buzzell, 1968; Hamel and Prahalad, 1985; Levitt, 1983; Martenson, 1987). These studies have, however, concentrated on a conceptualization of strategies for international markets but they provide little information on brand globalization itself. There has been little empirical work in determining the extent of international brand diffusion, the identification of markets served internationally, and the extent to which brand standardization occurs among consumer products firms in international markets (Rosen, Boddewyn and Louis, 1989). In a study of 651 US brands these authors report that about 80 per cent of sales were achieved in the United States itself with a high proportion of the remainder in Canada. "This modest foreign distribution is not compensated for by foreign production or export of similar products under different names." (Rosen, Boddewyn and Louis, 1987, p. 17) Timing and age of brands does not appear to be significant either. According to these authors "older brands are not more likely to be widely internationalized nor standardized than younger brands ... it appears that brands do not necessarily 'grow up' into standardized international brands over time." (Rosen,

Boddewyn and Louis, 1989, p. 17) In order to understand the issues better it will be necessary to carry out longitudinal studies of brand diffusion into many markets, originating in a number of countries.

## Developing international consumer brands

### Consumer products in international markets

For centuries consumers have sought choice in the things they buy. The growth in consumer products markets which is much discussed in the literature and in the popular media is not a phenomenon of the late twentieth century. Exotic products were in demand in Europe from the time they were discovered as a result of endeavours by trading companies to expand their business empires.

The general increase in living standards fuelled the demand for choice. As more products were produced better, faster and in greater quantities, and as the consumer was willing to pay for them, this led to continuous growth in consumer demand, interrupted by the slumps of the 1920s, the 1930s, the 1940s and the 1970s and in some countries in the 1980s.

Consumer products are usually associated with developed countries. Food, clothing, toys, cars, beer, and magazines are often cited as examples. Most developing countries also have a very high demand for the products mentioned, and the growth in many of these markets is faster than growth in developed country markets. Nevertheless, many consumer products are developed first in western style developed country markets but are rapidly transferred to developing country markets. Large multinational companies are usually at the centre of such activity.

The concept of a deterministic international life cycle model as proposed by Wells (1968) does not seem to have much to support it, however, in the 1990s. Japan is a leader in the production and international sale of electronic consumer products. Japan leads the world in the production and further development of calculators, TVs and watches. Japan has also developed products such as personal stereos and mini hi-fis. The United States and Europe are at present experiencing the dominance of Japan in these product markets. This is a trend which is likely to continue for some time with the development of the Pacific rim countries.

The completion of the internal EC market is also expected to give rise to growth in consumer choice as well as an increase in the penetration of consumer products from non-EC countries as internal and external trade barriers fall and as distribution channels are opened and developed.

International consumer products are usually developed sequentially from market to market or region to region, leading to the same products and services being available in many countries and even worldwide. A good example of the

**Table 15.2**   Generations of consumer products

Some products have been on the market for a long time in different forms:

| Laundry powder | Coffee | Vegetables |
|---|---|---|
| Conventional soap powder | Conventional ground coffee | Canned |
| Simple synthetic detergents | Tinned soluble coffee powder | Canned mixed vegetables |
| Synthetic detergents with bleaching and blueing additives | Soluble coffee powder in glass jar or vacuum packed | Fully prepared and frozen |
| Low sudsing detergents for washing machines | Concentrated soluble coffee: spray on | Freeze dried |
| Hot and cold water synthetic detergents | Espresso, caffeine free coffee powder | Concentrated |
| Biodegradable synthetic detergents | Freeze dried coffee granules | |
| Bioactive synthetic detergents | Freeze died coffee cubes and bags | |

development of a product over time and across different markets is laundry powder. Laundry powder initially began as bar soap and is still used in that form to wash clothes in many developing countries. The introduction of soap powder was followed by non- biological soap powder. When this product reached maturity in Western Europe, liquid detergent was introduced. It is likely that this product will also spread throughout world markets. These product generations may be seen over time in a single market and at a given point in time in different markets (Table 15.2).

## Products or brands

A product is something with a fundamental purpose; a brand offers something in addition. All brands are products or services in that they serve a functional purpose. Not all products or services are brands, however. A brand is a product or service that provides functional benefits and added values that some consumers value sufficiently to buy. Added values form the most important part of this definition of branding. Strong brands are balanced between motivating benefits and discriminating benefits. Motivating benefits are the functional benefits that prompt the consumer to use any brand in the product class, and discriminating benefits, i.e. those benefits that prompt the consumer to buy one brand rather than another (Jones, 1986, pp. 28–34). It is generally accepted that no brand can be all things to all consumers. Striving to cover too wide a field will result in a brand that is No. 2 or No. 3 over a wide range of attributes rather than No. 1 over a limited range.

---

**Exhibit 15.1   Selecting the brand name requires care**

---

*Getting the name right*

A brand's fortunes hang on its nomenclature. As international marketing grows, so does the importance of the product's starting point — its brand name. And the cost of getting it wrong grows, too.

Pricing can be changed — even the whole brand strategy, if necessary — but changing the name is virtually changing the product.

Yet, says John Murphy, of London-based Novamark/InterBrand, which specializes in developing and registering brand names, it is surprising how often the choice of a name for a product that is to be sold all round the world is made in the shower, by the company chairman.

But finding a brand name that is both attractive and usable internationally is becoming increasingly difficult. "Finding brand names, whether they are national or international, is one third strategy, one third creative and one third legal", says Mr Murphy.

A good brand name, he says, is not just a convenient label by which a product can be known. It can also be a protective halo around the product's identity, distinguishing it from competitors. Soft drinks company Schweppes named one of its products Bitter Lemon. The product was a success, but the name could not be legally protected and within a short space of time it had become a generic used by every other soft drinks manufacturer.

Mr Murphy spends quite a lot of time persuading people to think internationally, even though they might not be interested in international sales for the foreseeable future. Otherwise, they might have the same experience as Gillette in the US. It pioneered a swivel-headed razor in the US, which it named, logically, Swivel. But when Gillette decided to launch it in Europe the company ran into major branding problems, since to Germans the name Swivel, self-explanatory in English, meant absolutely nothing. Novamark/InterBrand came up with its European name, Slalom, which means the same thing in any language.

Similarly, Papermate's Erasa-mate pen was just as unintelligible and had to become Replay in Europe...

Source: *Focus*, October, 1985, p. 21.

---

Most companies attempt to achieve one or a combination of three things in branding. First, they may confirm the legal protection afforded by the inventor's patent. Second, they may guarantee quality and homogeneity in a period when buyers and sellers have lost face-to-face contact. The brand becomes a mark of assurance for a level of quality. Third, firms may try to differentiate their products and services in a competitive environment. Differentiation has traditionally attracted the attention of economists "... various brands of a certain article which in fact are almost exactly alike may be sold as different qualities under names and labels which will induce rich and snobbish buyers to divide themselves from poorer buyers." (Robinson, 1933, pp. 180–1) This view is supported by many consumer brand managers. Selecting the brand name becomes a very important decision requiring much care (Exhibit 15.1).

Branding is believed to add values to products and services. These added values arise from the experience gained from using the brand: familiarity, reliability and risk reduction; from association with the kind of people who are known users of the brand — rich and snobbish, young and glamorous; and from the belief that the brand is effective — branding of some proprietary drugs is thought to affect the mind's influence over body processes. There is some evidence to support this contention "... branding works like an ingredient of its own interacting with the pharmacological active ingredients to produce something more powerful than an unbranded tablet." (Lannon and Cooper, 1983, p. 206) Finally the added values which derive from the appearance of the brand are very strong. Herein lies the special role of packaging for consumer and industrial products.

## Managing consumer brands in international markets

### Long-term brand management

The life cycle concept applies to products and services and only through neglect by management does it apply to brands. It is the pressure of competition in the market which dictates the pace of innovation. There is nothing inevitable about it. This is not to deny that brands do not mature. Brands do reach maturity and maintain relatively constant permanent levels of market share in the face of competition. The decline stage of the brand life cycle is under management control. The life cycle is a dangerous self-fulfilling concept. Successful brand companies do not ignore the life cycle concept; they manage it. In recent years Guinness' United Distillers Group has endeavoured to rationalize and strengthen its portfolio of whisky brands. Many brands were amalgamated, dropped or rejuvenated and new products introduced (Exhibit 15.2). Products become obsolete but brands can be adapted functionally to remain competitive. Many companies allow their brands to lose market share by the conscious transfer of resources from old to new.

For longer-term growth and development of the brand it is necessary to ensure continued and growing promotional support. The emphasis should be on those added values that have become the brand's unique property. Sometimes firms have to relaunch their brands. With relaunching, product improvements can be evaluated alongside the established and accepted battery of functional benefits that the brand provides. Relaunching also provides an occasional opportunity to sharpen the attention of existing and potential users. During a

---

## Exhibit 15.2  Managing the life cycle and rejuvenating the brand

---

*Guinness licks its spirits into shape*

"We are not talking about a single business in a single market. We are dealing with a multitude of brands selling in many countries. We have got to the top of the table in marketing sales and bottom of the league in costs", claims Guinness Beverages managing director Victor Steel.

With this in mind, the Guinness group has pinpointed the spirits division as one to focus on, aiming at "mass niche marketing". Steel sums up the initiative as one of "creating brands which will be the driving force behind our success and developing a total brand image — one that will enhance a lifestyle whether it's in Japan, Kuala Lumpur or the UK.".

The importance of spirits to Guinness is shown in analysts' estimates that, in 1987, this area could generate some 10% of pre-tax profits for the group, which overall could hit £460m. Whisky looms large in the Guinness game plan. But it is a spirit that in many people's view has been a victim of its own success. It was the first international spirit, and as such is beginning to suffer an ageing consumer profile.

Guinness is now looking for the yuppie drinker. James Espey, the new deputy managing director of Guinness Beverages, is the first to admit that a change in brand positioning is long overdue.

The famous Johnnie Walker Red Label and Black Label are earmarked for change, with a possible merging of the brands, exploitation of Buchanans Reserve and an upgrading of the Black & White brand as well as geographic expansion for Dewar's.

The most controversial scheme is the possible dumping of the beleaguered VAT 69, which has always had a down-at-heel image. "This is a brand with a good history but not a good future", says Espey.

While Guinness wants to keep Bell's as its flagship whisky brand Espey points to malt whisky as a major area for expansion. The luxury single malt end of the Scotch market has weathered the 80s far better than the run-of-the-mill blended market.

Glenfiddich sales, for example, soared 50 percent to 6 million cases last year.

Espey predicts two major new brands in the coming year, and the pouring of funds into Pimm's. "Watch out", he warns the drink industry. "We are a sleeping giant."

**Source:** *Marketing,* 26 March, 1987, p. 16.

---

relaunch, firms sometimes introduce new versions, e.g. new types, flavours and colours which can add market share without cannibalizing existing sales.

### Branding for success

If a consumer product is unbranded it may be difficult for the manufacturer to be independent and to succeed internationally on a long-term basis. Unbranded products can be successful for products of low perceived value or low involvement, e.g. jelly confectionery for children. Sometimes such products are sold under a private label brand on a regional or country basis. The role of the manufacturer or private label in the branding process demonstrates that branding is very important in consumer products markets as it gives the consumer a reference point throughout the purchasing process.

By allowing others to control the branding means that the firm relinquishes the opportunity of creating the desired consumer and channel image. The goodwill associated with the brand is outside the manufacturer's control. The firm that controls the brand usually dominates the marketing of the product. For many firms, small enterprises in particular, it is usually easier to manufacture and to pay less attention to the international marketing aspects. Such an approach may have a lucrative financial payoff in the short term but in the longer term the firm is exposed.

Many firms with global brands refuse to share control of production, the product or the brand. Indeed, it is a feature of large branded products companies in the late 1980s and early 1990s that they attempt to own the entire distribution system for their brands, e.g. Coca-Cola in India, IBM in India and Brazil, International Distillers and Vintners, the beverages division of Grand Metropolitan, in all its principal markets.

Brands are perceived differently in different markets despite the product being the same. A Vauxhall in the United Kingdom, an Opel in West Germany and General Motors in the United States may be exactly the same except for the branding in order to maximize the goodwill from the consumer in each market in terms of brand recognition, country of origin stereotyping, social status of the brand and perceived performance (Johannson and Thorelli, 1985).

Variations in consumer applications are frequently found in international markets. Pain relievers, for example, are usually targeted at the housewife in the United States, at the busy executive in West Germany, and in a number of other countries at people with hangovers. In such circumstances it is difficult to adopt a universal marketing approach in each of these markets as the customer group and the purpose of use vary so greatly.

## Sustaining competitive advantage

Building and sustaining competitive advantage for the firm's product are continuous tasks throughout the life cycle of the product as the environment and competitors change and as new markets are entered and developed. A competitive advantage is based on an attribute or combination of attributes of the product or service which the consumer values more than competing offers. Firms compete on the basis of very specific attributes. In the washing-up-liquid market, for example, supermarket own labels compete on price, whereas Fairy Liquid, the Unilever brand, competes on softness for the hands and the claim that it "goes further." Quix, a Procter & Gamble brand, competes on performance and a luxury smell, while other brands compete on a claim of being fully biodegradable and non-toxic.

Each company chooses a different approach in order to be competitive. The approach must be changed among markets as the brand name may not be acceptable or the product attributes may not sufficiently differentiate the product or for some other reason the product may not be desirable. Manufacturers attempt to promote their competitive advantage to retailers and consumers to highlight actual or perceived differences whether that refers to the brand name itself, price, speed of delivery, convenience, product quality or effective advertising.

## Implementing international brand strategies

### Branding the competitive advantage

Most luxury products have built their reputation on quality and performance. They have been able to sustain that advantage over their competitors by transferring customer goodwill to a brand name or logo. The ability to make this transfer in one market has facilitated brand building across markets. The brand names Gucci, Louis Vuitton, Tessori, Bang & Olufsen, Giorgio, Simone and Hasselblad are readily identifiable throughout the world.

In attempting to build an international competitive advantage the firm first ensures that the featured attributes give a competitive advantage in every market. Luxury, country of origin and prestige are important factors in building the demand for many consumer brands in most markets. These factors are especially important in Japan (Exhibit 15.3). If the attributes featured are not desirable it may be a mistake to attempt to internationalize.

Over time competitive advantage can dissipate due to competitor activity. Competitive activity is usually not benign. It is also necessary to monitor consumers who change, sometimes unpredictably. In the toilet tissue market, for example, the Velvet brand dominated most western style markets in the 1950s and 1960s by introducing colours in its products. This advantage was eroded in the 1970s by Andrex, a softer paper promoted in association with the Labrador puppy. Velvet eventually offered even softer paper. Andrex responded with additional paper in each roll. At the end of the 1980s Andrex still held the edge on Velvet because it had built an image for itself in the toilet tissue market, even though the price of the brand was about 15 per cent more than the average priced toilet tissue in most markets.

In order to build a competitive advantage and internationalize it, the firm usually needs a brand to epitomize what the product is attempting to achieve.

It is also important that the firm understands the differences in the decision-making process between markets. In Canada, a French Canadian decision regarding the purchase of a car is more likely to be influenced by word of mouth with the result that their search process is shorter than that of their English-speaking Canadian neighbours (Muller, 1985). As a result the French Canadian

---

**Exhibit 15.3 Branding luxury, prestige and country of origin**

---

*The land of the rising brand name*

In many ways, Japan is the ideal market for prestige brands. Most middle-class Japanese are cash-rich, regular gift givers, obsessed with elite labels, and enamoured of traditional images. Usually the traditional image and the exclusive name come from Europe, which is still considered the source of Western culture in Japan.

"Our strength is that we're British", says Roger Wragby, general manager of Alfred Dunhill of London's Tokyo office. One third of Dunhill's total sales of £525 million last year ($866 million) were to Japanese customers.

Louis Vuitton sells 25 percent of its output in Japan and another 15 percent to Japanese customers in its shops elsewhere in the world. Gucci has 300 shops in Japan, while Rolex, Cardin, Cartier, Burberry, Wedgwood and scores of other prestige European brands are available in any upmarket department store.

Prices in Japan can be high even by luxury standards. A tiny Vuitton handbag called the Speedy, aimed at Tokyo's army of affluent "office ladies," working women in their 20s and 30s, costs an impressive ¥43,000 ($297). Rolex's most popular man's watch sells for ¥890,000 ($6,140).

Despite the rapid rise in the Japanese yen, prices of prestige items haven't dropped at all, primarily because high price is part of their attraction. Rolex watches sell for 40 percent less in Hong Kong.

"Imagery", says one Tokyo retailer. If a gift comes in the wrapping of a famous Tokyo store, it is much more impressive than if the box has a Hong Kong shop's name on it, even when the products inside are identical.

**Source:** *International Management*, December, 1987, p. 27.

---

car market requires more warranties and free maintenance services whereas the English-speaking market depends more on advertising and specific product characteristics. English-speaking Canadians are likely to be less disappointed with their purchases, as their search is longer and more intensive (Muller, 1985).

In such circumstances it is likely that the firm will have to modify the proportions of the elements within the total product offering in order to achieve the same result in two or more international markets.

## Competing with different marketing programmes

A firm may choose its competitive environment by changing its marketing programme in order to confront competitors directly in order to overtake and by-pass them. The international tussle for market share between Coca-Cola and Pepsi-Cola may be cited to illustrate the point. For many decades Coca-Cola had an almost unassailable lead in nearly every market of the world where it was distributed. When its share in the United States and Europe began to slip the company changed the taste of the product in the United States which undermined its greatest competitive advantage: "Coke is it." Pepsi immediately retaliated by claiming that Pepsi was the "Choice of a new generation." They accompanied the claim with taste tests and with discounts to wholesalers. Coca-Cola capitulated by offering its old recipe Coke as "Coke Classic" in the United States and by starting a large promotional campaign in the United States and Europe in order to reinstate its competitive advantage.

The above illustrations demonstrate how changing the marketing programme can affect the product not only in the market where it was changed but also in other related markets where goodwill can be lost, even though the marketing programme has not been changed in those markets. This domino effect can be very damaging but it may also be exploited to promote the product or brand especially in the fashion industry where success in New York, Paris, Milan, London, or Munich can easily transform a domestic brand into an international brand with the assistance of the media.

Sometimes the brand has to be changed when the firm enters a foreign market, even though all other aspects of the marketing programme, including the product, remain the same. A good example of such adaptation is the success of Irish Sugar, a Republic of Ireland firm, in Northern Ireland, geographically part of the same island but politically part of the United Kingdom. Irish Sugar exploited the neglect of the Northern Ireland market in the early 1970s by British Sugar which made very poor attempts to serve the market during and after a strike at its British based plants. Irish Sugar entered with the McKinney brand, a name acceptable to both sections of the divided community. The Irish Sugar brand, Siuicre Eireann, would have been acceptable to the Nationalist community but not to the majority Unionist community. The McKinney brand was quite successful and by the end of the 1980s had 45 per cent share of the white granulated sugar market in Northern Ireland.

In order to build a competitive advantage in a market, the firm must be aware of the differences between its home market and the foreign market. Adopting the 1950s and 1960s US general management view that it is as possible to sell abroad as at home can quickly lead to new competitors entering the market or even to the collapse of the firm. A way of avoiding large-scale failures in foreign markets is to enter a smaller market first, one which is culturally and economically similar to the larger target market. French, German and Italian speaking Switzerland could act as test markets for Germany, France and Italy respectively, if care is taken in making the comparisons.

Competitive activity in the domestic market can force a firm to internationalize. Well-known brands such as Ford, Nissan and Sony were forced to internationalize because of insurmountable competition at home. All three companies pursued very aggressive market building strategies abroad in order to thwart and delay their principal domestic competitors, General Motors, Toyota and Matsushita, respectively (Mascarenhos, 1986). These firms built their competitive advantage abroad rather than at home and have managed to sustain their positions. Colgate-Palmolive also developed its competitive advantage abroad but varied the theme. It copied Procter & Gamble's products which were successful in the United States, and pioneered them abroad. Colgate-Palmolive did not have a large R & D facility and always relied on Procter & Gamble ideas, though it was first to internationalize them. Colgate, the first fluoride toothpaste outside the United States, still dominates many world markets.

Developing competitive advantage may mean appreciating cultural differences and the different uses for products in different markets. Guinness stout is considered a mild aphrodisiac in the Caribbean, as an alternative drink with "Green" associations in West Germany, as a typical Irish drink in Ireland, Scotland and Wales but as a British drink in England. Consumers in each market consume Guinness for different reasons and the perceived benefits and images are also considered to be different.

## Quality standards in brand strategy

Quality and standards are important issues in developing competitive advantage for consumer products. Quality leadership is considered essential if the firm wishes to assure itself of long-term product supremacy, at home and abroad (Feigenbaum, 1986). Improved product and process quality improves market share and return on investment and helps to decrease overall production and inspection costs (Carroll, 1985). One of the most fruitful ways of sustaining competitive advantage, therefore, is by providing quality and meeting quality standards.

In Europe the EC Commission is attempting to harmonize product standards across its member countries. It does this by setting minimum product safety standards which must be accepted by all member countries. In many cases these standards will become acceptable throughout the world. In such circumstances it is necessary to meet these minimum standards in order to compete. As these standards refer to minimum levels of attainment, competitive pressure is likely to push the market standard very much higher. Herein lies the risk for smaller consumer products firms. They could be trapped between the minimum and the competitive quality standards without any of the scale effects. This shake-out normally occurs when markets and industries begin to mature, as has happened recently in the calculator and personal computer industries. Many companies in these industries suddenly found themselves with products which were less advanced and less reliable than those of their competitors but did not have sufficient resources to overcome the disadvantage. Many withdrew from the market, leaving it to the now dominant brands such as Sharp and Casio in calculators and IBM and Apple in personal computers.

One way for smaller firms to cope with competition on the basis of quality is to apply for the internationally recognized process and management quality standards such as the IS0 9000 to IS0 9002 quality standards. These standards are quality regulations for raw materials procurement, production and management. By using these standards the firm may eliminate waste and inefficiency and set itself up for continuous improvement in internal company quality, quality in the product itself and in the rest of the marketing programme. To be competitive, adherence to normal product standards, i.e. conformance standards, is not enough. The firm must continuously monitor its operations in order to minimize costs and increase quality.

The firm in international markets uses quality management along with the other elements of the marketing programme to create a total offering that is distinctive and has a competitive advantage in all markets entered. The task is easier if the firm faces the same competitors in each market as the adjustments in the marketing programme are likely to be similar.

The understanding of the customer's needs and their levels of satisfaction is central to the success of the international firm. In this context firms normally endeavour to operate with internationally compatible quality regulations and standards.

## Umbrella branding in international markets

A consumer product that is not targeted at a segmented market is unlikely to enjoy much success. A way of avoiding this, if the company or the product has a presence in the market, is to use the mechanism of umbrella branding. Letting a product benefit from the competitive advantage of an established product but using a variation of the marketing programme is a very popular approach by large consumer products companies. The car industry is a good example. Mercedes-Benz carries with it a very different connotation than Fiat or Toyota. Perhaps better known are the soft drinks umbrella brands used to include diet soft drinks. These products are priced and distributed in the same way as their ordinary counterparts but the product is changed. The image and promotion of the diet products are totally different from their non-diet counterparts. Some successful firms have used an umbrella brand to bring a range of new products to the market and to transfer the success from one market to another.

A different form of umbrella branding may be observed in Saab-Scania. Here cars are associated with sophisticated jet fighter aircraft through the use of advertising. This approach combines consumer and industrial promotion to good effect. The 1988 model year advertising campaign for Saab cars showed the 900 and 9000 car series and the supersonic fighter Saab JA-37 Viggen: "We'd like to make our cars the Rolex watch or the Gucci loafers of the industry," said Robert Sinclair, president of Saab-Scania of America, the US importer; "Distinctly different isn't enough. We have to communicate an aura around the name that goes on the product" said Mr Sinclair (*Advertising Age*, 9 November, 1987, p. 70).

## Traps in international marketing

There are many pitfalls in international markets for the unwary firm, especially in the area of consumer products and services. Packaging and labelling in foreign markets are particularly important decision areas not only in regard to compliance with local regulations but also in regard to product enhancement, information and promotion. Some markets place greater value on packaging than others. Far Eastern markets value the decorative value of packaging a great deal and even industrial products are packaged to a much greater extent in Japan than in other western style markets. A related area which gives rise to many problems is that of language and instructions. Examples of poor instructions or no translation of instructions in packaged products abound. In this respect Japanese or Korean language instructions on how to operate a cassette recorder or calculator, for example, are not very helpful to Europeans or Americans, especially if the product must be assembled. In these circumstances, the manufacturer is expecting too much and is also limiting the chances of success by not taking simple things, such as language, into consideration.

On the other hand, attempting to enhance the product by providing meaningless information is pointless, as was demonstrated by Volvo in West Germany and the United States, where the firm found that the projection of "Swedishness" and Swedish engineering did not help sales as the claims did not mean much to consumers in these markets.

Packaging is very important for consumer products because it provides the first impression, which if negative, can be very difficult to overcome later. Sometimes firms overplay their hand in this respect. Currys, a UK electrical retailer, tried to pass off some of its British-made products as Japanese. This practice is now being made illegal throughout the EC. Manufacturers of private label consumer products have also attempted to imitate well-known brands by using similar packaging, similar shapes and colours and other features which cause objections by the originator of the brand and its packaging (Exhibit 15.4).

After sales service is another mine field of traps for the unwary firm in international markets. A television or video player manufacturer, for example, causes severe dissatisfaction and even rejection among consumers if no provision is made for repair and replacement services in the target-market. An otherwise good product is not likely to sell if the consumer becomes aware beforehand of the absence of such services. The consumer must have after sales redress if required in order to feel assured of the quality of the product itself. The after sales service function also enables the manufacturer to monitor the performance of the product in the foreign market, which allows the firm to rectify any damage that may occur to the product due, for example, to conditions in the physical environment. The manufacturer may also be able to change the marketing programme in response to a discrepancy between the real and perceived cultural and social circumstances in the target market. The after sales service function for consumer durable products in particular is central to the success of the firm in international markets.

---

**Exhibit 15.4   Private label products sometimes infringe brands**

---

*Beecham hits back in the UK*

The UK's foods-to-pharmaceuticals major, Beecham, is hitting back at own-label goods in a test case against leading UK retailer J Sainsbury.

The case centers on those firm British culinary favorites — the Bovril and Marmite brands of yeast extract. For many years, these have been sold in distinctively shaped, brown-coloured jars. Until this year, Sainsbury sold its rival own-label yeast extracts in "anonymous" straight-sided jars. Recently, however, it has adopted a shape very similar to the "classic" Bovril and Marmite containers.

Beecham is alleging that the new packaging infringes its copyright in the shape of the jars (assuming that Beecham has, somewhere, an artist's drawing of the jar's dimensions), and amounts to Sainsbury "passing off" its own-label goods as Bovril and Marmite. Beecham has, however, failed to secure a court injunction requiring the immediate withdrawal of the offending jars, but is actively pursuing a civil action for damages. Manufacturers of everything from ketchup to cleaning products should check to see whether their container designs are derived from copyrighted blueprints; and keep track of the Beecham case.

**Source:** *Business Europe*, 4 May, 1987, p. 6.

---

## Protecting the firm and the brand

### Counterfeiting and forgeries

Competitive advantage can easily be eroded in some international markets due to counterfeits and forgeries. Counterfeiting means that another company uses the firm's competitive advantage to supply products to consumers at lower prices. Counterfeiting is a term frequently used generically to include a range of forged or faked products (Table 15.3). The principal focus of forgeries are luxury products such as branded shirts, suitcases, ladies handbags, and watches. Counterfeits usually occur only where the trademark holder receives relatively high margins, where the brand is international and where the competitive advantage reflects a worldwide interest in acquiring the best in the market, irrespective of origin. In such circumstances brand logos are easily recognizable. The strength of the brand logo rather than its quality, which is usually inferior, carries the fake. The trademark owner attempts to ensure that the exclusivity of the brand is preserved because that element of the marketing programme is likely to have become the firm's principal competitive advantage, even superior to the product quality attribute.

Counterfeiting is big business and a serious problem for many countries, especially in the developed world and for many brand companies in those

**Table 15.3**  The language of counterfeiting

Counterfeiting is the unauthorised copying of a product. It comes in many forms:

- *Associated counterfeit, imitation*: the illegal use of a name or product shape that differs from the original product but that the consumer will associate with the original
- *Diversion*: the distribution and sale of legitimate products through unauthorized dealers
- *Grey Market*: goods available through diversion, usually cheaper and without service guarantees
- *Knockoff*: a product that copies another design closely but carries its own name. Also used as slang for counterfeit
- *Look-alike, fake*: slang for counterfeit or knockoff
- *Parody*: the intentional mockery of a product through imitation that results in an infringement of the original product's trademark.
- *Passing-off*: the simulation of a trademark to closely resemble the original.
- *Piracy*: similar to counterfeiting but broader. The unauthorized publication, reproduction, use, or imitation of an invention, creation, or product with the objective of having the result pass as genuine
- *Re-entry*: purchasing goods from a domestic manufacturer, allegedly for overseas destinations, then returning them and selling them at lower cost in the domestic grey market
- *Replica, reproduction*: A close but not exact copy.

Source: *Business Week*, 1 June, 1987.

countries. The Counterfeit Intelligence Bureau in London estimates that up to $60 billion in annual world trade are fakes. The problem is far more costly than the mere market value of the bogus products. Counterfeits undermine legitimate business and obscure long-held legal distinctions about who own ideas and inventions. Disputes caused by counterfeits create tensions between a number of highly regulated industrialized countries and some developing countries.

Familiar counterfeits include: Gucci watches; Louis Vuitton bags; Cartier watches; Cabbage Patch dolls. Less familiar counterfeits include: chemicals; computers; drugs; fertilizers; pesticides; medical devices; hardware; and food. Most forgeries today come from the Far East, especially South East Asia. Many European distributors and retailers refuse to sell to these markets because they fear the potential emergence of fakes if their brands become quite successful there. On the other hand there are some products, such as the Rubik's Cube, which it is claimed could not have been successful without forgery. Because of the poor market development support for the original product other firms were left to develop the market. Although the product was successful, the Rubik brand, in terms of sales and profits, was not.

Copying some aspect of an already successful brand is very popular among cosmetics, perfume and food producers. They sometimes attempt to copy specific aspects of the original product's competitive advantage. In food and beverages, witness, for example, the worldwide proliferation of corn flakes, cream liqueurs, and cola products which clearly attempt to exploit some of the brand advantages built in the market by the brand leader.

In early 1987 Giorgio, a perfume recently acquired by Avon was selling for $135 an ounce, while a copy, Parfums de Coeur Ltd, was selling a Giorgio imitation called Primo at $7.50 an ounce. Primo is found in drug stores and discount outlets throughout the United States where the imitators mince no words: Parfums de Coeur declares on its packaging: "If you like Giorgio, you'll love Primo." (*Business Week*, 1 June, 1987) These direct references annoy the original designers who claim that the imitators are benefiting from their continued investment in the product and brand. Scents cannot be patented, however, so there is little they can do about it.

Furthermore, most imitators put disclaimers on their products: Lennox Laboratories Inc. sells an imitation of Giorgio called "The Great Pretender" with the disclaimer "Not Genuine Giorgio" on the packaging (*Business Week*, 1 June, 1987). Managers of designer brands report that the imitators damage moderately priced lines to a much greater extent than they harm those they imitate.

## Brands in the grey market

The most common activity in the grey market arises when an individual or firm buys products from a foreign distributor where wholesale prices are low and then diverts them to the lucrative high-priced US or European markets where domestic distributors who have paid a higher price are undersold. This issue of the grey market is intimately linked with attempts by firms to standardize some aspects of branding but to ignore or neglect others such as price and distribution policies. The wholesale prices that manufacturers charge for fragrances targeted at the US market can often be 25 per cent higher than the wholesale prices in Europe (Figure 15.1). To protect the US premium, perfume houses try to ensure that US distribution is through select dealers to exclusive outlets (*Business Week*, 7 November, 1988).

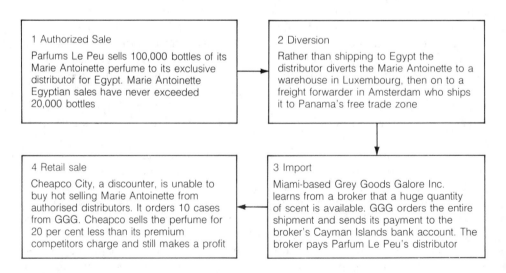

| 1 Authorized Sale | 2 Diversion |
|---|---|
| Parfums Le Peu sells 100,000 bottles of its Marie Antoinette perfume to its exclusive distributor for Egypt. Marie Antoinette Egyptian sales have never exceeded 20,000 bottles | Rather than shipping to Egypt the distributor diverts the Marie Antoinette to a warehouse in Luxembourg, then on to a freight forwarder in Amsterdam who ships it to Panama's free trade zone |
| 4 Retail sale | 3 Import |
| Cheapco City, a discounter, is unable to buy hot selling Marie Antoinette from authorised distributors. It orders 10 cases from GGG. Cheapco sells the perfume for 20 per cent less than its premium competitors charge and still makes a profit | Miami-based Grey Goods Galore Inc. learns from a broker that a huge quantity of scent is available. GGG orders the entire shipment and sends its payment to the broker's Cayman Islands bank account. The broker pays Parfum Le Peu's distributor |

**Figure 15.1**   The journey of a grey-market product — hypothetical example (Source: Adapted from *Business Week*, 7 November, 1988)

Because wholesalers in different markets are treated differently the manufacturers allow the grey market to develop. Publicly they argue that unauthorized imports of their products unfairly reduce their profits and damage their trademarks. Privately these companies may not sanction diversion but from time to time some of their sales people, in order to gain share or meet sales targets, will allow the grey market to develop. Some manufacturers, do, however, take a stronger line in some markets (Exhibit 15.5). Customers in the grey market defend the practice by asking why should they pay up to 20 per cent more than buyers in other markets. In most cases the trade is perfectly legal as may be witnessed by the increase in cross-trading of high-priced European motor cars among European markets encouraged by the open competition policy of the EC Commission.

To reiterate, product diversion to grey markets occurs when manufacturers offer very different wholesale prices to different customers in different international markets. In such circumstances manufacturers can protect themselves by insisting that major wholesale customers sign contracts preventing them from selling their products outside agreed territories, though this may come under scrutiny from the EC Commission.

Manufacturers design packaging for specific countries which runs counter to the advantages of standardization discussed above. Finally, they could also introduce regular audits of sales managers and distributors.

## Market value of a brand

Until recently branding was thought to have marketing value only. In particular, brands were considered to be psychological in nature and, therefore, not in any sense real. They were thought to be the material of advertising managers but not possessing financial worth. In addition, the accounting profession had difficulty with valuing brands. Accountants, and indeed the legal profession, prefer to deal with tangible assets such as factories, machinery and transport equipment. A market may be established for these items, their value can be assessed and their worth entered in the balance sheet. All this is changing with the spate of financial transactions involving brands.

The brands debate started in earnest in 1987 with the successful bid by Nestlé for the UK chocolate maker Rowntree Mackintosh, the owner of brands such as "After Eight," "Kit Kat" and "Rolo." Brand values depend on how these intangible assets should be treated. Nestlé paid £Stg2.5 billion to acquire Rowntree when the book value was £Stg668 million. Much of that premium can be considered the unaccounted value of the brands. The debate raises the issue of the firm's balance sheet: a reflector of company value or a historical record of costs not yet written off against revenues.

Irrespective of what accountants think, several large firms have begun to value brands in the balance sheet. In making a $US5.23 billion bid for Pillsbury, Grand Metropolitan reported that it would value newly acquired brands. Grand Metropolitan estimated that this could add over £Stg500 million to its balance

---

**Exhibit 15.5   Manufacturers sometimes take a strong line on grey markets**

---

*Colgate takes a diverter to task*

Colgate (UK) claims that the widespread practice of diverting is harming its reputation and undermining its market share.

Colgate (UK) sued Mr Juda Bak, a Belgian businessman operating in London, after he imported several large consignments of Colgate toothpaste to the UK from Brazil, where it was made under licence with an export market restricted to Bolivia, Paraguay, Chile and Nigeria. Colgate (UK) told the High Court that because of price restrictions and a shortage of raw materials in Brazil, the toothpaste made there relied on local chalk as a main constituent and was of "inferior" quality compared with the toothpaste made in the UK.

Mr Bak, who was found guilty in the High Court of passing off (one product as another) and infringement of trademark, said he was unaware that the consignments of toothpaste from Brazil to London had been granted an export licence on the understanding they were destined for Nigeria.

Mr Justice Falconer, the High Court judge, said Limatada, the company manufacturing the toothpaste in Brazil under licence from Colgate (US), "were deceived as to the real destination for which the products were intended." He agreed with Colgate (UK) that shoppers who bought the toothpaste in Britain, where it was sold to retailers at up to 15 per cent lower than the UK-produced Colgate, "had been deceived and being dissatisfied, had complained."

Mr Bak is appealing against the judgement. "Colgate cannot complain if it produces, throughout the world, products of different quality. This case shows that big companies now want to clamp down on diversion", said his solicitors S.J. Birwin & Co. of London.

Mr Bak's solicitors are confident of winning their appeal but Ms Ann Harper, a legal expert working for Colgate (UK), said the company would consider taking the case to the House of Lords, Britain's highest law court, if it lost the case. "We want to stop this happening again if we can. This toothpaste was coming in such large quantities that it was damaging our reputation and denting our market share."

The International Chamber of Commerce has also voiced its concern over diverting. Mr Giles Wyburd, ICC director in London, said: "We want to protect consumers against being misled. But we make it quite clear that it is contrary to European Community law for there to be any restrictions on parallel imports (diversions) within the community."

A spokesman for Revlon, which lost its case in the UK courts over what it claimed was illegal diversion of its shampoo from the US, suggested senior management in some multinationals turned a blind eye to diverting and on occasion took advantage of it. "A lot of the time diverters are used by companies to get rid of stuff which is old. It's a way of inventory clearance. A product which is a poor seller in one country may be sold to a known diverter to maintain turnover and sales. Nobody likes a diverter but everybody needs them."

**Source:** *The Financial Times*, Friday, 14 April, 1989.

sheet. The company's move was prompted by its purchase in 1987 of RJR Nabisco Inc's Heublein unit, which held Smirnoff, a premium vodka brand (*International Herald Tribune*, 8 December, 1988). Some commentators have argued that the debate is vacuous since the underlying economics of the firm are unchanged.

These commentators argue that companies are not valued according to their balance sheets but that share prices, a more sophisticated method of valuation, reflect the firm's value, i.e. share prices reflect the likely earnings the firm's assets, including its brands, would produce. The balance sheet and the share price are, of course, intimately linked. The debate on brand valuation is likely to continue for some time. Brand owners have clear multiple objectives for valuing their brands, which makes good managerial sense but causes problems for accountancy firms (Exhibit 15.6).

Brands are valued for reasons other than the profit they bring their owners. Sometimes, well-known brands are sought because the buyers believe that the firm's corporate image will improve or that the brand can be extended to an existing line of products or new products. Brand acquisition can also mean acquisition of the means of access to new and difficult markets. In 1988 Seagram won the battle for the world's second largest brandy brand, Martell. Not only did this give Seagram access to the brandy market, it also allowed the company distribution channel access for its maturing whisky brands to the rapidly growing Chinese speaking Far Eastern markets, traditional consumers of brandy.

Until recently property was treated as a depreciating asset in the balance sheet and was eventually written off. When this nonsense was discovered, property began to be revalued periodically and the balance sheet adjusted accordingly. Brands are the same, they are a property with legal protection and a value in the market. By including them, the firm's balance sheet is strengthened, its share price may be increased, its borrowing powers revised, and its vulnerability to predators decreased. In this context it is noteworthy that interest in brand valuation occurred in markets where strong brands have attracted bidders.

## Summary

Underlying this chapter is the view that consumer markets throughout the world are at different stages of development. It is recognized that a particular consumer market may be very advanced in one product area but less advanced in others. The opposite may be the case in other markets. This causes a high degree of fragmentation in consumer markets. Two forces are, however, very influential in bringing about consolidation in some consumer markets — the pressure of convergence of consumer tastes and preferences and the benefits to companies of brand building as a means of entering and competing in many international markets simultaneously.

Because tastes and preferences are different in different markets the management of the brand across markets becomes a significant issue within the consumer products firm. The issue of standardization of the marketing programme across markets becomes an issue and, frequently, companies accept the trade off between scale economies and niche strategies. The firm must ensure that featured attributes present it with a competitive advantage in every market in which it operates. This becomes a constant struggle as such time competitive advantage can erode due to competitor activity and poor brand management. Usually the firm must develop separate marketing programmes for its major international markets, though common elements may be found in a number of markets.

---

## Exhibit 15.6   Multiple objectives make it difficult to value a brand

*What's in a brand? UK accountants wonder*

Moves by British companies to value their product brand names in their balance sheets have caused concern and confusion among leading accounting firms in London. Accountants say they are worried about valuing things they have never had to value before, with no rules to guide them. The foods company Rank Hovis McDougall Plc set the example last month by putting a value of £678 million ($1.27 billion) on brands like Hovis and Mother's Pride bread, Mr Kipling cakes and Bisto gravy in its annual accounts. And a number of other companies are considering similar moves, accountants say.

"We are now getting an explosion of all sorts of things, all sorts of assets in balance sheets we have never had before", said David Tweedie of Peat Marwick McLintock. "There are going to be valuation problems." Peter Holgate of Deloitte Haskins & Sells said "A sizeable number of largish companies are actively considering valuing their brands. You are only talking about cosmetics in a sense. The underlying economics", he said, "are unchanged."

An incentive to put a figure on a brand has been strong in an environment where strong brands have attracted bidders, yet do not boost balance sheet value. Ranks Hovis was the subject of a failed bid from Goodman Fielder Wattie Ltd., the Australia-based food company, this year.

But predators, too, would find advantages. "We have this lunatic situation that a company buys a fabulous company with a world leader brand and yet they end up with an apparently weakened balance sheet", said John Murphy, chairman of Interbrand Group PLC, the brands marketing consultancy that valued Ranks Hovis's brands.

The brands debate arose recently in Britain, triggered by Nestlé SA's successful bid last summer for the chocolate maker Rowntree PLC, said Mr Murphy of Interbrand. Brands are valued by using property value techniques, Mr Murphy said. A brand's ability to generate profit is combined with a ranking related to its market position. Brand valuing is a sophisticated application of an accounting rule on how to treat a company's intangible assets, Mr Holgate said.

**Source:** *International Herald Tribune*, Thursday, 8 December, 1988.

The management of international brands absorbs a lot of management time and resources. Building and maintaining international brands represents a very heavy investment in marketing. Companies sometimes develop umbrella brands to be used in launching new products into markets.

There are many traps in international marketing related to branded consumer products. In the chapter a number of problems associated with packaging, labelling and after sales service were discussed. The chapter ended with a discussion on the need to protect the brand from counterfeits and forgeries and the developments of the grey market. A brief section was devoted to examining approaches to valuing brands and its importance in international markets.

## Discussion questions

1. Many consumer markets in the developed world are fragmented and consumer products firms develop programmes to consolidate these markets. It is argued that the natural convergence in these markets facilitates consolidation. Discuss.

2. What is branding and what are the key attributes of a good brand?

3. How do firms use brands to enter international markets?

4. Is there such a thing as a global brand? How would you recognize one? How do firms maintain such a brand?

5. Successful consumer products companies attempt to brand their competitive advantage. Discuss.

6. Protecting the brand from counterfeits and forgeries is becoming increasingly difficult as consumers throughout the world seek brands. Discuss.

7. How relevant is the concept of brand valuation? What are the implications for managers in the consumers products firm which has successfully developed an international brand? How would you determine the value of a consumer brand that you know?

## References

Buzzell, Robert D. (1968) 'Can you standardize multinational marketing,' *Harvard Business Review*, November–December, 103–13.

Carroll, Charles (1986) *Building Ireland's Business — Perspectives from PIMS*, Irish Management Institute, Dublin.

Feigenbaum, S.V. (1986) 'International quality leadership,' *Quality Progress*, September, pp. 21–3.

Hamel, Gary and Prahalad, C.K. (1985) 'Do you really have a global strategy?,' *Harvard Business Review*, July–August, pp. 139–48.

Johansson, Johnny K. and Thorelli, Hans B. (1985) 'International product-positioning,'

*Journal of International Business Studies*, **16** (3), 57–75.

Jones, John Philip (1986) *What's in a Name*, Gower, England.

Lannon, Judie and Cooper, Peter (1983) 'Humanistic advertising: A holistic cultural perspective,' *International Journal of Advertising*, **2** (3), July–September, 195–213,

Levitt, Theodore (1983) 'The globalization of markets,' *Harvard Business Review*, May–June, pp. 92–102.

Martenson, Rita (1987) 'Is standardization of marketing feasible in culture-bound industries? A European case study,' *International Marketing Review*, **7** (3), 7–17.

Mascarenhos, Briance (1986) 'International strategies of non-dominant firms,' *Journal of International Business Studies* **17** (1), 1–26.

Muller, Thomas E. (1985) 'Search behaviour of French and English Canadians in automobile purchase,' *International Marketing Review*, **2** (7), 21–30.

Robinson, Joan (1933) *The Economics of Imperfect Competition*, (reprinted 1950), Macmillan, London.

Rosen, Barry Nathan, Boddewyn, Jean J. and Louis, Ernst A. (1989) 'US brands abroad: An empirical study of global branding,' *International Marketing Review*, **6** (1), 17–19.

Wells, Louis T., Jr (1968) 'A product life cycle for international trade,' *Journal of Marketing*, **32**, July 1–6.

# *The industrial products firm in international markets*

## 16

Industrial marketing is far more complex than consumer marketing because organizational buying behaviour involves a more intricate network of buying influences. The technical nature of many of the products purchased adds to the complexity of industrial marketing. Generally the size of the purchase in money terms is greater and the buying relationship is more complex and long term.

In the marketing of industrial products technology is a more pervasive element which frequently produces a technologically driven production orientation rather than a marketing orientation. This production orientation is due to the greater amount of interaction and interdependence between marketing and other functional areas, especially manufacturing, R & D, inventory control, and engineering. This interdependence may mean that the marketing function is accorded a subservient role.

## Nature of industrial markets

Industrial products are frequently classified according to their application, whereas consumer products are classified according to the manner in which they are purchased. For example, industrial products have been classified as heavy equipment, light equipment, consumable supplies, component parts, raw materials, processed materials, and industrial services (Haas, 1986). Jackson and Cooper (1988), however, criticize most classification schemes due to their inadequate handling of industrial services. They propose a classification which includes both goods and services and which divides them into three major groupings (Figure 16.1).

In this classification capital products have a long life span and involve a major capital outlay: land; buildings; and major items of equipment. Operations products are products used in the operation of a business. These may be durable or non-durable. Finally, output products are absorbed by the products being manufactured in the firm.

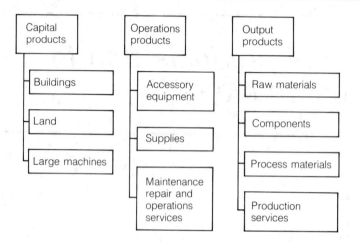

**Figure 16.1**   Classification of industrial products (Source: Based on Jackson, R.W. and Cooper, P.D. (1988) 'Unique aspects of marketing industrial services,' *Industrial Marketing Management*, **17** (2), 116)

Since an industrial product is purchased for business use and thus sought, not for itself, but as part of a total process, buyers value service, dependability, quality, performance and cost, since the output of their own business is dependent to a large extent on the inputs used. All customers do not place the same importance on each dimension and therefore this marketing orientation which, typically, industrial firms have been accused of lacking, is crucial in determining the product offering required by each customer.

The situation is further complicated when a firm operates in international markets where environmental factors differ. The level of economic development in a country is a major determinant of the demand for industrial products. The type of product needed and the level of demand are influenced by economic development (Day, Fox and Huszagh, 1988). Culture has much less impact on industrial products than on consumer products. Culture, however, affects usage patterns, product features and product specifications.

Product quality includes both the physical product and the array of essential supporting services. The ultimate measure of high quality is customer satisfaction. Industrial marketing firms frequently misinterpret the concept of quality, which is not an absolute measure but one relative to use patterns and standards. Since use patterns frequently differ from one country to another, standards will vary so that superior quality in one country may fall short of superior quality as determined by needs in another country.

The adequacy of a product must be considered in relation to the environment within which it is used rather than solely on the basis of technical efficiency. Equipment that requires a high degree of technical skill to operate, maintain or repair may be inadequate in a country that lacks a pool of technically skilled labour. This dilemma is particularly prominent in developing countries which demand the most up to date technology but lack the ability to absorb the high technology (Ford, 1984; Millman, 1983).

## Product development and standards

There is an extremely high product failure rate among industrial marketing firms. This high failure rate occurs because firms do not understand their customers, the competition and the market environment (Cooper, 1976). Furthermore, "technology-oriented" companies often overstate market responsiveness to their new product and underestimate the ability of existing competitors to retaliate (Doyle and Saunders, 1985). Pre-development activities have been identified as the most important part of the product development process (Cooper, 1988; Cooper and Kleinschmidt, 1988).

A new product strategy, however, need not be either "market pull" or "technology push" (Abeele and Christiaens, 1986). Instead, success determinants and their relationships to performance depend on the size of the firm. It seems that the small firm which is successful operates according to a "market pull" principle and success is mainly influenced by its technological innovativeness. The successful larger firm operates by the "technology push" principle and it is the strength of its marketing programme which determines the extent of its success. The pattern determining success is less clear for firms intermediate in size, according to these authors.

There appears to be a relationship between organization structure and the speed of introduction of new products abroad (Davidson and Harrigan, 1977). In functionally organized firms, 40 per cent of the innovations from firms with international divisions internationalized in two years or less as compared with 6 per cent of innovations that went abroad in functionally organized firms without international divisions. For product organized firms, the analogous figures were 33 per cent and 18 per cent respectively. For globally integrated organizations, 80 per cent of all products introduced in such organizations go abroad in two years or less and every innovation in their sample was introduced abroad in five years or less.

For firms serving global markets, important decisions need to be made regarding the amount and management of resources used in product development. The most important competitive weapon may prove to be the skilful management and deployment of technical resources rather than the resources themselves. A Booz-Allen Hamilton survey quoted in Perrino and Tipping (1989) produced the following findings concerning industrial product development:

1. Markets are global but technology development is not. Technological developments occur in "pockets of innovation" around the world.
2. There is a "critical mass" necessary for technology development, mainly because of dramatically rising costs and the need for interdisciplinary teams and specialized equipment.

3. External relationships, i.e. joint ventures, research consortia or technology acquisition programmes are becoming more important and more widespread than ever in an attempt to spread costs and risks.
4. Higher levels of R&D do not guarantee success in global markets. Research indicates that companies can get more out of their research by linking it more closely to market needs and customer needs.
5. The use of the global network where a network of technology core groups exists in each major market — managed in a co-ordinated way for maximum impact — is advocated.

A lack of universal standards is a problem in the international sale of industrial products. Within Europe the problem is likely to disappear or become less critical with the harmonization of standards after 1992. However, between the United States and Europe there is a lack of common standards for highly specialized equipment manufacturing such as machine tools, and also the use of the Imperial system of measurement in the United States compared with the metric system in Europe.

Efforts at universal standardization are being made through international organizations dedicated to the creation of international standards, e.g. the International Electrotechnical Commission (IEC) is concerned with standard specifications for electrical equipment in machine tools (Brown, 1985). The development of world standards is also the focus of attention of the International Organization of Standardization.

## EC Directive on product liability

Recent efforts have been made to set standards for industrial products in the EC with the introduction of the Council of Ministers Directive on product liability. All member states are required to bring their statutes and regulations into compliance with this Directive. Prior to the new Directive injured parties had to prove all elements of their claim under tort law, i.e. negligence, causation and damage. Consumers had to bear the risk of legal actions, including the costs of expert witnesses. In addition, legislation was quite fragmented across member states. This new Directive favours user protection placing greater obligations on industrial producers.

The following is a brief outline of the Directive and implications for producers. First, once a defect has been found to exist it is presumed to have existed at the time it left the producer's hands. The onus of proof now lies with the producer and not the customer. Second, defects in product design, manufacturing and product warnings may each be the basis of liability under the Directive. A producer may be found liable if he has not warned people adequately of a product's dangerous properties. This could require advertising to consumers by producers who have not done so previously. The content of producer and wholesaler advertising to the trade may be affected. The content of personal salesmanship and point of purchase displays may also be affected. Third, the injured person bears only the burden of proof that the finished product is defective.Thereafter it is up to each person along the channel, i.e. retailer, wholesaler, component manufacturer, raw material manufacturer, to prove that they are not liable. If any middlemen in the distribution channel cannot clearly identify the supplier that made the product, then the middleman takes on the legal role of producer and is so treated. Importers of products into the EC are also considered producers but not importers of products from another EC member country. In this way liability for defects will remain within the EC jurisdiction. Producers and constructive producers cannot exclude or limit their liability for defects by clauses in the contract with the customer.

Finally, the plaintiff customer has three years in which to file for recovery. Rights are extinguished, however, when the product is ten years old or more.

Unlike the United States, most West European cultures have ignored or given little emphasis to damages for pain and suffering. Damage done to business property may not be compensated. However, it is generally felt that the cost of business will rise significantly because of liability awards, many of which might reach the level which exists in the United States, due to high insurance premiums.

There is some concern that product innovation will decline in countries that choose to remove the state-of-the-art defence, i.e. where one can prove that the state of technical knowledge at the time the product was commercialized was insufficient to discover defect.

This directive is also relevant to non-EC countries, especially those with strong trade, investment and political ties with the EC. Product liability enforcement and regulation, therefore, represents a major force within the firm's macro environment which must be monitored and addressed if the firm is to survive and grow.

## Organization for buying

### Industrial buying process

The industrial product purchasing process is one of the foundations on which the marketing strategy in industrial firms is based. The other is an understanding of competitive behaviour. Research on the industrial buying process has focussed on multiphased decision making, the decision-making unit, the different purchasing situations and the degree of risk involved (Smith and Taylor, 1985). The buying process for industrial products is often conceptualised as a sequential process. Many classifications have been proposed. Ozanne and Churchill (1971) propose a five-stage model, while Wind (1978) prefers a twelve-stage model. Perhaps the most widely quoted classification, however, is the Robinson, Faris and Wind (1967) eight-buy stages model: awareness of the problem; deciding the appropriate product to solve the problem; searching for qualified suppliers; accepting offers; placing the order; and evaluating the outcome.

Classifications such as these suggest that the industrial marketing firm should be able to identify the type of decision and the decision stage and hence the key people to influence at a particular time. Before this can be done one needs to consider the make-up of the decision-making group as well as the differences that exist between purchasing situations.

One method of determining the make-up of a decision-making unit (DMU) or buying centre is to consider the roles that members fill. Roles have been classified in various ways: users; influencers; deciders; and gatekeepers (Webster and Wind, 1972). The importance of different organizational roles varies by the phase of the buying process. The make-up of a DMU or buying centre in terms of members and the roles fulfilled changes depending on organizational factors, the organization size and the buying situation (Wind, 1978).

The purchasing situation is believed to consist of four major components: the environment; interpersonal factors; organizational factors; and individual considerations. These factors dictate the type of situation encountered. By examining the purchase situation facing the individual firm Mattsson (1988) concludes that organizational buying is best considered as a set of interrelated variables cascading down from the environment to the transaction (Figure 16.2). In following this process the composition of the decision-making unit is identified.

Both domestic and international factors have a large impact both on the composition of the buying centre and on the manner in which the product is purchased. The business area in which the firm operates determines the importance of the purchasing function. Without an understanding of the customer's mission, other knowledge may be fruitless. Determining the mission is the first step in determining who in the buying firm will be interested in the decision-making process.

The issues which relate specifically to purchasing are how the product will be used, how the product benefits the buyer, the stage of the purchase decision, the buying process, the size of the purchase, and the duration of the purchased contractual commitment. The high functional interdependence among all departments of the buying firm requires the industrial purchaser to buy according to specifications developed elsewhere in the firm. Suppliers must therefore know the range of potential uses of the product and priorities in the buying firm.

The buyclass and buyphase variables are used by Robinson, Faris and Wind (1967) to determine the relative influence of purchasing managers in the buying process. Regardless of the industry or buyphase of the purchase, the decision-making process is shared for all but the smallest, most routine decisions. The firm in industrial markets must search for the individual who has the most influence at each stage rather than for the sole decision maker.

For Mattsson the money value of the purchase is relative across industries and firms. Money value is defined as the perceived impact of the purchase on organizational profitability and productivity (McQuiston, 1989). Purchasing departments use money values as a management intensity criterion. In very small companies the purchasing manager has little influence in most purchases because the amount is relatively large, thus involving senior management. In medium-sized firms more authority is delegated to the purchasing manager as the relative

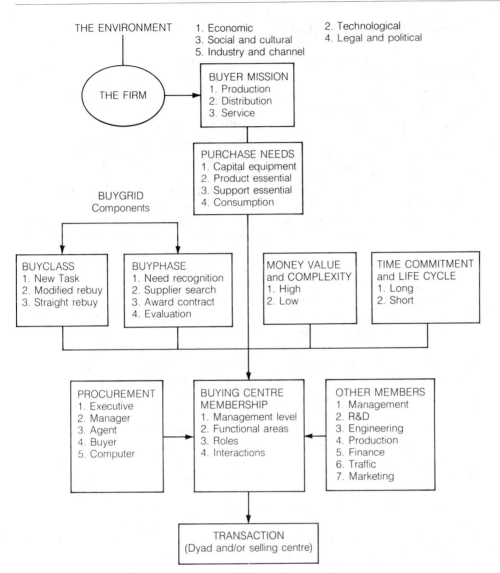

THE ENVIRONMENT     1. Economic     2. Technological
                    3. Social and cultural     4. Legal and political
                    5. Industry and channel

THE FIRM

BUYER MISSION
1. Production
2. Distribution
3. Service

PURCHASE NEEDS
1. Capital equipment
2. Product essential
3. Support essential
4. Consumption

BUYGRID
Components

BUYCLASS
1. New Task
2. Modified rebuy
3. Straight rebuy

BUYPHASE
1. Need recognition
2. Supplier search
3. Award contract
4. Evaluation

MONEY VALUE
and COMPLEXITY
1. High
2. Low

TIME COMMITMENT
and LIFE CYCLE
1. Long
2. Short

PROCUREMENT
1. Executive
2. Manager
3. Agent
4. Buyer
5. Computer

BUYING CENTRE
MEMBERSHIP
1. Management level
2. Functional areas
3. Roles
4. Interactions

OTHER MEMBERS
1. Management
2. R&D
3. Engineering
4. Production
5. Finance
6. Traffic
7. Marketing

TRANSACTION
(Dyad and/or selling centre)

**Figure 16.2**  Composition of buying centre in industrial marketing (Source: Adapted from: Robinson, P.J., Farris, C.W. and Wind, Y. (1967) *Industrial Buying and Creative Marketing*, Allyn and Bacon, Boston; and Mattson, Melvin, R. (1988) 'How to determine the composition and influence of a buying centre,' *Industrial Marketing Management*, **17**(3), 205–14)

size of each purchase gets smaller. Berkowitz (1986) believes that larger firms establish criteria and guidelines for individuals and departments, even for small purchases; therefore individuals have less flexibility.

The importance of the purchase decision to the firm is one of the factors that affects both the number of participants and their behaviour throughout the purchase process (Reve and Johansen, 1982).

## Commitment of the firm to industrial buying

Because demand in industrial markets is derived it is the life cycle of customer firms which should receive emphasis. The strategic changes of the buying firms during the life cycle of their products must be the focus of attention in an organizational buying model.

The buyclass variable suggests that the level of management involvement should decrease as products progress from a new task purchase class to a straight rebuy, but during both the design and product maturity stages, purchasing involvement tends to be high (Fox and Rink, 1978).

Time has two effects on the organization for industrial purchasing decisions that need to be measured. First, as the time horizon increases, interactions can be made routine and delegated down the managerial hierarchy. Second, as they become routine, decisions may start to exceed the time allocated for such activities in the firm.

The buying centre includes all members of the buying firm who are actively and significantly involved in the purchase decision process. Membership is fluid depending on product and buyphases. Five general areas in the buying centre must be examined. First, the management level is determined by the five purchase specific variables discussed above. Second, the functional area composition of the buying centre varies with the product being purchased and the buyphase. Third, roles accorded to members in the buying centre must be examined. Webster and Wind (1972) identified the roles of user, influencer, buyer, decider, and gatekeeper in the purchasing decision process.

Roles can be conceived fairly easily for the purchasing of products such as production materials. It is more difficult to specify roles for services, such as who within the firm is the user of transportation for inbound materials or outbound products, who is the gatekeeper, or who has the decider role. Fourth, there is the question of interaction which is mainly concerned with identifying who is involved in the decision process. The contribution of the interaction of members of the buying centre is of greater value when the identity of those involved is determined. Finally, the purchasing department through greater professionalism has become an important part of the firm's management team for product planning. Negotiating skills make the purchasing department a key element during the interorganizational steps of the purchasing process.

Industrial buying can no longer be studied as individual actions; rather it must be viewed as a multidimensional complex process which is diffused throughout the firm.

## Decision criteria for industrial buying

The numerous stages involved in industrial buying means that a cascading hierarchical dependency exists among the choice criteria. It is likely that numerous different sets of buying criteria are involved (Möller and Laaksonen, 1984). First, buyers use one set of criteria for selecting potential suppliers to submit bids. Because the intention is to restrict or screen suppliers, cut-off levels of criteria based on supplier reputation, technical specifications and delivery capacity dominate. In evaluating bids the same set of criteria may be used but now a rank order of preference among the suppliers is established. The relative importance of the criteria may change as those left meet the criteria imposed.

At the stage involving negotiations with one or two potential suppliers a third set of criteria may be used which contains only the most important attributes which still have some variation across the bidders after the first two stages. At this stage in the negotiations the buyer's aim is often to get the best possible price without jeopardizing quality and delivery.

Numerous stages in the industrial buying process are more in evidence for high value and complex buying situations where competitive offers are available. In simpler routinized buying situations the above stages will not normally be used. The stages phenomenon is complicated further by the presence of the buying centre influence on the criteria. The interaction of buying stages and buying centre members should also be assessed. In an attempt to generalize, Möller and Laaksonen (1984) develop a set of major criteria which might be used in industrial purchasing situations. These criteria, which should be applied in a differential manner at each of the three buying stages identified, consist of factors relating to the product itself, the supplier, the transaction, and the buyer–seller interaction (Figure 16.3). These authors warn, however, that no single list of criteria, despite the degree of generality, should be applied. A more rewarding approach would be to first define the type of buyer–seller relationship involved and then develop a set of purchasing criteria.

## Assessing competitive positions

### Segmenting industrial product markets

Industrial product markets are highly heterogeneous, complex and often hard to reach because of the multitude of products and uses as well as a great diversity among customers. Formulating a coherent marketing strategy can be extremely difficult in such an environment (Kluyver and Whitelark, 1986). The need for market segmentation becomes very important in such circumstances. As was seen in Chapter 9, market segmentation is the process of dividing a potential market into distinct subsets of consumers or users and selecting one or more segments as a market target to be reached with a distinct marketing programme.

Failure to properly segment an industrial market can result in missed opportunities, surprise competition and even business failures (Hlavacek and Reddy, 1986). It is also particularly important for the firm in international markets because the benefits that accrue from standardizing elements of the marketing strategy are realized only when similarities among countries are identified. Universal needs and similarities in buying processes are far more evident in

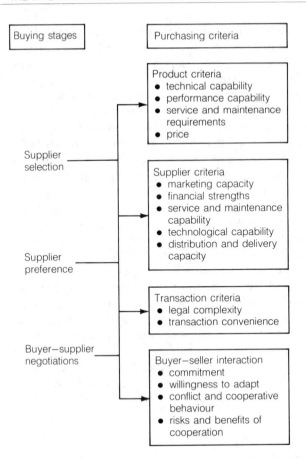

**Figure 16.3** Buying stages and purchasing criteria in industrial markets (Source: Adapted from Möller, K.E., Laaksonen, Kristian and Martti (1984) 'Situational dimensions and decision criteria in industrial buying: Theoretical and empirical analysis,' in *Proceedings of the International Research Seminar on Industrial Marketing*, Stockholm School of Economics, 29–31 August)

industrial markets than in consumer markets (Day, Fox and Huszagh, 1988; Kacker, 1975). In general the industrial purchasing process among managers at different functional levels in US, Australian, UK and Canadian firms is similar. Differences in the industrial purchasing process within these countries have more to do with what is being purchased than with the country of the buyer.

Before attempting to segment international markets Day, Fox, and Huszagh (1988) recommend that one should screen world markets in a preliminary manner in order to assess similarities among countries, thus making the task of segmentation more focussed and less complex. They propose the use of economic variables as a method of determining the level of economic development and hence the level of demand and the type of products needed. Scores are allocated to each country for each of the economic variables chosen. The factor scores thus represent the degree to which each country can be described by each of the underlying constructs. Subsequently, through cluster analysis countries are grouped according to similarities exhibited by the factor scores. The more favourable clusters are then selected for detailed examination. There are certain limitations to this approach, i.e. subjectivity in selecting the type and number of variables needed to cluster countries and the difficulty in finding accurate data on international markets being the more important. Once this process has been completed a typical segmentation technique can be employed.

Various market segmentation approaches have been proposed. A staged approach to the segmentation of industrial markets such as the two-step approach proposed by Wind and Cardoza (1974) or the nested approach (Shapiro and Bonoma, 1984) is recommended for a more comprehensive analysis. In these approaches macro variables such as type of industry, size of customer and product usage are relevant. Then these segments are sub-divided on the basis of micro variables such as the characteristics of the decision-making unit. Such approaches capture all the variables which help to make a particular segment unique.

Hlavacek and Reddy (1986) propose a four-step method:

(a) identification;
(b) qualification;
(c) attractiveness; and
(d) monitoring.

The identification phase involves classifying the particular product and segmenting the market for it on the basis of typical end uses employing industry classification codes such as the SITC or BTN (Figure 16.4). In the qualification phase, each segment is described in greater detail (Figure 16.5). In the attractiveness phase the requirements of the segment and the ability of the firm to meet those requirements are assessed.

Finally, once a segment is selected there is continuous monitoring of both competitive and technological changes which could dramatically change the boundaries and attractiveness of segments (Figure 16.6). An example of the need for monitoring may be found in the X-ray film market. DuPont concentrated on and achieved a large market share in the X-ray film market, but recent developments in nuclear magnetic resonance (NMR) technology may replace a portion of the need for X-rays.

## Developing market positions

In developing a marketing strategy to enter foreign industrial markets the firm must pay attention to how it wishes to be positioned in the market. A positioning strategy implies a frame of reference for the firm's image among its target customers, the reference point usually being the competition. A positioning strategy can provide a focus for the development of a promotional campaign.

IDENTIFY CUSTOMER FUNCTIONS FIRM CAPABLE OF PROVIDING

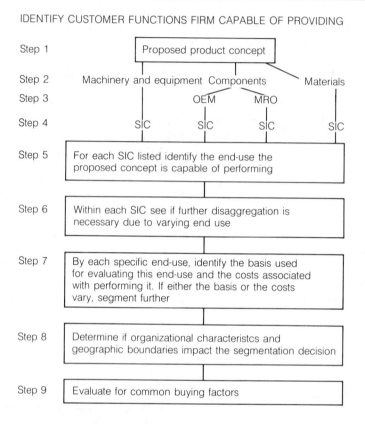

Step 1    Proposed product concept

Step 2    Machinery and equipment Components    Materials

Step 3    OEM    MRO

Step 4    SIC    SIC    SIC    SIC

Step 5    For each SIC listed identify the end-use the proposed concept is capable of performing

Step 6    Within each SIC see if further disaggregation is necessary due to varying end use

Step 7    By each specific end-use, identify the basis used for evaluating this end-use and the costs associated with performing it. If either the basis or the costs vary, segment further

Step 8    Determine if organizational characteristcs and geographic boundaries impact the segmentation decision

Step 9    Evaluate for common buying factors

**Figure 16.4** Identifying specific segments in industrial markets ( Source: Hlavacek, J.D. and Reddy, N.M. (1986) 'Identifying and qualifying industrial market segments,' *European Journal of Marketing*, **20** (2), 8–21)

The strategy is usually conceived and implemented in reference to the firm's attributes, the competition and types of customers involved, to name the more important. While there are many ways of measuring buyers' reactions to suppliers involving detailed lists of evaluative factors, managers frequently seek a parsimonious approach which would give useful managerial information in summary form. An example of such an approach is a study of industrial buyers who evaluated sixty international companies, the results of which were analysed using a multidimensional scaling technique (Bradley, 1986). In this study the preferences of twenty buyers of electric and electronic components used in industrial markets were examined. The basic idea behind multidimensional scaling of such data is that preferences, buyers and suppliers can be represented as points in space (Figure 16.7).

Decision: evaluate operational relevance of segments

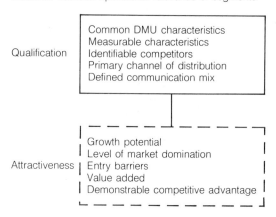

**Figure 16.5** Qualifying industrial segments (Source: Hlavacek, J.D. and Reddy, N.M. (1986) 'Identifying and qualifying industrial market segments,' *European Journal of Marketing*, **20** (2), 8–21)

In Figure 16.7, only average positions are reported. Hence, the various positions of all French companies in the study were averaged or pooled before being submitted to the multidimensional scaling model. A similar exercise was carried out for the remaining companies in the study. The twenty buyers, A–T, are positioned at their point of preference around the diagram. Ten buyers are located in Quadrant 3, five in Quadrant 2, four in Quadrant 4 and only one, Buyer H, in Quadrant 1. The positions of the companies are similarly evaluated and reflect buyer preferences. Thus the average position for French companies falls in Quadrant 1, while Swiss and Italian companies fall in Quadrant 2. The

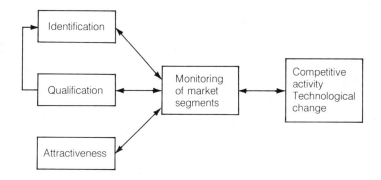

**Figure 16.6** Monitoring industrial market segments (Source: Hlavacek, J.D. and Reddy, N.M. (1986) 'Identifying and qualifying industrial market segments,' *European Journal of Marketing*, **20** (2), 8–21)

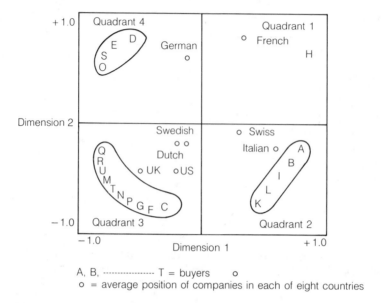

A, B, ----------------- T = buyers     o
o = average position of companies in each of eight countries

**Figure 16.7**   Multidimensional scaling of buyer preferences for suppliers (Source: Bradley, M. Frank (1986) 'Developing communications strategies for foreign market entry,' in Turnbull, Peter W. and Paliwoda, Stanley J. (eds.) *Research in International Marketing*, Croom Helm, London, pp. 35–61)

majority of companies fall in Quadrant 3, while West German companies fall in Quadrant 4.

From this study of preferences it appears that the French firms are preferred by a segment dominated by Customer H, while Swiss and Italian firms are preferred by a segment containing five customers. The Italian firms on average are most preferred in this segment. German firms located in a very different market segment are preferred by a segment containing four customers. The largest segment, which contains ten customers, prefers to work with Dutch, Swedish, US and UK firms, with UK firms being the most preferred and Swedish firms the least preferred of this group.

There are a number of important lessons arising from this study for the firm in industrial markets. First, the relative competitive positions are established. Second, the size and identity of the key market segments become evident. Third, the match or fit of customer segments and supplier firms is specified.

It becomes a managerial decision for the firm to choose to change position or otherwise alter it in the light of the information supplied by the analysis.

## Commitment to international markets

The commitment of the firm to international markets may be measured by the way in which the firm organizes its resources to reach the market. The character of the marketing organization through formal and informal marketing networks indicates the commitment to the market and the strategic choices open to the firm (Hallen, 1986, p. 242). This author identifies three basic types of marketing organization related to the degree of investment in the market. For major customers in international markets, direct selling from the home base may be the most appropriate organizational form. Alternatively, access to the market with only minor investments may be obtained by the use of agents. To obtain a long-lasting presence in the market, however, a sales subsidiary, perhaps with local production facilities, may be used according to Hallen. In a study of 120 suppliers located in France, the Federal Republic of Germany, Sweden and the United Kingdom, Hallen (1986) found a preponderance of direct selling in domestic markets.

In export markets the use of direct selling is less common, although there is some variation among the countries represented. High commitment, extensive experience or strategic ambitions are reflected in the establishment of subsidiaries. Regarding the choice between agents and subsidiaries the British and Swedish suppliers were very different, while the French and German were somewhere in the middle of the strategic spectrum. The dominance of agents in the British relationships reflects recent internationalization of these firms, while the dominance of subsidiaries among Swedish firms reflects their well-established position in international markets (Hallen, 1986, p. 243). In general the greater the use of subsidiaries the greater the investment in, and hence commitment to, the market in question.

## Pricing industrial products

International pricing has to take many variables into consideration. It is very rare to have the same price for one's product prevail in all world markets because

**Table 16.1**  International marketing organization in selected European countries

| Country | Market | Direct selling (%) | Agents (%) | Subsidiaries (%) |
|---|---|---|---|---|
| France | Domestic | 87 | 4 | 9 |
| (43 firms) | International | 12 | 42 | 47 |
| Germany | Domestic | 67 | 7 | 27 |
| (30 firms) | International | 21 | 46 | 33 |
| Sweden | Domestic | 62 | 5 | 33 |
| (20 firms) | International | 8 | 17 | 75 |
| United Kingdom | Domestic | 100 | 0 | 0 |
| (27 firms) | International | 9 | 64 | 27 |

Source: Adapted from Hallen, Lars (1986) 'Comparison of strategic marketing approaches,' in Turnbull, Peter W. and Valla, Jean Paul (eds.) *Strategies for International Industrial Markets*, Croom Helm, London, p. 242.

of currency fluctuations, different factor costs, different product requirements and government regulations, standards and official limits on pricing and discounting. At best this differential may be contained within a few percentage points across different markets. Otherwise, there is the ever-present danger of parallel exports taking place.

Fluctuating values in currencies pose considerable problems to the international firm. Due to fluctuations in currencies many companies seek to use forward foreign exchange markets. Foreign currency is sold either at the spot rate, which is the daily rate prevailing on the day of the requested exchange transaction, or for any number of months ahead, usually three, six or nine. The rate of exchange is specified and known to the exporter when the forward contract is made. Thus the buyer is relieved of exchange risk.

Government interventions and political interference is a second issue which can cause concern to the firm. Government legislation and regulations directly affect price. National government regulations concerning maintenance of good trade balances, development of national resource bases, promotion of national security, and provision of employment can all have a considerable impact on prices. Industrial goods are particularly susceptible since they are often the cannon fodder of economic wars being waged to win the political allegiance of developing countries (Rahman and Scapens, 1986). As a result, international marketing firms are sometimes confronted with impossible price competition because prices are shaded by a foreign government for political rather than economic reasons.

Dumping is the third concern which affects prices and revenues in international markets. This is an unfair trade practice, based on international price discrimination, which occurs when a product is sold abroad for a lower price than the seller charges for the same product in the home market. This normally occurs when the home country's demand is less elastic than is the foreign market.

Article 6 of the 1979 Gatt Agreement proclaims the act of dumping as illegal and authorizes the imposition of anti-dumping duties on dumped exports. The maximum amount of such a duty is the "margin of dumping," i.e. the difference between the price at which the products are sold in the exporter's home market and the price of the product when exported.

In recent years there has been a very large increase in anti-dumping action by the EC against Japanese exporters. Some of the products found to be dumped include electronic typewriters, photocopiers, hydraulic excavators and semi-conductor chips. Lately, an attempt has been made to extend the scope of the community anti-dumping measures beyond finished products to the components of products imported separately into the EC and assembled locally.

However, there has been widespread speculation that the EC has been using anti-dumping procedures as a substitute for safeguards (Norall, 1986; Piontek, 1987; Hindley, 1988). Safeguards are rules which permit, under agreed conditions, the postponement of previously agreed tariff reductions, the evaluation of tariffs or the introduction of qualitative restrictions. They are normally employed to protect weak or vulnerable domestic industries.

Hindley (1988) finds it difficult to see how dumping of the magnitude and scale claimed by the European Community could make commercial sense for

Japanese and Far Eastern exporters. In support of his argument Hindley argues that the EC Commission uses a flawed method in calculating the price differential.

The most usual method in the determination of the normal value of the product is by reference to the price on the domestic market of the country of origin. Normally one would use the ex-factory price. This is not normally available, however, so in most cases the price at the point of import is used, from which expenses that may have been incurred between the export of the product and its final importation are deducted. The Commission, however, refuses to make deductions for overheads and general expenses, including research and development costs, or advertising, when calculating the ex-factory domestic price. This flawed calculation method almost always arrives at a verdict of illegal dumping, according to Hindley. It may also be alleged that dumping incorporates hidden subsidies from the home government, perhaps in manufacturing location incentives and selective employment assistance.

The fourth concern is transfer pricing which refers to the prices at which products and services are transferred within the corporate family across national frontiers, as they move globally, division to division or to a foreign subsidiary or joint venture (Burns, 1980). Transfer pricing sometimes becomes a problem within the company. Where a profitable international division is an intermediary there will be an inevitable conflict over price when products move from the manufacturing division to the international division and from there to the foreign subsidiary. For the manufacturing division the price should be high enough to encourage a flow of products for export and build up an export trade. Low prices result in poor returns for the manufacturing division, and losses can have a very bad effect on morale. From the viewpoint of the international division, however, the transfer price should be low enough to enable it to be both competitive and profitable in the foreign market.

Market price is by far the most usual method of transfer pricing followed by standard unit full cost plus a fixed mark-up. Seven reasons may be identified which are likely to induce high transfer price above arm's length prices for flows from parents to foreign subsidiaries:

(a) corporate income tax higher than in parent's country
(b) pressure from workers to obtain greater share of profits;
(c) political pressure to nationalize or expropriate high-profit foreign firms;
(d) political instability;
(e) high inflation rate;
(f) price of final product controlled by government but based on production cost;
(g) desire to mask profitability of subsidiary operations to keep competitors out.

## Selling and promoting industrial products

## Personal selling

Personal selling is the most important method of promoting and selling industrial products. The reason that personal selling is so important in the industrial markets is inherent in the types of purchases that are made. The need for sales personnel who are well trained and experienced within their individual technical discipline when marketing high-technology industrial products is well documented in the literature and in trade journals. Most such purchases are large and processing the sale often takes considerable time. Often the purchaser is not exactly sure of what is available in a company's product line, or he requires a special item for which specifications need to be worked out and a price and delivery date negotiated. Those operating in another culture need to be familiar with various negotiation strategies employed there and how the negotiation process is similar to and different from that which exists in their own culture.

By dealing with a salesman, many of the final details concerning the product can be resolved. For new, maintenance, repair and operating service products end-users often determine which products are purchased and are most influenced by advertising, but closing a sale may still require many calls from the salesman to the organization's gatekeepers (Berkowitz, 1986).

## Promoting industrial products

Trade journals are the principal communications medium used by industrial products firms. Williams (1988) suggests the use of product publicity, i.e. free media coverage, as a useful promotional tool. It is particularly suitable when other promotional activities are greatly restricted or entirely prohibited, especially in international markets. Such a strategy enjoys the benefits of low-cost and high credibility over other promotional tools, provided press releases are well written and selectively sent to various credible trade journals for publication.

Trade fairs are also a valuable means for reaching the hidden buying influences not reached by regular salesmen or by trade publications. A salesman can talk to more prospects in a three or four day trade show than he could reach by personal calls in a much longer period. Other members of the buying centre frequently attend trade shows. In the marketing of high-technology industrial products, exhibitions and trade shows play a very important role at the interest-awareness stage as well as the evaluation and selection stage.

Mail brochures are popular, especially for technical products. While it is unknown what percentage of mail brochures are read or taken seriously, a low sales response rate is often sufficient to cover the cost of the mail campaign. Though often irritating to customers, it has remained a promotional technique for this reason. Improved targeting of customers can improve effectiveness of mail brochures.

Product sampling is a very effective way to introduce and stimulate interest among end-users and influencers for industrial supply items which are relatively inexpensive. More expensive products, however, may be promoted in this way by offering a free trial period.

Various restrictions are imposed on the industrial marketing firm's chosen communication mix in international markets. The EC directive on product liability influences the content of a particular communication mix. Another directive, the 1984 "Misleading Advertising" Directive, also governs message content.

Various laws exist within the EC, varying from country to country, which directly or indirectly restrict the choice of media chosen, e.g. time allocated to TV advertising is restricted to a few hours in some countries, while free sheets are banned in others. In such circumstances media availability for industrial products promotion becomes an issue.

## Summary

There are very great differences between marketing consumer products and industrial products. Industrial marketing is far more complex in that organizational buying involves a more intricate network of buying influences, the product is normally much more technical and therefore quite complex, the size of the purchase is greater in money terms and the buying relationship is more involved and continuous in nature. These differences influence how industrial products are marketed internationally. The complex interaction process is made even more complex when operating within different cultures. Finally, industrial products, because of their usage, are vulnerable to foreign government interference. Various laws and regulations often further restrict and determine how industrial products are marketed internationally.

## Discussion questions

1. Describe the main characteristics of industrial markets facing the international firm.

2. What are the key purchasing criteria in industrial products marketing? Are they different in domestic and international markets?

3. What effect have international product standards on the sale of industrial products abroad?

4. Outline the industrial buying process and demonstrate how it is complicated in international marketing.

5. What role do cultural influences have on the marketing of industrial products in international markets?

6. How might you apply segmentation analysis to international industrial markets?

7. How would the industrial products firm establish a position in international markets?

8. The pricing, selling and promotion of industrial products in international

markets is complicated by the intervention of governments and multinational regulatory authorities. Discuss.

## References

Abeele, Piet Vanden and Christiaens, Ivan (1986) 'Strategies of Belgian high-tech firms,' *Industrial Marketing Management*, **5**, 299–308.

Berkowitz, Marian (1986) 'New product adoption by the buying organization: Who are the real influencers?' *Industrial Marketing Management*, **15** (1), 33–43

Bradley, M. Frank (1986) 'Developing communication strategies for foreign market entry,' in Turnbull, Peter W. and Paliwoda, Stanley J. (eds.), *Research in International Marketing*, Croom Helm, London, pp. 35-61.

Brown, Derek (1985) 'EC Plan seeks standardization,' *Europe*, May–June, pp. 24–5.

Burns, Jane O. (1980) 'Transfer pricing decisions in US MNCs,' *Journal of International Business Studies'*, **2**, 23–38.

Cooper, Robert G. (1988) 'Predevelopment activities determine new product success,' *Industrial Marketing Management*, **17** (3), 237–47.

Cooper, R.G. and Kleinschmidt, E.J. (1988) 'Resource allocation in the new product process,' *Industrial Marketing Management*, **17** (3), 249–62.

Davidson, William H. and Harrington, Richard (1977) 'Key decisions in international marketing: Introducing new products abroad,' *Columbia Journal of World Businss*, **12** (4), 15–23.

Day, Ellen, Fox, Richard J. and Huszagh, Sandra M. (1988) 'Segmenting the global market for industrial goods,' *International Marketing Review*, **5** (3), 14–27.

Doyle, Peter and Saunders, John (1985) 'Market segmentation and positioning in specialized industrial markets,' *Journal of Marketing*, **49**, 24–32.

Ford, David (1984) 'Buyer–seller relationships in international industrial markets,' *Industrial Marketing Management*, **13**, 101–12.

Fox, Harold W. and Rink, David R. (1978) 'Purchasing's role across life cycle,' *Industrial Marketing Management*, **7** (3), 186–92.

Hallen, Lars (1986) 'A comparison of strategic marketing approaches,' in Turnbull, Peter W. and Valla, Jean Paul (eds.) *Strategies for International Industrial Markets*, Croom Helm, London, pp. 235–49.

Haas, R.W. (1986) *Industrial Marketing Management*, Kent Publishing Co., Boston.

Hindley, B. (1988) 'Dumping and the Far East trade of the European Community,' *World Economy*, **11** (4), 445–63.

Hlavacek, James D. and Reddy, N. Moham (1986) 'Identifying and qualifying industrial market segments,' *European Journal of Marketing*, **20** (2), 8–21.

Jackson, Ralph W. and Cooper, Philip D. (1988) 'Unique aspects of marketing industrial services,' *Industrial Marketing Management*, **17** (2), 111–18.

Kacker, P. Madhaw (1975) 'Export-oriented product adaption — its patterns and problems,' *Management International Review*, **15** 6), 61–70.

Kluyver, Cornelis A. de and Whitelark, David B. (1986) 'Benefit segmentation for industrial products,' *Industrial Marketing Management*, **15** (4), 273–86.

McQuiston, Daniel H. (1989) 'Novelty, complexity and importance as causal determinants of industrial buyer behaviour,' *Journal of Marketing*, **53** (2), 66–79.

Mattson, Melvin R. (1988) 'How to determine the composition and influence of a buying centre,' *Industrial Marketing Management*, **17** (3), 205–14.

Millman, A.F. (1983) 'Technology transfer in the international market,' *European Journal of Marketing*, **17** (1), 26–47.

Möller, K.E., Laaksonen, Marthi and Kristian (1984) 'Situational dimensions and decision criteria in industrial buying: Theoretical and empirical analysis,' *Proceedings of the International Research Seminar on Industrial Marketing*, Stockholm School of Economics, 29–31 August.

Norall, C. (1986) 'New trends in anti-dumping practice in Brussels,' *World Economy Watch*, **19** (1), 97–111.

Ozanne, U.B. and Churchill, G.A. (1971) 'Five dimensions of the industrial adoption process,' *Journal of Marketing Research*, **8**, 322–8.

Perrino, Albert C. and Tipping, James W. (1989) 'Global management of technology,' *Research Technology Management*, **32** (3), 12–19.

Piontek, Euganiusz (1987) 'Anti-dumping in the EEC — some observations by an outsider,' *Journal of World Trade Law*, **21** (4), 67–93.

Rahman, M. Zubaidur and Scapens, Robert W. (1986) 'Transfer pricing by multinationals: Some evidence from Bangladesh,' *Journal of Business Finance and Accounting*, **13** (3), 383–91.

Reve, Torger and Johansen, E. (1982) 'Organizational buying in the offshore oil industry, *Industrial Marketing Management*, October 11, pp. 275–82.

Robinson P.J, Faris, C.W. and Wind, Y. (1967) *Industrial Buying and Creative Marketing*, Allyn and Bacon, Boston.

Shapiro, B.P. and Bonoma, T.V (1984) 'How to segment industrial markets,'*Harvard Business Review*, **62** (3), 104–10.

Smith David and Taylor, Robert (1985) 'Organizational decision making and industrial marketing,' *European Journal of Marketing*, **19** (7), 56–71.

Wind, Yoram and Cardozo, R. (1974) 'Industrial market segmentation,' *Industrial Marketing Management*, **3** (3), 153–66.

Wind, Yoram, (1978) 'Organizational buying center: A research agenda,' in Zaltman, G. and Bonoma, T.V. (eds.) *Organizational Buying Behavior*, American Marketing Association, pp. 67–76.

Webster, Frederick E. and Wind, Yoram (1972) 'A general model for understanding buying behaviour,' *Journal of Marketing*, **36**, 12–19.

Williams, E. Cameron (1988) 'Product publicity: Low cost and high credibility, *Industrial Marketing Mangement*, **4**, 355–9.

# 17 *The services firm in international markets*

There are three reasons, stemming from the international marketing of products, why service firms have grown and internationalized. First, a manufacturing firm which pursues an international strategy requires detailed information on the size, composition and trends in foreign markets — information which is usually provided by specialized firms. Second, where it is essential to modify the product the firm will require engineering and design services and, frequently, after sales maintenance and servicing facilities. Third, as products moving across borders meet more obstacles than sales within the domestic market, e.g. distance, language, customs, laws and regulations, there is a growing demand for services to remove these barriers. Many of the added costs of internationalizing in manufacturing are service costs. Services are independent of, but related to, developments in product markets.

## Services in marketing

### *Nature of services*

A service firm develops a system to organize the production and implementation of a set of services for customers. A service is an organized integrated arrangement of diverse but interrelated and interdependent assets. A service may be described as any activity or benefit that a supplier offers a customer which is usually intangible and does not result in the ownership of anything. The provision of a service may or may not be tied to a physical product. Services, according to the International Standard Industrial Classification (ISIC), include wholesale and retail trade, restaurants and hotels; transport, storage and communications; financial, insurance, real estate and business services; personal, community and social services; and government services. The key asset managed by the firm in each of the above businesses is a system for interfacing people and machines or equipment.

These systems are developed by the firm over many years and are the result of investment in human, financial and physical resources. The unique blend of these assets in a system gives the service firm its competitive advantage.

"The effective service management system is characterized by harmony and by the good fit between its components. All the components enhance each other; and they must all promote the fundamental ideas which constitute the basic logic and success factors in any business." (Normann, 1984, p. 96) Normann develops these points by noting that it is the unique corporate culture in service firms which sets them apart. He notes the dangers which can arise when firms attempt to extend or transfer service systems to new markets or new customer groups. The corporate culture in the firm embraces people, values and skills which can be confused when extended to new situations:

> it is difficult to mix service management systems which represent delicate formulas for poised success without destroying or disturbing something valuable in the process. If diversification is to be devised, it must be done with the utmost sensitivity, so as to maintain the integrity of the existing service management systems." (Normann 1984, p. 98)

One of the principal factors causing an increase in the level of services is the change from "in-house" to "arm's-length" provision of services. This has occurred at two levels. At the household level it is reflected in increased participation by women in paid employment. At the level of the firm there has also been a pronounced shift to arm's-length sourcing of services as manufacturing industry reorganizes to take account of the changes in the working environment mainly brought about through technological change.

The growth in services internationally may be attributed to two principal factors: changing life styles affected by affluence, leisure time and women in paid employment; and the changing world affected by the increased complexity of life, ecological concerns and the variety and complexity of products available on the market (Figure 17.1).

In general, the production of services and products are usually very closely linked. Telecommunications services cannot be produced without the support of extensive technical equipment. Distribution services are essential for manufacturing to take place. To some extent the difference in the relative importance of services in developed and developing countries may be due to the lower prices of many services in developing countries (General Agreement on Tariffs and Trade 1989, p. 24). Services are very important in the gross domestic product (GDP) of most countries. In 1970 services represented 55 per cent of the GDP in developed countries and 45 per cent in developing countries. By 1987 these proportions had risen to 63 per cent and 49 per cent respectively. Among

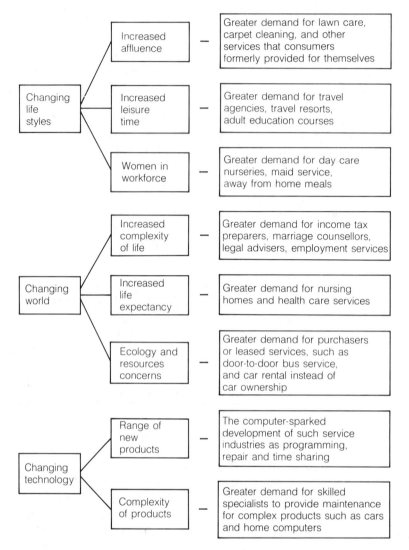

**Figure 17.1** Reasons for growth in service businesses (Source: Adapted from: Schoel, W.F. and Ivy, J.J. (1981) *Marketing: Contemporary Concepts and Practices*, Allyn and Bacon, Boston, Mass., pp. 277)

developed countries it appears that services are proportionately more important in the smaller countries. In Hong Kong and Singapore services are also very important (Table 17.1).

In some countries the shift to a service economy has not been very pronounced but the composition of services has changed dramatically. Finance, business and government services have gained share at the expense of personal and distribution services (General Agreement on Tariffs and Trade 1989, p. 24).

**Table 17.1** Importance of services in
gross domestic product, 1970 and 1987

| Areas and countries | Services 1970 (%) | 1987 (%) |
|---|---|---|
| Developed countries of which: | 55 | 63 |
|   Australia | 51 | 62 |
|   Belgium–Luxembourg | 54 | 67 |
|   Denmark[a] | 55 | 66 |
|   France | 55 | 66 |
|   Germany (FRG) | 44 | 60 |
|   Italy | 49 | 61 |
|   Netherlands | 57 | 66 |
|   Spain | 52 | 57 |
|   United Kingdom | 59 | 60 |
|   Canada | 62 | 62 |
|   Japan | 47 | 47 |
|   United States | 62 | 68 |
| Developing countries of which: | 45 | 49 |
|   Argentina | 47 | 44 |
|   Brazil | 51 | 51 |
|   Hong Kong | 62 | 70 |
|   India | 31 | 40 |
|   Korea (Rep of) | 45 | 46 |
|   Philippines | 43 | 43 |
|   Singapore | 67 | 62 |
|   Taiwan | 42 | 51 |
|   Thailand | 47 | 49 |

[a]1965 and 1986 respectively.

Sources: General Agreement on Tariffs and
Trade (1989): *International Trade 88–89*, Volume
1, Geneva, pp. 23–4.
World Bank (1988): *World Development Report*,
Oxford University Press, p. 227 .

The importance of the various kinds of services varies somewhat between
developed and developing countries and among service categories. In developed
countries the wholesale and retail trade and restaurants and hotels were responsible for 15 per cent of GDP in the period 1980–4 (Table 17.2). Government services
were of the same magnitude, while financial services were 14 per cent of GDP.
The wholesale, retail, restaurant and hotel category was more important in
developing countries, and government services were less significant.

Services marketing is very heterogeneous and consists of many disparate
activities. Services are provided by private and public firms which use low- and
high-skilled labour. Services provided are sold to final consumers and to the
industrial market. In the United States, firms in health care, education and
retailing sell more than 90 per cent of their output to consumers. In contrast over

**Table 17.2**   Importance of key services in gross domestic product[a]

| Types of service | Developed countries (%) | Developing countries (%) |
|---|---|---|
| Wholesale and retail trade restaurants and hotels | 15 | 17 |
| Transport, storage and communications | 7 | 6 |
| Finance, insurance, real estate and business services | 14 | 10 |
| Community, social and personal services | 7 | 7 |
| Government | 15 | 7 |
| Total services | 57 | 47 |

[a]Average for 1980–4.

Sources: General Agreement on Tariffs and Trade (1989): *International Trade 88–89*, Volume 1, Geneva, pp. 23–4; World Bank (1988): *World Development Report*, Oxford University Press, p. 26.

80 per cent of the output of accounting, engineering, advertising, equipment rental, computer and data processing, freight and air transport are sold to industrial buyers (General Agreement on Tariffs and Trade, 1989, p. 26).

According to the GATT (1989) study, as a rough rule of thumb, the transportation of merchandise and people, i.e. shipping, port and passenger services, account for about 30 per cent of world trade in commercial services. Expenditure by travellers at their destinations accounts for a further 30 per cent and other private services and income account for about 40 per cent (GATT, 1989, p. 31).

## Treatment of services in marketing

The usual way of examining services in marketing has been to attempt to overlay the success formulae of product marketing on service industries with little or no adjustment. The approach led one commentator to claim that "service industries remain dominated by an operations orientation that insists that each industry is different." (Lovelock, 1983, p. 10) Early attempts to develop a discipline of service marketing went astray. The relentless pursuit of segmentation, adaptation and differentation, as if such were a prerequisite for the recognition of service firms' unique needs was a failure to recognize the linkages between products and services and the need to treat both uniformly and within the same analytical framework. Not only were boundaries and demarcations being drawn up between services and products but also among service industries. This left the early enthusiasts open to attack from traditional marketing academics.

The development of service industries is also being hindered considerably by the failure to recognize commonalties among service industries. To date, they are treated as heterogeneous. The literature is replete with separate treatments of banks, airlines, insurance and hotels, to name the more common. It is not necessary, however, to consider various service industries as unique and separate from each other (Grönroos, 1978). By recognizing the common features of many service industries, a service marketing theory could develop more rapidly and, as Lovelock (1984) points out, such an approach would be conducive to some useful cross-utilization of concepts and strategies.

Defining a pure service business as one in which the service is the primary component on offer (similarly for a pure product); it becomes clear that few, if any, pure products or services exist. Products are not marketed. Only the benefits they offer are marketed and these include both tangible and intangible elements. By deduction, the same applies to services. Following along these lines is Levitt's (1972) view that "everyone is in service" becomes more acceptable. Levitt is saying that everyone is in services, not that everyone is in products, hence the focus of attention should be on the service component of the "thing" being marketed and this can only improve progress in the area of service marketing.

## Classifying services

Interest in developing classification schemes for services extends to practically every work in this area. Many have been criticized for not being based on "a sufficiently comprehensive theoretical foundation and strong definitional basis that clearly delineates between products and services." (Uhl and Upah, 1983) There are general marketing concepts, approaches and theories of universal applicability which must be adapted to suit different circumstances.

Although the marketing concepts and many of the techniques are universal, marketing practices are often unique to particular situations. It must be remembered, however, that because both product and services marketing are derived from the same general marketing theory, it follows that there are also many areas of commonalty. Nevertheless, a number of differences do arise.

In the literature four major characteristics of services distinguish services from products: (a) intangibility; (b) inseparability, i.e. simultaneous production and consumption; (c) heterogeneity, i.e. less standardization and uniformity; and (d) perishability, i.e. services cannot be stored; to which Cowell (1984) has added a fifth (e) ownership.

The view of most researchers is that intangibility is the critical product-service distinction from which all other differences emerge. It is wrong to imply that services are just like products except for intangibility. Schostack (1977) explains: "By such logic, apples are just like oranges except for their 'appleness'. Intangibility is not a modifier, it is a state."

## Product service continuum

The simplest approach in attempting to develop a continuum of services is to distinguish between pure service businesses on the one hand and product-orientated businesses on the other (Thomas, 1978). A market offering is classified as a service or a product on the basis of whether the essence of what is being sought is tangible or intangible. In this way, a continuum can be developed with varying degrees of dominance towards a product in one direction and a service in the other.

In this way, Schostack (1977) has developed a "molecular model" classifying products and services according to the degree to which ownership of a tangible object is transferred from buyer to seller in the market transaction: "This broader concept postulates that market entities are in reality combinations of discrete elements which are linked together in molecular-like wholes." This enables all "market-entities" or "product-service hybrids" (Uhl and Upah, 1983) to be positioned along the continuum, according to the weight of the mix of elements that comprise them.

For example, an apple is almost totally dominated by a tangible object, i.e. a product, whereas intangibility dominates in an airline flight. Many market offerings fall in between, e.g. food served in a restaurant has a considerable service component. Wilson (1972) uses the concept of tangibility to distinguish between producer and consumer services which are essentially intangible and those which are tangible (Table 17.3).

In tandem with Schostack's exposition, it is possible to represent the definitions of other researchers on a similar continuum. Services may be treated in a spectrum of people-based or equipment-based services (Thomas, 1978). According to Thomas, as a service business evolves, it moves along the spectrum from people-based to equipment-based (Figure 17.5). The middle ground is covered by the many businesses that are in more than one type of business, i.e. nearly all banks operate multiple service businesses: some equipment-based; and some people-based.

The extent of required customer contact in the creation of the service is another way of examining services (Chase, 1978). Customer contact is defined as the physical presence of the customer in the system. Extent of contact is defined

**Table 17.3**  Application of the concept of tangibility to services marketing

| Degree of tangibility | Producer services | Consumer services |
| --- | --- | --- |
| Services that are essentially intangible | Security communications systems, franchising, mergers, acquisitions and valuations | Museums, employment agencies, auctioneers, entertainment |
| Services providing added value to a tangible product | Insurance, contract maintenance, engineering, consultancy, advertising, packaging, design | Launderettes, repairs, personal care, insurance |
| Services that make available a tangible product | Wholesaling, transport, warehousing, financial services, architecture, factoring, contract R & D | Retailing, automatic vending, mail order, hire purchase, charities, mortgages |

Source: Adapted from Wilson, Aubrey (1972) *The Marketing of Professional Services*, McGraw-Hill, London, p. 8.

as the percentage of time the customer must be in the system relative to the total time it takes to serve him (Table 17.4). At the "high-contact" end of the scale, it is likely that supply will seldom match demand for the service, given the customized nature of each delivery. At the opposite end of the continuum the potential for supply and demand to exactly match is much greater.

Grönroos (1987) proposes a useful conceptualization of a service as a combination of the "core service," and "auxiliary or supporting services." Grönroos explains that the core service obviously cannot be left out. The other kind, auxiliary and support services, are optional.

These can be added to the service offering to increase its total value to make it more attractive. It is here that the competitive advantage may be found where the service marketing firm can differentiate its service from all other services but also, with some measure of imaginative application, standardize these peripherals and obtain some degree of standardization.

Grönroos further distinguishes auxiliary services into facilitating services and supporting services forming his "basic service package." Facilitating services are defined as additional services often required in order for the consumer to use the core service, e.g. a ticket issuer at a cinema. From these he distinguishes support services which are only there to increase the services' value and to differentiate them from the services of competitors, e.g. a restaurant in an hotel. Supporting services are competitive tools.

**Table 17.4** Alternative view of the provision of services

|  | Tangibility | Equipment | Contact |
|---|---|---|---|
| Production | Tangible dominant | Equipment-based | Low-contact |
| ↑ | Salt | Automated | Manufacturing |
|  | Soft drinks |  |  |
|  | Cars | Unskilled operators |  |
|  | Cosmetics |  | Quasi-manufacturing |
|  | Fast food restaurants |  |  |
|  | Advertising agencies | Skilled operators |  |
|  | Airlines | Unskilled labour | Mixed services |
|  | Investment management | Skilled labour |  |
|  | Consultancy | Professional | Pure services |
| ↓ | Teaching |  |  |
| Performance | Intangible dominant | People-based | High-contact |

Sources: Adapted from: Chase, Richard B. (1979) 'Where does the customer fit in a service operation?' *Harvard Busines Review*, November–December; Shostack, G. Lynn (1977) 'Breaking free from product marketing,' *Journal of Marketing*, April, pp. 73–80; Thomas, Dan R.E. (1978) 'Strategy is different in service business,' *Harvard Business Review*, July–August, p. 161.

Grönroos extends his model by building an augmented service offering to three dimensions: (a) service accessibility; (b) interactions, i.e. employees and consumers; and (c) consumer participation. Under "accessibility" Grönroos lists such factors as the following:

- number of skills of personnel;
- office hours, time tables and time used to perform various tasks;
- service location;
- office interiors and exteriors;
- tools and documents.

The "interactions" with the firm are listed as follows:

- the interaction communication of people which, in turn, depends on the behaviour of the workers, on what they say and how they say it;
- the interactions with various physical and technical resources of the service firms, e.g. documents, waiting rooms;
- interactions with systems, e.g. waiting systems.

"Consumer participation" is defined as the consumer himself and his own impact on the service, i.e. filling out documents, giving information.

The overall satisfaction with the service will depend on how prepared and willing the consumer is to become involved in the production process. Grönroos terms the whole service offering made up of the three elements of accessibility, interactions and consumer participation as the service concept. This is a very valuable conceptualization which greatly widens the scope open to the service marketing firm in attempting to successfully manage the service process internationally. It focusses attention on many aspects of the service and shows them to be interrelated.

**Table 17.5** Customer view of service

| Nature of service | Recipient of services | |
| | People | Possessions |
| --- | --- | --- |
| Tangible | Health care | Dry cleaning, laundry |
| | Hair styling | Landscaping, gardening |
| | Passenger transportation | Veterinary care |
| | Restaurants | |
| Intangible | Education | Financial |
| | Broadcasting | Legal |
| | Information | Accounting |
| | Theatres | Insurance |
| | Museums | Architectural |

Source: Lovelock, Christopher H. (1983) 'Classifying services to gain strategic marketing insights,' *Journal of Marketing*, **47**, 9–20.

Grönroos concludes by drawing attention to the highly integrated nature of developing a service offering; changes in any one element with impact on the others. But it also places the scope for obtaining competitive advantages in service marketing in clear perspective.

A framework to illustrate the nature of a service from the point of view of the customer has been developed by Lovelock (1983). The cultural issue can be conveniently incorporated into Lovelock's framework for our purposes. Lovelock notes that services are provided for people and their possessions. Observing whether these services are tangible or intangible allows him to develop a four cell framework (Table 17.5). Starting with the tangible classifications, the cultural dimension comes into play when the service is directed at "things" rather than at 'people." Cultural conditioning would be a major consideration in the marketing of such "tangible intangibles" as laundry, dry cleaning and landscaping.

Moving to Lovelock's intangible classifications, the social and cultural element appears strongest when "people" are the direct recipients of the services. Such services as education, broadcasting, theatres, and information services are highly culture bound.

## Role of technology in the services firm

Technology has the potential to make service industries more cost effective and it also supports quality control. Other potential benefits highlighted by Cowell (1984) include the ability to handle large volumes of services, to offer a wider range of services, and potential increases in management efficiencies. Employees also benefit considerably. Technological improvements enhance the status and motivation of employees (Normann, 1984). For example, secretarial work has become less tedious as word processors were introduced.

Services involve social actions and considerable customer interactions. Both are heavily dictated by cultural and social norms. With the introduction of technology, social interaction may be removed. The potential benefits from employing new technology will only be realized if they are favourably perceived by potential customers. For instance, many customers have reacted adversely to the introduction by banks of "face-less" ATMs. The banks may have a more efficient and controlled service but, in many cases, customers do not welcome such developments.

Once again, it is necessary to be constantly aware of the delicately balanced service process and management system. Any changes must be skilfully introduced and positioned to increase the likelihood of their trouble-free acceptance. If this could be achieved, i.e. "if the new technology could be skilfully employed to enhance and promote rather than to disturb the kind of social process that typifies effective service organizations, then the potential will be very great." (Normann, 1984, p. 71)

## Productivity in services

The importance of services in the United States may be judged by observing that service firms account for more than 70 per cent of private employment. As a result it is argued that "higher services productivity is clearly the key to securing a rising national standard of living. Moreover, it's a critical factor in improving the nation's competitiveness and shrinking the trade deficit." (*Business Week*, 22 May, 1989, p. 18). Pressure for increased productivity in services comes from the customers of services, the manufacturing firms who must also compete in international markets. Productivity in service firms has increased at different rates in different countries due mainly to differential investment levels in new technology to support workers in service firms.

Between 1979 and 1986 services output per person in Japan, the Federal Rupublic of Germany, France, Sweden and the United Kingdom increased by about 2 per cent per year compared with only 0.4 per cent in the United States. The increased capital investment in services industries in Europe has been driven by the high level and relative inflexibility of pay in service firms. While US private service workers are paid only 67 per cent of manufacturing wages, in Japan they receive 93 per cent as much and in the Federal Rupublic of Germany 85 per cent as much (*Business Week*, 22 May, 1989, p. 18).

Recent research on product and service marketing has been concerned not so much with the issue of differences between products and services, but with ways of integrating the treatment of the two. Arguments about differences have not been productive (Ryans and Wittink, 1977). Recent literature has attempted to integrate the two sets of treatment with a view to developing better strategic planning models to guide the service marketing firm. An important conclusion is drawn by Shostack quoting Wilson (1977): "The more intangible the service, the greater the difference in the marketing characteristics of the service," i.e. the nearer to the intangible end an entity is "the greater the divergence from product marketing both in priorities and approach." (Shostack, 1977)

Thomas (1978) discusses the apparent difficulty in service-based offerings of availing of economies of scale. The perishable quality of a service creates a need to decentralize the service production process to a local level. However, a little imagination provides considerable scope, i.e. by introducing wide-bodied jets, airlines could fly twice as many passengers with the same number of high-salaried pilots.

Service systems with high customer contact are more difficult to control and to rationalize than those with lower customer contact (Chase, 1978). In high-contact systems, the customer can affect the time of demand, the exact nature of the service and the quality of the service since, by definition, (s)he becomes involved in the process itself. In fact is is frequently better to view the marketing of services as the marketing of a system. The system consists of products which produce explicit benefits and services which produce tacit benefits (Figure 17.2). Emphasis on individual components of the system is associated with

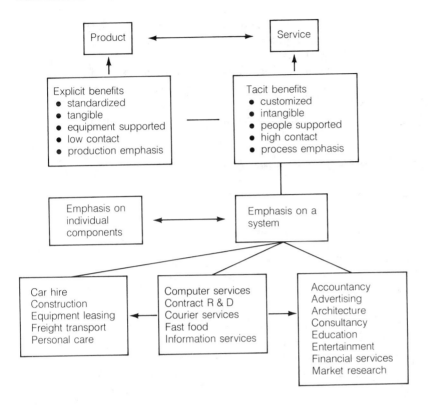

**Figure 17.2**  Services marketing is marketing a system

transportation, financial, and personal services. Emphasis on the system itself arises in education and professional services.

In services where the customer must be present, satisfaction with the service will be influenced by the interactions between customers and the service facilities themselves, and perhaps also by others using the system (Lovelock, 1983). At the opposite end, where the customer does not come in contact with the service facility, the outcome of the service remains very important but the process of service delivery may be of little interest. e.g. bank credit cards.

Service managers must be aware of the drawbacks of intangibles, or pure services, in any attempt to increase productivity through commonly accepted methods such as standardization or economies of scale. Many writers warn of the implications of bringing a highly intangible dominated "market offering" to the market. Such an approach must be weighed against the benefits of driving towards a more "tangible intangible" (Chase, 1978). Contrary to what managers might believe, service marketing has a lot of discretion in making this transformation both through the service marketing mix and by thinking creatively about the nature of the services provided. Chase provides two classic examples here: the use of ATMs by the financial service industry; and the UK's Open University system. The former transformed the delivery of certain traditional banking services from a human delivery mode, people-based and intangible, to a machine delivery mode, equipment-based and very tangible. Hence by weighing up the costs and benefits of a particular positioning on the scale, transformations involving a movement along the product service continuum can be made.

## International marketing of services

### Managing services marketing

To examine how best to approach the marketing of services, it is necessary to return to the unique characteristics of services: intangibility; inseparability; heterogeneity; perishability; and ownership. It is because services are performed, rather than produced, that they have many distinguishable characteristics which present the service firm with many problems.

In purchasing products, the product and its features provide enough evidence of what is being offered. In the case of a service, the "management of evidence" is vital (Shostack, 1977). This refers to the tangible cues surrounding the seller's capabilities to deliver the service. The literature is extensive on the importance of situational characteristics in purchase decisions for services (Berry, 1980; Shostack, 1977). Such things as the physical, environmental setting, e.g. doctor's waiting rooms, and the appearance of service, e.g. clothes and presentation, should receive very high management priority.

The importance of price should also be discussed here. The tendency for customers to use the price of a product as an indicator of its quality is well known. For services, it is even more pronounced. Berry (1980) explains that lawyers, consultants and even hairdressers can contradict signals they wish to communicate regarding quality by setting their prices too low. This is another "evidence" which must be managed carefully. Great emphasis is placed on ensuring that the distribution of products occurs at the "right time" in the "right place." With services, it is necessary to add: "in the right way." The "how" of service distribution is vital to get right. "How ... doctors, lawyers ... conduct themselves in the presence of the customer can influence future patronage decisions. Washing machines can't be rude or careless — but people providing services can and sometimes are." (Berry, 1980)

The whole issue of trust arises in service marketing but is seldom ever mentioned. Berry (1980) refers to it in what he terms the need for "internal marketing," particularly in high-contact service industries. He defines internal marketing as the need to apply the philosophy and practices of marketing to the people who serve the external customer so that: (a) the best people possible can be employed and retained; and (b) they will be the most effective in their work.

Presumably, by deduction, such employees exude an air of trustworthiness and reliability on which the customer places confidence and also, in the case of long-term relationships, a degree of loyalty.

Services are usually designed around the specific requirements of the individual customer. The degree of standardization possible in a service depends largely on the extent to which the service is "people-based" or "equipment-based." A service such as an automatic car wash raises the level of standardization as it removes the human element which has considerable bearing on the viability of the service function. Due to the inseparability factor, the service sector is one which is highly labour-intensive and therefore investment in good people and training is one approach to quality control. The difficulty of producing services of uniform quality which is necessary for successful branding, advertising, and other mass-marketing activities makes the successful and sustained marketing of services that much more difficult than is the case for products (Uhl and Upah, 1983). Trusthouse Forte, the international hotel chain, in considering expansion into new markets in Europe and the United States, recognized the value of branding its services while at the same time acknowledged that individual hotels could suffer under a general brand name (Exhibit 17.1).

The perishability associated with services creates a need for a careful matching of supply with demand (Sasser, 1976). Demand for services must be satisfied or lost (Uhl and Upah, 1983). Sasser has offered a number of possibilities for matching demand with supply: (a) peak load pricing, e.g. electricity, telephones; (b) developing non-peak demand, e.g. happy hours in bars; (c) in-house alternatives, e.g. ATMs at banks to minimize waiting; and (d) creating reservation systems for transportation companies. To adjust the supply of services to the demand for them, Sasser suggests the following:

- using part-time employees;
- maximizing efficiency (extending hours);
- sharing capacity (airlines share departure gates in airports);
- increasing consumer participation (self-service);
- increasing flow-through rates (spend less time with customers).

Obviously there are limits to how much capacity can be modified but the benefits would be so great to the service that a number of commentators expect to see much greater development in this area for the future.

Finally, there is the question of ownership. This additional characteristic is found in the work of Cowell (1984) who explains that it is a basic difference between service and product businesses. The buyer of a product has full use of it, but the buyer of a service only receives the use of or access to the service.

## Diversification in the services firm

When a service firm reaches a certain size or has spare capacity, it may consider

## Exhibit 17.1  Branding in an international hotel chain

*THF joins the search for brand identity*

On 25 March, the world's largest hotel owner will reach a decision on a subject it has been deliberating over for more than 20 years. Trusthouse Forte will decide how it is going to brand its products. It has dabbled in branding in the past and got its fingers burned; the brands that survive exist as internal communications vehicles only. The customer perceives no difference between them.

According to Denis Hearn, Forte's deputy, research should "identify the differences in our business hotels with an overall brand name for the UK. And because we're increasingly serving an international market, it should also come up with one or more international brand names."

Why the change of heart at THF? An aggressive hotel expansion programme is the key, the thrust of which is in continental Europe and the US. THF is now concerned that it stands to lose out on global brand recognition and will suffer in the referral bookings stakes.

The climate in the hotel industry has also changed and there is increasing evidence from the major players that branding, and brand segmentation, works. The US chains, for example, have already taken the route up-market: Renaissance from Ramada, Regency from Hyatt, Crowne Plaza from Holiday Inns and Towers from Sheraton. And several are dipping their toes in the water with no-frills products.

Hearn is keen to emphasise that THF's five-star properties, referred to as Exclusive hotels, will remain firmly outside the branding exercise. "We considered years ago, before the merger with Trust House, whether we'd put the name Forte on our top hotels, but we still draw back from the idea. The George in Paris, the Hyde Park in London and New York's Plaza Athenee are brands in themselves, and famous", says Hearn. "To superimpose a brand on those would take away their individuality."

**Source:** *Marketing,* 12 March, 1987, p. 14.

---

diversification as a growth strategy. The most common form of service companies' diversification is client-based diversification (Normann, 1984). The importance of establishing the confidence and trust of the client has already been discussed. This relationship with the client is an integral asset of a service firm. If clients indicate a need for complementary or additional services, this may be a strong motivator to the service firm to provide them. This is clearly illustrated in the financial services industry. Major companies such as Citicorp and Chase Manhattan now offer a complete range of banking or financial services.

Grönroos's earlier models provide the setting for the second form of diversification discussed by Normann: main; and auxiliary services. Viewing a service as more than just a "core" or "main" offering, diversification into auxiliary support and peripheral services makes good business sense. In some cases, as Normann points out, these auxiliary services can grow in importance in their own right.

A third common form advanced by Normann is the situation where basic knowledge exists in the company, making it capable of catering for different market segments. Such situations occur where there is no ambiguity in the image that the company presents to the public and employees.

In many ways the diversification of a services business is similar to diversifying in a product market. Service market diversification involves developing a new range of services for existing customers, transferring existing services to new customers in international markets. As in product markets, basic to the concept of growth through diversification is the idea of synergy. Synergy is usually based on financial benefits to the firm, better services to the established customer base or complementarity in services offered. Financial synergy arises when the service firm develops different businesses which have complementary cash flow patterns. As in many other areas of marketing, the established customer base constitutes a most valuable asset for the firm. In recent years, banks, insurance companies and building societies have each extended the kind of service they provide. It is reasonably easy for a transaction type business to diversify into providing several types of service based on such transactions.

The third type of diversification arises when a service firm develops an auxiliary service for its own core business and then commercializes this auxiliary business so that a wider customer group has access to it. Several examples may be cited to demonstrate the nature of this diversification. Airlines have developed their own catering and aircraft service and repair systems to such an extent that they are offered to other users, including competitors. American Express has developed a "front-office" and a "back-office" business. In the front office the traditional American Express business is carried on, while in the back office the company has developed its card billing and payments processing business to serve other proprietary credit card businesses. In these situations the service firm is using the same basic knowledge to cater for different market segments.

When a firm in the service business attempts to internationalize it must transfer an entire system abroad. It is not simply a matter of adapting a product to the needs of customers in international markets. It is necessary to transfer the entire system and the problem becomes one of adapting the system to new combinations. The issue of intangibility makes this process difficult to achieve. As in product markets, internationalization of a service business is frequently a condition for holding on to important customers.

## Internationalizing the service firm

With few exceptions, e.g. Cowell (1984) and Normann (1984), it is necessary to examine the work of economists on the structure of industries in the world to find any discussion of services in an international context. A random sample of a number of well-known standard international marketing text-books shows that little space is devoted to the treatment of service marketing, let alone considering the international dimension. The overall picture presented by the economists is, as Inman (1985) puts it, "a world economy predominantly involved in producing and trading services." Yet, it is difficult to find a more apparent neglect than that which the international marketing of services has suffered at the hands of marketing theorists (Cowell, 1984).

Many commentators believe that the principles of services marketing internationally are the same as those applied to domestic markets. Differences occur when considerations of environmental factors such as culture, legal, social and political factors are taken into account. Such beliefs have served product marketing reasonably well. With regard to services, however, an important difference needs to be examined. While domestic and international services are characterized by their range and complexity, the pattern of domestically traded services is, however, very different from those traded internationally (Staltson, 1985). Quoting the United States as an example, Staltson explains that the two major domestic service sectors — government and social services — hardly figure in the international arena where such services as transport, financial services and tourism are much more significant, even more so than in the United States itself. Staltson adds that high-tech sectors such as communications and data processing are likely to account for a significantly greater proportion of service revenues from abroad than they do domestically.

In 1970 and 1987 the United States was the largest exporter of services. In 1970 the United States exported $56 billion worth of services which represented 11.2 per cent of total world exports of services. Other important exporters are France, the United Kingdom, the Federal Republic of Germany and Italy (Table 17.6). In 1987 West Germany replaced the United States as the largest importer of services. In that year West Germany imported $64 billion worth of services or 12.4 per cent of the world total imports. With the addition of Japan the same countries dominated import activities.

World exports of commercial services were worth $505 billion in 1987. The most important category was private services and income. This includes financial services which constituted 40 per cent of the total in 1987. Travel and shipping were the other important categories. The fastest growing category is private services and income, the average growth of which was 14.5 per cent between 1970 and 1987. In the period 1980–7 passenger services was dominant in terms of growth (Table 17.7).

## Basis for internationalization in the service firm

In many cases the service offering is not conducive to "going international" or it is necessary to start out "large," e.g. the airline industry and some corporate

**Table 17.6**  Leading exporters and importers in commercial services, 1970 and 1987

| Rank (Exports) | | | 1970 Value $ billion | 1970 Share (%) | Rank (Imports) | | | 1987 Value $ billion | 1987 Share (%) |
|---|---|---|---|---|---|---|---|---|---|
| 1970 | 1987 | | | | 1970 | 1987 | | | |
| 1 | 1 | United States | 56 | 11.2 | 2 | 1 | Germany, Fed.Rep. | 64 | 12.4 |
| 3 | 2 | France | 53 | 10.6 | 1 | 2 | United States | 56 | 10.8 |
| 2 | 3 | United Kingdom | 43 | 8.6 | 5 | 3 | Japan | 52 | 10.1 |
| 4 | 4 | Germany, Fed.Rep. | 41 | 8.2 | 4 | 4 | France | 43 | 8.3 |
| 5 | 5 | Italy | 33 | 6.5 | 3 | 5 | United Kingdom | 33 | 6.4 |
| 6 | 6 | Japan | 28 | 5.5 | 6 | 6 | Italy | 26 | 5.0 |
| 6 | 7 | Netherlands | 23 | 4.5 | 8 | 7 | Netherlands | 23 | 4.5 |
| 8 | 8 | Spain | 22 | 4.3 | 9 | 8 | Belgium–Luxembourg | 17 | 3.3 |
| 10 | 9 | Belgium–Luxembourg | 19 | 3.8 | 7 | 9 | Canada | 16 | 3.1 |
| 15 | 10 | Austria | 15 | 2.9 | 15 | 10 | Switzerland | 12 | 2.3 |
| 12 | 11 | Switzerland | 14 | 2.8 | 10 | 11 | Sweden | 10 | 2.0 |
| 9 | 12 | Canada | 11 | 2.1 | 13 | 12 | Norway | 10 | 1.8 |
| 14 | 13 | Sweden | 9 | 1.7 | 44 | 13 | Saudi Arabia | 9 | 1.8 |
| 11 | 14 | Norway | 8 | 1.7 | 18 | 14 | Austria | 9 | 1.8 |
| 27 | 15 | Korea, Rep. | 8 | 1.7 | 16 | 15 | Spain | 8 | 1.6 |
| 16 | 16 | Denmark | 8 | 1.5 | 11 | 16 | Australia | 8 | 1.5 |
| 22 | 17 | Singapore | 7 | 1.5 | 17 | 17 | Denmark | 7 | 1.4 |
| 13 | 19 | Mexico | 7 | 1.3 | 32 | 19 | Korea, Rep | 5 | 1.0 |
| 17 | 20 | Australia | 5 | 1.0 | .. | 20 | Hong Kong | 5 | 1.0 |
| 26 | 21 | Taiwan | 4 | 0.9 | 12 | 21 | Mexico | 5 | 0.9 |
| 20 | 22 | Greece | 4 | 0.9 | 40 | 22 | Singapore | 5 | 0.9 |
| 18 | 23 | Yugoslavia | 4 | 0.9 | 20 | 23 | Yugoslavia | 5 | 0.9 |
| 33 | 25 | Thailand | 4 | 0.7 | 14 | 25 | South Africa | 5 | 0.9 |
| Total | | | 437 | 86.7 | Total | | | 444 | 86.0 |
| World | | | 505 | 100.0 | World | | | 515 | 100.0 |

Sources: General Agreement on Tariffs and Trade (1989) *International Trade 88–89*, Volume 1, Geneva, pp. 23–4; World Bank (1988) *World Development Report*, Oxford University Press, p. 34.

**Table 17.7**  World exports of commercial services

| Service category | Share in exports of commercial services 1970 (%) | Share in exports of commercial services 1987 (%) | Average annual change in value 1980–7 (%) | Average annual change in value 1970–87 (%) |
|---|---|---|---|---|
| Shipment | 22 | 13 | 1.5 | 9.5 |
| Passenger services | 5 | 6 | 7.5 | 14.0 |
| Port services | 12 | 11 | 0.0 | 12.0 |
| Travel | 29 | 30 | 6.5 | 13.0 |
| Other private services and income | 24 | 40 | 6.5 | 14.5 |
| Total commercial services (%) | 100 = $64 billion | 100 = $505 billion | 5.0 | 13.0 |

Sources: General Agreement on Tariffs and Trade (1989) *International Trade 88–9*, Volume 1, Geneva, pp. 23–4; World Bank (1988) *World Development Report*, Oxford University Press, p. 30.

banking activities. The international service marketing firm often cannot draw from small-scale domestic experience whereas the product marketing firm can usually develop the domestic market first — before going abroad.

The product-marketing firm can also "test the waters" — start into export markets initially by exporting a limited or reduced product line. Gradually, as success gathers momentum, the full product line can be introduced abroad. Market commitment can be extended by setting up overseas production units and subsidiaries. The process continues, constantly building from a position of strength. It is very different for the service marketing firm. It will have to "plunge straight in" as a service cannot be exported. Normann (1984) explains that few services can be exported without also exporting the full "service delivery system." Basically, the service offering must be available in full from the day of entry to the market.

As was seen in earlier chapters, among the many reasons why product marketing firms go international were: stagnant domestic market; growth in the market abroad; matching domestic competitors as they internationalize; opportunism; counteracting foreign firm action, i.e. threat in the domestic market; and exploiting a competitive advantage. These reasons also apply to service firms as they attempt to enter and develop international markets. Normann (1984) highlights two additional reasons: (a) a personal challenge to senior people in the firm; (b) the need to service customers who have internationalized. Unless three conditions are fulfilled, however, the full potential of international markets can never be realized (Normann, 1984):

1. A competitive advantage must exist in the service management system.
2. There must be a strong desire or ambition among senior management to internationalize.
3. The service firm must provide adequate commitment of time and resources.

The involvement of people in the process usually means that there is a degree of variability not experienced by the product-marketing firm. Cultural diversities and social norms quickly come into focus in service marketing.The effect of these elements obviously varies with the degree of intangibility of the service offering.

## Market entry modalities for services

In respect of market entry strategies, the options open to the service firm are similar to those available for the product marketing firm:

- exporting;
- competitive alliances;
- acquisitions/direct investment.

Exporting has already been shown to be difficult for the services firm since the delivery system must accompany the service. Forms of competitive alliance such as joint ventures abound and are used more often than in product marketing due to the cultural element of services and the different people involved. Locals can overcome many barriers confronting the service marketing firm.

The licensing of a service operation has never been as widespread as it is for products but, as was seen in Chapter 13, franchising of services operations is growing. Many are of the opinion that because of the very nature of services, a service firm cannot have patents or exclusive "manufacturing" processes to protect its offering, hence it is considered unsuitable for licensing. To overcome this problem, Winter (1970) demonstrates the need for the service firm to offer a substantial *quid pro quo* in return for the licence fee. He suggests that to avoid the foreign counterpart "taking the idea and going it alone", an acceptable arrangement should include the following:

- a strong name;
- a well-designed marketing strategy;
- a complete manualized operation system;
- substantial opportunity for profit.

The name of the firm and the goodwill attached to the trademark are crucial elements in the service offering process. When a product is taken to international markets, these markets are generally quite familiar with the product. For a service marketing firm such will not be the case; the firm's name and reputation are critical to selling the service successfully and these must be given much attention and be advertised or communicated in some way to the new market before purchase of the service can begin. The confidence of the prospective client or customer must be won initially. The firm's name and existing experience may not be sufficient, however. The conditions in the marketing environment must be conducive. Sears Roebuck discovered that its experience was not relevant to international trading and so dropped its aspirations in that direction. The firm acquired specialized firms to perform the tasks and reverted to consumer products in which it had experience (Exhibit 17.2).

In designing an international licensing agreement, Winters (1970) strongly advises that minimum sales performance standards be included. Otherwise, the licensee is unlikely to put much effort into the programme. Due to the nature of services, the licensee will need considerably greater legal, personnel, management and promotional support. The distance factor, language barriers and differences in business customers can often cause problems between the licensor and licensee. There may be a requirement for strong regional management structures that are constantly able to guide the licensee.

Franchising appears to be even better for service companies, affording a greater degree of control over the elements of the service component, as described in the Grönroos model. Franchising is frequently used in the fast food industry.

Acquisitions and foreign direct investment decisions for service firms, in

---

**Exhibit 17.2   Retailer sticks to the knitting but acquires specialist firms to trade internationally**

---

*Back to first base*

US corporations are unable to compete with their foreign counterparts because they are bloated, inflexible and protected by trade barriers, says US deputy treasury secretary Richard Darman. His attack came within days of the announcement by the giant retailer, Sears Roebuck and Company, that it was ending its ambitious experiment in international trade after running up losses of US$60 million.

The Chicago-based store and financial services company set up Sears World Trade (SWT) in 1982, modelled on Japanese trading houses such as Mitsubishi and Mitsui. Trading analysts looked to Sears to show that US companies could compete effectively in such areas as barter trade and compensation agreements. SWT's first chairman, a former Securities and Exchange Commissioner Roderick Hills, boasted that the company would help cash-strapped Third World countries get rid of primary commodities that were already glutting world markets.

But Hills and his team, encountered more problems than they bargained for. When SWT was launched, most US trade exporters believed that countertrade was on the verge of a big boom. In 1982, the Third World debt crises looked to be looming forever on the horizon and world trade was contracting. Countertrade, however, was no solution. Yoshi Tsurumi, a professor of international business at Baruch College in New York, sees other reasons for why SWT failed. "The American corporate culture is too legalistic and too mechanistic for a trading company", he said. "Trading companies' cultures must be flexible, entrepreneurial, fast, opportunistic."

Perhaps with this in mind, SWT began accumulating foreign companies that had more practice in the vagaries of export trade among Third World countries and in Eastern Europe. SWT acquired Hagemeyer NV, a big Dutch trading company, Price and Pierce, a British timber trader and two consultancy companies. It also got out of the business of trading primary commodities and stuck to looking for details on consumer goods that could be used by Sears' vast retail network.

**Source:** *South*, January, 1987, pp. 96–7.

---

the form of a branch or subsidiary, must consider the costs of the investment compared to other market entry modes, on the one hand, and the obvious scope for greater control, particularly quality control, on the other.

## *Public policy restrictions on international marketing of services*

Restrictions come into play much more rapidly for service firms than is usually the case for product-based firms. We have already dealt with two potential problems facing the international services firm: (a) the risk of plunging straight into the foreign market; and (b) the need to adapt to the new market.

Another problem, more strongly felt by service firms than by product firms, is that of barriers to trade and government restrictions. Restrictions by governments and public agencies are much more common for service firms than is the case for product firms. After primary resources, host governments see services as a way by which foreign companies can "take the most out of a country and leave little." (Carman and Langeard, 1979) The special nature of some services prompts governments into taking action — particularly when the service has some cultural, political or security sensitivity.

Staltson (1985) illustrates the extent of government regulation of services in the United States by drawing attention to "a voluminous inventory compiled by the Office of the US Trade Representative." She also highlights the service equivalent to tariff barriers used against products. Services can be controlled by measures such as licences, fees and special taxes. Administrative and investment-related barriers are quite common and are examined in detail in Cowell (1984). Administrative barriers may be in the form of:

- delays in granting licences;
- failure to certify certain professional services;
- discriminatory implementation of statutory regulations;
- inadequate access to local judicial bodies.

Investment-related barriers include:

- employment requirements that control the personnel practices of the foreign firm;
- restrictions on the extent of foreign ownership permitted;
- biased government regulation against foreign service companies;
- limitations on the firm's access to advertising and communications failures;
- discriminatory practices against specific service industries (i.e. higher reserve requirements for foreign bank subsidiaries or special capital requirements for foreign insurance firms).

## Internationalization in selected service industries

### Advertising services in international markets

Any service marketing firm attempting to tackle the complexities of advertising unequipped with a thorough understanding and appreciation of the uniqueness and abstract nature of a service is bound to pay a very heavy price as it attempts to advertise.

The product marketing firm enters the arena with a principal, tangible product to which the advertising process adds abstract qualities to enhance and sell the product. The service marketing firm enters with an intangible offering which cannot be physically evaluated or accessed. When combined with further abstract and intangible qualities by the advertising process, the result may be confusion, even a "money-for-nothing" image (Shostack, 1977). Shostack urges the service marketing firm to understand the need to make the service offered more "concrete" through advertising, rather than more "hazy." Merrill Lynch has developed a strong association between itself and the bull symbol. Also, its advertisements show photographs of tangible physical booklets and the TV screening of most advertisements finish by inviting customers to write for them. In this regard Merrill Lynch successfully associated its intangible service with some "tangible evidence" working against the media's abstracting qualities. Both domestic and international services marketing firms are well advised to acquaint themselves with Shostack's concluding principle: "Effective media representation of intangibles is a function of establishing non-abstract manifestations of them." (Shostack, 1977, p. 80)

The advertising agency world has gone through a number of changes in recent years, many of which can be attributed to international market trends and company responses. Many advertising agencies find that to service their clients properly they must follow them abroad. The European top ten advertising agencies were dominated by the Saatchi & Saatchi group in 1988 with its two networks, Backer Spielvogel Bates Worldwide and Saatchi & Saatchi Advertising Worldwide (Table 17.8). Other very large agencies are Ogilvy & Mather, McCann-Erickson and Young & Rubicam, each of which is reported to earn more than £200 million each year from European operations alone (*The Sunday Times*, 12 March, 1989).

It is not just the large agencies which have internationalized. Many smaller firms are also seeking partners and other ways into international markets. The smaller agencies seek partnerships due principally to the squeeze placed on them by the size of their clients, on the one hand, and the size of the international media groups, on the other.

The concentration of advertiser strength and the development of large media groups are together forcing many small- and medium-size advertising agencies to internationalize by seeking competitive alliances abroad. Other factors are also important in opening up international markets to advertising agencies. Deregulation of the television industry in Europe indicates that further growth in advertising is expected. Liberalization tends to increase the size of the market rather than just draw advertising away from other media such as newspapers or magazines. Satellite television also contributes to the growth in the international advertising market. Advertisers have access through satellite television to new and wider markets. The market in Europe is, however, at different stages of maturity depending on country. The United Kingdom is still the largest market for advertising (Table 17.8).

It will continue to be difficult to consolidate the European advertising industry for two reasons. Many of the advertising agencies sought as partners are private companies and therefore difficult to acquire through share

**Table 17.8** Europe's top ten countries and companies in advertising

| Advertising budgets, 1988 | | Advertising gross income, Europe 1987 | |
|---|---|---|---|
| Country | $ Million | Agencies | $ Million |
| 1. United Kingdom | 11,894 | 1. Backer Spielvogel Bates | 248 |
| 2. West Germany | 9,522 | 2. Saatchi & Saatchi AW | 230 |
| 3. France | 6,843 | 3. Ogilvy & Mather | 218 |
| 4. Italy | 4,981 | 4. McCann-Erickson | 215 |
| 5. Spain | 4,407 | 5. Young & Rubicam | 201 |
| 6. Netherlands | 2,438 | 6. Lintas: Worldwide | 186 |
| 7. Switzerland | 1,985 | 7. J Walter Thompson | 175 |
| 8. Finland | 1,443 | 8. BBDO Worldwide | 171 |
| 9. Sweden | 1,571 | 9. Publicis | 162 |
| 10. Belgium | 981 | 10. Grey Advertising | 151 |

Source: *The Sunday Times*, 12 March, 1989.

purchases. Furthermore, mergers or cooperative alliances between advertising agencies are intrinsically difficult to establish and maintain. Manufacturers of industrial or consumer products combine to serve a common purpose: to sell a product. The advertising agency is a service business where success depends greatly on its next campaign. There is no product to hold potential partners together. The need is greater for a coalition of people and perceptions and how they work together. It is the human factor and the nature of the business which can cause disharmony and instability in such partnership relations. A further complicating factor is that joining with another agency to serve a particular market can easily fall into the trap of a conflict of interest among customer groups. Rarely will competitor clients agree to being served by the same agency. In such circumstances, the newly formed joint groups frequently lose valued customers.

## Financial services in international markets

Between 1984–5 and 1986–7 the number of mergers and acquisitions recorded by the EC Commission Directorate General for Competition in distribution,

**Table 17.9** Acquisition of service businesses in the EC, 1986–7

| Service sector | Location of acquisition | | | Total (No.) |
|---|---|---|---|---|
| | Same EC country (No.) | EC cross-border (No.) | EC and non-EC country (No.) | |
| Distribution | 40 | 5 | 4 | 49 |
| Banking | 22 | 3 | 10 | 35 |
| Insurance | 17 | 7 | 4 | 28 |
| Total | 79 | 15 | 18 | 112 |

Source: Adapted from EC Commission (1988) *Seventeenth Report on Competition Policy*.

banking and insurance increased from 67 to 112. Most of these acquisitions occurred within the same EC country, which is similar to the situation in manufacturing discussed in Chapter 14. In 1986–7, EC cross-border acquisitions and mergers accounted for only fifteen of the total, while non-EC firms were involved in only eighteen situations (Table 17.9). Most of these acquisitions were in distribution, followed by banking and insurance.

Acquisitions and mergers in financial services have increased quite dramatically. As was seen above, the purpose of these acquisitions and mergers appears to be a broadening of the product range and market expansion. Financial institutions are able, through mergers and acquisitions, to quickly offer their customers an international network based on a wider range of services and at the same time to reduce costs of operation. The recent alliance between the Royal Bank of Scotland and the Banco Santander in Spain is an example of these developments (Exhibit 17.3).

Scale economies are not a key determinant of acquisitions in financial services as labour and interest expenses represent the most important costs of operation. Nevertheless, the EC is attempting to liberalize the financial services market. Recent directives are expected to turn the EC into a single financial market (Exhibit 17.4). Mergers and acquisitions, however, are not the easiest way of obtaining the benefits of integration of large financial markets such as the EC. Friendly competitive alliances involving cross-selling of selected products or joint ventures could be an attractive alternative.

## Internationalizing accountancy services

Accountancy firms are also going through a dramatic period of change for similar and different reasons. The growth of individual firms among the "Big Eight" accountancy firms has lead to much comment. The announcement by Ernst & Whinney and Arthur Young that they planned to merge has focussed attention on firms within and outside the "Big Eight."

The subsequent announcement by Price Waterhouse and Befec, part of the European based BDO Binder group, that they would also merge, raised the question of survival for smaller European accountancy firms. The importance of Befec to Price Waterhouse lies in the area of the market for audits (Exhibit 17.5). Price Waterhouse has a strong base in the United Kingdom and the United States but very little representation elsewhere in Europe. In 1988 in the United States, Price Waterhouse had an audit market share approaching 20 per cent of the market. In the United Kingdom its share was 15.5 per cent. But in other European markets its share was just over 9 per cent (Table 17.10).

Since audits change very infrequently among companies, success by Price Waterhouse in attracting such firms as Befec, complete with its own client bases, is a key way of building market position in the core accountancy business in Europe. When the merger is complete the share positions in the table will change. Two other interesting factors emerge from Table 17.10. First, two firms in the "Big Eight" already have very strong positions in Continental Europe:

---

**Exhibit 17.3    Offering customers an international service network**

---

*Taking stock of a pioneering alliance*

One of the few examples of banking alliances formed specifically to exploit a single European market is that between Royal Bank of Scotland and Banco Santander of Spain. The alliance, formed last October, was cemented by a cross-shareholding with Santander buying 9.9 per cent of Royal and Royal buying 2.5 per cent of Santander. The idea is to combine the strengths of two banks which are relatively small in Europe as a whole, but have similar features, such as a strong regional presence, and an ambition to enlarge their geographical reach.

    "This means we will have a presence in all the major markets of Europe, and will be sharing the costs", said Mr Matias Inciarte, Santander's finance director, who is pleased both by the level of co-operation and the return his bank has received on its investment in the Royal. The arrangements so far include:

- **Personal Banking**: RBS customers will be able to use 50 Santander branches in Spanish holiday resorts, with a similar arrangement for Santander customers at RBS's Knightsbridge branch in London. They are also linking cash machine facilities. A jointly owned bank is being formed to serve the UK expatriate community in Gibraltar and Spain.
- **Business Banking**: the two banks have appointed representatives in each other's capitals to speed the flow of banking services to corporate customers. They are also working together in corporate finance, venture capital and merchant banking.
- **Franchising, stock custody and settlement, and technology**: are further areas where the two banks see scope for co-operation. A joint approach to hardware and software purchases has been adopted, and ultimately the two banks hope customers will be able to access their accounts from any part of the alliance network.

In a new study of UK bank strategies in Europe, S.G. Warburg Securities takes quite a bullish line on the possibilities of the alliance. It estimates the profit potential to Royal Bank of some £10m ($16.7m) a year but adds: "This figure should be capable of doubling or tripling if the scale of co-operation at present envisaged can be realised."

**Source:** *Financial Times*, Tuesday, 9 May, 1989.

---

KPMG; and Coopers & Lybrand. Second, the planned merger between Ernst & Whinney and Arthur Young will make the new firm dominant in the US market but only the third largest in Europe (Table 17.10).

## Constraints on the growth of the international service firm

International service industries are fragmented. There are low entry barriers to service businesses as manifested by the many small firms sharing each market.

---

**Exhibit 17.4   A single financial market in the EC?**

---

*EC sets out bank licence proposals*

The European Commission has announced further details of its long standing plans to make the European Community a single financial market. The draft of the second banking directive announced on January 13, proposes that any bank based in an EC country, which is licensed to do business in that country, will be allowed to do business in any other EC country by virtue of that licence.

At the moment, banks can set up subsidiaries in other EC countries, but are not allowed to set up branches. The subsidiaries are subject to the laws and banking regulations of each country.

Under the proposed "single community licence", banks will be allowed to open branches in other EC countries, and these branches will be subject to the supervisory authority of the country of origin which granted the licence. Banks will still be allowed to set up subsidiaries in other EC countries, but those subsidiaries will come under the regulation of the country in which they operate.

The second directive also specifies new standards with which banks must comply in order to gain a licence. These are in addition to the standards set by the first banking directive in 1977. The new standards specify a minimum capital requirement of 5m ecus (US$6.3m); that information about major shareholders is to be disclosed; that not more than 50 per cent of the bank's own funds are to be used for non-banking activities and not more than 10 percent should be invested in one undertaking.

The single community banking licence will authorize a bank to do a wide range of banking related activities, including portfolio management, and advice and trading in securities. Significantly, the range of activities open to a bank will be those allowed in the country which issued its licence, irrespective of whether these activities are allowed in the country which issued its licence, irrespective of whether these activities are allowed by the country in which it is operating.

**Source:** *Retail Banks*, 25 January, 1988, p. 6.

---

There are few scale economies due to the relatively simple process involved, e.g. warehousing, or the inherently high labour content, e.g. personal care. In service businesses there are frequently very high transportation costs since services are usually produced at the customer's premises or the customer must visit the provider; because inventory is impossible, service businesses must usually be frequented. The problem is exacerbated for services with fluctuating demand. Firms with large-scale facilities have no advantage.

In many instances diseconomies of scale exist in service businesses. Small firms are more efficient where personal service is the key to the business.

**Exhibit 17.5 Acquiring a client base for market dominance**

*Future in balance for firms outside big eight*

While all eyes in the accountancy world have been on the "Big Eight" since Ernst & Whinney and Arthur Young announced that they plan to merge, the future of the largest firm outside the eight appears to have been thrown into the balance as well.

BDO Binder, which have revenues of $783m will lose its French associate, Befec & Associés to Price Waterhouse from the end of this year. The defection is a significant blow to BDO and symptomatic of the difficulties faced by firms its size.

In revenue terms, Befec is not a huge force in its home country. However, it has a powerful client list. According to figures in the French press earlier this year, it audits 162 of the country's public companies — just three fewer than the market leader, Fiduciaire de France.

Befec's client base, which includes household names such as Michelin, will give Price Waterhouse an important leg-up as the single European market draws closer. It will also go some way to making up for PW's weak client base elsewhere in Europe.

Befec's defection has been prompted by the same consideration that has forced similar moves in other European countries. As its domestic clients have become more international in outlook, accountancy firms on the Continent have had to pay more heed to the strength of their international networks.

They have also had to accept the unpalatable (to many) reality that in the US and UK, the financial community almost demands that large companies be handled by one of the big eight.

Befec has already lost some important clients in the past two years, including Banque National de Paris and Compagnie Financière de Suez. The link with Price Waterhouse, a "brand leader" in the auditing market, should help it to retain many of the others.

**Source:** *Financial Times*, 1 June, 1989, p. 15.

---

Individualized, responsive service declines with size after reaching a threshold, e.g. beauty care and management consulting.

Market needs in regard to services are diverse. Buyer tastes for many services are fragmented. This fragmentation arises due to local and regional differences in market needs. There is considerable need for customized products and services, e.g. most fire engines sold are unique. The problem with fragmentation in the marketing of services is that an industry in which no firm has a significant market share means that no firm can strongly influence the industry outcome. There is also considerable indeterminacy in the industry since there are no market leaders with the power to shape industry events.

It is the accessibility of the service that counts. A service may be intangible

**Table 17.10** Audit market shares of leading accountancy firms, Europe and the United States

| Firm | US *Fortune* 500 firms (%) | Audit market share among: UK *Times* top 1,000 firms (%) | European *Financial Times* top 500 (%) |
|---|---|---|---|
| Arthur Andersen | 17.0 | 6.7 | 4.3 |
| Arthur Young | 8.6 | 6.4 | 5.7 |
| Coopers & Lybrand | 11.6 | 8.1 | 12.5 |
| Deloitte Haskins and Sells | 8.8 | 8.9 | 8.1 |
| Ernst & Whinney | 14.6 | 7.3 | 6.4 |
| KPMG | 13.6 | 19.1 | 18.7 |
| Price Waterhouse | 19.4 | 15.5 | 9.4 |
| Touche Ross | 4.8 | 4.7 | 6.0 |
| Other | 1.6 | 23.3 | 28.9 |
| Total | 100.0 | 100.0 | 100.0 |

Source: Adapted from *The Financial Times*, Thursday, 1 June, 1989.

but the resources, human and equipment, influencing its accessibility transform the service into a concrete offering. A number of simple illustrations, as follows, demonstrate how accessibility is evaluated by customers in comparison with competing offerings:

- location of a bank and its interior;
- means of transportation and their condition;
- exterior of a restaurant and the waiters.

Stressing accessibility isolates direct distribution as just one way of reaching customers:

- insurance vending machines;
- hotel and restaurant franchising.

As with all aspects of marketing it is necessary for the service firm to research the market, identify its target customers very carefully, and aim its products and services at customer needs. For a retailer this means merchandising to meet consumer requirements. As Jaeger, a UK retailer, learned to its cost, it is also essential to select the right city and even the right environment in the city (Exhibit 17.6).

People are very important in service marketing. The administration of human resources is a key way of competing. Most people in a service firm act in a selling capacity; all are engaged in the personal market communication effort of the firm. In such circumstances marketing training, especially in the areas of communications and selling, is essential for success.

As all people in the service firm are engaged in marketing tasks, the firm must recognize the internal marketing task of service firms. The service must be successfully marketed to the people in the firm itself. This helps to avoid the

---

**Exhibit 17.6   Understanding the customer is essential for international retailing success**

---

*Shops miss the mark*

UK stores are keen to enter the German market. But some find it a hard nut to crack. Is the going too rough in the German textile retail market for UK firms? This is the question that arises following Jaeger's recent decision to close its 12 West German outlets. The announcement follows Next's withdrawal after a two-year trial; initially it planned to open around 50 stores.

Joro Hertwig, secretary-general of the Textile Retailers' Association (BTE) is adamant that the "market wind" in Germany does not discriminate against UK companies. If you want to survive and make a profit against 80,000 competitors, he says, "you must adhere to some rules that are not even particular to the German market: know your target group, make your target group recognize you, offer them the right goods in the right fashion at the right time and price. If I want to find critical criteria in which Next and/or Jaeger may have underrated their German engagements, I might say this: perhaps they did not realise that for their kind of commodity the market was saturated before they entered it."

"It would have taken something strikingly different in the shop windows to make buyers cross their thresholds. It would have taken a promotional effort to establish their names with consumers. And it would have taken — even with the strikingly different goods and the promotional campaigns — greater stamina."

The British commercial vice-consul in Dusseldorf, Chris von Massenbach, believes that the different structure of the German textile retail market is not seen clearly enough in the UK, where there are fewer shops specializing in clothing than in West Germany.

What should a retailer do when faced by the stiff competition in the German market? Von Massenbach urges thorough market research, close identification of the target group and merchandise oriented towards the target consumers. However, he also points out that it is essential to select the right city, and the right environment in that city.

In Hamburg, Munich or Dusseldorf, the undisputed fashion centres of Germany, the fashion aspect weights much more heavily than it does in Augsburg or Hanover.

**Source:** *Marketing*, 12 March, 1987, p. 47–9.

---

possibility that the service might fail in its ultimate target markets. The staff are simultaneously the producers and sellers of the service.


# Summary

The unique status of marketing in services offers rich potential for creative new approaches and analysis. Interest in service marketing has reached a considerable height. However, marketing theorists lag far behind, particularly when the international dimension is added to the discussion.

The need for the management of trade-offs to be addressed by marketing scholars has been highlighted. It is regrettable that this has not yet been done to any significant extent as these trade-offs are pertinent to the success of the service firm in international markets. Unless service marketing is perceived by managers to be at least as important as product marketing, opportunities in the international market place will continue to be lost.

The key characteristics of services are as follows:

- intangibility;
- direct contact between supplier and customer;
- customer participates in the production of the service ;
- production and consumption occur simultaneously.

The problems in service marketing which frequently arise are due to the following:

- physical display is impossible;
- patent protection is impossible;
- demonstration gives the service away;
- provision of warranties is difficult;
- packaging is marginal.

In recent years there has been a very considerable growth in the international marketing of services. Many of the motives for international product marketing can be found in services marketing. Most of the growth which has occurred in international services has been concentrated in a few key sectors such as advertising, accounting and financial services.

## Discussion questions

1. A service has been described as any activity or benefit which a supplier offers a customer, which is usually intangible and does not result in the ownership of anything. Discuss.

2. The growth in services internationally has been attributed to changing life styles and a changing world. Do you agree?

3. Why are services more important to the economies of some countries than to others? How reliable are statistics on services in different countries?

4. The problems and approaches to marketing of products and services are similar and there is no need to develop a separate treatment of services. Discuss.

5. For the firm in international markets is there any classification framework for its activities which is more appropriate than others?

6. What market entry options does the services firm have if it wishes to internationalize?

7. There are fewer barriers to international services marketing than to international product marketing . Do you agree?

8. Discuss the recent trends in the internationalization of firms in advertising and financial services businesses.

9. How useful can information technology be in removing constraints on the growth of the international services firm?

# References

Berry, Leonard L. (1980) 'Service marketing is different,' *Business*, May–June, 24–8.

Carman, James and Langeard, Eric (1979) 'Growth strategies for the service firm,' a paper presented to the *Eighth Annual Meeting of the European Academy for Advanced Research in Marketing*, Groningen, The Netherlands, 10–12 April.

Chase, Richard B. (1978) 'Where does the customer fit in a service operation?' *Harvard Business Review*, November–December, **56** (6), 137–42.

Cowell, Donald W. (1984) *The Marketing of Services*, Heinemann, London.

EC Commission (1988) *Seventeenth Report on Competition Policy*, Brussels.

General Agreement on Tariffs and Trade (1989) 'Guidelines for Advertising of Services,' *Business Horizons*, July–August.

Grönroos, Christian (1978) 'A service-orientated approach to the marketing of services'. *European Journal of Marketing*, **12** (8), 588–601.

Grönroos, Christian (1987) 'Developing the service offering — a source of competitive advantage,' *Working Paper 161*, Swedish School of Economics and Business Administration, Helsinki, Finland.

Inman, Robert P. (1985) *Managing the Service Economy, Prospects and Problems*, Cambridge University Press, Cambridge.

Levitt, Theodore (1972) 'Production-line approach to services,' *Harvard Business Review*, September–October, pp. 41–52.

Lovelock, Christopher H. (1983) 'Classifying services to gain strategic marketing insights,' *Journal of Marketing*, **47**, 9–20.

Normann, Richard (1984) *Service Management*, John Wiley & Sons, Chichester.

Ryans, A. and Wittink, D. (1977) 'The marketing of services categorization with implications for strategy,' in Barnett, A. *et al.* (eds.) *Contemporary Marketing Thought*, American Marketing Association, pp. 312–14.

Sasser, W. Earl (1976) 'Match supply and demand in service industries,' *Harvard Business Review*, November–December, pp. 133–40.

Shostack G. Lynn (1977) 'Breaking free from product marketing,' *Journal of Marketing*, April, pp. 73–80.

Staltson, H. (1985) 'US trade policy and international services transactions" in Inman, Robert P. (ed.) *Managing the Service Economy*, Cambridge University Press, Cambridge.

Thomas, Dan R.E. (1978) 'Strategy is different in service business,' *Harvard Business Review*, July–August, pp. 158–65.

Uhl, Kenneth P. and Upah, Gregory D. (1983) 'The marketing of services: Why and how it is different?' *Research in Marketing*, **6**, 231–57.

Winter, Elmer L. (1970) 'How to license a service,' *Columbia Journal of World Business*, September–October, pp. 83–5.

Wilson, Aubrey (1972) *The Marketing of Professional Services*, McGraw-Hill, NY.

# Managing international distribution channels

Though recognized as a subject of study in its own right it is important for the firm to avoid functional myopia by integrating decisions on distribution and channels with other key management decisions. Access to international markets is the key decision area facing companies in the 1990s. Companies which have invested heavily in developing new products and processes will need to seek international markets in which to exploit these developments. Accelerating product life cycles and increasing capital requirements for research and development in many product areas requires rapid international market entry to numerous markets. The ability to maximize the number of markets successfully entered requires the international firm to have access to a highly developed distribution system characterized by co-ordination between marketing and production.

## Nature of international channels of distribution

Definitions of business using the traditional product-market concept ignore the levels of business at which the firm should operate. Donnelly Mirrors, a manufacturer of prismatic rear view mirrors for road vehicles, and supplier to many well-known models, integrated forwards to enter the French market for prismatic mirrors for cars. Rank Xerox and IBM have established retail shops to reach small business customers. There is a trade-off between the increased control and the return gained from vertical integration in international distribution channels compared to the increased risk and loss of flexibility associated with the investment involved in the integrated system.

### Establishing channel relationships

The management of international channels of distribution refers to the myriad relationships which arise in the transfer of products and services from a        461 producer located in one country to a customer located in another. Marketing channels have been defined as "sets of interdependent organizations involved in the process of making a product or service available for use or consumption." (Stern and El-Ansary, 1988) The American Marketing Association defines distribution in a similar vein but uses the more specific phrase "intra-organizational units and extra-company units" instead of "interdependent organizations." (Goldstucker, 1968) In contrast, other writers have focussed on the legal nature of the transaction, concentrating on the movement of the title from manufacturer to user. This approach ignores the use of intermediaries in international channels who facilitate international marketing but who do not take title to the product. It also ignores the whole development of international marketing of services. There are many alternative channels for the firm in international markets to choose from (Kahler, 1983). This static picture has the advantage of identifying the many decision areas which need to be managed (Figure 18.1).

The recurring theme of the many studies which compare international distribution with distribution in the domestic market is that several key factors separate the two. The most "significant" difference between establishing a domestic or international system is the complexity of the variables involved in the choice of "international activities" (Slater, 1978, p. 243). In attempting to manage these issues the firm frequently finds that it must service each foreign market with a different distribution system. Thus, the key success factors which promote profitability in one market may not be transferable to another. Distribution networks in different countries may, however, have much in common so that planning should be based on observed similarities rather than

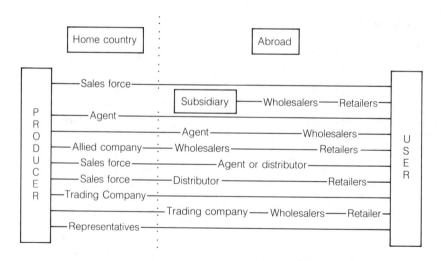

**Figure 18.1**  Selection of international marketing channels (Source: Kahler, Ruel (1983) *International Marketing*, 5th edn., Cincinnati, Ohio. Southwestern Publishing Company, p. 165)

differences (Goldstucker, 1968). Goldstucker argues that the distribution strategy should be modified to suit the country rather than attempting to change it completely. He further argues that culture also exerts an indirect influence on the costs of distribution through its direct effect on the marketing programme.

## Channel management as an interactive process

Much of the early research on channels of distribution has been descriptive and has considered structural issues such as the number and role of wholesalers and retailers in a particular channel. In the 1970s researchers focussed on issues such as the acquisition and use of power, the relationship between power and conflict and the consequences of conflict in the channel (Stern and Reve 1980). More recently, researchers have begun to focus on improved conceptualizations of management problems in distribution channels. By examining channel interactions, Frazier (1983) characterizes channel behaviour as occurring in three interactive processes: the initiation process; the implementation process; and the review process (Figure 18.2). The initiation process focusses on the reasons

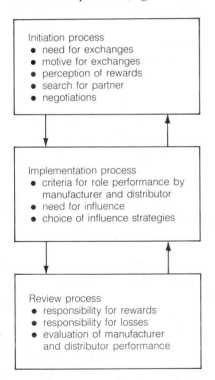

**Figure 18.2**  Interactive processes in channel behaviour (Source: Based on Frazier, G.L. (1983) 'Interorganizational exchange behaviour in marketing channels: A broadened perspective,' *Journal of Marketing*, Fall, 68–78)

why and the methods by which firms establish channel relationships with other firms. Key aspects of this relationship include the need and motive for exchanges, perceptions of deserved rewards, a search for a prospective partner and negotiations (Frazier, 1983). Frazier lists a number of reasons that start the initiation process: replacing an unsatisfactory distributor and adding a new distributor for a market, being the two more important.

The implementation process refers to the way in which independent firms manage and co-ordinate continuing channel relationships. It starts with the exchange of products, services and information in particular. Other aspects of the implementation phase deal with the interaction itself: role performance for the manufacturer and distributor; the need for influence; and the choice of influence strategies.

The review process examines the rewards and losses achieved by each firm in the relationship. The important aspect of such evaluation is the attribution of responsibility for the rewards and losses and a detailed evaluation of managerial performance on both sides.

## Marketing channel design

In designing a marketing channel the firm operates on a number of basic criteria which apply in many circumstances. First the choice of intermediary for manufacturers and the choice of supplier for middlemen is frequently very restricted due to the nature of the business and the size and geographical distribution of customers. To achieve sales volume and scale effects a new manufacturer would probably have to compete for private label business in most marketing situations. Likewise, wholesalers and retailers may find themselves cut off from suppliers because of marketing policies to by-pass such institutions.

Second, the number, size and geographical concentration of customers will have a direct effect on the design of the marketing channel. For industrial products, customers are likely to be few, large and geographically concentrated. Hence, a direct channel design might be appropriate. For consumer products with a diffuse market the opposite may be the case. A cumbersome distribution task calls for the use of intermediaries.

Third, perishable products require direct marketing or the use of intermediaries who can ensure rapid merchandize turnover and protected delivery. Manufacturers and producers of bulky products normally attempt to minimize shipping distance and handling costs, which also implies a direct selling approach. Non-standard products calling for technical expertise in selling require direct selling to allow for specialized attention by or on behalf of the manufacturing company. In contrast, non-perishable, non-bulky, standardized products indicate the use of indirect channels of distribution. Fourth, the characteristics of the environment facing intermediaries, competitors, and the firm itself also influence channel design.

Furniture intermediaries are particularly well adapted to serve manufacturers and customers because of their ability to carry a full line of complementary products assembled from a variety of manufacturers. For shopping goods, comparisons as to style, price, and suitability are important to consumers; therefore, the selection of appropriate channels is dictated, to a large degree, by the need to provide such comparisons.

Having assessed the constraints implied by these four criteria the firm must make two decisions, as follows:

(a)  determine the way in which products and services will be made available to designated user markets;
(b)  determine the number of intermediaries or suppliers the firm in the channel wishes to work with.

## Needs of channel members

Manufacturers and intermediaries in international channels have very different perspectives. It is necessary to achieve a subtle blending of the needs and objectives of all parties in the system: manufacturer; intermediary; and consumer (Proudman 1976, p. 15). These perspectives are manifested in the criteria that each uses to select the other (Figure 18.3).

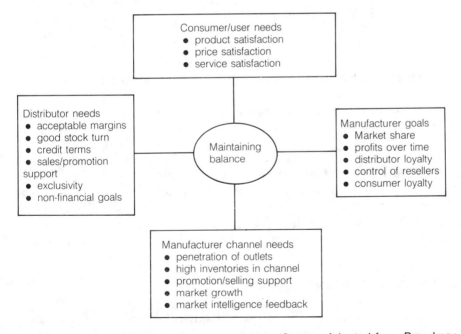

**Figure 18.3**  Balancing channel member needs (Source: Adapted from Proudman, A.J. (1976) 'Distribution channels: Analytical aspects of the marketing system,' *The Quarterly Review of Marketing*, Winter, pp. 8–16)

The factors which are important to the manufacturer in selecting intermediaries usually involve final consumer considerations, company strategic issues and financial returns. The manufacturer usually evaluates potential channel partners on the basis of their contacts and relationships with customers in target markets and their capabilities, reputation and past performance in respect of sales and service. The manufacturer normally checks that the functions provided by the intermediary complement those provided by the manufacturer. In this regard the manufacturer also evaluates the potential contribution of the product or service to the intermediary's needs; profit; contribution; and gaps in product line. Here the manufacturer is attempting to determine the probability of effective long-term working relations. Finally, it is necessary to examine the potential intermediary's financial status and management ability.

Factors which are important to intermediaries in establishing relationships with manufacturers usually involve the manufacturer's product and/or brand image, the support and assistance provided, and the compatibility of the product with the intermediary's existing line. The intermediary is also concerned with the trade reputation of the manufacturer and the potential profit contribution of the product to the intermediary. Sometimes it is difficult for a manufacturer to break into a distribution system for reasons well known only to the intermediary. The manufacturer will be concerned with the anticipated reaction of channel members to the attempted entry by the manufacturer to the channel system. Finally, intermediaries will examine the estimated start up or investment costs closely in adding the new product to the existing business.

## Structure and function in channels of distribution

Distribution channels vary enormously from one country to another on a number of dimensions. Traditions, culture, customs and legal requirements influence both the structure of distribution channels and the functions performed in the system. There are, however, a number of things which are usually common to all channels irrespective of product category or market. Actors in the channel usually include manufacturers, distributors and wholesalers, retailers and consumers. The nature of the activities and their direction is also usually constant (Table 18.1). The activities specified in the right-hand side of this diagram are found in all channels of distribution.

### Structure of distribution channels

In this section the structure of distribution channels for a variety of products in a number of countries is examined to identify similarities and differences. We start by observing distribution channels in the United States. There are three principal import channels in the United States for handbags, travel goods and

**Table 18.1**  Marketing flows in distribution channels

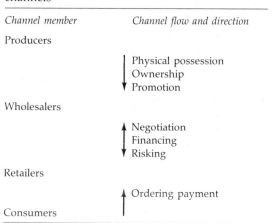

| Channel member | Channel flow and direction |
|---|---|
| Producers | |
| | Physical possession |
| | Ownership |
| | Promotion |
| Wholesalers | |
| | Negotiation |
| | Financing |
| | Risking |
| Retailers | |
| | Ordering payment |
| Consumers | |

small leather goods — specialized importers, manufacturers, and retailers including mail order and catalogue firms, department stores, chain stores and specialty footwear and luggage chains (Figure 18.4).

A very different import channel structure exists for flatware in the United States. Flatware is the term used in the United States to denote cutlery products consisting of knives, forks, spoons and ladles used for eating or serving at table. Approximately 95 per cent of the volume of imported flatware into the United States consists of stainless steel products. The major import channels are distributors, manufacturers, specialized importers and, to a lesser extent,

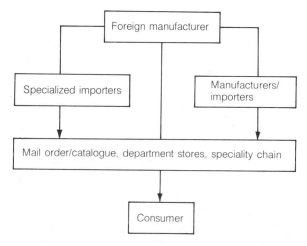

**Figure 18.4**  Distribution channels in the United States for handbags and leather products (Source: International Trade Centre (UNCTAD/GATT) *Monograph on Trade Channels: Handbags, Travel Goods and Small Leather Goods in the United States*, Geneva, 8 June, 1984)

buying groups and discounters (Figure 18.5). There is a very large number of flatware importers in the United States but less than twenty or thirty account for nearly 70 per cent of total imports.

By way of further contrast is the US import market for rattan furniture. Furniture made from rattan includes chairs, tables and occasional pieces, sold in the casual furniture market. The selection of import channels is greatly influenced by the specifications of the product offered: component or finished product; and the target market segment: upper or lower (Figure 18.6). The principal import channels which supply components and semi-finished furniture to the middle and upper market segments are manufacturers and specialized importers. Distributors and retailers supply the lower segment. Department stores and buying groups are less significant.

The European markets and distribution channels differ in many respects from those in the United States. The Belgian distribution channels for sports goods and the Italian channels for carpets serve to illustrate these differences. While Belgium is one of the smallest European markets for sports goods it is nevertheless very important as many of its distributors and manufacturers also sell to the neighbouring markets such as the Netherlands, France and the

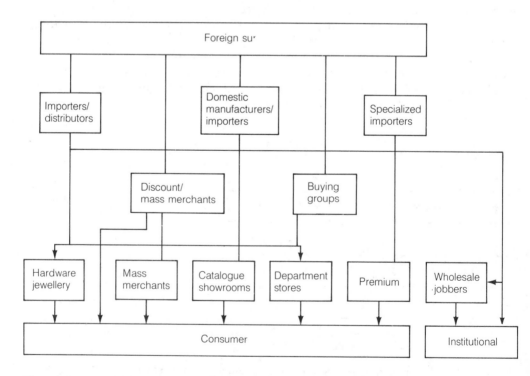

**Figure 18.5**  Distribution channels in the United States for flatware (Source: International Trade Centre (UNCTAD/GATT): *Monograph on Trade Channels: Flatware in the United States of America*, Geneva, 15 February, 1985)

northern part of the Federal Republic of Germany. About 65 per cent of imports of sports goods in Belgium go through distributors. Direct imports by domestic manufacturers such as Donnay SA and Snauwaert and Depla NV account for a further 15 per cent. Department stores, specialized large-scale retailers, mail order forms and discount houses also account for 15 per cent (Figure 18.7). Retail distribution is very fragmented: about 55 per cent of sales are made by a large number of small retailers, some of which are members of a buying cooperative which accounts for 5 per cent of imports.

In contrast, the Belgian market for jewellery is very fragmented: over 80 per cent of retail sales are made by specialized retailers. It is estimated that there are about 2,500 retail jewellery shops in the country. Most retailers are single shop enterprises. Department stores sell less expensive and imitation jewellery in specialized jewellery and accessories departments. Fashion boutiques also sell a small amount of jewellery (Figure 18.8).

Importers and wholesalers in Italy are the channels for 95 per cent of hand-knotted carpets imported. Specialist retailers account for most of the remainder. Between the importers and wholesalers and the final consumers there are a variety of channels of varying significance (Figure 18.9).

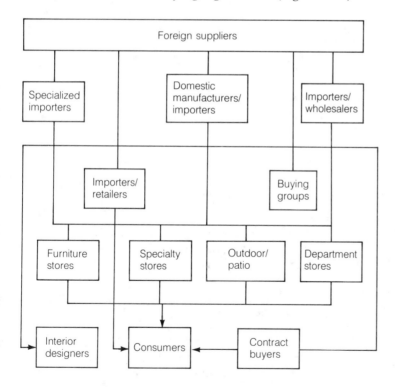

**Figure 18.6**   Distribution channel in the United States for rattan furniture (Source: International Trade Centre (UNCTAD/GATT), *Monograph on Trade Channels: Rattan Furniture in the United States of America*, Geneva, 18 February, 1985)

## Actors in the distribution channel

There are a number of features of distribution channels that the firm must consider. From the examples examined above it is clear that the product group influences the choice, as does the kind of market. The smaller European markets for the specialized products are very different from the large US market. Similarly, the role played by the various type of importer is a key consideration.

## Specialized importer and distributor

The role of the specialized importer in the distribution of handbags and small leather goods in the United States is very important. Because of the physical size of the country, transportation costs are high. The specialized importer exploits the large volume of business and holds large inventories, which allows it to compete successfully. Specialized importers generally work with specialized customers, e.g. the specialized importers of flatware in the United States distribute work in institutional and premium segments of the market. The

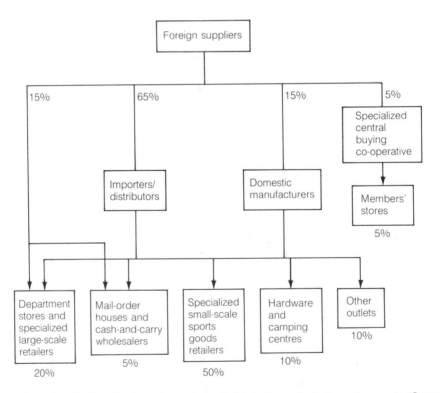

**Figure 18.7** Distribution channels in Belgium for selected sports goods (Source: International Trade Centre (UNCTAD/GATT), *Monograph on Trade Channels: Selected Sports Goods in Belgium*, Geneva, 22 July, 1983)

specialized importer of rattan furniture in the United States generally supplies the middle and more exclusive segments of the market. They import finished furniture of high quality.

In the Belgian import market for sports goods the specialized importers account for about 65 per cent of all imports. They also tend to specialize in equipment and clothing aimed at certain sports. Similarly, specialized importers or wholesalers in Belgium are responsible for over 75 per cent of jewellery imports. These specialized importers sell to specialized retailers who generally only keep a minimum of stock because of the high costs involved. The specialized importers and wholesalers are responsible for almost all the Italian imports of hand-knotted carpets.

Specialized importers, because of their knowledge of the market, frequently influence new product development and design. They often seek exclusive arrangements with the foreign firm.

## Manufacturer as importer

Some major manufacturers also import a complementary range of products to supplement their own product range. This is especially true in the leather goods market in the United States. Similarly, a number of US furniture manufacturers import unfinished rattan components for assembly, finishing and upholstering. Firms in this category dominate the upper market segment for rattan furniture. Domestic manufacturers as importers are also important in the Belgian sports goods market. Manufacturers are not important as importers of jewellery in Belgium or carpets in Italy.

Manufacturers who import pose a potential threat to the foreign supplier.

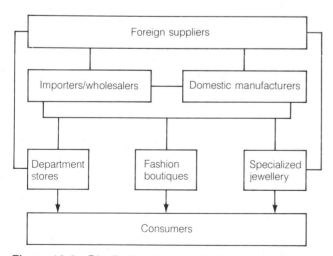

**Figure 18.8** Distribution channels in Belgium for jewellery (Source: International Trade Centre (UNCTAD/GATT), *Monograph on Trade Channels: Jewellery in Belgium*, Geneva, 11 July, 1985)

There is a distinct possibility that future growth could be limited due to the possible conflict of interests between competing products manufactured by the importing manufacturer and those manufactured by the foreign supplier.

## Retailers and importers

Many different types of retailers import directly. The principal types are department stores, specialized retailers, mail order houses and catalogue firms. Department stores are interested primarily in volume business because of the size of their own market and the financial terms involved. Department stores are active in leather goods, handbags in the United States and sports goods and jewellery in Belgium. Mail order houses play a very important role in the distribution of leather goods in the United States. These outlets plan their purchasing requirements up to one year in advance of seasons and make early

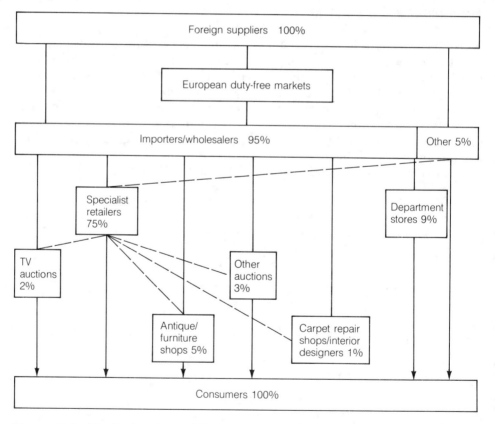

**Figure 18.9** Distribution channels in Italy for hand knotted carpets (Source: International Trade Centre (UNCTAD/GATT), *Monograph on Trade Channels: Hand Knotted Carpets in Italy*, Geneva, 6 June, 1984)

commitments for their requirements. Quality of merchandize and adherence to delivery dates are key factors when supplying to this type of foreign customer.

## Effectiveness of international distributuion channels

In deciding a distribution strategy for international markets or in assessing existing channels the firm must consider the cost of the alternative chosen, the barriers to entry in the market, the orientation of intermediaries, the ability of the channel to distribute the range of the firm's products and the characteristics of the product or service and the customer.

One very effective framework to analyse this situation is based on the Five Cs: coverage; character; continuity; control; and cost (Cateora, 1990). This framework allows the firm to establish its strategic goals with respect to channel management (Table 18.2).

Considerations of market coverage usually refer to the firm's objectives regarding market penetration and market share or merely sales. The firm attempts to find that channel which is optimal in terms of sales and the ability of the channel to service the product or product line.

In most cases the firm is intimately interested in the character or suitability of the channel for its particular product or product line. Occasionally this becomes an issue of whether the intermediary fits the overall positioning strategy for the product. Here concern lies in determining the suitability of the channel in the overall market positioning of the product. The character of the channel addresses the broader aspects of managing the channel.

Distributors frequently change their loyalties depending on the returns they receive. The contribution the intermediary receives is the principal determinant of the continuity of the channel. Small-scale exporters frequently complain of the lack of continuity in international channels.

Generally, control diminishes with the length of the channel. Control may be increased by investing in control systems which send information back to the firm.; it is usually proportional to the capital intensity in the channel. Longer

**Table 18.2**  Analysing channels of distribution: the Five Cs framework

| | |
|---|---|
| Coverage | Ability of channel to reach targeted customers to achieve market share and growth objectives |
| Character | Compatibility of channel with the firm's desired product positioning |
| Continuity | Loyalty of channel to the firm |
| Control | Ability of the firm to control total marketing programme for the product or service |
| Cost | Investment required to establish and maintain the channel — variable associated with sales level. Fixed costs required to manage the channel: inventories, facilities, training of salesforce |

Source: Cateora, Philip (1990) *International Marketing*, 7th edn, Irwin, Homewood, Ill.

distribution channels which are frequently found in developing country markets are typically weak in regard to control.

The firm tries to reduce or optimize the effect of cost. Here the firm is concerned with the capital cost, which refers to the expenditure by the firm on salesforce training, the investment in safety stocks and the initial marketing and distribution costs. These costs are generally fixed or at least periodic. The firm is also concerned with the cost or investment required to develop and maintain the distribution channels. Firms aim to minimize these costs, which are usually variable and associated with the level of sales.

Complicated channel systems which are long and involve margins at each stage are sometimes considered as barriers to entry to the market in question. In other situations multitiered distribution systems which have evolved over many generations make it very difficult for the international firm to penetrate. Sometimes foreign governments claim that such distribution structures prevent trade and are, therefore, a barrier to international competition. Sometimes it is a question of understanding the origins of the system. For many US firms the Japanese distribution system is archaic but is now beginning to be understood (Exhibit 18.1).

## Performance of the marketing channel

There are a variety of ways of improving the performance of distributors. The basic ways of improving general business performance also apply to intermediaries who are profit motivated. As in other parts of business, distributor performance is improved by the prospects of greater profits, less capital investment, fewer user complaints, lower training costs and more repeat business.

Small distributors, like small retailers, may need assistance in accounting, financing and inventory control. Manufacturers who can provide such assistance especially by way of computer software geared at reordering the manufacturer's products, can easily gain a strong competitive advantage in this sector.

The provision of various kinds of information to intermediaries can strengthen the position of the manufacturer. The firm usually tries to ensure the provision of regular information regarding the firm's products, margins, credit terms, and advertising support available. Successful firms provide such information for specific intermediaries or groups of intermediaries on a regional basis.

As a matter of dealing with contingencies, successful firms pay immediate personal attention to distributor grievances in international markets. The R & A Bailey & Company Limited, manufacturers of Baileys Original Irish Cream, recognize that excessive delegation of such tasks is dangerous. For this reason the Dublin based marketing sales executives travel immediately to all major customers on discovery of problems similar to those outlined here. Most firms employ a range of criteria to measure the performance of the marketing channel.

---

**Exhibit 18.1   It is necessary to understand the structure of distribution**

*Selling in Japan gets less befuddling*

Suddenly there is a lull in US-Japanese trade histrionics... But the imbroglio with Japan is bound to heat up again, and near the top of Washington's hit list will be Japan's Byzantine distribution and retailing system, which the US perceives as a structural trade barrier.

Washington says the multitiered system is inefficient, unwieldy, and expensive — and therefore difficult for importers to penetrate. Specifically, the US wants Japan to dismantle a law that limits the number of big stores, which, it says, sell more imports than the mom-and-pop shops the law is designed to protect. One result is that Japan has more than 1.6 million retail outlets. That's one for every 74 Japanese, compared with one for every 144 Americans. Last year the country's largest food retailer was Seven-Eleven Japan Co., a chain of convenience stores run under license from the US's Southland Corp. Then there are Japan's 1 million bars and restaurants — more than three times as many per person as in the US.

These shops and restaurants are usually much smaller than their Western counterparts and contain little, if any, storage space. More than half are independent operators, so they need frequent deliveries in small quantities. Campbell Japan Inc's typical delivery of soup to a retailer is minuscule by US standards: six cans. To wholesalers, Campbell's average shipment is three to five 24 can cases. That and a 19 percent duty help drive the price of a can of tomato soup in Tokyo to $1.45, compared with 39 cents in New York. The Seven-Elevens get same-day delivery of all products on orders placed before 10am and wholesalers of perishable foods make as many as three dropoffs a day.

This has given rise to a maze of 413,000 primary, secondary, and tertiary wholesalers — about half of which employ fewer than five persons. Most products must negotiate this labyrinth before they reach the consumer. Japan will never evolve a distribution system à la US, where plenty of space, a vast highway system, and the prevalence of chains allow most retailers to purchase goods in bulk.

A critical function of the primary distributor, often one of Japan's giant trading companies, is extending credit down the distribution channel to absorb some of the risk of unsold merchandise and business failures. And generous credit means that unsold products can be returned.

Distributors must also be prepared to satisfy the seemingly insatiable demand of the Japanese for premium service — and their willingness to pay for it.

Source: *Business Week*, 30 January, 1989, pp. 16–18.

---

At a minimum marketing channels should provide products/services as follows:

- in desired quantities (lot size);
- when needed (delivery time);
- at different locations (market—decentralization);

- where they are displayed and combined with complementary and substitutable items (assortment breadth) allowing for market demand.

Performance means measuring the outputs of the system against evaluative criteria: lot size; delivery time; market decentralization and assortment breadth. The approach adopted by Texas Instruments (TI) to improve the performance of its distributors is a valuable illustration of the issues just discussed. In the late 1970s TI was the largest manufacturer of semi-conductors sold on the open market. But by the end of 1986, the US firm had fallen behind Japan's Fujitsu and NEC in worldwide sales. According to David Klein, the business development group manager at TI in the United Kingdom, "there was an awareness within the company that our dominant position had led us into thinking that we knew what the customer wanted better than he did." (*Business International*, 31 August, 1987, p. 2) As a consequence, TI responded by changing the role of distributors and by investing in them to achieve a higher performance (Exhibit 18.2).

## The distribution audit

A distribution audit provides the basis for a change of distribution strategy that needs to be revised due to changed circumstances. The distribution audit provides management with details of inefficiencies and early warnings of possible obsolescence of channels. Methods of auditing the marketing channel might include a comparison of net sales to costs incurred in serving it effectively. The analysis would also include an examination of:

- different channels used by each product line;
- costs of maintaining each channel and cost trends;
- sales trends and sales volume of each channel;
- types and numbers of end-users served by each channel;
- number of middlemen involved in each channel;
- degree of control over channels and balance of bargaining power;
- contractual obligations, contract expiry dates, exclusivity rights;
- channels used by main competitors.

The distribution audit must be detailed and periodic to be effective. It requires considerable commitment of management time and resources.

## Integrated international distribution

In Chapter 1 the issue of deciding which activities should be performed by the firm itself and which should be performed by others outside the firm was discussed from the point of view of firm size and growth. Here the same issue is discussed from the point of view of effective control and cost regarding the

**Exhibit 18.2 Responding to the changing role of distributors by investing in them**

*How Texas Instruments is improving distributor performance*

In the late 1970s, TI was the largest manufacturer of semiconductors sold on the open market. But by the end of 1986, the US firm had fallen behind Japan's Fujitsy and NEC in worldwide sales. According to David Klein, the business development group manager at TI's UK headquarters, "There was an awareness within the company that our dominant position had led us into thinking that we knew what the customer wanted better than he did."

Senior TI executives decided that the company's network of independent distributors should play an important part in the company's move to get closer to its customers and respond better to their needs. They realized that the role of distributors in their industry had changed dramatically: whereas in the past distributors had operated primarily as holders of stock, they now have to provide a higher level of technical support if they want to stay ahead of the competition.

Thus, TI committed itself to improving the responsiveness of its distributors. According to Klein, "We wanted our distributors to move toward a technical, pro-active marketing role."

TI's efforts to improve its independent distribution network have concentrated on two objectives:

- increasing the technical knowhow of the independent distributors; and
- encouraging the distributors to better identify new customers and respond to their needs.

Moves to forge closer ties with distributors have included frequent consultations on new product development, product seminars and assistance from TI engineers in designing complex semiconductors and related components... the introduction of the Design Reward Scheme (DRS) in March of this year in order to make it profitable for distributors to work more closely with their customers and increase their level of technical support.

Under the DRS, each distributor recruits a minimum of three engineers to take part in training courses at Texas Instruments' UK R&D centre. Upon completing the course and a series of exams, the participating distributors are awarded an official "TI-approved" status.

Distributors who get this status are rewarded financially under the DRS scheme. The distributors encourage customers to use TI components in their products, and the "TI-approved" engineers assist in designing the components and providing any necessary technical support. The distributor in turn receives a higher profit margin on the sale.

TI's Klein believes that there are a number of important benefits of the DRS:

- The technical ability of the distributors is greatly improved

- The distributors have more motivation to increase technical support
- Customers are more assured about the distributor when they know that he has been certified by TI
- TI receives more regular and accurate information about customer needs
- TI engineers have more time to spend on a major direct-sales projects

David Klein believes that the DRS will increase TI's market share by more than 50 percent by 1990. There is little doubt that TI is pleased with the scheme's success so far: "The DRS was designed to give us the edge over other manufacturers in a very competitive market, and it is proving very successful."

**Source:** *Business International/Ideas in Action*, 31 August, 1987, pp. 2–4.

---

international channel. Internalizing international distribution within the firm gives rise to a trade-off between cost and control. Some firms, especially strong brand companies, insist on owning their international distributors where possible. This is the policy followed to ensure complete control of brand positioning in each international market. The choice of approach can be interpreted as a transactions costs problem (Ruekert, Walker and Roering, 1985). The balance of control and cost evaluated in terms of transactions costs determines whether international distribution should take place through subsidiaries of the firm or through independent distributors.

In calculating the transactions costs the firm also examines many other factors. Integration offers the benefit of having a captive outlet in each international market entered. Such extensive control implies the commitment of a lot of resources, which means that failure is thereby much more expensive. In contrast, the use of an independent distributor implies specialization and the associated benefits. The ready-made access to markets means that learning costs are low and entry is quickly and effectively expedited.

As already mentioned, the value of independent distributors in regard to channel loyalty and control of the marketing programme is questionable. Benetton, an Italian knitwear manufacturer, believes in distributing its products through its own agents wherever possible. This has allowed the firm to standardize its promotions and distribution: inventories; type of outlet; shipment; types and sizes. Sometimes, success depends on combining two moves at the same time. Hiram Walker, a whisky firm, whose principal brand is Ballantine's, combined advertising and distribution decisions to achieve the desired effect. Success in the US market for the Ballantine brand depended on good advertising and the use of the best distributors available (Exhibit 18.3).

Firms are sometimes advised to use independent distributors if the market is competitive. Other influencing factors include the cost of monitoring the performance of the intermediary, the stage of the life cycle for the product and the degree of standardization applied to the marketing programme. Integration

---

**Exhibit 18.3   Improved distribution and advertising for better market performance**

---

### Brands that scotched market problems

While the whisky market as a whole has been declining, not all manufacturers have suffered. Hiram Walker's main brand is Ballantine's, which has doubled its sales in the premium standard market in the past ten years.

Not being a big player in the US helped Ballantine's cause. In Japan it is the fourth largest and managed to maintain sales while the competition was losing out.

Brand development manager Richard Pudderphatt puts the success down to two main factors, advertising policy and the distributors. "We probably use the best liquor distributors in each market, so they normally have a good portfolio of drinks", he says.

Hiram Walker also uses a network of 25 area managers around the world who work for the company rather than the distributor. "They're mostly local people in the culture of that market, and they eat sleep and think the market, and get a smell of what's going on", adds Puddephatt. "They act as a link between the distributor and ourselves."

Ballantine's was also one of the first whiskies to be supported by lifestyle advertising, in the early 70s. "We are using aspirational lifestyle situations to go for the 25 to 30-year-old younger consumer, to establish a longer-term franchise", says Puddephatt.

**Source:** *Marketing*, 15 January, 1987, p. 24.

---

of services within the firm is more likely for US firms where the market entered is culturally similar, where the firm's product is innovative or highly differentiated, where the salesforce is specialized and where the firm wishes to control the marketing of its products closely (Anderson and Coughlan, 1987). In a study of ninety-four US overseas distributors these authors also found that the initial channel choice was very influential on all subsequent decisions.

Occasionally a firm may choose a dual strategy of distributing through its own distributors and through an independent company. This allows the market to be differentiated into two or more segments to be served differently. Problems sometimes arise if there is a delay in production or supply is limited for a period. In such circumstances integrated distributors tend to be favoured. The oil industry in the 1970s is an example of this situation: the major oil companies favoured their own outlets over independents when supplies were short.

A major issue in managing international channels of distribution is the degree to which they are susceptible to change and innovation. The highest level of innovation in marketing channels appears to arise in channels which are partially integrated. See Arndt and Reve, 1979. These authors, in a review of theoretical and empirical literature, found a U-shaped relationship between innovativeness and the degree of vertical integration in the distribution channel: intermediate levels of vertical integration may be the most congenial to innovativeness and adaptability (Arndt and Reve, 1979, p. 233). The hypothesis remains to be tested empirically.

Innovation may also arise in independent distribution systems. Creation of a completely new channel can lead to the firm obtaining a sustainable competitive advantage. The introduction by L'eggs Hosiery of its uniquely packaged hosiery, in (plastic egg-like containers) in supermarkets while competitors relied on conventional channels, e.g. department stores, is a good example of a firm exploiting a new distribution channel. L'eggs solved many supermarket problems: ordering and stocking; selling on consignment a product relatively difficult to shoplift; using space efficient vertical displays; and providing a high-quality low-priced product supported by heavy advertising. This is a difficult combination to beat.

## Conflict and control in international channels of distribution

Conflict in distribution channels arises when inter-organizational management breaks down. Cooperation is an essential ingredient of distribution because of the multiplicity of firms, many of which are usually independent decision makers and not under common ownership. The situation is complicated by culture, distance, legal factors and different business practices in international markets.

The exchange of assets in a marketing channel requires the specification of role relationship for each channel member. The ensuing inter-dependency may give rise to conflict, and the subsequent use of power. In such circumstances it is necessary to recognize that an inter-relation exists among role specification, conflict, use of power, conflict management, and channel performance.

### Cooperation in the marketing channel

Functional inter-dependence in the marketing channel requires a certain minimum level of cooperation to accomplish the channel task. Because of the complexity and number of levels in international distribution the issue of cooperation is even more crucial. It is especially true in international markets that firms seek to be autonomous. This is frequently supported by local government policies which attempt to prevent foreign ownership of too many local firms. The firms themselves seek to maintain a degree of interdependence while also attempting to link with other firms in the system. Hence, a mixture of cooperative and autonomous motives exists in firms. This mixture sometimes leads to conflict.

Channel conflict arises when one channel member perceives another to be impeding the achievement of its goals. The frustration arises from a restriction of role performance. There are three sources for such conflict. First, incompatible goals or objectives are frequently found between large manufacturers and small retailers. Second, domain conflict may be found in situations where manufacturers compete with some of their wholesalers. Third, different perceptions of reality arise when there are incongruent perceptions of reality attributable to technical communication problems. This gives rise to different bases for action in response to the same situation.

Some conflict in the channel is manageable but coping with too much is difficult. If conflict becomes destructive, i.e. pathological moves are made which impede the performance of the conflicting parties and the system itself, then the channel system is likely to disintegrate, even though channel objectives are attained in the short run. But channel conflict is highly positive so long as it does not pass the malignant threshold and impair the output of the system. Conflict at the functional end of the continuum strengthens the system and creates bonds for growth.

## Specifying channel tasks

By clearly specifying channel roles, cooperating firms in the marketing channel can reduce the potential for conflict and improve the situation of the channel system in its entirety. Roles define appropriate behaviour for firms occupying each position in the system: the firm selects a channel position which is a function of its goals, expectations, values and frame of reference. For example, a 20 per cent return or investment objective may suggest manufacturing as a more attractive position than, say, retailing.

Role prescriptions are determined by the norms the channel members set for each other; they indicate what each member desires from all channel members, including itself, relative to their respective degree of participation in the channel marketing functions. Role consensus enables channel members to anticipate the behaviour of others and to operate collectively in a unified manner.

Power may be used to achieve effective role congruence and performance and to keep conflict within the functional range. Power is the ability of one channel member to get another to do what the latter would not otherwise have done. It is important that the firm knows where power lies in the channel and is able to note changes in its location over time. In some industries there is evidence that power lies at a particular location. It is generally accepted, for example, that retailers possess the power in the apparel and furniture industries. In alcoholic beverages, cars, some appliances, especially washing machines, and microwave ovens, manufacturers have established brand names and greater relative power. Firms discover that it is strategically wise to avoid channels with undesirable power balances. Changes in power structure can have strategic implications: legislation for generic drugs shifted power to retail pharmacies.

## Using power in distribution channels

Firms use power in bargaining. Firms make commitments and concessions, provide rewards, make threats and sometimes compromise all part of a strategy to manage conflict. Channel leadership is often based on power relationships. One of the primary functions of the channel leader is to provide leadership. Channel leaders use power to co-ordinate and to specify and implement channel synergy. Power is correlated with asymmetrical dependence believed to arise from five source (Table 18.3).

Rewards refer to the belief by one firm that the second has the ability to mediate rewards for it, e.g. wider margins, promotional allowances in fast moving consumer products. Coercion refers to the belief that punishment will ensue if the firm fails to conform, e.g. margin reduction, slowing shipments, reduced territory rights. Frequently, manufacturers squeeze the margins of intermediaries who are not performing well. New agents are appointed to cover markets poorly served by established agents.

Expertise refers to the firm's perception that another possesses special knowledge, e.g. manufacturers providing managerial training for marketing intermediaries or detailed technical manuals for the salesforce of sophisticated industrial or medical product are examples of this form of power. As in human relations it is believed that firms sometimes wish to identify with other firms. The attraction of being associated with the other may stem from the worldwide reputation of the other firm or its well-known brands in particular markets. This

**Table 18.3** Sources of power in distribution channels

Rewards
- wider margins
- promotional allowances

Coercion
- reduced margins
- slow deliveries
- restricted market coverage

Expertise
- training for intermediaries
- manuals for salesforce

Referent
- affiliation and association

Legitimacy
- value system

is referent power in that the responding firm expects that the benefits of the association will have positive and important effects in the local market. The power of legitimacy stems from values internalized by one firm which produce the feeling that another firm has a right to exert influence and that the first firm has an obligation to accept it.

## Control of distribution channels

The ability of the firm to control its intermediaries internationally is a key part of any distribution strategy. Control in particular is an issue where the channel used is independent rather than integrated. Channel control is characterized by the degree of congruence between distributor goals and those of the supplier, the amount, and relevance, of market information feedback from the channel and whether the distributor conforms to certain standards determined by the supplier (Exhibit 18.4).

Smaller firms have particular problems in this area and often find that they must trade-off control with the cost of that control. One example is Alltech Biotechnology, a Kentucky-based biotechnology firm, whose rapid expansion within the US market led it to consider international markets only three years after its creation. Because it was small, and had few resources, the company's desire to exploit as many markets as possible was limited and it was forced to use independent agents, whereas it would ideally have chosen to use an internal distribution network. In order to control these agents the company tries to form a special relationship with them. Where the agent doesn't work closely with Alltech the agent is dropped.

Channel control is affected by whom the firm sees as the immediate customer, the intermediary or the final customer and user, and whether the firm takes a passive or an active interest in the international market.

Many authors have attempted to explain sources of power and the emergence of leaders within international channels of distribution. One author argues that channel leaders emerge when the environment is threatening (Etgar, 1977). These threats arise from the following:

- product-service demand characteristics;
- technology used and the risk of obsolescence;
- level of channel competition for space;
- need for control.

Successful firms use a variety of sources of power in controlling channel relationships. IBM's package of hardware and software allows it to avoid the cyclical problems experienced by other computer firms. The firm's leadership in technology has allowed IBM to dominate the channels of distribution internationally. Seiko used independent distributors when entering the US market, but made sure that these were exclusive deals, bringing a higher degree of trust and loyalty to the contract. This loyalty gave the company more market

## Exhibit 18.4   Linking marketing, manufacturing and distribution

### Benetton's hi-tech direct link to the consumer

Benetton owes its rapid rise to a handful of effective innovations...

Benetton is one of the few companies to have devised a formula that allows it to achieve "both variety and efficiency" in a market that is "a notorious headache for department stores and is littered with failed boutiques and speciality chains."

The company has installed state-of-the-art communications, manufacturing and distribution technology to give it flexibility and speed in adapting to market trends. Production is keyed to orders from its shops. Using advanced telecommunications, Benetton receives data on sales trends around the world 24 hours a day, every day of the year.

Manufacturing is heavily computerised, from the cutting of fabric to the assembly of the garments. "If everyone decided to wear nothing but hats tomorrow, we'd be ready to produce 50 million hats within a week", quips finance director Gilardi.

The group's network of shops has been another key element in its success. They are almost exclusively franchised to hasten the group's expansion and to keep the financial exposure to a minimum; but they differ significantly from most franchises. To avoid the usual quality problems, they are fully owned by carefully screened entrepreneurs.

The shop owners must follow a set of strict merchandising rules. For example, Benetton window displays are generally placed closer to the glass and include only two or three colours, so that they are immediately obvious... the franchises do provide Benetton with a captive distribution network without financial commitment, without expensive staff, and without the necessity to oversee day-to-day performance.

Benetton's integrated, high-tech production, distribution, sales and communication system has effectively removed much of the "fashion risk" from its business. In fact, the company's rather conservative styling policy ensures that it rarely sets a fashion trend, and rarely misses one.

**Source:** *International Management*, November, 1987, pp. 29–30.

control and ensured that the product was well represented in a highly competitive market.

Sears Roebuck in the United States developed "sole agreements" with its suppliers where it became the only purchaser of a particular supplier's products. This gives suppliers a steady source of demand in competitive markets but they also can become subject to coercive power plays which control their margins and products.

Any examination of channel control raises the question of bargaining power. The power structure in a channel requires a channel member to compare profits which it earns with its ability to tolerate restrictions on its activities

(Bucklin, 1973). Bucklin concluded that conflict arises when profits fall or when a channel member's stake falls low enough for it to reconsider the equity of the balance of power. This is the result of competition.

Legal restrictions have limited the effect that companies have on their intermediaries. Traditional use of penalties and rewards has become more difficult as anti-trust legislation restricts a firm's actions. Companies may still consider the options for control in terms of persuasion, authority, and coercion (Bucklin, 1973).

While the power of a company to influence the actions of its agents or intermediaries is primarily a function of its power sources and the dependence of the agent on the firm, a third factor must be considered; the intermediary's countervailing power. According to Etgar (1977) countervailing power is believed to arise from the following:

- customer loyalty;
- intermediary's volume;
- acquisitions of other intermediaries;
- advertising sales ratio; and
- the strength of an intermediary's associations.

If strong countervailing powers exist in an international channel, then a distributor will find that monetary rewards and threats will be more effective than the use of non-monetary reward systems (Etgar, 1977). In practical terms this means that the acceptance of controls will be easier where an exchange relationship exists, i.e. the intermediary accepts controls in return for a high level of service.

The question of conflict in the channel has been examined by Rosson and Ford (1980), who found that there was strong empirical support for the hypothesis that low levels of conflict are associated with high performance in the channel. Less support was found for the notion that conflict was linked to the stake of the intermediary.

## *Leadership in international distribution channels*

In many situations the imposition of rigid controls as a way of improving the control of the international channel is a weak solution. Likewise, developing a strategy for distribution which appears to provide a solution often fails because in distribution the firm is usually dealing with independent firms. Their interdependence, however, sometimes allows leadership to surface. Leadership is necessary to provide direction which also allows a degree of control. Much of the literature on leadership deals with managerial leadership within the firm, which is linked to corporate culture. The literature on strategy discusses the issue of price leaders, cost leaders and industry leaders who provide control in their industries.

It is much more difficult, however, to exercise such control in international markets, particularly among distributors that operate in their own country, on the basis of their own business traditions and practices. These ways of doing business may have been in operation for many years and may in some countries have obtained a high degree of legal protection. Within such constraints, however, firms do attempt to exercise leadership in international distribution channels. Successful firms recognize that they cannot simply transfer the approach used by one market into another market.

The relationship and trust between independent firms appears to have an over-riding influence on the leadership issue. In a 1980 study of manufacturers and their foreign distributors, three features characterized the better relationships (Rosson and Ford, 1980). First, little attempt was made by the manufacturer to establish the roles of foreign distributors. These were allowed to evolve depending on the needs of the market. Second, strategic market decisions become a joint endeavour between the manufacturer and the distributor rather than being imposed by one party or the other. Third, as found in most successful international business, a high degree of personal contact between manufacturer and distributor was established and maintained.

## Innovation in international channels of distribution

### Innovation in marketing channels

Channel innovation is the discovery of a new type of intermediary to use in distributing the firm's products or services. Innovation may be the result of the following:

- changing technology which allows a firm to use a type of intermediary previously unavailable;
- legislation allowing the creation of a certain type of intermediary; and
- experimentation with previously untried types of intermediary by the exporter.

The advent of satellite television has allowed the marketing of products for many markets simultaneously. In the EC this has allowed firms to market their products through advertising or "shopping programmes" which can reach customers throughout Europe. This differs from marketing through similar media, such as magazines for an EC market, since the product may be demonstrated visually.

Timex watches were distributed in the United States through discount stores, rather than through the conventional jewellers. The other elements of the marketing programme employed at this location also differed from those that would have been used in a "watch" shop: watches were priced considerably below competitor prices; the watches were sold in a standard display often placed beside the cashier's desk; and the watches sold were standardized. Unconventional approaches to distribution have also occurred in other industries. Austin Rover, the UK car manufacturer, used an unusual approach to strengthen its position in the Federal Republic of Germany: a combination of a mass marketing approach through a hypermarket with a comprehensive system of workshops and service units (Exhibit 18.5).

The channel structure is also affected by the societal and behavioural traits of the market. The uniqueness of international distribution patterns derives less from the structural alternatives, i.e. the possible set of middlemen to choose from than from the infinite range of operational and marketing variables which affect channel decisions (Cateora, 1990).

Strategic marketing demands that the firm examines whether the innovative distribution strategy is really more competitive than that of the other firms in the market. There is no point in pursuing an innovative strategy as an end in itself! Often a firm cannot employ an innovative distribution strategy, since the inertia of the channel is too difficult to overcome. Czinkota's description of the distribution of consumer products in Japan shows that not only do foreign companies have to "accept a degree of tolerated inefficiency" by providing a service which is higher than a cost–benefit analysis would allow, but they are often expected to provide a level of service which exceeds that given by local manufacturers (Czinkota, 1985).

## International direct distribution

Four sets of factors influence the firm's decision regarding direct distribution: the resources of the firm; the characteristics of the product or service; the market segments served; and the marketing programme developed by the firm.

In regard to the first factor, successful direct distribution presumes that the firm has sufficient resources available to support a direct marketing approach, e.g. establishment of a sales force. It is also necessary that the firm already possesses experience in the marketing of similar products to comparable market targets, i.e. that direct channels exist. There must also be sufficient time available to develop direct distribution before potential competition becomes a threat, e.g. patent protection.

Direct distribution is likely to be possible where the manufacturer's personnel are required to sell and service the product or service because of its complexity, e.g. computer sales and service.

Width of product line sufficient to support a direct marketing approach is another concern, e.g. Avon, Tupperware. In situations where product application assistance is required, direct distribution may be appropriate, e.g. steam turbines. Finally when product technology is changing rapidly, direct distribution may be favoured, e.g. computer turnkey services.

The direct distribution decision is also influenced by the nature of the market segments served. Market segments with relatively few customers, where the unit purchase is large in terms of quantity or price and where customers are concentrated geographically, tend to favour direct distribution. There must also be a sufficient margin to support personal selling or frequent mail shots. Finally, when the purchase decision is a major long-term commitment by the buyer, direct distribution may be an attractive proposition.

The marketing programme developed by the firm influences the decision

---

**Exhibit 18.5   Market relaunch through innovative distribution and after-sales service**

---

*Austin Rover links with retailer to break open German market*

In an attempt to double its sales in the notoriously difficult German car market, Austin Rover Deutschland GmbH (ARD, a wholly owned subsidiary of BL, the state-owned UK automaker) has decided to ignore conventional wisdom and sell through the huge Massa hypermarket chain.

Austin Rover is no newcomer to the German market. In a country, however, famed for the quality of its auto industry and preference for domestically produced cars, ARD has suffered from the "poor quality label" that became synonymous with UK-made products. Eight years ago it had a network of between 500 and 600 dealers. Today the number has dwindled to around 200, and in 1983 sales of the combined Austin and Rover lines totalled a mere 4,014; 0.15% of the market.

"It was obvious that something dramatic had to be done", explains Huw Jones, recently appointed managing director of ARD. "To capitalize on the Europewide success achieved by Austin Rover with the Metro and Maestro models, we knew we would have to rapidly renovate our image and revamp our distribution system. We needed an explosive, rather than an evolutionary approach."

An important element in ARD's decision to award Massa the franchise was the retailer's willingness to build separate showrooms and workshops on its hypermarket sites. The cars will not be sold within the hypermarkets, and the 22 outlets will function as full-fledged individual dealers. They will carry spare parts and offer warranty and maintenance services, each signing its own contract with ARD. In return, ARD will assist with sales seminars and technical training on the range of cars to be sold.

It is this comprehensive after-sales service, missing from the existing dealer network, which ARD believes will end customer dissatisfaction. As Jones points out: "People feel safer buying from a big name place. Massa cannot run away or suddenly close tomorrow. It has its reputation to think about and will therefore provide a very high standard of service to customers buying Austin cars."

Although the first Massa outlets opened only in November 1984, ARD as a whole already appears to be tasting success: in the first seven months of 1984, the company sold more cars than in the whole of the previous year. As the Massa dealership begin to make their presence felt, ARD looks likely to succeed its target of doubling sales in 1985.

**Source:** *Business Europe*, 18 January, 1985, pp. 17–18.

to distribute directly. It is favoured where personal selling is a major component in the marketing programme and where intermediary functions are not needed, e.g. storage, local credit inventory, and packaging. Where these services can be efficiently provided by the manufacturer, direct distribution may also be favoured. In most distribution channels there is a series of direct distribution relationships which characterize the situation described. The extensive set of direct relationships which exist in the distribution of rattan furniture are shown below in Figure 18.10.

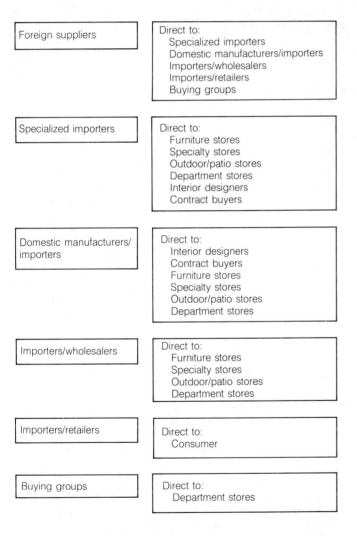

**Figure 18.10**  Direct marketing in distribution channels (Source: Adapted from International Trade Centre (UNCTAD/GATT) *Monograph on Trade Channels: Rattan Furniture in the United States of America*, Geneva, 18 February, 1985)

## Summary

Access to international markets is one of the key areas of management in the 1990s. Gaining and holding access to markets relies heavily on good distribution channel management, which must be seen as an interactive process between manufacturer and the intermediary who may dominate the path to the final consumer. The relationship is further complicated in international markets where different historical developments give rise to different distribution structures. The first task facing the firm in international markets is to understand the distribution channel for its products and services. This means understanding the needs of channel members as well as the needs of final users or consumers.

Increasingly firms are paying close attention to ensuring that channels perform according to objectives. Agreements between manufacturer and distributor will involve a range of factors including physical performance criteria related to the sale of the product or service and financial criteria related to profits and return on investment. Because objectives may be different at different stages in the distribution channel, conflict between the members can arise. The resolution of conflict requires one or a sub-set of channel members to use power to bring about inter-organizational harmony for the good of the entire channel. Specifying channel roles in advance can minimize channel conflict. It is not an easy task, however. The large consumer brand companies pay very close attention to control in distribution channels. The primary objective of this interest is in maintaining the position of their brand in the market. Frequently they go to the extreme of buying up their distribution partners to ensure this control.

By combining with other elements in the marketing programme firms can be very successful in innovating in the channel of distribution. A number of examples of innovations in international distribution channels are outlined in the chapter.

## Discussion questions

1. What is meant by a marketing channel? Describe the differences which exist between domestic and international channels of distribution.

2. What criteria should the firm apply when selecting channels of distribution?

3. Explain why different countries have different channel structures.

4. A number of examples of distribution channels were outlined in the text. What are their common elements? How are they different?

5. How can the firm motivate channel members?

6. Discuss the need for control and market coverage in selecting and managing a distribution channel.

7. Why does channel conflict occur? Is conflict more likely to occur in international marketing?

8. What role has innovation in international channel management? How can a firm maintain or gain market share by innovating in the channel of distribution?

# References

Anderson, E. and Coughlan, Ann T. (1987) 'International market entry and expansion via independent or integrated channels of distribution,' *Journal of Marketing*, **51**, 71–82.

Arndt, Johan and Reve, Torger Reve (1979) 'Innovativeness in vertical marketing systems,' in Fisk, George, Nasson, Robert W. and White, Philip D. (eds.) *Proceedings, Fourth Macromarketing Seminar*, Graduate School of Business Administration, University of Colorado, Colorado, pp. 223–37.

Bucklin, L.P. (1973) 'A theory of channel control,' *Journal of Marketing*, **37**, 39–47.

Cateora, Philip R. (1990) *International Marketing*, 7th edn, Irwin, Homewood, Ill.

Czinkota, Michael (1985) 'Distribution of consumer products in Japan,' *International Marketing Review*, **2** (3), 39–51.

Etgar, Michael (1977) 'Channel environment and channel leadership,' *Journal of Marketing Research*, **14**, 69–76.

Frazier, G.L. (1983) 'Interorganisational exchange behaviour in marketing channels: A broadened perspective,' *Journal of Marketing*, Fall, pp. 68–78.

Goldstucker, J.L. (1968) 'The influence of culture on channels of distribution,' *AMA Proceedings*, **28**, 468–73.

International Trade Centre (UNCTAD/GATT). *Monographs on Trade Channels*, Geneva, various issues.

Kahler, Ruel (1983) *International Marketing*, 5th edn, Southwestern Publishing Company, Cincinnati, Ohio.

Proudman, A.J. (1976) 'Distribution channels: Analytical aspects of the marketing system,' *The Quarterly Journal of Marketing*, Winter, pp. 8–18.

Rosson, Ph.J. and Ford, I.D. (1980) 'Stake conflict and performance in export marketing channels,' *Management International Review*, **20** (4), 31–7.

Ruekert, Robert, W. Orville and Roering, Kenneth (1985) 'The organisation of marketing activities: A contingency theory of structure and performance,' *Journal of Marketing*, **49**, 13–25 .

Slater, A.G. (1978) 'International logistics strategies,' *International Journal of Physical Distribution and Materials Management*, **8** (4), 228–44.

Stern, Louis W. and Reve, Torger (1980) 'Distribution channels as political economies: A framework for comparative analysis,' *Journal of Marketing*, Summer, pp. 52–64.

Stern, Louis W. and El-Ansary, Adel (1988) *Marketing Channels*, 3rd edn, Prentice-Hall, Englewood Cliffs, NJ.

# Implementing the international marketing programme

# Selling and negotiating in international markets

Marketing strategy is implemented through the salesforce, which is key to the growth and survival of the firm since it is the salesforce which directly interacts with customers in the market and becomes the eyes and ears of the company. In international markets, the salesforce must work with an additional constraint. In most circumstances, communication, especially through personal selling, is more difficult due to differing cultures and language and the interaction between the familiar and unfamiliar.

The role of the salesforce is emphasized since personal selling is a key function in most firms that are actively involved in international markets. In international marketing most marketing exchanges are between firms. The supplying firm in one market deals directly with a purchasing firm in another market but only indirectly with the consumer market. The strategy is one of pushing products and services down through the channel from producer to agent or intermediary or industrial user. Rarely does the international firm sell directly to the consumer mass market internationally. Frequently, it sells directly to industrial users. Hence, much of the emphasis on personal selling in this chapter applies to international business-to-business marketing.

## Marketing exchange through selling and negotiating

Marketing exchanges which occur internationally refer to the transfer of a wide range of assets including products, services, ideas, information, and myriad marketing agreements which arise in exporting, competitive alliances and foreign direct investment. The marketing exchange involves at least two parties, in this chapter referred to as the buyer and seller for convenience. Also for the sake of convenience the exchange of assets is referred to as buying and selling but at all stages it is recognized that a wide range of activities is involved in the process.

495

## Nature of marketing exchanges

Marketing exchanges are events and processes which arise between two or more parties which may be organizations, firms or individuals. Behind every marketing exchange is a network of individuals and groups who contribute in various ways to its implementation. In a marketing exchange we are concerned with the transfer of assets which may consist of products, services, ideas, information or rewards associated with the transfer of industrial and consumer products, licensing and joint venture agreements, distribution and agency agreements and information. Marketing exchanges are central to marketing as they represent the point of convergence of the selling process and the buying process.

In marketing exchanges concern rests with transactions involving the products of the exchange which include products, services, ideas and information and relationships. Concern also involves understanding the process of exchange including personal selling, marketing negotiations and managing the resulting relationships. The selling and buying firms are linked through these products and processes (Figure 19.1).

## Changing role of the salesforce

Marketing is an interactive function in the firm. The traditional emphasis on selling and purchasing as separate processes, often in conflict, is an inaccurate reflection of the task facing the firm.

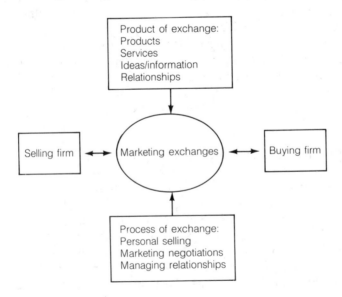

**Figure 19.1**  Nature of marketing exchange

Marketing as interaction in the systems exchange framework allows the company to embrace the resources of supplier and customer organizations to achieve mutually beneficial targets. The interaction perspective treats the development of relationships with other organizations as a necessary condition for the effective harnessing of resources across organizations.

These relationships are established through the negotiation process. For the purposes of this chapter negotiation situations are confined to those where buyers and sellers attempt to settle the basis of their future behaviour across national and cultural boundaries without the intervention of third parties. As was seen in Chapter 5, cultural boundaries include micro cultures, e.g. corporate philosophies and styles, and macro cultures, e.g. national, political and linguistic frameworks. It is argued that these cultural boundaries act as barriers to communication between the firm and its international customers.

A permanent presence in a foreign country requires a greater knowledge of both the national culture and the micro culture of individual firms and organizations. Where the stage of growth in international markets relies on the use of intermediaries, knowledge at the national culture level probably suffices but may be limiting. However, for the high-technology and high-value capital products manufacturer whose specialist marketing people deal with a few customers in each of a number of countries, a knowledge of the micro culture at company level may be essential.

Many companies are beginning to give the salesforce more marketing autonomy. A rapidly changing marketing environment, especially in Europe, is allowing firms to reassess the role of the salesforce. In many instances firms are reorganizing to give marketing autonomy to the product-market salesforce. This shift to a new organization form has broadened the role of the salesforce. From calling on distributors, retailers, industrial users and their customers the salesforce is now spending more time meeting country-based agency creative directors and media buyers to develop local advertising campaigns. The converted salesforce is better able to obtain good deals locally which result in more effective marketing. The salesforce by its nature can move quickly to respond to local conditions. In such circumstances the role of the salesforce is changing from concentrating on discrete marketing exchanges to the development of broad-based marketing relationships requiring sophisticated negotiation skills.

In marketing, the salesforce is given a focal position in the implementation of strategy. It negotiates relationships with its counterparts in customer firms and with their constituents and influencers. It seeks information about the needs and preferences of customers prior to formal negotiations. Sales people employ skills to elicit information in the course of a negotiation. This information is valuable in determining the source and location of power in the marketing relationship being established.

Marketing is concerned with exchange activities and the manner in which the terms of such exchange are established. We distinguish between discrete exchanges where only weak relationships are established between the parties, and negotiated exchanges where buyers and sellers are actively involved in a process which may result in the formation of longer lasting and deeper marketing relationships.

Negotiation has been defined as

> any sequence of written and or verbal communication processes whereby parties to both common and conflicting commercial interests and of differing cultural backgrounds consider the form of any joint action they might take in pursuit of their individual objectives which will define or redefine the terms of their interdependence (McCall and Warrington, 1989, p. 15).

Negotiations have a number of distinguishing features. At least two parties are involved and there is usually a conflict of interests. Buyers and sellers, however, come together in a voluntary relationship concerned with the exchange of tangible and intangible assets. The negotiations process is a sequence of activities involving the presentation of demands by one or both parties, their evaluation, possible concessions and counter proposals, closing with an agreement which, in an ideal situation, benefits both parties.

## Convergence of buying and selling

Individuals, companies and organizations are constantly seeking solutions to various problems which can only be solved by becoming involved in the buying and selling process. Potential buyers must search for information and they try to keep this search as simple as possible. Sellers are rarely passive in such circumstances. They frequently intervene with information to assist the buyer. The search is influenced by the background of the buyer and by a host of other intervening factors including the role of the potential seller. Motivated by the need to reduce uncertainty or to avoid conflict, companies and organizations frequently seek satisfactory solutions rather than optimal solutions. Individual buyers may seek optimal solutions in their buying. The interaction between buying and selling is acknowledged by firms that recognize the convergence of buying and selling processes to provide a solution.

## Identifying the buying process

The anatomy of the buying process consists of five discrete phases (Figure 19.2). First, buyers must recognize the need to buy: Stage One. At this stage the buyer identifies and defines a need. Need recognition may arise within the organization, e.g. the need for supplies of components. Alternatively need recognition may be stimulated through promotion by salespeople or advertising.

A new need is the most difficult of the three buying situations identified:

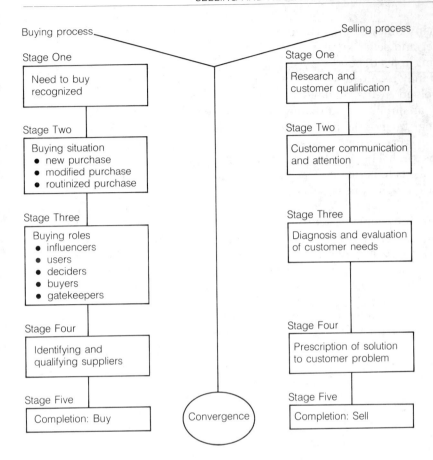

**Figure 19.2**  Convergence of buying and selling processes

Stage Two. A new need frequently arises from a very significant change in the operation of the company or organization. The introduction of a new product may require new materials, components, packaging and even capital equipment. The solution to such buying problems is usually complex and time consuming. The amount of interaction between the buyer and seller is also usually quite significant and takes place at several points in the respective organizations.

A change in a production process or a change in internal accounting procedures may give rise to a modified buying situation. The buyer may have to search for a new solution but because of a high degree of familiarity with the situation and experience the decision process is much simpler than the first time such a purchase was made.

Buying needs also reflect the buying situation and decision process. A routinized buying situation results in the purchase of a product that has been bought many times before. The buying process is simple and often automatic. Both buyer and seller know the solution to the buying problem.

Buying roles depend very much on the buying situation: Stage Three. A new need may require a number of people within the firm and outside the firm to be involved in the buying decision. For example, the purchase of a new aircraft by an airline would require considerable involvement from purchasing, engineering, finance, senior management, outside consultants, banks, leasing firms and even government departments. At the other extreme, for a routinized need, it is probably only necessary for the buyer to become aware that a purchase needs to be made. Depending on the situation, therefore, the buying decision will involve one or several people. In such circumstances it is important that the seller understands that there are important differences in the way in which different people search for information and make buying decisions.

Before buyers begin to search for information they develop criteria by which the information collected can be evaluated: Stage Four. The criteria serve as a guide in the search process. For the seller it is important to know and understand the buying criteria used. The search process is directed at identifying and qualifying potential suppliers.

Buyers frequently shortlist potential suppliers, particularly for industrial products. Selection criteria including credit rating, financial strength, management skills, experience in the product market, and quality control and performance standards are used to shortlist potential suppliers. Often at the same time the buying firm compares actual products on offer.

Specifications are prepared which establish criteria in terms of product performance, characteristics, quality, acceptable price ranges, repair, maintenance, installation and advice. The final step involves a comparison of competing offers to choose the best possible package of price, quantity, delivery, quality and service in making the purchase decision: Stage Five. At all stages there are valuable opportunities for interaction by the selling firm which assist in the problem solving process outlined.

## Identifying the selling process

The selling process may similarly be divided into five definable but interdependent stages. The first step is to qualify the customer to prepare for the ultimate sale: Stage One. At this stage the seller is interested in identifying possible problems in the customer firm. This also means attempting to specify a set of selling objectives which take account of the marketing environment and the specific situation in the customer firm. The selling firm begins to identify the nature and range of issues to be resolved in a possible encounter with the buyer. Intangible issues are also identified. At this stage, too, it is important to plan the negotiation strategy, to incorporate trade-offs and to allow for contingencies. The seller or salesforce will also establish authority limits for dealing with the potential customer. All activity at this stage is carried out before meeting the customer.

The attention phase is critical in international selling: Stage Two. Getting the buyer's individual attention is critical to success. Very often the sales person has very little time to do it and many factors can interfere in the process. The sales call may be in person, by telephone, at an exhibition stand in a trade fair, or even at the potential customer's premises. Many legitimate distractions and disruptions can interfere with obtaining the potential customer's individual attention. All subsequent stages in the selling process depend on successful completion of this one. Cross-cultural communications and differences in cognitive styles add to the possible distractions or interference in the communication between buyer and seller which reduces attention.

In the first communications with the potential customer the seller must complete a number of tasks. At this stage the selling firm attempts to test the limits to which it may go with the buyer in order to isolate key issues. At this stage, too, factors which affect the relative power of the parties are identified. The seller and the buyer begin to determine how best to approach the negotiation, whether it should be a competitive, a cooperative or a collaborative approach. Indeed, if the work of the first stage was not carried out accurately it may now be decided not to proceed or to adopt an avoiding posture. Both sides also attempt to establish the needs and preferences of the other party. Face-to-face communication is normal at various points in this stage of the process.

In Chapter 9 attention was given to ways of diagnosing customers and evaluating their needs and buying situation: Stage Three. This stage consists primarily of collecting facts and qualitative information about the potential customer, and analysing these to arrive at a diagnosis of the customer. Real needs are identified rather than perceived needs. It is important at this stage to establish the buyer's primary concerns in terms of the product or service sought. The seller must also attempt to identify the buyer's dominant buying urge, i.e. the reason for buying the product or service. Diagnosis and evaluation clearly indicates the problem solving aspect of selling.

At this stage, which should be highly interactive with a great deal of interpersonal communication, buyers and sellers become very aware of the other's problems. This stage is very demanding on interpersonal skills especially those concerned with communicating and influencing. It is important to maintain flexibility, and experienced buyers and sellers keep issues linked as proposals and counter proposals are made. It may be necessary at this stage to reformulate objectives and strategies in the light of new information on tangible and intangible issues.

The next step in the selling process is to begin to prescribe a range of possible solutions: Stage Four. A well-prepared and executed selling programme will convince the potential buyer of the seller's purpose and that he is the target. The seller at this point demonstrates that he understands the buyer's problem and that his range of products and services can help solve that problem. The seller attempts to dominate the buyer–seller negotiations by assuming a knowledgeable role and concern for and proper understanding of the buyer's problem.

At this stage it is necessary for both parties to consider details of the exchange package. It is important to determine how issues interact and to establish the effect of the interaction on results. The seller moves toward an agreement conditional on acceptance of a package of products, services and conditions for their exchange. It is essential at this stage to test the other side for understanding and agreement. Good negotiators attempt to keep options open and rarely allow the process to degenerate to the point where only a very limited number of factors are examined. Recent research on negotiation has shown differences between average and skilled negotiators (Exhibit 19.1).

Having obtained acceptance for the prescription offered, the seller must convince the buyer as to the appropriateness of the proposed solution. This means explaining the purpose, use, features and benefits of the product or service so clearly that the buyer completely understands and accepts what is said. Gaining conviction often requires the use of evidence from outside sources which support the selling firm's claims. Associated with the need to convince the buyer is the need to motivate or stimulate a purchase. This may mean an appeal to the buyer on a personal as well as a professional level. Such an appeal might contain an assurance that the proposed solution is most likely to be effective.

The final stage in selling is to close the sale, which means employing an effective approach to direct the buyer to the point of decision and also means recognizing when the buyer has made such a decision: Stage Five. The objective of closing is to influence the buyer to make a decision to purchase the product or service and to ensure that all formalities are completed. At this stage the seller resorts to an appropriate closing technique. In some situations it is more appropriate to close a sale by summarizing the agreement, while in other circumstances making a concession to the buyer is more appropriate. The choice depends on the situation, the product market and the circumstances.

In closing, the seller normally draws up an agreement which reflects the mutual understanding of the parties. It may also be necessary to acknowledge the basis for legal interpretation if such is warranted. Finally, good marketing relationships usually call for the provision for revision when circumstances change.

## Foundations for marketing relationships

### Buyer–seller communications

Communication is defined as a "process of convergence in which two or more participants share information in order to reach a better mutual understanding of each other and the world in which they live." (Barnett and Kincaid, 1983) Communication is at the heart of buying and selling negotiations in international markets. Effective communication is essential for understanding, for cooperation, and for completing exchanges. The importance of good

## Exhibit 19.1   Developing negotiating skills

*What distinguishing the good negotiators from the crowd*

According to research conducted by Neil Rackham and others of the Sheffield-based Huthwaite Research Group into actual negotiating performance, there are significant differences of technique between good and merely average negotiators.

No significant differences were found between the total planning time that skilled and average negotiators claimed they spent prior to actual negotiation, but there was a wide gap on other points:

- The skilled negotiator considered twice the number of outcomes or options for action compared with the average negotiator, and three times as much attention to common ground.
- The average negotiator took a shorter term view. Only one comment in 25 met the criteria of a long-term consideration. The skilled negotiator made twice as many long-term comments.
- The researchers also asked negotiators about their objectives and recorded whether their replies referred to single point objectives (e.g. "We aim to settle at $1.00") or to a defined range (e.g. "We hoped to get $2 but we would settle for a minimum of $1.50"). Skilled negotiators were significantly more likely to set their objectives in terms of a range. Average negotiators, in contrast, were more likely to plan their objectives around a fixed point.
- Skilled negotiators show marked differences in their face-to-face behaviour. They avoid irritating words and phrases like "generous offer" used by a negotiator to describe his own proposal. When the opposition puts forward a proposal, they generally avoid immediately making a counter-proposal.
- Average negotiators seem to believe that there is some special merit in quantity. Having three reasons for doing something is considered more persuasive than having only one reason. In contrast, skilled negotiators used fewer reasons to back up their arguments. They also do considerably more checking out, testing their understanding and summarising thoroughly during ... the negotiation and reviewing it afterwards.

Over two-thirds of the skilled negotiators claimed that they always set aside some time after a negotiation to review it and consider what they had learned. Just under half of the average category made the same claim.

**Source:** *International Management*, May, 1987, p. 69.

communication is emphasized in buying and selling in face-to-face meetings (Graham, 1985).

Communication is a two-way process of interaction involving a sender, a message and a receiver (Figure 19.3). The message may be conveyed verbally or otherwise by means of a code (Cooley, 1983). The code includes oral and written

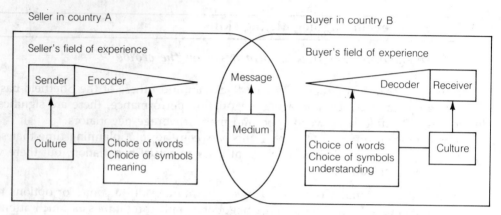

**Figure 19.3**  Factors affecting shared meaning in international marketing (Source: Adapted from Kotler, Philip (1988) *Marketing Management*, 6th edn, Prentice Hall International, Englewood Cliffs, NJ, p. 590; and Schramm, Wilbur (1971) 'How communication works,' in Schraum, Wilbur and Roberts, Donald F. (eds) *The Process and Effects of Mass Communications*, University of Illinois Press, Urbana, p. 4)

language accompanied by a set of paralinguistic features such as stress and loudness. It also contains non-verbal phenomena such as gestures and facial expressions. Coding and decoding are the ways in which participants in the buying and selling process negotiate and define new knowledge, new understanding, new joint priorities, and new values as a key to understanding the inter-cultural communication process. Throughout the communications process, especially in international marketing, many opportunities exist for distortion of messages.

Two principal factors which cause a distortion in a verbal communication, and thereby affect the buyer's or seller's ability to understand what the other is saying, have been identified (Gourlay, 1987). The first of these is filters and the second is referred to as "noise." Filters refer to forms of internal psychological distorting mechanisms which alter the counterpart's message. A number of examples will illustrate. In buying and selling in international markets it is very easy for a buyer or seller to assume that he or she knows instinctively what the counterpart seeks. Expectations can also lead to difficulties. If the seller expects the buyer to be difficult he or she may distort the buyer's communications to fit the expectation.

Another set of distorting factors which act as filters, called double messages, make listening difficult because one party picks up more than one message from the other. The listener should be concerned with what is genuinely meant, not necessarily with the words themselves.

The second set of factors referred to as "noise" in the system relates to background distraction which has nothing to do with the substance of the message but can complicate the communication process. Such "noise" is present in all markets, domestic and international, and includes physical noise, the presence of other people, a poor telephone connection and the habits and idiosyncrasies of the communicators. In an international marketing exchange the effect of such noise is exacerbated. Cross-cultural noise derives from gestures, behaviour seeming overly or insufficiently courteous, clothing, office surroundings and the speaking distance between the parties to the exchange. Noise may lead to conflict with expectations and may result in a misinterpretation of the situation, a change of intent on the part of the counterpart or even a change in the meaning of the message itself.

## Culture and communication

Communication, whether inter- or intra-cultural can only take place when the participants in the process share a set of affective meaning symbols. Such symbols are learnt: the whole range of symbols used in communication, from the more basic such as language to non-verbal cues and sets of ideological principles, beliefs, values and norms, are acquired and attributed meaning on the basis of experience. Interpersonal communication is at its most effective when those involved attribute very similar or identical affective meaning to the various communicative stimuli which feature in the process. The more divergent the experiences of individuals, the more difficult it is for effective communication to take place.

Symbolic meaning systems are, effectively, frames of references used to interpret information emanating from the environment or from the other human beings. It is these "networks of shared meanings" (culture) which Schramm (1971) refers to in his discussion of the conditions necessary for effective communication. The Schramm model conceives of participants in the communicative process as having separate frames of reference. These frames of reference comprise affective meaning sets, and include the four principal types of meaning. As may be seen in Figure 19.3, effective communication can only take place in the area of overlap between the two frames of reference. The greater the degree of overlap, the broader the range of issues about which the individuals can communicate. The area of common frames of reference also determines the possible depth of communication.

Cultural barriers militate against effective communication and increase the likelihood of total breakdown in communication. The reason for this is that such barriers lead one of the parties to ignore or fail to respond correctly to all of the cues in the situation — from the environment or from the other person. "Denial of critical cues from the environment and distortion of verbal or non-verbal cues from the other person" are the primary causes of communications breakdown (Barnlund, 1979).

The convergence of the buying and selling processes in international markets is greatly influenced by the ability of the parties to the exchange to communicate. At almost every stage in the buying and selling process there is a need to communicate. Buyers attempt to learn what is available that can solve their perceived problems, and the buying process involves many people at many stages. Similarly, sellers must communicate with potential buyers to obtain their attention to convey offers and to prescribe possible solutions to identified problems. Hence there are many opportunities for communications breakdown. Fisher (1980, p. 13) has identified three sets of constraints which cause some of the normal features of thought and perception to become booby traps in communication when two or more cultures are involved:

(a)  information processing;
(b)  internal consistency;
(c)  projection of meaning.

In buying and selling negotiations the human mind is an information processor which receives, stores, analyses and uses information. Though born with this capacity people also learn to behave in a certain way. Effective communication depends on there being a reasonable similarity of such learning among buyers and sellers. To a large extent, however, the cultural impact on learning is dominant. Where cultures differ, communication is more difficult and buyer–seller convergence is likely to be slower or distorted.

Within a culture it is necessary to have a certain degree of internal consistency among beliefs, images, and the way we understand phenomena around us in order to experience efficient communications. Because the mind resists any disturbance to this consistency it attempts to fit new pieces of information into the existing framework of ideas or beliefs. In some circumstances it may be impossible to understand something that conflicts with the way we expect to see it. Buying and selling negotiations in international markets almost certainly means having to cope with new and inconsistent information and very different behaviour by the counterpart to the negotiations.

The third difficulty arises when we assume that the implicit assumptions and habitual ways of thinking about our own circumstances have universal applicability. This self-reference criterion trap gives rise to many problems in international marketing (Hall, 1960; Lee, 1966). As a consequence confusion turns full circle in cross-cultural communications when the mind not only places its own stamp of meaning on an incoming message but begins to project that same meaning to the counterpart in the negotiations (Fisher, 1980, p. 15). One form of unconscious projection that wreaks havoc in negotiations according to Fisher is attribution of motive. Motives attributed reflect the buyer's or seller's experience in dealing with another. An example of an assumed motive that does not need to be thought through to complete an exchange when operating in single culture would be: "he is hesitating because he thinks that the price is too high or that my offer could improve." In such circumstances the probability of being correct in assuming motives is relatively high. The probability falls rapidly when a cross cultural situation is encountered and declines further when the subject matter is complex.

## Impact of culture on cognitive structure

A crucial aspect of the influence of culture on communication is the context in which it takes place (Hall, 1976). By context Hall refers to situation specific factors such as the roles of participants, their power and status, the physical environment and the subject of interest. The content of communication can be understood only in the context of these factors. For Hall the relevance of context also applies to negotiations. In high-context countries the content of the communication used in negotiation is not as important as the role of participants in the negotiation. In such situations communications depend greatly on the context or non-verbal aspects of the communications. In low-context countries focus of attention is on the content or words used. In this respect Campbell *et al.* (1988, p. 57) reports that context makes a difference in France. In a negotiations simulation involving business people they found that the role of the negotiator in France appeared to influence negotiation results, whereas in Germany role or context had no importance, leading these authors to claim support for Hall's (1976) characterization of Germany as a low-context culture.

At a more general level it is accepted that there are pronounced differences in cognitive structures or intellectual styles which influence international communications. For example, it is generally believed that there is a wide gulf between the ways in which people in the West and East think. Western cognition tends to be logical, and uses sequential connections and abstract notions of reality to represent universals. The emphasis is on causes rather than outcomes.

Oriental cognition, on the other hand, tends to be intuitive with more reliance on sense data. It is concrete and not abstract. It is non-logical in the Cartesian sense, with emphasis on the particular rather than the universal, highly sensitive to context and relationships, and expresses a concern for reconciliation, harmony, and balance in relationships.

For marketing and sales people the analysis of social structure in high-context countries is essential to obtain useful insights to a selling or buying situation. In such circumstances the firm must obtain sufficient knowledge of the culture to communicate understandably and acceptably.

As an example of the negotiations process it is instructive to examine Chinese cognitive structure and its effect on international negotiations. In business negotiations the Chinese tend to elicit as much information as possible before disclosing their hand to avoid losing face or displaying ignorance. In 1985 Boeing negotiated a deal with the Chinese, taking eight months to obtain an agreement in principle, i.e. the agenda for the negotiations was agreed. It is generally accepted that the Chinese assimilate data in intuitive lumps or bundles and understand in terms of systems. In such circumstances appreciation of technologies may be limited until they have grasped how the diverse elements fit into an entire system.

Establishing the negotiation range may be unimportant where the assimilation of information is a major element in the interaction. The problem solving element assumes a greater importance for the development of the relationships between the negotiators. It is not a gradual move but one of attaining an agreed position in one well considered step. In such a buying–selling regime the foreign negotiator must make his points as cogently as possible within the relationships that he can establish and hope that his package is accepted.

Following these guidelines suggests that the international firm should present a summary close involving a simple package which would be more suitable than a concession close, provided the timing is right. Finally, it is important to note that in dealing with the Chinese, business relations are based on harmony and friendship. The Chinese accept contracts as a basis of business relationships rather than in any strictly legal sense, as would be the case in the West.

## Buyer–seller interaction

The reality of international markets, especially for industrial products, is that the supplier cannot usually determine its product offering unilaterally. For this reason an interaction approach based on a longer-term relationship between buyer and seller seems more appropriate (Turnbull, 1987). Aspects of product development, product quality, delivery and service criteria, price, and other factors are all subject in many cases to a process of negotiation and adaptation. This negotiation and change process, whereby suppliers and customers adapt to each other, takes place through a complex interaction framework. Interaction can only occur where relationships have been established between people, and thus the challenge is often to establish relationships with potentially new partners, as well as to defend existing relationships (Cunningham and Homse, 1982). In the traditional view of marketing, the firm has a simple contract with a single unit within the customer company (Figure 19.4a). This naïve view must be modified for international markets to recognize that a decision-making unit (DMU) exists within customer firms to which the selling firm's marketing programme is aimed (Figure 19.4b). More recently, researchers have recognized that the complexity of the buying decision is often manifested by a large number of people being devoted to serving customers (Figure 19.4c).

Industrial products firms in international markets generally emphasize close relationships, even contractual relationships, rather than market relationships. The value of these relationships in terms of cost reduction or increased sales act to reduce the incentive of both buying and selling companies to seek additional or substitute partners (Ford, 1984). For consumer products firms the same may be said since in most cases the marketing exchange is between two independent firms located in different countries and hence has many of the trappings of an industrial market.

The interaction approach as discussed in Chapter 2 is particularly relevant in the international context. The development of relationships across national boundaries is often a very time consuming and resource intensive process. The seller is likely to be faced with considerable modifications to the products and services on offer to suit a foreign buyer. The demonstration of commitment may involve considerable travel costs and perhaps the establishment of an overseas sales and service subsidiary. The selling firm is usually faced with the task of overcoming the "business distance" which exists between itself and the buyer.

Trends in international markets in recent years have shown a move away from ownership of sources of production inputs towards greater channel cooperation. Adoption of the Japanese tradition of working closely with existing suppliers on a long-term basis rather than seeking new ones is widespread. The sharing of technology, new product, and financial information between manufacturer and long-term supplier is commonplace. Adoption of such

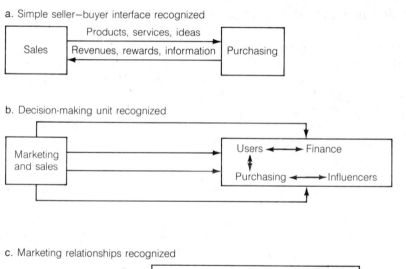

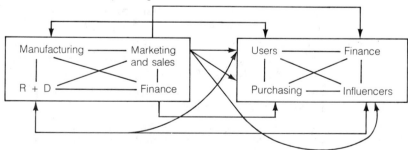

**Figure 19.4** Evolution of marketing relationships in international marketing (Source: Adapted from Turnbull, P.W. (1987) 'Interaction and international marketing: An investment process,' *International Marketing Review*, **4** (4), 7–19)

strategies as "just-in-time" requires close interaction and cooperation to succeed.

International customer firms expect very high commitment from their suppliers. Attributes used to select suppliers in France, West Germany, Italy, Sweden, and the United Kingdom were examined by Ford (1984) who found that there is a strong association between a buyer's assessment of the technical and commercial skills of its suppliers and the extent of commitment to it. Technical skill refers to the buyer's view of the seller's technical abilities in the area of product performance, production quality, or development. Commercial skill refers to the seller's commercial ability in the provision of sales service, in delivery and delivery information. Such types of commitment are especially important for international industrial markets where there are differences in national standards and procedures between the United States and Europe, for example.

## Relationships in international marketing

The interaction model of buyer–seller relationships proposed by the Industrial Marketing Purchasing Group (Hakansson, 1982) recognizes four sets of variables to be studied. First, the interaction process involves the exchange of products, services and ideas. Second, the parties to the exchange comprise individuals, groups, and formal organizations, i.e. a buying centre or a marketing and sales team. Third, it is necessary to examine the economic environment and market structure surrounding the exchange. Finally, the relationship between the supplier and the customer must be considered. The interaction model focusses on the last variable, recognizing that personal contacts between buyer and seller are used to initiate, develop, and maintain such relationships. "These contacts represent a scarce human resource in which is vested much of the expertise, credibilty and authority of the participating companies." (Cunningham, 1984, p. 5) To examine the importance of the relationships between buyer and seller, Cunningham analysed the extent of the human resources allocated to domestic and foreign customers by British suppliers. In his study Cunningham used as measures the number of meetings each year at supplier and customer premises, the number of supplier staff involved, the number of different management functions involved and the level of managers involved in the relationships (Table 19.1). There were fifty-nine companies in the study and the average scores are reported for firms supplying the domestic UK market and the export market.

In general, more meetings tended to occur at customer premises. This was slightly more pronounced in the case of export markets. The number of staff involved from both sides was about the same. The same was true for the number of functions involved. Senior managers were more likely to be involved on the supplier side and in the domestic market. The lower proportion of relationships involving senior customer managers might reflect the nature of products and the

**Table 19.1** Contact, breadth of contact and level of contact in buyer–seller relations in industrial markets

| Buyer–seller relations | Domestic (n=18) (No.) | Export (n=41) (No.) | All markets (n=59) (No.) |
|---|---|---|---|
| Meetings at suppliers' premises | 2.6 | 0.9 | 1.5 |
| Meetings at customers' premises | 16.6 | 5.2 | 8.7 |
| Supplier staff involved | 14.0 | 5.0 | 8.0 |
| Customer staff involved | 13.0 | 6.0 | 9.0 |
| Supplier functions involved | 4.2 | 2.8 | 3.2 |
| Customer functions involved | 3.7 | 3.2 | 3.3 |
| Relationships involving senior supplier managers (%) | 77.0 | 32.0 | 50.0 |
| Relationships involving senior customer managers (%) | 50.0 | 34.0 | 39.0 |

Source: Cunningham, Malcolm T. (1984) 'Controlling the marketing-purchasing interface: Resource deployment and organizational implications,' *Proceedings of the International Research Seminar on Industrial Marketing*, Stockholm School of Economics, 29–31 August.

market structure. A market structure dominated by the customer may not have required such an intensive presence of senior managers on the buying side. The relatively low representation of senior managers in supply relationships in the export market may reflect a lack of serious commitment to such markets. However, it is difficult to be so conclusive given the data provided.

Interaction between suppliers and customers in industrial markets is the key to developing a successful relationship. Such interaction occurs when suppliers and customers recognize the value of the other's assets. The actual context of the interaction is strongly influenced by the structure of the market (Cunningham, 1984). In markets which are concentrated, i.e. few buyers and few sellers, there is likely to be a close matching between customers and their preferred suppliers (Table 19.2). Where there are many suppliers and many customers the degree of mutual dependence may be low. Each party has a greater freedom to change partners as switching costs are lower. A degree of indeterminancy exists where there is an imbalance between suppliers and buyers. In such circumstances either the customer dominates the relationship or the supplier dominates.

## Selling and negotiating strategies

### Buyer–seller styles

In international marketing personal selling is the dominant demand-stimulating factor in the communications mix. This is especially true for industrial products and for products and services transferred between two firms in different international markets. In such situations sales people work primarily to stimulate demand while also providing a range of other customer services. Such

**Table 19.2**  Market structure and supplier–customer relationships

| | Suppliers | |
| Customers | Few | Many |
| --- | --- | --- |
| Few | Mutual dependence | Customer dominated |
| Many | Supplier dominated | Relative independence |

Source: Cunningham, Malcolm, T. (1984) 'Controlling the marketing–purchasing interface: Resource deployment and organizational implications,' *Proceedings of the International Research Seminar on Industrial Marketing*, Stockholm School of Economics, 29–31 August.

services are frequently crucial to the buyer–seller relationship in international markets.

In recent years the approach to selling has changed significantly. From once being an adversarial function selling has recently become much more cooperatively and collaboratively driven. Noting this trend for industrial products has led Hutt and Speh (1989, pp. 521–2) to refer to consultative selling, negotiative selling, systems selling and team selling. In consultative selling the sales person assumes the role of a consultant helping to improve the client's profitability. The sales person provides analysis and problem-solving assistance in an attempt to offer more value than competitors. A negotiations style is adopted to optimize the benefits of a marketing transaction for both the buyer and seller. The objective is to establish a partnership between buyer and seller with common objectives, mutually beneficial strategies, and a common defence against outsiders. Negotiation means talking about a relationship before doing something about it. Negotiations are mixed motive situations. Each party has a motive to enter into negotiation to reach a mutually acceptable solution while, simultaneously, each has a motive for competition.

In systems selling recognition is given to the likelihood that most buying and selling situations require a perspective beyond the product itself. A systems approach to selling would require a comprehensive package of products, recommendations on use and facilities, information and advice and even training and maintenance programmes. In team selling the firm provides a group of people with functional expertise that matches the specialized knowledge of key buying influences in the customer firm. The team is formed to serve the buying and selling process and members may contribute to that process in different ways at different times.

Many authors have examined buying and selling styles from different perspectives. These may be examined from the point of view of concern for the counterpart and concern for the sale or purchase (Blake and Mouton, 1976; McCall and Warrington, 1989). Concern for the counterpart measures the extent to which the buyer or seller seeks to satisfy the other's objectives, while concern for the sale or purchase seeks to satisfy the buyer's or seller's own objectives

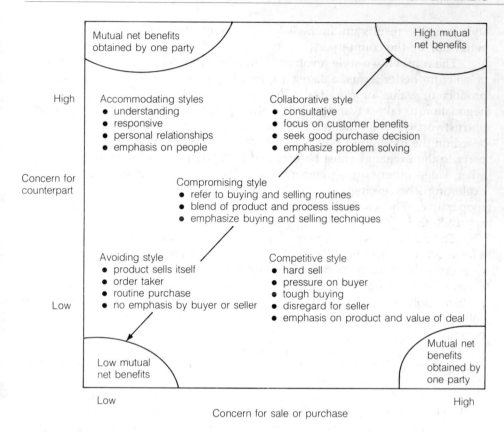

**Figure 19.5** Buyer—seller styles (Source: Adapted from Blake, Robert R. and Mouton, Jane S. (1976) *The Grid for Sales Excellence: Benchmarks for effective salesmanship*, McGraw Hill, NY; and McCall, J.B. and Warrington, M.B. (1989) *Marketing by Agreement — Cross Cultural Approach to Business Negotiations*, 2nd edn, John Wiley and Sons, Chichester)

(Figure 19.5). A low level of concern for both leads to an avoiding style where the product or service is expected to sell itself or where the purchase is a very routine affair in the customer firm. Neither buyer nor seller emphasize any aspect of the exchange. Avoiding behaviour frequently results in a breakdown of the exchange relationship and no exchange is likely to result. An accommodating style means an attempt to understand the counterpart, to be responsive, to think in terms of establishing and developing personal relationships and in general to emphasize people rather than things. Such a style displays a high concern for the counterpart and a lower concern for the sale or purchase. In these circumstances the buyer or seller enters the negotiation with a trusting posture and expects cooperative gestures to be reciprocated. If the other party is cooperative the relationship will flourish. An accommodating style usually results in immediate agreement through acceptance of this behaviour by the counterpart.

The competitive style revolves around the hard sell, pressure on the buyer or seller for better terms, a disregard for the other side and an emphasis on the product or value of the deal. The competitive buyer or seller enters the negotiation to take advantage of the other party and is usually suspicious and untrustworthy. The outcome of an exchange based on a competitive style is based on the location of power in the relationship. A competitive style by one party to the exchange must be matched by a complete accommodation by the other side, otherwise agreement is unlikely. A competitive style implies exploiting the exchange situation, especially when the other party is cooperative. The competitive style is often associated with the adversarial approach in buying and selling.

The collaborative style to buying and selling is based on consultation with a focus on customer benefits and the need to find a good result for both parties. Concern is high for both sides. The collaborative style seeks a good purchase decision and a good selling decision. Emphasis is on solving problems; a joint problem solving operation provides the best mutually attractive result. In collaborating, both parties recognize the possibility of increasing the shared benefits.

In a compromising style, buyers and sellers refer to routines established within their respective firms. Here a blend of product and process issues is emphasized through a mix of in-house buying and selling techniques. A compromising style resolves conflict by give and take on both sides. In general, the level of total benefits to both parties arising from a compromising style tends to be lower than in a strictly problem-solving style, as is found in collaboration. The reference to techniques and bureaucratic procedures introduces a degree of inflexibility which can restrict the level of the total benefits.

## Benefits of marketing relationships

In establishing a marketing relationship involving buying and selling it is necessary to recognize that a range of possible outcomes is possible. By examining the mutual expected net benefits of a marketing relationship, we can observe that in some situations the seller will attempt to dominate and manage the relationship, while in other situations the buyer will attempt to dominate and manage the relationship between buyer and seller (Dwyer, Schurr, and Oh, 1987). In other situations the relationship will be jointly managed (Figure 19.6). Where the expected net benefit from the relationship is equally high for both parties a joint arrangement is likely to operate. The seller manages where the pay-off is high for the seller but neither high nor low for the buyer. The buyer manages where the pay-off is high for the buyer and neither high nor low for the seller. A relatively large area remains which is designated as a buyer's or seller's market depending on the relative benefits which are likely to be

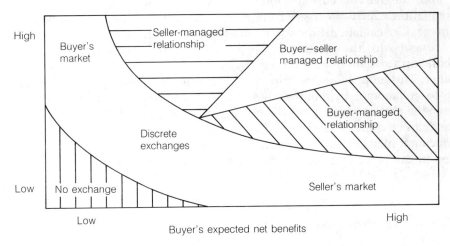

Seller's expected
net benefits

**Figure 19.6** Realm of buyer−seller relationships (Source: Adapted from Dwyer, F. Robert, Schurr, Paul M. and Oh, Seio (1987) 'Developing buyer−seller relationships,' *Journal of Marketing*, **51**)

dominated by discrete exchanges. In circumstances where the benefits or pay-offs are low to both parties it is unlikely that exchange will occur.

Marketing exchanges may be concerned with discrete transactions which lie in the realm of selling, or relationships which lie more in the area of negotiations. The latter involve a degree of dependence and once well developed lead to loyalty and repeat business. There is an increasing tendency for marketing exchanges to be conditioned by longer-term contractual or semi-contractual relations which bond buyers and sellers together (Arndt, 1979). Discrete transactions which fall into the selling mode are usually characterized as exchanges involving the transfer of money for an easily identified and quantified product. Discrete transactions usually involve limited communications and detail. A one-off purchase of a newspaper at a railway station in a strange city closely represents such a discrete transaction.

Firms that have developed a strong customer franchise or have become recognized as reliable and sought after suppliers have established marketing relationships. The key factor for such firms is that the basis for further collaboration may be supported by implicit and explicit assumptions and planning. Firms at this end of the continuum can be expected to derive complex, personal, non-economic satisfactions and engage in social exchange. Observing that duties and performance in such circumstances are relatively complex and occur over time lead Dwyer, Schurr, and Oh (1987, p. 12) to conclude that the parties to an exchange may direct much effort toward carefully defining and measuring the items of exchange.

Close relationships between two parties in a marketing exchange usually lead to a degree of customization of products and services leading to differentiation which can create barriers to switching and hence a competitive advantage. Close relationships also reduce uncertainty and significantly increase joint benefits to the parties arising from effective communication and collaboration to attain mutual objectives, i.e. profit for one and satisfaction for the other. This emphasizes the importance of a problem-solving approach in an effort to collaborate by both parties. Sometimes, however, conflict occurs between the parties which is not always easy to resolve. Conflict in international markets can be difficult to resolve. Considerable assistance in avoiding conflict or reducing it may derive from an understanding of buyer–seller styles, as was studied in the preceding section. Sometimes it is possible to develop a set of rules which can be applied to international marketing exchanges (Exhibit 19.2).

## Selecting the sales team

For the international sales person to succeed it is necessary to have a comprehensive knowledge of the business culture as well as an ability to adapt to a foreign culture if necessary. A number of skills have been identified as important in adapting to a new culture (Hutton, 1988). Most important among these are the following:

(a) tolerance of ambiguity and a willingness to change objectives;
(b) a low task orientation to allow flexibility to different circumstances;
(c) open-minded non-judgemental view of life;
(d) empathy;
(e) ability to communicate across cultures;
(f) self-reliance.

Flexibility does not mean that the salesforce relinquishes its own ways of doing business and goes "native" in the face of different circumstances. In such circumstances the role of language becomes important. A facility in the counterpart's language is a basic ingredient for successful interpersonal relations and affects results (Exhibit 19.3). In this regard, however, it is generally advised that if the sales person does not have a reasonable command of the counterpart's language he or she should consider not using it at all.

In attempting to be flexible there is the added danger of interference from the paralinguistic features of another tongue. The length of pauses between sentences uttered by orientals can be misleading, for example. In the East the time between conscious thought and speaking can be much longer than in the West. In other instances a seeming degree of exaggeration or overassertion of certain words may appear be misinterpreted. For example, in Arabic the apparent assertion of certain phrases and words is a natural means of expression.

The manager of a subsidiary or sales firm is a key figure since he or she absorbs the culture of the subsidiary and the wider national culture and

---

## Exhibit 19.2  Understanding buyer–seller styles to avoid conflict

---

### *Who makes the rules in cross-cultural conflicts?*

What is conflict? Simply stated, conflict begins when one perceives that the other has frustrated, or is about to frustrate, some right. This frustration may result from actions that range from intellectual disagreement to physical violence. If we add an international or intercultural perspective to conflict, however, there is added complexity. The frustration, which precipitated the conflict, may be based on a different cultural perception of the situation.

When participants in a conflict are from the same culture, they are more likely to perceive the situation in basically the same way and organise their perceptions in similar ways. The persons involved in cross-cultural conflicts must be careful not to assume that the perception and values of the persons involved in the conflict are the same.

Conflicts are usually resolved in one of five ways.

- Being competitive represents a desire to satisfy one's concern at the expense of the other
- Cooperative style attempts to satisfy the other
- Compromising style is a preference for moderate, but incomplete, satisfaction of both parties
- Collaboration attempts to satisfy fully the concerns of both parties
- Avoidance is an indifference to the concerns of either party.

The cooperative style is an Eastern mode of resolving conflict; assertive styles tend to be more Western. The twain have great difficulty meeting.

But let us never forget that the methods used by a society for dealing with conflicts reflect the basic values and philosophy in that society. In the Arab world, mediation is critical in resolving disputes. Confrontation almost never works — especially if the rules are made by those who have the gold. Mediation allows for saving face, mutual understanding, and is rooted in a realism that all conflicts do not have neat solutions.

The Chinese, on the other hand, have learned to internationalize conflict and seem to ignore it. To them, conflict is not healthy, desirable or constructive.

If we begin by trying to understand the basic values and philosophy of those involved we might then be able to develop acceptable means for solving some of the cross-cultural conflicts.

**Source:** *International Management*, January, 1986, p. 45.

---

interprets it for headquarters. Where response to the market and its culture is deemed to be more important than communication between the person in the field and headquarters, a national of the country is usually employed.

The key prerequisites for successful communication in international markets in an ideal world are awareness of the selling and negotiating process,

## Exhibit 19.3   Foreign languages are basic ingredients in successful interpersonal relations

*Why speaking English is no longer enough*

Although more and more people are learning English, companies are finding that buyers are beginning to insist on doing business in their own language.

As a business becomes more international, every bit of competition edge counts. More than ever, in the search for deeper penetration into foreign markets, global companies are encountering customers or potential customers unaccustomed to being approached by foreigners. Fluency in the local language thus becomes essential. And failure to communicate with these would-be clients can mean loss of business to a better-prepared company from another country — often Japan.

In Germany in the 1950s and 1960s, US and British businessmen could afford to have a take-it-or-leave-it attitude to learning German, recalls John D. Brennan, general manager of the American Chamber of Commerce there. But that has all changed, he says, partly because of new pressure from Asian competitors. "The Japanese are speaking very good German and so are the Koreans. You have to follow the competition", he says.

It is in France that the importance of knowing the local language is perhaps best understood by foreign businessmen. Only the major internationally oriented French business executives are comfortable in English.

At its most basic level, competence in the language makes life outside your own country more tolerable. Adjusting to a new culture is difficult enough. Having to rely on your secretary to help you buy shampoo, negotiate with your landlord and give directions to taxi drivers will not make you feel any more at home.

Athene Choy, headhunter for a major international group of management consultants in Hong Kong, is English, but is married to a Cantonese and speaks the language. She agrees that in this British colony, English is adequate for many purposes. "But getting hold of the person you want, leaving messages and so on can be frustrating unless you use Cantonese. I never have problems with immigration, taxi drivers are never rude, my phone messages are always passed on because I do it all in Cantonese. You break down barriers that way. It gives you better insight and more enjoyment if you speak Cantonese, whether it's in the market or to the watchman of your building. It enriches your experience."

**Source:** *International Management*, November, 1986, p. 39.

---

the ability to understand and use influencing behaviour, and empathy for the culture with which the sales person is dealing.

In dealing with the real world, stereotyping of approaches to selling and negotiating may sometimes be used to characterize the likely responses of counterparts. In this regard Fisher (1980) poses the following questions: Is there a national style in choosing negotiators and what kind of people are likely to be chosen to conduct business with foreign counterparts? He provides a series of answers for the United States, Japan, Mexico and France which demonstrate the differences involved. His approach relies on the choice of technical competence or social competence as a qualification for conducting business in international markets (Exhibit 19.4).

Fisher concludes that most negotiators will need a mix of technical

---

**Exhibit 19.4  Ensure a combination of technical and social competence in sales negotiators**

---

*Analysing the negotiating team*

Then there is the question: is there a national style in choosing negotiators; what kinds of people qualify to occupy positions that call for conducting business with foreign counterparts; how does their bureaucratic or business culture determine the team members' relationship to each other. This sets the internal dynamics of the team.

For Americans technical competence is basic. It is the position in the firm that supplies the authority for team members whose background is an egalitarian society. Competence is key; team members are not judged by other factors, e.g. negotiators' social egos are not placed on the line.

For the Japanese the team presents much more of a closed circle. Cultural conditioning that stresses orderliness in group dynamics rules the relationships among the members and defines their relationships with the non-Japanese world. The progression to leadership and status is by professional competence but also very much by seniority and experience. The team leader might be only marginally competent in the specific subject matter under negotiation but still be the obvious boss.

For Mexicans, individuals on a negotiating team stand out. The factors which bring them into a negotiating position are much more likely to reflect their personal qualities and social connections or leverage inside a political/business system in which personality is paramount — "ubicacion" — how the individual is "plugged in" in the system. Leaders of such teams do see their social egos more on the line.

For the French it is the social status or high academic qualification for entering the system that then stresses competence and adherence to standards. The typical senior negotiator in foreign business deals is likely to have studied at one of three or four business schools. Preparatory work will be done carefully. Typically self assured in international negotiations because his system prepared him for it and backs him up — it gives him prestige and authority — "the French have a highly sophisticated ability to make their opponents feel inadequate".

The understanding of the above "national identities" is important because it helps define a problem that often plagues international negotiation: conflicting expectations in role behaviour — a particularly useful conceptual tool in cross-cultural analysis.

**Source:** Based on Fisher, Glen (1980) *International Negotiation*, Intercultural Press, Chicago, pp. 17-26.

competence and social competence. The mix between the two tends to vary in emphasis, however, from place to place. Counterparts from traditional societies may operate much more on the basis of their social competence, i.e. who they are, their connections and social class. Most Americans tend to believe in technical competence when credentials are being checked. Thus Americans frequently find they are dealing with counterparts who place more stock on their social competence than seems reasonable to Americans. An underlying difference in this role definition helps explain some of the feeling of social distance in achieving rapport both within and without the negotiation process.

## Summary

Selling and negotiation strategies are developed by the firm to implement marketing strategy. The firm implements its strategy through the sales and marketing team. The interaction between buyer and seller in international marketing is a very complex activity. The marketing exchange may refer to a simple discrete transaction or, alternatively, it may refer to a long-standing, well-developed relationship between two firms operating in two very different cultures to attain mutually beneficial objectives. Understanding the selling and negotiations process is important whichever situation is present. Where sophisticated marketing relationships are involved it is important to understand the multifaceted aspects of the relationships.

The role of the salesforce in international markets is changing to include a deeper understanding of marketing and an acknowledgement of a degree of marketing autonomy in local markets. In deciding the appropriate roles for the salesforce it is necessary for the firm to acknowledge the existence of a buying process and a selling process which converge to produce a satisfactory result to both parties to the exchange.

The successful outcome of these processes of convergence is dependent, to a large extent, on there being a high degree of cultural understanding and affinity between the partners. This affinity arises through communications between the parties involved. The international marketing aspect adds a new and complex dimension to the communications process. Successful buying and selling strategies are based on establishing mutually beneficial marketing relationships.

## Discussion questions

1. Describe what is meant by marketing exchanges in international marketing. To what extent are marketing exchanges confined to products and services?

2. What is the role of the salesforce in the firm in international markets? Do you expect any changes in its role in the future?

3. A distinction was drawn in the chapter between discrete exchanges and exchanges which occur as a result of a longer-term relationship. What is your opinion regarding this distinction?

4. What is meant by the convergence of buying and selling processes?

5. Discuss the importance of communications in buying and selling in international marketing. What is the effect of culture on communications?

6. In developing a selling or negotiating strategy the firm may use a particular buyer—seller style. Outline the more important of these and discuss their relevance to the firm in international markets.

7. What are the key factors to consider in picking the international sales team?

# References

Arndt, Johan (1979) 'Towards a concept of domesticated markets,' *Journal of Marketing*, Fall, pp. 69–75.

Barlund, D.C. (1979) 'A transaction model of communication," in Mortensen, D. (ed.), *Basic Readings in Communications Theory*, Harper and Row.

Barnett, G.A. and Kincaid, L.D. (1983) 'Cultural convergence: A mathematical theory,' Chapter 10 in Gudykunst, W.B. and Hill, Beverly (eds.), *Intercultural Communication Theory*, Sage Publications.

Blake, Robert R. and Mouton, Jane S. (1970) *The Grid for Sales Excellence: Benchmarks for effective salesmanship*, McGraw Hill, NY.

Campbell, Nigel C.G., Graham, J.L., Jolibert, A. and Meissner, H.G. (1988) 'Marketing negotiations in France, Germany, the United Kingdom, and the United States,' *Journal of Marketing*, **52**, 49–62.

Cooley, R.E. (1983) 'Codes and contexts: An argument for their description,' Chapter 13 in Gudykunst W.B. and Hill, Beverly (eds.), *Intercultural Communication Theory*, Sage Publications.

Cunningham, Malcolm T. (1984) 'Controlling the marketing purchasing interface: Resource deployment and organisational implications,' *Proceedings of the International Research Seminar on Industrial Marketing*, Stockholm School of Economics, 29–31 August.

Cunningham, Malcolm T. and Homse, E. (1982) 'An interaction approach to marketing strategy,' in Hakansson, H. (ed.), *International Marketing and Purchasing of Industrial Goods: An interaction approach*, John Wiley, Chichester, pp. 358–69.

Dwyer, F. Robert, Schurr, Paul H. and Oh, Sejo (1987) 'Developing buyer—seller relationship,' *Journal of Marketing*, **51** 11–27.

Fisher, Glen (1980) *International Negotiation*, Intercultural Press, Chicago.

Ford, I. David (1984) 'Buyer—seller relationships in international industrial markets,' *Industrial Marketing Management*, **13**, 101–12.

Gourlay, R. (1987) 'Negotiations and bargaining,' *Management Decision* (UK), **25**, 3.

Graham, John L. (1985) 'The influence of culture on the process of business negotiations: An exploratory study,'*Journal of International Business Studies*, **26** (1), 81–96.

Hakansson, Hakan (ed.) (1982) *International Marketing and Purchasing of Industrial Goods: An interaction approach*, John Wiley and Sons, Chichester.

Hall, Edward T. (1960) 'The silent language of overseas business,' *Harvard Business Review*, May−June, 81−98.

Hall, Edward T. (1976) *Beyond Culture*, Anchor Press/Doubleday.

Hutt, Michael D. and Speh, Thomas W. (1989) *Business Marketing Management*, Dryden Press, 3rd edn, Chicago.

Hutton, J. (1988) *The World of the International Manager*, Philip Allan, Oxford.

Kotler, Philip (1988) *Marketing Management*, Prentice Hall International, 6th edn, Englewood Cliffs, NJ.

Lee, James A. (1966) 'Cultural analysis in overseas operations,' *Harvard Business Review*, March−April, 106−11.

McCall, J.B. and Warrington, M.B. (1989) *Marketing by Agreement*, John Wiley & Sons, Chichester.

Schramm, Wilbur (1971) 'How communication works,' in Schramm, Wilbur and Roberts, Donald F. (eds.), *The Process and Effects of Mass Communications*, University of Illinois Press, Urbana.

Turnbull, P.W. (1987) 'Interaction and international marketing: An investment process,' *International Marketing Review*, **4** (4), 7−19.

# Managing international marketing operations

Managing international marketing operations means ensuring that the programme developed for each international market is implemented and controlled. This means that in planning the programme the firm must pay attention to difficulties which may subsequently arise in implementing plans in the market. Successful firms institute control systems to complement and support their planning.

The key issues which arise in implementing international marketing plans and systems for controlling implementation are examined in this chapter. A hierarchy of control systems is introduced. First, we examine how firms develop and use operational control systems. This is followed by a section dealing specifically with financial control. Finally, the appropriate role for strategic control in the firm is discussed. The chapter ends with a short section on the need to review performance standards periodically as they apply to the management of international marketing operations.

## Effective implementation of the international marketing task

### Measuring marketing performance

The objective of the firm in international markets is to create a multidimensional management process capable of identifying and responding to diversity, dynamism, and complexity in the international environment. Only effective firms survive in this environment.

Effectiveness derives from the management of demands of the various interest groups upon which the firm depends for resources and support (Pfeffer and Salancik, 1978, pp. 2–3). As was seen in many earlier chapters the firm is linked to its environment by federations, associations, customer–supplier relationships, competitive relationships, the cultural and political–legal

523

framework which defines and controls the nature and boundaries of these relationships.

The behaviour of the firm depends upon the firm itself, its structure, its leadership, its procedures and its goals. It also depends on the environment and the particular contingencies and constraints deriving from that environment. The firm must manage these relationships. For the firm in international markets the task is more complex and difficult.

The task is all the more complicated since

> achieving a coherent view of the output or performance measures of marketing has remained a difficult and generally unrewarding business. Indeed, perhaps no other concept in marketing's short history has proven as stubbornly resistant to conceptualization, definition or application as that of marketing performance. (Bonoma and Clarke, 1988, p. 1).

Managers bring four implementation skills to the marketing task: interacting, allocating, monitoring and organizing (Bonoma, 1984, p. 75). Bonoma suggests that the marketing task by its nature is one of influencing others inside and outside the firm. There are internal and external conditions over which the manager has no direct control but which he must influence. The manager must also allocate time, assignments, and resources among the various tasks involved in implementing marketing strategy. Monitoring is a task which must be done; some firms cope very poorly with it, spending too much time collecting data and not enough time developing managerially useful information. Finally, good implementation means having the ability to develop informal networks and relationships both within the firm and outside it to address problems as they arise. According to Bonoma (1984, p. 75), customized informal organization facilitates good implementation.

Many of the issues which must be considered in implementing marketing strategies apply also for the firm in international markets. In assessing marketing performance, firms are concerned with measuring the efficiency of the use of marketing inputs, the influence of mediating factors, and the nature and level of marketing outputs (Bonoma and Clarke, 1988). Many of these, which Bonoma and Clarke derived from an extensive literature search, are already familiar. These authors identify eleven input measures, twenty-six mediating factors divided into market characteristics, product characteristics, customer characteristics and task characteristics, and twelve output measures (Figure 20.1). Very few firms measure all the variables outlined. Many firms use a subset of these variables and monitor their behaviour over time. How they are measured and the value firms place on them is the subject of the following sections in this chapter.

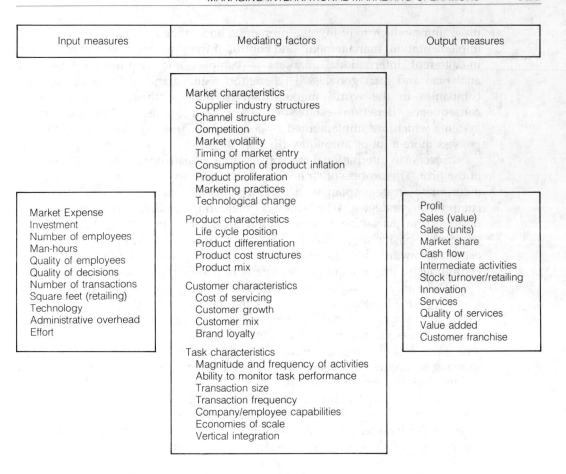

| Input measures | Mediating factors | Output measures |
|---|---|---|

**Market characteristics**
Supplier industry structures
Channel structure
Competition
Market volatility
Timing of market entry
Consumption of product inflation
Product proliferation
Marketing practices
Technological change

**Market Expense**
Investment
Number of employees
Man-hours
Quality of employees
Quality of decisions
Number of transactions
Square feet (retailing)
Technology
Administrative overhead
Effort

**Product characteristics**
Life cycle position
Product differentiation
Product cost structures
Product mix

**Customer characteristics**
Cost of servicing
Customer growth
Customer mix
Brand loyalty

**Profit**
Sales (value)
Sales (units)
Market share
Cash flow
Intermediate activities
Stock turnover/retailing
Innovation
Services
Quality of services
Value added
Customer franchise

**Task characteristics**
Magnitude and frequency of activities
Ability to monitor task performance
Transaction size
Transaction frequency
Company/employee capabilities
Economies of scale
Vertical integration

**Figure 20.1**   Measures of marketing efficiency, inputs, mediating factors and outputs
(Source: Bonoma, Thomas V. and Clarke, Bruce H. (1988) *Marketing Performance Assessment*, Harvard Business School Press, Boston, pp. 35–7)

## *Review of international marketing tasks*

The firm in international markets faces two major sets of tasks. First it must analyse and understand its customers, actual and potential. Second, it must provide products and services through a marketing programme to produce satisfaction for the customer and profits for the company. Managing international marketing operations is the planning and co-ordinating of all the activities implied above to arrive at a successful integrated marketing programme which may involve numerous and different foreign markets. The implementation, management, and control of the firm's marketing programme in different international markets is complex and requires sophisticated analytical and managerial skills. Benetton realized that it is easier to build companies in the world market than to manage them effectively. As a consequence Benetton established centralized strategies and supporting systems which are implemented by local subsidiaries or franchise firms who possess quite a lot of autonomy (Exhibit 20.1).

Success in international markets requires a strategic orientation on the part of the firm. The process of strategic marketing means working in the context of a corporate strategic plan with specified mission statements, objectives, and component strategies. The strategic marketing process, therefore, implies deciding the marketing strategy based on a set of objectives, target market segments, positioning, and policies. The firm in international markets is especially aware that its markets are dynamic; needs and wants change continuously; product markets evolve; and resources are not fixed.

There are three key components in formulating a marketing strategy. First, it is necessary to analyse the firm itself, the market, and the competition to understand the market and the competitive environment. Second, international marketing operations must have institutional support, i.e. organizational structures and processes, incentives and value systems, to allow strategic thinking to occur. Third, strategic thinking refers to creative, entrepreneurial insights into the firm, the industry, and the market.

As was seen in Chapter 4, international marketing strategy is an integrated set of activities which takes account of the firm's resources and is designed to increase the long-term well-being of the firm through securing a sustainable competitive advantage with respect to the competition in serving customer needs in one or more international markets.

## Financing international market expansion

Many firms following a growth strategy in international markets do not fully understand that profitability and solvency, though related, frequently follow very different paths during an expansionary phrase. The firm entering international markets for the first time or seeking to expand there must remain solvent. That is the firm's first financial objective. Its second objective is to ensure that funds for expansion are available when needed. This means deciding the sources of the funds and the capital and ownership structure of the firm in the longer term.

In costing the international marketing strategy the firm must identify costs under a number of headings: management; time; any reorganization required; any new staff employed and their training. It is also necessary to allow for the acquisition of know-how, development costs and any capital investment associated with expansion abroad. The firm must also ensure that production,

---

## Exhibit 20.1   Implement strategy through local autonomy

### *Benetton's global structure*

As many entrepreneurs have found to their cost, it is easier to build companies than to manage them effectively. Thus the Benetton brothers' decision, taken in 1982, to bring in outside management and then restructure their empire was one that most impressed outsiders. "The Benettons understood that it was important to have good management. They created the group, but could they manage it once it grew to be international? They had the honesty and the intelligence to know they could not", says an executive of a rival company.

According to Managing Director, Palmieri, "when I arrived (from the Bank of Italy in January 1983), I found a situation typical of most family businesses that have outgrown their entrepreneurial roots." If the company's growth required new management functions, he says, the Benettons had simply hired people without having any clear organizational structure in mind. "At the start 20 to 25 people reported directly to me." Now only a handful of senior executives dealing with marketing, finance and production report to Palmieri.

In addition, a major decentralization of the group's management has begun. Regional subsidiaries are being set up that will take over many of the central functions now based in Italy. For example, the company has created Benetton USA and plans other "subsystems" in the Far East, Latin America and Eastern Europe. "We will give the overall strategy and guidelines on fashion", asserts Palmieri. "Otherwise (the regional subsidiaries) will be entirely autonomous. They will have their own communications system, they will be the main source of analysis of their market areas."

**Source:** *International Management*, November, 1987, pp. 30–5.

---

distribution and marketing costs, any income forgone through reduced prices, and a contribution to overheads are met. Finally, the firm must decide whether the new international strategy involves an investment which is a budget item, an annual investment matter, or whether it should be considered part of the long-term development plan of the firm.

Expansion through self-financing has a number of benefits: the firm pays no interest on the money used though the opportunity cost of such money is relevant, the firm retains control over the financial strategy, and it is possible to retain the existing capital structure of the firm. In some instances, however, it may be desirable or necessary to seek external finance, especially for a new international marketing venture or an expansion in an existing international market. External financing requires the firm to estimate the feasibility of a number of possible growth rates and to judge the level and source of finance required to service such sales. In making the decision whether to finance a strategy internally or externally the firm must recognize the need to support its marketing strategy at every point with an appropriate financial strategy.

## Meaning of management control

In preceding chapters the emphasis on developing strategies for the firm in international markets focussed on controlled expansion into foreign markets and controlled growth. The need to pursue growth opportunities selectively raised the issue of finding an agreed strategic framework for international marketing control. Unfortunately, there has been very little interaction of concepts and theories in international marketing strategy and planning with those of finance and managerial accounting. While the importance of market share objectives, market size and growth rates, and the importance of good forecasts have been recognized, procedures for marketing control have not yet been successfully related to these key factors (Hulbert and Toy, 1984, p. 452). Good control systems are necessary for implementation of management strategies.

A framework for control

> provides a system for attempting to ensure that "things don't go wrong" during the implementation of strategies. During implementation, control should be continuously exercised through the application of the framework. The basis of this application is the achievement of organizational and business objectives, with profits being extracted for separate attention. (Greenley, 1989, p. 369).

Control and implementation are serious and complex management issues faced by the firm. In international markets they mean added complexity and are frequently very central to the growth and survival of the firm.

## Operational control in international markets

### Sales quotas and controls

Sometimes firms monitor foreign sales from one year to the next and use the trends to judge performance, good or poor depending on the trend. Other firms adopt a more formal sales control approach, where sales might be classified by country or region of a foreign market, by customer, and by product group. The next step would be to decide appropriate criteria for decide the sales level which should fall into each category. The firm might develop an index to measure the importance of each of the categories used. An analysis of previous sales might be used to establish quotas which, over time, are adjusted to accommodate changes in the market. Usually, effective sales control systems require a variable standard, as implied here. If economic activity in a particular country is very high and developing rapidly, sales in that market might also expect to grow. Similarly, a decline in the market should also be reflected in a downward adjustment of the quota. The assumption behind such a sales control system is that factors causing an expansion or contraction in the market beyond the influence of the firm should not be used in evaluating sales performance.

## Current earnings and profits

The managers of foreign operations evaluated on the basis of current earnings are likely to emphasize short-run profits and neglect long-run profits. This is particularly true if managers are frequently moved from market to market or are repatriated, which would allow them to avoid the longer-term consequences of their actions. These actions could involved reducing advertising and general marketing expenditures, reducing research and development work under their control, and not spending sufficient sums on staff training and development. Because circumstances can be different in different foreign markets and outside management control, performance measures based on sales, profits or return on investment can be misleading at best and inaccurate at worst. For this reason firms frequently compare actual results with budgeted estimates. Variances in costs and revenues can then be examined to determine whether these are affected by outside events such as changes in the exchange rate or caused mainly by management intervention.

## Financial control in international marketing

Having decided to enter or expand in international markets the firm must ensure that the strategy to be followed is costed properly. The firm must also decide how to finance the strategy, from internal resources or from selected external sources. Finally, good financial management dictates that the expansion strategy should not jeopardize the survival and growth of the firm.

As emphasized elsewhere in this chapter, growth and expansion in international markets are associated with considerable cost. The costs of entering and expanding in slow-growth markets are particularly high. Expansion for the firm in international markets, even in industries which are not capital intensive, requires large cash outlays, the postponement of income, and skilful marketing and financial management. For success it is thus necessary to co-ordinate marketing strategies and financial planning. Where the firm does not properly relate its marketing strategy to its financial resources this lack of co-ordination can lead to collapse.

The costing and financial control of international marketing strategies are difficult tasks for most firms and can be very complicated. International marketing strategies can be difficult to quantify; they refer to the longer term and consist of numerous steps with varying impacts. It is difficult in costing strategies to separate costs into fixed costs, variable costs, and cash flow projections. To overcome these difficulties, successful international firms attempt to ensure that control rests with financial, marketing, and general management people since such a team effort is likely to better understand the cost implications of an international marketing strategy.

## Importance of cash flow in international markets

The significance of cash flow to the firm in international markets may be gleaned by observing the difference between profits and cash flow. A brief review of these concepts will illustrate the point. There are two reasons why cash flow is very unlike profit. First, there is a lapse of time between obtaining raw materials and employing labour to produce the product for sale and the time of the actual sale of the product. Second, there is the influence of credit. Cash is not necessarily paid out for the materials and labour at the time they are used. Similarly, cash may not be received at the time the sale is made.

In contrast, profit is the difference between two sums: the price the customer pays; and the total of prices the firm agrees to pay for all the inputs used in preparing the product or service for sale. Profit is the difference between agreed prices.

Cash flow is money lodged to a bank account, less cash withdrawals from that account in any given period. Most deposits arise when customer receipts are received for products and services previously sold.

Disbursements generally arise when the firm pays for the goods and services previously purchased. Cash flow is the difference between money lodged in the bank and the money withdrawn from the bank. The size of the cash flow and its direction, positive or negative, depends every bit as much upon when the money is lodged or withdrawn as upon how much is deposited or withdrawn.

Profit is therefore very different from cash flow. As will be seen, it is possible to have a very profitable business in international markets but still fail due to poor cash flow performance.

The significance arises most dramatically as the firm expands into international markets. A major benefit of examining the firm's cash flow requirements related to an expansion is that the amount of financing required to carry out the anticipated expansion programme is determined. Associated with most international expansions are larger purchases of raw materials and other inputs, more sophisticated machinery, access to sources of finance, and additional sales people. An instinctive urge to grow through international market expansion has led many firms into the growth trap. Herein lies the dilemma for many international firms. The firm operationalizes international strategies, not just for increased sales in world markets; many firms also require the cash flow generated in world markets to support new product development, to support the acquisition of new technologies, and to invest in international marketing channels of distribution. According to Hamel and Prahalad (1985, p. 145), this is a real problem; companies that remain in the domestic market are likely to find themselves at a resource and cost disadvantage which will also prevent them from defending the home market.

In general a faster growth in sales should produce an attractive increase in profits. There may, however, be an adverse impact on cash flow. The firm may experience impressive growth in many of its international markets with an equally impressive growth in earnings and at the same time face a severe financial constraint. Sales growth in most businesses consumes cash. As we saw above, cash is needed to purchase items such as raw materials, services and merchandise when preparing the product or service for sale. Growth in sales requires that greater quantities of these items be bought in anticipation of future sales. Cash is also needed to support the business at its now larger size while awaiting payment from customers for larger sales. Consequently, during periods of rapid growth the cash flow is characteristically negative. It is perfectly normal to find that a business is growing profitably while bank balances are in the red.

The firm that introduces its products to a new foreign market usually finds that, initially, sales growth is slow, the firm incurs losses and cash flow is negative. While customers may be innovative there are few of them and the firm needs a lot of money to develop the market. At this stage the firm is attempting to move potential customers from awareness to adoption. Initial success brings with it rapid sales growth which requires considerable amounts of cash to service it. At this stage the firm may have to lower prices slightly and incur extra costs to improve the product in an effort to penetrate distribution channels. The costs of such expansion to establish preferences for the firm's products can be very high. Such developments exacerbate the pressure on cash flows in the firm.

While it is not possible to be precise about the exact nature of the relationships between sales, profits, cash flow, and bank balances for all businesses there are some general principles that apply and that can be examined (Figure 20.2).

Sales growth is generally believed to follow the traditional path of a life cycle, starting off relatively slowly and then rising rapidly in the new and growing phase, slowing down to the growth in population for consumer products and to the replacement sales rate for industrial products in the mature and stable phase and falling off rapidly in the decline phase. The life cycle of the profit loss curve is thought to parallel the sales curve starting out as a loss and only becoming positive in the growth phase. Greatest profits are believed to occur in the mature and stable phase of the market evolution.

These early losses give rise to a problem encountered by many firms which expand into international markets without adequate financial resources. The early losses, or negative cash flow, may cause a significant drain on the cash resources in the company's bank. As sales increase, investment by the firm in cash, debtors and stocks must grow proportionately, and fluctuations in sales, for whatever reason, would be followed by similar fluctuations in current asset

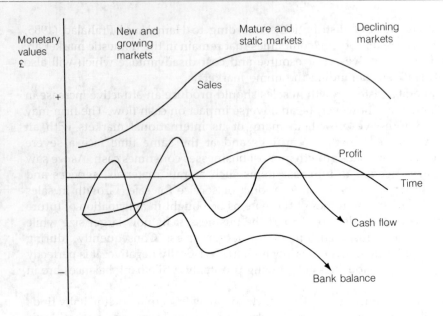

**Figure 20.2** Relationship among sales growth, cash flow and bank balance: Expansion into new foreign markets

requirements (Weston and Copeland, 1988, p. 243). For the small- to medium-size company the working capital management policy is likely to depend on the banking system. Assuming no external financing the cash flow position is likely to be negative for a considerable period of time, only becoming positive in the late period of the new and growing phase of the life cycle. Further expansions and the extra demands on cash, as discussed above, are likely to be reactivated, thereby pushing the cash flow curve down again. The process continues in such a cyclical fashion throughout the earlier phases of the life cycle, which causes great demands on the firm's cash resources. Under the conditions assumed the result on the company's bank balance is likely to be traumatic.

With the initial flurry of sales and first orders and sales perhaps being made out of inventory, bank balances are likely to be positive. The continued pressure on cash flow will, however, rapidly cause bank balances to become negative. While the cyclical pattern is likely to be repeated in the bank balances, most of the activity is likely to occur below the line in the negative or loss area (Figure 20.2). The size of the negative bank balance is indicative of the amount of external cash that must be injected into the business. The behaviour of the four variables: sales; profits; cash flow; and bank balances and their interrelation may be cited in support of government financial subsidy schemes for smaller businesses attempting to internationalize. The peculiar pattern of these four key variables also raise the important issue of an adequate equity in the firm contemplating an expansion in international markets.

## *Size of firm and cash flow*

The problem is greater for smaller firms than for larger firms. Smaller firms need proportionally more external financing and typically have much more difficulty obtaining it. It is relatively easy to double sales in one year if what is being doubled is small. It is a much more difficult task to double sales in one year if existing sales are very large. A small firm entering international markets for the first time could easily find itself in a position of doubling its sales if it chooses. Consequently, smaller firms are more likely to have a continuous and urgent need for proportionally more cash to overcome negative cash flow than larger firms.

Larger firms frequently find it easier to obtain the additional money under conditions of rapid growth. They usually have long-established relationships with banks and suppliers, good reputations, and historical evidence of their ability to survive. Lenders and investors feel reasonably safe in giving money to large firms that are growing profitably.

Smaller firms, and entrepreneurial firms especially, usually find that the additional money needed is difficult to obtain. They seldom have long-established relationships; they may have little or no reputation, and they may have only narrow evidence of their ability to manage the larger enterprise they hold as an aspiration for their firm. In such circumstances lenders and investors find it difficult to give money to smaller firms. Consequently, money that is made available to smaller firms often takes longer to procure, costs more and has conditions of control over management attached to it which may be unattractive. This is one of the major reasons behind the many government-sponsored export promotion and industrial development schemes involving financial incentives.

## Implementing performance standards

### *Financial performance criteria*

For the firm in international markets measuring the relevant returns on foreign operations is a difficult task since differences can arise between foreign market cash flows and cash flows back to the firm itself due to tax regulations and exchange controls. Furthermore, adjustment in transfer prices and credit can distort the true profitability of an investment by shifting profits and liquidity from one location to another (Shapiro, 1985). Firms use a variety of ways of measuring returns including foreign earnings, dividends, royalties and fees, interest, commissions and profits on exports. The key considerations in measuring returns in most circumstances are that they are incremental.

While non-financial criteria such as market share or sales growth may be used in determining the value of a foreign market investment, many firms employ a version of return on investment as the means of measuring the long-run profit performance of their foreign operations. We usually associate the former approach with Japanese firms and a virtual complete dependence on ROI by US and other Western firms.

Where return on investment is used, a number of comparisons are possible: comparisons with similar firms in the foreign market; with other foreign operations controlled by the firm; or with the firm's operations in the domestic market; or with targets established before entering the foreign market. Unless historical measures such as the above indicate the relative returns to be expected from future investments there is no point in using any of the above measures. The most important comparison that can be made is between actual results and *ex ante* budgeted figures since a post-investment audit can help a firm to learn from its mistakes as well as its successes (Shapiro, 1985).

The appropriate measures to use in evaluating and controlling foreign operations depend on the nature of the business. For marketing-oriented firms, market share, sales growth or the costs associated with generating a unit of sales revenue may be the most relevant measures. These measures would seem appropriate for the industrial products firms, the consumer products firm, and the service firm operating abroad in most circumstances. They are especially relevant when entry to foreign markets is made by exporting particularly.

A firm that enters foreign markets through foreign direct investment, however, may be more concerned about unit costs of production, quality control and labour productivity and labour related matters. Firms that enter foreign markets through the foreign direct investment mode and equity-based competitive alliances may find return on assets or a working capital to sales ratio most helpful.

The important point is to use those measures which experience has shown are the key indicators to evaluate the performance of the foreign business. An important objective in deciding on the approach to performance valuation is to ensure that managers are motivated to attain the firm's corporate objectives. A well-designed marketing strategy which does not capture the imagination and support of managers is likely to fail. It is thus necessary, in selecting the performance criteria, to anticipate managerial reaction. Ultimately, all performance measures are subjective since the choice of which measure to stress in particular circumstances is a matter of judgement for the individual firm (Shapiro, 1985, p. 231).

## Return on international investments

Financial analysis based on return on investment is frequently used by firms to measure annual performances of foreign operations. A detailed financial analysis can decompose the elements that affect the firm's return on investment.

In order to examine these issues it is necessary to recall that the formula for return on investment can be decomposed into two sub-ratios, one which measures cost control in the firm and the second which measures marketing effectiveness:

Return on Investment = (Cost Control)     (Marketing Effectiveness)

$$\frac{\text{Net Income}}{\text{Total Assets}} = \frac{\text{Net Income}}{\text{Sales}} \times \frac{\text{Sales}}{\text{Total Assets}}$$

The first ratio to the right of the equals sign, net income divided by sales, measures cost control in the firm, i.e. the amount of gross profit the firm obtains in the market. The second ratio, sales divided by total assets, measures marketing effectiveness in the firm, i.e. the level of sales the firm obtains from the total resources at its disposal. This formula owes its origins to the DuPont Company which developed it to measure new wealth created, i.e. net income, compared to all the resources the firm could employ in the creation of that wealth, i.e. total assets.

By plotting the firm's cost control performance against its marketing effectiveness we derive the firm's return on investment. Numerous combinations of cost control effort and marketing effectiveness produce a given return on investment. By plotting the ratios over a number of years the firm can determine whether its emphasis on marketing effectiveness or cost control have been more fruitful. To illustrate the principles involved, short historical performance of two hypothetical firms, ABC Technologies and XYZ Textiles adapted from Mobley and McKeown (1987a, 1987b) is shown in Figure 20.3. As can be seen, ABC Technologies, which entered a nearby foreign market for the first time during Year l, experienced a decline in cost control between Year 1 and Year 2, while marketing effectiveness did not change sufficiently to compensate for this loss. Understanding the costs of entering a market, and particularly the costs of product adaptation in high-technology firms, is a common problem. The result is that return on investment declined to 20 per cent. For such a business it is generally believed that a return of 20–25 per cent would be much too low and that the firm should attempt to raise its return to at least 40 per cent to satisfy profit and development requirements fully. Acknowledging this problem and the need for greater profits ABC Technologies plans a balanced growth of its operations to obtain a return on investment in Year 3 of 40 per cent. It plans to reach its target by improvements on the cost side and by improved marketing effectiveness.

The return on investment in Year 2 for ABC Technologies and XYZ Textiles was the same: 20 per cent. XYZ Textiles, however, achieved its 20 per cent ROI through a much more effective marketing effort; it made £3 of sales for every £1 of assets. The performance of ABC Technologies was £1 of sales for each £1 of assets but its productive efficiency was 25 per cent compared to 5 per cent for XYZ Textiles. As a result of this analysis and a decision to seek balanced growth, ABC Technologies might decide in Year 3 to increase its return on investment to 40 per cent.

The foreign operation which is evaluated on the basis of return on investment can, however, produce undesired results. In such an evaluative system longer-term performance may be ignored by managers. In order to boost returns essential equipment may not be replaced even when such investment

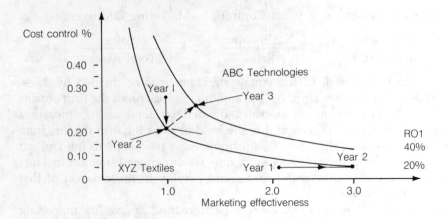

**Figure 20.3**  Cost control and marketing effectiveness for balanced growth (Sources: Mobley, Loy and McKeown, Kate (1987a) 'ROI revisited' in *Intrapreneurial Excellence,* a publication of American Management Association, April, pp. 1 and 4; Mobley, Loy and McKeown, Kate (1987b) 'Balanced growth plans - an ROI breakthrough,' in *Growth Strategies,* a publication of the American Management Association, June 3)

is required for longer-term growth. This is so because new investments increase the asset base, the denominator in the equation above, and also because return on investment measured on a historical cost basis will be greater than investment measured on a replacement cost basis.

## Strategic control of international marketing operations

Periodically the firm in international markets decides to undertake a critical review of its overall marketing effectiveness in its various markets. Because marketing suffers from rapid obsolescence of objectives, policies, strategies and operational programmes, the firm should regularly reassess its overall approach to the market (Kotler, 1988, p. 744). Strategic control for Kotler means auditing the firm's marketing activities to evaluate its marketing effectiveness. According to Kotler the marketing effectiveness of a firm is reflected in the degree to which it exhibits five major attributes of a marketing orientation: customer philosophy; integrated marketing organization; adequate marketing information; strategic orientation; and operational efficiency.

Successful entry to and performance in international markets usually means developing a marketing strategy involving a combination of initiatives by the firm under each of the above headings. These initiatives may involve new or redesigned products, different distribution channels, expanded or improved production facilities with an emphasis on cost competitiveness in international markets, pricing with an emphasis on the ability to retaliate to influence the behaviour of competitors, and even perhaps the acquisition or establishment of associated companies in the target market. All such initiatives require increased marketing expenditures.

Some of the above initiatives may be managed within the firm's long-term strategy, while others would fit into annual marketing plans. Some marketing expenditures and price changes would be tactical matters, the concern solely of a local manager or salesman. It is the combination of these initiatives which the firm uses to expand in international markets and which therefore comprise the cost of the strategy.

The manner in which firms cost international marketing strategies varies according to the size and nature of the expansion, size, corporate culture, and structure of the firm, and the type of management involved. Sometimes the chief executives of very large firms take the decision to internationalize and develop and monitor the marketing strategies developed. In other cases, even small subsidiaries of international firms are required to prepare detailed cost analyses of international market expansion strategies. Increasingly, larger firms take a greater interest in how they organize to implement strategies in various international markets. The emphasis appears to be away from country managers and marketing activities organized on a country basis to management for a region or group of countries on a product line basis. Much of this interest in redesigning organizational structures relates to the growth of large market groups, as is occurring with the completion of the internal EC market and the opening of markets in Eastern Europe. In recent years Gillette has reorganized to capitalize on new opportunities in international markets (Exhibit 20.2).

## Planning and control

It is generally believed that there is a positive correlation between planning and financial performance in the firm. Recall that marketing planning must answer six key questions for the firm:

- Where are we now?
- How did we get here?
- Where are we going?
- What must be done?
- Who should do it?
- When should it be done?

Answers to these questions should help to improve the firm's marketing performance in all aspects of its activities. The value of marketing planning stems from the observation that international marketing is complex and life cycle properties result in changes in marketing programme requirements in the firm over time. In the context of rapid growth and expanding markets as faces the firm on first entry to overseas markets, many firms may initially be profitable but experience cash flow problems as outlined elsewhere in this chapter.

**Exhibit 20.2   Effect of changing market structure on organizational structure**

*New multinational structures and operating units for Gillette*

Inspired by the growth of the EC market and a new ease in advertising across borders, Boston's Gillette Co last year switched from 15 country-based subsidiaries to a system organized along product lines. The new organization requires multilingual product-line managers who are sensitive to cultural differences. To avoid losing local managers who might feel their authority has been reduced, Gillette put those who once ran several product lines within one country in charge of one line in several countries. Despite the difficulties, Gillette's payoff is handsome: cost savings of up to 30% are possible on production runs of 1 million units, instead of five 200,000-unit runs.

As businesses of all types seek to move away from national strategies, managers will face wrenching changes. "Companies capable of evolving in the new open environment are going to have messy organization charts", says Eric G. Frieberg, managing director of McKinsey & Co in Brussels. "managers have to think through how they can become local insiders in ways that count.".

**Source:** *Business Week*, 31 August, 1987, pp. 30–1.

Gillette Co said Thursday it was adopting a new structure with the creation of two new operating units, Gillette North Atlantic and Gillette International/Diversified Operations. It said that Gillette North Atlantic would include the blade and razor, personal care and stationery products business in North America and Europe. Gillette International/Diversified Operations will include international operations outside Europe, as well as existing diversified units, Braun AG, Oral-B and Jafra, the company said. Gillette North Atlantic will be managed on a product line basis rather than on geographical lines, it added.

The two new units replace the three existing groups, which are Gillette North America, Gillette International, and Diversified Operations, the company said.

**Source:** *International Herald Tribune*, November, 1987, p. 15.

The day-to-day operational aspects of the business dominate at this stage in the development of the firm. As the market stabilizes and a more mature situation reigns, survival and continued growth may depend on the extent to which the firm has anticipated these changes, has recognized their present and future implications, and has developed strategic as well as operational skills to cope with them (Bracker, Keats and Pearson, 1988, p. 593).

In a study of 217 electronics firms in business for more than five years and employing no more that 100 people these authors found that strategic planning, what they refer to as "structured strategic planning procedures," returned a better financial performance than firms following operational planning methods only or no planning at all. According to these authors "one of the most important aspects of planning may be the level of planning sophistication ... [substantiating the finding] ... that the quality of planning is the most important determinant of financial performance." (Bracker, Keats and Pearson, 1988, p. 599) These authors conclude that structured strategic planners devote attention both to growth and cost control.

Most strategic planning starts with a static view of the firm, its customers and the competition: a static analysis means assessing the attractiveness of the market and the company's position compared to competitors. As was seen in earlier chapters, Chapter 10 particularly, many companies are very myopic in this regard. Companies, especially those defending domestic positions, are often shortsighted about the strategic intentions of their competitors. It has been argued that such companies will never understand their own vulnerability until they understand the intentions of their rivals and then reason back to potential tactics (Hamel and Prehalad, 1985, p. 143). With no appreciation of strategic intent these authors argue that defensively minded competitors are doomed to a perpetual game of catch-up. Key issues and problem areas are also identified at this stage. The next stage involves a dynamic analysis which is sometimes based on subjective judgements but usually supported by research. The firm must examine sets of factors in deciding likely future outcomes. There are a series of factors which affect customers, competitors, and the environment which impact on costs and the financial performance of the firm which must be considered in a dynamic analysis of the firm (Figure 20.4).

## Meeting and reviewing performance standards

Designing an effective implementation and control system is not an easy task. A range of possible controls were discussed in preceding sections. A comprehensive treatment of the subject would mean an evaluation of the effectiveness of the firm in international markets on the following criteria (Newman and Logan, 1976, p. 512):

(a) profitability (percentage of sales and return on investment);
(b) market position;
(c) productivity (costs and sales improvements);
(d) leadership in technological research;
(e) development of key people (technical and managerial);
(f) attitudes (employees and public).

The above list places considerable emphasis on strength for future company growth and current profitability. As may be judged, therefore, real control of marketing strategy implementation in the firm is more comprehensive than a simple examination of how well the firm performed in the past.

Unless corrective action is taken when performance standards are not met or when new opportunities appear, the process of implementation and control

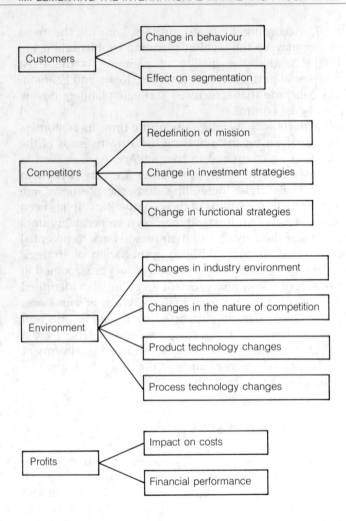

**Figure 20.4** Factors analysed in a dynamic analysis of the firm, customers and competitors

in the firm is an empty exercise. As soon as a deviation from standard is detected, the causes of the variation should be investigated. A number of causes may be identified: obstacles arising in operating conditions; poor communications leading to misunderstanding; inadequate training; lack of required basic skills; or inadequate incentives (Newman and Logan, 1976, p. 509). Corrective action sometimes leads to a change in the targets. An evaluation of the operating conditions, leadership training, and motivation may reveal unrealistic standards in relation to the firm and its markets. In such circumstances it would be important to revise the standards. In circumstances where the performance evaluation indicates results better than expected, new higher standards might be established if improved circumstances are likely to continue.

## Summary

Implementing international marketing strategy means paying attention to a number of closely related areas. First, it is important to understand the dimensions of effective implementation of strategy in the firm in international markets. Second, the firm must decide on the best approach to operational control in its markets. Finally, there is the issue of implementing performance standards in the firm. In examining the issue of implementation there is the added dimension of short-run tactical controls on implementation and long-term strategic control on the direction of the firm.

Measuring marketing performance is not an easy task. There are numerous measures of efficiency which can be applied to marketing inputs, intermediary factors, and marketing outputs. Firms select a number from among these measures which they monitor over time. Among the more common measures are sales quotas and controls, asset earnings and profits, market share and market growth. In addition, firms seek financial control in their international markets. One of the key variables to be managed in this regard is cash flow. The timing and sequencing of events in international markets are such as to put great pressure on cash flow. The effect is usually greater on smaller firms.

Financial controls in the form of return on investment are also used by firms which are short-term in nature. They have the advantage, however, that if applied over time the firm can monitor its performance and attribute any deviation from standard to cost or marketing factors.

Most firms attempting to develop and grow in international markets apply strategic controls to their international operations. Strategic control involves a much broader set of factors related to marketing, customers and competitors, and distinguishes the more successful companies from the less successful. It is also recognized that not only do strategies change from time to time but so too do performance standards. With more experience of international markets the firm may revise the performance standards it uses.

## Discussion questions

1. Why is the firm concerned with measuring marketing performance?

2. What is meant by strategy implementation for the firm in international markets? Describe the relationship between marketing strategy and its implementation?

3. Expansion into international markets must be accompanied with a financial strategy. Discuss.

4. Describe the more important operational controls which could be applied in international markets.

5. Short-term financial performance measures identify the likelihood of long-term survival in international markets. Discuss.

6. Most of the measures of strategic control are inappropriate, difficult to apply and too expensive. Discuss.

7. Increasingly, firms in international markets organize themselves on the basis of information networks to serve customers and compete. Discuss.

8. Marketing strategies evolve with time and circumstances so why not performance standards and approaches to implementation too?

## References

Bracker, Jeffrey, S., Keats, Barbara W. and Pearson, John N. (1988) 'Planning and financial performance among small firms in a growth industry,' *Strategic Management Journal*, **9**, 591–603.

Bonoma, Thomas V. (1984) 'Making your marketing strategy work,' *Harvard Business Review*, March–April, 69–76.

Bonoma, Thomas V. and Clarke, Bruce H. (1988) *Marketing Performance Assessment*, Harvard Business School Press, Boston.

Greenley, Gordon E. (1989) *Strategic Management*, Prentice Hall, NY.

Hamel, Gary and Prahalad, C.K. (1985) 'Do you really have a global strategy,' *Harvard Business Review*, July–August, 139–48.

Hulbert, James M. and Toy, Norman E. (1984) 'A strategic framework for marketing control,' in Weitz, Barton A. and Wensley, Robin (eds.), *Strategic Marketing*, Kent Publishing Company, Boston, pp. 452–65.

Kotler, Philip (1988) *Marketing Management*, Prentice Hall International, 6th edn.

Mobley, Lou and McKeown, Kate (1987a) 'ROI Revisited,' in *Intrapreneurial Excellence*, a publication of the American Management Association, April. pp. 1 and 4.

Mobley, Lou and McKeown, Kate (1987b) 'Balanced growth plans — an ROI breakthrough,' in *Growth Strategies*, a publication of the American Management Association, June, p. 3.

Newman, William and Logan, James P. (1976) *Strategy, Policy and Central Management*, South Western Publishing Company, Cincinnati, 7th edn.

Shapiro, Alan C. (1985) 'Evaluation and control of foreign operations' in Vernon, Wortzel, Heidi and Wortzel, Lawrence C. (eds.), *Strategic Management of Multinational Corporations: The Essentials*, John Wiley, NY, 225–39.

Pfeffer, Jeffrey and Salancik, Gerald R. (1978) *The External Control of Organizations*, Harper and Row, NY.

Weston, J. Fred and Copeland, Thomas E. (1988) *Managerial Finance*, 2nd edn, Cassel Educational Limited, London.

# Company index

543

# Name index

# Subject index

549